Discovering Christ In Exodus

Volume 1

# Discovering Christ

# In Exodus

## Volume 1

## Donald S. Fortner

Go *publications*

Go Publications
Gibb Hill Farm, Ponsonby, Cumbria, CA20 1BX, ENGLAND.


© Go Publications 2020




ISBN 978-1-908475-19-0

This Book is Dedicated to

Pastor David Pledger

# Table of Contents

7

As Moses wrote of Christ, we might be careful not to lose sight of Him through every chapter, but to be searching for Him in this field of scripture as for hidden treasure. And indeed as it appears from the many references which are made by the other sacred writers of both the Testaments to this book of God, that there are more types and shadows of the Lord Jesus in Exodus, than perhaps in any other of the writings of the Old Testament a more awakened attention, therefore, should be called forth, accompanied with earnest prayer to God the Spirit, that we may find Him, of whom Moses and the prophets did write, Jesus of Nazareth.

Robert Hawker

# Foreword

God's saints often stand amazed at the providential timing with which our sovereign Saviour arranges things in our lives. The time at which I was asked to write this foreword is no exception. Unbeknownst to Pastor Fortner, I had recently begun preaching through the book of Exodus. Therefore, not only has it been an honour to write my thoughts on his new commentary, it has also been a great help as I have referred to it weekly for the past two years.

'I want you to know Christ.' That is the first line that grabbed my attention in the preface. Having heard Brother Don faithfully preach the gospel of God's sovereign grace for over 30 years and having now used the commentary you hold in your hands, I can say, indeed, this is the heart of its author. You will see for yourself after reading only the overview in the first chapter where he shows the theme of Exodus to be God's Son, Jesus Christ our Lord.

From the names of the children of Israel in chapter 1 verse 1 to the cloud of the LORD in chapter 40 verse 38, you will find Christ set forth in simple language the youngest reader can understand. Where most commentaries skip over chapter 37 because it is a repetition of chapters 25 and 30, you will find the all-important lesson 'there is nothing in the Holy Word that can be said to be unnecessary or superfluous. And if, as it is written, our God does not forget our work of faith and labour of love, surely we can never think too often, remember too dearly, or speak too frequently of his great acts of mercy, operations of grace and works of love for our souls.' You will even find Christ exalted in the 'brass nails and linen cords' of the tabernacle's construction.

A faithful pastor is a miner. Here Pastor Fortner has dug deep to bring forth precious jewels by comparing scripture with scripture to make the shadows and types clear, and including the best quotes and excerpts from faithful men of the past, so it becomes easy for the reader to adore the multifaceted diamond that is our great Redeemer.

I am always eager to find a commentary written by men faithful to the word of God who, like Mary, understand 'one thing is needful'. After reading this book you will discover that Pastor Fortner's subject throughout this excellent commentary is 'that good part'.

Clay Curtis
Sovereign Grace Baptist Church
Ewing, New Jersey

# Preface

We live in the most religious day the world has ever known. Multiplied millions of dollars are given by people every year to build huge, elaborate 'church' buildings. In some places, thousands of people crowd into massive auditoriums every Sunday to sing the songs of Zion and listen to a man preach. Their sincerity cannot be questioned. They hope, by their religious efforts, to attain everlasting life and salvation. As I behold their devotions, I feel like Paul when he came into Athens and beheld the devotions of the Athenians on Mars Hill. I want to cry out to the world around me, 'God is not impressed with silver, or gold, or stone graven by art and man's device. God is Spirit. If you worship him, you must worship him in spirit and in truth. Outward religion, without heart faith in Christ, is damning!'

Paul tells us, 'bodily exercise profiteth little'. That is to say, the mere exercise of religious duties and devotions, even when performed with great sincerity and zeal, are of no benefit to your soul. 'But godliness with contentment is great gain.' Godliness is Christ in you. Godliness is knowledge of and faith in the Lord Jesus Christ. That is indescribably great gain. And that is what I want for you. I want you to know Christ.

Apart from living faith in Christ there is no pardon for sin, no cleansing from iniquity, no reconciliation with God, no access to him, no acceptance with him, no peace in your soul, no hope of heaven, no escape from hell, no salvation! Yet, it is by the outward means of public worship, by the preaching of the gospel that God the Holy Spirit conveys grace and salvation to our souls (Romans 10:17; Hebrews 4:12; 1 Peter 1:23-25).

We are infallibly taught that the preaching of the gospel is the divinely appointed means of spiritual life and blessing. There is no substitute for it.

> If Christless sermons fall on Christless crowds,
> Allured by music and bewitching show,
> The lifeless will remain lifeless,
> And the bubble burst in woe.

The blame for so much empty, lifeless religion in our day must be laid squarely at the pulpit. Multitudes of those men who fill pulpits Sunday after Sunday whose responsibility it is to preach Christ to eternity-bound sinners only scatter chaff. They never preach the pure wheat of the gospel, 'Jesus Christ and him crucified'. 'Christ is All' in the Book of God. 'Christ is All' in redemption. 'Christ is All' in salvation. And Christ will be All in eternity. Let Christ be All in the pulpit! My purpose in preaching and in all that I write is simple. I want you to know Christ. I have no other ambition. Therefore, I am determined to know nothing among you and to preach nothing to you, except 'Jesus Christ and him crucified'.

God cannot be known, sinners cannot be saved, except by God the Holy Spirit revealing the glory of God in the face of Jesus Christ.

Most people who are familiar with the Bible, when they think of the Book of Exodus, immediately think of three things: The exodus of the Children of Israel from Egypt, the giving of the law, and the wilderness wanderings of Israel. Few, very few, realize this blessed book of inspiration, in all its details, was written to reveal 'Jesus Christ and him crucified'. It is my hope and prayer that God the Holy Spirit will, in the following chapters, discover Christ to you in the Book of Exodus.

Donald S. Fortner
Grace Baptist Church
Danville, Kentucky

# Chapter 1

# Stand Still And See The Salvation Of The Lord

'And Moses said unto the people, Fear ye not, stand still, and see the salvation of the LORD, which he will show to you to day: for the Egyptians whom ye have seen to day, ye shall see them again no more for ever.'
(Exodus 14:13)

### An Overview of the Book of Exodus
The Book of Exodus is a book about redemption. Throughout the book, we are given picture after picture of our redemption and deliverance from sin and death by Christ. The theme of the book is found in verse 13 of the fourteenth chapter. 'Stand still and see the salvation of the Lord'. That is the way sinners are saved. God does it. We see it (2 Timothy 1:9, 10).

There are multitudes who, when they read the book of Exodus, see it as nothing but a book of religious laws and ceremonies. There are three basic reasons for that. First, many read the Scriptures as though they were two books; two revelations from God. They read the Old Testament as though it is an independent book, standing alone, and separate from the New. How often have you heard people refer to the Old Testament as 'the Old Bible'? The Old Testament is but the first part of God's written revelation of himself. The New Testament is the second and final part. But they are one Book of God, one revelation.

They must never be separated. Someone once helpfully said of the two Testaments, 'The New is in the Old concealed; the Old is in the New revealed.' Second, others attempt to interpret the New Testament by the Old. That is a terrible mistake, leading to terrible erroneous doctrine. The New Testament is the Holy Spirit's inspired commentary on the Old Testament. In the New Testament he explains that which is written in the Old Testament. Third, the vast majority of people read the Old Testament as though it has very little to say about the person and work of our Lord Jesus Christ. Some time ago, after listening to a large box of our audio-tapes given to her by her nephew, a lady who had been in church all her life wrote to me to say, 'The Old Testament has come alive with Christ.' Truly, the Old Testament comes alive to us when we see Christ in it. Until then, we see nothing but religious history, religious laws, and religious ceremonies.

## Moses' Gospel

We often speak of the gospel according to Matthew, Mark, Luke, or John. But Moses' writings are also gospel literature. The gospel is the proclamation of God's salvation in and by Christ. Matthew, Mark, Luke, and John tell us about the earthly life and ministry of our Redeemer. Yet, Moses wrote about our Saviour's person and work more systematically and in greater detail than they did. Only he tells us the story of redemption, grace, and salvation by Christ in types, and pictures, and shadows. Moses gives us the same story, the same gospel, the same good news as Matthew, Mark, Luke, and John. He continually holds before us God's election, our sin, Christ's atonement for sin, and the Holy Spirit's cleansing of our souls in regeneration. I want the Book of Exodus to come alive to you. In these forty chapters Moses wrote of Christ (Luke 24:27; John 1:45).

As we read the Old Testament we must never lose sight of him of whom the Old Testament speaks. Rather, let us search for him in this field of Holy Scripture as for hidden treasure. In particular, as we study the Book of Exodus, I want to show you Christ on every page. There are, perhaps, more types, shadows, and pictures of the Lord Jesus in Exodus than in any other book of the Old Testament. May God the Holy Spirit graciously bring to light the things of Christ in these forty chapters and show them to us, that we may find him 'of whom Moses and the prophets did write, Jesus of Nazareth'.

Exodus means 'going out'. This book is called 'Exodus' because it reveals God's great work of grace in bringing his covenant people out of Egyptian bondage. It covers a time frame of about 140 years, from the death of Joseph to the erection of the tabernacle.

## The Message

The whole Book of Exodus is a message of divine deliverance. As such, it portrays the great work of our God in redeeming us from the bondage of sin and death and bringing us into what Paul calls, 'the glorious liberty of the children of God' (Romans 8:21). Even as he gave Israel his law in ten commandments, God told them his intention in his dealings with them was that they might ever be reminded of this fact, 'I am the Lord thy God, which have brought thee out of the land of Egypt, out of the house of bondage' (Exodus 20:2).

Exodus shows us God's answer to our need, his remedy for our ruin, and his deliverance from sin and death by Christ. As such, it is a tremendous picture and conveys very instructive lessons about redemption; what it is and how it is accomplished. Here we see pictures of what our God has done for us, is doing for us, and will yet do for us in bringing us into 'the glorious liberty of the children of God'. His wondrous method of grace is the same in your life and mine as it was in Moses' day. He does not change; and his method of grace does not change.

Everything written in the Book of Exodus was written by divine inspiration to show us how God works in providence and grace, overruling evil for good, to teach us the gospel (Acts 10:43; Romans 15:4; 1 Corinthians 10:11). It focuses our minds on seven great events. Israel's Bondage in Egypt. The Birth of Moses. The Passover. The Crossing of the Red Sea. The Giving of the Law. The Making of the Tabernacle. The End of Moses' Work.

## Israel's Bondage

In chapter 1 we see Israel in Egyptian bondage. Israel was God's chosen nation, and typically represents all his elect, his 'holy nation' and 'royal priesthood', 'the Israel of God'. All these are terms used to describe God's church and kingdom. National Israel was but a type of true Israel.

Just as Israel was in bondage to Egypt for 400 years, so all God's elect, by the sin and fall of our father Adam, are by nature in a state of

bondage to sin and death, 'having no hope and without God in the world'. But it is very important for us to remember four things.
1. Israel's bondage in Egypt was according to God's purpose of grace toward Abraham (Genesis 15:13).
2. Israel's time of bondage was for a set time 400 years.
3. At the appointed time all Israel came out of Egypt.
4. And though they were bondmen in Egypt for 400 years, they lost nothing by their bondage, but gained much. They came into Egypt as 70 poor, starving souls. They came out as a mighty nation, upwards of 4 million people, carrying with them all the spoils of Egypt!

It shall be so with God's elect. For each one there is a set time of bondage; and at the time appointed, called 'the time of love', every chosen sinner shall come out of Egypt. In due time, in the fulness of time, Christ our Passover was sacrificed for us. At the appointed time of love, every blood-bought sinner is delivered by the power and grace of God the Holy Spirit in effectual calling. We will suffer no loss by reason of our bondage. Rather, when our Saviour gathers his elect unto himself in resurrection glory, we shall bring all the wealth of the earth with us into his heavenly kingdom. And, when the former things are passed away, we shall have all the fulness of all things forever with Christ. There shall be no sorrow, for there shall be no sin, only the glory of perfect redemption in and with Christ!

### Moses' Birth

The Lord God told Abraham he would send Israel into a stranger's land, where they would be afflicted for four hundred years. Then, he promised to deliver his people (Genesis 15:13, 14). The book of Exodus begins with Israel in bondage in the land of Egypt. They had been in bondage for four hundred years. But the time of deliverance had come, and God raised up a deliverer. Now, the time of deliverance was at hand. In chapter 2 we have the birth of Moses, Israel's deliverer.

Moses is a type of Christ. Without question, the name 'Moses' represents the law of God and is used, at times, as a synonym for the law (Acts 6:11; 15:21; 21:21; 2 Corinthians 3:15). But Moses was also a type of Christ (Deuteronomy 18:15-18; Acts 3:22; 7:37). As it was with the incarnation, birth, and life of our great Saviour, the Lord Jesus Christ, the hand of God was remarkably and undeniably manifest throughout Moses' life. Like the Lord Jesus, that Deliverer whom he typified, Moses appeared 'in the fulness of time'. When the 'due time' arrived, the deliverer arrived. His birth was at a time of great darkness and great need. When he was born, Pharaoh sought to kill him. But Moses was miraculously preserved until the time of his appearing as God's deliverer.

God often uses Satan's devices to accomplish his purposes. As I read the Scriptures, I cannot help thinking our Lord must have a sense of humour. I can hardly refrain from laughter as I read about him turning the tables on his enemies and overruling the evil ploys of men and devils to accomplish his great purpose of grace, the very thing they try to prevent. We see the ways of our God, as revealed in Psalm 76:10, displayed in the life of Moses and in the life of our Redeemer.

Though Pharaoh ordered the midwives to murder all the baby boys born among the children of Israel, Moses was not only saved, but Pharaoh's daughter hired his own mother to nurse him and take care of him! He grew up in Pharaoh's house, as his own grandson. He was trained in all the learning of the Egyptians and given the best education in the world at that time. As Pharaoh's adopted son, he had every privilege and every advantage of the world.

When he became a man, God revealed himself to him and showed him he was chosen and ordained to be the deliverer of Israel. Moses went out, trying to do his job, as he thought, and ended up killing an Egyptian and fleeing into the wilderness. He left the land of Egypt and tended sheep for forty years in the wilderness.

Then he was called, sent, and equipped of God to deliver Israel. The Lord God appeared to him in the burning bush and sent him back to Egypt to deliver Israel at the time appointed (chapter 3). But Moses was totally unfit for the task before him; and he knew it. He could not deliver Israel; but God could. Moses was only a typical redeemer (Exodus 3:7-22). The Lord told him, 'I am come down to deliver them' (v. 8).

Moses knew he was not able to articulate things as he should as God's spokesman. So the Lord assured him he would be his tongue and he would speak through him (Exodus 4:10-12). There was nothing wrong with that. In fact, it is commendable humility. God never uses anyone who thinks he is fit for the job. He always uses nothings and nobodies to do his work (Isaiah 6:1-8; 66:2; 1 Corinthians 1:26-31).

But then Moses said, 'Lord, can't you get someone else to do this work?' And we are told, 'the anger of the Lord was kindled against

Moses' (Exodus 4:14). We would be wise to lay this to heart. A sense of inability, inadequacy, and personal unworthiness is always commendable; but any lack of willingness, or even hesitancy, in doing what is clearly God's will is abhorrent rebellion.

Moses went back to Egypt with nothing but the rod (Word) of God in his hand to deliver Israel from the most powerful king the world had ever known (2 Corinthians 10:4, 5). Immediately, he ran into trouble. He came into conflict with Pharaoh. The conflict between Pharaoh and Moses, the representatives of Satan and God, was tremendous. No drama ever written by a man compares to this bit of history. As you read it, you can feel the intensity of it. Though the Lord God sent plague after plague upon the Egyptians, 'Pharaoh hardened his heart and refused to let the people go.'

There were ten plagues in all. Each one was directed against one of the gods of Egypt. By sending these plagues, God not only judged Egypt, but also, as he punished the Egyptians, showed the impotence of their idols and displayed himself as God alone, sovereign, omnipotent, majestic, and holy.

**The Passover**
Moses was typical and representative of Christ, our Saviour. The next great event in the Book of Exodus, the Passover (chapters 11 and 12), was typical of our redemption by Christ. It is so obvious the Passover represents our redemption by Christ that everyone who even claims to believe the Bible is the Word of God acknowledges it. Few understand what is taught by this great picture of redemption; but all acknowledge it is a picture of redemption. Let me call your attention to the highlights.

The Passover, like our redemption by Christ, was an act of God's free, sovereign, covenant mercy. It was God who put a difference between Israel and Egypt (Exodus 11:7). That shows us God's distinguishing grace (1 Corinthians 4:7). Then the message was spoken in the ears of God's chosen (Exodus 11:1). The call of God the Holy Spirit is a particular, distinguishing call (Romans 8:29, 30). God promised an effectual, glorious work, by which all (Egyptians and Israelites) would know he is God. Then the Egyptians thrust Israel out of the land; and they went out with a high hand, spoiling the land of Egypt, taking all the good of the land. Israel was under the special protection of divine providence. God promised, 'Against the children of Israel shall not a dog move his tongue, against man or beast' (Exodus 11:7). The Lord God raised up Pharaoh and hardened his heart. He specifically said, 'That my wonders may be multiplied in the land of Egypt' (Exodus 11:9; Romans 9:15-18). And we observe, Satan is God's servant, not his rival! When God gets done with him, he will dump his carcass in the sea of his fury, just as he did Pharaoh's; and all shall know that he alone is God.

The Passover, like our redemption, was a display of how God saves sinners by blood atonement. It was accomplished at God's appointed time (Exodus 12:2). It was for Israel the beginning of months (2 Corinthians 5:17). The paschal lamb portrayed Christ our Passover who is sacrificed for us (1 Corinthians 5:7). The blood sprinkled upon the door speaks of the effectual call of grace in which the Spirit of God applies Christ's atoning blood to the conscience, creating faith in the redeemed sinner (Hebrews 9:12-14). Particular, effectual redemption is displayed in the fact that all for whom a lamb was slain went out of Egypt (Exodus 12:37). And, as Israel spoiled the Egyptians (Exodus 12:36), we shall have the spoils of victory in resurrection glory, inheriting the earth.

**The Red Sea**
The story does not end there. Beginning in chapter 13, we see the fourth great event in Exodus, the crossing of the Red Sea. Really, the Passover and the crossing of the Red Sea are two parts of the same thing. They cannot be separated. Israel could never have crossed the Red Sea had the Passover not been kept. And the keeping of the Passover would have been meaningless, and useless, had Israel not crossed the sea.

The crossing of the Red Sea is a picture of our conversion by the power and grace of God the Holy Spirit in effectual calling. This is so closely connected with the sacrifice of Christ as our sin atoning Substitute, that the two cannot be separated. Christ's death effectually secured our conversion. And without the conversion of God's elect, Christ's death would have been a useless, futile, vain, and meaningless thing. Now, watch the type. May God make it dance with life.

The Lord went before them (Exodus 13:21). He led them through the way of the wilderness (Exodus 13:18). Israel was brought into terror and fear; but their fear only stirred the rebellion that was in them (Exodus 14:10, 11). Legal conviction is not saving. It takes Holy Spirit conviction to save (John 16:8-11). Yet, it seems to be the common experience of God's elect that a time of legal conviction (the terror of eternal death) precedes the blessed joy of faith. When Israel was utterly terrified, Moses said, 'Fear ye not, stand still, and see the salvation of the Lord' (Exodus 14:13).

'The Lord shall fight for you, and ye shall hold your peace' (Exodus 14:14). That is exactly the place to which God brings his own. He graciously forces us to cease from our own works and efforts to save ourselves. He makes us look to Christ alone for salvation.

Israel crossed the sea by the rod of Moses. That rod represents the whole Word of God; mercy and truth, justice and grace, holiness and love. 'By mercy and truth iniquity is purged.' The law of God, being satisfied by the blood and righteousness of Christ, opens the way before us to everlasting salvation, and the grace of God carries us through. Then, standing upon the shores of blessed deliverance, looking back upon their slain enemies, they believed, worshipped, gave praise to God, and started on their journey (Exodus 14:31-16:1).

**Baptism**
The Scriptures (1 Corinthians 10:1, 2) tell us plainly that the passage of Israel through the Red Sea was a baptism unto Moses. It signified the same thing as believer's baptism does today. It showed the distinction God put between Israel and Egypt. So does believer's baptism. It was an act of obedience to God's command. Both Israel's baptism unto Moses and the believer's baptism with reference to the finished work of Christ are acts of obedience performed to the command of God with reference to the promise of God (Exodus 14:13-16; Matthew 28:19; Mark 16:16). As Israel followed Moses through the Red Sea, so believers follow Christ through the waters of baptism, symbolically declaring salvation to be the work of God alone by Christ's fulfilling all righteousness as our Representative and Substitute.

**Marah**
No sooner had they crossed the Red Sea than they came to the bitter waters of Marah (Exodus 15:23-26). So it is with us. From its very inception, the life of faith is a life of trial. 'We must through much tribulation enter into the kingdom of God.' The Lord showed Moses 'a tree, which when he had cast into the waters, the waters were made

sweet'. Then he revealed himself in a singular way, declaring, 'I am the Lord that healeth thee'. Let us ever be assured that whatever trials of bitterness we must endure as we go through this wilderness of woe, the trials and bitter experiences are but means by which our God intends to reveal himself more fully. Those trials and bitter waters are made sweet to our souls because they flow to us as blessings of grace from the throne of our heavenly Father, through the blood of our crucified Mediator who died upon the cursed tree for us. The cross sweetens all. How it sweetens life's experiences! Pastor Scott Richardson[1] often said, 'There's no bad news once you get the good news.'

## Manna
As they made their journey through the wilderness, the Lord graciously fed the children of Israel with heavenly manna every day (chapter 16), and refreshed their bodies with water flowing from the smitten rock that followed them (chapter 17). Without question, these things were miraculous provisions for their physical sustenance. But they were much more than that. The manna that fell from heaven and the water that flowed from the smitten rock were pictures of God's provision for our souls, for time and eternity in Christ, our crucified Saviour (John 6:48-58; 1 Corinthians 10:1-11).

## Amalek
Perhaps the most difficult experience of God's people in this world, after being converted, is the constant, ever-increasing warfare between the flesh and the spirit. We see this portrayed in chapter seventeen as well. Amalek comes and fights with Israel; but God declares unending war with Amalek (Exodus 17:10-16). The fact is, the flesh lusts against the spirit and the spirit against the flesh, so we can never do the things we would. We can never walk with our God and serve him perfectly, without sin, while we live in this world. We constantly find ourselves to be wretched sinners (Romans 7:14-23; Galatians 5:17). This warfare will never end, or even abate, until we have dropped these bodies of flesh. We can never make peace with Amalek. Yet, Amalek will never cease to assail us. But, blessed be God our Saviour, Amalek shall never prevail! Because Christ is our Banner, because the Lord our God fights

---

[1] Former pastor of Katy Baptist Church, Fairmont, West Virginia.

for us, 'we are more than conquerors', and all our foes shall fall before us, even our sins!

## The Law
The fifth thing that stands out in the Book of Exodus is the giving of the law at Mount Sinai. In chapters 19-24 we find Israel at Mount Sinai, where the Lord God gave Israel his law in ten commandments and taught them how he must be worshipped. The law was a detailed revelation of God's immutable, unrelenting, perfect, glorious holiness. That is why the law and the giving of the law were terrifying to Israel. Nothing is so terrifying to sinful men and women as the realization God Almighty is absolutely and unchangeably holy, and nothing can change him. He will never be talked out of anything. He can never be bought-off. He will never lower his standards in any degree. The law is the absolute, irrevocable standard of God's character. It is also a declaration of the absolute sovereignty and utter solitariness of his being as God. Because he is who and what he is, the Lord our God demands perfection of all who are accepted of him.

At the very outset, the law of God taught Israel, and teaches us, that the holy, sovereign, unalterable Lord God cannot be worshipped by fallen, sinful, sinning men and women except through a mediator he has ordained, provided, and accepted (Exodus 20:18, 19), upon an altar of his own making, an altar to which man contributes nothing, and can never climb by degrees (Exodus 20:23-26). In other words, the law drives us away from Sinai to Calvary, away from Moses to Christ for refuge and salvation (Galatians 3:19-26).

## The Tabernacle
The sixth thing in Exodus is the erection of the tabernacle, the place of reconciliation and peace, with its altar, sacrifices, priesthood, and mercy seat (Exodus 25-40). In chapter twenty-five the Lord began to give Moses instructions about the tabernacle and priesthood, sacrifices and ceremonies, by which the children of Israel might come to him and find acceptance with him. The whole thing speaks of Christ and the believer's acceptance with God in him (Hebrews 9:1-10:22). Here we are taught by types and pictures how the Lord our God can be both a just God and a Saviour (Isaiah 45:20, 21). Through the sacrifice of our Lord Jesus Christ, the holy Lord God, in complete justice, holiness, and

truth, receives redeemed sinners in total reconciliation and declares, 'There is now no condemnation', none whatsoever. None whatsoever! Every believing sinner has perfect access to the Father through the Son. And God himself, by his Holy Spirit, has taken up his tabernacle in our hearts and lives. He will never leave us, and will never let us leave him! We are forever, immutably 'accepted in the beloved'!

**The End of Moses' Work**
The last thing we see in Exodus is the end of Moses' work. Once the tabernacle was finished and God and his people were ceremonially reconciled, Moses had finished his work (Exodus 40:33). And once the chosen, redeemed sinner has been brought to faith in Christ, the law of God has finished its work (Romans 6:14, 15; 7:1-4; 8:1; 10:4). Once God's elect are brought into the blessedness of reconciliation with him by faith in Christ, the law has nothing more to do with us. It no longer terrifies, condemns, or even frowns upon us. Rather, the law of God cries as fully as the grace of God, 'JUSTIFIED!' This is beautifully portrayed in the last paragraph of Exodus.

'Then a cloud covered the tent of the congregation, and the glory of the LORD filled the tabernacle. And Moses was not able to enter into the tent of the congregation, because the cloud abode thereon, and the glory of the LORD filled the tabernacle. And when the cloud was taken up from over the tabernacle, the children of Israel went onward in all their journeys: But if the cloud were not taken up, then they journeyed not till the day that it was taken up. For the cloud of the LORD was upon the tabernacle by day, and fire was on it by night, in the sight of all the house of Israel, throughout all their journeys' (Exodus 40:34-38). Philip Bliss wrote,

> Free from the law, O happy condition!
> Jesus hath bled, and there is remission!
> Cursed by the law and bruised by the fall,
> Grace hath redeemed us once for all.

> Now are we free, there's no condemnation!
> Jesus provides a perfect salvation!
> 'Come unto Me' O hear His sweet call!
> Come, and He saves us once for all.

25

Children of God, O glorious calling!
Surely His grace will keep us from falling!
Passing from death to life at His call,
Blessed salvation, once for all!

## Moses' Prayer

As we seek to worship, serve, and honour our God in this world, we would be wise to pray for the very same great boons of mercy and grace Moses sought from the Lord in chapter 33.

'Now therefore, I pray thee, if I have found grace in thy sight, show me now thy way, that I may know thee, that I may find grace in thy sight' (v. 13). If the Lord God will be pleased to show us his way, order our steps in his way, cause us ever to grow in the grace and knowledge of Christ, and ever give us his grace, we shall be blessed throughout our days upon the earth and forever in heavenly glory.

'Consider that this nation is thy people' (v. 13). Let us ever pray for the church and kingdom of God in this world. We cannot ask anything greater than that the Lord God ever consider his people are his people.

After the Lord promised Moses' his abiding presence, Moses sought it earnestly. 'And he said unto him, If thy presence go not with me, carry us not up hence' (v. 15). It is almost as if he felt he had neglected this before, or simply made the presumption that God's presence was his. Certainly every believer is promised the Lord's unfailing presence. But let us never presume upon it, or imagine we can function without it. Rather, let us constantly seek it. If the Lord is with us, no need is unsupplied.

Then, Moses prayed, 'I beseech thee, show me thy glory' (v. 18). And the Lord God granted his request. He showed himself to be a just God and a Saviour. Oh, may he be pleased ever to hold before our eyes his glory in the face of the Lord Jesus Christ, that our every thought may be consumed with it, that we may in all things do all for the glory of our God.

# Chapter 2

# The Counsel Of The LORD, That Shall Stand

' ... And all the souls that came out of the loins of Jacob were seventy souls: for Joseph was in Egypt already. And Joseph died, and all his brethren, and all that generation. And the children of Israel were fruitful, and increased abundantly, and multiplied, and waxed exceeding mighty; and the land was filled with them. Now there arose up a new king over Egypt, which knew not Joseph ... And Pharaoh charged all his people, saying, Every son that is born ye shall cast into the river, and every daughter ye shall save alive.'
(Exodus 1:1-22)

Knowing God's promises, that 'all things work together for good to them that love God, to them that are called, according to his purpose', that 'no evil shall happen to the just', that 'no weapon that is formed against thee shall prosper', how often have you looked at your circumstances and thought, 'I know those promises are true, but everything I see, everything I am experiencing, everything I feel appears to me to be evil and is telling me that all things are against me, every weapon formed against me is prospering'?

That is exactly how the children of Israel must have felt when they found themselves bondmen in Egypt, serving as slave labourers under cruel taskmasters, who made their lives bitter, according to the whims of Egypt's reprobate king, Pharaoh. God had promised that he would be with them, bless them in all things and at all times, that he would make them a great nation. He had promised to give them all the spoils of the land of Egypt. But Pharaoh ordered that the nation be destroyed, that every male child born to the children of Israel be drowned as soon as it was born. They must have thought the same thing their father Jacob thought when Joseph was secretly arranging to bring them down into Egypt. 'All these things are against me.' Read Exodus chapter 1 and you will see why they might have entertained such thoughts.

**Important Matters**
Let me call your attention to three things that appear to me to be matters of great importance as we study the Book of Exodus and the events recorded in these chapters by divine inspiration. And what I am saying here about Exodus applies to all the Old Testament Scriptures.

First, we should always remember the nation of Israel was chosen of God, used of God, and blessed by God for spiritual, not carnal, reasons. It was never God's intention that Christ would come to the earth to reign as a physical king over Abraham's physical descendants. Rather, God used Abraham's physical descendants (the nation of Israel) to accomplish his purpose of grace toward his elect, the spiritual seed of Abraham; his church, called in the New Testament 'the Israel of God'. Israel was, throughout the Old Testament, typical of God's church. All God's dealings with Israel as a nation have a spiritual meaning, and must be interpreted in a spiritual way as applying to you and me, the church of God. By preserving the nation of Israel, the Lord God graciously preserved Abraham's seed, through whom Christ, the woman's Seed, came into this world. As God fulfilled all his promises to the nation of Israel when he brought them into the land of Canaan (Joshua 21:43-45), so he will fulfil all the promises he has made to his elect, Abraham's spiritual seed, in Christ (Romans 11:25-27).

Second, the Holy Spirit tells us that everything that happened in the book of Exodus, indeed, everything that happened in the history of the Old Testament, was not only written for our instruction, but also happened for our instruction. Everything that came to pass was brought to pass by our God for our instruction, comfort, and edification in the knowledge of Christ (Romans 15:4; 1 Corinthians 10:1-6, 11).

Third, everything in the history of Israel is directly related to the redemption of our souls by Christ. Let me show you something very interesting in Luke 9:31. On the mount of transfiguration Moses and Elijah appeared with our Saviour. When they did, they spoke to him about 'his decease which he would accomplish at Jerusalem'. That means that our Saviour's substitutionary death at Jerusalem was not something that happened to him. It was something accomplished by him. Christ's death is the accomplishment of God's eternal purpose, all the prophecies, pictures, and types of the Old Testament, God's covenant promises, and our eternal redemption. However, the word decease in verse 31 is particularly instructive. The word translated 'decease' (εξοδοσ) is the word 'exodus'. The word means 'departing'. And the departing, the exodus, that our Saviour accomplished in his death was typically portrayed throughout the Book of Exodus.

**Israel in Egypt**
Now, let us look at Exodus chapter one. The first thing we see is the fact that Israel is now in Egypt. 'Now these are the names of the children of Israel, which came into Egypt; every man and his household came with Jacob. Reuben, Simeon, Levi, and Judah, Issachar, Zebulun, and Benjamin, Dan, and Naphtali, Gad, and Asher. And all the souls that came out of the loins of Jacob were seventy souls: for Joseph was in Egypt already' (vv. 1-5).

These verses show us that the Book of Exodus is a continuation of the Book of Genesis. It is but another part of God's unfolding drama of redemption set before us upon the pages of Holy Scripture.

As the word 'exodus' suggests, the theme of this book is redemption. In the Book of Genesis, the book of beginnings, we have first the creation, then the fall, and then the promise of redemption. In Genesis 3:15 God promised he would send his Son into the world, as the seed of woman, to crush the serpent's head and deliver his elect from the ruins of sin and death by the sacrifice of himself. He promised the coming of another Adam in and by whom his people would be redeemed (Galatians 4:4, 5).

After making the promise of redemption in Genesis 3:15, the Lord gave Adam and Eve a vivid picture of how he would accomplish it. He killed an innocent victim, stripped Adam and Eve of their fig leaves, and clothed them with the skins of the slain victim. When Abel came to worship God, he brought the firstlings of his flock, indicating his faith in God's promise, trusting Christ the Lamb of God, and was accepted.

29

Cain brought the fruit of his own labour, despising Christ, and was rejected. Because he was rejected and Abel was accepted, Cain hated his brother and murdered him. That was the first display of the enmity, the malice, and hatred the seed of the serpent has for the woman's Seed.

But God's purpose was not thwarted by Cain. The Lord brought another man into the world, Seth, by whom he would bring in the woman's Seed. Later, after the flood, he chose Noah's son, Shem, as the one through whom Christ must come. Then, he called Abraham, and declared that through him our Saviour must come into the world, and promised that by that One who would come he would give the blessing of his grace and salvation to all nations. Abraham believed God, built an altar, offered sacrifices, and worshipped. Then, God told Abraham that the things we see in the Book of Exodus would come to pass (Genesis 15:13, 14).

Abraham had two sons: Ishmael and Isaac. God chose Isaac. Isaac had two sons: Esau and Jacob. God chose Jacob. Jacob and his twelve sons, with their families (70 souls in all), came down to Egypt. That is where the Book of Genesis closes and the Book of Exodus begins. You can see why Genesis is very properly called 'the seed-plot of the Bible'.

As the book of beginnings, Genesis displays many, many things. Still, it ends with Joseph dead and Israel in Egypt. In Exodus there is just one subject – redemption. It vividly portrays the redemption of God's elect by the purpose of God, by the purchase of blood, and by the power of grace.

**Joseph Died**
Everything was going well for Jacob and his sons in Egypt. When Joseph brought them into the land, he was prime minister of Egypt, second only to Pharaoh. Joseph arranged for his family to dwell in Goshen, the richest, most fertile, well-watered place in Egypt. There they prospered. Then we read, 'And Joseph died, and all his brethren, and all that generation' (v. 6). Let me remind you of three things here. They are things we need to remember.

First, you and I must die. At God's appointed time, we shall leave this world of time and pass into another, everlasting, eternal world, either a world of eternal woe or a world of eternal bliss. 'It is appointed unto men once to die'. Let us be wise. May God teach us to number our days and apply our hearts to Wisdom, to Christ, who is our Wisdom.

Second, though we all must die, God's people lose nothing, and gain much by death. In fact, when our bodies die, we begin to live and never die (John 11:25). 'Blessed are the dead that die in the Lord.' 'Precious in the sight of the Lord is the death of his saints.' This means there is no reason for any ransomed soul to fear death.

Third, though God's servants die, God's purpose endures. Though God's servants die, God's promise stands. Though God's servants die, God's church survives. The loss of Don Fortner will be no loss to God's work, God's people, or God's purpose. When my appointed time has come, when my work is finished and I breathe my last mortal breath, my death will not make the slightest hesitation in the accomplishment of God's purpose. 'One generation passeth away, and another generation cometh: but the earth abideth for ever' (Ecclesiastes 1:4).

I laughed with thankful joy when I read John Trapp's comment on verse 6. 'God also maketh haste to have the number of his elect fulfilled; and, therefore, despatcheth away the generations.'

**Great Prosperity**
'And the children of Israel were fruitful, and increased abundantly, and multiplied, and waxed exceeding mighty; and the land was filled with them' (v. 7). While they were in the land of Egypt, the children of Israel grew into a great nation. They prospered greatly. The nation grew from 70 souls to 600,000 men, besides women and children (Exodus 12:37). That makes their number, I would imagine, about 4,000,000. And as long as we are in this world, God's church continues to grow and multiply.

Back in Genesis 1:28 God commanded Adam and Eve to be fruitful, to multiply, and to replenish the earth. That was his command in the original creation. God gave the same commandment to Noah when he came off the ark (Genesis 9:1). And he repeatedly promised Abraham he would make him fruitful, he would make his seed multiply, and he would make his seed a blessing to the earth (Genesis 17:2; 22:17).

A good many people take those commandments to Adam and Noah, and the promises to Abraham to mean that men and women are to produce as many children as possible, regardless of their ability to provide for and educate them. But they forget the command and the promise was given in connection with God's covenant promise of redemption. Its concern is not with physical descendants, but spiritual.

31

Our Lord's new-creation command to his church is to be fruitful, multiply, replenish the earth and subdue it (Matthew 28:18-20). And his promise is that we shall (Romans 11:26; Revelation 7:9; 19:6).

### Israel's Sorrows

Verses 8-22 describe a time of great sorrow for the children of Israel. The chosen seed is looked upon as an enemy to be destroyed. The people of God are despised, treated with horrible cruelty, and mercilessly persecuted.

'Now there arose up a new king over Egypt, which knew not Joseph' (v. 8). Nothing is so quickly forgotten as kindness and a magnanimous spirit. Joseph was now dead. The new Pharaoh and the Egyptians forgot all the benefits they had received from him. Had it not been for Joseph, they would have starved to death. But now, they looked upon Joseph and his descendants as their enemies. As Solomon tells us, 'Now there was found in it a poor wise man, and he by his wisdom delivered the city; yet no man remembered that same poor man' (Ecclesiastes 9:15). How often is that the case!

'And he said unto his people, Behold, the people of the children of Israel are more and mightier than we: Come on, let us deal wisely with them; lest they multiply, and it come to pass, that, when there falleth out any war, they join also unto our enemies, and fight against us, and so get them up out of the land. Therefore they did set over them taskmasters to afflict them with their burdens. And they built for Pharaoh treasure cities, Pithom and Raamses. But the more they afflicted them, the more they multiplied and grew. And they were grieved because of the children of Israel. And the Egyptians made the children of Israel to serve with rigour: And they made their lives bitter with hard bondage, in mortar, and in brick, and in all manner of service in the field: all their service, wherein they made them serve, was with rigour' (Exodus 1:9-14).

The enmity of the serpent and his seed against the woman and her Seed, the enmity of Satan and this world against Christ and his church is relentless (Revelation 12). It never ceases. It never abates, but only increases. Our Saviour tells us plainly, 'In the world ye shall have tribulation'. The enmity of this world against God and his people may vary in its outward manifestations, but it is ever the same. If we fail to recognize that, we bury our heads in the sand and court misery.

Satan's devices can never thwart God's purposes or hinder his work. Pharaoh's schemes did not hinder what God had purposed. Verse 12 tells us, 'the more they afflicted them, the more they multiplied and grew'. Pharaoh's efforts at suppression were completely neutralized by the abundant increase God gave. As David sang, so may we sing, 'Thou hast enlarged me when I was distressed' (Psalm 4:1).

Pharaoh and the Egyptians made the lives of the children of Israel 'bitter with hard bondage', but it was a great blessing. Egypt typifies the world. It was not until their lives were made bitter in Egypt that the children of Israel sighed by reason of their bondage and cried out to God. 'Therefore he brought down their heart with labour; they fell down, and there was none to help. Then they cried unto the LORD in their trouble, and he saved them out of their distresses' (Psalm 107:12, 13). Blessed is the soul made bitter by reason of sin and sin's bondage under the goodness of God. To such the Lord God makes every bitter thing sweet (Proverbs 27:7). Israel ate the Passover lamb with 'bitter herbs' (Exodus 12:8). And we eat Christ our Passover with bitter tears of repentance. No sooner did they come out of Egypt than they came to the bitter waters of Marah (Exodus 15:23). But those waters were made sweet to them by the tree Moses cast into the waters. So the Lord God makes the bitter things of this world sweet to us by the cross of Christ, by the glorious gospel of his free grace in Christ.

What a blessed evidence this is of our God's great love to us! Every persecution, every scoff, every sneer, every form of opposition we meet with in this world is but a source of blessedness for our souls! The believer will never meet with a pain, or a sickness, or a sorrow that our great God and Saviour will not convert into a cause of joy (Psalm 105:23, 24; Romans 8:28). Robert Hawker wrote,

'As Israel flourished more after Joseph's death, and under the oppression of another king which knew not Joseph: so the true Israelite now literally and truly abounds more in divine things in seasons of trouble, than in the sun-shine of life. And the church of Jesus hath abundantly increased since the Redeemer's return to glory, more than in all the time he was personally with his disciples here upon earth.'

**God's Rule**
The rest of this chapter describes Pharaoh's continued attempts to destroy the people of God. That is the thing we see outwardly. But

behind Pharaoh's wicked designs, we see Satan's relentless fury towards the Lord Jesus Christ and his malicious attempts both to thwart God's glorious purpose and to destroy our precious Redeemer, and thereby to destroy us.

'And the king of Egypt spake to the Hebrew midwives, of which the name of the one was Shiphrah, and the name of the other Puah: And he said, When ye do the office of a midwife to the Hebrew women, and see them upon the stools; if it be a son, then ye shall kill him: but if it be a daughter, then she shall live. But the midwives feared God, and did not as the king of Egypt commanded them, but saved the men children alive. And the king of Egypt called for the midwives, and said unto them, Why have ye done this thing, and have saved the men children alive? And the midwives said unto Pharaoh, Because the Hebrew women are not as the Egyptian women; for they are lively, and are delivered ere the midwives come in unto them. Therefore God dealt well with the midwives: and the people multiplied, and waxed very mighty. And it came to pass, because the midwives feared God, that he made them houses. And Pharaoh charged all his people, saying, Every son that is born ye shall cast into the river, and every daughter ye shall save alive' (Exodus 1:15-22).

Throughout the whole of this chapter, the eye of faith sees the hand of God working behind the scenes, secretly performing his will, graciously working out the salvation of his elect. Pharaoh was an absolute king in Egypt; but 'The king's heart is in the hand of the Lord, as rivers of water: he turneth it whithersoever he will' (Proverbs 21:1).

None of Pharaoh's subjects dared oppose his will. But here are two Hebrew midwives (Shiphrah and Puah) who defied the king's orders because they feared God. And the Lord God sustained them, protected them, and blessed them. C. H. MacIntosh wrote, 'The mightiest monarch in the world is powerless against God, and equally so against those who are identified with God and his people'. 'If God be for us, who can be against us?' (Romans 8:31).

**Lessons**

There are many things to be learned from this chapter, lessons we need to be constantly reminded of as we make our pilgrimage through this world. May God the Holy Spirit graciously inscribe them upon our hearts and constantly bring them to our memories. Here are some,

1. Satan and wicked men are utterly impotent before our God. Nothing and no one shall ever frustrate the purposes of God.
2. God's people, his church, his kingdom, and his cause are completely invincible!
3. The fear of God will deliver us from the fear of man, even as it did Shiphrah and Puah.
4. God always honours those who honour him, just as he dealt well with the midwives because they honoured him. Honour God and God will honour you.
5. Our God rules, everywhere, all the time, in all things!

## God Meant it for Good

Joseph was sold into Egypt by the wicked devices of his brothers; but he came there by the purpose of God 'to save much people alive'. Israel was forced to go to Egypt because of famine, famine the Lord God brought in order to accomplish his wise and good purpose and promise (Geneses 15:13, 14). I am continually filled with admiration, and made to repent of my horrid unbelief, when I pause to reflect upon these things. Whatever the deeds of men may be, even in wickedness and high-handed rebellion, they are subservient to God's everlasting purpose of grace and love. As Peter said on the day of Pentecost concerning Christ, 'Him, being delivered by the determinate counsel and foreknowledge of God, ye have taken, and by wicked hands have crucified and slain' (Acts 2:23), so it is now. Whatever men intend to do against us for evil is designed and brought to pass by God's purpose to do us good.

It is God's prerogative to bring good out of evil. Joseph's brothers sold him to the Ishmaelites. The Ishmaelites sold him to Potiphar. Potiphar cast him into prison. But all the while the Lord God was accomplishing his own gracious purpose. The wrath of man was working his praise. There are 'wheels within wheels' in the machinery of God's providence. He uses everything to perform his unsearchable designs. Potiphar's wife, Pharaoh's butler, Pharaoh's dreams, Pharaoh himself, the dungeon, the throne, the fetters, the royal signet, the famine, the order of Pharaoh to murder the baby boys born in Israel, the bricks, the mortar, and the taskmasters and tears, yes, even Satan himself, all were at God's sovereign disposal. All were instruments by which God wisely performed the good pleasure of his will.

Our great God, all-wise and almighty, is in all things performing his will, unfolding his counsels of redeeming love, and doing his people good. Infidels cannot see it. Religious will-worshippers despise the fact of it; but we rejoice to know it and pray for grace to walk in the light of blessed revelation all the days of our lives. 'The Judge of all the earth shall do right'. We rejoice to know he does it for the everlasting good of our souls. William Cowper wrote,

> God moves in a mysterious way,
> His wonders to perform;
> He plants His footsteps in the sea,
> And rides upon the storm.

> Ye fearful saints, fresh courage take;
> The clouds you so much dread,
> Are big with mercy and will break,
> With blessings on your head.

> Judge not the Lord by feeble sense,
> But trust Him for His grace.
> Behind the frowning providence,
> He hides a smiling face.

> His purposes will ripen fast,
> Unfolding every hour;
> The bud may have a bitter taste,
> But sweet will be the flower.

> Blind unbelief is sure to err
> And scan His works in vain;
> God is His own interpreter.
> And He will make it plain.

Surely, in the light of these facts, we ought to sing in the face of any evil, 'It is well with my soul'. Even the wrath of man is yoked to the chariot wheels of God's decrees. God give us grace to rest in his hands with childlike confidence, knowing 'the counsel of the Lord, that shall stand'.

# Chapter 3

# Pharaoh's Wisdom

'Now there arose up a new king over Egypt, which knew not Joseph. And he said unto his people, Behold, the people of the children of Israel are more and mightier than we: Come on, let us deal wisely with them; lest they multiply, and it come to pass, that, when there falleth out any war, they join also unto our enemies, and fight against us, and so get them up out of the land.'
(Exodus 1:8-10)

This was the wisdom of a man who not only 'knew not Joseph', but of one who knew not Joseph's God. Pharaoh's wisdom was but the wisdom of a fool. He was well educated. I do not doubt he was a brilliant man. But he was a fool. God was not in all his thoughts (Psalm 10:4). He had never learned to take God into his calculations. That is the case with every natural, unregenerate man. The unregenerate mind is a mind of complete darkness. The most brilliant reasonings of fallen men are rightly compared to blind men groping about in utter darkness. The worldly wise are just fools. Their greatest wisdom is vain folly.

It is absurd for us to be influenced by, or admire, the wisdom that has for its basis the total exclusion of our God and Saviour! To do so is to be influenced by and admire the wisdom of unbelief and atheism!

Pharaoh, according to the light of his darkness and the folly of his wisdom, calculated the children of Israel were multiplying rapidly, and so greatly increasing in strength, that they would soon take over the land. In fact, he stated this was already the case in verse 9. 'Behold, the people of the children of Israel are more and mightier than we.'

Dishonesty is another common trait of man's wisdom. By exaggerating the facts, Pharaoh knew he could more easily raise the hostilities of the Egyptians against the Israelites. He said, 'These immigrants will soon take over the country. If we do not do something, they will unite with our enemies and go to war against us.' With great sagacity, the king of Egypt took everything into consideration except God. Though he knew it not, that wrote 'ABSURD FOLLY' in capital letters across all his schemes. 'Let no man deceive himself. If any man among you seemeth to be wise in this world, let him become a fool, that he may be wise. For the wisdom of this world is foolishness with God. For it is written, He taketh the wise in their own craftiness. And again, The Lord knoweth the thoughts of the wise, that they are vain' (1 Corinthians 3:18-20). So all Pharaoh's wisdom was overturned. The wise man was taken in his own craftiness. 'Therefore they did set over them taskmasters to afflict them with their burdens. And they built for Pharaoh treasure cities, Pithom and Raamses. But the more the Egyptians afflicted them, the more Israel multiplied and grew. And they were grieved because of the children of Israel' (Exodus 1:11, 12). And so it shall ever be! Our God ever makes foolish the wisdom of this world (1 Corinthians 1:20).

### Infidels and Sceptics

The wisdom of Pharaoh is the wisdom of all infidels and sceptics. It is the wisdom of all unbelief. Human reason shuts God out and tries to keep him out of consideration. The very being of God is the death-blow to all scepticism and infidelity. Until God is acknowledged, the proud wisdom of infidelity and scepticism struts up and down the stage, displaying clever chains of 'logic', 'scientific' evidence, and 'irrefutable' facts, laughing at us poor, ignorant fools who believe God and his Word. If ever the thought of God's being is taken into consideration, the worldly wise man's 'logic', 'scientific' evidence, and 'irrefutable' facts all come falling to the ground like a house of cards.

Creation is no difficulty, if God is. The plagues in Egypt, the crossing of the Red Sea, manna falling from heaven, water flowing from a rock, and a rock following Israel through the desert for forty years are not difficulties, if God is. The virgin birth is no difficulty, if God is. Our Lord's miracles are not difficult, if God is. Redemption and righteousness by the God-man is no difficulty, if God is. The salvation of our souls by grace alone is no difficulty, if God is. Providence is no difficulty, if God is. The resurrection is no difficulty, if God is.

Like the Sadducees of our Lord's day, Pharaoh did 'greatly err' (Mark 12:27), not knowing God, his unalterable purpose, his sovereign power, or his sure word of promise. Pharaoh did not know that hundreds of years before he breathed the breath of mortal life, God's word and oath, 'two immutable things', had infallibly secured the full and glorious deliverance of Israel, the very people against whom Pharaoh now devised plans of annihilation in his great 'wisdom'. He was ignorant of God, of his purpose, and his promise. All his 'wise' thoughts and plans were founded on utter ignorance. He imagined vainly he could, by his 'wisdom', prevent the increase of those people of whom God had said, 'They shall be as the sand which is upon the sea-shore, and as the stars of heaven' (Genesis 22:17; 26:4). Pharaoh's ignorance of God made his 'wisdom' mere madness and folly.

### Sad Mistake

What a sad mistake it is for man to ignore God and his Word! Sooner or later, the fact of God's being, wisdom, and power will force themselves upon every man. Then, all their plans, and schemes, and hopes will come crashing down around them. C. H. MacIntosh wrote, 'All that is merely human, however solid, however brilliant, or however attractive, must fall into the cold grasp of death, and moulder in the dark, silent tomb'. 'Mortality' is engraved upon everything human. But God and his work are forever (Ecclesiastes 3:14). 'The counsel of the LORD standeth for ever, the thoughts of his heart to all generations ... His name shall endure for ever: his name shall be continued as long as the sun: and men shall be blessed in him: all nations shall call him blessed' (Psalm 33:11; 72:17).

All who set themselves up against the eternal God and devise their own way are fools. Pharaoh could as easily have stemmed the tide of the ocean as prevent the increase of Abraham's seed. Therefore, we read, though 'they did set over them taskmasters to afflict them with their burdens, ... the more they afflicted them, the more they multiplied and grew'.

## Our Peace

Thus it shall ever be. 'He that sitteth in the heavens shall laugh; the Lord shall have them in derision' (Psalm 2:4). Eternal confusion shall be inscribed upon all the opposition of men and devils to the will and purpose of our God. This is our peace. This gives sweet rest to the believing heart. Though everything around us appears so contrary to God's being, so contrary to his promises, and so contrary to faith in him, we are assured 'the wrath of man shall praise' him (Psalm 76:10).

But the moment we begin to look at anything from a mere rational standpoint, the moment we begin to act after the wisdom of the flesh, our hearts are troubled, our spirits sink, and we are cast down. We are urged to fix our eyes upon things above, not on things on the earth. 'If ye then be risen with Christ, seek those things which are above, where Christ sitteth on the right hand of God. Set your affection on things above, not on things on the earth. For ye are dead, and your life is hid with Christ in God' (Colossians 3:1-3). Let us, like the Apostle Paul, 'look not at the things which are seen, but at the things which are not seen: for the things which are seen are temporal; but the things which are not seen are eternal' (2 Corinthians 4:18). 'Rest in the LORD, and wait patiently for him: fret not thyself because of him who prospereth in his way, because of the man who bringeth wicked devices to pass' (Psalm 37:7).

The children of Israel only 'looked at the things that are seen', and it made their lives 'bitter with hard bondage' (v. 14). They saw Pharaoh's wrath, stern taskmasters, heavy afflictions, hard bondage, the mortar and the bricks. How different things might have been for them, even in such hard circumstances, had they looked 'not at the things which are seen, but at the things which are not seen'. If only they had looked stedfastly upon God's eternal purpose, his unfailing promise, and the rapidly approaching dawn of the day of salvation that was at hand, such blessed realities would have made their bitter cup sweet.

## Faith

It is faith and faith alone, God-given faith, God-wrought faith, faith in Christ our God and Saviour, our Lord and Redeemer, that looks beyond the temporal to the eternal. We are, right now, 'heirs of God and joint-heirs with Jesus Christ' (Romans 8:17). 'We walk by faith, not by sight'

(2 Corinthians 5:7). We are the children of God, heaven born citizens of another world (1 John 3:1, 2).

For now, we must live in, and pass through, Egypt. But we are Christ's freemen. In spirit, we are in the heavenly Canaan. With the eye of faith trusting Christ our Saviour, trusting God manifest in the flesh. By the power and grace of the Holy Spirit we set our hearts upon 'unseen things above'. Mounting up with wings as eagles, let us look down upon this time-world with disdain, where sin, and death, and darkness appear to reign. Let us be 'looking for the mercy of our Lord Jesus Christ unto eternal life' (Jude 21). Oh, that God the Holy Spirit might ever give us simple child-like faith to sit beside the pure and ever-flowing fountain of living waters, drinking in those deep and refreshing draughts that lift the fainting spirit and inspire confidence in him!

**Be Wise**
Now, let me ask you a question. Would you be wise? I mean truly wise. If you would be truly wise, if you would have spiritual wisdom, wisdom with which to discern all things, you must become a fool. 'Let no man deceive himself. If any man among you seemeth to be wise in this world, let him become a fool, that he may be wise' (1 Corinthians 3:18).

This world, all the world, especially the religious world, counts the gospel of Christ foolishness. If you would be wise, you must count the wisdom of the world foolishness, and trust Christ alone as your God and Saviour. If you can, God has given you 'wisdom that is from above' as James describes it (James 3:17).

**A Contrast**
Pharaoh was a man of great earthly wisdom; but his wisdom was folly. Moses was a man the whole world would count a fool. He turned his back on the riches of Egypt, and chose to suffer affliction with the people of God, because he believed God. But Moses was truly wise.

The natural man, though he may be very religious and learned, is utterly ignorant of all things spiritual. That is to say, he is truly ignorant of all things, understanding nothing. The man or woman who is born of God is taught of God. Having faith in Christ, the believer has 'an unction from the Holy One and knoweth all things' (1 John 2:20; 3:20). Let me show you what a great contrast there is between the wisdom God gives and the wisdom of the world (1 Corinthians 2:1-16).

In preaching the gospel we preach salvation by the crucified Christ, and do so in utter simplicity, 'That your faith should not stand in the wisdom of men, but in the power of God' (vv. 1-5). Yet, we preach that which is true wisdom (vv. 6-9). Now, look at the contrast between the wisdom of this world and the wisdom that God gives.

'But God hath revealed them unto us by his Spirit: for the Spirit searcheth all things, yea, the deep things of God. For what man knoweth the things of a man, save the spirit of man which is in him? even so the things of God knoweth no man, but the Spirit of God. Now we have received, not the spirit of the world, but the spirit which is of God; that we might know the things that are freely given to us of God. Which things also we speak, not in the words which man's wisdom teacheth, but which the Holy Ghost teacheth; comparing spiritual things with spiritual. But the natural man receiveth not the things of the Spirit of God: for they are foolishness unto him: neither can he know them, because they are spiritually discerned. But he that is spiritual judgeth all things, yet he himself is judged of no man. For who hath known the mind of the Lord, that he may instruct him? But we have the mind of Christ' (1 Corinthians 2:10-16).

There are several things stated here that make stark distinctions between the wisdom of the world and the wisdom of faith. Natural wisdom is just that; natural, carnal wisdom. Ours is revealed wisdom (v. 10). Natural wisdom cannot receive the things of God. God-given wisdom knows 'the things that are freely given to us of God' (vv. 11, 12, 14). Natural wisdom is communicated from person to person. Spiritual wisdom can be communicated only by the Spirit of God (v. 13). Natural wisdom, appears to understand (judge and discern) all things, but really understands nothing. 'He that is spiritual judgeth all things' (v. 15). Natural wisdom knows nothing of 'the deep things of God' (v. 10). Bible history it can grasp. Bible facts, religious creeds, and religious tradition it can assimilate. But it can never grasp anything taught in the Word of God. 'But we have the mind of Christ' (v. 16).

**Specifics**
Those general statements might be easily misunderstood. Let me show you some specifics. The natural man makes everything spiritual to be carnal. He thinks giving is about money, time, or labour, and is motivated to do it by his own carnal lusts. But giving begins with and

is but a reflection of faith in Christ, the giving of ourselves to him (Mark 12:44; 2 Corinthians 8:5), being motivated by gratitude and love (Mark 14:1-10; 2 Corinthians 8:7-9). The natural man thinks prayer is an act performed by his lips; but prayer is an act of the heart. He thinks prayer is asking God to gratify his lusts; but it is seeking to bow to the will of God. He thinks worship is nothing but 'bodily exercise', not knowing it is heart exercise. The natural man vainly imagines good works are conformity to moral, religious traditions. He has no clue what good works really are: works of faith, brotherly love, and forgiveness. The surest thing that can be said about good works is this: Those who think they have them do not; and those who perform them are fully convinced that they haven't (Matthew 25:31-46). The believer understands that all things relating to faith in Christ, the worship of God, and service to God, all things relating to godliness, are spiritual (Philippians 3:3).

There are many who know Christ after the flesh, by natural wisdom. Those who are taught of God know him after the Spirit (2 Corinthians 5:16-21). We know 'if any man be in Christ, he is a new creature'. We know 'all things are of God'. We know God has made him sin for us, who knew no sin. We know all who trust Christ are made the righteousness of God in him. All men, by nature, assume they must and can make some contribution toward salvation and acceptance with God (Proverbs 16:25). All are will-worshippers (Colossians 2:23). We know 'Salvation is of the Lord!' The wisdom of man understands that righteousness is something we must do. The wisdom of God teaches us righteousness is something Christ has done for us, and gives to us by his grace (Romans 3:23).

The wisdom of man thinks God's requirements are outward. We understand that everything God requires is inward (Micah 6:6-8). They think godliness is external. We know it is internal. 'The sacrifices of God are a broken spirit; a broken and a contrite heart, O God, thou wilt not despise.' God requires a whole burnt offering that cannot be marred, even the Lamb of God.

'Wherewith shall I come before the LORD, and bow myself before the high God? shall I come before him with burnt offerings, with calves of a year old? Will the LORD be pleased with thousands of rams, or with ten thousands of rivers of oil? shall I give my firstborn for my transgression, the fruit of my body for the sin of my soul? He hath showed thee, O man, what is good; and what doth the LORD require of thee, but to do justly, and to love mercy, and to walk humbly with thy God?' (Micah 6:6-8).

This is the good thing the Lord requires of man. God only requires what he gives; and he gives all he requires. The vast majority of men writing on these verses, or using them from the pulpit, tell us that God requires all men to do that which is just, right, merciful, and humble in all things regarding men and God. This we are told is the essence of all moral and spiritual uprightness. I have not so learned Christ! Have you? The Prophet Micah is not teaching us God requires a work to be performed by us in order to be accepted of him. He is teaching exactly the opposite. The requirement that we do justly, love mercy, and walk humbly is distinctly said to be 'with thy God', with an eye to him, with the eye of faith fixed upon him.

We do justly with our God when we confess we justly deserve his eternal wrath, by reason of our many sins (Psalm 51:4). We love mercy with our God when we love the Lord Jesus Christ, who is the Mercy promised in the Scriptures (Luke 1:72). All mercy is found in his blood and righteousness. He is 'the mercy' God promised (Deuteronomy 7:12). The person who honestly confesses his sin to God can and does say with David, 'I trust in the mercy of God forever and ever' (Psalm 52:8). And we walk humbly with our God when we walk before him as sinners, confessing our sins and looking to Christ alone for salvation (1 John 1:9; 1 Corinthians 1:30; John 16:8-11). All this bounteous grace and mercy comes to us by the omnipotent power and irresistible grace of God the Holy Spirit.

It all comes to this: faith in Christ is the fruit of the Spirit, the gift and operation of God the Holy Spirit. If you trust Christ, you do justly, and love mercy, and walk humbly with thy God. If you trust Christ, you are born of God, redeemed, justified, called, and sanctified in Christ. Faith in Christ is the fruit and evidence of eternal life bestowed upon you and wrought in you, 'not by might, nor by power, but by my Spirit, saith the Lord of hosts' (1 John 5:1, 9-13; John 3:36; Hebrews 11:1, 2).

# Chapter 4

# Our Pain And God's Purpose

'And he said unto his people, Behold, the people of the children of Israel are more and mightier than we: Come on, let us deal wisely with them; lest they multiply, and it come to pass, that, when there falleth out any war, they join also unto our enemies, and fight against us, and so get them up out of the land. Therefore they did set over them taskmasters to afflict them with their burdens. And they built for Pharaoh treasure cities, Pithom and Raamses. But the more they afflicted them, the more they multiplied and grew. And they were grieved because of the children of Israel. And the Egyptians made the children of Israel to serve with rigour: And they made their lives bitter with hard bondage, in morter, and in brick, and in all manner of service in the field: all their service, wherein they made them serve, was with rigour.'
(Exodus 1:9-14)

After coming into the land of Egypt, the children of Israel enjoyed, for about thirty years, a time of great abundance and prosperity. I say that this time of peace and prosperity lasted about thirty years, because the Lord God told Abraham that the Egyptians would 'afflict them four hundred years' (Genesis 15:13; Acts 7:6). Yet, we are told in Exodus 12:40 that 'the sojourning of the children of Israel, who dwelt in Egypt' was 'four hundred and thirty years'. So their time in Egypt was 430 years; and 400 of those years were years of bondage and affliction, pain and suffering, toil and bitterness as strangers in a hostile land. About 30 years after they first came into Egypt, 'there arose a new king over Egypt, which knew not Joseph' (v. 8); and Israel's woes began. We read about them in verses 9-14.

God promised his blessings upon the children of Israel. In his covenant with Abraham he swore he would drive out their enemies and give them the land of Canaan, making them possessors of that land flowing with milk and honey. And all of this was to be done as a typical picture of the redemption and salvation of God's elect by Christ.

In light of that fact, in light of the fact God had revealed his purpose of goodness and grace to the chosen people, I cannot help asking some questions. Why did God send Israel into Egypt? Why did he leave them there for 430 years? Why did he allow the Egyptians to treat them with barbaric cruelty for 400 years? Why did the Lord cause his people to suffer so much pain for so long, before fulfilling his promise and bringing them out by the mighty hand of his grace?

Find the answer to those questions, and you will get some understanding of God's wise and adorable providence. You will be able to see and see clearly that the pains we experience in this world by God's providence and grace are pains brought upon us by God's eternal purpose of grace toward us in Christ, by the purpose of him who 'worketh all things after the counsel of his own will that we should be to the praise of his glory, who first trusted in Christ'. I have searched the Scriptures and have found six answers to those questions.

1. God brought all of Israel into Egypt by one man, because he had purposed and promised to bring them out of Egypt by one man, to the praise of his glory.

How did the chosen seed, the covenant children of Abraham get into the mess they were in in Egypt? The answer is plainly stated in Exodus 1:1. 'Now these are the names of the children of Israel, which came into Egypt; every man and his household came with Jacob'.

'Every man and his household came with Jacob.' They came into this land of bondage and sorrow with their father Jacob. He was the one who brought them there. Note how in this place the Holy Spirit uses his name 'Jacob', not 'Israel'. Every time he does so throughout the Scriptures, there is a reason. 'Jacob' speaks of the natural man, fallen and sinful. It means 'supplanter'. 'Israel' speaks of the spiritual man. It is the new name God gave to Jacob, the new name given to all the sons of Jacob in free and sovereign grace in Christ. 'Israel' means 'God prevails'. Israel is a prince with God. The children of 'God prevails' were brought into Egyptian bondage by one sinful man. The spiritual significance is obvious. You and I were brought into the place of spiritual bondage and death with our father Adam. 'Wherefore, as by one man sin entered into the world, and death by sin; and so death passed upon all men, for that all have sinned' (Romans 5:12). And this was not accidental. Israel was brought into Egyptian bondage because God had purposed and promised, long before any of those who came into bondage were ever born, that he would bring them out by a mighty deliverer, in justice and grace to the praise of his glory. God's promise to Abraham was, 'That nation whom they shall serve will I judge: and afterward shall they come out with great substance' (Genesis 15:14). All this was connected with a sacrifice required, provided, and accepted by God (Genesis 15:8-11), and a covenant made with Abraham (Genesis 15:17-21).

So it has been with us. The sin and fall of Adam, and of all the human race in him, was no accident. It came to pass because God our Father, before ever the world was made, purposed to save his people by another Representative Man, by another Substitute, even his own dear Son, the Lord Jesus Christ, the Lamb of God, the Sacrifice he required, provided, and accepted, with whom he made for us an everlasting covenant, ordered in all things and sure, 'to the praise of the glory of his grace, wherein he hath made us accepted in the Beloved' (Romans 5:12-21).

The only reason Egypt existed was to provide a place for God to show his grace to Israel. The only reason God raised up Pharaoh was to display his sovereign power and goodness in saving his people (Romans 9:13-18). So it is with the entire world. The world is the cradle God created to receive his children, the house he created to provide for their carnal needs, the stage he created to display his wisdom, goodness, grace and glory in saving his people by his Son, for the praise of his glory.

2. God brought Israel into bondage in Egypt to show his great displeasure against sin.

The thing that Joseph's brethren did in selling him into bondage was precisely according to God's purpose. But the holy Lord God shows us repeatedly that though he uses the evil devices of men to accomplish his purpose (Psalm 76:10), he neither forces the wicked to do evil, nor approves of the evil done. Every man is responsible for his wicked works, and must suffer the consequences of them, either personally or in Christ, the sinner's Substitute.

Joseph's brethren sold him into bondage because they intended to do him evil; but God used it to perform good (Genesis 50:20). David murdered Uriah and took his wife; and his deeds displeased the Lord; but God used his evil deeds to bring his Son into the world. It was through David and Bathsheba that Christ came into the world. The Jews delivered our Saviour up to be crucified, performing their own wicked wills; but the Lord God used their deeds of wickedness to accomplish his purpose of grace in redeeming our souls (Acts 2:23).

3. The Lord God brought Israel into Egyptian bondage for 400 years, because, as he had told Abraham, he would not fulfil his promise to give Israel the land of Canaan, thereby destroying the Amorites, until they had filled their iniquity.

'But in the fourth generation they shall come hither again: for the iniquity of the Amorites is not yet full' (Genesis 15:16).

God told Abraham his seed should sojourn in a strange land for four hundred years, but in the fourth generation they would come out and take possession of Canaan, because only then would the iniquity of the Amorites be filled up. The time for God to deal with the Amorites in judgment was not fully ripe; their iniquities had not reached the bound God had appointed, until Israel had been in bondage for 400 years.

Divine judgment is always just. That fact is set before us throughout the Scriptures. God would not destroy the Amorites (vessels of wrath) in his wrath until they were 'fitted for destruction' by their wickedness. The Spirit of God would not allow the gospel to be preached to the Gentiles until the Jews had filled up their sins (1 Thessalonians 2:16). The Lord Jesus says to the reprobate, as he did to the Pharisees of his day, 'Fill ye up the measure of your fathers' (Matthew 23:32).

Ed Dennett once said, 'Whatever the actings of men in wickedness and high-handed rebellion, they are made subservient to the establishment of the Divine counsels of grace and love ... Even the wrath of man is yoked to the chariot wheel of God's decrees.'

4. Israel was brought down to Egypt and remained in that land of darkness, bondage, and bitterness for 430 years, because the Lord God was preparing for himself a people.

The Lord God gave the land to the chosen nation back in Genesis 15. But Abraham had no children to possess it. And the land of Canaan was a huge, rich land. It would take a huge nation to possess it. So the Lord gave Abraham a son, and through his son seventy more sons. And during the next 430 years, he gave him millions of sons, and made them willing and ready to take possession of Canaan at the appointed time.

So it is with us. All the boundless blessings of grace and glory were given to us in Christ before the world began (Ephesians 1:3-6). The New Jerusalem is a huge city to be inhabited and possessed by a multitude that no man can number. And it is written of our Lord Jesus Christ, 'A seed shall serve him; it shall be accounted to the Lord for a generation' (Psalm 22:30). Our God is here preparing for himself a people. When the number of his elect has been fulfilled, deliverance will come! He is not slack concerning his promise. He is not willing that any of his chosen perish; and they shall not perish (2 Peter 3:9). Our God is preparing his people for their prepared place. He prepares his elect to possess heavenly glory by redemption, by regeneration, and by the resurrection.

5. The Lord God left Israel in Egypt for 430 years so that he might display his sovereign goodness and grace in delivering them.

The deliverance of Israel from Egyptian bondage typified and foreshadowed the redemption of sinners by Christ. The land of Egypt vividly portrays the place and the state of God's people in this world. Here we are, by nature, in a place and state of darkness, rebellion, and death, in total opposition to God. But as God stepped into that place and brought Israel out, so he steps into this world and delivers the objects of his love, snatching us as brands from the burning, 'to the praise of the glory of his grace'.

6. And the Lord God left Israel, toiling in bondage in Egypt, to suffer hatred, oppression, and bitterness to teach us something about our trials in this world.

Their bitter experiences in Egypt and many trials in the wilderness were designed by God to make them long for the land that flowed with milk and honey, and to make that fair and happy land more glorious, and them more thankful, once they took possession of it. Therefore, the Lord God graciously, wisely, and with deliberate measure used the malice of Pharaoh and the Egyptians to make his people 'serve with rigor. And they made their lives bitter with hard bondage'.

## Holy Spirit Conviction

When the appointed time of love has come, when the Lord God will deliver chosen, redeemed sinners from the kingdom of this world and translate them into the kingdom of his dear Son, he begins his work of grace by making their lives bitter. By providence and by grace, he graciously, sweetly, forces them and makes them willing in the day of his power to come to Christ, trusting him. Our God knows how to bring sinners down, that he may lift them up (Psalm 107:1-43; Lamentations 3:1-32).

## The Believer's Trials

After saving us by his grace, the believer continually lives in this world; and the longer we live in this body of flesh, the more we find this to be a land of bondage and bitterness, from which we long to be free. And that is precisely the intention of our God in sending trials (2 Corinthians 4:17).

Whenever I begin to think my burden is too heavy, my pains are too many, my trials are too great, and my sorrows are too much to bear, I try to remember that these are but my 'light afflictions'. They are 'light afflictions' when I recall what my blessed Saviour endured to save me (Lamentations 1:12). They are 'light afflictions' when I remember what I deserve! They are 'light afflictions' when I think about the things others have suffered and are suffering. They are 'light afflictions' when I realize the glory awaiting me (1 Peter 1:3-9).

Unto us are given 'exceeding great and precious promises' and these are the promises of God who cannot lie. 'Why art thou cast down, O my soul? Why art thou disquieted in me? Hope thou in God' (Psalm 42:11). Rest, then, my soul, with implicit confidence on the sure Word, forever settled in heaven, of the Lord God, my Saviour! 'For I reckon that the sufferings of this present time are not worthy to be compared with the glory which shall be revealed in us' (Romans 8:18).

How happy we should be to give thanks to our God for every pain, as well as for every pleasing thing, because both are performed by our God, according to his good purpose of grace; and by these things he is working for us a far more exceeding and eternal weight of glory than we have ever imagined.

# Chapter 5

## Shiphrah And Puah

'And the king of Egypt spake to the Hebrew midwives, of which the name of the one was Shiphrah, and the name of the other Puah: And he said, When ye do the office of a midwife to the Hebrew women, and see them upon the stools; if it be a son, then ye shall kill him: but if it be a daughter, then she shall live. But the midwives feared God, and did not as the king of Egypt commanded them, but saved the men children alive. And the king of Egypt called for the midwives, and said unto them, Why have ye done this thing, and have saved the men children alive? And the midwives said unto Pharaoh, because the Hebrew women are not as the Egyptian women; for they are lively, and are delivered ere the midwives come in unto them. Therefore God dealt well with the midwives: and the people multiplied, and waxed very mighty. And it came to pass, because the midwives feared God, that he made them houses. And Pharaoh charged all his people, saying, every son that is born ye shall cast into the river, and every daughter ye shall save alive.'
(Exodus 1:15-22)

In the Scriptures there are several examples showing us that faith in Christ, obedience to our God, and love for his people have often required that those who feared God deceive men. And the act of deception is set before us in such cases as an act of faith. One such act of faith is well known. When the spies came into Jericho, Rahab the harlot hid them. When the king of Jericho sent his men to Rahab's inn to get the spies, she said, 'Those men did come into the inn; but I didn't know who they were. They left just a little while ago. If you hurry, I am sure you can catch them.' Then she secretly let the spies down by a rope and sent them away (Joshua 2). Trusting the crucified Son of God to save her, she saved the Hebrew spies and her own house.

I realize some reprobate men seek to use Rahab's behaviour as an excuse for their own self-serving dishonesty. Others, self-righteous moralists, look upon what Rahab did as an enigma, and pass it off as something that cannot be explained, but that her behaviour can never be justified. They tell us that, though she may have acted in faith, Rahab should not have lied. She should have told the truth and trusted God to work things out as he would. But God the Holy Spirit tells us that what Rahab did was an act of faith in Christ, exactly the same as the faith by which Abel worshipped God, Noah built the ark, Abraham received Isaac as one raised from the dead, Moses refused to be called the son of Pharaoh's daughter and led Israel across the Red Sea, and David slew Goliath (Hebrews 11:31).

Just as Rahab believed God, and by her act of faith delivered both Jericho, and ultimately the land of Canaan into the hands of Israel, Moses tells us about two women God graciously used, who by their faith in Christ saved his life, brought Israel out of Egypt, and were instruments by which he brought our Saviour into this world. Like Rahab, these two women were instruments in the hands of God, whose faith and faithfulness God used to accomplish our salvation in Christ. We who now know Christ in the blessed experience of his saving grace owe them much. Were it not for these two women and their acts of faith, we could never have been redeemed. Let their names forever be honoured. 'The name of the one was Shiphrah (fair, beautiful), and the name of the other Puah (splendid, glittering)'. Let us look at these two women, singularly honoured of God, and see what we can learn from them about faith in Christ.

### Pharaoh's Determination

Pharaoh was determined to destroy Israel; and Pharaoh was no ordinary man, or even ordinary king. Pharaoh considered himself a god, and was looked upon by his people as a god. He was a little tyrant, who thought he was a god, and treated his subjects with such cruelty that, whether they wanted to or not, they obeyed him as their god. When he gave an order, he expected it to be obeyed; and it was. His orders to Shiphrah and Puah were crystal clear (vv. 15, 16).

'And the king of Egypt spake to the Hebrew midwives, of which the name of the one was Shiphrah, and the name of the other Puah: And he said, When ye do the office of a midwife to the Hebrew women, and see them upon the stools; if it be a son, then ye shall kill him: but if it be a daughter, then she shall live'.

Pharaoh did not just represent the law; he was the law. To defy him was to court the full force of his fury. When he told these Hebrew midwives to murder every male baby born among the children of Israel, they understood his intent was to destroy the nation God had chosen. And they understood that if they did not do as he commanded them, they would suffer the consequences.

I have no doubt there were many other midwives who served the women of Israel. It would take more than two to deliver all the babies of several million women. So, I presume Shiphrah and Puah were the two women who ran the business of delivering babies. So Pharaoh gave his orders to the two women responsible for the work.

But there is more here than Pharaoh's rage against a people he feared might destroy him. Pharaoh was but an instrument by which Satan hoped to prevent the Son of God, the Seed of woman, our Lord Jesus Christ, from coming to redeem us. What we have here is a vivid picture of Satan's rage against Christ and his people, Satan's rage against the woman's Seed, by whom God Almighty has purposed to destroy him (Genesis 3:15). If he could, Satan would destroy God himself. He tried to destroy Christ when he inspired Cain to murder his brother Abel, and again when he inspired Pharaoh to order the murder of the male children of Israel, and again when he inspired Herod to give the same order hundreds of years later (Matthew 2:16). Were it possible for him to do so, the fiend of hell would destroy every one of God's elect as soon as they are born (Revelation 12:4, 5).

Let us never imagine that Satan's rage has ended. It has not. He still uses men, often people in powerful places, ever seeking to destroy the church of God. He stalks the earth as a roaring lion, ever seeking to devour the spiritual seed of Christ. Therefore, the Holy Spirit teaches us to ever cast our care upon God our Saviour, who is able to and will deliver us from the enemy (1 Peter 5:6-11).

53

Have you ever thought about what the result would have been had Pharaoh succeeded in murdering all the male babies born to the Israelites in Egypt? The chosen line through which the promised Redeemer was to come would have been destroyed. If all the male children of the Hebrews were destroyed, Boaz would never have appeared, Jesse would never have been born, David could never have drawn breath, David's Son the Lord Jesus Christ, would never have come into the world, and redemption could never have been accomplished. But such a supposition can never be more than that, just a supposition. When Satan, Pharaoh, Herod, and all the nations of the earth combine in opposition to the purpose of God, the Lord God, 'he that sitteth in the heavens', roars with laughter and says, 'the counsel of the Lord, that shall stand'. He declares, 'Surely as I have thought, so shall it come to pass; and as I have purposed, so shall it stand.'

**Satan Foiled**
Satan's schemes were once more foiled and Egypt's god, like all the gods of men, was frustrated. How? By what means could the most powerful forces in the world be defeated? How could the plans of the mightiest king in the world be overturned? How could a people so hated as the Hebrews were by the Egyptians be delivered from such cruel hatred? Read verse 17, and you will see. 'But the midwives feared God, and did not as the king of Egypt commanded them, but saved the men children alive.'

The fear of God delivered those two women from the fear of man. Because they believed God, they could not and would not obey the king's command, regardless of cost. 'Behold, the fear of the Lord, that is wisdom' (Job 28:28). 'The fear of the LORD is the beginning of knowledge' (Proverbs 1:7).

Charles Buck defined the fear of God as, 'That holy disposition or gracious habit formed in the soul by the Holy Spirit, whereby we are inclined to obey all God's commands, and evidences itself: (1) By a dread of his displeasure. (2) Desire of his favour. (3) Regard for his excellencies. (4) Submission to his will. (5) Gratitude for his benefits. (6) Sincerity in his worship. (7) Conscientious obedience to his commands (Proverbs 8:13; Job 28:28).'

When God the Holy Spirit here tells us that these women 'feared God', he is not telling us they were afraid of God. They might well be afraid of Pharaoh; but they 'feared God'. That is simply another way of saying they worshipped God, they believed God (Psalm 31:19; 115:11; Job 1:1; 13:15; 19:25).

**Faith's Acts**
Read verse 17 again, and read verses 18 and 19 with it. I want you to see, and see clearly, that these two great women acted according to their fear of God.

'But the midwives feared God, and did not as the king of Egypt commanded them, but saved the men children alive. And the king of Egypt called for the midwives, and said unto them, Why have ye done this thing, and have saved the men children alive? And the midwives said unto Pharaoh, because the Hebrew women are not as the Egyptian women; for they are lively, and are delivered ere the midwives come in unto them.'

Faith is not merely believing facts about God. Faith is not merely believing facts revealed by God. Faith involves life. Faith is the fear of God by which we live. Faith involves acting upon God's revelation, acting upon what we believe. Here, the Holy Spirit tells us that these Hebrew midwives performed three great acts of faith.

'They did not as the king of Egypt commanded them.' That is, itself, a remarkable thing, showing great confidence in God. But, the next line tells us of a greater, more bold act of faith. They not only did not kill the babies, they 'saved the men children alive'. Then they did more. Because they believed God, they lied to Pharaoh.

Because they believed God, Shiphrah and Puah lied to Pharaoh. They did not lie to protect themselves. They did not lie for personal gain. They did not lie from any self or personal interest. Shiphrah and Puah lied to Pharaoh as Abraham did to Abimelech, and Rahab did to the king of Jericho, because they believed God. They trusted Christ as their Saviour and Redeemer, believing that he would and must come as Abraham's promised Seed (Galatians 3:13, 14). They believed God would fulfil his covenant promise, deliver his people, and send his Son to redeem them, and he would do it through Abraham's Seed. They believed all the blessedness, and all the blessings of grace, salvation, eternal life, and everlasting glory are to be found only in that Blessed One God had promised (1 Corinthians 1:30; Ephesians 1:3-6). Their faith in Jesus Christ and their love for him delivered them from the fear

55

of the king, and enabled them to overcome the world (1 John 4:4, 18, 19; 5:4, 5).

It is written, 'Faith worketh by love'. And these two women lied to Pharaoh, hazarding their own lives, because their faith in Christ caused them to love his people (1 John 5:1). Shiphrah and Puah risked their lives for you and me. They lied to Pharaoh because, loving Christ, they loved us, the members of his body, their brothers and sisters in Christ, looking upon us as one with Christ. Let us never forget their names! The name of one was Shiphrah. She was fair and beautiful. The name of the other was Puah. She was splendid and glittering.

I think it significant that the first time the name of God is mentioned in the book of Exodus is here in verse 17. His sovereignty is evident in every verse and every event. But Moses does not mention his name until he tells us about these two Hebrew midwives who 'feared God'. Why? Because the Holy Spirit here holds them before us as examples of faith, calling upon you and me to believe God. Whom will we serve, God or Pharaoh? Where is our confidence, in God or in Pharaoh? Whom do we fear, God or Pharaoh? Who is sovereign, God or Pharaoh? Shiphrah and Puah said, 'As for me and my house, we will serve the Lord'.

**Highly Honoured**

Just in case you are wondering whether I have accurately interpreted what these women did, read verses 20 and 21. Here we are specifically told that God highly honoured Shiphrah and Puah for their great deeds of faith. He promises, 'Him that honoureth me I will honour', and he always does.

'Therefore God dealt well with the midwives: and the people multiplied, and waxed very mighty. And it came to pass, because the midwives feared God, that he made them houses.'

The Lord honoured them in two ways. First, he used these two believing women to increase his kingdom. 'The people multiplied, and waxed very mighty.' What an honour that is (1 Corinthians 1:26-29; 2 Corinthians 4:7). And, because they feared God, 'he made them houses'. As Rachel and Leah are said to have built the house of Israel by their fruitful wombs (Ruth 4:11), God caused the midwives wombs to be fruitful. Our God is not unrighteous to forget any work and labour of love performed in his name and for his people (Hebrews 6:10). John Trapp wrote, 'God is a liberal paymaster: and his retributions are more than bountiful.' Therefore, 'be ye stedfast and unmoveable, always abounding in the work of the Lord, forasmuch as ye know that your labour is not in vain in the Lord' (1 Corinthians 15:58).

## Blessed Consolation

What a blessed source of consolation this whole chapter should be to our souls! God's purpose is sure. All the forces of earth and hell combined shall neither alter it, nor thwart it, nor hinder it! 'Hath he said, and shall he not do it? or hath he spoken, and shall he not make it good?' (Numbers 23:19). The creature shall never resist or hinder the will of the Creator! 'If God be for us, who can be against us?' It is written, 'There is no wisdom nor understanding nor counsel against the LORD' (Proverbs 21:30).

All that is recorded in this chapter is designed to teach us to patiently wait upon the Lord in all things. His promises are sure, though he appears (to our feeble apprehensions) to perform them ever so slowly. Abraham's seed did not seem to increase for a long, long time. God did not bring Israel out of Egypt for 430 years. But he brought them out, and brought them out at the best time and in the best way.

> Ye fearful saints, fresh courage take,
> The clouds ye so much dread,
> Are big with mercy and shall break,
> With blessings on your head!

The promises of our God are 'all yea and amen in Christ Jesus', 'The Lord is not slack concerning his promise, as some men count slackness'. The 'vision is for an appointed time; it shall come, it will not tarry'.

## Enmity Still

Let me show you one more thing. Though the Lord God had foiled his plans by the faith of two insignificant midwives, Pharaoh hardened his heart still more against the children of Israel, commanding all his people to drown every male child born in Israel in the Nile River. 'And Pharaoh charged all his people, saying, Every son that is born ye shall cast into the river, and every daughter ye shall save alive' (v. 22).

The enmity God put between the seed of the serpent and the woman's Seed will never cease, or even diminish, but only increases, so long as the world shall stand. The offense of the cross has not ceased, and will not cease until Christ comes again. We must never expect it to be otherwise. We must never be deluded into thinking it has ceased.

Just as Pharaoh, representing the political powers of the world, wanted nothing less than the destruction of God's church in Egypt, the political powers of this world are now, always have been, and always will be bent upon the destruction of God's church in their midst. Just as Pharaoh, representing the gods and religion of this world, wanted nothing less than the total destruction of Israel, the religion of this world (all freewill, legalistic, works religion) wants nothing less than the total destruction of Christ and his kingdom.

Then, just as surely as the Lord God caused Israel to triumph over Egypt, saving all the elect nation by his mighty hand and outstretched arm, the Lord our God always 'giveth' us the victory through our Lord Jesus Christ, and shall cause us to triumph over all our foes, saving all his elect by his mighty hand and stretched-out arm, to the praise of the glory of his matchless grace!

# Chapter 6

## The Birth Of Moses

'And there went a man of the house of Levi, and took to wife a daughter of Levi. And the woman conceived, and bare a son: and when she saw him that he was a goodly child, she hid him three months. And when she could not longer hide him, she took for him an ark of bulrushes, and daubed it with slime and with pitch, and put the child therein; and she laid it in the flags by the river's brink. And his sister stood afar off, to wit what would be done to him. And the daughter of Pharaoh came down to wash herself at the river; and her maidens walked along by the river's side; and when she saw the ark among the flags, she sent her maid to fetch it. And when she had opened it, she saw the child: and, behold, the babe wept. And she had compassion on him, and said, This is one of the Hebrews' children. Then said his sister to Pharaoh's daughter, Shall I go and call to thee a nurse of the Hebrew women, that she may nurse the child for thee? And Pharaoh's daughter said to her, Go. And the maid went and called the child's mother. And Pharaoh's daughter said unto her, Take this child away, and nurse it for me, and I will give thee thy wages. And the woman took the child, and nursed it. And the child grew, and she brought him unto Pharaoh's daughter, and he became her son. And she called his name Moses: and she said, Because I drew him out of the water.'
(Exodus 2:1-10)

In these ten verses God the Holy Spirit has preserved for us the historic account of Moses' birth. Here, he shows us how God raised up the man by whom he would deliver Israel. This passage gives us a good picture of the way God always works in providence; noiselessly accomplishing his eternal purpose, and secretly preparing his instruments for their appointed work. Then, at the time he has appointed, he makes bare his mighty arm and performs his wondrous work, displaying his presence, power, and glory in the salvation of chosen sinners to the praise of his glory and the confusion of the whole world.

We do not have to guess what the spiritual instruction of these ten verses might be. God the Holy Spirit has given us that in Hebrews 11:23. 'By faith Moses, when he was born, was hid three months of his parents, because they saw he was a proper child; and they were not afraid of the king's commandment.'

## Moses' Birth

'And there went a man of the house of Levi, and took to wife a daughter of Levi. And the woman conceived, and bare a son: and when she saw him that he was a goodly child, she hid him three months' (vv. 1, 2).

What a natural, beautiful, tender scene this is! Our hearts immediately enter into the joy and concern of this Jewish mother. Pharaoh had commanded that every son that was born in Israel be cast into the river (Exodus 1:22). But what mother could endure such cruelty upon her new born child? All the affections of her heart must have revolted at the thought of the tyrant's decree. But how could she, a poor, feeble woman of a despised race, resist the will of an absolute monarch? We have read the answer already. Both she, her name was Jochebed, which means 'Jehovah is Glory' (Exodus 6:20), and her husband, Amram, whose name means 'exalted people' (Exodus 6:18) believed God (Hebrews 11:23).

Not only was the king's decree repulsive to Moses' parents, more importantly, it would have required them to wilfully defy their God. Trusting him, they defied the king and overcame what must have been great fear of his wrath and power. By faith they hid their child, the child God had given them, for three months. Believing God, who never leaves nor forsakes those who trust in him, they were not confounded.

With the eye of faith fixed upon God our Saviour, they dared to disobey Pharaoh's wicked command; and they were fearless of the consequences. Like Shadrach, Meshach, and Abednego in Daniel's day, they believed the God whom they served was able to deliver them out of the king's hand (Daniel 3:16, 17). May God give us grace to learn that the rulers and powers of this world are powerless before our God, and powerless before his people. The gates of hell have never prevailed, and can never prevail, against the church of Christ.

### 'Goodly Child'

We are told that Moses was a 'goodly child'. He was, as we are told in Acts 7:20, 'exceeding fair', a beautiful baby. There was much in his outward appearance that was attractive to the eye. Yet, we read that our Lord Jesus, the Son of God, our Saviour, had no form nor comeliness, that there was no beauty in him that would cause any who saw him to desire him (Isaiah 53:2). If there is meaning in those contrasting physical features of Moses and the Saviour, and I am sure there is, the meaning should be obvious. The law and salvation by works is 'goodly' and 'exceeding fair' in the eyes of every natural man. But Christ and the gospel of God's free grace in him, that is, salvation by grace alone, is repulsive to all natural men. But, once a sinner is given life by God the Holy Spirit, he sees things differently. To every regenerate soul, the law is alarming and the gospel is 'goodly' and 'exceeding fair'.

After three months, Jochebed and Amram could no longer hide their baby. They had done all they could. Now, they must cast him into the arms of God. How wisely, how confidently, how calmly they seem to have cast all their care upon him who ever cares for his own!

'And when she could not longer hide him, she took for him an ark of bulrushes, and daubed it with slime and with pitch, and put the child therein; and she laid it in the flags by the river's brink. And his sister stood afar off, to wit what would be done to him' (vv. 3, 4).

Just as Abraham sacrificed Isaac to the Lord, and Hannah gave Samuel to God, Jochebed and Amram, by an act of confident faith, gave Moses to the Lord. What a blessed privilege it is for parents to cast their children into the Saviour's arms, giving up all parental claims to God and his grace, trusting him alone for their everlasting good! What a blessed child that child is whose parents give it up to God! What a blessed and joyous thing it is for parent and child, when the Lord God graciously receives the gift!

### Three Arks

Jochebed took her child, by an act of faith, believing God, trusting Christ, and cast him into an ark. That this was an act of faith in Christ will be obvious if we consider that this ark was itself a type of Christ and our salvation by him. There are three arks spoken of in the Word of God. Each was a place of refuge, shelter, and safety. The word 'ark' used to describe them means both 'vessel' and 'coffin'. Each ark was a vessel in which something was safely carried; and each was a coffin, connecting it with death. Each of these three arks was typical of the Lord Jesus Christ and God's salvation in and by him.

The ark that Noah built secured those who were in it from the vengeance and violent wrath of an angry God. That is Christ our Substitute. Noah and his family suffered under all the anger and fury of God's holy wrath that the rest of the world suffered, yet no anger and fury touched them. The ark absorbed it all. They were saved when all the world was drowned in the wrath of God. That is what Christ did for all God's elect. He absorbed all the fury of God's holy wrath for us, and extinguished it for us forever! In Christ all God's elect shall be eternally saved when all the world is drowned forever.

The ark of the covenant sheltered the two tables of God's holy law, and, being covered with blood, was the place of atonement, mercy, and acceptance with God for sinners through the sacrifice and death of an innocent lamb. Where the ark went, God went. That ark is Christ our Mercyseat. In him we have perfect righteousness and atonement. He kept the law for us in his life of obedience to God as our Substitute, and satisfied its justice by his death in our place at Calvary as the Lamb of God. In the Ark, Christ Jesus, God is reconciled to us, and we to him.

The ark in which Moses was hidden was a basket made of bulrushes. It protected Moses, God's chosen, from the murderous designs of the wicked ruler, Pharaoh. That ark is Christ, into whom chosen sinners were placed by our loving Father from eternity. As that ark of bulrushes was the means by which Moses was saved from drowning in the Egyptians' river, God's elect are saved from drowning in that infernal lake of his wrath, which burns forever with fire and brimstone.

### Pitch and Pitch

This ark of bulrushes was 'daubed with slime and pitch'. There is something important here I must mention. The word translated 'ark' in

Exodus 2:3 is exactly the same as the word used to speak of the ark Noah built. We are told in Genesis 6:14 that Noah covered his ark, inside and out, with pitch, just as Jochebed did this ark. But the word translated 'pitch' in Genesis 6:14 and the word translated 'pitch' in Exodus 2:3 are not the same. Noah, acting by divine direction, used a pitch that was different. The word translated 'pitch' in Genesis 6:14 comes from a word that means 'ransom'. It is the word commonly translated 'ransom' in the Old Testament (Exodus 30:12; Job 33:24), and is used with reference to the atonement. That pitch clearly had reference to the redemption of our souls by Christ. Moses' mother used pitch of another kind. The word used for 'pitch' in Exodus 2:3 is the word we would expect. It means 'tar'.

She, too, was acting by faith in the Lord Jesus Christ, as we are told in Hebrews 11:23; but she did not have as full a revelation of the matter, or did not understand the revelation she had been given as clearly as did Noah. By her act of faith, she confessed her need of a deliverer and her confidence that God would send her a deliverer. In fact, I am confident that Amram and Jochebed understood that Moses was the deliverer God would send.

Their deed in hiding Moses was not so much a parental act of love as it was the act of two people who believed God. What motivated the faith of these godly parents was that which the Lord God had made known to them. 'They saw he was a proper child.' The Holy Spirit is not merely telling us that Moses was a physically handsome child, as if he were too good looking to murder! No, this was an act of faith. They saw a deeper beauty, that Moses was beautiful to God, chosen of God to be Israel's deliverer (Acts 7:20). The word 'proper' means more than 'good looking'. Its fuller meaning is 'precious and favoured'.

It is obvious in the latter part of this chapter that they taught him this from his youth. Had this not been a matter of divine revelation, something specifically made known to them by God, it would not have been an act of faith, but of desperation to hide him. They believed God's word, the promise he had given to Abraham and Joseph, and had confirmed to them. Yet, it appears they did not understand clearly that the deliverance brought by Moses, typically, and the deliverance to be accomplished by Christ involved blood atonement. I do not suggest they did not believe in blood atonement, but that they simply did not grasp the fulness of it as Noah did.

Yet, Jochebed, being moved by faith in Christ, just as Noah was, made an ark of bulrushes, daubed it with slime and pitch, and sent him floating away, amid the flags in the river of death. She may have had less knowledge than Noah, but her faith was the same, and was fixed upon the same Deliverer, our Lord Jesus Christ.

## Great Faith

Great faith is often found where there appears to be much less knowledge. I do not mean to cast any evil aspersion upon, or in any way vilify knowledge. Knowledge is always good. The more the better. But let no one imagine that a person must have great knowledge and understanding to have great faith. What we have before us in this passage is a clear display of great faith, faith by which Jochebed calmly left her infant son Moses in the care of her omnipotent God alone. 'This she did', wrote John Trapp, 'by the force of her faith; casting the child upon God, and against hope believing in hope.'

That is remarkable faith! Faith God alone can give and sustain! Notice in verse 4 that Moses' 'sister stood afar off, to wit what would be done to him', but not his mother, and not his father. Believing God, having committed their darling son to him, they seem to have calmly walked away in peace. That baby boy was dearer to them than life itself; but they left him exposed to all the dangers and beasts of the wild in an ark and walked home in peace. They left their child in the arms of Christ and rested in him (Matthew 11:28-30; Isaiah 26:3).

## Divine Intervention

Will we ever learn that absolute faith and confidence in our great God is always sensible and well founded? Let me show you how the Lord God intervened, how he always intervenes for his weak, helpless, defenceless people in this world.

'And the daughter of Pharaoh came down to wash herself at the river; and her maidens walked along by the river's side; and when she saw the ark among the flags, she sent her maid to fetch it. And when she had opened it, she saw the child: and, behold, the babe wept. And she had compassion on him, and said, This is one of the Hebrews' children' (vv. 5, 6).

It is always wise and instructive to observe how our God works unseen and behind the scene, arranging everything according to his own purpose, for his own glory and for the salvation of our souls. Pharaoh's daughter came to take a bath, as I suppose she needed one. But there was another reason why she came at this time, and came to this place. The Lord God had ordained to make her one of the instruments by which he would save his people. She was totally ignorant of it. No doubt she is cursing him for it in hell to this day; but she was no less God's appointed instrument, accomplishing his good pleasure, than Gabriel himself! According to God's blessed purpose and by the direction of his sovereign providence 'the daughter of Pharaoh came down to wash herself at the river'. There, according to God's blessed purpose and by the direction of his sovereign providence she 'walked along by the river's side', looking for a good place to take a bath, and as she did, 'she saw the ark among the flags'. And according to God's blessed purpose and by the direction of his sovereign providence, when she opened the ark, 'the babe wept!'

Even the tears of the baby had their object; they were not shed in vain. Moses' crying stirred compassion in Pharaoh's daughter toward 'one of the Hebrews' children'. Moses was not only to be preserved from danger, but to be preserved by the daughter of the very man who sought his life. 'Whoso is wise, and will observe these things, even they shall understand the lovingkindness of the LORD' (Psalm 107:43).

While we admire and adore the goodness of God causing Pharaoh's daughter to be moved with compassion toward Moses by the irresistible cry of a baby, we ought to remember the far greater compassion of our God and Saviour toward us, when we were cast out to perish, when no eye pitied us but his, in our lost estate. His compassion was not moved toward us by our cry for him. His compassion was moved by his compassion. It was his love, his compassion toward us that gave us life and caused us to cry after him (Ezekiel 16:5, 6).

**Unexpected Mercy**
Moses' sister, who had been anxiously watching to see what might become of her baby brother, was moved by the Spirit of God to speak with God-given wisdom to Pharaoh's daughter (vv. 7, 8).

'Then said his sister to Pharaoh's daughter, Shall I go and call to thee a nurse of the Hebrew women, that she may nurse the child for thee? And Pharaoh's daughter said to her, Go. And the maid went and called the child's mother' (vv. 7, 8).

65

Moses, who had been exposed to horrible danger by Pharaoh's decree, is now restored to his mother under the protection of Pharaoh's daughter. And there he remained until he was grown. Anyone who is not blind can see God's wisdom and sovereign goodness in this, graciously arranging everything for his glory, Jochebed's joy, and the salvation of his chosen people.

What an unexpected blessing this was! Jochebed received her child back from the dead. She hoped confidently that God would save him, but never dreamed she would nurse him and raise him. That is a pretty clear picture of the unexpected recovery of every lost sinner. Watched over by divine providence throughout the days of spiritual death, 'sanctified in Jesus Christ' (Jude 1), each one is unexpectedly restored by omnipotent grace, when called of God (Luke 15:32). I can almost see Jochebed smothering Moses with kisses, just as our heavenly Father smothers returning sinners with kisses of love and grace (Luke 15:20).

## Drawn Out

'And the child grew, and she brought him unto Pharaoh's daughter, and he became her son. And she called his name Moses: and she said, Because I drew him out of the water' (v. 10).

When Moses was grown, his mother brought him to Pharaoh's daughter, and she named the young man 'Moses', because she drew him out of the water. His name means, 'Drawn Out', or 'Saved out of Water'.

Again, the Spirit of God here gives us a beautiful and blessed picture of God's free, sovereign, saving grace in Christ. God, who had saved Moses from death, brought him out of the waters of judgment by his sovereign grace and love. Thus, the man of God's choice, the one he had ordained as his chosen instrument for the deliverance of Israel, the man he had chosen to be the mediator of his covenant, finds shelter under the roof of Pharaoh. During this period, he became 'learned in all the wisdom of the Egyptians, and was mighty in words and in deeds' (Acts 7:22).

As Moses was drawn out of death to save Israel, so our Lord Jesus Christ was drawn out of death to save the Israel of God. As Moses was drawn out of death by the most unlikely means, so the Lord God draws chosen, redeemed sinners out of death by the most unlikely means imaginable to man, by that which all men think is utter foolishness, by the preaching of the gospel (Romans 10:17; 1 Peter 1:23-25). And as Moses found shelter under Pharaoh's roof, so the Lord God causes the very world that would destroy his people to supply us with all our needs.

May God the Holy Spirit give us such faith and such joy in believing that we may cast all our care upon our God who cares for us, and find sweet rest for our souls in our God and Saviour.

# Chapter 7

## Moses Flees Egypt

'And it came to pass in those days, when Moses was grown, that he went out unto his brethren, and looked on their burdens: and he spied an Egyptian smiting an Hebrew, one of his brethren. And he looked this way and that way, and when he saw that there was no man, he slew the Egyptian, and hid him in the sand. And when he went out the second day, behold, two men of the Hebrews strove together: and he said to him that did the wrong, Wherefore smitest thou thy fellow? And he said, Who made thee a prince and a judge over us? intendest thou to kill me, as thou killedst the Egyptian? And Moses feared, and said, Surely this thing is known. Now when Pharaoh heard this thing, he sought to slay Moses. But Moses fled from the face of Pharaoh, and dwelt in the land of Midian: and he sat down by a well.'
(Exodus 2:11-15)

If we would understand what we have just read, we must read two more passages of Holy Scripture (Acts 7:22-29; Hebrews 11:24-27) in which God the Holy Spirit explains what we have read here in Exodus 2.

'And Moses was learned in all the wisdom of the Egyptians, and was mighty in words and in deeds. And when he was full forty years old, it came into his heart to visit his brethren the children of Israel. And seeing one of them suffer wrong, he defended him, and avenged him that was oppressed, and smote the Egyptian: For he supposed his brethren would have understood how that God by his hand would deliver them: but they understood not. And the next day he showed himself unto them as they strove, and would have set them at one again, saying, Sirs, ye are brethren; why do ye wrong one to another? But he that did his neighbour wrong thrust him away, saying, Who made thee a ruler and a judge over us? Wilt thou kill me, as thou didst the Egyptian yesterday? Then fled Moses at this saying, and was a stranger in the land of Midian, where he begat two sons' (Acts 7:22-29).

'By faith Moses, when he was come to years, refused to be called the son of Pharaoh's daughter; Choosing rather to suffer affliction with the people of God, than to enjoy the pleasures of sin for a season; Esteeming the reproach of Christ greater riches than the treasures in Egypt: for he had respect unto the recompense of the reward. By faith he forsook Egypt, not fearing the wrath of the king: for he endured, as seeing him who is invisible' (Hebrews 11:24-27).

Moses is held before us by divine inspiration as a picture of God's saints in this world, a very clear and vivid picture of the lives of sinners saved by God's free grace in Christ. He is now a grown man, forty years old. He is not an old man, but he is not a young man. He is now a man in the prime of life, full of strength, well established in the world, and in the position of highest possible honour, advantage, and usefulness.

### A Man of Faith
Moses was a man of faith. He believed God. 'By faith he forsook Egypt, not fearing the wrath of the king.' It is obvious Moses' parents had taught him what God had revealed to them, that he was the deliverer ordained of God to save his people. What his parents taught him, the Lord God had revealed to him as well. Like the Lord Jesus Christ, of whom he was a type, Moses was a man chosen out of the people to save the people of God's choice. 'And when he was full forty years old, it came into his heart to visit his brethren the children of Israel.' It came into his heart to visit his brethren, because God put it into his heart.

### Moses' Supposition
I stress the fact that Moses believed God. He trusted Christ. He acted in faith. But Moses the believer, the saint, the redeemed, the blood-washed righteous man, while acting in faith, while living by faith, while seeking to serve God and his people, was still just a man of sinful flesh, just like you and me. He knew he was the man chosen and appointed of God to deliver his people; and he chose to identify himself with God's afflicted people.

Who could question his devotion? Who could question his zeal? Moses knew full well what the consequences of his actions would be if

Pharaoh found out what he had done. When he saw an Egyptian beating one of his brethren, Moses stepped in, slew the Egyptian, buried him in the sand, and sent his brother safely home. That is a blessed picture of what our Lord Jesus Christ has done for us (John 12:31-33; Revelation 20:1-3).

Yet, Moses made a grave mistake. He made a supposition. 'For he supposed his brethren would have understood how that God by his hand would deliver them: but they understood not.' Go through the Scriptures, looking at how the word 'supposed' is used (Matthew 20:10; Mark 6:49; Luke 2:44; 12:51; 13:2; 24:37; John 20:15; Acts 2:15; 7:25; 14:19; 16:27; Philippians 1:16; 1 Timothy 6:5). Whenever a man supposes something, his supposition is wrong. Faith is not an act of supposition, but of confidence.

Moses knew he was the man chosen of God and appointed to deliver Israel. He knew it by divine revelation. But he supposed the time had come for Israel's deliverance forty years before God had determined to deliver his people, forty years before he was prepared by God to be their deliverer, and forty years before they were prepared by God to be delivered. His supposition got him into trouble.

What a lesson there is here for preachers and those who would be preachers! As in everything else, God's ways are not our ways. Moses ran before he was sent. And when a man does that, he is sure to run into trouble. Moses thought he was ready to deliver Israel; but he was only ready to be withered. Moses was ready to work; but he must first learn to wait. God's time had not yet come to judge Egypt and deliver Israel. God had chosen to prepare Moses by putting him in Pharaoh's palace for forty years, and by putting him in the Midian desert for forty years. He will not have a novice to do his work. Still, the Holy Spirit is specifically talking about this very event in the life of Moses, when he tells us, 'By faith Moses, when he was come to years, refused to be called the son of Pharaoh's daughter'.

Like you and me, Moses made mistakes, displayed infirmities, was sometimes impatient, sometimes rash, and sometimes hesitant. All these facts are plainly exhibited the more to magnify the infinite grace and inexhaustible mercy of our God. You see, Moses was a man who was saved by God's free grace in Christ, accepted in the Beloved, and a man who lived by faith just like us.

## Moses' Fear

His deeds of faith were also deeds that showed the terrible weakness of fear. Moses acted with boldness, but with fear; with confidence, but with uncertainty. 'And he looked this way and that way, and when he saw that there was no man, he slew the Egyptian, and hid him in the sand' (v. 12). He was hoping for the favour of his brethren; and he feared the wrath of Pharaoh. Yet, the Spirit of God tells us he acted in faith. How can this be true?

Have you ever noticed how when the Spirit of God gives us the history of God's saints in the Old Testament, he always presents them to us as they are, warts and all? He makes no attempt to hide any of their sins, weaknesses, failures, or imperfections. But, when he relates the same history of the same people in the New Testament, he never talks about their sins and failures. In the New Testament he only talks about their faith, their righteousness, and their triumphs. In Exodus we read, 'Moses looked this way and that way', that 'he feared and said, surely this thing is known', and that he 'fled from the face of Pharaoh'. In Hebrews we are told that everything he did, he did by faith in Christ, 'not fearing the wrath of the king, for he endured as seeing him who is invisible'. There is a reason for that. In the Old Testament, under the law, sin is always exposed. In the New Testament, in this gospel day, in this age of grace, God always covers the sins of his people.

## Two Natures

Again, Moses was, just like God's saints in the world today, a man born of God, a sinner saved by grace. And a regenerate man or woman is a person with two natures, flesh and spirit. One is natural and sinful, and one is spiritual and holy. That which is born of flesh can do nothing but sin. And that which is born of God cannot sin (Romans 7:14-8:4; 1 John 3:5-9).

Yes, God's people sin. Sin is mixed with all we do, even our greatest deeds of faith; but the sin is not what we really are! And our God, having put away our sins by the sacrifice of his dear Son, will never impute sin to his own, but only righteousness (Romans 4:6, 8). More than that, he accepts our deeds of faith as deeds of perfect righteousness through the merits of Christ's blood and righteousness (1 Peter 2:5). In fact, he accepts our works and sacrifices as works of righteousness, perfect and pure. It is what he declares them to be (1 John 3:7). He shall, in the last day, reward us for them as works of perfect righteousness when 'the Lord comes, who both will bring to light the hidden things of darkness, and will make manifest the counsels of the hearts: and then shall every man have praise of God' (1 Corinthians 4:5).

## Moses' Faith

Let me show you what Moses did for the glory of God, by faith, because he believed God, because he trusted Christ, and because he endured as seeing him who is invisible. He 'refused to be called the son of Pharaoh's daughter'. He chose 'rather to suffer affliction with the people of God, than to enjoy the pleasures of sin for a season'. He esteemed 'the reproach of Christ greater riches than the treasures in Egypt'. He preferred the cross of Christ and the gospel of Christ to the crown of Egypt. 'He had respect unto the recompense of the reward'. Moses lived for eternity. 'By faith he forsook Egypt, not fearing the wrath of the king for he endured, as seeing him who is invisible'.

By faith, because he believed God, Moses despised all the pleasures, attractions, and honours of Pharaoh's court. Faith caused him to relinquish what could have been a wide sphere of usefulness. Human reason would have led him down another path. It would have led him to use his influence on behalf of the people of God, to act for them instead of suffering with them.

Human wisdom might very well have said, 'Moses, God's providence has opened a wide door before you. Look what you can do for Israel as Pharaoh's grandson. This must be the will of God.' But faith does not interpret God's revelation by his providence. Faith interprets God's providence by his revelation

Faith caused him to think differently. Human reason and faith are always opposites. They never agree about anything. Perhaps, there is nothing about which they differ so widely as in what we think of as the 'openings of providence'. Human reason always regards such openings as opportunities for self-indulgence. I have known many who, when offered a better paying job, moved to a place where there was no gospel church, no place of public worship, attempting to justify forsaking the assembling of themselves together with God's saints by asserting that it was 'a providential thing'. Faith looks upon such 'providential' things as opportunities for self-denial. Jonah found a ship going to Tarshish, because it was what he wanted to find. What he might have thought was a 'providential' opening was, in reality, the path of disobedience. 'So he paid the fare thereof' (Jonah 1:3).

It is truly the believer's privilege and wisdom to see our Father's hand and hear his voice in everything; but we are never to be guided by circumstances. Our God promises, 'I will guide thee with mine eye' (Psalm 32:8). He guides us by his Spirit through the eye of Scripture's instruction and teaching. 'Be ye not as the horse, or as the mule, which have no understanding: whose mouth must be held in with bit and bridle, lest they come near unto thee' (Psalm 32:9).

Moses refused to be called the son of Pharaoh's daughter and forsook Egypt by faith, believing God's revelation (Romans 10:17). Had he acted according to sight and reason, he would have grasped the throne of Egypt. But he walked by faith, not by sight. Therefore, he is held before us as a noble example to follow.

Because he believed God, he esteemed 'the reproach of Christ greater riches than the treasures in Egypt'. It was not merely reproach for Christ but 'the reproach of Christ'. The Lord Jesus Christ, in indescribable grace, identified himself with his people. He came down from heaven, assumed human flesh, and bore our sins in his own body on the tree. Being made sin for us, he cried, 'The reproaches of them that reproached thee have fallen upon me' (Psalm 69:9). He confessed our sins to be his own sins (Psalm 40:12; 69:5), and bore the wrath of God in our place, being made a curse for us, when he hung upon the cursed tree. He did not merely act for us. He made himself one with us, and became all that we are, that we might be made all that he is, even the righteousness of God in him (2 Corinthians 5:21; Jeremiah 23:6; 33:16). When Moses esteemed 'the reproach of Christ greater riches than the treasures in Egypt', he esteemed the gospel of Christ; he esteemed his crucified Saviour, 'greater riches than the treasures in Egypt'. That is what faith does.

He possessed all the ease, wealth, and dignity of Pharaoh's house, where 'the pleasures of sin' and 'the treasures of Egypt' were scattered before him. Had he chosen to do so, he could have lived and died in that splendour. But faith in Christ would not allow such a choice. Moses saw his brethren bowed down beneath the heavy burden of cruel bondage; and faith in Christ demanded he identify himself with them and take his place with them, in all their reproach, bondage, degradation, and sorrow. Had he merely acted in benevolence, philanthropy, or patriotism, he might have used his position and influence on behalf of his brethren. He might have succeeded in inducing Pharaoh to lighten their burden, and make their lives easier. But that is not what faith requires. Faith demands identification with Christ, his gospel, and his people. Today, that initial act of identification is believer's immersion; baptism, by which we publicly confess our faith in Christ and identify ourselves with him, his gospel, and his people (Romans 6:4-6).

We must never be satisfied with merely patronizing God's saints, wishing them well, or speaking kindly of them. We must always identify ourselves with God's despised people. A patron is one thing; a martyr is something else. This distinction is apparent throughout the entire book of God. Darius was so attached to Daniel that he lost a night's rest on his account; but Daniel spent that same night in the lion's den, nonetheless, as Christ's martyr. Nicodemus spoke well of Christ, but Paul longed to know Christ, being identified with him in the fellowship of his sufferings and made conformable to him in his death.

**A Type**
In all this Moses was also typical of our blessed Saviour, who identified himself with us at the heavy cost of all that love could give. Had he not done so, had he remained 'in the bosom of the Father', we could never have been united to him. Like Moses, because of his love for us, the Son of God 'gave himself for us, that he might redeem us from all iniquity, and purify unto himself a peculiar people, zealous of good works' (Titus 2:14). The Jews tried to take him by force and make him their king; but he refused the glory offered to him by man, for the joy set before him, for which he endured the cross, despising the shame. His infinite heart of love for God's elect could be satisfied only by bringing his chosen sons and daughters into everlasting union with himself, by the blood of his cross, bringing 'many sons' with him to glory. 'Father', he says, 'I will that they also whom thou hast given me be with me where I am, that they may behold my glory, which thou hast given me; for thou lovedst me before the foundation of the world' (John 17:24). Praise be his adorable name forever!

# Chapter 8

## Moses: A Type Of Christ

'And it came to pass in those days, when Moses was grown, that he went out unto his brethren, and looked on their burdens: and he spied an Egyptian smiting an Hebrew, one of his brethren. And he looked this way and that way, and when he saw that there was no man, he slew the Egyptian, and hid him in the sand. And when he went out the second day, behold, two men of the Hebrews strove together: and he said to him that did the wrong, Wherefore smitest thou thy fellow? And he said, Who made thee a prince and a judge over us? intendest thou to kill me, as thou killedst the Egyptian? And Moses feared, and said, Surely this thing is known. Now when Pharaoh heard this thing, he sought to slay Moses. But Moses fled from the face of Pharaoh, and dwelt in the land of Midian: and he sat down by a well. Now the priest of Midian had seven daughters: and they came and drew water, and filled the troughs to water their father's flock. And the shepherds came and drove them away: but Moses stood up and helped them, and watered their flock. And when they came to Reuel their father, he said, How is it that ye are come so soon to day? And they said, An Egyptian delivered us out of the hand of the shepherds, and also drew water enough for us, and watered the flock. And he said unto his daughters, And where is he? why is it that ye have left the man? call him, that he may eat bread. And Moses was content to dwell with the man: and he gave Moses Zipporah his daughter. And she bare him a son, and he called his name Gershom: for he said, I have been a stranger in a strange land.'
(Exodus 2:11-22)

There are several striking contrasts in the life of Moses. He was both the son of a slave, and the son of a king. He was born into poverty, but raised in a palace. He was both the leader of a great army, and a shepherd. He was a mighty warrior, and the meekest of men. He was educated in Pharaoh's court, and ordained to be Pharaoh's destroyer. He possessed all the wisdom of Egypt, but lived by the faith of a child. He was both a fugitive from Pharaoh's wrath, and God's ambassador. He was the giver of the law, and the forerunner of grace. He died alone on mount Nebo, and appeared with Christ in the mount of transfiguration. He was the faithful servant of God; yet died under the judgment of God. But, that which I find more striking than anything else is the fact that while Moses, as the representative of the law, is constantly held before us in Scripture as the very opposite of our Lord Jesus Christ, for example, 'the law came by Moses, but grace and truth came by Jesus Christ' (John 1:17), yet Moses is specifically held before us in Holy Scripture as a great type of our Lord Jesus (Deuteronomy 18:15-18). A. W. Pink, in his *Gleanings in Exodus*, identified 75 points in which Moses may be viewed as a type of Christ. I have inserted Pink's 75 points at the end of the chapter, so you can study them.

**A Type of Christ**
I want you to see that Moses is set before us in this passage as a tremendous type and picture of the Lord Jesus Christ. Three things particularly stand out in Exodus 2:11-22, showing him to be typical of our Saviour. First, Moses visited his brethren because it was in his heart to deliver them (vv. 11, 12; Acts 7:22-29).

'And it came to pass in those days, when Moses was grown, that he went out unto his brethren, and looked on their burdens: and he spied an Egyptian smiting an Hebrew, one of his brethren. And he looked this way and that way, and when he saw that there was no man, he slew the Egyptian, and hid him in the sand.'

'And Moses was learned in all the wisdom of the Egyptians, and was mighty in words and in deeds. And when he was full forty years old, it came into his heart to visit his brethren the children of Israel. And seeing one of them suffer wrong, he defended him, and avenged him that was oppressed, and smote the Egyptian' (Acts 7:22-24).

Just as Moses visited his brethren to deliver them, our Lord Jesus Christ visited and redeemed his people because of his great, infinite, everlasting love for us (1 John 3:16; 4:9, 10). Oh, that our hearts may ever be ravished with his love!

Second, when Moses came to his own, his own received him not, but despised and rejected him (vv. 13-15).

'And when he went out the second day, behold, two men of the Hebrews strove together: and he said to him that did the wrong, Wherefore smitest thou thy fellow? And he said, Who made thee a prince and a judge over us? intendest thou to kill me, as thou killedst the Egyptian? And Moses feared, and said, Surely this thing is known. Now when Pharaoh heard this thing, he sought to slay Moses. But Moses fled from the face of Pharaoh, and dwelt in the land of Midian: and he sat down by a well.'

So, too, our Saviour was 'despised and rejected of men; a man of sorrows, and acquainted with grief: and we hid as it were our faces from him; he was despised, and we esteemed him not' (Isaiah 53:3). Yes, we hid our faces from him, refusing to look to him, refusing to trust him, until he graciously forced us to do so, revealing himself in us by his omnipotent, irresistible mercy. 'He came unto his own, and his own received him not' (John 1:11). Just as the Jews received him not, we would not receive him, until he made us willing in the day of his power. Blessed be his name, he would not leave us to ourselves. How we ought to thank God our Saviour that he refused to take 'no' from us for an answer to his call. Now, because he would not leave us to ourselves, we are among the 'many' who have gladly 'received him', to whom he has given 'power to become the sons of God, even to them that believe on his name: Which were born, not of blood, nor of the will of the flesh, nor of the will of man, but of God' (John 1:12, 13).

Third, when he was despised and rejected of Israel, Moses went among the Gentiles, became a shepherd, and found a wife for himself among the Gentiles (vv. 15-22). Just as our Saviour did after him, Moses found a woman by a well (v. 15; John 4). Moses's wife was a despised, black Ethiopian (Numbers 12:1; Song of Solomon 1:5). Moses stood up to help her, delivered her from her enemies, and gave her water (vv. 16, 17). Moses went home with that black Midianite woman and married her; and he was content (vv. 21, 22). That is precisely what the Lord Jesus has done for us (Isaiah 62:1-5, 11, 12).

**As A Prophet**

Moses is specifically identified as a type of our Lord Jesus Christ in his prophetic office. The Scriptures clearly teach that our Lord Jesus Christ is our Prophet to teach us, our Priest to make atonement and intercede for us, and our King to rule over us. No other man ever held all three of these offices. Yet, Moses typified Christ in all three of his offices.

Being God's prophet to Israel, by whom God made known his will to his people, Moses was typical of Christ our Prophet (Matthew 1:23; 17:5). What a Prophet our Saviour is! He is not just a teacher come from God, as Nicodemus supposed (John 3:2). He is Immanuel, God with us, God come to teach. And all who are taught of him come to him. Without him we must forever have been left to perish in darkness (2 Corinthians 4:3-6).

They are blessed of God who hear and believe him (John 5:24); all who refuse to hear him are without excuse (John 3:18). Christ is that Prophet raised up from the midst of his brethren (Psalm 89:19; Romans 1:1-3; 9:4, 5). This Prophet, our Lord Jesus Christ, is both the Word of God and the One by whom God gives his Word (John 1:1-3). He is both God himself and the revelation of God (John 1:14, 18; Hebrews 1:1-3).

The Lord God declared, 'I will put my words in his mouth' (John 7:16; 8:28; 17:6-8). His words are the words of life, not just true facts concerning God and the kingdom of heaven; but he speaks and men live (John 5:21, 24; James 1:18; 1 Peter 1:23), even as he spoke and Lazarus came forth from the grave. His words are the words of truth (John 1:14-17; 14:6; 18:37). His words are the words of grace. Our Saviour is full of grace and truth. His words bring peace, pardon, life, and salvation from sin.

This great Prophet, our Lord Jesus Christ, came not to condemn the world, for the world stood condemned; but he came that we might have life more abundantly. He is the gospel (the good news), and he came bringing the gospel. If any man hears his words and believes on him, he shall never die (John 8:51; 14:23, 24).

All other prophets were inspired by Christ and were sent by Christ. He is more than a prophet. He is 'God with us' (Matthew 1:23). All other prophets pointed to Christ and spoke of Christ (Acts 10:43). Christ is the sum and substance of their prophecies. He fulfilled and completed all they foretold (John 1:45; Colossians 2:9, 10). All other prophets wrote the holy books of the Inspiration, and proclaimed the message of grace. Christ fulfilled their prophesies and performed the work of grace (Hebrews 1:1-3). All other prophets spoke of God by inspiration and learning. Christ spoke of the Father as One who is his equal, as One who is himself God (Proverbs 8:29, 30; John 1:18; Matthew 11:27). All other prophets have left their work and are gone. Christ abides forever! Being typical of Christ our Prophet, 'Moses came and told the people all the words of the LORD, and all the judgments' (Exodus 24:3).

## As Our Priest
Though he was not officially a priest, Moses was, also, typical of Christ our Priest. 'Moses and Aaron among his priests, and Samuel among them that call upon his name; they called upon the LORD, and he answered them' (Psalm 99:6). As a priest he stood between God and his people as a mediator (Deuteronomy 5:5; 1 Timothy 2:5). As a priest, he offered sacrifice upon God's altar (Leviticus 8:15). As a priest, he interceded for Israel, and 'brought their cause before the Lord' (Numbers 27:5; Hebrews 7:25). As a priest, Moses washed Aaron and his sons with water, and ceremonially purified the priesthood, consecrating them with blood (Leviticus 8). And as a priest, he blessed the people (Exodus 39:43; Luke 24:50).

## As A King
Though he was not officially a king, Moses was typical of Christ as king in Jeshurun, the upright and righteous people of God. 'Moses commanded us a law, even the inheritance of the congregation of Jacob. And he was king in Jeshurun, when the heads of the people and the tribes of Israel were gathered together' (Deuteronomy 33:4, 5).

## As A Saviour
Moses was typical of Christ as a Saviour, too. Like our Saviour, Moses was transfigured in the mount of God (Exodus 34:29, 35). Like our Lord Jesus, Moses finished all the work for which he was sent to Israel (Exodus 40:33; John 17:4). Like our Saviour, Moses had to die before Israel could enter into Canaan (Joshua 1:2; John 12:24). Like our blessed Saviour, Moses gave Israel an inheritance (Joshua 1:14; Ephesians 1:11). Like our dear Redeemer, Moses suffered and died for the people upon whom his heart was set, bearing the wrath of God for

them (Psalm 106:32; Deuteronomy 3:26). And like our Saviour, Moses, who died in humiliation and shame, appeared a second time in glory (Matthew 17).

---

# Seventy-five Types Of Moses And Christ

## A. W. Pink

1. His Nationality. Moses was an Israelite (Exodus 2:1, 2). So, according to the flesh, was Christ.
2. His Birth. This occurred when his nation was under the dominion of a hostile power, when they were groaning under the rule of a Gentile king (Exodus 1). So the Jews were in bondage to the Romans when Christ was born (Matthew 2:1 cf. Luke 24:21).
3. His Person. 'In which time Moses was born, and was exceeding fair to God' (Acts 7:20). How blessedly did he, in this, foreshadow the Beloved of the Father! His estimate of the 'fairness' of that Child which lay in Bethlehem's manger, was evidenced by the sending of the angels to say unto the shepherds, 'Unto you is born this day in the city of David a Saviour, which is Christ the Lord' (Luke 2:11).
4. His Infancy. In infancy his life was endangered, imperilled by the reigning king, for Pharaoh had given orders that, 'Every son that is born ye shall cast into the river' (Exodus 1:22). How this reminds us of Matthew 2:16: 'Then Herod ... sent forth and slew all the children that were in Bethlehem, and in all the coasts thereof.'
5. His Adoption. Though, previously, he was the child of another, he yet was made the son of Pharaoh's daughter: 'And became her son' (Exodus 2:10). Thus he had a mother, but no father! What anointed eye can fail to see prefigured here the mystery of the Virgin-birth! Christ was the Son of Another, even the Son of God. But, born into this world, He had a mother, but no human father. Yet was He, as it were, adopted by Joseph: see Matthew 1:19-21.

6. His Childhood. This was spent in Egypt. So also was Christ's: 'Behold the angel of the Lord appeareth to Joseph in a dream, saying, 'Arise, and take the young Child and His mother, and flee into Egypt, and be thou there until I bring thee word'' (Matthew 2:13). Thus was fulfilled God's ancient oracle, 'And called My Son out of Egypt' (Hosea 11:1).

7. His Sympathy for Israel. He was filled with a deep compassion for his suffering kinsmen according to the flesh, and he yearned for their deliverance. Beautifully does this come out in Acts 7:23, 24, 'And when he was full forty years old, it came into his heart to visit his brethren of the children of Israel. And seeing one of them suffer wrong, he defended him.' So too Christ was filled with pity toward His enslaved people, and love brought Him here to deliver them.

8. His Early Knowledge of his Mission. Long years before he actually entered upon his great work, Moses discerned, 'how that God by his hand would deliver them' (Acts 7:25). So as a Boy of twelve, Christ said to His perplexed mother, 'Wist ye not that I must be about My Father's business?' (Luke 2:49).

9. His Condescending Grace. Though legally the 'son of Pharaoh's daughter', yet he regarded the Hebrew slaves as his brethren: 'And it came to pass in those days, when Moses was grown, that he went out unto his brethren' (Exodus 2:11). So it is with Christ: 'He is not ashamed to call them brethren' (Hebrews 2:11).

10. His Great Renunciation. 'By faith Moses, when he was come to years, refused to be called the son of Pharaoh's daughter; Choosing rather to suffer affliction with the people of God, than to enjoy the pleasures of sin for a season; Esteeming the reproach of Christ greater riches than the treasures in Egypt' (Hebrews 11:24-26). What a foreshadowing was this of Him 'Who, being in the form of God, thought it not robbery to be equal with God; But made Himself of no reputation, and took upon Him the form of a servant' (Philippians 2:6, 7). Like Moses, Christ too voluntarily relinquished riches, glory, and a kingly palace.

11. His Rejection by his Brethren. 'And the next day he showed himself unto them as they strove, and would have set them at one again, saying, Sirs, ye are brethren; why do ye wrong one to another? But he that did his neighbour wrong thrust him away, saying, Who made thee a ruler and a judge over us?' (Acts 7:26, 27). This is very sad; sadder still is it

to read of Christ, 'He came unto His own, and His own received Him not' (John 1:11). This same line in the typical picture was before us when we considered Joseph. But mark this difference: In the case of Joseph, it was his brethren's enmity against his person (Genesis 37:4); here with Moses, it was his brethren's enmity against his mission. Joseph was personally hated; Moses officially refused 'who made thee a ruler and a judge over us'? So it was with Christ. Israel said, 'We will not have this Man to reign over us' (Luke 19:14).

12. His Sojourning among the Gentiles. 'But Moses fled from the face of Pharaoh, and dwelt in the land of Midian' (Exodus 2:15). Following Christ's rejection by the Jews, we read, 'God at the first did visit the Gentiles, to take out of them a people for His name' (Acts 15:14).

13. His Seat on the Well. Away from his own land, we read of Moses, 'And he sat down by a well' (Exodus 2:15). So the only time we read of the Lord Jesus seated by the well, was when He was outside Israel's borders, in Samaria (John 4:4, 6).

14. His Shepherdhood. 'Now Moses kept the flock of Jethro his father-in-law' (Exodus 3:1). This is the character which Christ sustains to His elect among the Gentiles: 'And other sheep I have, which are not of this fold, them also I must bring, and they shall hear My voice; and there shall be one flock, one Shepherd' (John 10:16).

15. His Season of Seclusion. Before he entered upon his real mission, Moses spent many years in obscurity. Who had supposed that this one, there 'at the backside of the desert', was destined to such an honourable future? So it was with the incarnate Son of God. Before He began His public ministry, He was hidden away in despised Nazareth. Who that saw Him there in the carpenter's shop, dreamed that He was ordained of God to the work of redemption!

16. His Commission from God. He was called of God to emancipate His people from the house of bondage: 'Come now therefore, and I will send thee unto Pharaoh, that thou mayest bring forth My people the children of Israel out of Egypt' (Exodus 3:10). So Christ was sent forth into this world to 'seek and to save that which was lost' (Luke 19:10).

17. His Apostleship. Thus he was God's apostle unto Israel, for 'apostle' signifies one 'sent forth': 'Now therefore go' (Exodus 4:12). So Christ was the Sent One of God (John 9:4 etc.); yea, in Hebrews 3:1 He is designated 'the Apostle'.

18. His Credentials. His commission from God was confirmed by power to work miracles. So also Christ's mission was authenticated by wondrous signs (Matthew 11:4, 5). It should be noted that Moses is the first one mentioned in the O.T. that performed miracles; so is Christ in the N.T., John the Baptist performed none (John 10:41).

19. His First Miracles. Moses wrought many wonders, but it is most striking to observe that his first two miraculous signs were power over the serpent, and power over leprosy (Exodus 4:6-9). So after Christ began His public ministry, we read first of His power over Satan (Matthew 4:10, 11), and then His power over leprosy (Matthew 8:3).

20. His Return to his Own Land. In Exodus 4:19 we read, 'And the Lord said unto Moses in Midian, Go, return into Egypt: for all the men are dead which sought thy life.' The antitype of this is found in Matthew 2:19, 'An angel of the Lord appeareth in a dream to Joseph in Egypt, saying, Arise, and take the young Child and His mother, and go into the land of Israel: for they are dead which sought the young Child's life'!

21. His Acceptance by his Brethren. This is recorded in Exodus 4:29-31. How different was this from his first appearing before and rejection by the Hebrews (Exodus 2). How beautifully it prefigured Israel's acceptance of their Messiah at His second appearing!

22. His Powerful Rod. Moses now wielded a rod of mighty power: see Exodus 9:23; 10:13; 14:16. So also it is written of Christ, 'Thou shalt break them with a rod of iron' (Psalm 2:9).

23. His Announcing Solemn Judgments. Again and again he warned Pharaoh and his people of the sore punishment of God if they continued to defy him. So also Christ declared, 'Except ye repent, ye shall all likewise perish' (Luke 13:3).

24. His Deliverance of Israel. Moses perfectly fulfilled his God-given commission and led Israel out of bondage: 'The same did God send to be a ruler and a deliverer' (Acts 7:35). So Christ affirmed, 'If the Son therefore shall make you free, ye shall be free indeed' (John 8:36).

25. His Headship. Remarkably is this brought out in 1 Corinthians 10:1, 2, 'All our fathers were under the cloud, and all passed through the sea; and were all baptized unto Moses'. So obedient Christians are 'baptized unto Jesus Christ' (Romans 6:3).

26. His Leadership of Israel's Praise. 'Then sang Moses and the children of Israel' (Exodus 15:1). Of Christ too it is written, 'In the midst of the congregation will I praise Thee' (Psalm 22:22).

27. His Authority Challenged. This is recorded in Numbers 16:3; the antitype in Matthew 21:23.

28. His Person Envied. See Psalm 106:16, and compare Mark 15:10.

29. His Person Opposed. Though Israel were so deeply indebted to Moses, yet again and again we find them 'murmuring' against him: Exodus 15:24, 16:2, etc.. For the N.T. parallel see Luke 15:2, John 6:41.

30. His Life Threatened. So fiercely did the ungrateful Hebrews oppose Moses that, on one occasion, they were ready to 'stone' him (Exodus 17:4). How this brings to mind what we read of in John 8:59 and 10:31!

31. His Sorrows. Moses felt keenly the base ingratitude of the people. Mark his plaintive plea as recorded in Numbers 11:11, 14. So too the Lord Jesus suffered from the reproaches of the people: He was 'the Man of sorrows and acquainted with grief'.

32. His Unwearied Love. Though misunderstood, envied, and opposed, nothing could alienate the affections of Moses from his people. 'Many waters cannot quench love, neither can the floods drown it' (Song of Solomon 8:7). Beautifully is this seen in Exodus 32. After Israel repudiated Jehovah and had worshipped the golden calf, after the Lord has disowned them as His people (Exodus 32:7), Moses supplicates God on their behalf, saying 'Oh, this people have sinned a great sin, and have made them gods of gold. Yet now, if Thou wilt forgive their sin ; and if not, blot me, I pray Thee, out of Thy book which Thou hast written' (vv. 31, 32). How this reminds us of Him who 'having loved His own which were in the world, He loved them unto the end' (John 13:1)!

33. His Forgiving Spirit. 'And Miriam and Aaron spake against Moses … Hath the Lord indeed spoken only by Moses? Hath He not spoken also by us'? (Numbers 12:1, 2). But he answered not a word. How this pointed to Him who, 'when He was reviled, reviled not again' (1 Peter 2:23). When Miriam was stricken with leprosy because of her revolt against her brother, we are told, 'Moses cried unto the Lord, saying, Heal her now, O God, I beseech Thee' (Numbers 12:13).

34. His Prayerfulness. An example of this has just been before us, but many other instances are recorded. Moses was, pre-eminently, a man of prayer. At every crisis he sought unto the Lord: see Exodus 5:22; 8:12; 9:33; 14:15; 15:25; 17:4; etc.. Note how often in Luke's Gospel Christ is also presented as a Man of prayer.

35. His Meekness. 'Moses was very meek, above all the men which were upon the face of the earth' (Numbers 12:3) cf. Matthew 11:29.

36. His Faithfulness. 'Moses verily was faithful in all his house' (Hebrews 3:5). So Christ is 'The faithful and true witness' (Revelation 3:14).

37. His providing Israel with water. See Numbers 20:11 and compare John 4:14, 7:37.

38. His Prophetic office. Deuteronomy 18:18, compare John 7:16, 8:28.

39. His Priestly activities. 'Moses and Aaron among His priests' (Psalm 99:6). Illustrations are found in Leviticus 8: 'And Moses took the blood, and put it upon the horns of the altar ... and he took all the fat ... and burned it upon the altar' (vv. 15, 16 and see 19:23). So Christ, as Priest, 'offered Himself without spot to God' (Hebrews 9:14).

40. His Kingly rule. 'Moses commanded us a law, even the inheritance of the congregation of Jacob. And he was king in Jeshurun' (Deuteronomy 33:4, 5). So Christ is King in Zion, and will yet be over the Jews (Luke 1:32, 33).

41. His Judgeship. 'Moses sat to judge the people: and they stood by Moses from the morning until the evening' (Exodus 18:13). Compare 2 Corinthians 5:10.

42. His Leadership. Moses was the head and director of God's people, as He said to him, 'Lead the people unto the place of which I have spoken' (Exodus 32:34). So Christ is called, 'The Captain of their salvation' (Hebrews 2:10).

43. His Mediation. What a remarkable word was that of Moses to Israel, 'I stood between the Lord and you' (Deuteronomy 5:5): 'There is one God, and one Mediator between God and men, the Man Christ Jesus' (1 Timothy 2:5).

44. His Election. In Psalm 106:23 he is called, 'Moses His chosen'. So God says of Christ, 'Behold My Servant, whom I uphold, Mine elect' (Isaiah 42:1).

45. His Covenant-engagement. 'And the Lord said unto Moses, Write thou these words: for after the tenor of these words I have made a covenant with thee and with Israel' (Exodus 34:27): so Christ is denominated, 'The Mediator of a better covenant' (Hebrews 8:6).

46. His sending forth of the Twelve. 'These are the names of the men which Moses sent to spy out the land' (Numbers 13:16 see previous verses). So Christ sent forth twelve apostles (Matthew 10:5).

47. His Appointing of the Seventy. 'And Moses went out and told the people the words of the Lord, and gathered the seventy men of the elders of the people' (Numbers 11:24). So Christ selected seventy (Luke 10:1).

48. His Wisdom. 'Moses was learned in all the wisdom of the Egyptians' (Acts 7:22). Compare Colossians 2:3.

49. His Might. 'And was mighty in words and in deeds' (Acts 7:22). Behold the antitype of this in Matthew 13:54: 'They were astonished, and said, Whence hath this Man this wisdom, and these mighty works'?

50. His Intercession. 'And Moses brought their cause before the Lord' (Numbers 27:5). Compare Hebrews 7:25.

51. His Intimate Communion with God. 'And there arose not a prophet since in Israel like unto Moses, whom the Lord knew face to face' (Exodus 34:10). So, on earth, Christ was 'The only-begotten Son, which is in the bosom of the Father' (John 1:18). It is striking to behold in Exodus 31 to 34 how Moses passed and re-passed between Jehovah in the mount and the camp of the congregation: expressive of his equal access to heaven and earth. Compare John 3:13.

52. His Knowledge of God. See Psalm 103:7 and compare John 5:20.

53. His Holy Anger. See Exodus 32:19 and compare Mark 3:5, etc..

54. His Message. He was mouthpiece of God: 'And Moses came and told the people all the words of the Lord' (Exodus 24:3). Hebrews 1:2.

55. His Commandments. See Deuteronomy 4:2 and Matthew 28:20.

56. His Written Revelation. See Exodus 31:13 and Revelation 1:1.

57. His Fasting. See Exodus 34:28 and compare Matthew 4:2.

58. His Transfiguration on the mount. See Exodus 34:29, 35 and compare Matthew 17:2.

59. His Place Outside the Camp. See Exodus 33:7 and compare Hebrews 13:13.

60. His Arraigning of the responsible head. See Exodus 32:21 and compare Revelation 2:12, 13.

61. His Praying for Israel's Forgiveness. See Numbers 14:19 and compare Luke 23:34.

62. His Washing his Brethren with Water. 'And Moses brought Aaron and his sons, and washed them with water' (Leviticus 8:6). Who can fail to see in that a foreshadowing of what is recorded in John 13:5: 'After that He poureth water into a basin and began to wash the disciples' feet'!

63. His Prophecies. See Deuteronomy 28 and 33 and compare Matthew 24 and Luke 21.

64. His Rewarding God's servants. See Numbers 7:6, 32:33, 40 and compare Revelation 22:12.

65. His perfect Obedience. 'Thus did Moses according to all that the Lord commanded, so did he' (Exodus 40:16). What a lovely foreshadowing was this of Him who could say, 'I have kept My Father's commandments' (John 16:10).

66. His erecting the Tabernacle. See Exodus 40:2, and compare Zechariah 6:12.

67. His Completing of his Work. 'So Moses finished the work' (Exodus 40:33). What a blessed prefiguration was this of Him who declared, 'I have finished the work which Thou gavest Me to do' (John 17:4).

68. His Blessing of the People. 'And Moses blessed them' (Exodus 39:43). So too we read in Luke 24:50, 'And He led them out as far as to Bethany, and He lifted up His hands, and blessed them.'

69. His Anointing of God's House. 'And Moses took the anointing oil (the O.T. emblem of the Holy Spirit), and anointed the tabernacle and all that was therein' (Leviticus 8:10). Carefully compare Acts 2:1-3, 33.

70. His Unabated Strength. 'His eye was not dim, nor his natural force abated' (Deuteronomy 34:7): compare Matthew 27:50, and note the 'loud voice'.

71. His Death was for the benefit of God's people. 'It went ill with Moses for their sakes' (Psalm 106:32); 'But the Lord was wroth with me for your sakes' (Deuteronomy 3:26). What marvellous fore-shadowing of the Cross were these!

72. His Appointing of another Comforter. Moses did not leave his people comfortless, but gave them a successor: see Deuteronomy 31:23 and compare John 14:16, 18.

73. His giving an Inheritance. 'The land which Moses gave you on this side of Jordan' (Joshua 1:14): in Christ believers 'have obtained an inheritance' (Ephesians 1:11).

74. His Death necessary before Israel could enter Canaan. 'Moses My servant is dead; now therefore arise, go over this Jordan, thou, and all this people, unto the land which I do give to thee' (Joshua 1:2). 'Except a corn of wheat fall into the ground and die, it abideth alone: but if it die, it bringeth forth much fruit' (John 12:24).

75. His Second Appearing. Moses was one of the two Old Testament characters which returned to this earth in New Testament times (Matthew 17:3), a type of Christ's second coming to the earth.

Our space is already exhausted so we shall leave it with our readers to search the Scriptures for at least twenty-five other points in which Moses foreshadowed our Lord. The subject is well nigh exhaustless. And a most blessed subject it is, demonstrating anew the Divine authorship of the Bible. May the Lord bless to many this very imperfect attempt to show that 'in the volume of the Book' it is written of Christ.

# Chapter 9

## Moses' Faith

'And it came to pass in those days, when Moses was grown, that he went out unto his brethren, and looked on their burdens: and he spied an Egyptian smiting an Hebrew, one of his brethren. And he looked this way and that way, and when he saw that there was no man, he slew the Egyptian, and hid him in the sand. And when he went out the second day, behold, two men of the Hebrews strove together: and he said to him that did the wrong, Wherefore smitest thou thy fellow? And he said, Who made thee a prince and a judge over us? intendest thou to kill me, as thou killedst the Egyptian? And Moses feared, and said, Surely this thing is known. Now when Pharaoh heard this thing, he sought to slay Moses. But Moses fled from the face of Pharaoh, and dwelt in the land of Midian: and he sat down by a well.'
(Exodus 2:11-15)

Here the Spirit of God tells us about the faith of a man just like us, a sinner washed in the blood of Christ, robed in the righteousness of Christ, and saved by the grace of Christ. If we read this passage by itself, we might think, 'That does not look like faith to me. It looks like presumption and fear.' But we must interpret Scripture by Scripture, not by our own reason and experience. And in Hebrews 11:24-27 God the Holy Spirit points to this very event in the life of Moses and says, 'Look at this. This is what faith is.'

'By faith Moses, when he was come to years, refused to be called the son of Pharaoh's daughter; Choosing rather to suffer affliction with the people of God, than to enjoy the pleasures of sin for a season; Esteeming the reproach of Christ greater riches than the treasures in Egypt: for he had respect unto the recompense of the reward. By faith he forsook Egypt, not fearing the wrath of the king: for he endured, as seeing him who is invisible.'

Moses is an example of faith that is very well suited to us. There are many examples of faith held before us in Holy Scripture, examples we follow in spirit, but not in deed. God has not called us to offer up a literal sacrifice, like Abel. He has not called us to build a literal ark, like Noah. And the Lord has not called us to literally leave our homeland and families, to dwell in tents, or to offer up our Isaac, like Abraham. But Moses' faith exactly tallies with the experience of all God's saints. Moses' faith made him walk in the same path, make the same sacrifices, and endure the same trials as true faith requires of us today. As it was with Moses, so it is with all believers. True faith in the heart manifests itself by the same characteristics of life demonstrated by Moses.

**Identified With Israel**
Moses identified himself with Israel (Exodus 2:11, 12).

'And it came to pass in those days, when Moses was grown, that he went out unto his brethren, and looked on their burdens: and he spied an Egyptian smiting an Hebrew, one of his brethren. And he looked this way and that way, and when he saw that there was no man, he slew the Egyptian, and hid him in the sand'.

The reason Moses went out unto his brethren at this time, when he was forty years old, is clearly stated by God the Holy Spirit in Acts 7:23. He did so because 'it came into his heart to do so'. It came into his heart to identify himself with God's people, and thereby to identify himself with the God of Israel, because God put it in his heart to do so.

Moses openly and publicly took the part of the Israelite against the Egyptian. God the Holy Spirit tells us that when he did so, and slew the Egyptian, he did it as an act of faith. In a similar way, this is what we do in believer's baptism. We publicly identify ourselves with Christ, his gospel, and his people. Moses preferred Israel to Egypt. He preferred being an Israelite to being the most prestigious, powerful man in the world. He preferred the care of God's church and people to his own honour and wellbeing. Has it come into your heart to identify yourself with Christ, his gospel, and his people? Has the Lord God given you faith in Christ? If so, 'Why tarriest thou? Arise and be baptized'.

**Things He Refused**
When it came into his heart to visit his brethren, Moses gave up some things any man would naturally prefer not to give up. Specifically, we are told that Moses gave up three things for the sake of his soul. He could not have followed Christ, he could not have been saved had he kept them. So he gave them up. He sat down, counted the cost of following Christ, and willingly paid the price of doing so. Moses made three of the greatest sacrifices a man could ever make.

He gave up rank, position, and greatness. 'When he was come to years, he refused to be called the son of Pharaoh's daughter.' We are told, by tradition, that Pharaoh had but one daughter, his only child; and that Moses was her only child. She had adopted him as her son. He was next in line for the throne of Egypt, the greatest nation in the world. He could have been a great man, the most powerful, influential man in the world. But Moses refused it. This was a very great sacrifice. He refused the throne of Egypt. He forsook his family and a mother whom he loved. And he made the decision to do so when he was a man of forty years of age.

Moses gave up earthly ease and pleasure. The pleasures he gave up would have been for other men matters of indifference, involving no sin in themselves. They were simply the pleasures of wealth, security, comfort, luxury, and ease of life. But for Moses, they would have been 'the pleasures of sin', because they were contrary to the will of God. This, too, was a great sacrifice. Moses gave up that which all men and women of all ages and social conditions most naturally seek, their own personal pleasure!

Moses gave up great, great riches. 'The treasures of Egypt' were his. He had more wealth than any of us can imagine in his hand; but when God put it into his heart to visit his brethren, he dropped it all, every penny. This, I dare say, was his greatest, most difficult sacrifice. Most men are far more willing to give up both position and pleasure than give up prosperity. Yet, Moses did not give away only a portion of his wealth. He gave up all his wealth.

Let me show you something of how great Moses' sacrifices were. He gave up all of these things: position, pleasure, and prosperity, all at one time. He gave them up deliberately, as a wise, well educated, mature man, a full forty years old (Acts 7:22). His was not a hasty, rash decision made in an emotional moment, but a deliberate, wilful, calculated choice. He knew exactly what he was doing. He knew what he was giving up. He knew what he was choosing.

Nothing obliged Moses to give these things up, except the fact he believed God. Pharaoh had not disowned him. The children of Israel did not want him to become their leader. He was not a dying man who was about to leave the world, and, therefore, willing to give it up. He was not a beggar who had no rightful claim to or hope for these things. He was not an old man who could no longer enjoy these things. Moses willingly made these sacrifices for the honour of God and the good of his people, hoping for and expecting nothing in return.

**His Choices**

Moses choices were as great as his sacrifices. He chose to walk in a path completely contrary to the flesh, contrary to worldly wisdom, and contrary to personal desire. The Holy Spirit tells us Moses chose three things: 'Choosing rather to suffer affliction with the people of God, than to enjoy the pleasures of sin for a season' (Hebrews 11:25). Moses' choices were hard, costly choices. But they were necessary to the salvation of his soul. The things Moses chose did not in any way merit, earn, or cause his salvation. But had he not done these things, he could not have been saved. Though we choose to obey our Saviour, and obey him willingly, obedience is not an option with God's people. It is essential. We see that clearly in Exodus 4:24-27.

First, Moses chose a path of affliction and suffering. He chose conflict instead of comfort, adversity instead of advantage, sorrow instead of satisfaction, pain instead of peace, suffering instead of solace. Second, he chose the company of God's people. He left his family and friends and became one with the people of God. Their troubles became his troubles, their sorrows his sorrows. Moses not only preferred God's despised people to the people of this world, he preferred God's people to himself. Third, this man believed God and chose a path of reproach and scorn. He was, no doubt, mocked, belittled, ridiculed, and laughed at. He must have been the joke of Egypt. He saw reproach and scorn before him, and deliberately chose them. Most of us can face almost anything easier than we can face scorn and ridicule.

It is true, he was chosen of God to be one of his own; but Moses chose to be numbered among God's people. At first glance, this might not seem to be a very difficult choice for anyone to make. After all, these were the chosen, redeemed, peculiar people of God. These were the people to whom alone God gave his Word and ordinances of divine worship. God himself was with them. And Canaan was promised to them. But Moses was fully aware of the consequences of his choice. He counted the cost and chose rather to suffer the afflictions of God's elect than to enjoy the pleasures that were his in Egypt. He knew the afflictions God's people endured were hard afflictions indeed; but he also knew they were afflictions endured as the people of God. He knew they were divinely appointed, fatherly chastisements, that they were for the glory of God, that they were only temporary, and that they were spiritually and eternally beneficial (1 Peter 1:3-9).

There has never been a man, except the God-man, who made such sacrifices and choices as Moses made. He gave up a king's throne and chose a slave's rags. He gave up the king's palace for a place among God's people. He gave up riches for poverty. He gave up respectability and chose reproach.

### Motivated by Faith

Why would any sane, reasonable man make such choices? What compelled Moses to act as he did? What motivated him? The Holy Spirit tells us it was 'by faith Moses' did these things. Moses believed God. Faith motivated him. Faith directed him. Faith controlled him. Moses did what he did because he believed God.

Moses believed on Christ. He believed God's promise that he would send a Deliverer, a Redeemer, a Saviour, a King of the seed of Abraham in whom all the nations of the earth would be blessed. He believed God would keep his promise. He would fulfil his covenant. He would deliver his people. He would never forsake his own. Moses believed that with God nothing is impossible. The deliverance of Israel and the overthrow of Pharaoh seemed impossible. But Moses believed God! He believed in the wisdom and goodness of God's providence. Like Joseph before him, he was in the place of God, and he knew it. Moses believed God is faithful (Lamentations 3:21-26).

Blessed be his name, our God is faithful to his purpose, to his promise, and to his people. It was faith in Christ that caused Moses to see things that had not yet come to pass. Faith caused him to see temporal things as temporal and eternal things as eternal. Faith, remember, is the response of the believer's heart to God's revelation (Romans 10:17). Because he believed God's Word, Moses knew what God would have him to do; and faith in Christ gave him strength to do it. Yet, marvellous as Moses' sacrifices and choices seem to be, they are really not very marvellous at all. He believed God and acted accordingly.

**The Reproach of Christ**
Because he believed God, Moses esteemed the reproach of Christ to be far greater riches than the treasures of Egypt. 'Esteeming the reproach of Christ greater riches than the treasures in Egypt: for he had respect unto the recompense of the reward' (Hebrews 11: 26). The Scriptures do not declare that Moses esteemed reproach for Christ greater riches than the treasures of Egypt. He esteemed the reproach of Christ, that is to say the reproach the Lord Jesus Christ endured, the reproach Christ bore for him upon the cursed tree, as his Substitute, when he suffered and died under the wrath of God, being made sin for him (Psalm 69:9, 2 Corinthians 5:21).

Moses considered it his greatest wealth and honour to be allowed to identify himself with Christ and bear the reproach of Christ his Substitute (Philippians 3:10). He gladly bore the reproach of the gospel, the reproach God's people endured, and the reproach of worshipping his unseen God and Saviour. May God make us willing, always willing, to bear the reproach of Christ (1 Peter 2:19-24).

He was all the more willing to bear the reproach of Christ, because he had respect to the promises God had made in his Word. Believing God, 'he had respect unto the recompense of the reward' (Hebrews 11:26). That is to say, he believed God would do what he promised, and he looked for the recompense of reward. He expected it and anticipated it (2 Timothy 1:7-12). He was 'looking for the mercy of our Lord Jesus Christ unto eternal life'. Moses was looking for the deliverance of Israel out of their bondage, the blessings of Canaan, the blessedness of eternal glory with Christ.

## Fear, but No Fear

There appears to be a contradiction between Exodus 2:14 and Hebrews 11:27. Exodus 2:14 tells us that Moses was afraid of Pharaoh. But Hebrews 11:27 tells us he was not afraid of him. That is an obvious contradiction; but it is not a contradiction in the Scriptures. It is a contradiction of flesh and spirit. When Moses thought the thing was known to Pharaoh, he was, to put it mildly, afraid. I suspect he was utterly terrified. His heart must have quaked within him. But he overcame his fear of Pharaoh by his fear of God. Faith triumphed over fear. He fled from Egypt, not in fear, but in faith (1 John 4:4; 5:4, 5).

Moses made no effort to appease Pharaoh's wrath. His fleeing was not an act of cowardice, but of obedience to the will of God. There he must wait for God to send him for the work to which he was ordained. He must be trained in the prophecy-school of hardship, isolation, and trouble in the Midian desert. 'Temptation, prayer, and meditation', wrote Luther, 'make a minister.'

Pharaoh was a roaring lion; but Moses did not fear him. So, too, those who are called by the grace of God, out of a state of darkness and bondage, out of a strange land, forsake this world and all that is near and dear, when it is in competition with Christ, not fearing the wrath of any temporal king or prince, nor of Satan, the prince of this world.

## Enduring Faith

Moses' faith was enduring faith. 'He endured' says Hebrews 11:27. Faith perseveres. Faith never quits. Faith endures, and endures to the end. It endures the trials of providence, the afflictions of the gospel, the rod of chastisement, the warfare in our souls, and even countless falls. And the thing that causes faith to endure in God's saints today is the same thing that caused Moses' faith to endure. Being 'kept by the power of God through faith', it endures 'as seeing him who is invisible'. The cause of Moses' great faith, the thing that sustained him to the end was just that. Moses had seen God and lived seeing him who is invisible.

This was not a one-time sight, but an ever-increasing sight, a sight which guided, sustained and refreshed this man Moses unto the end. He saw the Lord God in Christ. He saw the invisible God in Christ. He saw Christ in the Word of God taught to him by his parents. He saw the Saviour in the bush. His life was ruled by 'the good will of him that dwelt in the bush'. He saw Christ our Passover sacrificed for us in the paschal lamb and sprinkled blood. He saw Christ in the salvation wrought for him and Israel at the Red Sea. His sight of God was the sight of faith, just like ours. It was entirely the spiritual sight of faith. It was a glorious, but humbling sight. It was a transforming sight. It was a separating sight. It was an inspiring sight. It was a sustaining sight. And it was a costly, but satisfying sight (Exodus 33:13-19).

**Some Lessons**
What lessons are we to learn from this man who believed God? We have seen what Moses did. He denied himself, took up his cross, and followed Christ. And we have seen why he did it. He believed God. But what does all of this have to do with us? What does the Spirit of God intend for us to learn from Moses' example?

If we would be heirs of eternal life, we must deny ourselves, take up our cross, and follow Christ (Luke 14:25-33). Where there is no cross, there is no crown. Where there is no sowing, there is no reaping. Where there is no battle, there is no victory. Where there is no struggle, there is no triumph. Nothing will cause a man in his heart to deny himself and forsake this world, except faith in Christ. If we believe Christ, we can and will follow him, regardless of cost or consequence.

If we live for ourselves and refuse to forsake this world, we cannot have faith, we cannot have Christ, we cannot have eternal life (Mark 8:34-38). If I prefer my will to God's will, if I seek my way rather than my Lord's way, if I prefer the world to Christ, if I place the things of time before the things of eternity, if I live for the comfort of my body, rather than for the welfare of my soul, if in my heart I prefer myself to Christ, I do not know Christ and I have no faith. No man can serve two masters. We will either serve self, or serve Christ. We will either deny self, or deny Christ. We will either live for the world, or live for Christ. Choose you this day whom you will serve. If we believe Christ, follow Christ, and seek the will of and glory of Christ, our God will take care of all our earthly and eternal interests (Matthew 10:28-33).

This faith, the faith Moses had, the faith all God's elect have in this world, is the gift of God. Only the Spirit of God can create true faith in a sinner's heart (Ephesians 2:8-10). Has God given you faith? Has the Lord given me faith? Surely, then, it is a most reasonable thing for us to give ourselves to him.

# Chapter 10

# 'God Remembered'

'And it came to pass in process of time, that the king of Egypt died: and the children of Israel sighed by reason of the bondage, and they cried, and their cry came up unto God by reason of the bondage. And God heard their groaning, and God remembered his covenant with Abraham, with Isaac, and with Jacob. And God looked upon the children of Israel, and God had respect unto them.'
(Exodus 2:23-25)

When someone says to me, 'I will remember you', I take that to mean the person loves me and is concerned for me. I often receive letters from people around the world, who tell me, 'I remember you in prayer every day'. Whenever I do, I am humbled and filled with gratitude. What a great blessing! I take those words to mean, I am loved and prayed for by someone who knows that I need God's constant grace, protection, direction, and care. Frequently, particularly when I am preparing to leave for preaching engagements, members of our church family remind me they remember me in prayer before the throne of grace. Words cannot express what that fact means to me. It tells me the people I serve love me, are concerned for me, that they have a real interest in the work God has trusted to our hands, and they know something of both my weakness and inability, and God's greatness and infinite ability.

To be remembered by God's saints in prayer before the throne of God is, to me, a wonderful blessing of God's goodness. It is of indescribable value. Yet, there is a blessing of God's goodness that surpasses that infinitely. Great as it is to be remembered before God, this is better: We are remembered by our God. Our heavenly Father remembers us. God our Saviour remembers us. We are engraved upon his heart. He never forgets us. He purposefully remembers us, always, in all our circumstances. All he does, he does because he remembers us in infinite grace, in tender mercy, and in faithful, lovingkindness. What could be more wonderfully glorious? That is what we read in Exodus 2:23-25.

'It came to pass in process of time, that the king of Egypt died.' God raises up kings and destroys them as he will. While they live, he rules them absolutely. When he is done with them, he puts them down. And the mightest of kings, just like the most insignificant worms of the human race, die at the time appointed by God from eternity. In the process of time Pharaoh died; and so shall we.

'And the children of Israel sighed by reason of the bondage.' Another king was on the throne; but God's people were still in bondage and bitter affliction. Political changes never change human nature. Cain hates Abel, Ishmael despises Isaac, and the serpent's seed afflicts the woman's seed in all nations, at all times, relentlessly. That fact will not be altered until the offense of the cross ceases to enrage the hearts of men.

'And they cried, and their cry came up unto God'. They sighed and groaned by reason of their bondage and affliction. It is a great blessing of grace for the God of glory to hear the cries of our hearts when we call upon his name in prayer (Psalm 18:6). That is truly a blessing indescribable. But the children of Israel did not cry to him. They only sighed and groaned by reason of their bondage and affliction. There is no indication of any repentance. They had learned the ways of the Egyptians, and cried to the gods of the Egyptians (Joshua 24:14). They cried to the river gods, frog gods, and calf gods of their captors. Yet, their God, the only Lord God, heard their cry, not because of them, but in spite of them. 'And their cry came up unto God by reason of the bondage'. He heard them, because they needed him, though they looked to other gods. That is called free grace; unconditional, immutable, indestructible!

'And God heard their groaning.' Yes, he hears the very groans of our hearts! 'And God heard their groaning, and God remembered his covenant with Abraham, with Isaac, and with Jacob' (Genesis 15:14; 46:4; Exodus 6:5; Psalm 105:8, 42). 'And God looked upon the children of Israel.' He looked upon them with pity and compassion, and beheld their bondage and affliction. 'And God had respect unto them.' He favoured them as the objects of his tender mercy, love, and grace.

## God's Respect

Throughout the Word of God we are told that God is 'no respecter of persons'. How often have you heard some ignorant Arminian throw those words at you, as if that statement denies of God's free, sovereign, electing love and discriminating grace? Yet, here we read that God had respect to the children of Israel. We see that frequently in the Book of God. There are some people who are distinctly respected, favoured, loved, and accepted by God (Genesis 4:4, 5; Romans 9:11-13).

True, God respects no man's person. That is to say, God does not show partiality to anyone because of anything in man. Those things that cause us to be prejudicial and show partiality, for example, race, wealth, education, morality, etc., God Almighty sees through. He sees all men exactly the same. He sees every man as he really is, nothing but filth and sin. Therefore, he is no respecter of persons. Race, place, and face mean nothing to God (Acts 10:34, 35; Romans 2:9-11; Ephesians 6:8, 9; Colossians 3:25; James 2:1, 2; 1 Peter 1:17). And they should mean nothing to us. Social, economic, racial matters ought never have any place in our esteem of others (Colossians 3:11).

While it is certainly true that God respects no man's person, never imagine God does not show partiality, favouring some and not others, being gracious to some and not others, loving some and not others. The Scriptures universally declare that there are some to whom God shows infinite, eternal, distinguishing favour and respect (Exodus 2:23-25; Leviticus 26:9; 2 Kings 13:23; Psalm 74:19, 20). If you will read these references, you will see in each of them God's respect of men is based not upon their persons, but upon his covenant. God shows favour to some and passes by others because of, and only because of his covenant. It is on the basis of God's covenant of redemption and grace made with Christ before the world began that he deals favourably with, and receives, sinners in time. It is this covenant of which David sang on his deathbed. It is by this covenant that all things are brought to pass in God's providence. And it is by this covenant that all the blessings of grace flow to chosen, redeemed sinners in Christ (2 Samuel 23:5; Romans 8:28-31; Ephesians 1:3-6). Thank God for the covenant!

## God Remembers

Thank God, he remembers his covenant! That is the delightful thing revealed in Exodus 2:23-25. 'God remembered his covenant with Abraham, with Isaac, and with Jacob'. That covenant God made with Abraham and confirmed to Isaac and Jacob was but a typical picture of the covenant of grace made with Christ before the world was, ratified and fulfilled by our Surety's blood, and confirmed to us by the gift of faith in Christ.

Without question, David had this passage of Scripture in mind when he was inspired of God to write Psalm 136. This psalm is distinct from others because of the chorus repeated in each verse, 'for his mercy endureth for ever'. It is a song of praise for God's enduring mercy. The chorus, 'for his mercy endureth for ever', we are told was a favourite among the Old Testament saints. They often sang it when giving praise for the display of God's great goodness in the performance of his wondrous works.

This psalm was probably written by David when he brought the ark of the covenant to Jerusalem. In 1 Chronicles 16:34 David said, 'O give thanks unto the Lord; for he is good; for his mercy endureth for ever'. Solomon repeated those words when he dedicated the temple. When the glory of the Lord filled the temple and the people fell with their faces upon the pavement, Solomon led them in a chorus of praise, 'The Lord is good, for his mercy endureth for ever'. Then, again in 2 Chronicles 20:21, when Jehoshaphat led Judah out against the overwhelming armies of Ammon and Moab, who had come up from the valley of Tekoa, he appointed singers to sing praise to God, saying, 'Praise the Lord; for his mercy endureth for ever'. In this great psalm, David calls for all who have experienced his grace to give thanks to God because of his greatness, his great goodness, and his great works of goodness for his people. Then, in verses 23 and 24 he refers to that which Moses wrote in Exodus 2:23-25. 'Who remembered us in our low estate: for his mercy endureth for ever: And hath redeemed us from our enemies: for his mercy endureth for ever.'

What thanks! What praise! What wonder! What comfort fills our hearts when we meditate upon the boundless mercy of our God! That he pities us in our misery and is determined to do us good, that his mercy endures forever, without abatement, that his mercy is from eternity to eternity; constant, immutable, and sure. Oh, what a cause this is for wonder and praise! Psalm 136 is a psalm of praise to God for his unfailing mercy, 'who remembered us in our low estate: for his mercy endureth for ever: And hath redeemed us from our enemies: for his mercy endureth for ever'. Do you sense something of the wonder of those words?

## Contrast

Moses wrote 'God remembered his covenant with Abraham, with Isaac, and with Jacob'. The Holy Spirit translates that to mean, that he 'remembered us in our low estate: for his mercy endureth for ever'. What a contrast there is between our God and us! We forget. He remembers! We are able to retain in our memory the most trivial, most useless, and even the most abominable things with ease. Try as we may, we just cannot forget worthless things. But that which is good, useful, profitable, spiritual, and meaningful, we forget very quickly, though try as we may to remember. I can remember jokes I heard as a child; but I quickly forget a passage of Holy Scripture I read this morning!

More tragically by far, how often, how quickly, how easily we forget God our Saviour and his countless mercies! In order to help us remember him, knowing our infirmity, our Lord gave us the blessed ordinance of the Lord's Supper, and told us to keep the ordinance often in remembrance of him. But, blessed be his name, our God never forgets us. He is, as A. W. Pink put it, 'The Faithful Rememberer'.

I found it very interesting and instructive to discover that the first five times the word 'remember' is used in Holy Scripture, we see God remembering his chosen (Genesis 8:1; 9:15, 16; 19:29; 30:22). The first time the word 'remember' is used with reference to man is in Genesis 40:23. There we read, 'Yet did not the chief butler remember Joseph, but forgat him'.

## Israel in Egypt

David tells us God 'remembered us in our low estate'. Israel was a nation of slaves, groaning under the lash of merciless task-masters, oppressed by a cruel, heartless king. But when there was no other eye to pity them, the Lord God looked upon them, heard their cries of distress, and 'remembered' them in their low estate. 'And God heard their groaning, and God remembered his covenant with Abraham, with Isaac, and with Jacob. And God looked upon the children of Israel, and God had respect unto it'.

This blessed word of grace is not to be limited to the physical seed of Abraham. It is God's word to us, to the whole 'Israel of God' (Galatians 6:16). We unite with God's saints of old, and sing, 'Who remembered us in our low estate: for his mercy endureth forever!' How 'low' our 'estate' was by nature! Fallen, sinful, and corrupt, we were in bondage and misery, wretched, ruined, and lost, unable to deliver, or even to help ourselves. But, in wondrous grace, God took pity on us. His strong arm reached down and rescued us. He came to where we were, saw us, and had compassion on us, and ran to us (Luke 15:20). Therefore we sing, 'He brought me up also out of an horrible pit, out of the miry clay, and set my feet upon a rock, and established my goings' (Psalm 40:2).

**Why?**
Why did He 'remember' us? The word 'remember' does not imply that God had forgotten us. That is never the case with Almighty God. 'Known unto God are all his works from the beginning of the world' (Acts 15:18). He declares, 'Behold, I have graven thee upon the palms of my hands; thy walls are continually before me' (Isaiah 49:16). Jeremiah the prophet assures us of God's constant knowledge of his elect. 'For I know the thoughts that I think toward you, saith the LORD, thoughts of peace, and not of evil, to give you an expected end' (Jeremiah 29:11).

The word 'remembered' tells us of God's previous thoughts of love and mercy toward us. As it was typically with the children of Israel in Egypt, so it was with us in our low estate. He 'remembered' his covenant, that covenant into which he had entered with Christ our Surety from old eternity. In that covenant, eternal life was promised to us in Christ, all the blessings of grace were bestowed upon us, and we were 'accepted in the Beloved', that is, we were respected and favoured, because the Lord God trusted our Surety Jesus Christ, the Lamb slain from the foundation of the world (Titus 1:2; Ephesians 3:3-6; Romans

8:28-31; Ephesians 1:12; Revelation 13:8; 17:8). God 'remembered' he had 'chosen us in him before the foundation of the world' (Ephesians 1:4). Therefore, in due time, Christ died for the ungodly, redeeming us with his precious blood, and, at the appointed time of love, sent his Spirit to redeem us from the bondage of our spiritual death by the power of his grace (Psalm 136:23, 24; Galatians 4:4-6), bringing us from death unto life by his omnipotent grace.

## Israel in the Wilderness

As David sings about this word recorded by Moses, he takes God's remembrance of our souls beyond our initial experience of his free, saving grace in Christ, and applies it to the wilderness wanderings of his people as they made their way from Egypt to Canaan. As you know, Israel's experiences in the desert were typical of our pilgrimage through this hostile world of woe. The Lord's remembrance of them was manifested in the daily supply of their every need. When the waters at Marah were bitter, he sweetened them. To feed his people, the Lord God poured manna from heaven for forty years. The Rock that followed them gushed with water to refresh them. Protected by God's presence, and so richly supplied by his hand, their clothes and shoes never wore out. Israel walked through the waste and howling wilderness for forty years and lacked nothing!

But all those historic facts pale into insignificance, when we realize they were things performed by our God only to typify, represent, and foreshadow the rich provisions of his boundless grace for us while we journey to our home on high. True, our present estate is but a lowly one. Yet, the Lord our God is ever mindful of us, and richly provides for us, ever remembering his covenant, so that having Christ we have all and lack nothing (Romans 8:28-32).

We do not always dwell upon the mountain top. We are often in deep valleys. Bright and sunny days give place to dark and cloudy ones. Summer is followed by winter. Disappointments, losses, afflictions, bereavements come our way; and we are brought low. Frequently, just when we most need the comfort of friends, they fail us. Those we count on to help, often forget us. But, even then, our great God and Saviour remembers us, and shows himself to be 'the same yesterday and today and forever'. 'O give thanks unto the LORD; for he is good; for his mercy endureth for ever' (1 Chronicles 16:34).

Yet, how often we forget him! How often our hearts turn cold and hard; and we forget our first love! How low our estate is then! Yet, he remembers his covenant, and comes to us in grace, awaking our hearts, and causing us to seek him anew with all our hearts (Song of Solomon 5:1-7). Then, we sing with David, 'He restoreth my soul; he leadeth me in the paths of righteousness for his name's sake' (Psalm 23:3).

In the hour of death we may be in a very low estate. When this heart and flesh shall fail, when the cold sweat of death is on our brow, our 'estate' may be low. But then the Lord God shall still remember his covenant and remember us, for 'his mercy endureth for ever'. It has often been said, 'Man's extremity is but God's opportunity'. His strength is made perfect in our weakness. In that hour our God will remember his covenant, though we may forget, and he will remember us. Though we may forget him, yet he will make good his promises (Isaiah 41:10; 43:1-7; 25:9).

'God remembered his covenant'. How we shall praise him in heaven's glory for his covenant faithfulness, his matchless grace, and his lovingkindness for having 'remembered us in our low estate!' Then we shall know, even as we are known. Our memories will be renewed, perfected, and we shall remember all the way the Lord our God has led us (Deuteronomy 8:2), recalling with gratitude and joy his faithful remembrance of our souls, acknowledging with adoration that, 'His mercy endureth for ever'. He remembers his covenant, and remembers us, because 'his mercy endureth forever!' 'O give thanks unto the God of heaven: for his mercy endureth for ever' (Psalm 136:26).

# Chapter 11

# God Remembers His Covenant

'And it came to pass in process of time, that the king of Egypt died: and the children of Israel sighed by reason of the bondage, and they cried, and their cry came up unto God by reason of the bondage.' (Exodus 2:23)

The children of Israel had been oppressed under Pharaoh for many years. At last, Pharaoh died. They must have hoped for relief from the new Egyptian king. But their miseries were only increased. They had, no doubt, sighed, and groaned, and cried much during their bondage in Egypt. But we are not told they cried unto God until now. Is it the case with you? How often it is! We all sigh, and groan, and cry because of trouble. But our heavenly Father's chastening rod is intended to graciously force us to pour out our souls to him. When our trials bring us to our Saviour's feet, lay us low, and keep us there, then our trials have been blessed and sanctified to our souls (Hebrews 4:16).

Many cry because of trouble and groan because of sorrow, without regard to their sin, which is the great cause of trouble and sorrow. Theirs is a repentance to be repented of. Job tells us they cry, but cry not to God (Job 35:9, 10). There is no crying to God, without crying because of sin. Do we cry out to our God in repentance; or do we just cry? Do our troubles lead us to repentance, or do they only lead us to sorrow? Blessed are they who are constrained by God's grace to cry out to him, looking to him alone for deliverance by his own free grace in Christ.

'And God heard their groaning, and God remembered his covenant with Abraham, with Isaac, and with Jacob. And God looked upon the children of Israel, and God had respect unto them' (vv. 24, 25).

Here we see the order by which God's grace comes into our souls. God's covenant is the source and cause of all mercy and grace. God remembers his covenant. He hears the cries of his chosen, looks on us in mercy, has respect to his elect, because he has respect to his covenant. 'The Lord was gracious unto them, and had compassion on them, and had respect unto them, because of his covenant' (2 Kings 13:23).

God remembers his covenant. He may chasten us; but he always remembers his covenant. He often hides his face; but he always remembers his covenant. He sometimes appears to forget us, and even appears to forsake us; but he always remembers his covenant (Isaiah 54:4-10; Psalm 89:28-34). Though we often forsake him, he will never forsake us. Though we often forget him, he will never forget us. Though 'we believe not, yet, he abideth faithful: he cannot deny himself' (2 Timothy 2:13).

## Psalm 106

I want you to see, and see it clearly for yourself, that I have not stretched the meaning of the words stated and the promises implied in our text beyond the intent of God the Holy Spirit. If you will turn to Psalm 106, you will see how David was inspired to praise God for his goodness and mercy, ever remembering his covenant, in spite of the many sins and failures of his saints. In verses 1 and 2 he calls us to praise our God and give thanks to him. Then, he asks God to remember him, and teaches us to do the same (vv. 4, 5).

Next, David begins to confess the sins of Israel, celebrating God's faithfulness and goodness, his mercy and grace to such a sinful, undeserving people (vv. 6, 7, 13-15, 19-25, 28, 29, 36-39, 43). Remember, throughout this Psalm, David is talking about our experience of God's grace in this world. Israel's whole experience typified ours. In verses 8, David tells us why God is so faithfully gracious to us. 'Nevertheless he saved them for his name's sake, that he might make his mighty power to be known.' And in verses 44, 45, David refers to our text in Exodus 2:24, 25. 'Nevertheless he regarded their affliction, when he heard their cry: And he remembered for them his covenant, and repented according to the multitude of his mercies.'

108

**Prayer**

There is something very powerful about the cry of a child to its father and mother. There is something very powerful about our cries to our God, the most tender of all fathers. 'Like as a father pitieth his children, so the LORD pitieth them that fear him' (Psalm 103:13). Let us kiss the hand that wounds us, and that hand will bind us up. Cry out to your heavenly Father, and he will turn unto you in lovingkindness, because God remembers his covenant.

'And God heard their groaning, and God remembered his covenant with Abraham, with Isaac, and with Jacob. And God looked upon the children of Israel, and God had respect unto them'.

Why did the Lord hear the cries of his afflicted children in Egypt? Why did he have respect to his people in their trouble? 'God remembered his covenant with Abraham, with Isaac, and with Jacob.' He looked to the covenant he had made of old with their father Abraham, when he said, 'Surely blessing I will bless thee, and multiplying I will multiply thee'. Because that promise had gone out of his mouth, he would not withdraw it! Here is a cause for great joy. Our God finds the reason for his mercy to us in himself, and in himself alone! Therefore, we have reason to believe and to believe confidently, he will ever be gracious to us. He remembers his covenant. Though there is nothing in us to fetch his mercy, there is everything in the covenant. He remembers his own covenant and, for his own name's sake, he deals with us in mercy.

Our text does not say, 'God remembered their covenant'. They broke every covenant they made, just as we do. Our text says, 'God remembered his covenant'. 'Nevertheless, for their sake, he remembered his covenant'. And his covenant is a covenant of pure, free, sovereign grace.

The Lord said to Abraham, 'I will establish my covenant between me and thee and thy seed after thee in their generations for an everlasting covenant, to be a God unto thee, and to thy seed after thee'. That same covenant, after being made more fully known in his promises to Moses and many others, was stated anew in Psalm 89. 'I have made a covenant with my chosen, I have sworn unto David my servant, Thy seed will I establish for ever, and build up thy throne to all generations. Selah'. Since then the Lord has given us promises by his Prophets and

Apostles, and particularly in the Person and ministry of his own dear Son, affirming that same, blessed, and everlasting covenant, ordered in all things and sure. It is this covenant God remembers. It is the great foundation upon which all our hopes are built.

**The Covenant**
Blessed be his name, our God has made for us an everlasting covenant, ordered in all things and sure. And this is all our salvation, and all our desire. The covenant God remembered was made long before the mercy was needed. Our text speaks of a covenant remembered. It could not have been remembered had it not been made beforehand. In love he remembered the covenant as an abiding thing. Our God declares, 'My Covenant will I not break, nor alter the thing that is gone out of my lips'. What shall I say about this covenant? How does the Word of God describe it?

This covenant is an everlasting covenant (2 Samuel 23:5). This covenant, which our God has made for us from eternity, is a covenant of pure, free, grace. Everything in it speaks of grace (Jeremiah 31:3, 31-34; 32:37-41). This everlasting covenant of grace is a covenant made in anticipation of, not as a reaction to, our needs (Isaiah 48:4-8).

When God chose Abraham and made him his friend, he knew what failures there would be in Abraham and in his seed. He made his choice deliberately, knowing the end from the beginning and foreseeing all the provocations which he would endure for 40 years in the wilderness, and how they would provoke him to anger again and again in the Land of Canaan. So, too, God's choice of his redeemed was made deliberately; and the promises made to us in Christ were given in the full knowledge of all our unbelief, lukewarmness, backsliding, selfishness and sin!

'I have declared the former things from the beginning; and they went forth out of my mouth, and I showed them; I did them suddenly, and they came to pass. Because I knew that thou art obstinate, and thy neck is an iron sinew, and thy brow brass; I have even from the beginning declared it to thee; before it came to pass I showed it thee: lest thou shouldest say, Mine idol hath done them, and my graven image, and my molten image, hath commanded them ... Yea, thou heardest not; yea, thou knewest not; yea, from that time that thine ear was not opened: for I knew that thou wouldest deal very treacherously, and wast called a transgressor from the womb' (Isaiah 48:3-8).

The covenant is not according to what we deserve, but according to the greatness of God's grace and the immutability of his promise. This covenant of grace was sealed and ratified, made sure and certain by Christ our Surety, the Lamb slain from the foundation of the world. When God revealed his covenant to Abraham, Abraham was commanded to offer sacrifices which were later identified as sin offerings (Leviticus 1-5). The sacrifices were slain and divided. Then, the image of a burning lamp passed between the pieces. What a solemn night that was! When Abraham awoke from his sleep, he saw vultures attempting to devour the sacrifices, and drove them away.

Thus the covenant was symbolically ratified before him. But when the triune God made his covenant for us, the seal he gave was infinitely greater and infinitely more precious. He took his only-begotten Son and gave him to be a Covenant to us (Isaiah 49:8).

The covenant was made sure by 'the blood of the everlasting covenant', by the blood of the Lamb, our Surety, accepted and trusted from eternity. Our Saviour says, as we hold the cup at the Table, 'This cup is the new covenant in my blood.' His blood, accepted before God and accepted by our God from everlasting, has made us accepted, and has procured for us all mercy and grace from everlasting (Romans 8:29, 30; Ephesians 1:3-6).

Can God deny his promise to his bleeding Son? Can he turn his back from the promise he made to the Son of his love in his death? Never! 'By his knowledge shall my righteous Servant justify many; for he shall bear their iniquities.' Can these promises fail? Impossible! The very thought of such a possibility is blasphemous! This covenant, ratified and made sure by the death of our great Surety and Sacrifice, can never be repealed, neglected, changed, or forgotten.

This everlasting covenant of grace will and must stand forever, because the very glory of the triune God stands or falls with it (Ephesians 1:3-14). He declares, 'This people have I formed for Myself: they shall show forth My praise' (Isaiah 43:21; Micah 7:17, 18; Ephesians 2:7). C. H. Spurgeon, wrote:

'God is more glorified in the Covenant of Grace than in creation, or in Providence. In fact, creation and Providence are but the temporary scaffold of the great house which God is building, even the God who inhabits the praises of Israel! The Lord cannot break His Word, nor forego His designs, nor forget His promises. Do not even think it! The

111

crown jewels of God are staked and pawned upon the carrying out of the Covenant of Grace!'

Blessed be his name, it is not possible for God to break his covenant, no matter what strain is put upon it, even by us! The covenant and purpose of our God to save his own stands fast; come what may. 'If we believe not, yet he abideth faithful: he cannot deny himself.' They that trust in the Lord, notwithstanding all the enormous weight of their sin, shall find him faithful to his covenant. He will keep his covenant forever.

## We Forget

God ever keeps his covenant; but how often we forget! It appears that the children of Israel had forgotten the covenant while they were in Egypt. Whether that is absolutely so or not, this is. We often forget! How often, because of sin and sorrow, when we are laid low, we say, 'The Lord has forsaken me, and my God has forgotten me.' When we do, the Lord our God, our covenant-keeping God asks, 'Can a woman forget her sucking child, that she should not have compassion on the son of her womb? yea, they may forget, yet will I not forget thee' (Isaiah 49:15). These are the terms of our marriage covenant with God our Saviour:

'And in that day will I make a covenant for them with the beasts of the field, and with the fowls of heaven, and with the creeping things of the ground: and I will break the bow and the sword and the battle out of the earth, and will make them to lie down safely. And I will betroth thee unto me for ever; yea, I will betroth thee unto me in righteousness, and in judgment, and in lovingkindness, and in mercies. I will even betroth thee unto me in faithfulness: and thou shalt know the LORD' (Hosea 2:18-20). And, though we forget him and his covenant, he declares:

'Nevertheless I will remember my covenant with thee in the days of thy youth, and I will establish unto thee an everlasting covenant. Then thou shalt remember thy ways, and be ashamed, when thou shalt receive thy sisters, thine elder and thy younger: and I will give them unto thee for daughters, but not by thy covenant. And I will establish my covenant with thee; and thou shalt know that I am the LORD: That thou mayest remember, and be confounded, and never open thy mouth any more because of thy shame, when I am pacified toward thee for all that thou hast done, saith the Lord GOD' (Ezekiel 16:60-63).

He is still God in covenant with us. Though he causes grief, yet will he have compassion. He has said, 'All things work together for good to them that love God', and he will keep his Word. He has also said, 'When thou passest through the waters, I will be with thee, and through the rivers, they shall not overflow thee; when thou walkest through the fire, thou shalt not be burned, neither shall the flame kindle upon thee.' Depend upon it. He will preserve you. 'Cast thy burden upon the LORD, and he shall sustain thee: he shall never suffer the righteous to be moved' (Psalm 55:22).

> What cheering words are these! Their sweetness who can tell?
> In time and to eternal days, 'Tis with the righteous well.

In wrath, our God ever remembers mercy. Oh, that we could learn to say with Job, in the darkest night of our most difficult trials, 'Though he slay me, yet will I trust in him'.

'Although the fig tree shall not blossom, neither shall fruit be in the vines; the labour of the olive shall fail, and the fields shall yield no meat; the flock shall be cut off from the fold, and there shall be no herd in the stalls: Yet I will rejoice in the LORD, I will joy in the God of my salvation' (Habakkuk 3:17, 18).

**Their Groanings**
Though, to our shame, we often forget, our God always remembers his covenant. Because he remembered his covenant, when the children of Israel groaned in Egypt, 'God heard their groanings'. Because the covenant is always before him, he remembers it, stands to it, and performs it. Because he remembers his covenant, the Lord our God hears the groanings of our hearts (Romans 8:22-27). He ever looks upon us with tenderness and compassion, with the pity of a loving father (Psalm 103:13, 14). Because he remembers his covenant, our great God always has respect unto his own. That is to say, he always loves us, knows us, owns us as his own, accepts us, approves of us, and cares for us (Isaiah 63:9). Because of Christ, with whom the covenant of grace was made, in whom it stands, who is forever the Father's delight, the Father has compassion on us. God remembers the covenant, because he remembers Christ; and he would have us ever looking to Christ, to remember his covenant (Hebrews 9:15; 10:9-14).

Jesus, spotless Lamb of God,
Thou hast bought me with Thy blood,
I would value none beside,
Jesus – Jesus crucified.

I am Thine, and Thine alone,
This I gladly, fully own;
And in all my works and ways,
Only now would seek Thy praise.

Help me to confess Thy name,
Bear with joy Thy cross and shame,
Only seek to follow Thee,
Though reproach my portion be.

When Thou shalt in glory come,
And I reach my heavenly home,
Loudly still my lips shall own –
I am Thine, and Thine alone.

James G. Deck

# Chapter 12

# 'The Mountain Of God'

'Now Moses kept the flock of Jethro his father in law, the priest of Midian: and he led the flock to the backside of the desert, and came to the mountain of God, even to Horeb. And the angel of the LORD appeared unto him in a flame of fire out of the midst of a bush: and he looked, and, behold, the bush burned with fire, and the bush was not consumed. And Moses said, I will now turn aside, and see this great sight, why the bush is not burnt. And when the LORD saw that he turned aside to see, God called unto him out of the midst of the bush, and said, Moses, Moses. And he said, Here am I. And he said, Draw not nigh hither: put off thy shoes from off thy feet, for the place whereon thou standest is holy ground. Moreover he said, I am the God of thy father, the God of Abraham, the God of Isaac, and the God of Jacob. And Moses hid his face; for he was afraid to look upon God. And the LORD said, I have surely seen the affliction of my people which are in Egypt, and have heard their cry by reason of their taskmasters; for I know their sorrows; And I am come down to deliver them out of the hand of the Egyptians, and to bring them up out of that land unto a good land and a large, unto a land flowing with milk and honey; unto the place of the Canaanites, and the Hittites, and the Amorites, and the Perizzites, and the Hivites, and the Jebusites. Now therefore, behold, the cry of the children of Israel is come unto me: and I have also seen the oppression wherewith the Egyptians oppress them. Come now therefore, and I will send thee unto Pharaoh, that thou mayest bring forth my people the children of Israel out of Egypt.'
(Exodus 3:1-10)

Moses was about as far out of the loop as a man can get. He was not in Egypt, but in Midian. He was not involved in some great work, but tending his father-in-law's sheep. What a contrast to his former life in Pharaoh's court. There he was surrounded with all the luxury and refinement of his age. Now he is a nobody, an insignificant outsider, living upon the charity of his father-in-law. In Egypt, Moses had been very zealous for the children of Israel; but he had now been in Midian for forty years (Acts 7:30). He appeared to be on the fast track to nowhere. He probably long ago concluded God had left him to live out his days in obscurity. He could not have been more mistaken.

### The Mountain of God

One day, while taking care of his father-in-law's sheep, he came to a place called Mount Horeb, 'the mountain of God'. Mount Horeb is another name for Mount Sinai. Moses called Mount Sinai, 'the mountain of God' (v. 1), because this is the place where the Lord Jesus came to Moses and revealed himself to him. It was here, in 'the mountain of God', that he learned 'the good will of him that dwelt in the bush'. Truly, any place where the Son of God manifests himself to us is 'the mountain of God'. But we must not forget that Moses gave this name, 'the mountain of God', to Mount Sinai by the inspiration of God the Holy Spirit. It seems to me he was inspired to do so to teach him and us, even before God gave his law from Mount Sinai, that Mount Sinai's fiery law had only one purpose. Its purpose is to bring us to Christ (Galatians 3:19-25).

### The Burning Bush

Suddenly, while he was tending Jethro's sheep, Moses saw an astonishing thing before him. He would in the days to come see many other astonishing things; but nothing would have such a lasting, life-long impression upon him as this. What he saw that day would alter and control his life forever. He never forgot it. In fact, he spoke of this event and the things he saw and heard on this day when he was about to die (Deuteronomy 33:16). Suddenly, he saw a bush burning with fire, and 'the bush was not consumed'.

'And the angel of the LORD appeared unto him in a flame of fire out of the midst of a bush: and he looked, and, behold, the bush burned with fire, and the bush was not consumed. And Moses said, I will now turn aside, and see this great sight, why the bush is not burnt' (vv. 2, 3). This revelation of God in the burning bush was not given just to astonish Moses. It was not given just to give him a hair-raising, thrilling, sensational, experience. The Lord God appeared to Moses in the bush to teach him vital lessons about Moses himself, about his God, about his people Israel, and about his personal salvation, lessons he would need to both motivate and sustain him throughout the rest of his life. Moses had been educated as the Son of Pharaoh in Egypt. He had the best education the world had to offer. But he was about to get a lesson in the school of grace. There he would get an education that cannot be gained anywhere else.

### The Angel

First, 'the Angel of the Lord appeared unto him in a flame'. The word 'angel' means 'messenger'. We do not have to guess who this Angel, this heavenly Messenger, is. It is none other than the Lord Jesus Christ himself who appeared to Moses in the flame, that One in whom and by whom alone God is revealed (Malachi 3:1; John 1:18).

What was that bush in which the Lord God revealed himself to Moses? The word translated 'bush' refers to a prickly bush, or a thorn bush. This bush is that which came as the curse of God upon the ground because of man's sin (Genesis 3:18). The Lord God revealed himself to Moses in the thorn bush, as if to show that he overrules and uses even the consequences of man's sin to make known and accomplish his purpose of grace toward fallen sinners through the Lord Jesus Christ. It is God's purpose of grace that Moses later describes as 'the good will of him that dwelt in the bush' (Deuteronomy 33:16).

What Moses saw was a type and picture of God the Son dwelling in our nature. Here we see our God, who 'is a consuming fire' (Hebrews 12:29), appearing in a bush, a thorn bush, that burned with fire and was not consumed. So the Lord of Glory, in due time, appeared on this earth in human flesh, in our nature, as one of us, God in our nature, that he might suffer all the fire of God's holiness, justice, and wrath as our Substitute (John 1:14; Philippians 2:5-8)

When the Lord Jesus bore our sins in his own body on the tree, and bore all the wrath of God for us, he was, like the sacrifices on the brazen altar, burned with the fire of God's offended justice, but with this great

117

difference, those sacrifices were consumed by the fire. Christ, our great Sacrifice, was not consumed by the fire, but consumed the fire forever (Isaiah 53:4-10; 2 Corinthians 5:21; Colossians 2:9-14).

What is our nature, at best, but a worthless, dry thorn bush, fit for burning? Yet, as the bush Moses saw burned with fire, the very fire of the shekinah glory of God, and was not consumed, so in our nature the glory of the God-man shone. 'We beheld his glory, the glory as of the only begotten of the Father, full of grace and truth.'

**God's People**
When Moses saw the bush burning with fire, and yet not consumed by it, he had before his eyes a lively picture of God's people in this world. The Lord Jesus Christ now dwells in our nature by grace. 'Christ in you, the Hope of glory'. Yes, the Son of God dwells in such prickly thorn bushes as we are. These bushes that burn with the fiery lusts of the flesh, the corruption of an evil heart, the fiery darts of the devil, and the fiery opposition of the world, shall not be consumed. From ashes to ashes and dust to dust we must go, yet the bushes shall not be consumed. We shall be resurrected in glory by 'the good will of him that dwelt in the bush'.

As he stood staring at the burning bush, Moses must have thought about his brethren in Egypt. They were, at that moment, in a fiery furnace of affliction. But they would not be consumed by it. The church of the Lord Jesus is, in all ages, like a bush burning with the fires of affliction and trouble, opposition and persecution, yet thriving in the flames, because of Christ's abiding presence and support. The furnace of affliction could not destroy the people of Israel, because God had bound himself to them by covenant. And so it is with us (John 16:33; Isaiah 43:1, 2).

**God's Character**
Moses was a believer. He had left Egypt 40 years earlier in faith. He knew God, and knew much about him. He knew the One who spoke to him out of the bush. He knew about God's promise to Eve. He knew about God's covenant with Abraham. He knew about God's promise to deliver his people out of Egypt. And he knew that the centrepiece of all God's purpose, work, covenants, and relations with men was and is the woman's promised Seed. But no one in this world ever knows God

completely and perfectly, though some seem to think they do. Moses still had much to learn, and we do, too.

What did this bush reveal about our God? It certainly revealed something of his sovereign power, the power by which he rules and overrules even what we call 'the laws of nature'. Here is a dry, thorn bush burning with fire, but unconsumed by the fire. Here is fire without heat.

The bush also revealed something of God's self-sufficiency as God. God himself, like that bush, is never used up. His power is never depleted. His wisdom is never lessened. His grace is never exhausted. He is God all-sufficient, all-sufficient for us!

As Moses watched the burning bush, he heard God's call. 'And when the LORD saw that he turned aside to see, God called unto him out of the midst of the bush, and said, Moses, Moses. And he said, Here am I' (v. 4). As the Lord later spoke to Samuel in the temple and to Mary at the tomb, here he called Moses by name; and Moses heard his voice (John 10:3). What a great and gracious thing that is! Nothing is sweeter than the special, distinguishing grace of our God and special, personal manifestations of our Saviour. These are things for which we constantly long. Are they not?

The bush also revealed something of God's great holiness. As Moses began to approach the bush, the Angel of the Lord said, 'Draw not nigh hither: put off thy shoes from off thy feet, for the place whereon thou standest is holy ground' (v. 5). God is of such a holy nature that the slightest particle of dust from Moses' shoes would contaminate the ground upon which God revealed himself. Taking off his shoes symbolized reverence and godly fear (Numbers 5:1-3; Joshua 5:15).

This word from God does not mean we must not approach God. David says, 'It is good to draw nigh unto God'. But it does mean we cannot approach God except in and through a Mediator (John 14:6). True, he is the God of all grace and all mercy; and God is love; but he is all these because he is holy; and he could never have manifested himself in all these blessed attributes of his being had it not been that in the cross of our Lord Jesus Christ mercy and truth met together and righteousness and peace kissed each other. Until our feet are unshod, remembering the holiness of him with whom we have to do, we can never draw near unto him except by faith in Christ.

119

**God's Salvation**

Then the Lord Jesus showed Moses that he is the eternal God, the God of covenant grace by whom his people would be raised to everlasting life. He is the God of all grace who will assuredly save his people. 'Moreover he said, I am the God of thy father, the God of Abraham, the God of Isaac, and the God of Jacob. And Moses hid his face; for he was afraid to look upon God' (v. 6).

Abraham, Isaac, and Jacob were all dead; yet God was, is, and ever will be, their God. He is God of the living. That means these men who had long ago died were really still alive and would live forever with, in, and by Christ. In a word, the Lord Jesus was saying to Moses, 'I am the resurrection and the life' (John 11:25). How vast the Word of God is! We could never have known the fulness of this single verse had not our Saviour used it to confound the Sadducees in Luke 20:37, affirming the resurrection of the dead in the last day. He who is the God of the living is the God who gives life eternal to chosen sinners (John 5:25-28).

In verse seven, we see a delightful picture of our great God and Saviour's compassion and pity for us. In verse 6 our Saviour reveals himself as the God of Abraham, Isaac, and Jacob, suggesting his own character is the foundation of all his works. His motive is always in himself. He always acts on the basis of what he is, not on the basis of what we are (Romans 8:28-30; Ephesians 1:3-6; 2 Timothy 1:9, 10). Grace is not God's reaction to our need. Our need is but the background upon which he shows forth the glory of his grace. 'And the LORD said, I have surely seen the affliction of my people which are in Egypt, and have heard their cry by reason of their taskmasters; for I know their sorrows' (v. 7).

Our God repeats his assurances of mercy that we may be the more confident of his mercy (Hebrews 6:17-19). What infinite tenderness! Our misery touches his heart. He knows our sorrows, and comes down to deliver us. So 'God commendeth his love toward us, in that, while we were yet sinners, Christ died for us' (Romans 5:8). 'In all their affliction he was afflicted, and the angel of his presence saved them: in his love and in his pity he redeemed them; and he bare them, and carried them all the days of old' (Isaiah 63:9). How sweet it is to hear the God of Glory call us, 'my people'. Those words assure us of his pity. 'Like as a father pitieth his children, so the LORD pitieth them that fear him' (Psalm 103:13).

Read verse 8, and you will see that what I said about the bush speaking of Christ's incarnation is exactly what was intended by this typical vision. 'And I am come down to deliver them out of the hand of the Egyptians, and to bring them up out of that land unto a good land and a large, unto a land flowing with milk and honey; unto the place of the Canaanites, and the Hittites, and the Amorites, and the Perizzites, and the Hivites, and the Jebusites.'

Our Saviour's heart was set upon our redemption from eternity. 'For the day of vengeance is in mine heart, and the year of my redeemed is come' (Isaiah 63:4). In the fulness of time the Lord Jesus Christ actually came down into this world of barrenness to bring us up to the heavenly Canaan (John 14:1-3).

You will notice nothing is mentioned about the forty years of wandering Israel endured between Egypt and Canaan. In Romans we read, 'Whom he justified, them he also glorified', with nothing between justification and glorification. There is a reason for that. In the mind and purpose of our God, there is nothing between our eternal redemption and everlasting glory.

'Now therefore, behold, the cry of the children of Israel is come unto me: and I have also seen the oppression wherewith the Egyptians oppress them. Come now therefore, and I will send thee unto Pharaoh, that thou mayest bring forth my people the children of Israel out of Egypt' (vv. 9, 10).

The Holy Spirit gives the best commentary on these two verses in Acts 7:35, 36. 'This Moses whom they refused, saying, Who made thee a ruler and a judge? the same did God send to be a ruler and a deliverer by the hand of the angel which appeared to him in the bush. He brought them out, after that he had showed wonders and signs in the land of Egypt, and in the Red sea, and in the wilderness forty years.'

Moses was sent to deliver Israel by the will of God. And he, who was sent by God to deliver Israel out of Egypt, actually brought them out by mighty wonders. So it is with our blessed Saviour. He was sent of God to save his people (Matthew 1:21). And he who was sent of God to save his people actually saved them by the mighty wonders he accomplished upon the cursed tree (Hebrews 9:12). And he is still doing it! He is still saving sinners by the mighty wonders of his omnipotent, irresistible grace. 'And so all Israel shall be saved' (Romans 11:26).

**Application**

What does all this have to do with us? The burning bush speaks to us, just as it did to Moses, about the greatness of our God and the need to reverence him. Pastor Roger Ellsworth wrote, 'No truth is more urgently needed by the church. This is the day of easy and breezy familiarity with God.' The burning bush tells us that the God of all grace ever sustains his elect. The fires of temptation, affliction, and adversity often burn in our lives. Indeed, as long as we are in this world, they will never cease. But the fires will never harm us in any way. Our God will bring all his people home to heaven in the perfection of holiness. Not one will be missing.

As our Lord stooped to reveal himself in the thorn bush, so he stooped to take upon himself our nature. He is God; yet he stooped to become a man. He is man; yet he is God over all, and blessed forever. Were he not God, his blood could not atone for our sins. Were he not man, he had no blood with which to atone. Someone once said, 'God could not suffer and man could not satisfy; but the God-man has both suffered and satisfied.' 'Behold, the bush burned with fire, and the bush was not consumed.'

As fire burned in the bush, so the fire of divine justice burned in the body and soul of our Lord Jesus Christ when he died as our Substitute. Yet, as the fire could not destroy the bush, so Christ was not destroyed by his sufferings and death, but arose triumphantly over death, hell and the grave as Lord over all.

The Son of God, our all-glorious Christ, went to the cross for the express purpose of redeeming sinners. Now, having accomplished eternal redemption for us, he freely receives and saves forever all who come to God by him.

# Chapter 13

# The Gospel Of The Burning Bush

'Now Moses kept the flock of Jethro his father in law, the priest of Midian: and he led the flock to the backside of the desert, and came to the mountain of God, even to Horeb. And the angel of the LORD appeared unto him in a flame of fire out of the midst of a bush: and he looked, and, behold, the bush burned with fire, and the bush was not consumed. And Moses said, I will now turn aside, and see this great sight, why the bush is not burnt. And when the LORD saw that he turned aside to see, God called unto him out of the midst of the bush, and said, Moses, Moses. And he said, Here am I. And he said, Draw not nigh hither: put off thy shoes from off thy feet, for the place whereon thou standest is holy ground. Moreover he said, I am the God of thy father, the God of Abraham, the God of Isaac, and the God of Jacob. And Moses hid his face; for he was afraid to look upon God.' (Exodus 3:1-6)

### Moses the Shepherd

'Now Moses kept the flock of Jethro his father in law, the priest of Midian: and he led the flock to the backside of the desert, and came to the mountain of God, even to Horeb' (v. 1). Moses is on the backside of the desert in the land of Midian, the land of Cush, the land of Ham, among a cursed people, from whom he was pleased to take his wife. He was tending sheep as a shepherd. Those facts are not insignificant. They are intended by the Spirit of God to teach us more than a few, scanty details of Moses' life in Midian. In all these things as we have seen,

Moses typifies our blessed Saviour. The Son of God came into this world to live among a cursed people in this cursed land, and to be numbered among the cursed. The Lord of Glory was pleased to take his bride from the cursed people. Like Moses, our dear Saviour assumed the despised roll of a shepherd (Genesis 46:34; John 10:14-18).

### The Angel of the Lord

'And the angel of the LORD appeared unto him in a flame of fire out of the midst of a bush: and he looked, and, behold, the bush burned with fire, and the bush was not consumed' (v. 2). In verse 4 we are specifically told the Angel of the Lord who appeared to Moses is our Saviour. He is called both 'LORD' (Jehovah) and 'God' (Eloheem).

The Hebrew word translated 'bush' is only used one other time in the Word of God. It is found only here and in Deuteronomy 33:16, where Moses speaks of 'the good will of him that dwelt in the bush'. The word translated 'dwelt' in Deuteronomy 33:16 appears to have reference to the 'shekinah'. In a word, what Moses saw in the bush was the Shekinah glory of God. He saw Christ in his glory, just as Isaiah did in the year that king Uzziah died, just as Paul did on the Damascus road.

Before Moses could be sent forth to deliver Israel, and before any man is able to preach the gospel, he must be made to behold the ineffable glory of the Lord God. That glory is seen only in the face of the crucified Christ, in whom and by whom redemption has been accomplished (Isaiah 6:1-8; 2 Corinthians 4:4-6). Until a man sees what Moses saw that day in the Mountain of God, he has nothing to preach; everything he has to say, insofar as spiritual matters are concerned, is less than irrelevant. He who is God's Messenger, the Angel of the Lord, is God's Message 'Jesus Christ and him crucified' (1 Corinthians 2:2).

### The Bush

'And the angel of the LORD appeared unto him in a flame of fire out of the midst of a bush: and he looked, and, behold, the bush burned with fire, and the bush was not consumed. And Moses said, I will now turn aside, and see this great sight, why the bush is not burnt' (vv. 2, 3).

Here was a wonder that all the magicians of Pharaoh's court could never imitate, a miracle that baffles all human wisdom. The Lord God our Saviour performed a miracle to make himself known as our God and our Saviour. Truly, there is much to be seen in 'this great sight'.

I do not doubt Moses was, at first, inspired by nothing but curiosity to turn aside to look at the bush; but, once he turned to look, he saw that which would forever change his life. He saw Christ in his glory! There are many who, like myself, first come to hear the gospel for the most insignificant reasons, and turn aside to consider the things of God only because of idle curiosity, like the Jews did to see John the Baptist, and to see the Lord Jesus performing miracles, who are caught by what they see. Hugh Latimer urged people to come hear the gospel, saying, 'Though thou comest to sleep; it may be, God may take thee napping.'

Christ was in the bush; and Christ is in the gospel. That may appear terribly simplistic to some; but in my eyes it is profoundly wondrous. The burning bush appeared to Moses that he might see the glory of Christ as set forth in the gospel of God's saving grace. The symbolism was startling.

The bush burned with fire, and yet the bush was not burned. That is profound, mysterious, and miraculous. But the mystery of the gospel is indescribably more profound, mysterious, and miraculous. Fire in Scripture is the symbol of God's holiness and of divine judgment. 'Our God is a consuming fire' (Hebrews 12:29). This is the mystery: how can God, who is 'a consuming fire', burning up all that is contrary to his holy nature, reveal himself to fallen men without consuming us? How can he who is 'of purer eyes than to behold evil and canst not look on iniquity' (Habakkuk 1:13), have anything to do with fallen, sinful, vile, depraved men and women, except in judgment and wrath? The mystery is revealed and resolved in the gospel, which tells us 'grace reigns through righteousness', not at the expense of righteousness, but 'through righteousness unto eternal life by Jesus Christ our Lord' (Romans 5:21).

How can that be? 'Grace reigns through righteousness unto eternal life by Jesus Christ our Lord', only by Christ who is the Righteousness of God, being made a curse for us (Galatians 3:13; 2 Corinthians 5:17-21). Remember, the word 'bush' means 'bramble bush' or 'thorn bush'. It is a vivid reminder of God's curse upon the earth because of Adam's transgression (Genesis 3:18).

The Son of God, our all-gracious, all-glorious Substitute and Saviour, entered into the place of the curse for us. The fierce flames of God's holy and furious wrath engulfed him; but they did not, and could not consume him. The 'Root out of a dry ground' not only survived the fire, he consumed it! It was not possible that death should hold the Prince of life. Three days after he died in our place, he came forth triumphant over death, hell and the grave, and is now alive for evermore, King of kings and Lord of lords! He is not only God of the resurrection, he is the Resurrection and the Life! And, by virtue of his accomplished redemption, he has power over all flesh to give eternal life to whom he will (John 17:2; Romans 14:9; Luke 20:37, 38). That which Moses saw in the bush is the gospel we believe and preach (2 Corinthians 5:17-21; Galatians 3:13, 14).

**The Gospel of the Bush**
What is the gospel of the burning bush? It is the gospel of Christ. It is the revelation of him who is the revelation of the invisible God. It is God assuming and forever dwelling in humanity. Here is 'the tender plant, the Root out of dry ground', in whom resides 'all the fulness of the godhead bodily'. God is here; and he is God come to save.

The gospel of the burning bush is the gospel of atonement by a suffering Substitute. Fire was in the bush and engulfed it, just as the fiery hot assaults of divine wrath fell upon God's dear Son when he died in our place at Calvary.

The gospel of the burning bush is the gospel of an irresistible, almighty, omnipotent, justice satisfying Sacrifice. The fire assailed the bush in vain. The bush was unharmed by the fire that engulfed it. So it was with Christ our Sacrifice. Every blow recoiled from Immanuel. Sustained by his eternal deity, he trod the winepress alone, and trod all his foes and ours beneath his feet. He burst the bands of death. He smashed the iron gates of the grave. He stood victorious upon the ruins of hell defeated. He rode triumphantly into the heaven of heavens, having obtained eternal redemption for us.

The gospel of the burning bush is the gospel of the eternal security of God's elect. Who can fail to see that, as this bush represents our Lord Jesus Christ, it represents the whole election of grace? Persecutions and trials are the fire which assails us with ceaseless fury. But God's saints thrive and gain strength, bud, blossom and flourish in the fire. How can that be? God indwells us; and where God resides there is unceasing, ever-springing life.

In all ages, though afflicted and distressed, God's people are like to a thorn bush, in ourselves weak and without strength, contemptible and low, covered with the thorns of corruptions and temptations within and without, often in the fires of afflictions and persecutions. Yet, they are not, and never can be consumed by the fire, for Christ is with us, among us, around us, and in us. Satan roars but Christ is ours. Hell opposes us but Christ is in us. We are weak but he is strong. The world allures us but Christ keeps us. Our very flesh would destroy us but my Saviour keeps us. Christ in us defies all and everything who oppose us.

Christ's church is the chosen home of his unbounded love. Here his all-protecting might, his all-preserving care, his full delights repose. He received it from his Father as his spouse, his jewels, his peculiar treasure, and his portion. We are the fulness of his body, 'the fulness of him that filleth all in all' (Ephesians 1:23), the completeness of his mediatorial glory. He is engaged to present his body, the church, holy, unblameable, unreproveable, and complete before his Father's throne. If one member be injured, Christ is marred. If one is absent, Christ is maimed. And Christ our God and Saviour is ever with us. Someone once said, 'He is all heart to love, all eye to watch, all hand to help, all wisdom to direct, and all power to beat back our foes.' Let the fire rage! Until Christ is consumed by the flame, we cannot be!

**Goodwill**

Child of God, think much of the 'goodwill of him who dwelt in the bush'. Fears will flee away. If we stood alone it would be presumption to hope; but because you are not alone it is unbelief to tremble. Though you have passed through many fires the flame has never harmed you. How is that? In Paul's words, 'The Lord stood with you and strengthened you.' 'The bush burned with fire, and the bush was not consumed.' You may now be enduring some great trial; but your Saviour says, 'Fear not, for I am with you.' The bush burns with fire; and the bush is not consumed. You may yet be required to endure great trials; but that same voice gives cheering assurance. 'Fear not, for I am with you; when thou walkest through the fire, thou shall not be burned.' The bush shall burn with fire; but it shall not be consumed.

May God the Holy Spirit cause you to now turn aside and see this great sight and trust him who reveals himself in the gospel of the burning bush. May he be pleased to reveal himself to you in the glory of his saving grace in Christ, as God in covenant with you and for you, as he did to Moses.

# Chapter 14

## 'The Angel Of The Lord'

'And the angel of the LORD appeared unto him in a flame of fire out of the midst of a bush: and he looked, and, behold, the bush burned with fire, and the bush was not consumed.'
(Exodus 3:2)

'The Angel of the LORD', who appeared to Moses in 'a flame of fire out of the midst of a bush', was our Lord Jesus Christ. To say that Christ is 'the Angel of the LORD' does not in any way contradict the fact of his eternal Deity. He is both Jehovah and Jehovah's Messenger. In his eternal Deity our Saviour is God himself, over all and blessed forever. In his mediatorial capacity, as our Surety and Substitute, he is 'the Angel of the LORD'. When the Scriptures speak of our Saviour as 'the Angel of the LORD' appearing in the form of a man before he actually assumed our nature in the incarnation, they are telling us that God's own Son, the Surety and Mediator of the covenant, the man Christ Jesus, is the Revelation of God. Jesus Christ, our Mediator, is, always was, and ever shall be the only one in whom and by whom God makes himself known to men. Christ is God's Message; and Christ is God's Messenger.

### Other Angels
Sadly, multitudes of religious people are caught up in superstition, sentimentality and idolatry. Some people pray to and worship angels.

Many wear idolatrous little 'angel' pins as good luck charms to keep them from evil. Of course, anyone who reads the Word of God knows these things are without foundation in Holy Scripture, and are acts of idolatry. Foolishly, there are multitudes who even imagine that when babies and little children die, they become angels.

Yet, the Word of God teaches us much about angels. The word 'angel' means 'messenger'. When we think of angels, the first thing that comes to mind are those of the angelic order. Those heavenly spirits are God's servants, sent forth to minister to those who shall be the heirs of salvation (Psalm 103:20; Hebrews 1:14).

Before the completion of Holy Scripture, before the entire canon of this Sacred Volume was written, God spoke to men by angels and visions, and by prophets and apostles (Matthew 2:13, 19; Luke 1:19, 26; Hebrews 1:1). He confirmed the word spoken in such a miraculous manner by miracles, signs, and wonders. But those days are over. Since that which is perfect has come, that which was in part has been put aside. We now have the complete revelation of God in Holy Scripture. There is no need for, nor can there be, any inspired prophets or apostles with a new word from God. Because we have no new word from God, we do not now live in the age of miracles, signs, and wonders. Those things were needed in the church's infancy to confirm the apostles as the messengers of the Messiah. For the same reasons, the Lord no longer sends angels in visible or audible manifestations to direct us in his will and ways. We have God's Word for that purpose.

However, that does not mean the ministry of God's angels has ceased. Not at all! The angels of God are just as active today as ever. Without question, there is a specific order of heavenly beings called 'angels'. The fallen angels (Revelation 12:4) are commonly referred to as 'devils' or 'demons' (James 2:19). Those fallen angels are messengers of Satan, bent upon the destruction of our souls. Whereas the angels of God are described as 'ministering spirits, sent forth to minister for them who shall be heirs of salvation'.

We have far more friends than we know. As we make our pilgrimage through this world, as we seek to serve our God and walk through the midst of our enemies in this world of darkness, if only we could hear, we would hear the rush of angels' wings, 'God's hosts', at our side and round about us. If we had eyes to see, we would see 'the mountain full of horses and chariots of fire round about' us. 'Jacob went on his way, and the angels of God met him … And when Jacob saw them, he said, This is God's host: and he called the name of that place Mahanaim' (Genesis 32:1, 2).

## Gospel Preachers

In Revelation 1:20 we read, 'The mystery of the seven stars which thou sawest in my right hand, and the seven golden candlesticks. The seven stars are the angels of the seven churches: and the seven candlesticks which thou sawest are the seven churches.' In chapters two and three the pastors of local churches are called 'angels', because faithful men, gifted and called of God to the work of the ministry, are God's messengers to his people. Not all pastors are designated 'angels', but all who are truly God's messengers to the souls of men are to be esteemed as such. Why? Because God has ordained the salvation of his elect by hearing of the gospel (Romans 1:16, 17; 10:17; 1 Corinthians 1:21-24; James 1:18; 1 Peter 1:23-25).

Let no one despise or lightly esteem the ministry of the Word. Gospel preachers are the gifts of the risen Christ to his church. They are instruments in the hands of the Saviour, by which he calls chosen, redeemed sinners to life and faith by his Spirit and edifies, comforts, and instructs his church (Ephesians 4:11-16).

It is important for us to recognize what the Scriptures teach about the angelic creatures and about gospel preachers. But both those heavenly creatures and every gospel preacher would have us first focus our attention on Christ.

## Christ the Angel of the Lord

Our Lord Jesus Christ, the Son of God, our Saviour is 'the Angel of the Lord', who appeared to Moses 'in a flame of fire out of the midst of a bush'. 'The Angel of the LORD' is clearly identified for us in this passage and throughout the Scriptures as our God and Saviour, the Lord Jesus Christ. In verses 3 and 4 he is called 'LORD' (Jehovah) and 'God' (Elohim). In verse 6 the Angel of the Lord, who spoke to Moses out of the bush declared, 'I am the God of thy father, the God of Abraham, the God of Isaac, and the God of Jacob'. In verse 14 the Angel of the Lord is still speaking to Moses out of the bush, and says, 'I AM THAT I AM'. That simply means, 'I AM WHO I AM', and expresses his eternal self-existence as our God, the great 'I AM'. Again, in verses 15-18 and in chapter 4 (vv. 4, 5) the Angel of the Lord identifies himself as God our Saviour.

In Genesis 16:13 Hagar spoke to the Angel of the Lord, and called his name, 'God who sees', 'Thou, God, seest me'. In Judges 6:22 when Gideon spoke to the Angel of the Lord, he called him 'Lord GOD'. In Judges 13:18 Manoah and his wife asked the Angel of the Lord to tell them his name. He said, 'It is Secret', it is 'Wonderful' (Isaiah 9:6, 7).

The Angel of the Lord, who appeared to Moses in the bush, performed what none but he who is himself God could perform. He promised that when Pharaoh would refuse to release the Israelites from bondage, 'I will stretch out my hand and smite Egypt with all my wonders which I will do in the midst thereof' (3:20); a promise he ultimately fulfilled in ten plagues (Exodus 7-12). He miraculously caused Moses' rod to change into a serpent, then back into the rod (4:1-5). He miraculously caused Moses' hand to become leprous, then restored it (4:6-8). Then, he identified himself as the Creator, and as he who causes man to be deaf and dumb, seeing or blind (4:11).

**Worshipped as God**
When Moses saw the Angel of the Lord and heard him speak, he worshipped him, reverencing him as God. 'Moses hid his face, for he was afraid to look upon God' (3:6). If ever a man sees God in his absolute holiness and sees his own complete sinfulness, he will hide his face before him (1 Kings 19:13; Judges 13:22). Even the cherubs cover their faces in God's presence (Isaiah 6:2). God is too holy to look upon sinful man (Habakkuk 1:13); and man is too sinful to look upon the holy God (Exodus 33:20). God must either veil his glory, as in Exodus 19:9, or we must cover our faces. Else we cannot look upon God, and he will not look upon us, except in the person of Christ, the Angel of the Lord. Then he sees us washed in blood, robed in righteousness, and accepted in him who is made of God unto us 'Wisdom, and Righteousness, and Sanctification, and Redemption' (1 Corinthians 1:30).

It is clear, unmistakably clear, that the Angel of the Lord who spoke to Moses is God our Saviour, the Lord Jesus Christ. He appeared to Moses, as he did to chosen sinners throughout the Old Testament, in the form of a man, identifying himself as the Mediator who would, in the fulness of time, be made flesh, made of a woman, made under the law, that he might redeem us from the curse of the law.

## God's Messenger

Remember, the word 'angel' means 'messenger'. As the Angel of the Lord, 'the Messenger of the covenant', the Son of God comes to men to reveal and fulfil all the stipulations of the covenant of grace for us (Jeremiah 31:31-34; Hebrews 8:6-13), thereby securing our 'eternal redemption' (Hebrews 9:12). Having fulfilled all the requirements of the covenant as our Substitute, our Saviour now sits upon the throne of universal monarchy ruling all things according to the purpose of God as our God-man Mediator to give eternal life to his people (John 17:2; Revelation 10:1-6).

He and he alone is able to fulfil the book of God's decrees (Revelation 5:1-7). He who rules the universe is God in human flesh, our Saviour and Redeemer, 'the Angel of the covenant'. Rejoice! Our Lord Jesus Christ is pre-eminently the Angel of the Lord. He is the Angel who came with a great chain of omnipotent power and bound Satan (Revelation 20:1-3). He is the Angel by whom all the earth shall be judged at last (Revelation 20:11-15). He is the Angel who sits upon the throne and will, at last, bring all the universe to its divinely ordained completion (Revelation 21:6).

## The Archangel

Our Lord Jesus is Michael the Archangel, who contended with and conquered Satan, when he delivered us from the hands of divine justice and the curse of the law (Jude 9; Zechariah 3:1-5). 'Michael' means 'One who is as God'. 'Archangel' means 'Chief of Angels', or 'Prince of Angels'. Our Saviour; 'The Prince of Angels', the Man who is God!

He is the Angel of the covenant (Malachi 3:1). In Isaiah 63:9 our Saviour is called 'the Angel of his presence'. He is that One who is our Redeemer and Saviour, the great Lover of our souls, who constantly watches over and protects us in this world. Pastor Daniel Parks wrote, 'His presence is Jehovah's presence because God's name and nature and perfections are manifested in him. He is indeed 'the brightness of (God's) glory and the express image of his person' (Hebrews 1:3).

Our blessed Saviour, the Lord Jesus Christ, is called 'the Messenger of the Covenant' (Malachi 3:1). He is Messenger of the New Covenant, the Everlasting Covenant of Grace, because he is the Surety and the Fulfiller of it (Hebrews 7:22). God delivered the Old Covenant to Israel by Moses, through angels (Acts 7:53; Galatians 3:19). But the New Covenant, the 'better covenant', which has abrogated and replaced the Old Covenant (Hebrews 8:6-12), came by Christ, 'the Messenger of the Covenant', the Mediator and Surety of it (Hebrews 7:22; 9:15). It is Christ, the Messenger, the Angel of the Covenant, who is the Revelation of God (John 1:1-3, 14, 18; Hebrews 1:1-3; 2 Corinthians 4:4-6).

**The Message**
Our great Saviour, the Lord Jesus Christ, is not only God's Messenger, he is God's Message. He is the divine Word of God (John 1:1) incarnate in human flesh (John 1:14). As words are vehicles of communication by which the thoughts of the mind are made known to others, the triune God has communicated to man the thoughts and intents of his own mind in the person of his Son, our Mediator, the Man Christ Jesus. He is the complete, full, final revelation of God. 'In him dwelleth all the fulness of the godhead bodily' (Colossians 2:9). All that God is, is revealed and evidenced in the Man Christ Jesus. All that can be known of God is revealed in him. He is the great 'I AM', who revealed himself to Moses in the bush (John 8:58).

John's primary object in writing his gospel narrative was to demonstrate our Saviour's eternal deity as one with the Father and the Holy Spirit in the Trinity (John 1:1-3; 14:9). Therefore, it is not surprising he constantly tells us that the Lord Jesus called himself the 'I AM', both directly and indirectly. He said to the Jews, 'Before Abraham was I AM'. He could not have been more direct in the assertion of his Godhood. Here are twelve instructive examples of the same thing in the Gospel of John.

1. 'I am the bread of life' (6:35, 50-58). If any man eat of this Bread, he shall live forever.

2. 'I am the light of the world' (8:12). He who follows Christ, the Light, no longer walks in the darkness of sin, tradition, superstition and idolatry, but walks in the light of the knowledge of the glory of God.

3. 'I am the door' (10:9). Christ is the only Door of entrance into the kingdom of God. He is the Door of the sheep. And all who enter in by him shall be saved.

4. 'I am the good shepherd' (10:11, 14-16). The Good Shepherd gave his life for his sheep, knows his sheep, gathers his sheep, and keeps his sheep.

5. 'I am the Son of God' (10:36). Thus the man Christ Jesus asserted his divinity (10:33), his eternality, the plurality of Persons in the Godhead, and the unity of the divine Persons.

6. 'I am the resurrection' (11:25). Those who believe on him shall never die.

7. 'I am he' (13:19) He of whom the prophets spoke, whose name is I AM, who came to save his people.

8. 'I am the way'. Without him we cannot come to God.

9. 'I am the truth'. Without him we cannot know God.

10. 'I am the life' (14:6). Without him we cannot live before God.

11. 'I am the vine' (15:1-10). We are the branches. The branches bear fruit in, by and of the vine.

12. 'I am King' (19:19-22). He is King everywhere, over all things, forever. 'He must reign!' The Father decreed it. He deserves it. And all his saints desire it and delight in it.

## Immanuel

Our Saviour is called the Angel of God's Presence, because his name is 'Immanuel', 'God with us' (Matthew 1:23; Isaiah 7:14). He is, as Thomas declared, 'My Lord and my God' (John 20:28). The Lord Jesus Christ is God with us, God in our nature, God our Saviour, who has delivered us from a bondage worse than Egypt and a foe mightier far than Pharaoh! The horse and his rider he has cast into the sea, triumphing over sin and Satan, and making us more than conquerors in him (Exodus 15:1-18).

Soon, the Angel of the Lord, Christ Jesus our Saviour, the mighty Archangel, shall come to bring us into the land of our everlasting inheritance in resurrection glory.

'For this we say unto you by the word of the Lord, that we which are alive and remain unto the coming of the Lord shall not prevent them which are asleep. For the Lord himself shall descend from heaven with a shout, with the voice of the archangel, and with the trump of God: and the dead in Christ shall rise first: Then we which are alive and remain shall be caught up together with them in the clouds, to meet the Lord in the air: and so shall we ever be with the Lord. Wherefore comfort one another with these words' (1 Thessalonians 4:15-18).

These are the things he revealed to Moses, when 'the Angel of the LORD appeared unto him in a flame of fire out of the midst of the bush'.

135

# Chapter 15

# Christ In The Flame Of Fire

'And the angel of the LORD appeared unto him in a flame of fire out of the midst of a bush: and he looked, and, behold, the bush burned with fire, and the bush was not consumed.'
(Exodus 3:2)

When the Lord appeared to Abraham and confirmed his covenant to him, fire passed between the divided pieces of the sacrifice and consumed them (Genesis 15:17, 18). In Exodus 3 the Lord God is about to send Moses back to Egypt to deliver his people, in fulfilment of that covenant promise he made to Abraham in Genesis 15:13, 14. When he was about to fulfil his covenant by delivering his people from Egypt, we read in Exodus 3:2, 'The Angel of the LORD appeared to him in a flame of fire'. Here we see Christ in the flame of fire, and have a clear example of fire being used in a typical way and portraying our blessed Saviour.

We have before us a vision of Christ, the Angel of the Lord, in a bush burning with fire; and we are told specifically that our Saviour appeared to Moses 'in a flame of fire'. The afflictions of Israel were great, but the Lord's mercies were greater. The Son of God appeared in a flame of fire, displaying his incomprehensible deity, majesty, and glory as our Deliverer and Saviour.

### Light

Fire is a good, instructive type of our Saviour, the Lord Jesus Christ. Light is always associated with fire; and our Saviour declares, 'I am the Light of the world' (John 8:12). He is the brightness of the Father's glory and the express image of his person (Hebrews 1:3). His brightness is described as 'the glory as of the only begotten of the Father, full of grace and truth' (John 1:14). All who follow the Lord Jesus, all who believe him, walk in the light as he is in the light. Walking in the Light, we confess our sins and confess that Christ alone is our Light and our Righteousness (1 John 1:1-2:2).

### Warmth

Fire provides heat and warmth. When the Lord Jesus comes to us, opens the Scriptures to us, and shows us things concerning himself out of the Book, he causes our hearts to burn within us. 'Did not our heart burn within us while he talked with us ... and while he opened unto us the scriptures?' (Luke 24:32). When our hearts are cold as ice and hard as a stone, if Christ will appear, we are melted before him immediately.

### Purifies

We commonly associate purity and purification with fire. And, when Christ the Sun of Righteousness arises in our hearts with healing in his wings (Malachi 4:2), giving us life and faith in him, we stand with him and in him pure before our God with 'a pure conscience', clothed in the pure, white linen of his righteousness (1 Corinthians 6:9-11).

### Consuming

We all know that fire is consuming. When our Lord Jesus comes in grace, he is our Light and our Purification. By his presence and his grace, we are warmed. But when he comes upon his enemies in wrath and judgment, he comes to consume. He is a consuming fire for us, going before us to destroy our enemies (Deuteronomy 9:3; Hebrews 11:29).

### No Harm

Yet, there was something in this appearance of Christ to Moses that was startling and great. 'He looked, and, behold, the bush burned with fire, and the bush was not consumed'. How beautiful that is! How blessed!

Although the fire completely engulfed the bush, possessing it entirely, it did not harm even its most tender twig or most delicate bud! The same divine fire, which consumes the wicked, blesses us. It was in fire the Lord appeared at Sinai in the giving of the law (Exodus 19:18, 19). Yet, it was in that same fire he appeared in saving mercy to Isaiah (Isaiah 6:4), and to Ezekiel at the river Chebar (Ezekiel 1:4), and to John on the Isle of Patmos (Revelation 1:14). Malachi tells us, in all his works as our great High Priest, he is 'as a refiner's fire' (Malachi 3:2), not to destroy, but to refine, cleanse, purify, and perfect.

John the Baptist asserted, though he shall burn up the chaff with unquenchable fire, he baptizes his own with the Holy Ghost and with fire (Matthew 3:11). God the Holy Spirit is the 'Spirit of judgment and the Spirit of burning' (Isaiah 4:4; 28:6). As the Spirit of judgment, he illuminates and convicts us of sin, righteousness, and judgment. As the Spirit of burning, he enflames our souls by shedding abroad in our hearts the love of God for us, making us, like John, 'burning and shining lights' (John 5:35) in a world of darkness. William Huntington wrote,

'In the light of the Spirit there are such views of Christ's person, loveliness, and fulness, and such beauties in God, his Word, and ways, as give heat and fervour to all our devotions, while the promises which flow into the heart, come as live coals from the altar, and increase the ardour. And the joy that springs from love is, at times, like the visible flames which on the altar, ascending to God from the hallowed fire within, which is pent up in the heart till the flames of joy give it vent.'

## Other Appearances

The Lord Jesus frequently appeared in the Old Testament in a flame of fire. Each appearance, like those given to Abraham in Genesis 15 and this one to Moses in Exodus 3, are full of instruction. As he led Israel through the wilderness, 'the LORD went before them ... by night in a pillar of fire to give them light' (Exodus 13:21). Our blessed Saviour will never leave us in darkness.

When he entered into a covenant with Israel at Mount Sinai, 'the LORD descended upon it in fire' (Exodus 19:18; 24:17). The fire at Sinai is an emblem of justice and of unapproachable holiness, teaching us we must come to God only by faith in Christ, upon his altar, without any works of our own (Exodus 20:24-26). There was an unceasing representation of the Lord Jesus on the altar in the 'holy fire that never went out' (Leviticus 6:13), typically assuring us of the everlasting efficacy of Christ as our sin atoning sacrifice, by which we are perpetually accepted in him

But of all the Old Testament appearances of our Lord in a flame of fire, none is more delightful to consider than his appearance to Manoah and his wife (Judges 13:17-20). If you look in the marginal reference of your Bible, you will notice the word 'secret' in verse 18 is really 'Wonderful'. You know whose name that is. It belongs to our Saviour (Isaiah 9:6), for whom and by whom are all things. Everything is designed to bring honour and glory to him whose name is Wonderful. Most particularly, the work of redemption and salvation is to the praise, honour, and glory of his Wonderful name (Revelation 4 and 5). When Manoah and his wife made a sacrifice to him, 'the Angel of the LORD ascended in the flame of the altar' (Judges 13:20). Similarly, the intercessions of Christ ascend to heaven with our prayers (Revelation 8:3; Romans 8:26-28).

When Solomon dedicated the temple, 'fire came down from heaven and consumed the burnt offering and sacrifices; and the glory of the LORD filled the temple' (2 Chronicles 7:1-3). The Lord God hereby shows us his acceptance of our sacrifices, including those of our bodies (Romans 12:1) and praise (Hebrews 13:15; 1 Peter 2:5), by Christ Jesus.

When he revealed himself in his initial vision to Ezekiel, he had 'the appearance of fire all around' (Ezekiel 1:27). So our Lord Jesus Christ reveals himself in light and glory (John 1:14), as the Lord of all providence, doing all things with wisdom and purity.

And, today, as he walks in the midst of his churches, our blessed Saviour has 'eyes like a flame of fire' (Revelation 1:14; 2:18). In his house, by the preaching of the gospel, our Saviour gives his light to purify and warm, to refine and comfort, to guide and to protect his own.

The Lord God makes his servants 'a flame of fire'. And the Word of God is compared to fire. 'Is not my word like a fire, saith the Lord, and like a hammer that breaketh the rock in pieces?' (Jeremiah 23:29). Our Saviour declared, 'I am come to send fire on the earth'. And so he does.

Once more, when Christ comes again, his eyes will be 'like a flame of fire' (Revelation 19:12). He comes as a consuming fire of wrath upon the ungodly. The torments of the damned are uniformly described in Scripture under the image of fire. 'A fire is kindled in mine anger, and shall burn unto the lowest hell; and shall consume the earth with her increase, and set on fire the foundations of the nations' (Deuteronomy 32:22). 'The sinners in Zion are afraid; fearfulness hath surprised the hypocrites: who among us shall dwell with the devouring fire? who among us shall dwell with everlasting burnings?' (Isaiah 33:14). The Son of God speaks repeatedly of a worm that never dies and a fire that never is quenched. In his solemn description of the last day, in the tremendous judgment of it, he has already recorded the very words with which he will speak to the damned. 'Depart from me, ye cursed, into everlasting fire, prepared for the devil and his angels' (Matthew 25:41). What terrible language is used to speak of the fire of God's wrath in that last great day in Revelation 20!

Men have, through the ages, hotly debated about whether the fires of hell and of judgment are literal or figurative. But the question is altogether insignificant. Whatever the fires of hell are, they are exactly suited to their purpose, the execution of God's furious wrath. It is written, 'The wicked shall be turned into hell, and all the nations that forget God'. At the same time we read, 'For the needy shall not always be forgotten; the expectation of the poor shall not perish for ever' (Psalm 9:17, 18). That is sufficient.

'Seeing it is a righteous thing with God to recompense tribulation to them that trouble you; And to you who are troubled rest with us, when the Lord Jesus shall be revealed from heaven with his mighty angels, In flaming fire taking vengeance on them that know not God, and that obey not the gospel of our Lord Jesus Christ: Who shall be punished with everlasting destruction from the presence of the Lord, and from the glory of his power; When he shall come to be glorified in his saints, and to be admired in all them that believe (because our testimony among you was believed) in that day' (2 Thessalonians 1:6-10).

Does Christ's fire enlighten, warm, and purify you? Or will it consume you? Brothers and sisters, 'Give diligence to make your calling and election sure'.

# Chapter 16

## 'The Angel Of The Lord Appeared'

'Now Moses kept the flock of Jethro his father in law, the priest of Midian: and he led the flock to the backside of the desert, and came to the mountain of God, even to Horeb. And the angel of the LORD appeared unto him in a flame of fire out of the midst of a bush: and he looked, and, behold, the bush burned with fire, and the bush was not consumed. And Moses said, I will now turn aside, and see this great sight, why the bush is not burnt. And when the LORD saw that he turned aside to see, God called unto him out of the midst of the bush, and said, Moses, Moses. And he said, Here am I. And he said, Draw not nigh hither: put off thy shoes from off thy feet, for the place whereon thou standest is holy ground. Moreover he said, I am the God of thy father, the God of Abraham, the God of Isaac, and the God of Jacob. And Moses hid his face; for he was afraid to look upon God. And the LORD said, I have surely seen the affliction of my people which are in Egypt, and have heard their cry by reason of their taskmasters; for I know their sorrows; And I am come down to deliver them out of the hand of the Egyptians, and to bring them up out of that land unto a good land and a large, unto a land flowing with milk and honey; unto the place of the Canaanites, and the Hittites, and the Amorites, and the Perizzites, and the Hivites, and the Jebusites. Now therefore, behold, the cry of the children of Israel is come unto me: and I have also seen the oppression wherewith the Egyptians oppress them. Come now therefore, and I will send thee unto Pharaoh, that thou mayest bring forth my people the children of Israel out of Egypt.'
(Exodus 3:1-10)

## Angel of the Lord

'The Angel of the LORD' appeared to Moses. As we have already seen, 'the Angel of the LORD' is our Saviour, the Lord Jesus Christ. There is no question about this. The Angel identifies himself clearly. He is the eternal 'I AM'. The One who is speaking from the burning bush is the same, yesterday, today, and forever. 'The Angel of the LORD' announced he is Elohim, the self-existent God; and beside him there is none else. He is the absolute 'I AM'. He said, 'I AM THAT I AM'.

This was a manifestation of God himself. Moses hid his face from him because he was afraid to look upon God. The same Angel of the LORD had appeared to Sarah, Hagar, Abraham, and Isaac four hundred years earlier. The Angel of the LORD speaks of himself as God, while at the same time declaring he is One sent from God. The Angel of the LORD is described throughout the Old Testament in exactly the same way our Lord Jesus is described in the New Testament. He guides and protects his people (Exodus 14:19). He is the constant Companion of his chosen in the wilderness, the One who keeps us in the way (Exodus 23:20-33; Numbers 20:16). He punishes sin (2 Samuel 24:15-17). He is seen ministering to his servant Elijah (1 Kings 19:7). The Angel of the Lord fights our battles and wins them (2 Kings 19:35; 2 Chronicles 32:21). The angel of the Lord is always dependent upon the Lord, and always subordinate to his commands (1 Chronicles 21:27), showing that he is the Servant of the Lord.

Yet, he is addressed as the Lord himself, showing that he is himself God (Exodus 23:23). The Angel of the LORD exercises prerogatives that belong to God alone in forgiving sin and commanding obedience. His deity is never left in doubt. In Exodus 23:20-33 he is the Angel of the Covenant. When he revealed himself in the Old Testament, people always recognized him as God and responded to him as God. Joshua 5:13-6:2 shows him possessing the attributes and authority of God. The name Jehovah is never rightly applied to anyone other than the God of Israel (Isaiah 42:8). Yet, the Angel of the LORD bears all the titles of deity. He is called Jehovah and Elohim. And, throughout the Old Testament, he was worshipped as God, because he is God.

In addition to all these things, we see the Angel of the LORD talking, walking, and eating with men as a man in the Old Testament Scriptures. Yet, even when he appeared in the form of a man, speaking of the Lord

God in the third person, his Godhead is clearly revealed and known. People recognized that he is God, praying to him and honouring him as God as they worshipped him, offering sacrifices, which he accepted. This Angel of the Lord is himself God over all and blessed forever (Exodus 33:20; Genesis 16:13; 32:30; Exodus 33:11).

Clearly, the Angel of the Lord is one of the persons of the eternal Godhead. He is not a created being, but God himself. He is the Shekinah, the Glory. The glory of God is seen in him, because he is Jesus Christ our Saviour, in whose face the glory of God shines forth.

The Angel of the Lord, in all those pre-incarnate appearances recorded in the Old Testament, appeared in the form of a man, recognizable by men. Yet, he appeared in such glory that he was always recognized as God in human form. They seem to have been like the appearances of our Lord in the Gospels, after his resurrection, like his appearance to the apostle Paul on the road to Damascus, and like his appearance on the Mount of Transfiguration before Peter, James and John (Matthew 17:1-8). In other words, they were pre-incarnate revelations of Christ in his resurrection glory, that glory which is the reward of his accomplishments as our Redeemer. He appeared to men in the Old Testament, as he did to John in Revelation 4 and 5, as being exalted because he had finished his work of redemption as the complete, full revelation of the triune God (John 1:18).

**Distinct yet Identical**

Let me briefly reprise what the Scriptures reveal about the Angel of the Lord. The Angel of the LORD is distinct from God, yet, identical with God as he revealed himself in the Old Testament. His name is Jehovah (Exodus 23:20, 21). His presence is the presence of the Lord (Exodus 32:30, 34; 33:14). The Angel of the LORD is the pre-existent 'Word of God', the Lord Jesus Christ, the second person of the holy Trinity (John 1:14-18; Colossians 1:15; 2:9). The Angel of the Lord appeared to men many, many times in the Old Testament age. Then, in the fulness of time he appeared once in the end of the world, in the Man Jesus Christ, to make atonement for our sins, to put away sin by the sacrifice of himself (Hebrews 1:1-3; 9:23-28).

The Angel of the LORD was and is none other than the Word, who, not only was 'with God', but 'was God', and 'was made flesh' and 'came unto his own'. By our Saviour's incarnation and accomplished redemption, everything revealed by the Angel of the LORD in the Old Testament was performed. But when he came into the world, our Saviour was not a newcomer on the earthly scene. The prophet declares of him, his 'goings forth have been from of old, from everlasting' (Micah 5:2). In the first chapter of Revelation the resurrected, ascended, glorified Son of Man was seen by the apostle John walking in the midst of the churches.

The Angel of the LORD in the Old Testament is revealed perfectly in the person and work of the Lord Jesus Christ when he took upon himself human flesh. God manifest himself fully in visible form in the person of our Saviour, his darling Son.

This is he whom Isaiah saw in the year King Uzziah died (Isaiah 6), sitting on his throne, high and lifted up, who filled the temple with his glorious presence. As the seraphs sang the song of his holiness, the temple filled with smoke, the foundations trembled, and Isaiah exclaimed, 'Woe is me, for I am undone! I am a man of unclean lips: and I dwell in the midst of a people of unclean lips: for my eyes have seen the King, the LORD of hosts'. Who did Isaiah see on the throne? He saw the pre-incarnate Son of God. He saw Christ in his pre-incarnate glory on the throne. 'These things said Esaias, when he saw his glory, and spake of him' (John 12:41).

The angel of the Lord in the Old Testament is the Christ of the New Testament, the eternal God, our Saviour. John followed our Redeemer every day for three years and describes him this way in 1 John 1:1-3.

'That which was from the beginning, which we have heard, which we have seen with our eyes, which we have looked upon, and our hands have handled, of the Word of life; (For the life was manifested, and we have seen it, and bear witness, and show unto you that eternal life, which was with the Father, and was manifested unto us;) That which we have seen and heard declare we unto you, that ye also may have fellowship with us: and truly our fellowship is with the Father, and with his Son Jesus Christ.'

**Appeared to Moses**
It is Christ, the Angel of the Lord, who appeared to Moses in Mount Horeb forty years after he fled from Egypt. All that time he had been secretly preparing his servant in obscurity for the great work of delivering his people out of the hand of Pharaoh. William Law wrote,

'God frequently ordains that early obscurity should lead to most distinguished work. Dark hours precede the break of day. Joseph rises from prison to sit beside the king. From the sheepfolds David is called to occupy the throne.'

The set time had now arrived. Deliverance must be accomplished. Therefore, 'the Angel of the Lord appeared to him in a flame of fire out of the midst of a bush'. The bush blazed with fire; but it was not burned. The flame had no ability to destroy, or even harm the bush. The fire blazed in fury; but the bush defied the flame. At first Moses was stunned; but, soon, his amazement turned to awe, and 'God called unto him out of the midst of the bush' (vv. 4-6).

'And when the LORD saw that he turned aside to see, God called unto him out of the midst of the bush, and said, Moses, Moses. And he said, Here am I. And he said, Draw not nigh hither: put off thy shoes from off thy feet, for the place whereon thou standest is holy ground. Moreover he said, I am the God of thy father, the God of Abraham, the God of Isaac, and the God of Jacob. And Moses hid his face; for he was afraid to look upon God'.

God's presence made the place holy. The One who appeared to Moses in human form as the Angel of the Lord spoke to him as God. Who can this be except Christ our Mediator? God the Father never appeared as man. God the Holy Spirit never appeared as a man. But our ever-gracious Saviour, the Son of God, anticipating the time when he would come to save us from our sins, appeared to Moses as the God-man, our Mediator.

**Afflictions Seen**
What brought our Saviour to the burning bush? What moved his holy heart to appear? The answer is given (vv. 7, 8).

'And the LORD said, I have surely seen the affliction of my people which are in Egypt, and have heard their cry by reason of their taskmasters; for I know their sorrows; And I am come down to deliver them out of the hand of the Egyptians, and to bring them up out of that land unto a good land and a large, unto a land flowing with milk and honey; unto the place of the Canaanites, and the Hittites, and the Amorites, and the Perizzites, and the Hivites, and the Jebusites.'

What blessed tenderness there is in those words! What assured compassion! Our Saviour ever appears to comfort the sorrowing. The

Son of God ever appears to meet the needs of his people. The Lord Jesus Christ is always God at hand (Philippians 4:4, 5). Let us never faint in the hour of trial, and never doubt in time of trouble and sorrow. You may walk through a dark valley. Your road may be rough. You may be called to lay your head on the hard pillow of sorrow. Troubles may roll over you, wave upon wave. But the eye of Christ's infinite, eternal love ever watches over you. His heart of love ever throbs with sympathy for you. The ear of his love hears your cry. The hand of his love will, in due season, be outstretched to deliver you. Yes, our Saviour ever appears to comfort the sorrowing. At his own appointed time, he will bring you forth into a large place and deliver you, because he delights in you (Psalm 18:19).

**Moses' Ebenezer**
This appearance of the Lord Jesus Christ as the Angel of the LORD was deeply engraved upon Moses' heart. He never forgot it. Moses' path through the wilderness was not easy. His toils were hard and his afflictions grievous. But in his trials he was constantly sustained by this experience, by what God showed him in the bush. The remembrance of this checked his fears, revived his strength, and refreshed his soul. This was his Ebenezer. He never forgot it. It was his lifelong comfort.

After forty more years had passed, and the man of God reached the conclusion of his appointed time and service, just before his lips are silenced in the grave, he pronounced a legacy of precious gifts, brilliant with prophetic splendour, upon God's people; gifts of boundless mercy, crowned with 'the good will of him that dwelt in the bush' (Deuteronomy 33:16). As he was about to leave this world of woe, Moses remembered 'the Angel of the LORD', and declared him to be the source of all blessedness to his people, according to 'the good will of him that dwelt in the bush'. May God ever give us grace to bask beneath the sunshine of his good will. His favour is life. His smile is deliverance from all woe. His good will is everything.

**The Mediator**
It is obvious that the name, 'the Angel of the LORD', primarily means that Christ is Mediator between God and man, the One by whom and in whom God is revealed to men. He is the channel of communication between God and men, between heaven and earth.

In Eden's happy hours, before sin and the fall of Adam, God and man walked together in sweet communion. As a loving child, Adam drew near. As a loving Father, God welcomed his presence. No barrier stood between God and man. No obstacle separated. All was light, without darkness, joy without sorrow, sweetness without bitterness.

Then our father Adam by transgression fell, and sin entered. Instantly a breach was made between God and man. Man was separated from God. How can that breach be removed? How can the wall of separation be taken away? How can man be reconciled to God? 'The Angel of the LORD appeared.' In his mission we have the answer. When he appeared, the Lord God said, 'Deliver him from going down to the pit: I have found a ransom' (Job 33:24).

Our God-man Mediator, the Lord Jesus Christ, spans the gulf between the holy God and fallen man. He brings heaven to earth, and raises earth to heaven. Thus the mountains separating us from God are swept away. Our Saviour is the Ladder constructed by our God, resting on earth and soaring into heaven. By this Ladder, God comes down to Man and man ascends up to God (Genesis 28:10-12).

**The God-man**
I remind you, again, that he who is our Saviour, the only Mediator between God and man, the Man Christ Jesus, the Angel of the LORD, is both God and man in one glorious Person. He is very God of very God, co-equal with the Father in being, in eternality, in majesty, in dignity, in power, and in glory. In him is all preeminence. Take away his eternal Godhead and the whole fabric of salvation crumbles into dust. No expiation can be made, no sin pardoned, no soul saved. But that can never be! All his mighty deeds on earth are stamped with Deity. His footprints are the footprints of God. His voice is the voice of God. Everything written of him in the Book of God says, 'Behold your God'! Of all things revealed in the Bible, nothing is more distinctly clear than this: 'The Angel of the Lord' is himself God over all, blessed forever. What God is, he is. What God knows, he knows. What God wills, he wills. What God does, he does.

If he were only God or only man, we would be without hope, or, as Paul puts it, 'of all men most miserable' (1 Corinthians 15:19). Reconciliation to God would be impossible. But without ceasing to be God, without diminishing his absolute Deity, God the Son became a man. He humbled himself to be 'the firstborn among many brethren' (Romans 8:29), that he might be our Saviour (Hebrews 2:14, 17). Being both God and Man, this mighty Daysman, our Kinsman Redeemer, the Mediator between God and Man, is able to lay his hands upon both God and man and unite the two.

## The Revealer

As 'the Angel of the LORD', he reveals God to men. He lived our life, died our death, suffered our sufferings, paid our every debt, bore our every curse, made atonement for our every transgression, redeemed us from all iniquity, and worked out for us a heaven-deserving robe of perfect righteousness. Glorious as that is, there is more. The Lord Jesus came to open out the Father's heart, to tell us the Father's will, to shine before us as the express image of his Father's person.

He is 'the Messenger of the Covenant'. Almost the very last word given in the Old Testament was, 'Behold, I will send my messenger, and he shall prepare the way before me: and the Lord, whom ye seek, shall suddenly come to his temple, even the Messenger of the Covenant, whom ye delight in: behold, he shall come, saith the LORD of hosts' (Malachi 3:1).

It is the great privilege of all who are taught of God to know that before time was, an everlasting covenant secured our everlasting salvation. And everything in that covenant so hangs upon Christ, so fully hangs upon him, that he is himself the covenant (Isaiah 42:6; 49:8).

He is the Surety of the Covenant, who was trusted with our souls by our heavenly Father, and the Surety in whom we trust our souls (Ephesians 2:12). But not only is he the Surety, he is also the Messenger of the Covenant, 'the Angel of the Covenant', the One by whom and in whom its mysteries are revealed and its wonders are opened in the sweet revelation of boundless grace.

Through him, the Eternal Word, the eternal counsels and purposes of the triune God are revealed. The Lord God declares of him, 'This is my beloved Son, in whom I am well pleased; hear ye him' (Matthew 17:5). We are urged with sweet promises of mercy by the Father, the Son, and the Holy Spirit to hear, come to, and trust Christ, the Angel of the LORD, our Covenant Surety (Isaiah 55:1, 2; Matthew 11:28-30; Revelation 22:17).

In him 'are hid all the treasures of wisdom and knowledge' (Colossians 2:3). He has come, who is the Light of the world, that those who follow him should not walk in darkness, but should have the Light of life. The Sun of Righteousness is never eclipsed. The door of heaven's storehouse of grace is never shut. Does your soul thirst for God? Would you know God as he really is? Then, fly away to 'the Angel of the LORD'. He says, 'Look unto me'. 'He that hath seen me, hath seen the Father' (John 14:9). He is the Light of life. May God the Holy Spirit cause us ever to gaze upon the Light (2 Corinthians 4:6).

**Divine Attributes**
In the face of Jesus Christ, 'the Angel of the LORD', all the attributes of God shine forth as sunbeams shining from the Sun of Righteousness. In this world of woe we see nothing but 'lamentations, and mourning, and woe' (Ezekiel 2:10). Misery stalks us through the earth. Wretchedness sits beside every hearth. Tears are ever flowing from every eye, burning the cheeks of every soul. Every mortal heart sighs and heaves with sorrow. Pain is the constant companion of every man born of woman. Earthquakes, and storms, and floods, and famine, wars and rumours of wars, sickness, sorrow, and death are the things we have seen and the things we expect to see in this world.

Multitudes ask, where is the God of love and the love of God? Then, 'the Angel of the LORD' appears, and all is bright. In him, and in him alone we see that 'God is love'. The proof is his own mission (1 John 4:9, 10; John 3:16; 1 John 3:16). Beholding the crucified Christ, we know that 'God is love'. And, as we see the love of God shining from the wounds of our dying Redeemer, we see shining through his bleeding wounds every attribute of our God, and see them conspicuously glorified. Justice is fully honoured. All that justice demands, Christ gave. Not one debt remains. All is satisfied. Truth is triumphant. Not one word falls to the ground. Not one promise is unfulfilled. Not one threat is put aside. It is declared that, 'Without holiness no man shall see the Lord'. But 'the Angel of the Lord' appears and assures us perfect holiness is ours in him, that we are made new creatures in him, that old things have passed away, and all things have become new.

Blessed Angel of the Lord, our God and Saviour, we adore you as the Way, the Truth, and the Life. Ever appear to us and fulfil in us your own word.

'O righteous Father, the world hath not known thee: but I have known thee, and these have known that thou hast sent me. And I have declared unto them thy name, and will declare it: that the love wherewith thou hast loved me may be in them, and I in them' (John 17:25, 26).

Fulfil in us 'the good will of him that dwelt in the bush'. You, and you alone have the words of eternal life.

Here I raise mine Ebenezer;
Hither, by thy help I've come;
And I hope by thy good pleasure
Safely to arrive at home.

Robert Robinson

# Chapter 17

## Barefoot On Holy Ground

'And he said, Draw not nigh hither: put off thy shoes from off thy feet, for the place whereon thou standest is holy ground.'
(Exodus 3:5)

How does a sinner come to God? How can I, a poor, worthless, doomed, damned, guilty, vile and helpless sinner come to the holy Lord God and find acceptance with him? How can I approach the Lord and obtain his mercy? How can I come to God and stand before him? In Exodus 3:5, God the Holy Spirit shows us exactly how we can and must come to God, if we would find acceptance with him.

'Now Moses kept the flock of Jethro his father in law, the priest of Midian: and he led the flock to the backside of the desert, and came to the mountain of God, even to Horeb. And the angel of the LORD appeared unto him in a flame of fire out of the midst of a bush: and he looked, and, behold, the bush burned with fire, and the bush was not consumed. And Moses said, I will now turn aside, and see this great sight, why the bush is not burnt. And when the LORD saw that he turned aside to see, God called unto him out of the midst of the bush, and said, Moses, Moses. And he said, Here am I' (vv. 1-4).

Moses drew near to the Lord; but, before he did, the Lord appeared to Moses. No sinner will ever come to God, until God first comes to the sinner. First, the Lord 'appeared to Moses in a flame of fire out of the midst of a bush'. Then Moses turned aside to see the Lord. That is always the order. God first came seeking Adam. Then Adam came to God. The Lord God first came to Abram. Then Abram came to the Lord. The Lord Jesus first appeared to Saul of Tarsus. Then Saul came to the Saviour.

Next, we are told in verse 4, 'God called unto him out of the midst of the bush, and said, Moses, Moses'. God called him personally, and called him effectually. It is obvious the Lord called him personally, for he said, 'Moses, Moses'. And we know his call was effectual, because Moses answered the call. No sinner will ever come to God, except he is called; personally, effectually, irresistibly called by grace to come. Faith in Christ is always the result of God's call. No sinner will ever come to Christ until the Lord Jesus Christ reveals himself to the sinner. You can no more trust an unknown Saviour than you can come back from where you have never been. Faith, true saving faith, is always the result of divine revelation, the result of the revelation of the glory of God in the face of Jesus Christ (Zechariah 12:10; 2 Corinthians 4:4-6).

In verse 5, the Lord God said to Moses, 'Draw not nigh hither: put off thy shoes from off thy feet, for the place whereon thou standest is holy ground'. The only way Moses could draw near to God was barefoot, on holy ground. And that is how we must come, barefoot, on holy ground.

**A Prohibition**
When Moses answered God's call and was about to approach him in the bush, the Lord God said, 'Stop. Do not take another step. You cannot come to me.' He said, 'Draw not nigh hither.'

What a strange thing that is. Does God call a man, only to tell him he cannot approach him? Indeed he does!

You and I cannot approach God, come to God, stand before God, and obtain acceptance with God in our natural, fallen, sinful state. It is written, 'Whosoever offereth a sacrifice of peace offerings unto the LORD to accomplish his vow, or a freewill offering in beeves or sheep, it shall be perfect to be accepted; there shall be no blemish therein' (Leviticus 22:21). Without holiness; perfect, absolute, unblemished holiness, no man shall see the Lord (Hebrews 12:14).

Not only does God prohibit us from coming to him as fallen, sinful men and women, he warns us plainly, if only we had ears to hear his warning, that if we dare attempt to make ourselves holy before him, we shall be slain by him. When the Lord God gave his law on Mount Sinai, it was not given to show men what they must do to be accepted of him. It was given to tell us plainly that we can do nothing to make ourselves acceptable to him (Exodus 19:11-13, 16-19; 20:18, 19, 22-26). When the Lord appeared to Moses in the mount, he told Israel to come up to the mount, to see it and hear his voice, but demanded they come no closer. They were not even to touch it with their polluted hands, lest they be slain. How thankful we ought to be that God does not require us to produce righteousness for ourselves! We have not come up to Mount Sinai, but unto Mount Zion (Hebrews 12:18-24).

**A Prerequisite**
That is the prohibition. 'Draw not nigh.' But blessed be his name, God's word does not end there. It is a prohibition that makes way for an open door of hope, giving us a prerequisite, a requirement that will allow us to come to God. 'Put off thy shoes from off thy feet.' God required Moses to come to him barefoot. In Exodus 40, he required Moses, and Aaron, and Aaron's sons to wash their hands and feet in the holy water of the holy laver of brass, as they came into the tabernacle. Then they went into the house of God barefoot, always barefoot, before the Lord. No man was allowed to enter God's house, do service in God's house, or offer sacrifice in God's house, until he was washed in the laver and was barefoot before the Lord. What does it mean?

It is customary in Asian countries for people to remove their shoes before entering a home. It is an act of courtesy, a show of respect, much like that shown by a gentleman taking off his hat when he enters a building, or greets a lady. Certainly, respect is one thing God required of Moses, and requires of all, when he says, 'Put off thy shoes from off thy feet'. The Lord God demands we reverence him. The holy Lord God cannot and will not be worshipped by any who do not sanctify his name and reverence him. Yes, we must reverence God. We can never come to him without reverence. 'God is greatly to be feared in the assembly of the saints, and to be had in reverence of all them that are about him' (Psalm 89:7). But there is more in this matter of being barefoot before the Lord than reverence.

In Deuteronomy 25 God's law uses barefootedness as a symbol of shame. If a man refused to take his dead brother's wife and raise up children to his brother, he was brought before the elders and in an act of public humiliation, the widowed wife took off his shoe and spit in his face. From that day, until the day of his death, he wore the title, 'him that hath his shoe loosed', as a shamed man (Deuteronomy 25:9, 10).

Do you see the picture? God requires all who come to him do so as shamed sinners. As people who are ashamed of themselves, ashamed to approach him, acknowledging themselves as utterly unworthy to lift their face in his direction.

Another thing associated with being barefoot is nakedness. We read in Isaiah 20:2, 'At the same time spake the LORD by Isaiah the son of Amoz, saying, Go and loose the sackcloth from off thy loins, and put off thy shoe from thy foot. And he did so, walking naked and barefoot'. I am confident that Isaiah was not completely naked for three years. That would have been indecent. But he was required to walk for three years without the sackcloth that covered his upper body and barefoot, exposed and defenceless. That is how we must approach the Lord God, as barefoot and defenceless, and shamefully naked, just like the publican our Lord described in Luke 18 (Luke 18:13; 1 John 1:9). The Lord God will never put the shoes of grace on our feet, as sons in his house (Luke 15:22), until we take off the shoes of our own filthy righteousness in the mountain of his holiness.

### A Place

Now, read the last line of Exodus 3:5 and you will see why we must come barefoot to God. 'And he said, Draw not nigh hither: put off thy shoes from off thy feet, for the place whereon thou standest is holy ground'. If we come to God, if we draw nigh to God, we come barefoot to stand upon a place called 'holy ground'.

The ground was called holy, because the Lord God was there, because it was the place chosen by God to meet this sinful man in mercy. He had sanctified it, set it apart from all other ground, as the place where he would meet Moses, reveal himself to Moses, and allow Moses to come to him. I did not just pull that idea out of my hat. I pulled it from the Book of God. Jerusalem was called God's holy hill of Zion (Psalm 99:9), because God put his temple there. That was the place of his sacrifice, his priest, and his worship. The holy of holies was separated from the holy place and called 'the most holy place' (Exodus 26:33, 34), because the mercy seat was there, the glory of God was there, and mercy was dispensed there. The Lord God said, 'And there I will meet with the children of Israel, and the tabernacle shall be sanctified by my glory' (Exodus 29:43). The one place, the only place where God meets with men, and men come to God, is the Lord Jesus Christ, of whom all things in the tabernacle and temple were types. Christ is the Holy Ground upon which we draw nigh to God and stand in grace (Hebrews 7:24-27; 10:14, 17-22).

Holiness is that attribute of God spoken of throughout the Scriptures by which he is entirely distinct and separated from all his creatures. It refers to his whole glorious and perfect being. God's holiness is his supreme perfection. This is 'the message', John tells us, 'God is light, and in him is no darkness at all.' That which is holy is perfect, pure, sinless, and undefiled.

As God is holy, he cannot and will not accept any who are not holy, perfect, pure, and undefiled (Psalm 24:3-5). He says, 'Walk before me and be thou perfect ... Be ye holy; for I am holy' (Genesis 17:1; 1 Peter 1:15, 16). Coming to God by faith in Christ, we stand barefoot on holy ground, and are made holy by him who is that 'holiness without which no man shall see the Lord' (Hebrews 12:14). Our Lord Jesus Christ is that Holy Ground by which we are made perfectly holy before our God (John 17:15-19).

Let me show you something of the blessedness of being barefoot on Holy Ground before the holy Lord God. When the Lord God says to poor sinners like us, 'Pull off your shoes and come in', he is expressing his open heart of hospitality to all who come to him by Christ Jesus. He is saying, "Sinners, come and welcome!" (Matthew 11:28-30). As a rule, the only time you see grown people barefoot is at home, or where they are so comfortable they feel at home. I cannot think of a better way to describe what I want to say than that. I am completely comfortable and at home with God in Christ! Find me a person who is running around barefoot, and I will show you someone who is completely confident that there is no danger before him. Look at the little child running through the grass, playing in its father's yard barefoot, or the housewife running around her house barefoot. There is not a more irenic, peaceful picture in the world, except this, a sinner standing barefoot on Holy Ground before God Almighty, 'accepted in the Beloved'. That is the only way to stand before the Captain of the Lord's hosts, the Captain of our salvation (Joshua 5:13-15).

The law demands holiness. Christ gives holiness. The law says, 'Cursed is every one that continueth not in all things which are written in the book of the law to do them.' The gospel says, 'Blessed is the man whose iniquities are forgiven, whose sin is covered; blessed is the man to whom the Lord will not impute iniquity'. The law says, 'Thou shalt love the Lord thy God with all thy heart, and with all thy mind, and with all thy strength.' Grace says, 'Herein is love: not that we love God, but that he loved us, and sent his Son to be the propitiation for our sins.' The law speaks of priestly sacrifices offered year by year continually, which could never make the comers thereunto perfect. The gospel speaks of Christ who, 'after he had offered one sacrifice for sins forever … by one offering hath perfected forever them that are sanctified.' The law declares that as many as have sinned in the law, shall be judged by the law. Grace proclaims, 'There is therefore now no condemnation to them that are in Christ Jesus', for all who are in Christ have forever passed from death unto life. The law says, 'Draw not nigh'. Christ says, 'Pull off your shoes and come in.' Joseph Hart wrote:

> Come, ye sinners, poor and wretched,
> Weak and wounded, sick and sore;
> Jesus ready stands to save you,
> Full of pity joined with power:
> He is able, He is able,
> He is willing; doubt no more.
>
> Come, ye needy, come and welcome,
> God's free bounty, glorify;
> True belief and true repentance,
> Every grace that brings you nigh.
> Without money, without money
> Come to Jesus Christ and buy.
>
> Let not conscience make you linger,
> Nor of fitness fondly dream;
> All the fitness He requireth,
> Is to feel your need of Him;
> This He gives you, this He gives you,
> 'Tis the Spirit's rising beam.

Come, ye weary, heavy laden,
Bruised and broken by the fall;
If you tarry till you're better,
You will never come at all:
Not the righteous, not the righteous,
Sinners Jesus came to call.

View Him grovelling in the garden;
Lo! Your Maker, prostrate lies;
On the bloody tree behold Him,
Hear Him cry before He dies:
"It is finished!" "It is finished!"
Sinner, will not this suffice?

Lo! th' incarnate God, ascended,
Pleads the merit of His blood;
Venture on Him, venture wholly,
Let no other trust intrude.
None but Jesus, none but Jesus,
Can do helpless sinners good.

Saints and Angels joined in concert,
Sing the praises of the Lamb;
While the blissful seats of heaven
Sweetly echo with His name;
Hallelujah! Hallelujah!
Sinners here may sing the same.

-------------

I will arise and go to Jesus,
He will embrace me in His arms.
In the arms of my dear Saviour,
O there are ten thousand charms!

# Chapter 18

# Christ Our Resurrection

'Moreover he said, I am the God of thy father, the God of Abraham, the God of Isaac, and the God of Jacob. And Moses hid his face; for he was afraid to look upon God.'
(Exodus 3:6)

When Moses turned aside to see the great sight that was before him, when the Lord God appeared to him in the burning bush, God made a tremendous revelation of himself. He said, 'I am the God of thy father, the God of Abraham, the God of Isaac, and the God of Jacob'. What is revealed in those words? What do they teach? There are several things here revealed by our God that are as obvious as they are delightful and precious.

First, the Lord God declared, 'I am the God'. He, and he alone is God. There is none like him and none beside him. He who is the God is eternal, sovereign, holy and self-existent, the Creator, Ruler and Sustainer of all things. Next, the Lord God identified himself as the God of Moses' father. 'I am the God of thy father', the God his father and mother trusted, the God they taught him to trust. What a blessed privilege and honour it is for a child to be born into the home of a man and women chosen, redeemed, and saved by the God of all grace, and to be raised in the nurture and admonition of the Lord!

Then, the Lord God identified himself as 'the God of Abraham'. Abraham was the eminent reminder to Israel, and should be to us, of

God's covenant, and all the promises and blessings of it. The Lord was saying, 'Moses, you can count on me; you can trust me; you can believe me. I am the God who is faithful and true, the God who ever remembers his covenant.

Then, the Lord revealed himself to Moses as 'the God of Isaac'. What do you think of when you think of Isaac? The first thing that comes to my mind every time I hear or read the name 'Isaac' is substitution and provision. Isaac is forever a picture of Christ our Saviour as Jehovah-jireh, The Lord will Provide. Isaac is forever fixed as an emblem of substitutionary redemption and the bounteous, unfailing mercy, love, and grace of God flowing to our souls through the precious blood of Christ, the Lamb of God!

And I love the next word by which the Lord God revealed himself to Moses. 'I am the God of Jacob'. He chooses to identify himself in his glory as 'the God of Jacob'. He does so because 'He delighteth in mercy!' When I think of Jacob, I think of grace, free, unmerited, undeserved grace, the grace of sovereign, electing love; omnipotent, conquering, irresistible, saving grace; immutable, indestructible, preserving grace!

**The God of the Living**
Those things, it seems to me, are obvious. But, in Luke 20 our Lord Jesus Christ, the One speaking to Moses in Exodus 3, explains the meaning of his words. The Herodians, the Pharisees, and the Sadducees tried to entrap our Saviour with what they thought were questions he could not answer without either denying his doctrine or giving them a justified excuse for killing him. What fools little men are when they imagine they are smarter than God!

The Sadducees, who denied the doctrine of the resurrection, dreamed up an incredible situation, and asked the Lord Jesus whose wife a woman would be in the resurrection if she had been married to seven brothers who had died. Our Saviour did not honour their foolish question by answering their imaginary quibble. Instead, he seized the opportunity to teach us what he revealed to Moses in Exodus 3:6.

'And Jesus answering said unto them, The children of this world marry, and are given in marriage: But they which shall be accounted worthy to obtain that world, and the resurrection from the dead, neither marry, nor are given in marriage: Neither can they die any more: for

162

they are equal unto the angels; and are the children of God, being the children of the resurrection. Now that the dead are raised, even Moses showed at the bush, when he calleth the Lord the God of Abraham, and the God of Isaac, and the God of Jacob. For he is not a God of the dead, but of the living: for all live unto him' (Luke 20:34-38).

He who is God, he who is our God is the God of the living, not of the dead. Abraham, Isaac, and Jacob were thought by all to have been dead for a very long time. As far as the eye of man could see, they were dead. They certainly appeared to be dead; but they were and are living. I find something personally sweet and glorious in that. When it appears to all others, and more so to me than to anyone else, that I am dead, Christ is my life, and I live in him and by him! When I was spiritually dead in myself, I was alive in him (Ephesians 2:4, 5). And now, though I often appear dead, I live, because Christ who is my Life lives.

In Luke 20 the Lord Jesus Christ declares that his people, God's elect, all who trust him, are a people who shall be accounted worthy to obtain the next world of heavenly glory, being made by grace equal to the angels of God, and more, being the children of God (John 1:12), we are 'the children of the resurrection'. Then he says, 'That is what I showed Moses at the bush; if you knew the Scriptures and the power of God, you would know that.' What Moses later spoke of as 'the good will of him that dwelt in the bush' is the complete salvation of all God's elect in and by the Lord Jesus Christ in resurrection glory. This is exactly what the Lord Jesus taught Martha in John 11.

'Then said Martha unto Jesus, Lord, if thou hadst been here, my brother had not died. But I know, that even now, whatsoever thou wilt ask of God, God will give it thee. Jesus saith unto her, Thy brother shall rise again. Martha saith unto him, I know that he shall rise again in the resurrection at the last day. Jesus said unto her, I am the resurrection, and the life: he that believeth in me, though he were dead, yet shall he live: And whosoever liveth and believeth in me shall never die. Believest thou this?' (John 11:21-26)

Martha's response to the Saviour's words demonstrated her confident faith in him as the long expected Messiah. 'She saith unto him, Yea, Lord: I believe that thou art the Christ, the Son of God, which should come into the world' (John 11:27). Because I have seen the good will of him that dwelt in the bush, because I know and believe Jesus of Nazareth is the Christ, the Son of God, I live in hope of the resurrection.

With Paul, I say, 'If in this life only we have hope in Christ, we are of all men most miserable' (1 Corinthians 15:19). That does not mean the believer's life in this world is a sad, morbid existence. Neither does it mean it is really more delightful and pleasurable to live in this world without faith. And it certainly does not mean, that were it not for the hope of eternal glory, the people of God would prefer not to live as they do in obedience and submission to our heavenly Father. We do not serve God for gain!

When Paul says, 'If in this life only we have hope in Christ, we are of all men most miserable', he simply means this: If there were no eternal life in Christ, no eternal bliss of life with Christ in glory, and no resurrection, then the believer would be the most miserably frustrated person in the world. We would never have what we most earnestly desire. We would never see the end of our hope. We would never embrace Christ, or be embraced by him. We would never see our Redeemer. Such a thought is the most distressing thought I have ever entertained. Nothing could be more cruel and miserable than to live in hope of seeing Christ, being like Christ, and spending eternity in the presence of Christ, only to die like a dog!

'If in this life only we have hope in Christ, we are of all men most miserable'. What a horrible, unbearable thought! What a tormenting supposition! But it is not so. I live in hope of the resurrection; and my hope is both sure and stedfast. 'For I know that my Redeemer liveth, and that he shall stand at the latter day upon the earth: and though after my skin worms destroy this body, yet in my flesh shall I see God: whom I shall see for myself, and mine eyes shall behold, and not another; though my reins be consumed within me' (Job 19:25-27). In sickness I am calm, in sorrow I am peaceful, in trial and affliction I am at ease, in bereavement I am confident, and I hope to die in confidence and joy, because I live in hope of the resurrection.

Our assurance of the resurrection is much more than belief in a point of orthodoxy. It is faith in and hope in a Person. Christ is himself our Resurrection. This is not some fool's philosophy. It is not a mere religious tranquilizer by which we are able to cope with the trials of life. This is the calm, confident assurance of the believer's heart. It is the necessary, inevitable result of God given faith in Christ. The Lord Jesus Christ is the resurrection and the life of all who trust him; and all who trust him shall in the last day be resurrected with him.

**Representative Resurrection**

We have been resurrected with Christ representatively, both as our covenant Surety before the world began and as our covenant Surety in time (Romans 8:29, 30; Ephesians 2:5, 6). When the Lord Jesus Christ rose from the grave, he rose as our Representative. All he has done and all he has experienced, all of God's elect have done and experienced in him, by virtue of our representative union with him. His obedience to the law was our obedience (Romans 5:12, 18-21). His death as a penal sacrifice for sin was our death (Romans 6:6, 7, 9-11; 7:4). This is our atonement. His resurrection was our resurrection. This is our life!

The resurrection of Christ is an indisputable fact of revelation and history, upon which we rest our souls (1 Corinthians 15:1-8). Disprove the resurrection, and you disprove the gospel. 'If Christ be not raised, your faith is vain; ye are yet in your sins' (1 Corinthians 15:17). And the bodily, physical resurrection of the Lord Jesus Christ necessitates the resurrection of all who are in Christ. That which has been done for us representatively must be experienced by us personally. We are members of Christ's mystical body, the church. If one member of the body were lost, the body would be maimed (1 Corinthians 12:12, 27). If one member of the body were lost, the Head would not be complete (Ephesians 1:22, 23). These bodies of ours must be fashioned like unto his glorious body (Philippians 3:21; John 17:24). Christ was raised as the firstfruits of them that sleep (1 Corinthians 15:20). The full harvest must follow. Christ is the last Adam. As we have borne the image of our first covenant head, we must bear the image of the second (1 Corinthians 15:21-23, 47-49). And Christ has obtained the victory over all that could hinder the glorious resurrection of his people: sin, death, hell, the grave, and the devil (Colossians 2:13-15; Hebrews 2:14, 15). The covenant engagements of Christ, as the Surety of God's elect, will not be complete until the hour of our resurrection (John 6:37-40).

**Experienced Resurrection**

We live in hope of the resurrection, because we have experienced the resurrection of Christ in regeneration. The new birth is resurrection from the dead. To be born again by the Spirit of God is the first resurrection (Revelation 20:6; John 5:25; 11:25, 26; Ephesians 2:1-4). Having been raised from spiritual death to spiritual life in and by the Son of God, we live in anticipation of resurrection glory.

**God's Revelation**

We live in hope of the resurrection, because we believe the revelation of God concerning the resurrection (John 5:28, 29). 'Whosoever liveth and believeth on me shall never die'. God's elect never die. There shall be a resurrection of life at the second coming of Christ (1 Corinthians 15:35-44, 51-58; 1 Thessalonians 4:13-18). This is not some imaginary secret rapture, but a glorious resurrection.

There shall also be a resurrection of damnation (John 5:29). The wicked and unbelieving shall be raised by the power of Christ in order to be judged and condemned. The believer shall be raised by virtue of his union with Christ in order to be judged and rewarded with everlasting glory. The wicked shall be raised in wrath. The believing shall be raised in love. The wicked shall be raised for execution. The righteous shall be raised for a wedding. 'Prepare to meet thy God!' Soon we will stand before the living God in judgment (2 Corinthians 5:10, 11). I am 'looking for the mercy of our Lord Jesus Christ unto eternal life', because of 'the good will of him that dwelt in the bush', because Christ is the Resurrection and the Life.

# Chapter 19

## 'Moses Was Afraid'

'Moreover he said, I am the God of thy father, the God of Abraham, the God of Isaac, and the God of Jacob. And Moses hid his face; for he was afraid to look upon God.'
(Exodus 3:6)

When I read that 'Moses hid his face; for he was afraid', the words appear to be totally contrary to everything we know about Israel's great deliverer. Was Moses afraid? Moses who slew the Egyptian, confronted Pharaoh, the most powerful king in the world in his own court, led Israel across the Red Sea, went up into the Mountain of God at Sinai as all the children of Israel trembled, led the children of Israel in battle after battle against the mightiest kings and mightiest armies in the world, and calmly walked up Pisgah to die, to see the Promised Land and die by the hand of God, was he afraid?

Indeed, he was. We read here that 'Moses was afraid'. There must be something different about this man and the fear that possessed him as he looked on the burning bush and heard God speak out of the bush.

In the Book of Malachi, the Lord God asks, 'Where is my fear?' (Malachi 1:6). That is the question I have for this religious generation. That is the question I want to ask the churches of this day, when I see all the tomfoolery that passes for worship in our day. And that is the question I ask you. Where is God's fear? Where is the fear of the Lord?

I know this. No sinner has ever had Christ revealed to him and walked away the same as he was before. When Christ reveals himself to a person, something happens. The result of such a revelation is always pretty much the same. The flesh always withers before Christ, when he is pleased to reveal himself in his saving glory and grace. We see this throughout the Scriptures.

When the Lord God came seeking Adam, Adam hid himself and was afraid, because he was naked (Genesis 3:9, 10). When the Lord revealed himself to Abraham, 'Lo, an horror of great darkness fell upon him' (Genesis 15:12). When the Lord appeared to Israel in the tabernacle, when 'the glory of the Lord appeared to all the people, and there came a fire out from before the presence of the Lord, and consumed upon the altar the burnt offering', the people shouted and fell on their faces (Leviticus 9:22-24). When the preincarnate Christ, the Angel of the Lord, appeared to Manoah and his wife, they 'fell on their faces to the ground' (Judges 13:20). When the Angel of the Lord appeared to David and the elders of Israel, they 'fell upon their faces' (1 Chronicles 21:16). That is what happened to Isaiah, when he saw the Lord (Isaiah 6:1-6; John 12:37-41). When Ezekiel saw Christ on his throne and the glory of the Lord appeared to him, and he heard the Saviour's voice, he said, 'I fell upon my face' (Ezekiel 1:26-28). When the Lord showed himself to Daniel, he said, 'there remained no strength in me: for my comeliness was turned into corruption, and I retained no strength ... And behold a hand touched me, which set me upon my knees and upon the palms of my hands' (Daniel 10:8-10). When the Lord Jesus was gloriously transfigured before his disciples, 'they fell on their faces and were greatly afraid' (Matthew 17:6). When the Saviour revealed himself to John the Beloved, the Apostle said, 'when I saw him, I fell at his feet as dead' (Revelation 1:17).

### Blessed Withering

How blessed it is to fall at his feet as one who has been slain in his glorious presence! We are never so much alive as when we are dead at his feet. We are never so truly living as when our flesh withers in death before our great and glorious Saviour. Every believer wants, more than anything else, the death of all that is sinful and rebellious in him.

The Lord Jesus Christ, who slays the flesh, will raise and revive those he slays by the hand of his almighty grace, just as he did John.

'And he laid his right hand upon me' (v. 17). He who is God, kills and makes alive! He wounds then he heals. He brings down then he lifts up. He abases then he exalts. He strips then he robes. He brings you down to the dunghill then sets you among princes. It is never the other way around! Life comes out of death. Revival comes out of withering. If you fall at his feet in the humiliation of broken-hearted repentance, he will raise you up by his grace.

The Lord Jesus Christ, who slays the flesh, will always raise and revive those he slays by the hand of his almighty grace. And Christ revealed in the heart always brings a word of comfort and assurance to the one to whom he reveals himself. He says to those who fall before his glorious majesty, 'Fear not, I am the first and the last: I am he that liveth and was dead; and behold, I am alive evermore, Amen; and have the keys of hell and of death' (Revelation 1:17, 18).

That is exactly what we see in Exodus 3:1-10. The God of Glory, the Angel of the Lord, the preincarnate Christ, appeared to Moses in the burning bush (vv. 1-5). When he did, 'Moses hid his face; for he was afraid to look upon God' (v. 6). Then, the Lord spoke a word of redemption, grace, and salvation to his servant (vv. 7-10).

**Our God**
The Lord Jesus revealed himself to Moses as the covenant-keeping God of Israel, the God of all grace. When he picked out Abraham, Isaac, and Jacob, and made them the fathers of his chosen people, it was not because of any excellence in them, but because of his free grace. His choice of those men, and the covenant made with them, was a matter of pure sovereignty and boundless grace. Now, he has come to redeem Israel from the land of bondage, not because of any good in them, or because of any good expected from them. Redemption, like the grace that inspired it, is absolutely free.

The Lord God appeared to Moses, wrote A. W. Pink, 'as the God of Abraham the sovereign Elector; the God of Isaac the almighty Quickener; the God of Jacob the long-suffering One; who is about to bare His arm, display His power and deliver His people.' Blessed be his name, that is exactly how he comes to sinners in saving grace today! The God of Abraham is our God, the One who sovereignly chose us in Christ before the foundation of the world. The God of Isaac is our God, who by his own miraculous power makes us new creatures in Christ.

The God of Jacob is our God, the One who bears with us in infinite patience, who never forsakes us, and who has promised to perfect that which concerns us (Psalm 138:8).

## Reverent Fear

'Moses hid his face: for he was afraid to look upon God'. Moses hid his face before the Angel of the Lord, concealed his face in the presence of Christ's manifest glory because 'he was afraid to look upon God'. What is the meaning of that word 'afraid'? What does the Holy Spirit here teach us? In what sense was Moses 'afraid to look upon God'?

The word 'afraid', as we commonly use it, expresses the idea of a distressing emotion that comes from a sense of impending danger. It means 'to shudder with terror, to quake and tremble with horror'. Certainly there is a natural, slavish fear, a dreadful apprehension of God that possesses all our fallen race. All men, because of guilt, shudder with terror before God. All, because of sin, quake and tremble with horror at the thought of God. You may not admit it; but, if you are without Christ, you are terrified of God. And your fear, your dread, your terror at the very thought of God is inescapable, so long as you are plagued with the guilt of sin. But that is not the word used here. The word here is a word meaning to 'revere'. It can be translated 'fearful', or 'reverent'. This is the fear God the Holy Ghost gives to all who are born again by grace. This is the fear of faith. This word rendered 'afraid' is used throughout the Old Testament (Job 28:28; Psalm 19:9; 34:11; 111:10; Proverbs 1:7; 2:4, 5; 8:13; 9:10; 16:6; 23:17).

This is a fear not to be feared, but craved. Blessed is that sinner who learns the fear of the Lord with which Moses was overcome at the bush, when he hid his face because he was afraid to look upon God! 'Come ye, my children, hearken unto me: I will teach you the fear of the LORD' (Psalm 34:11).

When a sinner is awakened from the sleep and death of sin, and brought forth into the light and life of grace in Christ, 'perfect love casteth out fear'. Therefore, we read in the Book of God, 'Ye have not received the Spirit of bondage again to fear; but ye have received the Spirit of adoption, whereby we cry, Abba, Father' (Romans 8:15). It is a blessed thing to be freed from slavish fear, to be given that child-like fear that comes by the revelation of God's saving grace and glory in Christ. This is the sweet promise of the covenant (Jeremiah 32:40).

## The God we Fear

Now, let me show you why we fear, revere, adore, exalt, magnify, venerate, and worship the Lord Jesus Christ, our God and Saviour. As we have seen already, the God who spoke to Moses here, the Angel of the Lord, is our blessed Saviour. In fact, in this sixth verse of Exodus 3, he calls himself God, using the plural name for the triune God, (Elohim), three times in this one verse. Three times, he says to Moses, 'I am the God, the triune God.' 'And Moses hid his face because he was afraid to look upon (the) God (the triune God).'

That God, the triune God, the triune Jehovah is seen, known, and revealed only in that One who is called 'The Angel of the LORD', the Lord Jesus Christ, the incarnate God (Colossians 2:9, 10). We bow before Christ in reverent fear as the God of Glory (1 Timothy 6:13-17).

He is the blessed and only Potentate (Psalm 41:13; Isaiah 40:12-31; Daniel 4:35). The 'only Potentate' is the Sovereign, the only Sovereign, the all-sovereign God of heaven and earth. Christ declares he is that God, saying, 'All power is given unto me in heaven and in earth' (Matthew 28:18). Christ our God is the only being in the universe who possesses the absolute right and power to do as he pleases.

Our Lord Jesus Christ alone is the 'King of kings and Lord of lords'. This title is expressly ascribed to him, and only to him (Deuteronomy 10:17; Psalm 136:3; Revelation 17:14; 19:16). Only he who is God is the Immortal and has immortality (Psalm 36:9; Isaiah 40:28; Daniel 4:34). When the Spirit of God tells us Christ is he 'Who only hath immortality', he means for us to understand not only that he can never die, but also that he is life's never-failing Fountain of Life (John 1:1-4).

Christ our Saviour is immortal God who dwells in unapproachable light, 'light which no man can approach unto' (Psalm 104:2). The glory of Christ is as unapproachable as the light of the sun. He is the brightness of the Father's glory and the express image of his person (Hebrews 1:3). Christ is the 'Sun of righteousness' (Malachi 4:2). He is God, so glorious that none can even look upon him, unless that person is veiled like Moses in Exodus 33:18-22, or God veils himself in human flesh. His glory is the glory of God (John 1:14).

This Christ is our God, 'whom no man hath seen, nor can see' (Exodus 33:20; Deuteronomy 4:12; John 1:18; 4:24). Because his divine essence is too glorious to be seen by mortal eye, he assumed our nature, that he might be known by us (1 John 3:1-3).

To him alone, who is God our Saviour, 'be honour and everlasting power. Amen'. To him be glory and dominion forever and ever, because he who is God our Saviour is the eternal God, 'which is, and which was, and which is to come ... the faithful witness, and the first begotten of the dead, and the prince of the kings of the earth', and he 'loved us and washed us from our sins in his own blood, and hath made us kings and priests unto God and his Father' (Revelation 1:4-6).

We bow before our all-glorious Christ, hiding our faces with awe and reverence because he is God. We reverence him because of who we are, recognizing that our only fitness to stand before him is his fitness, the fitness he gives us by his grace; his blood, his righteousness, and his beauty (Isaiah 6:1-7; Ezekiel 16:6-16; Colossians 1:12-14).

**A Message Given**
Every sinner to whom Christ reveals himself receives a message from him, a message to declare to others like himself in need of mercy. It is the sweet and glorious message of redemption and grace. 'I am come down to deliver' (v. 8). The message is always the same. It is from Christ and about Christ. All who receive it understand it. It is the message of a perfect Redeemer, perfect righteousness, a perfect Sacrifice, perfect grace, and perfect love (1 John 4:17-19).

When Christ is revealed in the heart of a sinner, that sinner who once cringed in fear before God, afraid of his wrath, is freed from such fear, and is delightfully overcome with a fear of reverence, faith, and love that bows before his throne in humble adoration. We who have seen the Lord are his witnesses (Isaiah 6:8; Acts 1:8). Let all who know him, young and old, men and women, go tell the world what a great and glorious Saviour our Lord Jesus Christ is!

**Be Not Afraid**
It is the fear of God, this fear that Moses experienced at the bush, the fear of faith in Christ, that delivers us from all other fear. Hear me, child of God. 'Be strong and of a good courage; be not afraid, neither be thou dismayed: for the LORD thy God is with thee whithersoever thou goest' (Joshua 1:9). Christ says, 'Be not afraid, only believe' (Mark 5:36).

If Christ is my God I have no reason to fear. I do not mean to suggest to you that I am free of fear. I am not. But my fear is my shame. I know if Christ is my God I should be free of all fear. I have no reason to fear

Satan, men, or the world. And I have no reason to be afraid of my God! 'Behold, God is my salvation: I will trust and not be afraid'. That is my desire. I want to trust Christ and not be afraid (John 3:14-16). Trusting Christ, I need not be afraid concerning all my past sins (Romans 8:1; 1 John 1:9). Trusting Christ, I need not be afraid even regarding my present corruption and sin (Romans 4:8; 1 John 2:1, 2). Trusting Christ, I need never be afraid of my future sins (Psalm 89:31-34). Trusting Christ, I need never be afraid of anything that concerns the welfare of my immortal soul (John 14:1-3).

Whatever my God may call me to do or to suffer for his name's sake, I ought to trust him and not be afraid. He will supply all my needs (Matthew 6). He who supplied the children of Israel with 100,000 bushels of manna every day for 40 years, will have no trouble feeding me! He will protect me in all my ways (Matthew 10:30). He will preserve me in his grace. He will receive me into glory when I die.

This I know. It is the fear of the Lord, this fear of faith in Christ that produces true meekness (Numbers 12:3; 1 Corinthians 6:19, 20; Romans 12:1, 2). Moses was meek above all men who lived upon the earth, because 'Moses was afraid'. Because he feared God, he was meek above all other men. He knew who he was, a sinner, loved, chosen, redeemed, and saved by the Lord Jesus Christ. Jehovah's Servant! He knew whose he was. He belonged to God! He knew why he was here. To do the will of God! To honour God! To serve the people of God! Because he feared God, he feared no one else and nothing else!

O Spirit of God give me such fear! The more fully the Lord our God makes himself known to us, the more we will humbly bow before him in reverence and godly fear. And the more we fear him, the less we will be afraid (Isaiah 12:1-6).

# Chapter 20

## The Making Of A Prophet

'Now Moses kept the flock of Jethro his father in law, the priest of Midian: and he led the flock to the backside of the desert, and came to the mountain of God, even to Horeb. And the angel of the LORD appeared unto him in a flame of fire out of the midst of a bush: and he looked, and, behold, the bush burned with fire, and the bush was not consumed. And Moses said, I will now turn aside, and see this great sight, why the bush is not burnt. And when the LORD saw that he turned aside to see, God called unto him out of the midst of the bush, and said, Moses, Moses. And he said, Here am I. And he said, Draw not nigh hither: put off thy shoes from off thy feet, for the place whereon thou standest is holy ground. Moreover he said, I am the God of thy father, the God of Abraham, the God of Isaac, and the God of Jacob. And Moses hid his face; for he was afraid to look upon God. And the LORD said, I have surely seen the affliction of my people which are in Egypt, and have heard their cry by reason of their taskmasters; for I know their sorrows; And I am come down to deliver them out of the hand of the Egyptians, and to bring them up out of that land unto a good land and a large, unto a land flowing with milk and honey; unto the place of the Canaanites, and the Hittites, and the Amorites, and the Perizzites, and the Hivites, and the Jebusites. Now therefore, behold, the cry of the children of Israel is come unto me: and I have also seen the oppression wherewith the Egyptians oppress them. Come now therefore, and I will send thee unto Pharaoh, that thou mayest bring forth my people the children of Israel out of Egypt.'
(Exodus 3:1-10)

Here we have a detailed account of Moses' call to be God's spokesman, his response to God's call, and the responsibility he had as a man called of God to be his prophet to his people.

## Salvation Sure

Let me state, as clearly as I can, that the salvation of God's elect is sure. The Lord our God has decreed from eternity to save a great multitude of sinners for the glory of his own great name; and they must and shall be saved (Ephesians 1:3-6; 2 Thessalonians 2:13, 14). They are elected, adopted, and predestinated heirs of God. God's servants do not hedge when it comes to the preaching of God's sovereignty in grace. Election and predestination are Bible terms in which God's people rejoice. God's elect must be saved. What fact could be more joyful?

The Lord Jesus Christ has redeemed that elect multitude, God's chosen seed, and must have them with him in heaven for the satisfaction of his soul's travail (Isaiah 53:9-12; Hebrews 2:13; 12:1, 2). The Son of God did not shed his blood in vain. The cross of Christ shall never be discovered a miscarriage. Every sinner for whom atonement was made shall be with Christ in heaven.

God the Holy Ghost sovereignly and irresistibly regenerates, calls, and preserves every sinner chosen by God and redeemed by Christ (Psalm 65:4; 110:3; John 6:63). 'Salvation is of the Lord'. Grace never fails. The Holy Spirit has been sent into this world to savingly apply the benefits of Christ's finished work to those for whom he lived and died. Without question, every sinner who comes to God by faith in Christ has everlasting life, and shall never perish (John 6:37-40; Romans 10:9-13). But no sinner can or will be saved apart from the preaching of the gospel (Romans 10:14-17). You cannot call upon Christ, if you do not believe in Christ. You cannot believe in Christ if you have not heard of Christ. You cannot hear of Christ without a preacher. And a man cannot preach Christ, until he is sent of God to preach him. C. H. Spurgeon observed:

'The word of this salvation avails not until it is declared in the ear; it must be published, or men cannot hear it; and not hearing, they cannot believe; and not believing, they cannot be saved.'

The men and women of this world are perishing all around us for lack of knowledge; and it is our responsibility, yours and mine, to tell them how God saves sinners by his dear Son, the Lord Jesus Christ.

All of God's people are missionaries, people sent on a mission. And our mission in this world is to preach the gospel of Christ to all men. I am calling for volunteers, volunteers sent of God, to tell the world about God's dear Son and his saving grace in his Son. I am calling for us, you and me, to give ourselves up to our Saviour, to be used of God wherever and however he sees fit to use us.

**God's Gift**
In Ephesians 4:11, the Holy Spirit tells us that Christ's ascension gifts to his church include apostles, pastors, teachers, evangelists, and prophets. The passage in Ephesians 4 is a quotation from Psalm 68. It is a declaration of the accomplishments of Christ as our Mediator. Redemption has been accomplished by the blood of Christ. His resurrection declares the sins of God's elect, which he bore in his own body on the tree, to have been put away by the sacrifice of himself as their Substitute. The Man who died for us at Calvary is now enthroned in glory and has received gifts of grace, gifts which he daily bestows upon his church for the salvation of his people.

'The chariots of God are twenty thousand, even thousands of angels: the Lord is among them, as in Sinai, in the holy place. Thou hast ascended on high, thou hast led captivity captive: thou hast received gifts for men; yea, for the rebellious also, that the LORD God might dwell among them. Blessed be the Lord, who daily loadeth us with benefits, even the God of our salvation. Selah. He that is our God is the God of salvation; and unto GOD the Lord belong the issues from death' (Psalm 68:17-20).

These ascension gifts of Christ, as I said, include apostles, pastors, teachers, evangelists, and prophets. It is obvious there are no continuing apostolic or prophetic offices in a strict sense. The last apostle was Paul, and the last prophet was John the Baptist. Evangelists are not itinerant preachers, but what we now call missionaries, church planters. Pastors and teachers are those men called and gifted of God for the work of the ministry, preaching the gospel in a local church, building up the saints in the faith, edifying the body of Christ. Pastors and teachers are not two separate offices, but one. Every God-called pastor is God's appointed teacher in the church he serves. The pastor-teacher called and sent of God is God's angel (messenger) to the local church over which the Holy Ghost places him.

177

**Prophets**

Because the term 'prophet' is used to describe one of the ascension gifts of Christ to his church, it is obvious the word does not apply in this context to an office that was terminated before the Lord's ascension.

It is next to impossible to find anything useful said or written in our day about the ministry of these men. What is a prophet? The word, as it is used regarding the New Testament era, seems to refer to men with extraordinary gifts of ministry, men who to have a remarkable, God-given understanding of the Scriptures, men who have a keen awareness of the times in which they live and the message required to meet the need of the hour (1 Chronicles 12:32).

A prophet, may be an evangelist, or a pastor-teacher, but he is also distinctly a prophet, a man distinctly gifted of God to lead his people in crucial times with boldness and authority, which only God can give. Clearly, there were such men in the early church (Acts 11:27; 13:1). At least six are named in Acts 11:27, 28 and 13:1.

There have never been many prophets, at least not many true prophets. But our times cry for such men. Is there not a prophet? Are there none today to stand in the gap and dare to speak for God? Never was the need greater and the supply smaller than today.

The prophet is a voice in the wilderness. It is his business to sound the trumpet, proclaim the Word of God, and press the claims of the sovereign God upon the hearts and lives of men. He does not work on details or set up programs. He does not devise ways and means. He does not belong on boards and committees. He is the voice of God to men in his day! He is not a parrot, a puppet, or a promoter. A prophet is never a team player. He is not a religious politician. He is a voice, a lone, dogmatic, unrelenting voice.

He is nothing but a prophet. If he tries to be or do anything else he is an embarrassment to himself and to everyone around him. He is not a politician; and he is never popular with politicians either in the state house or the church house. He is not cowed by dignitaries. If needful, he will call Herod a fox, even when he knows it may cost him his life.

A prophet is an unreconstructed rebel, an odd number in a day of regimentation. He has no more patience with religious nonsense than Isaiah had when he thundered against Judah and Jerusalem, or Amos when he rebuked Israel at Bethel, or Elijah when he mocked the

178

prophets on Mount Carmel, then mocked their gods. It is the prophet's business to say what others cannot, will not, or at least dare not say. The politician has his eye on the next election instead of the nation's welfare. I fear most preachers are more politician than prophet. They are more interested in your approval than your soul. They have their eyes on denominational promotion, the next rung of the ladder, a high seat in the synagogue, and being called a rabbi.

The prophet has no axe to grind, but an axe to wield. He lays the axe of Holy Scripture to the root of every tree in the groves of the world's idolatry. He does not know the meaning of the word 'compromise'. His subject never varies. His relentless message is, 'Repent, for the kingdom of heaven is at hand!' 'All flesh is grass!' 'Behold, your God!' 'Behold, the Lamb of God, which taketh away the sin of the world!' 'Salvation is of the LORD!'

As far as God's prophet is concerned, the grass is no greener in the next pasture. He seeks no man's office, position, or honour. His concern is for the will, and glory, and truth, and kingdom of God. Churches today are looking for scholars, specialists, socializers, and showmen. We need some seers, some prophets who, like Isaiah, have seen God in his glorious holiness, themselves in their shameful sinfulness, and the land in its idolatrous uncleanness.

The prophet does not pack the house, nor produce impressive statistics. He may get but poor response, but whether they hear or not, those who hear him know that a prophet has been among them. People do not crowd churches to hear prophets. In an age of ear-itch religionists, most everyone calls God's prophets 'troublers of Israel'. And wherever a prophet's voice is heard, trouble, of one kind or another, is sure to follow. Whenever John the Baptist, or the Apostle Paul came to town, whether they preached in the church-house, the jail-house, or the open fields, either a revival or a riot broke out. Nobody ignores a prophet.

The prophet is never popular with the Pharisees, and does not want to be. Organized religion is never more organized than when it attempts to silence a prophet. 'Which of the prophets have not your fathers persecuted?' 'Ye are the children of them that killed the prophets'. So said the greatest of the prophets to the Pharisees of his day. From Abel to Zacharias, our Master said, prophets have been stoned while living, and honoured when dead. Let no one be misled by the monuments men build to dead prophets. They are only the gestures and attempts of one generation to cover up the crimes of their fathers in earlier generations.

The prophet is never popular at home. In all four gospels we read our Lord's pronouncement, 'A prophet is not without honour save in his own country and in his own house.' But prophets do have their reward, and so do those who befriend them, even with a cup of cold water. God will not overlook the prophet's chamber, where his unpopular servant has been made to feel at home.

There are not many candidates for Elijah's mantle. His path is not an easy path to follow. There are many ways of getting rid of prophets. John the Baptist's head is not brought in on a charger these days. There are smoother and more skilful ways of silencing lone dissenters like Micaiah in these days of refined malice against God. Some can even be promoted into silence. Success has stopped many mouths when persecution failed.

Like John the Baptist, the prophet is out to pull down the high places, build up low places, and make a way for the Lord. His business is not to impress, but to pierce. He does not lecture about mustard. He makes a mustard poultice and lays it next to the sore. Others comfort the afflicted. The prophet afflicts the comfortable. We are trying to accomplish now by pep, publicity, propaganda, and promotion what once was done by preaching.

The woods are full of trained religious professionals. They are called 'preachers'. But this age cries for prophets, men in whom the Word of the Lord burns like fire, men who carry and are weighed down with 'the burden of the Word of the Lord'. Any young Elisha in line for Elijah's mantle will need the mind of a scholar, the heart of a child, the hide of a rhinoceros, the courage of a lion, and a backbone of steel. He may irk those who like to preserve the status quo, for he is a disturber of Israel; but no one else can take his place. Oh, that God may raise up some prophets in our midst in this dark, dark day!

Maybe some who read these lines are Samuels who will hear what the Lord says and who will speak what he hears. There is not much prospect as to pay, promotion, or prestige. But there has always been 'yet one man' who will scorn the hatred of Ahab and seek the honour of God. Read Exodus 3:1-10, and you will see how prophets are made. Prophets are made, called, gifted, and raised up by God at the time and in the place where they are needed, to 'prepare the way of the Lord'!

**Man of Faith**

First, it must be understood that a prophet is a man of God-given faith, God-given faith in Christ. Exodus 3 does not describe Moses' conversion. He was converted long before this. We are plainly told Moses left Egypt 40 years earlier by faith, because he believed God (Hebrews 11:24-27). No man can ever speak for God until he believes God. No man is called of God to preach the gospel who does not know the gospel. No man can follow Christ who does not trust Christ. Exodus 3 does not describe Moses' conversion. Here Moses himself tells us how he became God's prophet.

**Tending Sheep**

The second thing I want to point out is that when the Lord God called Moses to be his prophet, he was tending sheep, he was faithfully doing what God had put into his hands to do.

'Now Moses kept the flock of Jethro his father in law, the priest of Midian: and he led the flock to the backside of the desert, and came to the mountain of God, even to Horeb' (Exodus 3:1).

Moses was a shepherd, and appears to have been a shepherd for a long time. His job was tending the flocks of Jethro. By the arrangement of Divine providence Moses was a shepherd. The Lord made him a shepherd to prepare him to be a shepherd. It was the work of a shepherd to feed and water the sheep, to guide the sheep, to seek and save the sheep who got lost, and to protect the sheep.

It took a man with unique qualities to be a shepherd. His heart had to be both tough and tender, hard and compassionate, disciplined and soft. In addition to this, the shepherd had to spend a great deal of time alone out in the countryside. While alone, he could, of course, just allow his mind to wander about from thought to thought or he could utilize the time to worship God and learn of him. That appears to be what Moses did. For forty years he worshipped and served God as a shepherd. All the while God was preparing him to be a prophet.

Those men who are called of God to be prophets are men who are willing to do anything God puts in their hands to do for his glory, men who are found faithfully serving him where they are. No man is called of God to be a prophet in Israel who does not know what it is to worship and serve God where he is (Jeremiah 3:15; 23:4).

## Glory Revealed

Third, a prophet is a man who has seen the glory of God in the face of Christ, a man to whom God has revealed the glory of his grace. 'And the angel of the LORD appeared unto him in a flame of fire out of the midst of a bush: and he looked, and, behold, the bush burned with fire, and the bush was not consumed. And Moses said, I will now turn aside, and see this great sight, why the bush is not burnt' (Exodus 3:2, 3).

When God calls a man to be his prophet he causes that man to be possessed by 'the good will of him that dwelt in the bush'. His life is lost in the cause of the gospel. He surrenders everything to the cause of Christ, and is utterly consumed by it. God's prophets are men separated unto the gospel. They are separated by the call of God and the revelation of Christ (Galatians 1:15-17) and by their own determined purpose (Romans 1:1). That man whose life is consumed with 'the good will of him that dwelt in the bush' seeks to make the gospel of Christ and the glory of Christ the thing that determines everything about his life. Faithful men take their work seriously and mould their lives to it. A pastor does not need to wear tailor-made suits; but he better wear one that is clean and pressed. He does not need to drive a new car; but he ought to drive a clean one. He does not need to live in the largest or finest house; but his house ought to be clean and well maintained. Everything in his life says something about his attitude toward his work.

## Called

Fourth, the prophet is a man who is called of God to be his prophet. He is personally and distinctly called and sent by God for the deliverance of his people. We see this in verses 4-10. Here the one speaking is Christ himself, the God of Glory, who appeared to Moses. Here Moses is telling us how he was called and why. It was the Lord himself who called Moses (vv. 4, 5).

'And when the LORD saw that he turned aside to see, God called unto him out of the midst of the bush, and said, Moses, Moses. And he said, Here am I. And he said, Draw not nigh hither: put off thy shoes from off thy feet, for the place whereon thou standest is holy ground' (Exodus 3:4, 5).

When he called Moses to be his prophet, the Lord Jesus identified himself with his people, as if to say, 'Moses, I am trusting to your care the people I have loved, chosen to be my own, and redeemed with my blood' (v. 6). 'And Moses hid his face; for he was afraid to look upon God.' I understand that. 'Who is sufficient for these things.'

Then, the Lord assured Moses he is ever tender and affectionate to his people. 'And the LORD said, I have surely seen the affliction of my people which are in Egypt, and have heard their cry by reason of their taskmasters; for I know their sorrows' (v. 7). God's elect are the apple of his eye. That means they better be the apple of my eye!

Next, the Lord promised Moses he would save his people, exactly as he had said he would (v. 8). And, with that blessed word of assurance, God sent Moses to deliver his people (vv. 9, 10).

Moses had a mandate from God! He was sent to Pharaoh and to Israel with the authority of God upon him, confident of 'the good will of him that dwelt in the bush'. And you know the rest of the story. Moses brought Israel out of Egypt. God brought Israel out of Egypt with the high hand of sovereign omnipotence and the stretched out arm of mercy, by the hand of his servant, his prophet, Moses. Oh, that God may yet be pleased to raise up prophets in this generation! May he be pleased yet to give prophets to his church 'For the perfecting of the saints, for the work of the ministry, for the edifying of the body of Christ: Till we all come in the unity of the faith, and of the knowledge of the Son of God, unto a perfect man, unto the measure of the stature of the fulness of Christ: That we henceforth be no more children, tossed to and fro, and carried about with every wind of doctrine, by the sleight of men, and cunning craftiness, whereby they lie in wait to deceive; But speaking the truth in love, may grow up into him in all things, which is the head, even Christ: From whom the whole body fitly joined together and compacted by that which every joint supplieth, according to the effectual working in the measure of every part, maketh increase of the body unto the edifying of itself in love' (Ephesians 4:12-16)!

# Chapter 21

# God's Prophet

'Come now therefore, and I will send thee unto Pharaoh, that thou mayest bring forth my people the children of Israel out of Egypt. And Moses said unto God, Who am I, that I should go unto Pharaoh, and that I should bring forth the children of Israel out of Egypt? And he said, Certainly I will be with thee; and this shall be a token unto thee, that I have sent thee: When thou hast brought forth the people out of Egypt, ye shall serve God upon this mountain.'
(Exodus 3:10-12).

Like the prophets of old, gospel preachers are men chosen, called, gifted, and sent of God to deliver his people (Acts 7:35, 36).

## A Man Sent to Deliver

That man who is called of God is one who has learned and experienced the things God taught Moses in this chapter. He is a man to whom the Lord Jesus Christ has been revealed (vv. 1-5). No man is called and sent of God to preach the gospel, except that man to whom and in whom Christ has been revealed as God our Saviour, glorious in holiness, determined to save, and mighty to save. When Moses saw Christ in his glory, he understood 'the good will of him that dwelt in the bush'.

In verses 6-8, we see how the Lord God reminded Moses of his covenant relationship with his elect. That man who is called and sent of God, who speaks for God, is one who knows God's purpose of grace, and his determination to save his people (v. 6). He knows something of the Saviour's love and care, his compassion for his own (v. 7). And he knows the Lord Jesus will assuredly save his people (v. 8).

That man who is sent of God to preach the gospel, like Moses, knows he is sent on an errand sure to succeed, to do a work that cannot fail. The gospel of Christ cannot be preached, and is not preached, with uncertainty. The trumpet of God does not give an uncertain, but a certain, sound. God says, 'Behold, I will save my people'. The Lord Jesus 'shall save his people from their sins'. He says, 'I am come down to deliver them'. And deliver them he will, by the preaching of the gospel (Isaiah 55:11).

### Christ Prophesied

The man who is called and sent of God to deliver his people is a man who knows who Christ is, knows why he came into this world, and knows what he accomplished. This was clearly revealed to Moses as he stood before Christ in the burning bush (v. 8). Who can fail to see that this is a clear, prophetic picture of our blessed Saviour, the Lord Jesus Christ? Because he saw the affliction of his people by reason of sin and death, in due time, the Lord Jesus came down here to bring us up to the heavenly Canaan (Isaiah 63:4; John 14:1-3).

He said to Moses, 'I am come down'. Fifteen hundred years later, Jehovah-Jesus left his Father's House on high and came down into this world of sin and sorrow (2 Corinthians 8:9). Christ in our nature came down from heaven to earth to save his spiritual Israel out of the hands of all their enemies.

The purpose for which he came was 'to deliver' his people and 'bring them up out of that land'. He came to seek and to save that which was lost, to seek and to save his sheep, to bring all that the Father gave him in eternal love with him into eternal glory. Our blessed Saviour came down here to 'bring' us 'into a good land and large, unto a land flowing with milk and honey', to bring us by resurrection, both spiritual resurrection in the new birth and bodily resurrection in the last day, into a land of boundless grace.

### Moses Sent

In verse 10 the Lord Jesus Christ sends Moses to deliver his people. We are taught that the man who is used of God for the deliverance of his people is one who has been sent by the Lord Jesus Christ himself

(Romans 10:13-17). Moses was here commissioned by God to be his prophet, a man sent for the salvation of Israel, God's typical covenant people in the Old Testament. Moses was sent to deliver them from their physical bondage in Egypt. In precisely the same way, the Lord Jesus Christ commissions gospel preachers to be his messengers for the salvation of the Israel of God, his elect, to deliver them from their spiritual bondage into 'the glorious liberty of the children of God' (Matthew 28:18-20; Mark 16:15-18; John 20:19-23; Acts 1:8).

Christ sent Moses specifically to deliver Israel, only Israel (v. 10). 'I will send thee unto Pharaoh, that thou mayest bring forth my people the children of Israel.' There were other slaves in bondage in Egypt; but Moses was sent only to deliver Israel.

Moses was sent for the salvation of God's chosen people. He calls them 'My people, the children of Israel'. They became his people in a national and temporal sense when God entered into a covenant with their father Abraham in Genesis 15, the covenant he confirmed to them at Mount Sinai (Exodus 19:1-8). Today, the Son of God sends gospel preachers specifically to deliver and save his elect. No, preachers are not Saviours. They can save no one. But they are, by the gospel they preach, the instruments by which God saves his elect. God saves his elect through the instrumentality of gospel preaching (Romans 10:17; 1 Corinthians 1:23; Hebrews 4:12; 1 Peter 1:23-25; Isaiah 6:1-7).

Our Saviour sent Moses to the place where his people were, to the place of their bondage. He said, 'I will send thee unto Pharaoh', in whose land they were enslaved. So the Lord Jesus sends his preachers with his message to the place where his people are found in bondage. Though chosen by grace and redeemed by his blood, God's elect are by nature in bondage, just like all other people (Isaiah 61:1-3). Since this bondage is universal, God sends his servants 'into all the world' (Mark 16:15), even 'to the end of the earth' (Acts 1:8). Yet, by his Spirit, in the orderly disposition of his providence, in due time, at the appointed time of love, he sends them to each of his elect. 'He sends his Word and heals them'. He says, 'Fetch him!'

The Lord Jesus sent Moses to deliver his people from oppression and to overthrow their oppressors. 'I will send thee ... that thou mayest bring forth my people ... out of Egypt'. The oppressed cannot be saved unless their oppressors are defeated. So the Lord assured Moses that he would overthrow the Egyptians (vv. 16-20). So it is that our blessed

Saviour sends his servants out to preach the gospel of God's boundless, free grace, assuring each that he will foil our foes before us (1 Timothy 4:11-16; 2 Timothy 3:1-9; 1 Corinthians 15:58). O Spirit of God, give us grace that we may ever assault the very gates of hell with the gospel, knowing that the gates of hell shall not prevail against us!

There is a day coming when 'God shall judge the secrets of men by Jesus Christ according to my gospel' (Romans 2:16). The Son of God will judge all according to their response to the gospel, the gospel he has sent his church in every age to proclaim. All who trust Christ, all who believe the gospel, shall be forever saved. All who refuse to believe the gospel, all who refuse to trust the Son of God, shall be forever damned. There is no middle ground!

## Now

Be sure you do not fail to observe that little word, 'now'. 'Come now … and I will send thee'. God always sends his servants to his chosen at the time appointed for their deliverance. Forty years earlier, Moses became impatient. He decided to take matters into his own hands. What a horrible mistake! But 'now' the four hundred years of servitude and affliction God had appointed had run their ordained course. 'Now' the time for divine intervention had come. 'Now' the hour of grace had arrived. 'Now' God would prepare his people to receive his Word. The pleasant pastures of Goshen were made bitter to them. That is always the way God works (Psalm 107:10-16). He abases before he exalts. He strips before he clothes. He wounds before he heals. He kills before he makes alive. God will not be rushed. His grace is always on time.

## Moses' Response

Verse 11 gives us Moses' response to God's call. Can you imagine how excited he must have been? Can you picture him chomping at the bit? Not hardly. 'Moses said unto God, Who am I, that I should go unto Pharaoh, and that I should bring forth the children of Israel out of Egypt?' At eighty he was not so eager as he was at forty. Experience had sobered him. Keeping sheep had tamed him. He saw himself now as one completely inadequate, totally insufficient for such a great work. That is always the response of men who are called of God to preach the gospel (2 Samuel 7:18; 2 Chronicles 2:6; Isaiah 6:5; 2 Corinthians 2:14-16; 3:4-6).

When a man acts in self-appointed service as a preacher, by his own will, he is completely confident in himself; but the man who is called of God has seen Christ in his glory and knows the awesome task to which he is called, and knows he has no ability whatsoever in himself to perform the work.

**Moses' Assurance**
Yet, that man who is sent of God is sent forth with the confident assurance that the work is God's and God will bless his labour with success (v. 12). The Lord said to Moses, as he did to Paul. 'My grace is sufficient for thee!' What blessed comfort this is! God did not send Moses to go alone. The Almighty promised to accompany him. So it is now. The Lord Jesus says to his servants, 'Lo, I am with you always'.

'How beautiful upon the mountains are the feet of him that bringeth good tidings, that publisheth peace; that bringeth good tidings of good, that publisheth salvation; that saith unto Zion, Thy God reigneth! Thy watchmen shall lift up the voice; with the voice together shall they sing: for they shall see eye to eye, when the LORD shall bring again Zion' (Isaiah 52:7, 8).

# Chapter 22

## Israel's Misery And God's Mercy

'And the LORD said, I have surely seen the affliction of my people which are in Egypt, and have heard their cry by reason of their taskmasters; for I know their sorrows; And I am come down to deliver them out of the hand of the Egyptians, and to bring them up out of that land unto a good land and a large, unto a land flowing with milk and honey; unto the place of the Canaanites, and the Hittites, and the Amorites, and the Perizzites, and the Hivites, and the Jebusites. Now therefore, behold, the cry of the children of Israel is come unto me: and I have also seen the oppression wherewith the Egyptians oppress them. Come now therefore, and I will send thee unto Pharaoh, that thou mayest bring forth my people the children of Israel out of Egypt'. (Exodus 3:7-10)

God's ways are never our ways; and our ways are never his ways. If we had our way, we would never do things the way God does them. That fact is never more evident than it is in God's method of grace. But God's way is always best; and, when it is understood by experience, it is sweet beyond description.

The Lord God chose the nation of Israel as a typical picture of his people in this world; and all that nation experienced in Old Testament history exemplifies what chosen sinners experience in grace.

## God's Purpose for Israel

God chose Abraham's seed and determined to make of them a great nation and a peculiar people, to whom he would communicate the law and testimony, a people by whom he would keep the heavenly lamp burning until Christ should come. In time, Jacob and his family went down into Egypt. For a long, long time they and their descendants were very happy there.

The land of Goshen was fruitful, and the Israelites were greatly favoured by the Egyptian king. No one living as Israel lived in Egypt would ever dream of leaving. And, I am sure they never thought of leaving that country. They had settled permanently. They became as much like the Egyptians as they could. They were a part of the Egyptian nation. In time, they forgot their origin, forgot God's word to Abraham, and melted into the Egyptian culture. They lost all identity as God's chosen, covenant people. They adopted all the superstitions, idolatries, and iniquities of Egypt. Israel loved the land of Pharaoh and all its ease, wealth, and pleasure.

Though they had forgotten it, the Lord God had declared that their sojourn in Egypt would be for a set time; and when the appointed time had come he would bring them out of that land (Genesis 15:13, 14). All the time Israel was in the land of Israel, though they forgot him, the Lord God was determined to bring them out of Egypt by his mighty, outstretched arm. He was determined to separate the precious from the vile, to separate the chosen from the reprobate, to separate Israel from Egypt. He had made a difference between Israel and Egypt; and he meant to make the difference evident to both.

## The Parallel

The parallel is obvious to all who know the Scriptures. Scattered among the ruins of Adam's fallen race God has a people whom he has chosen to be his own peculiar people. At present, they are mixed up with the world. They are in the world and appear to be of the world. Like all others, they are 'children of wrath'. They love the world, love darkness, and love sin. They are happy the way they are. They have no desire to be separated from their lusts, separated from their companions, and separated unto the Lord. They love life in Egypt. But the Lord God has appointed a time, he calls 'the time of love', when he will bring his redeemed out from the rest of mankind.

He who bought them with blood will deliver them by the power of his omnipotent, irresistible grace. The Lord Jesus Christ did not make atonement for nothing. He did not die in vain. It is written, 'he shall see of the travail of his soul, and shall be satisfied'. The Lord God will yet call each of his sons and daughters out of Egypt, even as he called his Firstborn. He will bring his chosen out of the midst of the people among whom they sojourn until the time appointed for their emancipation.

## Blessed Misery

As the appointed day approached, when Israel must come out of Egypt, the Lord graciously prepared them for deliverance by making them want it. God does not save sinners against their will. He makes them willing in the day of his power (Psalm 110:3). And he did not drag Israel out of Egypt. He made them so miserable in Egypt that they wanted to leave, so miserable that they had to leave. He made them so sick of Egypt that they rejoiced and sang as they left the land they once loved.

How was that accomplished? God sent the Egyptians a king who knew not Joseph. This new Pharaoh was a petty little man, who feared that someday, when Egypt was at war, Israel might side with Egypt's enemies. He looked upon the Jews as a great danger, and determined, if he could, to thin their ranks. He issued a barbaric order to slaughter all the male children born in Israel. Then, hoping to break their spirit effectually, he put them to hard labour, making bricks without straw and building huge structures in the treasure cities of Egypt.

The Israelites became abject slaves. Under brutal taskmasters, the whip fell often and heavily upon their backs. They were required to labour and toil relentlessly, without the slightest reward or reprieve. At last, the yoke of bondage became intolerable, 'and the children of Israel sighed by reason of the bondage'.

'And it came to pass in process of time, that the king of Egypt died: and the children of Israel sighed by reason of the bondage, and they cried, and their cry came up unto God by reason of the bondage. And God heard their groaning, and God remembered his covenant with Abraham, with Isaac, and with Jacob. And God looked upon the children of Israel, and God had respect unto them' (Exodus 2:23-25).

'And the LORD said, I have surely seen the affliction of my people which are in Egypt, and have heard their cry by reason of their taskmasters; for I know their sorrows; And I am come down to deliver them out of the hand of the Egyptians, and to bring them up out of that land unto a good land and a large, unto a land flowing with milk and honey; unto the place of the Canaanites, and the Hittites, and the Amorites, and the Perizzites, and the Hivites, and the Jebusites. Now therefore, behold, the cry of the children of Israel is come unto me: and I have also seen the oppression wherewith the Egyptians oppress them. Come now therefore, and I will send thee unto Pharaoh, that thou mayest bring forth my people the children of Israel out of Egypt' (Exodus 3:7-10).

Reading those words, I cannot help thinking of David's words in Psalm 107:11-16.

'Because they rebelled against the words of God, and contemned the counsel of the most High: Therefore he brought down their heart with labour; they fell down, and there was none to help. Then they cried unto the LORD in their trouble, and he saved them out of their distresses. He brought them out of darkness and the shadow of death, and brake their bands in sunder. Oh that men would praise the LORD for his goodness, and for his wonderful works to the children of men! For he hath broken the gates of brass, and cut the bars of iron in sunder.'

Do you have a heavy heart, full of soul-trouble, sorrow, and distress? Maybe, just maybe, the Lord God is graciously making you sick of the world and sick of sin. If the Lord God has brought your soul into bondage perhaps it is because the appointed time of love has come for you, perhaps he will bring you out by his grace, as you read these lines!

### Israel's Misery

First, the Holy Spirit describes Israel's misery. What a mercy it was for them that God brought them into such misery! Their misery squeezed from their hearts a cry to God, a cry that would otherwise never have been heard. 'The children of Israel sighed by reason of the bondage, and they cried, and their cry came up unto God by reason of the bondage. And God heard their groaning' (Exodus 2:23, 24).

They began to sigh and to cry, because their time of prosperity was over. The land of Goshen was still very fruitful, but Israel was no longer enriched by it. The country was fair to look upon, but they could not enjoy it. All their prosperity and happiness had departed.

Does that describe you? Once you were very happy, completely satisfied with your life in this world. Now everything has changed.

There is no longer any joy to be found in that which once elated you. In fact, everything you once lived for now causes you nothing but distress and pain. If that is your case, I do not know what God has in store for you; but I do know when God is about to give a man to drink from the cup of salvation, he makes him thirst for it first. And he often does that by making every sweet thing bitter to his taste. When he is about to bring a poor sinner into his banqueting house of grace, he makes him hungry. When he is about to give rest, he fixes it so you can find none. When he is about to set the captive free, he makes his chains heavy and his soul dark.

Israel lost their former prosperity. And they began to feel that they were in bondage. They had been in Egypt for four hundred years. But up until now they were noblemen. They were all blood-kin to Joseph, the Prime Minister of Egypt. He was second only to Pharaoh himself. Every Jew walked through Goshen as an aristocrat. Then, Joseph died, and everything changed. Now, they are slaves in bitter bondage, completely controlled by others.

Laws were made against them. Taskmasters were given authority to enforce those laws. They woke up when they were told to wake up, worked when they were told to work, and slept when they were told to sleep. They were totally under the yoke of cruel oppressors. I know exactly what they felt at that time. I have been there. Have you? I was once a slave to men and to the world, a slave to every obscene lust, taken captive by Satan at his will, and under the heavy yoke of God's holy law, every word of it written against me!

The children of Israel began to feel the heavy weight, and their burdens were too heavy to bear. They had worked and toiled hard; but now they were made to serve with rigour. The pain of their bondage was unbearable. Their burden was crushing. They were now in a position where they must have help, help that God alone could give. O blessed, blessed misery!

As long as you can get along without Christ, you will. As long as you can get along without God, he will let you. As long as you can do for yourself, he will let you 'do' your own way to hell! But, oh what mercy it is, when he fixes it so that you must have him!

'When I kept silence, my bones waxed old through my roaring all the day long. For day and night thy hand was heavy upon me: my moisture is turned into the drought of summer. Selah. I acknowledged my sin unto thee, and mine iniquity have I not hid. I said, I will confess my transgressions unto the LORD; and thou forgavest the iniquity of my sin. Selah' (Psalm 32:3-5).

I remember all that painful time so vividly that I can speak to you like an experienced friend who is well acquainted with the dark road you walk. I know all about your pain and grief. And I know that this is God's way of fetching his own out of Egypt.

Once they were utterly helpless, completely without strength, when there was no help to be had from any other source, then, and only then, did the children of Israel cry out to God for help. So it is with every sinner. No sinner will ever seek the Lord until he has come to an end of himself. You will not come to the throne of grace until you need grace. You will never sue for mercy until you have no other suit to make in the court of heaven. Joseph Hart wrote,

> To understand these things aright,
> This grand distinction should be known:
> Though all are sinners in God's sight,
> There are but few so in their own.
> To such as these our Lord was sent;
> They're only sinners who repent.
>
> What comfort can a Saviour bring,
> To those who never felt their woe?
> A sinner is a sacred thing;
> The Holy Ghost hath made him so.
> New life from Him we must receive,
> Before for sin we rightly grieve.

Look back at Exodus 2:23 again. Notice the order in which things are stated there. First, 'the children of Israel sighed by reason of the bondage'. Then, 'they cried, and their cry came up unto God by reason of their bondage'. And, 'God heard their groaning'. Blessed is that misery that brings us to God! Blessed is that misery that forces us to the Throne of Grace! Blessed is that misery that makes us willing to look to Christ!

## God's Mercy

'They cried, and their cry came up unto God by reason of the bondage. And God heard their groaning, and God remembered his covenant with Abraham, with Isaac, and with Jacob. And God looked upon the children of Israel, and God had respect unto them'. Their misery was the forerunner of God's mercy.

Listen, 'their cry came up unto God'. When it rose up, sharp, and shrill, and intense, it burst through the gates of heaven, and 'came up unto God' (Hebrews 4:16; Jeremiah 29:10-14; Luke 11:5-13). Next, 'and God heard their groaning'. The God of all grace hears the hearts of needy sinners. He hears the sighs, and groans, and cries of his people.

Tell God your misery now, and he will hear your story. Tell him all, for he will hear you. Tell him what it is you want, what great mercy, great forgiveness, and grace you need. Spread your heart before him.

Having heard their groaning, 'God remembered his covenant'. He looked on the children of Israel, but he did not remember their idols, their declensions, or their transgressions. He remembered his covenant! If he were to look on you to all eternity, he would see nothing in you but that which he is bound to punish. But when he remembers his covenant, he looks on his dear Son whom he loves, the Lamb of God, and remembers mercy!

'And God looked upon the children of Israel.' He had given them his ear. He had given them his memory. Now he gives them his eyes. He stood still and looked upon his chosen people in pity and in love; and it is further said, 'and God had respect unto them'. The margin renders it, 'God knew them'. He looked upon them and said, 'I know them. They are mine!'

## God's Appointed Man

When he looked upon them in mercy, the Lord God sent the man he had appointed to deliver them. That is what we see in Exodus 3. That man, Moses, was Israel's Saviour. As such, he is held before us as a delightful type of Christ our Saviour.

'And the LORD said, I have surely seen the affliction of my people which are in Egypt, and have heard their cry by reason of their taskmasters; for I know their sorrows; And I am come down to deliver them out of the hand of the Egyptians, and to bring them up out of that land unto a good land and a large, unto a land flowing with milk and

197

honey; unto the place of the Canaanites, and the Hittites, and the Amorites, and the Perizzites, and the Hivites, and the Jebusites. Now therefore, behold, the cry of the children of Israel is come unto me: and I have also seen the oppression wherewith the Egyptians oppress them. Come now therefore, and I will send thee unto Pharaoh, that thou mayest bring forth my people the children of Israel out of Egypt' (Exodus 3:7-10).

One who is infinitely greater than Moses has come to deliver us. He is the Son of God, the Lord Jesus Christ. First, remember that Christ, the Saviour, is a man like ourselves, full of sympathy for needy souls.

This Moses, a man, yet clothed with divine authority, gave himself up to the people entirely. He was such a lover of Israel that he lived entirely for the people, and once, you will remember, he even said, as he pleaded for them, 'Oh, this people have sinned a great sin, and have made them gods of gold! Yet now, if thou wilt forgive their sin ; and if not, blot me, I pray thee, out of thy book which thou hast written' (Exodus 32:31, 32). That is Christ. Our Lord Jesus Christ, whom it is our joy to trust, was really made a curse for us. He actually stood in the sinner's stead and bore the penalty of the sinner's guilt.

Moses brought all Israel, the people of God's choice, out of Egypt, every one of them. He left not one little baby in Egypt, not so much as a sheep or a goat remained there. He said, 'There shall not a hoof be left behind' and not a hoof was left behind. All that belonged to Israel went marching out when Moses led the way.

And God's elect, all the Israel of God, all Christ's redeemed shall come out of Egypt. Pharaoh's power, the devil's power, cannot hold the very least of them in captivity; not even a bone of one of God's children shall be left in the grasp of death and hell. They shall come again from the hand of the enemy, come out completely, and come out with great substance! The Lord God has laid help upon One who is mighty and exalted, One chosen out of the people, the Lord Jesus Christ. Oh, may he give you grace to trust him!

Till God in human flesh I see, my thoughts no comfort find;
The holy, just, and sacred Three are terrors to my mind.
But if Immanuel's face appear, my hope, my joy begins;
His name forbids my slavish fear, His grace removes my sins.

# Chapter 23

## Ten Words Of Comfort From Our Saviour

'And the LORD said, I have surely seen the affliction of my people which are in Egypt, and have heard their cry by reason of their taskmasters; for I know their sorrows; And I am come down to deliver them out of the hand of the Egyptians, and to bring them up out of that land unto a good land and a large, unto a land flowing with milk and honey; unto the place of the Canaanites, and the Hittites, and the Amorites, and the Perizzites, and the Hivites, and the Jebusites. Now therefore, behold, the cry of the children of Israel is come unto me: and I have also seen the oppression wherewith the Egyptians oppress them. Come now therefore, and I will send thee unto Pharaoh, that thou mayest bring forth my people the children of Israel out of Egypt. And Moses said unto God, Who am I, that I should go unto Pharaoh, and that I should bring forth the children of Israel out of Egypt? And he said, Certainly I will be with thee; and this shall be a token unto thee, that I have sent thee: When thou hast brought forth the people out of Egypt, ye shall serve God upon this mountain. And Moses said unto God, Behold, when I come unto the children of Israel, and shall say unto them, The God of your fathers hath sent me unto you; and they shall say to me, What is his name? what shall I say unto them? And God said unto Moses, I AM THAT I AM: and he said, Thus shalt thou say unto the children of Israel, I AM hath sent me unto you. And God said moreover unto Moses, Thus shalt thou say unto the children of Israel, The LORD God of your fathers, the God of Abraham, the God of Isaac,

and the God of Jacob, hath sent me unto you: this is my name for ever, and this is my memorial unto all generations. Go, and gather the elders of Israel together, and say unto them, The LORD God of your fathers, the God of Abraham, of Isaac, and of Jacob, appeared unto me, saying, I have surely visited you, and seen that which is done to you in Egypt: And I have said, I will bring you up out of the affliction of Egypt unto the land of the Canaanites, and the Hittites, and the Amorites, and the Perizzites, and the Hivites, and the Jebusites, unto a land flowing with milk and honey. And they shall hearken to thy voice: and thou shalt come, thou and the elders of Israel, unto the king of Egypt, and ye shall say unto him, The LORD God of the Hebrews hath met with us: and now let us go, we beseech thee, three days' journey into the wilderness, that we may sacrifice to the LORD our God. And I am sure that the king of Egypt will not let you go, no, not by a mighty hand. And I will stretch out my hand, and smite Egypt with all my wonders which I will do in the midst thereof: and after that he will let you go. And I will give this people favour in the sight of the Egyptians: and it shall come to pass, that, when ye go, ye shall not go empty: But every woman shall borrow of her neighbour, and of her that sojourneth in her house, jewels of silver, and jewels of gold, and raiment: and ye shall put them upon your sons, and upon your daughters; and ye shall spoil the Egyptians.'
(Exodus 3:7-22)

This chapter gives a brief account of some of the circumstances that preceded God's deliverance of the children of Israel from their captivity and bondage in Egypt. But we must not forget these things were written 'for our learning, that we through patience and comfort of the scriptures might have hope' (Romans 15:4). 'They are written for our admonition, upon whom the ends of the world are come' (1 Corinthians 10:11). The One speaking to Moses is speaking to us; and the One speaking is our Lord Jesus Christ, the Angel of the Lord. In these verses, our Saviour speaks ten sweet, comforting words to and about his people.

### Christ's Words of Comfort
1. 'I have surely seen the affliction of my people' (v. 7). Deprived of liberty, the children of Israel were slaves to the king of Egypt. They were compelled to work in the open air, beneath the burning desert sun, in one of the hottest climates in the world. They were forced to make

bricks without straw, having to walk great distances each day to gather the straw (stubble) needed to make the bricks. Their work was performed under the eye of vigilant and rigorous task-masters, who constantly upbraided and beat them. Their food was meagre and contained little nourishment. It consisted only of the sheep they raised and the leeks and onions that grew like wild weeds in Egypt.

Degraded and oppressed, they had been in bondage for four hundred years. Who can imagine the anguish of heart caused by such sufferings? We cannot begin to understand their sorrows. To them the morning sun rose without hope; and the setting sun yielded no comfort. The beauties of new life budding forth in the spring had no charm for their eyes. The bounties of harvest only reminded them of their poverty and emptiness. Even ordinary charms of domestic life were made bitter to them. The expectation of a child being born was heart-wrenching torture. To them everything was misery, grief and despair!

Though they knew it not, and would not have believed it had they heard it, the Lord God says, 'I have surely seen the affliction of my people'. In their great sorrow they had forgotten God; but they were not forgotten of God. Though, for wise and gracious reasons, he delayed to appear in their behalf for four hundred years, he was not indifferent to their sufferings. He saw their affliction and heard their cries. His eye was upon them, his ear constantly open to their sobbing hearts. Every tear they shed was observed by him. Every groan they uttered he recorded.

These words of our Saviour, 'I have surely seen the affliction of my people', might be read, 'In seeing, I have seen the affliction of my people', indicating much more than his omniscience. The words express the clear, distinct, and full sight he had of their affliction, his sympathy toward them in their trouble, an affectionate concern for them, and the fixed, settled, determination in his heart to deliver them. He observed their affliction; and he was moved by what he saw. 'In all their afflictions, he was afflicted' and he was bent upon delivering them from it.

Child of God, ever remember this: Our God sees us. His eye is upon us. He watches over us with all the affection of a tender father, and all the goodness of his holy being. 'Thou God seest me' (Genesis 16:13). What a word of comfort that is to my soul! Though men oppress me, though Satan assails me, though sorrows crush me, though my own heart condemn me, 'Thou God seest me'! He sees you. He sees you perfectly. He sees you always. He sees you where you are. He sees you with the eye of his perfect love.

> Within Thy circling power I stand,
> On every side I find Thy hand;
> Awake, asleep, at home, abroad,
> I am surrounded still with God!

2. 'I have heard their cry' (v. 7). What an indescribable blessing! When we cannot put our cries into words, our Saviour hears the groans of our hearts (Romans 8:26). 'And it came to pass in process of time, that the king of Egypt died: and the children of Israel sighed by reason of the bondage, and they cried, and their cry came up unto God by reason of the bondage. And God heard their groaning, and God remembered his covenant with Abraham, with Isaac, and with Jacob' (Exodus 2:23, 24). The time of affliction is the time for supplication; and our extremity is God's opportunity. The God of Glory hears the cries of our hearts. 'In my distress I called upon the LORD, and cried unto my God: he heard my voice out of his temple, and my cry came before him, even into his ears' (Psalm 18:6). The doors of mercy are always wide open for our needy souls. And the King of Heaven says to us, 'Let me hear thy voice' (Song of Solomon 2:14; Hebrews 4:16).

Prayer is not eloquence, but earnestness. It is not the definition of helplessness, but the feeling of it. It is the cry of faith to the ear of mercy. By the merit and efficacy of Christ's precious blood, the cries and groans of our hearts penetrate the very heart of our God!

3.'I know their sorrows' (v. 7). No man can truthfully make such a statement. The tender feelings of another's heart no human sympathy can touch. But our blessed Saviour, the Prince of Sufferers, he who led the way in the path of sorrow, 'knoweth our frame' and remembers that we are dust. When crushing sorrow lies like ice on your heart, when the dearest earthly friend cannot enter into the grief you bear, Christ can and does! He who once bore my sins and carried my sorrows is touched with the feeling of my infirmity. His tender eyes were once dim with weeping, too.

'I know their sorrows!' He may at times hide his face, causing it to appear as though he has forsaken us and forgotten us, causing us to cry,

'Is his mercy clean gone for ever? Hath God forgotten to be gracious? Hath he in anger shut up his tender mercies?' (Psalm 77:8, 9). Even then, he is bending over us in tender love. He often allows our needs to attain their extremity so he may stretch forth his omnipotent hand to help and reveal the sufficiency of his grace.

Our blessed Saviour takes great care to comfort his people in their many trials and sorrows in this world. He says to his preachers, 'Comfort ye, comfort ye my people' (Isaiah 40:1). Here are three things described in the Word of God to be of great comfort to every believer.

## A Bag

He has made a bag for our sins. Job said, 'My transgression is sealed up in a bag, and thou sewest up mine iniquity' (Job 14:17). In bygone times, when a man died at sea, his body was placed in a weighted bag, which was sewn together and sealed. Then he was cast into the depths of the sea. That is what God has done with our sins. They are cast 'into the depths of the sea'. When Christ died, by his one sacrifice, he put away all our sins. They were buried in the sea of God's infinite forgiveness, put away, never to be brought up again. God Almighty will never charge us with sin, impute sin to us, remember our sins against us, or treat us any the less graciously because of our sin. That is forgiveness! 'Blessed is the man to whom the Lord will not impute sin.'

## A Book

The Lord God has written a book for our names. Take heart, child of God. Your name is written in the book of God! Before the worlds were made, the Lord God inscribed the names of his elect in the Lamb's book of life. In that book God has recorded, not only the names of the chosen heirs of heaven, but also all things pertaining to them. 'In thy book all my members were written' (Psalm 139:16; Philippians 4:3; Revelation 13:8; 17:8). The Lamb's book of life is the book of God's eternal purpose of grace, predestination, and election. The fact our names are written in that book means our salvation is a matter of absolute certainty, and all things work together for our good, by God's arrangement, to secure our predestined end, which is perfect conformity to Christ (Romans 8:28-30). When our Lord says, 'Rejoice because your names are written in heaven', he is telling us we have nothing to fear. All is well for those whose names are written in heaven.

## A Bottle

Moreover, the Lord God keeps a bottle for our tears (Psalm 56:8, 9). It was customary at ancient Egyptian funerals for mourners to have a small cloth or sponge to wipe away their tears. Then, they were squeezed into a small vial, a tear bottle, and placed in the tomb with the dead, symbolizing the care the mourners had for the one who had died. Even so, the Lord our God, our heavenly Father, our almighty Saviour, and our holy Comforter, tenderly cares for us. In all our afflictions he is afflicted. We are the very apple of his eye.

Could anything be more comforting in this world of sin, sorrow, and death? The Lord our God has put our sins in a bag and buried them, our names in a book to remember them, and our tears into a bottle to show his tender care for us. Each one is counted, drop by drop, tear by tear. They are sacred things among the treasures of God! Sorrow may have entered deep into our souls, yet we have reason to rejoice. Great is our honour. We are partakers with Christ in his sufferings. Our tender, sympathizing Saviour knows our sorrows. Our heavenly Father knows. John Trapp wrote, 'That is a sweet support to a sinking soul, that God knows all, and bears a part.' My Father knows. That is enough!

> I am a pilgrim and a stranger,
> Rough and stormy is my road,
> Often in the midst of danger;
> But it leads to God.
> Clouds and darkness oft distress me:
> Great and many are my foes;
> Anxious cares and thoughts oppress me:
> But my Father knows.
>
> Oh, how sweet is this assurance,
> 'Midst the conflict and the strife!
> Although sorrows past endurance,
> Follow me through life.
> Home in prospect still can cheer me;
> Yes, and give me sweet repose,
> While I feel His presence near me:
> For my Father knows.

Yes, He sees and knows me daily,
Watches over me in love;
Sends me help when foes assail me,
Bids me look above.
Soon my journey will be ended,
Life is drawing to a close;
I shall then be well attended:
This my Father knows.

I shall then with joy behold Him,
Face to face my Saviour see;
Fall with rapture and adore Him
For His love to me.
Nothing more shall then distress me
In the land of sweet repose;
Jesus stands engaged to bless me:
This my Father knows.

Mrs Maxwell

4. 'And I am come down to deliver them' (v. 8). He who sees our affliction, hears our cries, and knows our sorrows rises from his throne, not to command the armies of angels that surround his throne to fly to the relief of his suffering children, but to come down from heaven in his own Person to deliver us! God the Son came into this world in human flesh, that he might deliver us from our sins by his obedience as our Substitute. He sends his Holy Spirit, at the appointed time of love, to deliver his redeemed from spiritual death in regeneration. And he graciously comes down to restore and revive our souls with his grace. 'Clouds and darkness are round about him', but 'righteousness and judgment are the habitation of his throne' (Psalm 97:2).

'O sing unto the LORD a new song; for he hath done marvellous things: his right hand, and his holy arm, hath gotten him the victory. The LORD hath made known his salvation: his righteousness hath he openly showed in the sight of the heathen. He hath remembered his mercy and his truth toward the house of Israel: all the ends of the earth have seen the salvation of our God. Make a joyful noise unto the LORD, all the earth: make a loud noise, and rejoice, and sing praise. Sing unto the LORD with the harp; with the harp, and the voice of a psalm. With trumpets and sound of cornet make a joyful noise before the LORD, the King' (Psalm 98:1-6).

5. Our blessed Saviour declares, 'Certainly, I will be with thee' (v. 12). He will be with you, child of God, in all your afflictions to encourage and protect you, to strengthen and help you, to support and comfort you, and to sustain you by his grace (Isaiah 41:10; 43:1-5; Hebrews 13:5). He says to you, 'Fear thou not; for I am with thee: be not dismayed; for I am thy God: I will strengthen thee; yea, I will help thee; yea, I will uphold thee with the right hand of my righteousness' (Isaiah 41:10). 'I will never leave thee, nor forsake thee' (Hebrews 13:5). That is God's promise to every believing sinner in this world. It is given to us that we may, as Isaiah puts it, 'Suck, and be satisfied with the breasts of her consolations; that ye may milk out, and be delighted with the abundance of her glory' (Isaiah 66:11).

'But now thus saith the LORD that created thee, O Jacob, and he that formed thee, O Israel, Fear not: for I have redeemed thee, I have called thee by thy name; thou art mine. When thou passest through the waters, I will be with thee; and through the rivers, they shall not overflow thee: when thou walkest through the fire, thou shalt not be burned; neither shall the flame kindle upon thee. For I am the LORD thy God, the Holy One of Israel, thy Saviour: I gave Egypt for thy ransom, Ethiopia and Seba for thee. Since thou wast precious in my sight, thou hast been honourable, and I have loved thee: therefore will I give men for thee, and people for thy life. Fear not: for I am with thee: I will bring thy seed from the east, and gather thee from the west' (Isaiah 43:1-5).

6. In the last line of verse 12. Our Saviour declares, 'Ye shall serve God upon this mountain'. The Lord God promised Moses he and the children of Israel would serve him upon Mount Horeb, or Sinai, as they did at the giving of the law. There they built an altar upon a hill and offered burnt offerings and peace offerings (Exodus 24:4, 5). So it shall be with all who trust him. The high mountain of sorrow and trouble that rises before you shall be made a mountain of praise, upon which you shall offer sacrifices of thanksgiving and praise to your God.

7. In verse 14 we have the most powerful incentive possible to believe it shall be so. He who made these promises declares, 'I AM THAT I AM'. That is his name. Our Lord Jesus Christ is the eternal,

self-existent, self-sufficient God, the being of beings. He comprehends the past, the present, and the future. I do not merely mean he knows the past, present, and future. I mean he comprehends it. It all exists in him! Yet, there is more. This name, by which our God reveals himself, 'I AM THAT I AM', means, not only I am what I am at present, but I am what I have been and I am what I shall be, and shall be what I am. In a word it declares he is the constant, invariable, immutable, faithful God. Our Saviour here declares that his name, 'I AM THAT I AM', is the sure foundation upon which we may rely. The mighty I AM will do all that he has said!

8. 'I will bring you up out of the affliction' (v. 17). He purposed it. He promises it. And he will do it. And when he does, he will bring you into 'a land flowing with milk and honey'. Our God squeezes milk and honey out of every hard rock of adversity and causes the milk and honey to flow with such abundance into our souls that the rock of adversity from which it flows is soon forgotten.

9. The Lord God promises to give his people favour, even among the Egyptians, and he says, 'Ye shall not go empty' (v. 21).

The Egyptians loaded the sons of Jacob with everything they would need in the wilderness when the Israelites fled from them. So it shall be, believer, with you, when the Lord God delivers you from any trial by which he may momentarily crush your heart. You shall not go out empty, but enriched by the experience (2 Corinthians 4:17, 18; 1 Peter 1:3-9; James 1:12; Romans 8:28). Your light, momentary affliction will work for you 'a far more exceeding and eternal weight of glory'. The trial of your faith is more precious than perishing gold, and shall 'be found unto praise and honour and glory at the appearing of Jesus Christ'. 'All things are for your sakes, that the abundant grace might through the thanksgiving of many redound to the glory of God' (2 Corinthians 2:10). 'For all things are yours: the world, life, death, things present, things to come; all are yours; and ye are Christ's; and Christ is God's' (1 Corinthians 3:21-23).

10. There is one more word of comfort I want you to see in the last line of verse 22. God our Saviour says, 'And ye shall spoil the Egyptians'. Just as Israel took everything worth having out of Egypt, so it shall be with us at last. In that great day that knows no night, when God our Saviour has made all things new, when all his elect have at last been made possessors of their heavenly Canaan, they shall come from

207

all the nations of the earth, bringing the spoils of the nations with them (Revelation 21:22-27; Zechariah 14:1, 9, 20, 21). 'In that day shall there be upon the bells of the horses, HOLINESS UNTO THE LORD; and the pots in the LORD'S house shall be like the bowls before the altar. Yea, every pot in Jerusalem and in Judah shall be holiness unto the LORD of hosts: and all they that sacrifice shall come and take of them, and seethe therein: and in that day there shall be no more the Canaanite in the house of the LORD of hosts'.

# Chapter 24

## Do You Know His Name?

'And Moses said unto God, Behold, when I come unto the children of Israel, and shall say unto them, The God of your fathers hath sent me unto you; and they shall say to me, What is his name? What shall I say unto them? And God said unto Moses, I AM THAT I AM: and he said, Thus shalt thou say unto the children of Israel, I AM hath sent me unto you. And God said moreover unto Moses, Thus shalt thou say unto the children of Israel, The LORD God of your fathers, the God of Abraham, the God of Isaac, and the God of Jacob, hath sent me unto you: this is my name for ever, and this is my memorial unto all generations.' (Exodus 3:13-15)

Anytime one man presumes to tell another what he must do, it is likely he will be asked, 'Who sent you to me? By what authority do you speak? Who gave you the right to tell me what I must do?' Such a response is as reasonable as it is likely. When the Lord Jesus sent Moses to deliver Israel out of Egypt, Moses anticipated that the children of Israel would ask him by what authority he came to them. Though God sent him to Pharaoh (v. 10), and he was to command Pharaoh to let Israel go in the name of the Lord, he was not concerned about Pharaoh's response. But he was concerned about how to speak to the children of Israel. How could he assure them God would, indeed, deliver them? By what authority could he speak, that they might believe his message and trust God to save them? That is the question he raised in Exodus 3:13, and the question God answered in verses 14, 15.

All who call upon the name of the Lord shall be saved; but none can call upon his name who do not know his name. Do you know his name?

## Moses' Question

Look at Moses' question in verse 13.

'And Moses said unto God, Behold, when I come unto the children of Israel, and shall say unto them, The God of your fathers hath sent me unto you; and they shall say to me, What is his name? What shall I say unto them?'

Many see something evil and unbelieving in this question, and reproach Moses for asking it; but the Lord to whom he spoke did not reprove him or, in any way, indicate disapproval. Knowing his own insufficiency for the work to which the Lord God had sent him, Moses said, 'Who am I? I can't do that' (v. 10). And the Lord said, 'I am not sending you to do it. The work is mine. You are merely the instrument through which I have chosen to do the work.'

Remember the mission upon which Moses was about to embark. Any man sent upon such a mission, must (if he is wise) be personally assured that he goes in the name of God. The Lord promised, 'I will be with thee', but he would have no visible God or representation of God to accompany him. Insofar as others could tell, Moses would go to the enslaved Israelites and to Pharaoh alone, yet claiming to be a divinely sent deliverer. He was to tell them that the God of their fathers had promised to set them free. But the people to whom he was sent had, for the most part, embraced the idolatries of the Egyptians.

Moses knew they would want to know, 'Who is this God you speak of? What is his name? What is he like?' In those days and in that land, as in all the nations of the Gentiles, there were many gods, each having a name that indicated the particular power ascribed to him. So, Moses asked the Lord God to tell him his name. Add to that the fact that Moses, no doubt, remembered what happened forty years earlier when he had come to deliver Israel in his own name (Acts 7:27, 35).

So it is with God's servants today and in every age. We are sent to proclaim redemption and grace in the name of our God to a people who have never known him. With Paul, every faithful gospel preacher cries from his inmost soul, 'Who is sufficient for these things?' And by the

Spirit of God he is made to know that our sufficiency is not of ourselves, 'but our sufficiency is of God, Who also hath made us able ministers of the new covenant' (2 Corinthians 2:16; 3:4, 5; 5:17-21).

Let none go forth in the service of our Saviour until he has, like Moses, gone to the throne of grace (Ezekiel 2:1, 2, 6, 7).

**God's Revelation**
In verse 14, we see God's revelation to Moses. Here we see our Lord's answer to Moses' question. Here the Lord God our Saviour reveals himself in his great redemptive character.

'And God said unto Moses, I AM THAT I AM: and he said, Thus shalt thou say unto the children of Israel, I AM hath sent me unto you' (Exodus 3:14).

Those words by which God reveals himself here 'I AM THAT I AM', contain all three tenses of the verb of being, all three tenses of the words 'to be'. They might be translated, 'I was, I am, and I shall always continue to be'. God's name represents his character. When we call upon the name of the Lord, we worship him as he really is. When we pray in Christ's name, we pray upon the basis of all he is and all he has done. When we gather to worship in his name, we gather to worship trusting him in all his character as our God and Saviour.

When the Lord Jesus Christ, the Angel of the LORD, declares 'I AM THAT I AM', he is revealing himself as God, the only eternal, self-existent, self-sufficient, unchanging, immutable, constant, faithful One. He is saying, 'I am now what I have always been and what I shall forever be. I am the Lord, I change not.'

Remember, the One speaking to Moses is our great God and Saviour, Jesus Christ the Lord, the unchangeable Jehovah, 'the same yesterday, and today, and forever', the only wise and eternal God (Hebrews 13:8; John 8:58; Revelation 1:8, 17, 18). Our Lord Jesus Christ made this claim no less than fourteen times in John's Gospel. Fourteen times he publicly took to himself this title which belongs to none but God 'I AM' (4:6; 6:20; 8:24, 28, 58; 13:19; 18:5). He said 'I AM ...

'The Bread of Life' (6:35).
'The Light of the World' (8:12; 9:5).
'The Door' (10:7, 9).
'The Good Shepherd' (10:11, 14).

211

'The Resurrection and the Life' (11:25).
'The Way, the Truth, and the Life' (14:6).
'The Vine' (15:1, 5).

## 'I Am He'

This name 'I AM' is our Saviour's declaration that he is God come to save. He makes himself known to chosen sinners as that One of whom the Scriptures speak (John 4:22-26). I make no attempt to prove that he is. He cannot be known by human reason, or made known by the words of man's wisdom. Our business is simply to proclaim him as he has revealed himself in all his glorious character. The 'I AM' of the burning bush is the God-man Mediator, our Saviour, the Lord Jesus Christ, 'the same, yesterday, and today, and forever'. From everlasting to everlasting he is God. We declare, with Paul, 'By the grace of God I am what I am'. But he simply declares, 'I AM THAT I AM!' Well may he challenge all the earth, saying, 'To whom will ye liken me?' (Isaiah 46:3-5, 9, 10; 45:5, 7, 11, 20-25; 40:25-31). 'And it shall be said in that day, Lo, this is our God; we have waited for him, and he will save us: this is the LORD; we have waited for him, we will be glad and rejoice in his salvation' (Isaiah 25:9).

## 'Moreover'

In Exodus 3:15 our great God and Saviour gives us one of his great 'moreover' words. In verse 14 he tells us what he is in himself. Here he tells us what he is to his people. 'And God said moreover unto Moses, Thus shalt thou say unto the children of Israel, The LORD God of your fathers, the God of Abraham, the God of Isaac, and the God of Jacob, hath sent me unto you: this is my name for ever, and this is my memorial unto all generations.'

It is as though the Lord said, 'I have told you all that I am, the only eternal, self-existent, self-sufficient, unchanging, immutable, constant, faithful One. I am now what I have always been and what I shall forever be. I am the Lord, I change not.' And, 'moreover', all that I am is yours. I am your God. I have made myself your God, bound to you by my own covenant. I am the sovereign God who chose Abraham, Isaac and Jacob in sovereign mercy. I am the God who has pledged himself to the salvation of my people by an unconditional promise of unconditional grace.

**The Triune God**

Here is a threefold declaration of covenant grace from the three persons of the Holy Trinity. The Lord God does not say, 'I am the God of Abraham, Isaac and Jacob'. He says, 'I am the God of Abraham, the God of Isaac, and the God of Jacob.' He did not say that just to fill up space. There is much more here than is commonly observed.

We worship one God in three Persons: the Father, the Son and the Holy Ghost (1 John 5:7). The Lord Jesus Christ is himself God, the only God our Saviour. All the fulness of the triune God dwells in the God-man, our Saviour (Colossians 2:9, 10). Yet, all three Persons in the Godhead are engaged in the salvation of our souls (Ephesians 1:3-14). And the work of one is just as essential and just as glorious as the work of the others. The triune God is revealed and known, worshipped and adored, only in the Person and work of our blessed Saviour (John 1:18). All God is, as well as all he does for us in and by Christ, is ours because of a covenant made before the world was, an everlasting covenant full of divinely glorious, sweet 'moreovers' (Ezekiel 37:26-28; Romans 5:1-21; 8:28-32).

Moses asked the Lord to show him his name; and the Lord Jesus said 'I AM THAT I AM' the covenant God of Israel. We have a fuller declaration in Matthew 1:21. 'And she shall bring forth a son, and thou shalt call his name JESUS: for he shall save his people from their sins.' 'Neither is there salvation in any other: for there is none other name under heaven given among men, whereby we must be saved' (Acts 4:12). 'And they that know thy name will put their trust in thee: for thou, LORD, hast not forsaken them that seek thee' (Psalm 9:10). He whose name is I AM THAT I AM, JEHOVAH-JESUS, is able to save. He declares, 'Behold, I am the LORD, the God of all flesh: is there anything too hard for me?' (Jeremiah 32:27). 'Wherefore he is able also to save them to the uttermost that come unto God by him, seeing he ever liveth to make intercession for them' (Hebrews 7:25). And he will do it! 'Give unto the LORD the glory due unto his name; worship the LORD in the beauty of holiness' (Psalm 29:2).

# Chapter 25

## 'What Is His Name?'

'And God said moreover unto Moses, Thus shalt thou say unto the children of Israel, The LORD God of your fathers, the God of Abraham, the God of Isaac, and the God of Jacob, hath sent me unto you: this is my name for ever, and this is my memorial unto all generations.' (Exodus 3:15)

Throughout the Word of God names given to children had special meaning and significance. Sometimes a person's name would be changed, or a name would be ascribed to him, either by God or by someone else, indicating a radical alteration of life. For example: Adam means 'red earth', indicating his being created by God from the dust of the earth. Jacob means 'cheat, supplanter', but God changed his name to Israel, which means 'prince with God'. Moses means 'drawn forth'. He was so named because Pharaoh's daughter drew him out of the water. In the Bible, the name given to a person says something about that person.

When the Lord Jesus appeared to Moses in the burning bush and sent him to deliver Israel, Moses knew the children of Israel would require him to tell them exactly who sent him to deliver them, to tell them his name, thereby identifying his distinct character as God. So Moses asked the Lord to show him his distinct name, the name by which he distinguishes himself from all others, by which he especially distinguished himself from the gods of the Egyptians (Exodus 3:13). In verse 14, the Lord Jesus, our great God, identified his distinct character as God, the eternal, self-existent, self-sufficient 'I AM'. Then, in verse 15, he told Moses his name. Once they knew his name, the Lord told Moses, they would trust him and worship him (vv. 16-18).

**The Basis of Faith**
The whole basis of our faith in Christ is his name. It is written, 'Whosoever shall call upon the name of the Lord shall be saved'. We call upon people everywhere to trust and worship Christ our God. In all things, I say to you and to myself, trust him. I call upon my own heart and yours, saying, trust Christ. But I know that no one can trust him whom they do not know. You cannot trust an unknown God. So, I want to tell you who he is. In Exodus 3:15 our God and Saviour tells us his name that we might trust him.

First, the Lord Jesus here tells us, 'The LORD God' (i.e. Jehovah-Elohim, Jehovah-God, Jehovah to be Worshipped, Jehovah who Rules) is my name forever'. Second, he identifies himself as our covenant God and Saviour, 'the God of Abraham, the God of Isaac, and the God of Jacob'. Then, he says, 'This is my memorial unto all generations'. That is to say, 'This is the name by which I shall be known, worshipped, trusted and remembered forever'. It is only as we know his name that we trust and worship him (Psalm 9:10; Proverbs 18:10).

**Honour God**
It is my desire to exalt, magnify, extol, honour, praise, and glorify the name of the Lord our God in all things. I have every reason for doing so. With the Psalmist, my heart is resolved 'I will praise thee, O Lord my God, with all my heart: and I will glorify thy name for evermore. For great is thy mercy toward me: and Thou hast delivered my soul from the lowest hell' (Psalm 86:12, 13).

God's great mercy toward me compels me to magnify his name alone. As I think of the mercies of the Lord, my heart cries, 'not unto us, O Lord, not unto us, but unto thy name give glory, for thy mercy, and for thy truth's sake' (Psalm 115:1). God's mercy toward us is great! It is eternal, covenant mercy; immutable, electing mercy; redeeming, saving mercy; preserving, keeping mercy; daily, providential mercy.

Truly, his mercies are great! 'It is of the Lord's mercies that we are not consumed' (Lamentations 3:22). Therefore, 'I will bless the Lord at all times: his praise shall continually be in my mouth. My soul shall make her boast in the LORD: the humble shall hear thereof, and be glad.' I say, to you who know my God, 'O magnify the Lord with me, and let us exalt his name together' (Psalm 34:1-3).

In this day of contemptible (contemporary) worship, in which the whole purpose of church meetings appears to be pleasing, humouring and honouring the flesh, it needs to be stated clearly, emphatically, and frequently that in the house of God, God alone is to be honoured! In our songs, in our prayers, in our attitude, and in all that is preached and taught from the pulpit the triune Jehovah, and the triune Jehovah alone, is to be honoured.

I want all who read these lines to trust our God and Saviour, the Lord Jesus Christ. The surest way I know to persuade sinners to trust him is simply to tell them who he is. If God the Holy Ghost will show you who he is, you will trust him. If you knew my God, you would trust him. All who ever knew him trusted him. 'This is life eternal, that they might know thee, the only true God, and Jesus Christ, whom thou hast sent' (John 17:3). 'They that know thy name will put their trust in thee' (Psalm 9:10).

## His Name

Our God reveals himself by many, many names in Holy Scripture. But his most famous name, his redemptive, covenant name, is Jehovah. This is the name of the great I AM, the name of him who alone is the necessary and self-existent being. The name, Jehovah, implies God's eternality. The words 'I AM' come from a root word which signifies 'to be'. Jehovah is, God who is, who was, and who is to come (Revelation 1:4). This is God's personal, proper, and incommunicable name. 'That men may know that thou, whose name alone is JEHOVAH, art the Most High over all the earth' (Psalm 83:18). Other names of God are sometimes applied to creatures, but Jehovah is used exclusively to speak of the true and living God.

This name, Jehovah, is frequently used as a compound with other words to set forth specific aspects of our Saviour's character and work as our God and our Saviour in meeting the needs of his elect. There are fifteen of these Jehovah titles in the Scriptures.

JEHOVAH-JIREH – 'The LORD will provide' (Genesis 22:14). 'And Abraham called the name of that place Jehovah-jireh: as it is said to this day, In the mount of the LORD it shall be seen.'

This name by which Abraham taught Isaac to worship God means, 'The LORD will see. The LORD will provide. And the LORD will be seen in the provision he gives'. Obviously, Abraham was talking about God's manifold and gracious providential provisions for his elect, his daily looking after their needs, by which he shows himself gracious, wise, and good. But it is equally true that Abraham's words of instruction were prophetic, speaking of God's great provision of grace in the sacrifice of his darling Son, the Lord Jesus Christ (2 Corinthians 5:21). In the substitutionary, sin atoning sacrifice of Christ, the Lord God shines forth in all his glory as 'a just God and a Saviour'.

JEHOVAH-RAPHA – 'The LORD that healeth thee' (Exodus 15:26). 'If thou wilt diligently hearken to the voice of the LORD thy God, and wilt do that which is right in his sight, and wilt give ear to his commandments, and keep all his statutes, I will put none of these diseases upon thee, which I have brought upon the Egyptians: for I am the LORD that healeth thee.' The Lord Jesus Christ is the Great Physician, the Lord our Healer. 'With his stripes we are healed.' He is the Healer of our sicknesses, the Healer of our troubles, and the Healer of our souls.

JEHOVAH-NISSI – 'The LORD our Banner' (Exodus 17:15). 'And Moses built an altar, and called the name of it Jehovah-nissi'. Our dear Saviour is our Ensign, the rallying point of his people, the Banner lifted up for the gathering of his people (Isaiah 11:10).

JEHOVAH-ELOHEKA – 'The LORD thy God' (Exodus 20:2, 5, 7). 'I am the LORD thy God, which have brought thee out of the land of Egypt, out of the house of bondage' … 'Thou shalt not bow down thyself to them, nor serve them: for I the LORD thy God am a jealous God, visiting the iniquity of the fathers upon the children unto the third and fourth generation of them that hate me; And showing mercy unto thousands of them that love me, and keep my commandments. Thou shalt not take the name of the LORD thy God in vain; for the LORD will not hold him guiltless that taketh his name in vain.'

JEHOVAH-M'KADDESH – 'The LORD which doth sanctify you' (Exodus 31:13). 'Speak thou also unto the children of Israel, saying, Verily my sabbaths ye shall keep: for it is a sign between me and you throughout your generations; that ye may know that I am the LORD that doth sanctify you.'

Again, we read in Leviticus 20:8, 'And ye shall keep my statutes, and do them: I am the LORD which sanctify you'. Sanctification is God's work, not ours. We were sanctified by the decree of God our Father in eternity (Jude 1), by the precious blood of Christ our Redeemer at Calvary (Hebrews 10:10), and by the regenerating work of God the Holy Spirit, our Divine Comforter (1 Corinthians 1:30; 2 Thessalonians 2:13).

JEHOVAH-SHALOM – 'The LORD our Peace' (Judges 6:24). 'Then Gideon built an altar there unto the Lord, and called it Jehovah-shalom: unto this day it is yet in Ophrah of the Abiezrites.' Christ is our Peace! He is our peace with God. He is our peace with one another. And he is our peace within.

JEHOVAH-TSEBAHOTH – 'The LORD of Hosts' (1 Samuel 1:3). 'And this man went up out of his city yearly to worship and to sacrifice unto the LORD of hosts in Shiloh. And the two sons of Eli, Hophni and Phinehas, the priests of the LORD, were there.'

This name is expressive of God's sovereign dominion and power over all his creatures (Romans 9:29; James 5:4). The Lord of Hosts has 'his way in the armies of heaven and among the inhabitants of the earth; and none can stay his hand, or say unto him, what doest thou?'

JEHOVAH-HELEYON – 'The LORD Most High' (Psalm 7:17). 'I will praise the LORD according to his righteousness: and will sing praise to the name of the LORD Most High.' 'For the LORD Most High is terrible; he is a great King over all the earth' (Psalm 47:2). 'For thou, LORD, art high above all the earth: thou art exalted far above all gods' (Psalm 97:9). We have every reason to pray and trust our God with complete confidence, for he alone is Governor of the universe.

JEHOVAH-RA-AH – 'The LORD my Shepherd' (Psalm 23:1). 'The LORD is my shepherd; I shall not want.' He is the Good Shepherd who died for us (John 10:11, 15). He is the Great Shepherd who rules for us (Hebrews 13:20). And he is the Chief Shepherd who is coming for us (1 Peter 5:4).

JEHOVAH-HOSEENU – 'The LORD our Maker' (Psalm 95:6). 'O come, let us worship and bow down: let us kneel before the LORD our maker'. He made us. He made us for himself. He made us his people. He made us new in Christ (2 Corinthians 5:17).

JEHOVAH-ELOHEENU – 'The LORD our God' (Psalm 99:5, 7, 8). He who is Jehovah, the self-existent, eternal God of all grace is our God, because he made himself our God and made us his people.

'Exalt ye the LORD our God, and worship at his footstool; for he is holy. Moses and Aaron among his priests, and Samuel among them that call upon his name; they called upon the LORD, and he answered them. He spake unto them in the cloudy pillar: they kept his testimonies, and the ordinance that he gave them. Thou answeredst them, O LORD our God: thou wast a God that forgavest them, though thou tookest vengeance of their inventions' (Psalm 99:5-8).

JEHOVAH-TSIDKENU – 'The LORD our Righteousness' (Jeremiah 23:6). 'In his days Judah shall be saved, and Israel shall dwell safely: and this is his name whereby he shall be called, THE LORD OUR RIGHTEOUSNESS.' Christ is our righteousness in justification. Christ is our righteousness in sanctification. And we are made the righteousness of God in him.

I told you in the beginning of this chapter that the name Jehovah is always restricted to God, that none are ever called by that name except our great God. But there is an exception in Jeremiah 33:16. There, all God's elect are called by the very same name as God our Saviour, Jehovah-tsidkenu, The Lord our Righteousness. Oh, what a wonder! Our union with Christ is mystical; but it is real! We are one with God our Saviour, the Lord Jesus Christ, our God-man Mediator!

'In those days shall Judah be saved, and Jerusalem shall dwell safely: and this is the name wherewith she shall be called, The LORD our righteousness' (Jeremiah 33:16).

JEHOVAH-SHAMMAH – 'The LORD is there' (Ezekiel 48:35). 'It was round about eighteen thousand measures: and the name of the city from that day shall be, The LORD is there' (Ezekiel 48:35). Our Saviour's name is Immanuel, God with us! Wherever you are, child of God, the Lord is there. 'Rejoice in the Lord alway: and again I say, Rejoice. Let your moderation be known unto all men. The Lord is at hand. Be careful for nothing; but in every thing by prayer and supplication with thanksgiving let your requests be made known unto God' (Philippians 4:4-6).

JEHOVAH-ELOHAY – 'The LORD my God' (Zechariah 14:5). 'And ye shall flee to the valley of the mountains; for the valley of the mountains shall reach unto Azal: yea, ye shall flee, like as ye fled from before the earthquake in the days of Uzziah king of Judah: and the LORD my God shall come, and all the saints with thee.'

Zechariah tells us that this great day of God's grace flowing to sinners far exceeds the glory that appeared upon Mount Sinai, at the giving of the law, when the mountains skipped like rams, and the little hills like lambs (Psalm 114:6). So terrible was that sight, that Moses said, 'I exceedingly fear and quake' (Hebrews 12:21).

The Lord Jesus Christ, our great Josiah, has taken away both the curse of Sinai's law and the corruptions of his people by his finished work of redemption. By coming to the earth in our nature, obeying all the will of God, dying as our Substitute, and ascending from the Mount, he has split open the mountain where our offenses abounded and created the mighty river of mercy and grace for our souls in 'the valley of the mountains'! Let the sweet tidings of grace vibrate through the earth! Because Christ has come and finished his work, 'Whosoever shall call upon the name of the Lord shall be saved.'

Yet, Zechariah's vision reaches even further. It reaches to that day when our Saviour shall appear in his glory, descending again to the earth with all his saints (Acts 1:9-12; Jude 14, 15; Job 19:25-27). This is Jehovah-elohay. The LORD my God!

JEHOVAH-JESUS – 'The Lord will save' (Matthew 1:21). 'And she shall bring forth a son, and thou shalt call his name JESUS: for he shall save his people from their sins.'

He who is the incarnate God has a people in this world. They were his people long before he came into the world. These people were given to him in eternity by his Father. He came here specifically to save his people; and save them he shall. Every one of them!

God's glorious redemptive name is 'JEHOVAH'. The word 'Jehovah' means 'Saviour' or 'Deliverer' (Exodus 6:3). God in Christ is God mighty to save. Our Lord Jesus Christ is the eternal God of salvation, redemption, and deliverance. He is able to save unto the uttermost all who come to God by him.

**Honour His Name**

May God the Holy Spirit give you grace to believe on his name. 'For there is none other name under heaven given among men, whereby we must be saved'. As many as receive him, to them he has given power to become the sons of God, 'even to them that believe on his name'.

If ever you come to know his name, you will sing with all saints, 'Because of the savour of thy good ointments, thy name is as ointment poured forth' (Song of Solomon 1:3). When you are made to know your loathsomeness, and are made to see the greatness, glory, and grace of our triune God in Christ, his great and glorious name will be to you more fragrant than all the costly perfume of the sanctuary. Then you shall enter into the enjoyment of all the constellation of the names of Jehovah-Jesus by which the prophet Isaiah describes him. 'His name shall be called Wonderful, Counsellor, the Mighty God, the Everlasting Father, the Prince of Peace!'

There is infinite fulness in him, whose name is Jehovah. All the fulness of the Godhead is in him. All the fulness of grace is in him. All the fulness of all things is in him.

'This glorious and fearful name, THE LORD THY GOD' (Deuteronomy 28:58) is not to be taken in vain, used in common speech, or spoken with any levity. 'Thou shalt not take the name of the LORD thy God in vain; for the LORD will not hold him guiltless who taketh his name in vain' (Exodus 20:7). He who sent redemption to his people and commanded his covenant forever is to be reverenced by us. 'Holy and reverend is his name' (Psalm 111:9). Let us ever extol, honour, praise, and magnify the name of the Lord our God. 'I will praise thee, O LORD my God, with all my heart: and I will glorify thy name for evermore. For great is thy mercy toward me: and thou hast delivered my soul from the lowest hell' (Psalm 86:12, 13). 'Not unto us, O LORD, not unto us, but unto thy name give glory, for thy mercy, and for thy truth's sake' (Psalm 115:1). Soon, all men shall praise his name (Philippians 2:9-11).

# Chapter 26

# 'I AM THAT I AM'

'And God said unto Moses, I AM THAT I AM: and he said, Thus shalt thou say unto the children of Israel, I AM hath sent me unto you.' (Exodus 3:14)

**The God We Trust**

God's elect are called to a life filled with adversity, heartache, and sorrow. Those who follow 'the man of sorrows and acquainted with grief' must never expect to be free of sorrow and grief in this world of woe. 'In the world ye shall have tribulation.' That is our Saviour's word to all his disciples. It is in this context the apostle Paul writes to us: 'Only let your conversation be as it becometh the gospel of Christ: that whether I come and see you, or else be absent, I may hear of your affairs, that ye stand fast in one spirit, with one mind striving together for the faith of the gospel; And in nothing terrified by your adversaries: which is to them an evident token of perdition, but to you of salvation, and that of God. For unto you it is given in the behalf of Christ, not only to believe on him, but also to suffer for his sake; Having the same conflict which ye saw in me, and now hear to be in me' (Philippians 1:27-30).

If we would follow Christ, we must take up our cross daily, and follow him. We are in a daily warfare, a warfare that rages without and within. It is a warfare that will never cease, or even become less violent, but only increase, until we drop this mortal frame and enter into rest with Christ in Glory. Our daily experience of these things causes the heaven-born soul to cry out, 'Who shall deliver me from the body of this death?' 'How long shall I take counsel in my soul, having sorrow in my heart daily? how long shall mine enemy be exalted over me?' 'O God, how long shall the adversary reproach?' 'How long shall the land mourn, and the herbs of every field wither?'

Here is a word of encouragement 'to them that mourn in Zion', a word of consolation to God's pilgrims in this dark world. In every hour of need, support is sure. Look at God's servant Moses. The ground he must tread is slippery ground. The obstacles he must overcome are huge. The task before him is immense. The hill of difficulty set before him is rough and steep. The foes opposing him are many. But he found a staff of strength and a shield of defence, a guiding light and a shelter of protection in the God he served, in the Christ he followed. 'God said unto Moses, I AM THAT I AM: and he said, Thus shalt thou say unto the children of Israel, I AM hath sent me unto you.'

### Infinite Help

Here is infinite help for our souls. Knowing the apparent impossibilities before him, Moses asked, 'What is thy name?' It is as though the Lord Jesus said, 'I AM THAT I AM, cast on me all the burden of your soul, all the cares of your heart, all the fears you have, and all the pains that trouble your soul and perplex your life.'

Blessed are they who can lean upon this staff, ever mighty, ever near! O child of God, lean the whole weight of your immortal soul upon Christ, and like Mount Zion you shall not be moved. Like Moses, you will scatter your adversaries like dust. 'Humble yourselves therefore under the mighty hand of God, that he may exalt you in due time: Casting all your care upon him; for he careth for you' (1 Peter 5:6, 7).

'I AM THAT I AM' is the voice of the burning bush. The One speaking to us is our God and Saviour, the Lord Jesus Christ, the Angel of the Lord, the Angel of the everlasting Covenant. It is our great Redeemer. He speaks to establish us upon the firm rock of comfort, assuring us that all the majesty, all the supremacy, all the glory of absolute and essential Deity are his inherently.

O my soul, into what specks of insignificance must our troubles dwindle before his greatness! The breadth of our minds cannot imagine such greatness as resides in him. The words of our mouths cannot describe it. Had we the wings of eagles the ever-widening circle of Christ's infinite greatness can never be comprehended by us. Vain is the effort! Its height is on heaven's summit. What mortal arm can reach it? It is as space which has no boundary. Immeasurable! Our mortal eyes cannot pierce the infinite expanse. The scales of our judgment cannot weigh the mountain. Our minds cannot fathom the depths of this infinite ocean. 'I AM THAT I AM!'

**Fear Not**
If he who is our God is the eternal 'I AM', if we trust him who is 'I AM THAT I AM', we have nothing to fear in this world or in the world to come. No wonder our Saviour says so often to his people, 'Fear not'. Hear what God said to the children of Israel, when he sent them forth to conquer Canaan and possess it forever.

'Behold, the LORD thy God hath set the land before thee: go up and possess it, as the LORD God of thy fathers hath said unto thee; fear not, neither be discouraged.'

'When thou goest out to battle against thine enemies, and seest horses, and chariots, and a people more than thou, be not afraid of them: for the LORD thy God is with thee, which brought thee up out of the land of Egypt. And it shall be, when ye are come nigh unto the battle, that the priest shall approach and speak unto the people, And shall say unto them, Hear, O Israel, ye approach this day unto battle against your enemies: let not your hearts faint, fear not, and do not tremble, neither be ye terrified because of them'. 'Be strong and of a good courage, fear not, nor be afraid of them: for the LORD thy God, he it is that doth go with thee; he will not fail thee, nor forsake thee. And Moses called unto Joshua, and said unto him in the sight of all Israel, Be strong and of a good courage: for thou must go with this people unto the land which the LORD hath sworn unto their fathers to give them; and thou shalt cause them to inherit it. And the LORD, he it is that doth go before thee; he will be with thee, he will not fail thee, neither forsake thee: fear not, neither be dismayed' (Deuteronomy 1:21; 20:1-3; 31:6-8).

Shall we fret and fear, shall we murmur and complain before our God? Fret because our God is so great? Fear because our Saviour is so immense? Murmur because our Redeemer is so strong? Complain because his riches are unsearchable? What folly! What unbelief!

His treasures are such that gold is but dust in his deep mines! The riches of his grace fall like manna before our tent doors every day. May God the Holy Ghost allow us to drink the refreshing waters of this bottomless, ever-springing artesian well. 'I AM THAT I AM'. O Spirit of God, show us the things of Christ.

### Eternality

'I AM THAT I AM'. The first thing revealed in this name of our Saviour is his eternality. Here the Lord Jesus robes himself in eternity. He knows no past. He knows no future. He lives unmoved in one unmoving present. He stretches through all ages past and all ages future. He is, in all his glorious being, in all his indescribable majesty; infinite, immeasurable, boundless, and eternal! Before time was born, he is 'I AM THAT I AM'. When time is no more, he remains 'I AM THAT I AM'.

Were he not eternal, if there had been a time when he began to be, his name would be, 'I am what I was not'. If there could be a time when he ceases to be, his name would be, 'I am what I shall not be'. But he is! That means, he is 'I AM THAT I AM'. He treads first and last beneath his feet. He sits upon the unbroken circumference of existence, as he who ever was, and ever is, and ever shall be. Let your mind fly back, until it faints in weariness; let it look onward until all vision fails; and you will ever find him the same 'I AM'.

Look down now from this astounding height of glory and fix your eye on Bethlehem's manger. There lies a baby in a cowshed, in an insignificant town, the child of an insignificant couple. That child is the eternal 'I AM'. He who is eternal, he who never had birth, who never began to be, is born 'the woman's Seed'. He who encompasses eternity is contained within an infant's body. He who never began to be, here begins to be.

Can that be? Did the great 'I AM THAT I AM' take our flesh, as one born yesterday? Is it so? It is indeed! The Lord God promised it. Prophets foretold it. Types prefigured it. An angel announced it. Heaven rings with rapture at it. Faith sees it. All the redeemed rejoice in it (Genesis 3:15; Isaiah 7:14; 9:6, 7; Galatians 4:4, 5). 'And without controversy great is the mystery of godliness: God was manifest in the flesh, justified in the Spirit, seen of angels, preached unto the Gentiles, believed on in the world, received up into glory' (1 Timothy 3:16).

But why was this wonder of wonders performed? Why is eternity's Lord a child of time? He thus stoops, that he may save poor wretched sinners such as we are. Could he not do so by his will or by his word? No, he could not. He willed, and all things were. He speaks, and all obey. But he must die, as man, that lost sinners may live in him. To rescue us from the guilt of sin and the curse of the law, the Eternal must take the sinner's place, be made sin for us, made a curse for us, pay our debt, suffer all the wrath of God that we deserve, and die our death with our sin, our guilt, and our curse made his own. There is no other way for atonement to be made, no other way for salvation to come, no other way for sin to be put away, no other way for him to be 'a just God and a Saviour'.

'I AM THAT I AM' alone could do this. 'I AM THAT I AM' alone has done it (2 Corinthians 5:21; Galatians 3:13, 14; Romans 4:25-5:11). What self-denial, what self-abasement, what self-emptying is here! What infinite greatness of humility! 'For ye know the grace of our Lord Jesus Christ, that, though he was rich, yet for your sakes he became poor, that ye through his poverty might be rich' (2 Corinthians 8:9).

Royalty in rags and angels in prison would be nothing compared to this descent of Deity in flesh! But almighty, eternal love moved the Son of God, our Lord Jesus, the Christ, to despise all shame and to lie down in misery's lowest pit. Through ages past his 'delights were with the sons of men'. Eternity to come would be but an empty void, unless his people are made to possess his glory with him. Therefore, he humbled himself and became obedient unto death, even the death of the cross, that worms of earth might be raised to heaven's immortality.

We rejoice in prospect of living with him in his glory forever. But why is there such rapture in the thought? It is this that gives us such ecstasy in hope: eternity will allow us to gaze with steady look on the Saviour's face, to see his glory, to sing with unwearied hymn his praise, to bless with perpetual blessing his everlasting name, and to learn with ever-expanding knowledge his matchless worth!

## Immutability

'I AM THAT I AM'. There is another note in this glorious name, which sounds with special sweetness in the believer's ear. This great name, 'I AM THAT I AM', melodiously declares that our Lord Jesus Christ cannot change. It speaks of his absolute immutability (Malachi 3:6;

Hebrews 13:8). Our great Saviour is as constant as he is great. As surely as he ever lives, so surely he ever lives the same. He is an infinity of never-varying oneness. He sits on the calm throne of eternal serenity.

Change is the defect of all things below. Immutability is the glory of all things above, for immutability is the essence of perfection. Our brightest morning often ends in storm. Summer's radiance gives way to winter's gloom. The budding flower is soon withered. The friend who smiles today may soon become a relentless foe. Bereavement weeps where once the family beamed with domestic joy. Gardens wither into deserts. On all things here we must read a sad inscription 'Fleeting! Transient! Vanishing!' 'Time flaps a ceaseless wing', wrote Henry Law, 'and from the wings decay and death drop down. "I AM THAT I AM" sits high above all this. He is "the same yesterday, and today, and forever".'

> Change and decay all around me I see,
> O Thou Who changest not, abide with me!

**His Love**

'I AM THAT I AM'. The unchangeableness of our God and Saviour is the unchangeableness of his attributes. Every divine attribute shines brightly in this bright mirror. Take just a glance at his love, his power, and his grace.

His infinite love is infinitely and eternally perpetual. Its roots are deeply buried in himself. My brother, my sister, drink constantly from this cup of joy. Ever draw the sweet waters of this deep well into your soul. Do not allow Satan to infuse a poisonous doubt. Christ loved you fully when, in the councils of eternity, he took you as his own. He loved you truly when, in the fulness of time, he took upon himself your sin and your curse, and drank the cup of your damnation. He loved you tenderly when he showed you, by the Spirit, his hands and his feet, and whispered to you that you were his. He loves you faithfully as he ceases not to intercede on your behalf, and scatters the blessings of his grace upon your soul. He will love you intensely in heaven when you are manifested as his precious purchase and crowned as his bride!

To each doubting question; Has he loved me? Does he love me? Will he love me? the one reply is, 'I AM THAT I AM'. Do not raise the objection, if he thus loves, why am I thus? Why is my path so rugged, and my heart like flint? We will soon know that our most bitter trials and our most severe pains are sure tokens of his love. The father corrects because he loves. In attentive care the physician deeply probes the wounds. Thus our sweet, loving Saviour makes this world bitter, that we may long for heaven's blessed rest. He shows us our vileness that we may cherish his cleansing blood. He allows us to stumble that we may cling more closely to his side. He makes the world emptiness that we may seek all in him. If he appears to change, it is that we may be changed. He hides his face, that we may seek him. He is sometimes silent, that we may cry more loudly for him. His desertion prevents our desertion. He saves from real hell, by causing us to sometimes experience what seems like hell. But his compassions fail not. They are new every morning. All he does is the ever-flowing, overflowing tide of his infinite love. Let us with the eye of faith read upon his providence, 'I AM THAT I AM'.

## His Power

Our blessed Saviour's power, his infinite omnipotence, goes hand in hand with his infinite, everlasting love. They co-exist and co-endure. It was a mighty voice that said, 'Be', and all things were. It was a mighty hand that framed this wondrous universe. It is a mighty arm which turns the wheel of providence.

That power still is, and ever will be, what it always has been. Time does not make it feeble. Use does not make it weak. Christ is our Rock. The Word of God everywhere encourages the 'worm Jacob' to 'be strong in the Lord, and in the power of his might'. He still parts the sea for his own. He still opens the window of heaven and pours out his blessing. He still causes hurricanes and tempests to be a calm. He still makes straight the crooked path. He still levels the mountains that seem too high for us. He still stops the mouths of lions. He still quenches the fiery darts of the wicked one. In the face of all Goliaths, he cheers us on to victory, under the banner of 'I AM THAT I AM'.

## His Grace

'I AM THAT I AM' What more can I say? I have not touched the edges of the shadow of this glorious name. But I must remind you of one more thing about our infinite, eternal Saviour. His grace, his infinite, eternal grace is immutable grace. Grace never changes! What a glorious fact! Grace never changes! That means many, many things, but none more delightful than this: Our Saviour's grace is sufficient to meet our every need. He says to every soul that trusts him, 'My grace is sufficient for thee' (2 Corinthians 12:9).

God's elect are assured of his grace in Christ and the absolute sufficiency of it always and in all things. One of the names of our great God is El-Shaddai, which means 'God All Sufficient'. The grace of God in Christ, and that alone, is our sufficiency.

It is sufficient grace because it is effectual grace. Today there is much talk about grace; but those who talk about it talk about a grace that lacks efficacy. That is not the grace of our God. God's grace is effectual grace. It is always sufficient because it is always effectual. John Gill rightly observed,

'Nothing short of the grace of Christ is sufficient grace; and this is sufficient for all the elect of God, Jews and Gentiles, Old and New Testament saints, the family in heaven and in earth, the people of God that are already called, and are yet to be called, and even for the worst and vilest of sinners.'

Let us ever remember that God's grace in Christ is sufficient for us for everything and at all times. It is sufficient to accomplish all his saving purposes, sufficient to pardon, justify, regenerate, sanctify, and preserve us, sufficient in every time of need, sufficient in health and sufficient in sickness, sufficient life and sufficient in death, sufficient in judgment, and sufficient to present us faultless before the presence of his glory forever!

'The eternal God is thy refuge and underneath are the everlasting arms.' 'I AM THAT I AM' must perish or must change, before our names can be torn from his heart. Some greater power must arise, before we can be plucked from the grip of his omnipotent hand. The bare idea is folly. Blessed are those sinners the Lord God calls 'my people'. 'I AM THAT I AM' loves them, and they are loved. He calls them, and they follow him. He sanctifies them, and they are sanctified. He blesses them, and they are blessed. He gives them life, and they live. He gives them glory, and they are glorified.

# Chapter 27

## Christc: The God Of Israel

'And God said moreover unto Moses, Thus shalt thou say unto the children of Israel, The LORD God of your fathers, the God of Abraham, the God of Isaac, and the God of Jacob, hath sent me unto you: this is my name forever, and this is my memorial unto all generations. Go, and gather the elders of Israel together, and say unto them, The LORD God of your fathers, the God of Abraham, of Isaac, and of Jacob, appeared unto me, saying, I have surely visited you, and seen that which is done to you in Egypt: And I have said, I will bring you up out of the affliction of Egypt unto the land of the Canaanites, and the Hittites, and the Amorites, and the Perizzites, and the Hivites, and the Jebusites, unto a land flowing with milk and honey. And they shall hearken to thy voice: and thou shalt come, thou and the elders of Israel, unto the king of Egypt, and ye shall say unto him, The LORD God of the Hebrews hath met with us: and now let us go, we beseech thee, three days' journey into the wilderness, that we may sacrifice to the LORD our God.' (Exodus 3:15-18)

Far too often we read the Word of God with only a carnal eye, dwelling too much on the letter of the Word and missing the spirit, missing the message of the Spirit in the Word, dwelling too much on the literal and missing the spiritual application to our souls, dwelling too much on the type and missing Christ of whom the type speaks. Multitudes miss that which a passage is intended to teach, because they are consumed by a desire to define and understand the words by which the person and work of Christ are set before us in the Book of God. It is Christ of whom the Scriptures speak. We should always look first for him, as we read the pages of Holy Scripture. When we open the Book of God, we should always do so looking for our blessed Saviour. It is only when we see Christ in the Book that the Book of God lives.

That is what I want for you. I want you to see Christ and see him clearly. He who appeared to Moses in the burning bush, the Angel of the Lord, is throughout this chapter called God. In verse 14, he identifies himself as the great 'I AM', who, as we have seen is Christ our Lord (John 4:6; 6:20; 8:24, 28, 58; 13:19; 18:5). This appearance of our Saviour to Moses was one of the most enlightening and instructive of his pre-incarnate manifestations of himself in the Old Testament.

### The God of Our Fathers
The One who commissioned Moses at the burning bush declares his name in this remarkable way: 'I AM That I AM', and called himself 'Jehovah'. Then, lest there be any mistake about his meaning, he told Moses that he is 'the God of our fathers'. Specifically, he asserted that he is 'the God of Abraham, the God of Isaac, and the God of Jacob'. These three men are held before us throughout the Scriptures as the eminent patriarchs in the family of faith, the church, kingdom and family of God. He who is the God-man our Saviour, is the God of our fathers. What he was to them, he is to us. What he is to us he was to them when they walked through the earth as we do now. Let us look into several passages of Scripture and see what our Lord here tells us about himself, and about his relationship to us, as the God of our fathers.

### The God of Abraham
First, the Lord declares himself to be the God of Abraham. Our Lord Jesus is 'the God of glory [who] appeared to our father Abraham' (Acts 7:2). We know it was not God in his essential glory who appeared to Abraham, because 'No man hath seen God at any time' (John 1:18). It was the Lord Jesus Christ who appeared to Abraham. He declares, 'he that hath seen me hath seen the Father' (John 14:9). In a word, the Lord Jesus is the 'God of glory'. He is not just the Revealer of God, he is God, 'the brightness of his glory and the express image of his person'

(Hebrews 1:3; John 1:14). Our blessed Saviour, the One we trust, he who died as our Substitute at Calvary is the 'Lord of glory' (1 Corinthians 2:8; James 2:1; John 5:23; 1 Timothy 3:16).

## God Most High

In Genesis 14:19 we are told that the Christ who appeared to Abraham is 'the most high, God, possessor of heaven and earth'. It is God Most High, the Possessor of heaven and earth who blessed Abraham. Christ, is the most high God, the sole Possessor of heaven and earth because he is God, the 'King of kings and Lord of lords' (Revelation 19:16). Indeed, the Book of God declares that he is the 'God of gods' (Deuteronomy 10:17). And Christ is the 'Possessor of heaven and earth' because he has been given the nations for his inheritance, and the ends of the earth for his possession, by virtue of his accomplishments as our Mediator (Psalm 2:8; Matthew 28:18; John 17:4, 5; Romans 14:9; Philippians 2:8-11; 1 Corinthians 15:25).

## God the Word

We read in John 1:1, 'In the beginning was the Word, and the Word was with God, and the Word was God'. And that is how our Lord Jesus Christ appeared to Abraham. 'After these things the word of the LORD came unto Abram in a vision, saying, Fear not, Abram: I am thy shield, and thy exceeding great reward' (Genesis 15:1). The Word of God here refers not to what God speaks, but to God speaking. Christ is the visible Word of God. He came to Abraham in a vision, a revelation. That is how we come to know him (John 1:1-3, 14; 1 John 1:1-3). The Word who appeared to Abraham made himself known to Abraham as God, just as he has to us. He identified himself as Jehovah, and Abraham acknowledged him as God (Genesis 15:7, 8). That is exactly how God revealed himself to Saul of Tarsus on the Damascus Road (Acts 9). It is how sinners come to know God today (2 Corinthians 4:3-7).

## Our Shield and Reward

Be sure you do not miss that the Lord Jesus Christ, our God and Saviour, is our Shield and our 'exceeding great reward'. He became Abraham's Shield and Reward, in the experience of his grace, when he revealed himself and Abraham believed him; but he was his Shield and Reward long before that. Abraham came to experience his grace and believed him because he stood as Abraham's Shield in eternity and was his Reward before the worlds were made by him (Ephesians 1:3-6).

So it is with us. To believe God is to trust and confide in Christ alone for salvation, forsaking all other refuges. 'He is a shield unto them that put their trust in him' (Proverbs 30:5; cf. Psalm 5:12; 18:35; 28:7; 30:3; 33:20; 59:11; 84:9, 11; 115:9-11; 119:114; 144:2). Oh, what a Shield our Lord Jesus Christ is! He hides us behind his blood. He clothes us with the garments of salvation, with his own righteousness. He encompasses us in himself. 'The angel of the LORD encampeth round about them that fear him, and delivereth them' (Psalm 34:7). He holds us in his hands. He carries us in his bosom. He intercedes for us in heaven.

As our Lord Jesus revealed himself to Abraham as his 'exceeding great reward', so he is ours! Abraham forsook all his heathen gods, all earthly portions, his home and his family for Christ (Genesis 12:1-4); but he lost nothing. He lacked nothing. Oh, no! He gained everything. He gained Christ! So it is with us. The Lord Jesus Christ, the God of our fathers, is All, and we have all in him and abound. All things are ours, because we are Christ's and Christ is ours! He is our 'exceeding great reward'.

## Almighty God

The Lord Jesus, whom we trust, is El-Shaddai, 'the Almighty God', who blessed Abraham. 'And when Abram was ninety years old and nine, the LORD appeared to Abram, and said unto him, I am the Almighty God; walk before me, and be thou perfect' (Genesis 17:1).

This name emphasizes his omnipotence. He who demands we walk before him and be perfect is God possessing all power, and the God-man to whom all power has been given. That means many things, but none sweeter than this: He is able to make us what he demands we be! Perfect before him! El-Shaddai means 'God all-sufficient'. It expresses more than the power of God alone. It expresses the power and sufficiency of God to bestow his grace and fulfil his promises. El-Shaddai is God able to save, able to do his will, and able to shed his blessings upon his people. He is able to make sinners like us walk before him in faith; and he is able to make us perfect in the person and by the work of his dear Son, our Saviour (1 Corinthians 1:30).

## The Judge

In Genesis 18:25, Abraham extolled our God and Saviour as 'the Judge of all the earth' (John 5:22, 27; Acts 10:42, 43; 17:31; Romans 14:10-12; 2 Corinthians 5:10, 11). Let us, like Abraham, bow to him, acknowledging in all things, 'Shall not the Judge of all the earth do right?'

## The Everlasting God

In Genesis 21:33, Abraham worshipped the Lord Jesus as Jehovah, 'the everlasting God', the Eternal One. This name belongs to our Redeemer, because he is 'the Alpha and the Omega, the Beginning and the End, the First and the Last' (Revelation 1:8, 11, 17; 2:8; 21:6; 22:13), 'the true God and eternal life' (1 John 5:11, 20), 'the Everlasting Father' (Isaiah 9:6), 'whose goings forth have been from of old, from everlasting' (Micah 5:2). He is 'That which was from the beginning' (1 John 1:1; John 1:1). 'He is before all things' (Colossians 1:17), eternal and unchangeable!

## The God of Isaac

Our Lord Jesus Christ is the God of Isaac, Jehovah-Jireh. That is how Abraham describes him in Genesis 22:14. 'The Lord Will Provide'. That is his name! He who provided for Isaac's need has provided and will provide for all our need (Philippians 4:19). Christ has provided himself 'an offering and sacrifice for sin' (Ephesians 5:2) He is 'the Lamb of God which taketh away the sin of the world' (John 1:29). Because Christ is our divine Shepherd (John 10:11), we sing with David, 'The LORD is my Shepherd; I shall not want'. Christ is both our Provider and our Provision.

## The God of Jacob

Christ is the God Jacob extolled at Peniel (Genesis 32:24-31), saying 'I have seen God face to face, and my life is preserved'. And this God is also the 'Man who wrestled with him' as 'the Angel' of the Lord, the One who prevailed over Jacob and the One over whom Jacob prevailed once he confessed his name (Hosea 12:4). So it is with us. When Christ our God and Saviour wrestles with us, and conquers us by his Spirit, graciously forcing us to confess our sin we are made to prevail with him, seeing 'the glory of God in the face of Jesus Christ'.

Our Lord Jesus Christ is El Bethel, the God of the house of God, whom Jacob worshipped (Genesis 35:7). Jacob named that place Bethel because of the presence of God there, in the Ladder, which extended from earth to heaven, making it the house of God (Genesis 28:10-22). The presence of God there was in the person of both God the Father, who was at the top of the ladder (v. 13), and God the Son, who was himself the Ladder (John 1:51).

## The God of Israel

Our Lord Jesus is the God of Israel 'Elelohe-Israel' (Genesis 33:20), God, the God of Israel. It is he who chose Jacob and named him Israel, 'a prince with God', assured him of his covenant, and of his faithfulness, making all things new for him. And so it is still with all whom he makes his own (2 Corinthians 5:17). Christ our Saviour is the God of Israel. That means 'all Israel shall be saved' (Romans 11:26). He who redeemed Israel from all evil shall save Israel from all evil.

# Chapter 28

# 'Wonders In The Land Of Ham'
# Distinguishing Grace Displayed

'And I am sure that the king of Egypt will not let you go, no, not by a mighty hand. And I will stretch out my hand, and smite Egypt with all my wonders which I will do in the midst thereof: and after that he will let you go.'
(Exodus 3:19, 20)

'The Lord God of the Hebrews' sent Moses to Pharaoh, determined to harden Pharaoh's heart, that he might perform wonders in Egypt by which he would manifestly display himself as the God of the Hebrews and manifestly display his distinguishing grace, by which he ever distinguishes and separates his elect from the rest of Adam's fallen race.

Noah's cursed son Ham is held before us as the representative all the reprobate of the earth whose existence is to the end that they might serve and be instruments of benefit to God's elect (Genesis 9:18-27). The deliverance of Israel out of Egypt is specifically spoken of in Holy Scripture as that which the Lord God accomplished by performing his 'wonders in the land of Ham' (Psalm 105:23-27). That is exactly how God always saves his elect. He openly displays his sovereign love and distinguishing grace toward his chosen by performing 'wonders in the land of Ham'.

This is held before us as a matter of unceasing praise among God's saints of old. Moses, Nehemiah, David, and Jeremiah all hold these wonders of distinguishing grace before us as encouragements to faith and reasons for praise. Stephen, the first martyr of the New Testament church, just before he was stoned to death by those who were Jews after the flesh, spoke of God's wonders in the land of Ham, by which he saved (and still saves) the sons of Abraham (Deuteronomy 6:20-24; Nehemiah 9:5-10; Psalm 135:3-9; Jeremiah 32:17-21; Acts 7:36).

The Lord God said to Moses, 'And I am sure that the king of Egypt will not let you go, no, not by a mighty hand' (v. 19). He was sure of it because he had so ordered it from eternity (Romans 9:17). No mighty hand could bow the heart and bend the will of the obstinate king of Egypt, except one, the omnipotent hand of the omnipotent God! In fact, the opening words of verse 19 might be translated, 'And I am sure that the king of Egypt will not let you go, except by a mighty hand', as the next phrase indicates. The Lord God does not say, 'but I will stretch out my hand'. He says, 'and I will stretch out my hand'. Pharaoh was raised up by God and his heart was hardened by him for this specific purpose, that God might show his mighty hand and the mighty power of his hand upon him in the deliverance of his people.

'And I am sure that the king of Egypt will not let you go, no, not by a mighty hand. And I will stretch out my hand, and smite Egypt with all my wonders, which I will do in the midst thereof: and after that he will let you go'. May God the Holy Spirit be our Teacher and graciously show us the things of Christ as we look at his 'wonders in the land of Ham'.

## The Ten Plagues
Let us look at the ten plagues God brought upon the Egyptians. We will look at them in more detail individually, as we come to them in chapters 7-13. But I think you will find it helpful to look at them together as the signs and wonders by which the Lord God brings judgment upon the wicked, while performing the salvation of his elect.

These ten plagues are held before us in the book of Revelation (chapters 5-8 and 11) as things which typified the wonders of God in the land of Ham throughout the ages and by which he brings judgment upon the reprobate and displays his distinguishing grace upon his elect. These wonders are manifested again and again as our mighty Saviour, the Lord Jesus Christ, goes forth throughout the ages, 'conquering and to conquer', subduing all his enemies beneath his feet, either by the irresistible power of his saving grace or by the irresistible power of his holy wrath. The Lord God said to his Son, our all-glorious Saviour, this One who appeared to Moses in the bush, 'Sit thou on my right hand, until I make thine enemies thy footstool' (Hebrews 1:13; 10:9-14; Isaiah 45:20-25).

The Lord God performed ten wonders in the land of Ham, and brought ten plagues upon the Egyptians. They came in succession, one after another, with a brief space between each, giving Pharaoh and the Egyptians space for repentance. Each plague was more severe than the one preceding it, but to the very last Pharaoh hardened his heart in obstinate rebellion and God hardened his heart in judgment. Judgment never brings repentance! 'The goodness of God leadeth thee to repentance' (Romans 2:4). 'For godly sorrow worketh repentance to salvation not to be repented of: but the sorrow of the world worketh death' (2 Corinthians 7:10). By these ten wonders in the land of Ham God destroyed the Egyptians and all Israel was saved. So it is now; and so it shall be forever, to the praise of the glory of his grace!

**Water to Blood**

The first wonder God performed in Egypt was the turning the waters of the River Nile into blood and death.

'Thus saith the LORD, In this thou shalt know that I am the LORD: behold, I will smite with the rod that is in mine hand upon the waters which are in the river, and they shall be turned to blood. And the fish that is in the river shall die, and the river shall stink; and the Egyptians shall loathe to drink of the water of the river' (Exodus 7:17, 18).

The first wonder wrought by Moses was the of turning water into blood; but the first miracle performed by our Lord Jesus Christ was that of turning water into wine (John 2:11). Everything in the law, just as the waters of the Nile were turned into blood, is made a source of condemnation and death to all men, by reason of our sin. It is called 'the ministration of death' (2 Corinthians 3:7). But everything in the gospel brings life and liberty.

What is touched by the rod of Moses is smitten with death. Under the law, everything is a curse. But what is touched by the gracious hand of Christ is made to live. Under the gospel, Christ makes everything a blessing, putting his blessing upon everything, sanctifying everything to the blessedness of his people.

### Frogs

The second plague of Egypt was that of the frogs (Exodus 8:1-15).

'And the LORD spake unto Moses, Say unto Aaron, Stretch forth thine hand with thy rod over the streams, over the rivers, and over the ponds, and cause frogs to come up upon the land of Egypt. And Aaron stretched out his hand over the waters of Egypt; and the frogs came up, and covered the land of Egypt' (Exodus 8:5, 6).

There was a striking progression in the plagues God sent upon Egypt. The first was remote and distant, confined to the rivers and water; but this second plague came much closer to each person. Frogs came into their houses, even into their bed-chambers. 'Their land brought forth frogs in abundance in the chambers of their kings' (Psalm 105:30). When men harden their hearts and refuse to hear the voice of God warning them in one judgment, another often follows. Usually, the second is worse than the first.

### Lice

In the third wonder God sent lice to cover the Egyptians. All the dust of the land was turned into lice, covering man and beast.

'And the LORD said unto Moses, Say unto Aaron, Stretch out thy rod, and smite the dust of the land, that it may become lice throughout all the land of Egypt. And they did so; for Aaron stretched out his hand with his rod, and smote the dust of the earth, and it became lice in man, and in beast; all the dust of the land became lice throughout all the land of Egypt' (Exodus 8:16, 17).

What a horrible, disgusting plague of filth! The first two plagues had been on their water and their property. This one brought judgment upon every man, woman, and child among the sons of Ham, and upon every animal in their land. Pharaoh's magicians were stumped. They had imitated the previous wonders of God. But this one they could not even pretend to imitate. They were compelled to confess, 'This is the finger of God'. But no change was wrought in Pharaoh's heart. 'Pharaoh's heart was hardened, and he hearkened not (even to the voice of his magicians); as the Lord had said' (Exodus 8:19).

### Flies

Next, the Lord smote the land of Egypt with swarms of flies. 'And the LORD said unto Moses, Rise up early in the morning, and stand before

Pharaoh; lo, he cometh forth to the water; and say unto him, Thus saith the LORD, Let my people go, that they may serve me. Else, if thou wilt not let my people go, behold, I will send swarms of flies upon thee, and upon thy servants, and upon thy people, and into thy houses: and the houses of the Egyptians shall be full of swarms of flies, and also the ground whereon they are' (Exodus 8:20, 21).

Flies were everywhere, filling the land and every house with flies, so much so that even the ground was covered with dirty, smelly, biting flies! The plague of lice was great, but this of flies was indescribably greater. At last, Pharaoh seemed affected. His heart was not changed; but in order to get relief from torment, he finally consented to let Israel go. But as soon as the torment was over, he hardened his heart and refused to let Israel go (v. 32).

I said, 'Flies were everywhere', but that is not exactly right. They were everywhere, except in the land of Goshen, where the Israelites lived. The Lord God of the Hebrews made an open display of his discriminating grace, putting an invisible (though clearly obvious) net over all the land of Israel, as he plagued the land of Ham (vv. 22, 23).

'And I will sever in that day the land of Goshen, in which my people dwell, that no swarms of flies shall be there; to the end thou mayest know that I am the LORD in the midst of the earth. And I will put a division between my people and thy people: tomorrow shall this sign be'.

There were no flies in Goshen. How wondrously protected and blessed the Israelites were! How wondrously protected and blessed God's elect are in this world! What evident tokens of God's distinguishing mercy, love, and grace we witness every day of our lives!

'And they shall be mine, saith the LORD of hosts, in that day when I make up my jewels; and I will spare them, as a man spareth his own son that serveth him. Then shall ye return, and discern between the righteous and the wicked, between him that serveth God and him that serveth him not' (Malachi 3:17, 18).

**Pestilence**
God's fifth wonder in the land of Ham, his fifth plague upon Egypt, was even more severe and terrifying. Because Pharaoh still hardened his heart and refused to let Israel go, at an appointed time, the Lord God sent pestilence upon all the cattle of the Egyptians, identifying it as the

work of his own hand in an undeniable way. He again made an obvious display of his distinguishing grace upon Israel. Not one calf or lamb in the flocks and herds of the Hebrews was found dead.

'Then the LORD said unto Moses, Go in unto Pharaoh, and tell him, Thus saith the LORD God of the Hebrews, Let my people go, that they may serve me. For if thou refuse to let them go, and wilt hold them still, Behold, the hand of the LORD is upon thy cattle which is in the field, upon the horses, upon the asses, upon the camels, upon the oxen, and upon the sheep: there shall be a very grievous murrain. And the LORD shall sever between the cattle of Israel and the cattle of Egypt: and there shall nothing die of all that is the children's of Israel. And the LORD appointed a set time, saying, Tomorrow the LORD shall do this thing in the land. And the LORD did that thing on the morrow, and all the cattle of Egypt died: but of the cattle of the children of Israel died not one. And Pharaoh sent, and, behold, there was not one of the cattle of the Israelites dead. And the heart of Pharaoh was hardened, and he did not let the people go' (Exodus 9:1-7).

How we ought to rejoice in our God's discriminating, providential goodness!

'He that dwelleth in the secret place of the Most High shall abide under the shadow of the Almighty. I will say of the LORD, He is my refuge and my fortress: my God; in him will I trust. Surely he shall deliver thee from the snare of the fowler, and from the noisome pestilence. He shall cover thee with his feathers, and under his wings shalt thou trust: his truth shall be thy shield and buckler. Thou shalt not be afraid for the terror by night; nor for the arrow that flieth by day; Nor for the pestilence that walketh in darkness; nor for the destruction that wasteth at noonday. A thousand shall fall at thy side, and ten thousand at thy right hand; but it shall not come nigh thee. Only with thine eyes shalt thou behold and see the reward of the wicked' (Psalm 91:1-8).

'For this shall every one that is godly pray unto thee in a time when thou mayest be found: surely in the floods of great waters they shall not come nigh unto him' (Psalm 32:6).

As the earth bore a part in the curse upon man's disobedience, God makes the earth itself to bear a part in our deliverance from the curse, of which Israel's deliverance out of Egypt was a type (Romans 8:20-23).

## Boils

In the sixth plague upon the Egyptians we see the hand of God's judgment even more heavily in 'boils breaking forth with blains upon man and upon beast'.

'And the LORD said unto Moses and unto Aaron, Take to you handfuls of ashes of the furnace, and let Moses sprinkle it toward the heaven in the sight of Pharaoh. And it shall become small dust in all the land of Egypt, and shall be a boil breaking forth with blains upon man, and upon beast, throughout all the land of Egypt. And they took ashes of the furnace, and stood before Pharaoh; and Moses sprinkled it up toward heaven; and it became a boil breaking forth with blains upon man, and upon beast. And the magicians could not stand before Moses because of the boils; for the boil was upon the magicians, and upon all the Egyptians. And the LORD hardened the heart of Pharaoh, and he hearkened not unto them; as the LORD had spoken unto Moses' (Exodus 9:8-12).

Throughout the land a universal, previously unheard of epidemic broke out upon every man and beast of Egypt. Their bodies were covered with running sores. I cannot imagine such a thing. But there it stands. The work of divine judgment. Nothing this side of hell could be compared to this plague for the misery it caused in Egypt. Read Deuteronomy 28:15-68 and see what a horrible thing it is to have the Lord God of the Hebrews for your enemy.

## Hail and Fire

The seventh plague of Egypt was the 'thunder, lightning, rain, and hail'.

'And the LORD said unto Moses, Stretch forth thine hand toward heaven, that there may be hail in all the land of Egypt, upon man, and upon beast, and upon every herb of the field, throughout the land of Egypt. And Moses stretched forth his rod toward heaven: and the LORD sent thunder and hail, and the fire ran along upon the ground; and the LORD rained hail upon the land of Egypt. So there was hail, and fire mingled with the hail, very grievous, such as there was none like it in all the land of Egypt since it became a nation. And the hail smote throughout all the land of Egypt all that was in the field, both man and beast; and the hail smote every herb of the field, and brake every tree of the field. Only in the land of Goshen, where the children of Israel were, was there no hail' (vv. 22-26; Exodus 9:13-35).

Before sending this horrible storm in the fury of his wrath, God plainly told Pharaoh that there would be a continual succession of plagues upon him until he was cut off from the face of the earth. Then he told him he had raised him up for that very purpose, to show his power in him, that the Lord's name should be declared throughout all the earth (vv. 14-16).

Again, the Lord graciously displayed his love and mercy upon his chosen (v. 26). And there is another great display of distinguishing grace recorded here. Some of the Egyptians were converted by the Word of God (v. 20). We are told that those among them who feared the Word of the Lord, called their servants home and put their cattle in their stalls. Later, when Israel went out of Egypt by the high hand of God, a mixed multitude went with them. They were numbered by God as true Israelites, marked by grace as his own. These converted Egyptians were typical of God's elect among the Gentiles, given to the Lord Jesus before the world was made (Isaiah 49:6).

**Locusts**

The eighth plague was a plague of locusts covering the land, devouring all the vegetation of Egypt (Exodus 10:1-20).

'And the LORD said unto Moses, Go in unto Pharaoh: for I have hardened his heart, and the heart of his servants, that I might show these my signs before him: And that thou mayest tell in the ears of thy son, and of thy son's son, what things I have wrought in Egypt, and my signs which I have done among them; that ye may know how that I am the LORD' (vv. 1, 2).

'And the LORD said unto Moses, Stretch out thine hand over the land of Egypt for the locusts, that they may come up upon the land of Egypt, and eat every herb of the land, even all that the hail hath left. And Moses stretched forth his rod over the land of Egypt, and the LORD brought an east wind upon the land all that day, and all that night; and when it was morning, the east wind brought the locusts. And the locusts went up over all the land of Egypt, and rested in all the coasts of Egypt: very grievous were they; before them there were no such locusts as they, neither after them shall be such. For they covered the face of the whole earth, so that the land was darkened; and they did eat every herb of the land, and all the fruit of the trees which the hail had left: and there remained not any green thing in the trees, or in the herbs of the field, through all the land of Egypt. Then Pharaoh called for Moses and Aaron in haste; and he said, I have sinned against the LORD your God, and against you' (vv. 12-16).

'But the LORD hardened Pharaoh's heart, so that he would not let the children of Israel go' (v. 20).

Moses, the man of God, was commanded to tell Israel that the Lord had hardened Pharaoh's heart, that he might openly display his love toward Israel in showing these signs and wonders before them. How greatly the Lord God delights in his in distinguishing grace! He would have us ever aware of the manifold proofs of it, that we might rejoice in it too! He says, 'Tell it in the ears of thy son, and of thy son's son, what things I have wrought in Egypt, and my signs which I have done among them, that ye may know how that I am the LORD'. The plague of locusts was so grievous that the earth was covered with them, and the sky was darkened by them. But there were no locusts found in Goshen.

**Darkness**

The ninth plague was darkness covering the land of Egypt; but, again, the Children of Israel were spared. The land of Goshen, the habitation of Israel, was full of light.

'And the LORD said unto Moses, Stretch out thine hand toward heaven, that there may be darkness over the land of Egypt, even darkness which may be felt. And Moses stretched forth his hand toward heaven; and there was a thick darkness in all the land of Egypt three days: They saw not one another, neither rose any from his place for three days: but all the children of Israel had light in their dwellings' (Exodus 10:21-23).

For three days there was unrelenting darkness in Egypt. For three days no human being saw another. For three days no one in Egypt dared stir out of his house. For three days God sent such darkness in the land of Ham that it was felt darkness! Who can imagine such a thing? Never before or since, in all the history of the world has there been such a thing. What a picture that darkness is of the darkness of heart and soul and mind in fallen humanity! What a picture that darkness is of the everlasting torments of the damned in hell! Yet, Israel was spared. What a picture of grace!

**Firstborn Slain**

At last, in his tenth wonder wrought in the land of Ham, in his tenth display of distinguishing grace, the Lord God of the Hebrews destroyed the firstborn both of man and beast in every house of the Egyptians.

'And it came to pass, that at midnight the LORD smote all the firstborn in the land of Egypt, from the firstborn of Pharaoh that sat on his throne unto the firstborn of the captive that was in the dungeon; and all the firstborn of cattle. And Pharaoh rose up in the night, he, and all his servants, and all the Egyptians; and there was a great cry in Egypt; for there was not a house where there was not one dead' (Exodus 12:29, 30).

Who can imagine the horrors of that Egyptian midnight? Who can imagine the shrieks and cries that must have been heard in Egypt that night? There was not a house in Egypt where there was not one dead.

All this was done to manifestly display God's distinguishing grace in the salvation of his elect by Christ. The lamb the Israelites were commanded to slay, called by God himself, the Lord's Passover, was typical of Christ our Passover sacrificed for us. The blood sprinkled on their houses portrayed the sprinkling of Christ's blood upon our hearts by the Spirit of God in the blessed gift of life and faith in Christ. The eating of the paschal lamb typified faith in Christ, the eating of Christ's flesh and blood by faith (John 6:48-58). In a word, the whole of Egypt's destruction was performed by God to vividly portray the salvation of our souls by the sacrifice of Christ our Passover.

**Substitution**

There is something stated in verse 30 that is commonly missed. The Spirit of God distinctly tells us there was not a house in Egypt where there was not one dead. In the other plagues, the land of Goshen, the place of Israel's habitation, was specifically exempted. Why not here? Because even in the land of Goshen, there was not a house where there was not one dead. In the land of Goshen, the firstborn died under the wrath of God, too. The firstling of the flock died in the place of the firstborn son. Behold, the Paschal Lamb slain, God's Firstborn, 'the firstling of the flock' (Exodus 13:2, 3). Behold, Christ our Passover sacrificed for us! That is the zenith of distinguishing grace. The zenith of God's wonders wrought for us in the land of Ham. The zenith of his love for his own. No lamb was provided for the Egyptians; but Christ our Passover was sacrificed for us; and when he died for us we died in him (1 John 4:9, 10). This is our salvation. 'Christ our Passover is sacrificed for us'. This is our security forever. 'Christ our Passover is sacrificed for us'.

'And the blood shall be to you for a token upon the houses where ye are: and when I see the blood, I will pass over you, and the plague shall not be upon you to destroy you, when I smite the land of Egypt' (Exodus 12:13).

Eat this Passover, live forever!

# Chapter 29

## 'Wonders In Egypt'

'And I am sure that the king of Egypt will not let you go, no, not by a mighty hand. And I will stretch out my hand, and smite Egypt with all my wonders which I will do in the midst thereof: and after that he will let you go.'
(Exodus 3:19, 20)

In Psalm 106 David calls upon God's elect to praise and give thanks to the Lord God.

'Praise ye the LORD. O give thanks unto the LORD; for he is good: for his mercy endureth forever. Who can utter the mighty acts of the LORD? who can shew forth all his praise?' (Psalm 106:1, 2).

Then the psalmist teaches us to confess our sin, our iniquity, and our wickedness, and that of our fathers. We will never confess our own sin if we refuse to acknowledge and confess the sin of our fathers. But the confession David leads us to make begins very strangely. He begins not with open acts of unbelief, rebellion, ungodly behaviour, idolatry, or even the horrible evil of sacrificing children to idols. Rather, David was inspired of God to confess 'Our fathers understood not thy wonders in Egypt; they remembered not the multitude of thy mercies' (v. 7).

Failure to remember what God has done for us, failure to remember or constantly to keep in mind God's 'wonders in Egypt' leads to nothing but unbelief, rebellion, love of the world, and ungodly behaviour. The greatest preservative of, and inspiration for, consecration to our God is the constant remembrance of his 'wonders in Egypt'.

In the previous chapter we saw how the plagues our God brought upon the Egyptians portrayed his distinguishing grace upon his elect. I want us to look at God's 'wonders in Egypt' again and observe a few more lessons from those wonders.

God the Holy Ghost tells us it was because 'our fathers understood not thy wonders in Egypt' that they 'provoked him at the sea, even the Red Sea' (Psalm 107:7). Failure to observe and remember those great wonders led Israel to unbelief and revolt at the Red Sea. Oh, my God, help me ever to remember your 'wonders in Egypt', that I may give myself relentlessly to you, for Christ's sake (Romans 12:1, 2; 1 Corinthians 6:9-11, 19, 20).

Remember, those things that were plagues upon the Egyptians were wonders of grace wrought in the land of Egypt for the deliverance of God's people (Psalm 105:23-27).

It is the natural tendency of men to look upon things like earthquakes, tornadoes, hurricanes, and tsunamis as terrible, freak accidents that have no explanation. Even believers are sometimes lulled into such thinking. When terrorists attack us, or nations make war against us, our immediate response is to retaliate against the enemy. And such retaliation by a nation is both demanded and just. But, if anyone dares suggest that the hand of God is in such things, he is looked upon as a religious crack-pot and denounced as a bigot. Why? Because the whole world prefers not to hear God speak. The whole world prefers to deny God's existence. I grant that most everyone acknowledges God's being, and tips his head toward deity of some kind. But to deny that God rules all things, and has his way in all things is really man's way of denying that God is. It is man's attempt to silence the voice of God in his conscience.

Let us ever pray for grace to listen for and hear God's voice in all things: in his Word, in the preaching of the gospel, and in providence.

### Divine Providence

Read the Book of Revelation. Begin in chapter 5, where the Lord Jesus takes the seven-sealed book of divine predestination, and begins to open the seals of the book, and read through to the end of chapter 19. Those seven seals do not refer to seven imaginary dispensations. They refer to the whole, perfect, complete, purpose of God. The opening of those seals by the Lord Jesus Christ, our Redeemer, is the accomplishment of God's eternal purpose of grace in predestination and in providence (Revelation 10:1, 2).

When we get to Revelation 10, six trumpets have sounded and the seventh, the final trumpet is about to sound. Just before John sees the final, consummate judgment of God fall upon the earth, the Lord Jesus Christ appears with one last word of warning. He stood 'upon the sea and upon the earth (and) lifted up his hand to heaven, and sware by him that liveth for ever and ever that there should be time no longer' (vv. 5, 6). Because he could sware by no greater, he swore by himself.

It is as though the Lord says, 'No more delay! Prepare to meet thy God!' If you read chapters 8-11 at one sitting, you cannot fail to see that chapter 10 is an abrupt interruption of events. It is almost parenthetical. It stands as both a word of warning to God's enemies of the certainty of divine judgment and a word of comfort to God's elect. It portrays and assures us of the providential rule of Christ. What could be more comforting than the fact that he who loved us from eternity and died to redeem us at Calvary, and saves us by his almighty grace, also sovereignly rules all things according to God's eternal purpose for us? This is the picture we have before us in God's 'wonders in Egypt'.

## Speaks in Judgment

God speaks in acts of judgment as well as in acts of mercy. He speaks both to warn his enemies and to comfort his people. The wonders he performed in the land of Ham, the plagues he wrought in Egypt, were both acts of judgment to warn his enemies and acts of mercy to comfort his people. There is a distinct parallel between those ten plagues and the opening of the seals portrayed in the Book of Revelation.

I am often asked, 'What does it take to save a sinner?' The answer is clearly given in the Scriptures. It takes God's sovereign election and predestination, Christ's blood atonement, the Holy Spirit's regeneration, God's gift of faith in Christ, the relentless preservation by his grace, and all things in providence (Romans 8:28-31).

## Typical Picture

God's dealings with Egypt and Israel in the Book of Exodus were typical. They portrayed both divine judgment upon the ungodly and the

251

salvation of God's elect by his out-stretched arm of omnipotent grace. The Egyptians represent all the reprobate of the world. They represent the whole world, the political world, the economic world, the civil world, the educational world, the scientific world, and the religious world, that is ever opposed to God and opposed to his people.

The Angel who spoke to Moses was Christ who came down to deliver Israel out of Egypt. He is 'the God of Abraham, of Isaac, and of Jacob' (v. 6), the great 'I AM' (v. 14), the Lord Jesus Christ our Saviour. The Angel of the Lord is the pre-incarnate Christ (Isaiah 63:9; Malachi 3:1; Revelation 20:1).

God's people Israel were suffering in Egyptian bondage (3:7). The Lord Jesus sends Moses to deliver them (3:8-10). He knew the Egyptian Pharaoh would refuse to let his people go (3:19). So he told Moses, 'I will stretch out my hand and smite Egypt with all my wonders which I will do in its midst thereof: and after that he will let you go' (3:20).

### The Plagues

The 'wonders' the Lord Jesus determined to perform in the land of Ham were the ten plagues with which he afflicted the Egyptians in chapters 7-12. We have already mentioned them:

Water was turned to blood (7:14-25). Frogs covered the land (8:1-15). Lice plagued people and beasts (8:16-19). Swarms of flies covered the land (8:20-32). Pestilence smote livestock (9:1-7). Boils broke out on people and beasts (9:8-12). Hail and fire struck people and livestock, and destroyed vegetation (9:13-35). Hordes of locusts devoured vegetation (10:1-20). Felt darkness covered the land (10:21-29). The firstborn of people and livestock were slain (11:1-12:50; Psalm 78:43-51; 105:26-36).

These ten plagues teach us much about our Lord Jesus Christ and his sovereign providence. They typify his work among the nations today in providence, as set forth in the Book of Revelation under seven seals (5:9-8:1-6), seven trumpets (8:7-9:21 and 11:15-19), and seven vials (15:1-19:8). The opening of the seven seals portrays the work of our sovereign Christ in providence throughout history, as the world constantly persecutes his people. The trumpet judgments are set before us as God calling people who deserve his wrath to repentance. The vial judgments portray our Saviour dispensing his wrath upon a world that will not hear his voice, hardening its heart, and refusing to repent.

The judgments portrayed in John's vision are not to be viewed as successive prophetic events, but as parallel events of providence, occurring throughout history, from the first advent of Christ until his second coming. The seals, the trumpets, and the vials were all typified in the wonders God performed in Egypt, among those cursed people whom he made servants to his chosen.

**Plagues and Seals**
In the ten plagues, as in the seven seals of Revelation, the Lord Jesus Christ 'went out conquering and to conquer' the world (Revelation 6:1-8:1). In Revelation 6, as in the Book of Exodus and throughout both Scripture and history, we see the world described as a world hell-bent on the slaughter of God's saints. But our blessed Saviour is a mighty man of war who declares, 'I will build my church and the gates of hell shall not prevail against it'. As the Egyptians slaughtered the Israelite babies (Exodus 1:8-22), the world ever persecutes and murders God's people. As the Egyptians imposed great economic hardships on Israel, forcing them into slavery and requiring the Jews to provide straw to make bricks for them, so the world ever imposes hardships upon God's people, seeking to enslave the Church of God to its philosophies, customs, and obscenities. But, even in such opposition, our blessed Saviour is riding forth in all the majesty of divine sovereignty, 'conquering and to conquer', as our mighty Saviour (Exodus 15:1-13).

**No Harm Done**
Not only does our Lord Jesus assure us he will avenge the blood of his saints (Revelation 6:9-11), he assures us his chosen shall not be harmed by all that men do, and that his elect will not be harmed by all the judgments he pours out upon the wicked (Psalm 91; Isaiah 11). It is written, 'There shall no evil happen to the just' (Proverbs 12:21). Does that mean none of God's elect are killed or even physically harmed by what we call 'natural disasters', persecution, sickness, or terrorism? Of course not. What it does mean is this: not even the most terrible things that occur in the world can harm one of God's chosen.

**Revelation 7**
Did you never notice that in the Book of Revelation, as John sees the opening of the seals, just as he is about to see the trumpet judgments,

his vision is interrupted by another sight? What a glorious revelation it is! John said, I saw an 'angel ascending from the east, having the seal of the living God: and he cried with a loud voice to the four angels, to whom it was given to hurt the earth and the sea, Saying, Hurt not the earth, neither the sea, nor the trees, till we have sealed the servants of our God in their foreheads. And I heard the number of them which were sealed: and there were sealed an hundred and forty and four thousand of all the tribes of the children of Israel' (Revelation 7:2-4). What a glorious interruption! God's elect are sealed by him. But really, that is not an interruption. Everything going on around that vision is the way he is sealing and saving his Israel.

Our all-glorious Christ has prepared his awesome deeds against the nations (Revelation 8:1-6), just as he prepared his plagues against the Egyptians; but the plagues and awesome deeds he has prepared for the wicked he performs for the salvation of his chosen (Isaiah 45:5-9).

### Trumpets and Vials

The seven trumpets and the seven vials of Revelation were also typified by the ten plagues upon Egypt. The earth is stricken with hail and fire which destroy vegetation (Revelation 8:7), and with sores which afflict that part of mankind worshipping the beast (Revelation 16:2), just as Egypt was (Exodus 9:1-25). The sea is stricken with death, turning it to blood (Revelation 8:8; 16:3), just as the Nile was turned to blood and death (Exodus 7:20, 21). The heavens are stricken with darkness (Revelation 8:12), God turning light to darkness (2 Thessalonians 2:11, 12). Darkness covered Egypt for three days, while the light shined still in Goshen (Exodus 10:21-23; 2 Thessalonians 2:11-14). The wicked are afflicted with locusts (Revelation 9:1-4) and with darkness and pain (Revelation 16:10), just as the Egyptians were (Exodus 8-10), turning everything that had been their pleasure to a bitter curse; yet there was no pain, or bitterness, or curse in Goshen. As the firstborn in every house of the Egyptians was slain (Exodus 12:29), so we are told the Lord God our Saviour commands his angels to kill 'the third part of men' dwelling on the earth (Revelation 9:13-19).

Yet, still, even after the slaughter of their firstborn, neither Pharaoh nor the Egyptians repented, but hardened their hearts the more, so it is today. Wrath and judgment never produce repentance (Revelation 9:20, 21).

## The End

In the end, the announcement is made that 'the kingdoms of this world are become the kingdoms of our Lord and of his Christ' (Revelation 11:15-19). We read, 'It is done' (Revelation 16:17-21), and the saints of God redeemed and saved out of all the earth are brought forth, singing the song of Moses and of the Lamb (Exodus 15:1-21; Revelation 15:1-3; 19:1-6; 1 Corinthians 15:24-28).

## The Lessons

What are we to learn from these things? Why are they written in the Book of God? The Spirit of God tells us (1 Corinthians 10:11; Romans 15:4). The plagues God brought upon the Egyptians and the wonders he is performing today in this land of Ham, are intended to teach us.

The Lord Jesus Christ, our God and Saviour, is the God of gods (Deuteronomy 10:17; Joshua 22:22; Psalm 136:2; Daniel 2:47; 11:36). The plagues performed in Egypt were, our Saviour said, executed 'against all the gods of Egypt (Exodus 12:12). 'Also on their gods the LORD had executed judgment' (Numbers 33:4). Egypt was a land of such great idolatry that throughout their dark land ignorant men worshipped the sun, the Nile River, cows, sheep, goats, cats, dogs, jackals, lions, hippopotami, apes, birds, and frogs. As Elijah mocked the dung gods of Baal on Mount Carmel, so the Lord God mocked the gods of the Egyptians by the plagues. And he mocks and humiliates the gods of the nations in the salvation of his people (Psalm 115:3-8).

Our great God and Saviour afflicts and even sacrifices men and nations upon the altar of his love for his elect (Proverbs 11:8; 21:18; Isaiah 43:1-7). Distinguishing grace is displayed everywhere!

Antichrists and false prophets, like Pharaoh's sorcerers, Jannes and Jambres will not thwart, or even slightly impede, the purpose of our great God and Saviour (2 Timothy 3:1-9; 1 Corinthians 11:19). They only serve to accomplish it.

'Salvation is of the Lord!' Our great God and Saviour, by every act of providential judgment warns sinners of judgment to come and gives them 'space to repent' (Revelation 2:21); but the heart of man is only hardened, until he is regenerated by God the Holy Spirit and granted repentance by the goodness of God (Romans 2:4).

The ten plagues inflicted upon Egypt teach us that Christ uses his plagues to convince men of their sinfulness and his own righteousness

(Psalm 107). Many will, in times of dread and fear, cry like Pharaoh, 'I have sinned … the LORD is righteous, and I and my people are wicked' (Exodus 9:27); but, instead of repenting unto salvation, they only harden their hearts to greater condemnation, as Pharaoh did (Exodus 7:22; 8:15, 19, 32; 9:7, 34, 35).

O sinner, does that describe you? How often have you said, 'I have sinned. God is righteous. If he sends me to hell, he will be right. I deserve his wrath', only to harden your heart the more? The Lord God says, 'As I live, saith the Lord GOD, I have no pleasure in the death of the wicked; but that the wicked turn from his way and live: turn ye, turn ye from your evil ways; for why will ye die, O house of Israel?' (Ezekiel 33:11). But it will take something more than judgment, even something more than preaching to bring you to repentance. It will take the revelation of Christ in you (Zechariah 12:10; 2 Corinthians 4:4-6).

O Spirit of God, come! Blow upon the poor sinner reading these lines, yet dead in sin. Reveal Christ that the poor soul might live!

The ten plagues Christ inflicted upon Egypt teach us that Christ is merciful to his own people even in times of trouble. Having sworn to Pharaoh 'I will make a difference between my people and thy people' (Exodus 8:23; 9:4-7; 10:23; 11:7; 12:13), he separated the precious from the vile by omnipotent mercy.

God's wonders in the land of Ham, the ten plagues he performed in Egypt, declare in bold capital letters 'ALL ISRAEL SHALL BE SAVED!' The Lord God Almighty will save all his elect. He will save all his chosen. He will save his chosen through the instrumentality he has ordained, by the prophets he sends. There is no need and no excuse for compromise. Compromise never accomplishes anything but compromise. Pharaoh repeatedly offered Moses a compromise. But each time, in strict obedience to God's word, Moses refused to alter God's message (Exodus 10:24-26). When Israel went out of Egypt, there was not so much as a hoof left behind (Exodus 12:40-42).

The Lord God has sworn, 'I am the LORD, and I will bring you out from under the burdens of the Egyptians, and I will rid you out of their bondage, and I will redeem you with a stretched out arm, and with great judgments' (Exodus 6:6). He has promised, 'Behold, I will save my people' (Zechariah 8:7); and save them he shall, 'by a stretched out arm, and by great terrors, according to all that the LORD your God did for you in Egypt before your eyes' (Deuteronomy 4:34).

# Chapter 30

# 'Ye Shall Not Go Empty'

'And I will give this people favour in the sight of the Egyptians: and it shall come to pass, that, when ye go, ye shall not go empty: But every woman shall borrow of her neighbour, and of her that sojourneth in her house, jewels of silver, and jewels of gold, and raiment: and ye shall put them upon your sons, and upon your daughters; and ye shall spoil the Egyptians.'
(Exodus 3:21, 22)

In Exodus 3:16-22 the Lord God gives a detailed account of the whole history of his controversy with Pharaoh and the Egyptians and of the final redemption of his people before it happened. The Lord was about to visit Israel in grace; but he told Moses to declare that he had already visited them in grace. 'The LORD God of your fathers, the God of Abraham, of Isaac, and of Jacob, appeared unto me, saying, I have surely visited you.' Because he had visited them in his purpose of grace, he was sure to visit them in the blessed experience of his grace.

## Done and Sure
Moses was sent to Israel and commanded by God to announce to his people that their deliverance was accomplished, that redemption was done, and that redemption accomplished is redemption sure. That is exactly what God's servants are sent to preach. Redemption done and

sure to be done is salvation finished and sure to be finished (Isaiah 40:1, 2; Romans 8:29-31; 2 Timothy 1:9, 10). The Lord God assured Moses that his people would hear and believe his message (v. 18). 'They shall hearken to thy voice'. God never sends his servants on a useless mission. He will bless his word (2 Corinthians 2:14-16; Isaiah 55:11).

Next, the Lord told Moses to go with the elders of Israel to ask permission from Pharaoh that they might go three days' journey into the wilderness to worship 'the LORD our God'. 'And thou shalt come, thou and the elders of Israel, unto the king of Egypt, and ye shall say unto him, The LORD God of the Hebrews hath met with us: and now let us go, we beseech thee, three days' journey into the wilderness, that we may sacrifice to the LORD our God' (v. 18).

Then, the Lord plainly told Moses that Pharaoh would not let Israel go, but he would harden his heart (v. 19). And, the Lord again assured his servant that he would, by the performance of his wonders in Egypt, compel Pharaoh to let his people go (v. 20).

**According to Purpose**
All these things are written for us, to assure us that all things move according to the eternal purpose of our great God. He who declares the end from the beginning performs all his pleasure. What a sweet, blessed source of consolation this is for our fearful hearts! We shall never meet a difficulty or an enemy, in the world or in our own hearts, that was not purposed by our God. We shall never face a foe that he will not conquer. We shall never endure a trial from which he does not deliver us.

The Lord God knew beforehand what Pharaoh would do. He knew it because he had predestined it, that he might show his glory in Pharaoh's destruction and Israel's salvation. It is thus with every trial, every foe, and every hardship in the path he has marked out for us through this world. All has been prearranged for our final triumph and our victorious exit from this scene of woe, by the accomplishment of our redemption by Christ. 'Faithful is he that calleth you, who also will do it' (1 Thessalonians 5:24). 'He which hath begun a good work in you will perform it until the day of Jesus Christ' (Philippians 1:6).

**God's Promise**
This was God's promise to Moses and to Israel. 'When ye go, ye shall not go empty ... And ye shall spoil the Egyptians'. And that which was

promised regarding Israel after the flesh and the typical redemption of Israel out of Egyptian bondage is true concerning the redemption of God's elect, 'the Israel of God', by the blood of his Son and the power of his grace. 'It shall come to pass, that, when ye go, ye shall not go empty ... Ye shall spoil the Egyptians.'

## Blessed Bondage

We must not forget, as we read the Book of Exodus, that Israel's redemption from Egyptian bondage was a picture of the Lord Jesus Christ coming from heaven to redeem and save his people. Our blessed Saviour has seen, heard, and known the afflictions of his children in the land of bondage. More than that, he ordained our bondage as well as our deliverance, to display and make known to us and in us the greatness of his grace and glory in our deliverance (Ephesians 2:4-7).

Blessed is that bondage by which our Saviour displays the glory of his grace in deliverance! Had there never been a fall, there would never have been redemption from the fall. Had we never been in captivity, we could never have been set free. If the first Adam had not sinned, the last Adam would not have been revealed. Christ came to seek and to save that which was lost. Had we not been lost, he would never have come to save. The whole need not a physician, but they that are sick.

The same thing is true with regard to our present trials, even our present faults. Let no one mistake my meaning. I do not excuse Adam in his sin; and I do not excuse myself in my sins, or you in yours. Yet, I do assert, and assert with delight, that our God has ordained the falls of his people, that he might the more show in us the glory of his grace and the more enrich our lives by the experience of his grace. I fully agree with C. H. Spurgeon who said: 'O happy fault, which has thus made manifest the abounding mercy of God! Looked at in one aspect all sin is an unutterable calamity; but as it has had the effect of displaying still more of the matchless mercy of God in the person of Jesus Christ, we see how God brings forth good out of evil.'

That was the meaning of Samson's riddle (Judges 14:14-18). Peter was made better by the Lord Jesus sifting him in Satan's sieve; and we are made better by the sifting. It is especially when we have been sifted that we are called by our Saviour to trust him (John 13:38-14:3).

Our dear Saviour, the Lord Jesus Christ, is the almighty I AM. He is 'the same yesterday, and today, and forever!' May he give us grace, by his Holy Spirit, to trust him, even in the midst of terrible adversity. How blessed it is that, when our souls are bowed down and brought low by the bondage and oppression of sin and we cry, 'My strength and my hope is perished from the Lord', he enables us to remember, even in our lowest conditions, 'His mercy endureth forever!' That is what Jeremiah teaches us (Lamentations 3:18-30).

## Unexpected Favour

These are the things taught and illustrated in Exodus 3:21, 22. In verse 21, the Lord Jesus told Moses he would cause the Egyptians to show unexpected favour toward his people. 'I will give this people favour in the sight of the Egyptians: and it shall come to pass, that, when ye go, ye shall not go empty.'

Did the Lord God say that Israel would be given 'favour in the sight of the Egyptians', who hated, enslaved, persecuted, and murdered them? Verse 21 is not a misprint. That is what he said, and what he promised he performed (Exodus 11:3; 12:36; Psalm 105:38; 106:42-46). And what he has done he still does. The world that hates, persecutes, and would destroy God's church, is made to favour and help his church (Proverbs 16:6, 7; Revelation 12:13-16).

## Borrowed Wealth

The Lord promised, 'when ye go, ye shall not go empty'. But how were they to obtain everything they needed to live in the wilderness? How could they ever get everything they needed to worship and serve God in the wilderness? Where could they ever expect to get the wealth with which to offer such costly sacrifices as God would require? Later, they would be required to build a tabernacle with the richest furnishings imaginable, furnishings of brass, silver, and pure gold! How could a rag-tag bunch of slaves get such wealth? Verse 22 gives us the answer to those questions: 'But every woman shall borrow of her neighbour, and of her that sojourneth in her house, jewels of silver, and jewels of gold, and raiment: and ye shall put them upon your sons, and upon your daughters; and ye shall spoil the Egyptians.'

Some foolishly imagine God here commanded the women of Israel to steal the wealth of the Egyptians. That is not the case. The word translated 'borrow' in verse 22 simply means 'to seek, ask, or desire a favour'. In 1 Samuel 1:20, Hannah used this word when she asked the

Lord to give her a son. Then when Hannah brought Samuel to the temple, she told Eli she had asked, or begged, God to give her the son she now brought to the Lord (1 Samuel 1:27, 28).

In Exodus 12:36 we are told 'And the LORD gave the people favour in the sight of the Egyptians, so that they lent unto them such things as they required'. That is the same word Hannah used when she told Eli that she had 'lent' Samuel to the Lord forever. He was not loaned to the Lord, but given to him, unconditionally, forever. The Egyptians gave the Israelites their wealth unconditionally, forever (Exodus 12:35, 36).

Though the children of Israel departed carrying away their jewels of silver, their jewels of gold, their clothes, and their cattle, the Scriptures declare, 'Egypt was glad when they departed'. The Lord God made the Egyptians happy to give his people Israel everything they required. Do you suppose, child of God, he will let you go naked, homeless, or hungry? That he will leave you unprotected, and not provide for you everything you require? (Romans 8:32).

**Egypt Spoiled**

Exodus 3:21, 22 was God's promise to Moses and to Israel. 'It shall come to pass, that, when ye go, ye shall not go empty ... Ye shall spoil the Egyptians'. What he promised, he performed (Exodus 12:35, 36).

All of this would be as meaningful, or as meaningless, to us as any other piece of history, except for one thing. This is God's promise to you and me, his promise to all his elect, his promise to every believing sinner. 'It shall come to pass, that, when ye go, ye shall not go empty ... Ye shall spoil the Egyptians'. If you will read Exodus chapter 35, you will see how all the riches Israel brought with them out of Egypt were used to make and adorn the tabernacle in the wilderness, used in the worship and service of God to the praise of his glory, in the perpetual celebration of redemption. This is a covenant promise. God made this promise in a covenant long before any of these people were ever born (Genesis 15:14). And with regard to God's true Israel, this is a promise of universal application (Job 27:13-17; Proverbs 13:22; 1 Corinthians 3:19-23; Romans 8:28-32; Revelation 21:1-4, 22-27).

**All Nations**

How is it God's elect spoil the Egyptians? How are we made rich by that which once was our ruin? First, when Israel went out of Egypt there were numerous Egyptians who were delivered with them. 'A mixed multitude went up also with them; and flocks, and herds, even very much cattle' (Exodus 12:38). Those Egyptians who were saved with Israel were a beautiful prophetic picture of the fact that the Lord God has purposed to save a great multitude out of every nation, even from Egypt itself (Isaiah 19:1, 18-22; Zechariah 8:23).

**Christ's Death**
When the Lord Jesus redeemed us by his blood, he spoiled the prince of darkness and all the evil represented by Pharaoh and Egypt, 'blotting out the handwriting of ordinances that was against us, which was contrary to us, and took it out of the way, nailing it to his cross; and having spoiled principalities and powers, he made a shew of them openly, triumphing over them in it' (Colossians 2:14, 15; John 12:32; Revelation 20:1-3; Isaiah 53:12). He restored what he took not away.

We read in Isaiah 53:12 the words of God the Father, promising his Son that he would have a great, large, and ample, portion given to him and that he would make him higher than the kings of the earth, giving him a name above every name in this world and in the world to come. 'And he shall divide the spoil with the strong.' That is to say, 'He shall divide the strong as a spoil'.

**Saving Operations**
When the Lord God comes in the power of his saving grace to set captive sinners free, he causes his ransomed ones to spoil the Egyptians. 'For the LORD will plead their cause, and spoil the soul of those that spoiled them' (Proverbs 22:23). 'They shall spoil those that spoiled them, and rob those that robbed them, saith the Lord GOD' (Ezekiel 39:10; Isaiah 33:22-24; Jeremiah 30:16-22; Isaiah 40:1-5).

**Law of Restitution**
In the Book of Leviticus the law of God demanded that anyone wronged by another should not only have the wrong repaired but also be made to benefit and gain by the injury done. The thing must be restored with increase. 'Add the fifth part more thereto' (Leviticus 5:15, 16; 16:2-7).

It is God primarily who has been wronged in all his rights by sin. Yet, man too has been wronged. But the Lord God has, in infinite wisdom, fixed it so both he and his people shall be made to gain from the injury done. As the children of Israel were enriched by their bondage in Egypt, as the fall of Israel has been overruled by our heavenly Father for the riches of the world (Romans 11:12), so the fall of Satan and the entrance of sin into the world by the fall of our father Adam has been, is being, and shall yet be made to redound to the everlasting riches of God's elect and the glory of his great name.

Yes, the God of glory works all things together for the good of his people and the everlasting glory of his own great name. Satan will gain nothing by the havoc he has wrought in the world. He will achieve absolutely nothing! God's elect will lose nothing, absolutely nothing! I have chosen my words deliberately. This is the great glory of the cross. 'Where sin abounded, grace did much more abound!' Both God and his people have gained more by the forgiveness of sin through the blood of Christ than was lost by the sin and fall of our father Adam and the long years of our Egyptian bondage.

The Lord God has arranged all things, even the sin and fall of our father Adam, for the everlasting good and happiness of his people. I repeat myself deliberately. We shall lose nothing, but only gain by what happened in the garden. We are made gainers not by sin but by redemption. Indeed, the sin and fall of Adam was itself, by divine purpose, a picture of redemption by Christ (Romans 5:12-20). Martin Luther said with regard to Adam's sin in the Garden, 'O blessed fall!' Had there been no fall, no sin, no condemnation, we could never have known the wonders of redemption. Had there been no fall, no sin, no condemnation, we could never have known the glories of grace. Grace not only pulls up sin by the roots and ultimately destroys it, grace makes chosen sinners to be eternal beneficiaries of Satan's work!

There is more. The holy Lord God has gained more by redemption than ever he lost – if I can be permitted to use such language – by the fall. The Lord God reaps a richer harvest of glory in the fields of grace than he could ever have reaped in the garden of innocence (Ephesians 1:3-14; 2:7). The sons of God raise a more lofty song of praise around the empty tomb of the crucified Christ than we could have raised in the Garden of Eden. The injury done by sin has not only been perfectly atoned for and remedied by the blood of Christ, but our great God has gained by the cross the praise of the glory of his grace (Psalm 76:10).

This is a stupendous truth. God, the eternal, triune, holy Lord God, has gotten himself great gain by the work accomplished by our all-glorious Christ at Calvary! Who could ever have conceived such a thing? When we see man and the creation over which he was lord laid in a heap of ruins at the feet of Satan, how could we ever imagine that from those ruins the great God of Glory would gather a crown for his holy head which could not be gotten in any other way?

It was ever the immutable purpose of the all-wise God to glorify himself and reveal his glory to all creation by the accomplishments of his darling Son at Calvary. That is precisely what he tells us in the fortieth chapter of Isaiah's prophecy.

'Comfort ye, comfort ye my people, saith your God. Speak ye comfortably to Jerusalem, and cry unto her, that her warfare is accomplished, that her iniquity is pardoned: for she hath received of the Lord's hand double for all her sins. The voice of him that crieth in the wilderness, Prepare ye the way of the LORD, make straight in the desert a highway for our God. Every valley shall be exalted, and every mountain and hill shall be made low: and the crooked shall be made straight, and the rough places plain: And the glory of the LORD shall be revealed, and all flesh shall see it together: for the mouth of the LORD hath spoken it' (Isaiah 40:1-5).

**Final Restitution**
In the end, when all things are finished, in that day called 'the times of restitution of all things, which God hath spoken by the mouth of all his holy prophets since the world began' (Acts 3:11), all the glory and honour of the nations shall be brought to the feet of our blessed Saviour to the everlasting praise of the triune God (Revelation 21:26; Philippians 2:9-11; 1 Corinthians 15:24-28).

Soon, very soon, child of God, we shall go out of this land of Egypt. 'And it shall come to pass, that, when ye go, ye shall not go empty!' 'For so an entrance shall be ministered unto you abundantly into the everlasting kingdom of our Lord and Saviour Jesus Christ' (2 Peter 1:11).

# Chapter 31

## Signs Of Deliverance

'And Moses answered and said, But, behold, they will not believe me, nor hearken unto my voice: for they will say, The LORD hath not appeared unto thee. And the LORD said unto him, What is that in thine hand? And he said, A rod. And he said, Cast it on the ground. And he cast it on the ground, and it became a serpent; and Moses fled from before it. And the LORD said unto Moses, Put forth thine hand, and take it by the tail. And he put forth his hand, and caught it, and it became a rod in his hand: That they may believe that the LORD God of their fathers, the God of Abraham, the God of Isaac, and the God of Jacob, hath appeared unto thee. And the LORD said furthermore unto him, Put now thine hand into thy bosom. And he put his hand into his bosom: and when he took it out, behold, his hand was leprous as snow. And he said, Put thine hand into thy bosom again. And he put his hand into his bosom again; and plucked it out of his bosom, and, behold, it was turned again as his other flesh. And it shall come to pass, if they will not believe thee, neither hearken to the voice of the first sign, that they will believe the voice of the latter sign. And it shall come to pass, if they will not believe also these two signs, neither hearken unto thy voice, that thou shalt take of the water of the river, and pour it upon the dry land: and the water which thou takest out of the river shall become blood upon the dry land.'
(Exodus 4:1-9)

After forty years in the backside of the desert, the Lord God appeared to Moses at Horeb in the burning bush and declared that he had chosen him to go to Pharaoh and deliver his people from Egyptian bondage (Exodus 3:10). Moses responded to God's revelation with astonishment and humility, saying, 'Who am I, that I should go unto Pharaoh, and that I should bring forth the children of Israel out of Egypt?' (v. 11). Then the Lord assured his servant of his presence, saying, 'Certainly, I will be with thee (v. 12).

Then, Moses asked the Angel that spoke to him what his name is. 'And God said unto Moses, I AM THAT I AM: and he said, Thus shalt thou say unto the children of Israel, I AM hath sent me unto you. And God said moreover unto Moses, Thus shalt thou say unto the children of Israel, The LORD God of your fathers, the God of Abraham, the God of Isaac, and the God of Jacob, hath sent me unto you: this is my name for ever, and this is my memorial unto all generations' (vv. 14, 15).

The Lord then promised Moses that he would deliver his people from their affliction and bondage in Egypt, and bring them into the land of Canaan. He commanded his servant to appear before Pharaoh and beseech the Egyptian king to allow the Hebrews to go a three days' journey into the wilderness that they might hold a feast unto the Lord their God. At the same time, the Lord informed Moses that Pharaoh would not grant this request. Still, he assured Moses that he would bring Israel out of Egypt, that he would do so by smiting Egypt with his wonders. Not only that, he also assured him that Israel would spoil the Egyptians, and they would be greatly enriched by them when he had accomplished their deliverance.

**Moses' Unbelief**

Still Moses' mind was occupied with difficulties and obstacles that appeared too great to be overcome. We pick up the story in Exodus 4:1.

'And Moses answered and said, But, behold, they will not believe me, nor hearken unto my voice: for they will say, The LORD hath not appeared unto thee.'

Surely, Moses had seen and heard all that could possibly be needed to dispel his fears. Had he not? He had seen the bush burning with fire, yet unharmed by the fire. He had seen Christ, the Angel of the Lord, and heard his voice. The Lord God revealed himself in and by the most assuring and endearing titles and names to be the covenant God of Israel. He had assured Moses of his favour, his grace, his presence, and of Israel's deliverance. He assured him his people would hear him and Pharaoh would, at last, let his people go. After all that, 'Moses answered and said, But, behold, they will not believe me, nor hearken unto my voice: for they will say, The LORD hath not appeared unto thee'.

How hard it is to overcome the unbelief of our hearts! What evils are engendered by our unbelief! God plainly told Moses that the people would hearken to his voice (3:18); but Moses did not hearken to God's voice. However, lest we think too severely of Moses, let us judge ourselves. What horrible unbelief rages in our own hearts!

How difficult it is, even for believing men and women, to believe God! Do you not find yourself constantly crying, like the man who brought his demon-possessed son to the Saviour, 'Lord, I believe; help thou mine unbelief?' I am ashamed to confess it, but I do. How slow I am to believe the naked promise of God. The most slender reed that the human eye can see is trusted, but the unseen 'Rock of ages' is not. I find myself quick to run to any creature stream or broken cistern, rather than abide by the unseen 'Fountain of living waters'.

Almost everything I have read, almost every commentary, sermon, or even the briefest comment severely criticized Moses for his unbelief (and rightly so, I suppose); but I cannot help noticing that the Lord did not! It is true, as we see in the latter verses of this chapter, that the Lord was ultimately provoked to anger by Moses' continued unbelief; but here we see nothing but patience, forbearance, and grace. When I read Moses' words of unbelief in this first verse, and hear the sweet sound of God's silence concerning it, I am filled with gratitude and praise, as the sweet words of Psalm 103 ring in my heart:

'He made known his ways unto Moses, his acts unto the children of Israel. The LORD is merciful and gracious, slow to anger, and plenteous in mercy. He will not always chide: neither will he keep his anger for ever. He hath not dealt with us after our sins; nor rewarded us according to our iniquities. For as the heaven is high above the earth, so great is his mercy toward them that fear him. As far as the east is from the west, so far hath he removed our transgressions from us. Like as a father pitieth his children, so the LORD pitieth them that fear him. For he knoweth our frame; he remembereth that we are dust' (vv. 7-14).

## Three Signs

In response to the third difficulty raised by Moses, the Lord gave his reluctant servant the power to perform three great wonders or signs, which were to be wrought before his people to convince them he was truly God's ambassador to them. There is deep meaning to these three signs, which were designed to teach important lessons to Moses, to Israel, and to us all. The first was a sign of power. The second was a sign of cleansing. The third was a sign of judgment. These three signs were given as signs by which the Lord God assured Moses and his people of their deliverance from Egypt by his omnipotent grace. And they give even greater assurance to us of the greater deliverance of our souls by Christ. Let me show you these three signs of deliverance, as they are set before us in verses 2-9.

## Moses' Rod

The first sign was the turning of Moses' rod into a serpent, and that back again into a rod.

'And the LORD said unto him, What is that in thine hand? And he said, A rod. And he said, Cast it on the ground. And he cast it on the ground, and it became a serpent; and Moses fled from before it. And the LORD said unto Moses, Put forth thine hand, and take it by the tail. And he put forth his hand, and caught it, and it became a rod in his hand: That they may believe that the LORD God of their fathers, the God of Abraham, the God of Isaac, and the God of Jacob, hath appeared unto thee' (vv. 2-5).

Just three verses are devoted to the description of this wonder; but they are full of spiritual riches. We are not left to guess what this rod is. In verse 20 we are specifically told it is 'the rod of God'. 'The rod of God' was upon Israel to deliver and defend them. By 'the rod of God', the red sea was parted (Exodus 14:16). By 'the rod of God', Pharaoh and his armies were drowned in the sea (Exodus 14:26, 27). It was by 'the rod of God' Israel prevailed over Amalek (Exodus 17:9). 'The rod of God' was upon Israel; but we read of the wicked in Job 21:9, 'neither is the rod of God upon them'.

The rod in Moses' hand was the shepherd's staff upon which he leaned. As such it was that which he trusted, which upheld him, comforted him, and defended him. You are familiar with that rod, are you not? It is the rod of which David sang in the twenty-third Psalm.

'Yea, though I walk through the valley of the shadow of death, I will fear no evil: for thou art with me; thy rod and thy staff they comfort me' (Psalm 23:4).

The rod of God upon which we lean is his almighty grace that is ours in Christ Jesus, and the Word of his grace in Scripture. Cast away his grace, cast away his Word, and we are helpless before that old serpent the devil. The only way we can stand before him and withstand his wiles is by simple dependence upon God's grace revealed in his Word.

The rod, being cast to the ground, became a serpent, and 'Moses fled from before it'. That shows the helplessness of man to cope with Satan. The sinner is completely under his power, 'taken captive by him at his will' (2 Timothy 2:26). That was Israel's condition in Egypt. They were subject to bondage and utterly incapable of freeing themselves. Nothing less than divine intervention and omnipotent power could set them free.

Notice this too: this power, 'the rod of God', was placed in the hands of a mediator Moses, the one who stood between Israel and God. He, and he alone was given power to deliver Israel. His power over the serpent was manifested by taking it by the tail and reducing it to nothing. The serpent disappeared when it became a rod again. So our blessed Saviour, the one Mediator between God and men, of whom Moses was a type, is our only hope. He alone has all power in his hands to save us (John 17:2; Romans 14:9). When Adam cast away the rod of God, the Word of God, in the garden, the serpent began to slither through God's creation. But he who is greater than Moses, our Lord Jesus, the Word of God, has conquered Satan, and shall destroy all his influence in this world (Psalm 2:8, 9; Revelation 2:27).

In a word, this rod represents Christ himself, who is called the Rod of God's Strength in Psalm 110. When he came into the world, when the Word was made flesh and dwelt among us, the Rod of God's Strength came here to be made a serpent. The 'serpent' is inseparably connected with the curse (Genesis 3). When he who knew no sin was made sin for us, the Son of God was 'made a curse' for us, that we might be made the righteousness of God in him (2 Corinthians 5:21; Galatians 3:14). Our Lord Jesus said to Nicodemus, 'As Moses lifted up the serpent in the wilderness, even so must the Son of Man be lifted up' (John 3:14). But, blessed be God, that is all past! The Lord Jesus, the Rod, is now exalted to God's right hand, and he declares, 'Now is the judgment of this world: now shall the prince of this world be cast out.

And I, if I be lifted up from the earth, will draw all men unto me. This he said, signifying what death he should die' (John 12:31-33). Blessed be his name, he crushed the serpent's head forever! He who is the Rod of God's Strength rules the serpent of hell absolutely!

Yet, there is more. Our conquering Saviour has made us more than conquerors in him; and the serpent of hell shall never do us harm (Psalm 91:13; Mark 16:18). 'And the God of peace shall bruise Satan under your feet shortly' (Romans 16:20).

## Moses' Hand

The second sign God gave Moses was just as significant, and just as important, as the first. As the first was a sign of power, the second was a sign of cleansing.

'And the LORD said furthermore unto him, Put now thine hand into thy bosom. And he put his hand into his bosom: and when he took it out, behold, his hand was leprous as snow. And he said, Put thine hand into thy bosom again. And he put his hand into his bosom again; and plucked it out of his bosom, and, behold, it was turned again as his other flesh. And it shall come to pass, if they will not believe thee, neither hearken to the voice of the first sign, that they will believe the voice of the latter sign' (vv. 6-8).

Moses was required to put his hand into his bosom, to slip his hand under his garment and lay it over his heart. 'And when he took it out, behold, his hand was leprous as snow.' It was not Moses' hand that defiled his heart. It was his heart that defiled his hand. What a vivid picture that is of our hearts (Mark 7:21-23).

Then, as commanded, Moses put his defiled hand to his heart again, and it was restored whole as the other. Here, again we see a picture of our Lord Jesus in his great substitutionary work, by whom alone we can be made clean before God. First, Moses is seen as whole, then as leprous, then whole again. That is exactly how the Scriptures portray our Saviour. Ineffably holy in himself, he had no sin (Hebrews 4:15), did no sin (1 Peter 2:22), and knew no sin (2 Corinthians 5:21). But in infinite grace Christ took our place and 'was made sin for us' (2 Corinthians 5:21). 'He bare our sins in His own body on the tree' (1 Peter 2:24).

Being made sin for us, our adorable Saviour was leprous as snow before God, defiled and unclean. The leper's place was outside the camp (Leviticus 13:46), as one cast away from God. On the cross the Lord Jesus Christ was separated for three infinitely terrible hours from his holy Father, crying, 'My God, my God, Why hast thou forsaken me?' But after the awful penalty of sin had been endured and the work of atonement was finished, the Forsaken One is seen again in communion with God, saying, 'Father into thy hands I commend my spirit'. It was as 'the Holy One' (Psalm 16:10) that he was laid in the sepulchre. Thus, after Moses thrust his leprous hand into his bosom, he drew it forth again perfectly whole, every trace of defilement gone.

As the first sign intimated that the great Deliverer would 'destroy the works of the devil' (1 John 3:8), the second signified that he would 'take away our sins' (1 John 3:5) by the sacrifice of himself.

This also pictures God's work of grace in us by his Spirit in regeneration, as he effectually applies our Saviour's blood to his redeemed. He, and he alone can bring a clean thing out of an unclean. The cleansing begins in the heart and is unseen. Only by this inward cleansing can the hand, which is seen, be made clean. Our Saviour says to every heaven born soul, 'Ye are clean' (John 13:10).

The law entering our hearts, represented by Moses' hand, defiled us and made us leprous as snow before God, and slew us (Romans 7:9). That same law, fulfilled and satisfied by Christ, entering our hearts, pronounces us clean (John 15:3; 1 Corinthians 6:9-11; Titus 3:3-7). Now, being made clean in Christ, by Christ, and with Christ, the very works of our hands are made clean and acceptable to God by him, 'an odour of a sweet smell, a sacrifice acceptable, wellpleasing to God' (Philippians 4:18; 1 Peter 2:3-7). God says to every believing sinner, 'Go thy way, eat thy bread with joy, and drink thy wine with a merry heart; for God now accepteth thy works' (Ecclesiastes 9:7).

### Water to Blood

Now, look at the third sign.

'And it shall come to pass, if they will not believe also these two signs, neither hearken unto thy voice, that thou shalt take of the water of the river, and pour it upon the dry land: and the water which thou takest out of the river shall become blood upon the dry land' (v. 9).

Moses was required to take water from the Nile and pour it out upon the ground. When he did, it became blood, a preliminary picture of the first plague that fell upon Egypt (Exodus 7:19). This was a sign of simple judgment. The river Nile was the natural source of Egypt's fertility and prosperity. If they refused to hear God's messenger, the earthly fountain of their life would become death; their blessing should be made a curse. Instead of life, God would make their river bring forth death; instead of fruitfulness, corruption; instead of blessing, a curse.

This third 'sign' is very solemn. It shows us the consequences of refusing to believe the gospel typified by the first two. If sinners reject the testimony of God, they heap to themselves 'wrath against the day of wrath and revelation of the righteous judgment of God' (Romans 2:5). The water turned into blood speaks of life giving place to death. It anticipates 'the second death', that eternal death, 'the Lake of Fire', which awaits every Christ-rejecting unbeliever. Be warned and flee to Christ for refuge before the storm of God's wrath overtakes you.

'Believe on the Lord Jesus Christ and thou shalt be saved.' 'Now then we are ambassadors for Christ, as though God did beseech you by us: we pray you in Christ's stead, be ye reconciled to God. For he hath made him to be sin for us, who knew no sin; that we might be made the righteousness of God in him. We then, as workers together with him, beseech you also that ye receive not the grace of God in vain. (For he saith, I have heard thee in a time accepted, and in the day of salvation have I succoured thee: behold, now is the accepted time; behold, now is the day of salvation)' (2 Corinthians 5:20-6:2).

# Chapter 32

## An Unbelieving Servant
## (And His Ever Gracious God)

'And Moses said unto the LORD, O my Lord, I am not eloquent, neither heretofore, nor since thou hast spoken unto thy servant: but I am slow of speech, and of a slow tongue. And the LORD said unto him, Who hath made man's mouth? or who maketh the dumb, or deaf, or the seeing, or the blind? have not I the LORD? Now therefore go, and I will be with thy mouth, and teach thee what thou shalt say. And he said, O my Lord, send, I pray thee, by the hand of him whom thou wilt send. And the anger of the LORD was kindled against Moses, and he said, Is not Aaron the Levite thy brother? I know that he can speak well. And also, behold, he cometh forth to meet thee: and when he seeth thee, he will be glad in his heart. And thou shalt speak unto him, and put words in his mouth: and I will be with thy mouth, and with his mouth, and will teach you what ye shall do. And he shall be thy spokesman unto the people: and he shall be, even he shall be to thee instead of a mouth, and thou shalt be to him instead of God. And thou shalt take this rod in thine hand, wherewith thou shalt do signs.'
(Exodus 4:10-17)

When Moses was a young man, he chomped at the bit to deliver Israel from Egyptian bondage. In those days, a forty-year-old man was a young man. When he was a young man, Moses presumed God had sent him, presumed he was ready, and presumed he was able to do the work.

He was zealous and bold; but he wound up fleeing from the face of Pharaoh like a whipped pup, his tail between his legs (Exodus 2:12-15).

Forty years later, the Lord God appeared to him in the burning bush and said, 'Come now therefore, and I will send thee unto Pharaoh, that thou mayest bring forth my people the children of Israel out of Egypt' (Exodus 3:10). When that happened, Moses was 80 years old; and he had learned a few things. He was not so anxious to go. He was not so confident in his abilities. He had spent forty years learning that he was weaker than water, and as useless as a bucket without a bottom. 'And Moses said unto God, Who am I, that I should go unto Pharaoh, and that I should bring forth the children of Israel out of Egypt? And he said, Certainly I will be with thee' (Exodus 3:11, 12).

**Our Sufficiency**
Any man who thinks he is able to speak for God, able to preach the gospel, and able to minister to the needs of God's people is altogether unfit for the work of the ministry. Any man who is chomping at the bit to be a preacher has not been called, gifted, and sent of God to preach the gospel. Any man who is sent of God knows something of the magnitude of the work of the ministry, and knows that the business of speaking for God to eternity bound sinners is a work for which he is totally insufficient. He cries with the apostle, 'Who is sufficient for these things?' Does a sinful man dare to imagine he can interpret the Word of God by his own brilliance? Dare a mere mortal think he can speak as God's ambassador, fetching a message from God himself to deliver to the hearts of men? Dare a man presume he can speak to the hearts of men? Dare any man presume that God the Holy Spirit will speak through his lips? 'Who is sufficient for these things?' Yet, these are the very things that every man sent of God to preach the gospel does and must do.

**Three Wonders**
Moses had to learn, he had to be convinced, as every prophet, apostle, and preacher must be convinced, by God himself, that 'our sufficiency is of God'. And the people to whom he was sent had to learn and be convinced that the work of deliverance is altogether God's. So the Lord performed three great wonders, signs by which he assured him that his work would be efficacious (Exodus 4:1-9).

The Lord told Moses to throw his rod on the ground. When he did, it became a serpent; and Moses fled from before it. Then God commanded him take the serpent by the tail. When he did, it became a rod in his hand again. Thus, the Lord assured Moses that Satan's power would be turned against Satan himself. Rejoice, child of God. The serpent of hell is entirely under the control of our Redeemer's hand. When Satan has reached the highest point in his mad career, he shall be hurled into the lake of fire, there to reap the fruits of his work throughout eternity's countless ages. He shall be eternally crushed beneath the rod of God's Anointed. And the God of peace shall crush him beneath your heels!

> Then the end, beneath His rod,
> Man's last enemy shall fall;
> Hallelujah! Christ in God,
> God in Christ, is all in all.

Then the Lord commanded Moses to put his hand into his bosom. When he took it out again, his hand was leprous as snow. God told him to put his hand into his bosom again. When he took it out, his hand was perfectly whole. His clean hand, placed in his bosom, was made leprous; and his leprous hand replaced there was made clean.

What an instructive picture that is! 'By man came death, by man came also the resurrection of the dead' (1 Corinthians 15:21). The first man, Adam, brought in ruin. The last man, Christ, the last Adam, brought in redemption. Man brought in guilt; and Man brought in pardon. Man brought in sin; and Man brought in righteousness. Man brought death; and Man abolished death.

Blessed assurance this is! Not only shall the serpent himself be forever defeated and confounded, every trace of his abominable slime shall be eradicated and wiped away by the atoning sacrifice of Christ, who 'was manifested that he might destroy the works of the devil'.

The third sign was a sign of judgment. Moses was commanded to take water out of the Nile River and pour it on the ground. When he did, the water became blood. All who refuse to bow to the authority of our Lord Jesus Christ, trusting him alone for redemption, righteousness, and cleansing from sin, trusting him alone as their Saviour, shall be forever damned.

**Unbelieving Reluctance**

Now, I want you to see Moses' response to these wonders. Up to this point, his reluctance seems to have been the commendable reluctance of sincere modesty. But Moses was still reluctant to do what God called him to do. He said, 'Lord, send anyone you want to, anyone but me. I cannot go back to Egypt. I cannot deliver Israel.' We see the reluctance of unbelief, by which he provoked God to anger in verses 10-17.

'And Moses said unto the LORD, O my Lord, I am not eloquent, neither heretofore, nor since thou hast spoken unto thy servant: but I am slow of speech, and of a slow tongue' (v. 10). When the Lord God himself said, 'I will be with thee', that was the infallible assurance of Moses' security and success in reference to everything for which he was sent. If an eloquent tongue had been necessary, Jehovah had declared, 'I AM'. Life, eloquence, wisdom, might, energy, everything is contained in that inexhaustible treasury.

'And the LORD said unto him, Who hath made man's mouth? or who maketh the dumb, or deaf, or the seeing, or the blind? Have not I the LORD? Now, therefore, go, and I will be with thy mouth, and teach thee what thou shalt say' (vv. 11, 12). Profound, adorable, matchless grace! Grace worthy of our God! There is none like unto our God, whose patient grace surmounts all our difficulties, and proves itself sufficient for us in all our needs, even when the need arises from our unbelief and sin.

'I the LORD' ought to silence forever the reasonings of our carnal hearts; but the rebellion and unbelief of our hearts is not easily subdued. The monstrous unbelief and rebellion of our hearts rises again and again, like a multi-headed snake, to disrupt our peace and dishonour our Saviour, who is Faithful and True, full of grace, and ever ready to help.

If the Lord is with us, our very deficiencies and infirmities are, for him, but an opportunity to display his all-sufficient grace. Moses' lack of ability, his lack of eloquence should not have troubled him. But that is easy enough to say when you are not the one being sent to confront the most powerful king in the world.

**Grace All-sufficient**

Like Moses, we need to know our weakness and, in our weakness, to rely upon our Saviour's all-sufficient grace (2 Corinthians 12:8-10). Let us ever remember that God's grace in Christ is sufficient for us for

276

everything, and at all times. God's grace is sufficient, abundantly sufficient to accomplish all his saving purposes; sufficient to pardon, justify, regenerate, sanctify, and preserve us, sufficient in every time of need, sufficient in health and sufficient in sickness, sufficient in life and sufficient in death, sufficient in judgment, and sufficient to present us faultless before the presence of his glory forever!

'Most gladly therefore will I rather glory in my infirmities, that the power of Christ may rest upon me' (2 Corinthians 12:9). It is only when we are brought to acknowledge our weakness, infirmity, frailty, nothingness, and insufficiency that the power of Christ and his all sufficient grace rests upon us. The moment we flex our muscles, straighten our backs, lift our chins and say, 'I can do this', we are in trouble.

## Your Mouth

The knowledge of all that the Lord had revealed to him, both by word and by the wonders he performed, and all he had experienced of God's free grace should have made Moses confident, and should have enabled him to overcome his unbelief. Still, rather than upbraiding him, the Lord said, 'I will be your mouth' (vv. 11, 12; Proverbs 16:1; Psalm 124:8; Isaiah 32:4; Jeremiah 1:6-9; Matthew 10:19; Luke 21:15).

He who made man's mouth could fill it with the most commanding eloquence, if such were needed. But our poor, unbelieving hearts place far more confidence in an eloquent tongue than in the One who created it. We want learned, well educated, highly respected preachers, men who are able to present the gospel with intellectual argument and irrefutable logic. Yet, the one man who had such abilities in the New Testament made it his business never to employ them, 'lest the cross of Christ should be made of none effect' (1 Corinthians 1:17-2:5).

## Provoked Anger

Next, we read that Moses provoked the Lord to anger, by his persistent unbelief. 'And he said, O my Lord, send, I pray thee, by the hand of him whom thou wilt send. And the anger of the LORD was kindled against Moses' (vv. 13, 14).

Moses became the meekest of men; but this was not an expression of meekness and humility. Let us ever seek grace to 'be clothed with humility'. But that cannot be called humility which refuses to obey

God's will, walk in the path his hand marks out for us, and do what he has commanded us. Moses' problem was fear; and fear is never identified with true humility, only with the pretence of humility. The fact that Moses provoked the Lord's anger by this makes it clear he was not speaking in humility.

Unbelief is not humility, but pride. It refuses to believe God, because it finds nothing in self to make faith reasonable. That is the utmost expression of pride. If, when God speaks, I refuse to believe, because of something in myself, or the lack of something in myself, I make him a liar (1 John 5:10) When God promises salvation to all who trust his Son, and I refuse to trust him because of anything in me, or the lack of anything in me, I make him a liar. When he declares his unconditional love for me in Christ, and I refuse to believe because I do not deem myself worthy of his love, I make him a liar and exhibit the utmost pride of my heart.

When he asserts his care for me, and bids me cast all my care on him, and I refuse, I make him a liar. Our acceptance with our God is altogether in Christ, because of Christ, and for Christ's sake. It has nothing to do with anything in us, or the lack of anything in us. His mercy, his love, his tender care, his grace, and his protection are all unconditional.

Christ got what I deserved, that I might have what he deserves. It is only when self is set aside that humility begins. Finding redemption, life, righteousness, and salvation in Christ alone, finding grace, mercy, peace, and acceptance with God in him alone, we begin to learn something of humility before God, but not until then. Then, and not until then we begin to sing from our hearts.

'Not unto us, O LORD, not unto us, but unto thy name give glory, for thy mercy, and for thy truth's sake' (Psalm 115:1).

**Gracious Still**
Thank God, Moses' story does not end with the words, 'The anger of the Lord was kindled against Moses'. Though provoked to anger, the Lord God was gracious still, 'and he said, Is not Aaron the Levite thy brother? I know that he can speak well. And also, behold, he cometh forth to meet thee: and when he seeth thee, he will be glad in his heart' (v. 14) 'For he knoweth our frame; he remembereth that we are dust' (Psalm 103:14).

Instead of being the singular voice of God to Israel and the sole instrument of their deliverance, Moses got the 'privilege' of having Aaron's help. Aaron who mocked him because he had married an Ethiopian! Aaron who led Israel to worship the golden calf!

Moses was a highly honoured servant of God. He 'was verily faithful in all his house, as a servant, for a testimony of those things which were to be spoken after' (Hebrews 3:5). And I dare not say more about his failure than God has said. Yet, I cannot say less. Because he refused to believe God, because he provoked the Lord to anger, Moses forfeited the great dignity God had put upon him when he made himself known and made his goodwill known in the bush, because 'the anger of the Lord was kindled against' him.

What a warning this passage ought to be to us! No doubt, the fellowship of a brother is most valuable. 'Two are better than one', whether in labour, rest, or war. The Lord Jesus, in sending forth his disciples, 'sent them two by two', because unity is always better than isolation. Still nothing was gained; there was no greater virtue or efficacy in Aaron's mouth than in Moses', no greater work was done because Aaron accompanied him, and much evil was the result. We are all more ready to trust anything than the Lord our God and his gracious Word! How much we lose by our unbelief! What dignity we forfeit! What evil we cause!

'Thus saith the LORD, thy Redeemer, the Holy One of Israel; I am the LORD thy God which teacheth thee to profit, which leadeth thee by the way that thou shouldest go. O that thou hadst hearkened to my commandments! then had thy peace been as a river, and thy righteousness as the waves of the sea: Thy seed also had been as the sand, and the offspring of thy bowels like the gravel thereof; his name should not have been cut off nor destroyed from before me' (Isaiah 48:17-19).

'The anger of the Lord was kindled against Moses'. But when I read the rest of verse 14 and those following, I cannot help remembering, Paul's words to the Romans. Up to this point, we have been reading about Moses, Moses who represents the law; and from the law we can expect nothing but frustration, failure, and sin. But where sin abounds under the law, grace much more abounds through Christ.

'Moreover the law entered, that the offence might abound. But where sin abounded, grace did much more abound: That as sin hath reigned unto death, even so might grace reign through righteousness unto eternal life by Jesus Christ our Lord' (Romans 5:20, 21).

That is what I see set before us in the Lord God providing Aaron for Moses in verses 14-17.

'And the anger of the LORD was kindled against Moses, and he said, Is not Aaron the Levite thy brother? I know that he can speak well. And also, behold, he cometh forth to meet thee: and when he seeth thee, he will be glad in his heart. And thou shalt speak unto him, and put words in his mouth: and I will be with thy mouth, and with his mouth, and will teach you what ye shall do. And he shall be thy spokesman unto the people: and he shall be, even he shall be to thee instead of a mouth, and thou shalt be to him instead of God. And thou shalt take this rod in thine hand, wherewith thou shalt do signs' (Exodus 4:14-17).

Aaron was Moses' near kinsman, his brother. Christ is our near Kinsman, our Brother. Aaron came to Moses gladly. Christ comes to us gladly. Aaron was Moses' high priest. Christ is our High Priest. Aaron made atonement for Moses. Christ made atonement for us. Aaron was Moses' mediator. Christ is our Mediator. Moses put words of law in Aaron's mouth, and words of grace (Numbers 6:22-27). And the Lord God put both words of law and of grace in the mouth of our Saviour, law to be honoured by him, and grace to be bestowed by him (Psalm 45:1, 2). Aaron could speak well, but not in comparison with our blessed Saviour!

# Chapter 33

# 'I Will Harden Pharaoh's Heart'

'And Moses went and returned to Jethro his father in law, and said unto him, Let me go, I pray thee, and return unto my brethren which are in Egypt, and see whether they be yet alive. And Jethro said to Moses, Go in peace. And the LORD said unto Moses in Midian, Go, return into Egypt: for all the men are dead which sought thy life. And Moses took his wife and his sons, and set them upon an ass, and he returned to the land of Egypt: and Moses took the rod of God in his hand. And the LORD said unto Moses, When thou goest to return into Egypt, see that thou do all those wonders before Pharaoh, which I have put in thine hand: but I will harden his heart, that he shall not let the people go.'
Exodus 4:18-21

The Lord God appeared to Moses in the burning bush and sent him to bring Israel out of Egypt (Exodus 3:1-4:17). In order to accomplish the work he sent him to perform the Lord gave Moses miraculous powers (4:1-9). In addition to those miracles, the Lord promised to send Aaron with him to be his spokesman to Pharaoh. Moses then took his wife, his two sons, and 'the rod of God in his hand', and started toward Egypt. 'And the LORD said unto Moses, when thou goest to return into Egypt, see that thou do all those wonders before Pharaoh, which I have put in thine hand'.

Then the Lord God said, with regard to Pharaoh, 'but I will harden his heart'. And he did so repeatedly. In judgment upon that wicked tyrant, and in great mercy toward his chosen people God hardened Pharaoh with a judicial, penal hardness. Nineteen times in the Book of Exodus the Holy Spirit tells us about the hardening of Pharaoh's heart. Obviously, he intends for us to sit up and pay attention. This is no light thing to consider. Three times we are told that Pharaoh hardened his own heart (Exodus 8:15; 8:32, and Exodus 9:34). Sixteen times his heart is said to have been hardened by just judgment of God (Exodus 4:21; 7:3, 13, 14, 22; 8:19; 9:7, 12, 35; 10:1, 20, 27;11:10; 14:4, 8, 17).

God hardened Pharaoh's heart, giving him up to the hardness of his heart in judicial reprobation (Romans 1:28-32). Giving him no grace, the Lord God left Pharaoh to the corruptions of his own heart and nature and the power of Satan, and sent him strong delusions to believe the lying miracles of his magicians.

How do these things apply to us? What are we to learn from the hardening of Pharaoh's heart? What does the hardening of Pharaoh's heart teach us about ourselves? About our God? About his grace? About his judgment? These are the questions I hope to answer in this chapter.

### Heart of Stone

The very first thing we learn from the picture God the Holy Spirit holds before us in this passage is the fact that the human heart is a heart of stone; dead and hard. How hard the heart of man is since the fall of our father Adam! Our Lord Jesus tells us that the law God gave by the hand of Moses was given because of the hardness of our hearts (Matthew 19:8; Mark 10:5). The heart of man is so hard that the only thing that keeps the unregenerate from performing all the evil in his heart is the utter terror of God's law (1 Timothy 1:8-11). Believers are motivated sweetly and ruled by the love of Christ that constrains them (2 Corinthians 5:14). But the unbeliever's wickedness is checked only by the terror of God's law stamped upon his conscience by divine creation.

Though terrified of God and his wrath, though tormented in his conscience by fear of everlasting damnation, though his very heart is horrified by the thought of hell, so hard is the heart of man that God the Holy Spirit declares that all men by nature treasure up unto themselves wrath against the day of wrath and revelation of the righteous judgment of God, after the hardness and impenitence of their hearts (Romans 2:5).

Nothing can ever change the heart of man except God himself. If ever we are saved, it will be by God the Holy Spirit taking away our hard heart of stone and giving us a new heart by his grace (Ezekiel 11:19; 36:26). In the new birth God gives chosen, redeemed sinners a new heart called, 'an heart of flesh', that is to say, a soft, tender, penitent heart of faith, a sanctified, spiritual heart. This new heart of flesh is the heart of Christ formed in us by the Spirit of God, 'the new man, which after God is created in righteousness and true holiness' (Ephesians 4:24). It is only by this mighty operation of God's efficacious grace that we are enabled to trust the Lord Jesus Christ, and love God and one another. It is only when Christ is revealed in us that our hearts are broken and made new by his grace (Zechariah 10:12).

> My heart, like flint, before your law
> Was hard and would not break;
> But when in Christ I saw your love,
> This heart began to ache.
>
> Though Sinai's wrath, like thunder, rolled
> And terror seized my soul,
> I would not bend my stubborn will
> And yield to your control.
>
> But mercy has my heart subdued,
> Your grace has broken in:
> A bleeding Saviour I have seen,
> And now I hate my sin.

Never was there a clearer picture of man's hardness of heart than that which the Holy Spirit holds before us in the Book of Exodus in Pharaoh, the king of Egypt.

Hard as man's heart is toward all things good, it is a heart that burns with lust and enmity against God. 'Because the carnal mind is enmity against God: for it is not subject to the law of God, neither indeed can be' (Romans 8:7). Nothing more quickly stirs the enmity of man's corrupt, depraved heart against God than the revelation of his righteous judgment and absolute sovereignty. Unless God himself, by his almighty grace, removes the enmity of a man's heart against him, every renewed display of his justice and sovereignty increases the enmity and hardness of his heart.

This fact is set before us in the increasing hardness of Pharaoh's heart by the miracles Moses wrought before him by God's command. Each succeeding miracle was blessed of God to convince the children of Israel that the Lord was about to deliver them from Pharaoh's hand and Egypt's bondage. Yet, Pharaoh and the Egyptians were hardened increasingly by them, becoming more callous to conviction with each miracle Moses performed. So it is to this day. The same heat that melts the wax hardens the clay (Isaiah 6:9; Romans 1:28-32; 9:14-18, 11:5-10; 2 Corinthians 4:3, 4; 2 Thessalonians 2:8-12; Hebrews 3:12, 13).

Like you and me, Pharaoh was born with a heart of stone; hard, cold, and dead. The longer he lived in hardness the harder it became. The more he despised God and his Word, the more his heart was hardened. We read in Exodus 7:14, 'Pharaoh's heart is hardened'. Notice the word 'is' is in italics, it was added by the translators. The text should read, 'Pharaoh's heart hardened'. We see this more clearly in the New King James translation of verse 22. 'Then the magicians of Egypt did so with their enchantments; and Pharaoh's heart grew hard, and he did not heed them, as the LORD had said.'

**Judicial Reprobation**
Now, be sure you learn this. Pharaoh's heart was hardened by God in judgment, in judicial reprobation. It did not simply happen. Because Pharaoh refused to bow to Christ and his Word, as sent to him by his servant Moses, his heart grew hard (Exodus 7:3, 13, 14).

'And I will harden Pharaoh's heart, and multiply my signs and my wonders in the land of Egypt … And he hardened Pharaoh's heart, that he hearkened not unto them; as the LORD had said. And the LORD said unto Moses, Pharaoh's heart is hardened, he refuseth to let the people go.'

Throughout the Scriptures God's judgment is presented to us as coming upon the ungodly because of what they do. His judgment is always a matter of justice. It is never arbitrary, capricious, or without cause. Just as Adam's heart was hardened in spiritual death because of his sin, Pharaoh's heart was hardened because of his unbelief.

Why is this point so important? It is important for two reasons:
First, let it be clearly understood that God is not the author of sin.
'Let no man say when he is tempted, I am tempted of God: for God cannot be tempted with evil, neither tempteth he any man: But every

man is tempted, when he is drawn away of his own lust, and enticed' (James 1:13, 14).

The Lord God did not cause Pharaoh to disobey his Word. The hardening of Pharaoh's heart required no positive action on God's part. All the Lord has to do to harden the hearts of men in reprobation is leave them to the corruption of their nature. If God leaves a sinner alone, he is forever damned! As surely as the removal of the sun would result in the seas being hardened into ice, so the removal of God's grace in Christ results in the hardening of man's heart.

In hardening Pharaoh's heart our Lord did not harden a heart that otherwise might have become soft toward him. Pharaoh's hard-heartedness is emphasized from his first appearance in Scriptures (Exodus 1:8-22). And we are told he continued to harden his own heart (Exodus 8:15, 32), before the Lord hardened it (Exodus 9:12). When the Lord God hardened Pharaoh's heart, he simply gave him what he wanted. He left him to himself. He did not violate Pharaoh's will. Rather, he granted Pharaoh's desire.

Second, this is a matter of tremendous importance, because God still hardens the hearts of those who refuse to bow before his sovereign throne and trust his Son. Pharaoh's heart was hardened as the just penalty of his wilful, obstinate rebellion against the Son of God. God, ever just and true, hardens even to everlasting damnation those who despise him, his word, his law, his gospel, and his Son. Moses' word wrought faith in Israel while hardening Pharaoh's heart. The gospel of free grace in Christ melts the hearts of his elect, and hardens the hearts of all who despise it (Proverbs 29:1; 2 Corinthians 2:14-16).

In other words, if anyone goes to hell it will be his own fault, and his own fault alone. 'For the wages of sin is death; but the gift of God is eternal life through Jesus Christ our Lord' (Romans 6:23; Proverbs 1:23-33).

### God's Purpose
Having said all that, let no one imagine that the hardening of Pharaoh's heart was contrary to the will, purpose, and decree of God. I cannot explain the mysteries of divine predestination, and will not attempt to do so. The secret things belong to God; and I am completely happy to leave secret things secret. But those things that are revealed belong to us. And these things are clearly revealed in the Book of God.

God purposed the fall of the first Adam, that he might show forth the glory of his grace in saving his elect by the last Adam, our Lord Jesus Christ (Romans 5:14-17; 1 Corinthians 15:21, 22, 45). And God raised up Pharaoh and purposed the hardening of his heart that he might show forth the glory of his grace in bringing Israel out of Egypt (Romans 9:14-18), typically showing forth the glory of his grace toward his elect in Christ.

The hardening of Pharaoh's heart and the deliverance of Israel out of Egyptian bondage were precisely according to the sovereign will and purpose of God. And the everlasting ruin of the damned, as well as the everlasting salvation of his elect, is precisely according to the sovereign will and purpose of our God (Romans 11:5-12, 25, 26, 33-36).

**The Method**
How did God harden Pharaoh's heart? As we have already seen, he left Pharaoh to himself. Yet, he did something more. Because Pharaoh refused to receive his Word, and would not receive the love of the truth, the Lord God sent him a strong delusion that he should receive a lie and be damned by it. Every time Moses performed a miracle before Pharaoh, Pharaoh's preachers, his magicians, entertained him with a miracle. We have an obvious and striking parallel to this in the New Testament in 2 Thessalonians 2:7-12. 'For the mystery of iniquity doth already work: only he who now letteth will let, until he be taken out of the way. And then shall that Wicked be revealed, whom the Lord shall consume with the spirit of his mouth, and shall destroy with the brightness of his coming: Even him, whose coming is after the working of Satan with all power and signs and lying wonders, And with all deceivableness of unrighteousness in them that perish; because they received not the love of the truth, that they might be saved. And for this cause God shall send them strong delusion, that they should believe a lie: That they all might be damned who believed not the truth, but had pleasure in unrighteousness.'

God's stated purpose, his plainly revealed design in all that he did with Pharaoh and Egypt was the salvation of his people and the glory of his name (Exodus 6:7; 7:5; 14:4). Even so, God's stated purpose, his plainly revealed design in all things is the salvation of his elect and the glory of his own great name (Ephesians 1:3-14). Just as the Lord God accomplished his purpose in Pharaoh, Egypt, and Israel, getting himself the glory, he is accomplishing his purpose in heaven, earth, and hell. When all things in time are finished, all God's Israel shall be saved, and 'God shall be all in all' (Exodus 14:30, 31; 15:1, 2; 1 Corinthians 15:24-28; Revelation 15:2-4).

## A Difference

But did not the children of Israel harden their hearts repeatedly against the Lord? Indeed, they did, murmuring against his Word, his providence, and his servant again and again. In fact, it appears to me they were even more guilty than Pharaoh. They sinned and hardened their hearts against far greater light than God gave Pharaoh and the Egyptians. Why, then, did God not harden the hearts of the children of Israel? Only one answer can be given; it is the answer God himself has given. 'The LORD doth put a difference between the Egyptians and Israel' (Exodus 11:7).

'For he saith to Moses, I will have mercy on whom I will have mercy, and I will have compassion on whom I will have compassion. So then it is not of him that willeth, nor of him that runneth, but of God that sheweth mercy. For the scripture saith unto Pharaoh, Even for this same purpose have I raised thee up, that I might shew my power in thee, and that my name might be declared throughout all the earth. Therefore hath he mercy on whom he will have mercy, and whom he will he hardeneth' (Romans 9:15-18).

We who believe, whose hearts the Lord God has refused to harden, to whom he has given a new heart and a new spirit, ought never cease to praise him and give thanks to him for his boundless, sovereign, and free grace bestowed upon us in Christ Jesus. The only difference between you and me, and sinners forever damned under the wrath of God's holy justice is the difference grace has made, because 'the LORD doth put a difference between the Egyptians and Israel'. 'For who maketh thee to differ from another? and what hast thou that thou didst not receive? now if thou didst receive it, why dost thou glory, as if thou hadst not received it?' (1 Corinthians 4:7). 'What shall we then say to these things? If God be for us, who can be against us?'

# Chapter 34

# Christ The Firstborn

'And thou shalt say unto Pharaoh, Thus saith the LORD, Israel is my son, even my firstborn.'
(Exodus 4:22)

Here is the authority and power by which a true prophet of God speaks. 'Thus saith the LORD'. This is the first time we find the expression in Holy Scripture. From this point on, throughout the Old Testament, inspired prophets frequently prefaced their declarations with these words. 'Thus saith the LORD.' But this is the first mention of the phrase. With those words, Moses was commanded to declare to Pharaoh that he stood before him as God's ambassador with God's message. God's preachers are men who come with boldness, because they come with the authority of God to proclaim the Word of God.

Here is the name by which God's people are identified: 'Israel'. The name was first given to the patriarch Jacob. It was given to him because, when the Lord wrestled with him and prevailed over him by his mighty grace, he prevailed with the Lord (Genesis 32:28). Israel means 'Prince with God'. It conveys the idea of one who has power with God. Those who are conquered by Christ, over whom grace so prevails that they confess their sin (1 John 1:9), as when Jacob was compelled to confess, 'My name is Jacob', have power, authority with God, and prevail. We are more than conquerors with Christ, in Christ, and by Christ.

Next, the Lord God declares, 'Israel is my son'. With those words, the God of Glory identifies his special relationship with the descendants of Jacob. Specifically, he is here talking about Jacob's physical descendants. He chose Israel from among the nations of the earth and bestowed special privileges and blessings upon them (Deuteronomy 7:6-8; 14:2). But its broader, fuller reference is not to Jacob's physical descendants, but to believing sinners, his spiritual descendants, 'the Israel of God' (Galatians 6:16; Romans 9:4-8).

And there is a definite reference here to our Lord Jesus Christ. When the Lord God said, 'Israel is my Son', he was not just talking about his covenant people; he was talking about the Lord Jesus Christ. We know this is the case because the Holy Spirit tells us so in Hosea 11:1 and when we compare Matthew 2:15. Hosea and Matthew tell us that when God said, 'Israel is my son', he was not talking about the nation of Israel, or even his elect alone. He was talking about the Lord Jesus Christ, our Saviour, that baby boy brought up from Egypt by Joseph. He was telling us the man Christ Jesus is God the Son.

This is the message God gave Moses to declare to Pharaoh. Indeed, this is the message God gives to every man who is his ambassador among men, the message God's servants must proclaim to all men everywhere throughout the ages. 'Israel is my Son, even my Firstborn'. Israel typified Christ, here said to be God's Firstborn, that One man who is 'above all people that are upon the face of the earth' (Deuteronomy 7:6). The Word of God has much to say of Christ the Firstborn, as typified in Israel and throughout the Old Testament.

**God's Purpose**
In all things the triune God has purposed and determined that his Son, the Lord Jesus Christ, have preeminence as the God-man Mediator, the Saviour of his people. Therefore, he is declared to be 'the firstborn'. The Holy Spirit tells us that God's purpose in saving his elect is that his Son, the Lord Jesus Christ, 'might be the firstborn among many brethren' (Romans 8:28, 29). We read in Colossians chapter one that our Saviour 'is the image of the invisible God, the firstborn from the dead ... the head of the body, the church: the beginning, the firstborn from the dead; that in all things he might have the preeminence'. And in Hebrews 12:23 the church of God is called 'the church of the firstborn'. The Lord our God is determined that his Son, our Saviour,

the Lord Jesus Christ, be exalted and have all preeminence as his Firstborn. He says, 'Also I will make him my firstborn, higher than the kings of the earth' (Psalm 89:27).

## Old Testament Types

Throughout the Old Testament, the preeminence of our Lord Jesus Christ as our Saviour is typified as the first, the firstborn, the firstfruits, and the firstlings of the flock, and of the herd. Indeed, everything recorded in the Old Testament foreshadows him who is the Alpha and the Omega, the First and the Last, and the Sum and Substance of all things in the salvation of his people (Luke 24:25-27, 44). There is nothing in the Book of God that does not speak of our all-glorious Christ, nothing that does not, in one way or another, set forth his supremacy, excellence, and glory as God our Saviour. Nowhere is this fact more evident than in those passages dealing with the firstborn.

The firstborn symbolized a father's strength, 'the excellency of dignity and the excellency of power' (Genesis 49:3). In that awesome night, when the Lord God slew the firstborn of man and beast among the Egyptians (Exodus 12:29), he claimed the firstborn of man and beast in Israel as his own, requiring they be sanctified to him (Exodus 13:2).

## The Difference

It was God himself, and God alone who put a difference between the firstborn in Egypt and the firstborn in Israel that night. We are taught by the Spirit of God that everything on that passover night was typical of Christ, who as 'our Passover was sacrificed for us' (1 Corinthians 5:7). The sprinkling of the blood of the lamb of the first year, without blemish, and without spot, on the houses of the Israelites, was the one thing that put a difference between the firstborn of Israel and the firstborn of Egypt. The blood of the lamb alone saved Israel's firstborn from destruction. This we are plainly told in Exodus 11:7.

As it was on that great night of judgment and mercy, so the year of Christ's redeemed is both the day of vengeance and the day of salvation (Isaiah 63:3-5). When the Son of God died as our Substitute upon the cursed tree he bore all the vengeance of God's holy wrath for us to the full satisfaction of divine justice, and obtained eternal redemption and salvation for us (Hebrews 9:12). At the same time, he declares, 'The day of vengeance is in my heart'. Yet, there is a day, appointed and fixed by him, when our God will execute judgment upon his enemies, as well as mercy upon his people (Acts 17:31; 2 Corinthians 5:10; Revelation 20:11-15.

## The Birthright
The birthright belonged to the firstborn among the children of Israel, and gave him preeminence in the family. To him belonged the right of priesthood (Numbers 3:12, 13, 40-45; 8:15-18). The firstborn was given a double portion among his brethren (Deuteronomy 21:17). And to the firstborn it was promised, 'Thou art he whom thy brethren shall praise: thy hand shall be in the neck of thine enemies; thy father's children shall bow down before thee' (Genesis 49:8). All these Old Testament declarations were intended to show the majesty of Christ as 'the firstborn among many brethren'. All the offerings required of God for every male that opened the womb pointed to our Lord Jesus (Exodus 13:2; 34:19, 20; Leviticus 12:6; Luke 2:21-24).

## Opens the Womb
Robert Hawker suggested that the Scriptures, when speaking of 'the firstborn that openeth the womb', must have been prophetic of the virgin birth of our Saviour. 'For strictly and properly speaking, none but the Lord Jesus ever did open the womb ... In every other instance, from the creation of the world, as anatomists well know, it is accomplished at the time of conception.'

Our blessed Saviour, 'the firstborn', was conceived in Mary's virgin womb by the overshadowing power of God the Holy Spirit. He opened Mary's virgin womb when he came forth from it to accomplish our redemption. Thus, throughout the Levitical dispensation, the firstborn of man and beast directed the eye of faith to him whom the triune God appointed to have everlasting preeminence as 'the firstborn'. In all things it is, was, and forever shall be the will of the eternal God that Christ have preeminence as the God-man, our Mediator and Redeemer.

## Firstborn Redeemed
Yet, the law of God required redemption of the firstborn among the children of Israel (Numbers 18:15, 16). The firstborn was brought to the priest, along with 'five shekels, after the shekel of the sanctuary'. The priest received the child in the name of the Lord as his own. Then,

the priest returned the child to the care of its parents; but it belonged to the Lord. All the firstborn had to be redeemed. And we who are called 'the church of the firstborn' had to be redeemed to our God by the blood of Christ, either redeemed or killed.

However, the firstborn of the Levites were not redeemed (Numbers 1:47, 48; 3:12, 13). Why was this exemption made? Why did God require that the firstborn of the Levites not be redeemed? Because the Levites represented Christ our Redeemer; and he, who is our Redeemer, did not need to be redeemed. Though our Saviour came, as a man, from the tribe of Judah, the Levites, being chosen as the priestly tribe, portrayed the whole election of grace as a people holy and accepted in the Beloved, 'a kingdom of priests' and 'a chosen generation, a royal priesthood, an holy nation, a peculiar people', redeemed and called in Christ (Exodus 19:6; 1 Peter 2:9). And the whole Levitical priesthood typified Christ our Priest and Mediator, whom God took in the stead of his firstborn ones. The Redeemer need not be redeemed.

**Fulfilled in Christ**
The law of God distinguished a man's firstborn in all these ways. While these distinctions were to be observed ceremonially throughout the Mosaic dispensation, they are all gloriously accomplished in Christ, the Firstborn. Let me show you how.

The firstborn was considered 'the beginning of his [father's] strength' (Deuteronomy 21:17; Genesis 49:3; Psalm 78:51). The firstborn was particularly near and dear to his father. So the Lord Jesus Christ, as the God-man Mediator, because of his accomplishments as the Firstborn, is precious in God's sight and beloved of the Father (John 10:17; Proverbs 8:22, 30; Matthew 3:17; Hebrews 1:9).

The firstborn was consecrated to the service of God (Exodus 13:1, 2, 12). It was because he was consecrated to God that the firstborn had to be redeemed (Exodus 13:13; 34:20). Israel was 'redeemed from the house of bondage, from the hand of Pharaoh', because they were, typically, Jehovah's firstborn (Deuteronomy 7:8; Exodus 15:13), and were consecrated to the service of God (Exodus 19:1-6; Romans 9:4). The priestly duties of the firstborn were transferred to the Levites (who ceremonially and typically became the tribe of the firstborn) in Numbers 3. The Levitical priesthood typified that of our Saviour (Hebrews 8-10), whose priesthood is the priesthood of God's Firstborn.

The firstborn received a double portion of his father's estate (Deuteronomy 21:17; 2 Kings 2:9). All nations and people receive a goodly portion from our Father, in that he bestows physical blessings upon them (Matthew 5:45). But God's Israel has been doubly blessed, not only with physical blessings, but also with 'all spiritual blessings' in Christ (Ephesians 1:3). We have received of the Lord's hand double for all our sins (Isaiah 40:2). Our Lord Jesus, the Firstborn, is gloriously blessed. The Father has given all things to the Son, 'whom he has appointed heir of all things' (Hebrews 1:2). Truly, we who are 'the church of the firstborn' are given the double portion of the firstborn in Christ. We are heirs of God and joint-heirs with Christ (Romans 8:17).

The firstborn could never be deprived of his birthright (Deuteronomy 21:15-17). Christ the Firstborn will never be deprived of his birthright (Psalm 2:8; 1 Corinthians 15:24-28; Revelation 11:15). And God's Israel, the firstborn nation of his elect (Romans 11:1-5), the church of the firstborn, who are grafted into and made one with Christ (Romans 11:13-26), will never be deprived of its birthright (Exodus 19:5-16 and 1 Peter 2:9, 10).

The firstborn succeeded his father as head of the family (2 Chronicles 21:3). The Lord our God, by reason of his eternality, will never be succeeded, yet he nevertheless has appointed Christ his Son, his Firstborn, to be head of the nations, 'a special treasure above all the people that are upon the face of the earth' (Deuteronomy 7:6). He has appointed Christ to be Head over his family the church (Ephesians 3:14-22; 5:23), and the Head over 'every man' (1 Corinthians 11:3), the Head over 'all principality and power' (Colossians 2:10), the Head over 'all creation' (Colossians 1:15), even the Head over 'all things' forever and ever, to the praise of his glory (Ephesians 1:22).

'Christ', the Firstborn, 'is the end of the law for righteousness to everyone that believeth' (Romans 10:4). May God graft you into Christ, his Firstborn, giving you faith in him, that you may be counted his firstborn with Israel his Son, his Firstborn! As God destroyed Egypt, and many nations since, for not honouring His Firstborn, so he will destroy all who refuse to honour his Son, his Firstborn, the Lord Jesus Christ. Honour him by trusting him, even as the Father has trusted him with all things from eternity; and God will honour you with everlasting life before him. If you refuse to trust him, God will destroy you with everlasting destruction in hell.

# Chapter 35

# How Important Is Obedience?

'And it came to pass by the way in the inn, that the LORD met him, and sought to kill him. Then Zipporah took a sharp stone, and cut off the foreskin of her son, and cast it at his feet, and said, Surely a bloody husband art thou to me. So he let him go: then she said, A bloody husband thou art, because of the circumcision. And the LORD said to Aaron, Go into the wilderness to meet Moses. And he went, and met him in the mount of God, and kissed him. And Moses told Aaron all the words of the LORD who had sent him, and all the signs which he had commanded him. And Moses and Aaron went and gathered together all the elders of the children of Israel: And Aaron spake all the words which the LORD had spoken unto Moses, and did the signs in the sight of the people. And the people believed: and when they heard that the LORD had visited the children of Israel, and that he had looked upon their affliction, then they bowed their heads and worshipped.'
Exodus 4:24-31

How important is obedience? Is it really necessary for you and me to obey God in the details of our lives? Since we are saved by grace alone, justified freely through the blood of Christ, and assured that God will not impute sin to those who trust his Son, is it really necessary for us to obey God?

Turn to Exodus 4 and you will find the answer to that question. Having been called of God to go down to Egypt to deliver his people from the oppressive bondage of Pharaoh, Moses took his wife and his two sons and started for Egypt. Along the way they stopped at an inn to rest for the night. 'And it came to pass by the way in the inn, that the LORD met him, and sought to kill him. Then Zipporah took a sharp stone, and cut off the foreskin of her son, and cast it at his feet, and said, Surely a bloody husband art thou to me. So he let him go: then she said, A bloody husband thou art, because of the circumcision' (vv. 24-26). I think it is safe to say, God requires obedience in his children!

### Saved Man

Let me begin by showing that Moses was a saved man, a true believer, a child of God. The Holy Spirit tells us in Hebrews 11 that he was already a believer before he slew the Egyptian and fled from Egypt. Indeed, his slaying the Egyptian and his deliberate rejection of the throne of Egypt were acts of faith (Hebrews 11:24-26).

The Lord God revealed himself to Moses in the burning bush in his great redemptive name Jehovah (Exodus 3:2-14), and revealed his purpose of grace and redemption toward his afflicted people. Without question, Moses was already a believer. He was righteous and justified in Christ; pardoned, forgiven, and sanctified by faith in the blood of the Lamb, the Seed of the woman, the same Lord Jesus Christ, who spoke to him out of the bush. I stress this fact, because I do not want there to be any mistake about Moses. He was a child of God. My point is this: God's people in this world, though complete in Christ, are sinners still.

None who know the grace of God by experience need proof of that sad fact. In the disposition and direction of his life Moses walked by faith and was obedient to God. This is true of all who are born of God. Believers walk with God! Yet, this man Moses was not without sin.

The Word of God speaks plainly about the sins of even the most eminent saints. It never seeks to conceal the faults of God's people. Why? These things are not revealed in the Book of God to make us think less of God's saints than we would if we were not informed of their sins. God the Holy Spirit shows us the sins of the most eminent among his saints in this world to teach us salvation is by grace alone, ever reminding us the whole of our acceptance with God is in Christ, our Substitute, to keep us looking to Christ, and to keep us from being proud, self-righteous, and severe in dealing with our fallen brethren.

## Called of God

Not only was he a saved man, Moses had been called, equipped, and sent of God to do a great work (Exodus 4:18-23). God called him, saying, 'I will send thee unto Pharaoh, that thou mayest bring forth my people' (3:10). Moses knew his inability for the work of a prophet, much less a deliverer, so the Lord God assured him of his presence and his success (3:11, 12). Then, he gave Moses special powers from heaven to authenticate him as one sent of God (4:1-9).

When God sends a man to do a work for him, he will equip him and demonstrate his power in him. And every man sent of God is sent with a message. So God gave Moses a message. 'And thou shalt say unto Pharaoh, Thus saith the LORD, Israel is my son, even my firstborn: And I say unto thee, Let my son go, that he may serve me: and if thou refuse to let him go, behold, I will slay thy son, even thy firstborn' (4:22, 23). The message with which Moses was sent was a message of grace to his people. 'Israel is my son'. It was a message of judgment to Pharaoh and Egypt. 'I will slay thy son, even thy firstborn.' And it was a message proclaiming redemption by the Lord God. 'I will bring them out of Egypt' (Zechariah 10:10).

## Moses' Sin

Moses had taken Zipporah, his wife, and his sons, Gershom and Eliezer, and started out for Egypt in obedience to God's command. But Moses was guilty of a great evil, a terrible evil against his God and Saviour. It may be that Moses thought it really did not matter whether or not he circumcised his son. I say that because he appears to have circumcised one of his boys, but did not circumcise the other. He knew that it was the will of God for him to circumcise his sons. He simply chose not to do it. But the evil began much earlier. After leaving Egypt, Moses had married a Midianite wife. Midianites were the descendants of Ishmael. Moses had taken a wife from those who were not the people of God. That was in itself a shameful thing.

Though Moses was in a strange land, he should have restrained himself from taking a pagan woman to be his wife. No doubt he convinced himself that circumstances made his choice justifiable, if not necessary; but he knew better. The wrath of God had once been provoked against the earth for this great sin (Genesis 6:2). Such an unequal yoke of a believer to an unbeliever begins with compromise, and can only be continued with compromise, unless God is pleased to save the unbeliever (2 Corinthians 6:14, 15). Those who believe on the Lord Jesus Christ are free to marry whom they will, but 'only in the Lord' (1 Corinthians 7:39).

This passage, if I understand it correctly, makes it obvious that the reason Moses had neglected his known duty was the fact that he was married to Zipporah. Their firstborn son, Gershom, had apparently been circumcised when he was eight days old, as God required; but Zipporah despised the ordinance of God as a needlessly painful and bloody rite. She appears to have been a fiery, hot-tempered woman, who got what she wanted by tantrums and fits. And Moses simply caved in to her. But in trying to please Zipporah, he greatly displeased the Lord.

Let this man Moses be a beacon of warning to us all. We must each carefully watch his own heart. We must not allow our fondness for anyone, or our relationship with anyone keep us from obedience to our Lord. Eli honoured his sons more than he honoured God (1 Samuel 2:29). So God killed his sons. Moses in this area showed more fear for Zipporah than for God. So the Lord sought to kill him. If we would follow Christ, our earthly relations must be given no consideration when it comes to obedience (Matthew 10:36-38).

Moses had been obedient in many things. He had followed Christ, regardless of cost or consequence. He was now on his way to meet Pharaoh, king of Egypt, armed with nothing but the promise of God. But there was this one area where he was not in obedience to his Master, one matter in which he had not yet surrendered to the rule of Christ. He had not circumcised his son, Eliezer, because he wanted to please Zipporah more than he wanted to please the Lord. This issue had to be settled. Our Lord demands absolute and universal surrender. He will not allow us to pick and choose what we will give him, what we will do for him, or what we will surrender to him.

### Sought to Kill
This was such a serious matter that the Lord sought to kill Moses because of his sin (v. 24). We are not told how the Lord sought to kill him. And we are not told that Zipporah was even aware of what was going on between God and Moses. Maybe she was. Maybe she was not. But Moses knew what was going on. God met him at his point of rebellion and said, 'Before you make another move we are going to

settle this issue. You will either bow to me and obey me, or I will kill you right here!' God's displeasure was revealed against Moses, not Zipporah, because the worship, discipline, and direction of his family were Moses' responsibility. He was the head of the house, not Zipporah.

It is not unusual for a man to be united to a woman who opposes him at every step as he seeks to lead his family in the worship and service of Christ, and seeks to maintain discipline and rule over his children. But that does not absolve him of his responsibility. Zipporah's wickedness was no excuse for Moses' disobedience. Before Moses would be allowed to go on to be God's spokesman and representative to his people, he was required to set his own house in order. No man can be allowed to undertake the rule and government of God's house who does not rule his own house (1 Timothy 3:1-4).

The neglect of any known duty is as great an evil in God's sight as the commission of any transgression. 'Behold, to obey is better than sacrifice, and to hearken than the fat of rams' (1 Samuel 15:16-22). There are sins of omission as well as sins of commission. If I fail to do that which I know is the will of God, I have sinned against my God, just as surely as if I had committed adultery, murder, or even an act of base idolatry. Any time I fail to do something I know God would have me do, the cause is pride, covetousness, and unbelief. It would cost me something I am not willing to give. If that is the case, there is an idol somewhere in my heart that must be torn out, a rebel lurking in my soul that must be destroyed, some realm of my life that is not brought into subjection to Christ. Whatever it is, that is to me a point of rebellion; and that is the place where God will cross my path. Surrender to Christ is not a once-for-all act. It goes on as long as we live in this world. Whatever comes up between me and my God must be slain.

The Lord God takes notice of and is displeased with the sins of his people. Thank God, he has forgiven our sins and removed them from us as far as the east is from the west, through the blood of Christ. We rejoice to know we are so fully forgiven in Christ that our God will never impute sin to one who trusts his Son. In a judicial sense, we shall never be charged with or punished for sin. But God, as our heavenly Father, is grieved by the sins of his people. As a grieved Father, full of love, he takes his rod to correct his erring children (Hebrews 12:5-11).

If we behave as rebels, we will hear about it. Our heavenly Father will not allow his children to live in rebellion to him. He will sharply reprove our consciences by his Word and his Spirit. If we persist in disobedience, he will chasten us in providence.

In this place we are plainly told 'the Lord sought to kill' Moses. I will leave it to others to argue about how we are to relate this to God's absolute purpose in predestination to deliver Israel out of Egypt by the hand of Moses. Moses knew more about that than any of us. He was there when God revealed himself and revealed his purpose. But Moses, who wrote these words, and his wife Zipporah were both convinced 'that the LORD met him (in the inn), and sought to kill him'. Rolfe Barnard once said, 'The only way God will ever kill a Christian is when he is done with him, or when he gets in his way.' And he was right. Disobedience to Christ is a serious matter!

## Costly, but Necessary

After God met him and sought to kill him, Moses repented. He now did what he had refused to do before. Moses' obedience to the Lord was very costly, but absolutely necessary. Moses knew God meant business. He knew he had been wrong. Therefore, he quickly circumcised his son. He surrendered to his Master. Actually, Zipporah did the act. Either Moses was physically incapable of doing it because the Lord sought to kill him, or he assumed the reins of his house and commanded his wife to do it. Either way, Zipporah did the act, and the Lord God spared Moses' life, because he was now obedient.

His obedience was immediate. Eliezer must be circumcised, then and there, even if it must be done with a rock (a piece of flint). Moses' life depended on it, because God's honour depended on it. Someone once said, 'Understanding can wait; obedience cannot.'

I repeat, it was Zipporah, not Moses, who performed the act of circumcising their son. But she did it because Moses now demanded she do it. She appears to have been as much opposed to it now as she had been before. When she had finished, she took the boy's foreskin, threw it down at Moses' feet, and said, 'Surely a bloody husband art thou to me!'

Moses' obedience was costly, very costly. When this thing was over, the rift between Moses and Zipporah was so strong, that he was compelled to send her, with their two sons, back to Midian to stay with her father Jethro, until he had done what God sent him to do. We know that, because we read in Exodus 18:1-6 that Jethro brought her and her two sons back to Moses in the wilderness, where he was camped at the Mount of God, after he heard 'that the Lord had brought Israel out of Egypt'. Moses faced the fact that Zipporah would be a constant hindrance to him. And he knew he could not relinquish God's commission. Therefore, he sent her back home. Contending with Pharaoh and with Israel would be enough. He did not want to have to go home every night and contend with Zipporah. He did not divorce her. He did not cease to provide for and care for her. He simply resolved he could not allow her and the boys to keep him from obeying God. Once Israel was out of Egypt, Moses sent for his family again.

**Moses Bowed**
Once Moses bowed to the will of God, God let him go and greatly used him for the good of his people and the glory of his own great name. When Moses bowed to the will of God, he escaped the rod and the sword, and found himself once again in sweet fellowship with his Father. When he was reconciled to God, God showed himself merciful. It was the grace of God that subdued Moses' heart; but God did not show himself gracious until Moses' was subdued.

Once his rebellion was broken, though his obedience cost him much heartache and pain, the Lord proved himself gracious. Moses was now alone in the wilderness, going back to Egypt just like he had gone out, with nothing but faith in God. Then the Lord sent his brother, Aaron, whom he had not seen in forty years, to meet him and cheer him. 'And the LORD said to Aaron, Go into the wilderness to meet Moses. And he went, and met him in the mount of God, and kissed him. And Moses told Aaron all the words of the LORD who had sent him, and all the signs which he had commanded him' (vv. 27, 28). The cheek God burns with tears from one quarter, he soothes with kisses from another.

Moses and Aaron came to Israel to declare what God had determined to do. 'And Moses and Aaron went and gathered together all the elders of the children of Israel: And Aaron spake all the words which the LORD had spoken unto Moses, and did the signs in the sight of the people. And the people believed: and when they heard that the LORD had visited the children of Israel, and that he had looked upon their affliction, then they bowed their heads and worshipped' (vv. 29-31).

What a story they had for the poor, oppressed people of God. Their message to Israel was good news, the gospel of deliverance by God.

301

And, 'when they heard that the Lord had visited the children of Israel and that he had looked upon their affliction', they believed. Believing, they bowed before the Lord, surrendered to him, and worshipped in praise, adoration, thanksgiving, and hope.

## Do It

Do you remember what Mary said to those servants who stood before the Lord Jesus at the wedding feast in Cana? 'Whatsoever he saith unto you, do it' (John 2:5). That is the message of this passage to us. 'Whatsoever he saith unto you, do it.' Consult not with flesh and blood, just do it. And 'whatsoever thy hand findeth to do, do it with thy might', for the glory of God. Moses brought Israel out of Egypt. Failure is an impossibility to obedience to God. All heaven waits to help anyone who knows God's will and does it.

Obedience to Christ is essential. True, saving faith is always accompanied by obedience. Our Lord Jesus both demands and deserves that obedience be universal. Salvation begins with surrender to Christ, bowing to him as Lord; and he constantly demands surrender. He never relinquishes his rule. Let us never despise the will of God. Let us never be hardened against the direction of God's Spirit (Ephesians 4:30).

O God, my Saviour, will you graciously hold my heart and soul in compliance with your will! Allow nothing and no one to keep me from following and obeying you.

If we obey God, we will often meet with much opposition, even from those who are dearest to us. We will be misunderstood. Our actions will be misrepresented. Our motives will be misjudged, just as Joseph was misjudged by his brothers, Moses was opposed by Zipporah, David was despised by Michal, and our Saviour was misunderstood by his kinsmen. But displeasing men is nothing compared to displeasing and dishonouring him who loved us and gave himself for us.

'Whatsoever he saith unto you, do it.' When God calls you to do anything in the service of Christ and his kingdom, put away everything that might hinder you. 'Let the dead bury their dead'. And send Zipporah back to Midian! 'Whatsoever he saith unto you, do it.'

# Chapter 36

## How Is Deliverance Accomplished?

'And it came to pass by the way in the inn, that the LORD met him, and sought to kill him. Then Zipporah took a sharp stone, and cut off the foreskin of her son, and cast it at his feet, and said, Surely a bloody husband art thou to me. So he let him go: then she said, A bloody husband thou art, because of the circumcision. And the LORD said to Aaron, Go into the wilderness to meet Moses. And he went, and met him in the mount of God, and kissed him. And Moses told Aaron all the words of the LORD who had sent him, and all the signs which he had commanded him. And Moses and Aaron went and gathered together all the elders of the children of Israel: And Aaron spake all the words which the LORD had spoken unto Moses, and did the signs in the sight of the people. And the people believed: and when they heard that the LORD had visited the children of Israel, and that he had looked upon their affliction, then they bowed their heads and worshipped.'
Exodus 4:24-31

The Scriptures instruct us in the gospel by prophecy, by type, and by illustration. The Old Testament gives us the prophetic and typical revelation of the gospel. In the Gospel narratives our Lord Jesus declared the gospel and illustrated it by numerous parables. In the Book of Acts and the New Testament Epistles, God the Holy Spirit expounds the things of Christ to us by the inspired writings of the Apostles.

Using the typical deliverance of Israel out of Egyptian bondage, I want to show you God's method of grace as it is set before us throughout the Book of God. On his way to Egypt, God met Moses in an inn and sought to kill him, because he had not circumcised one of his sons. 'Then Zipporah took a sharp stone, and cut off the foreskin of her son, and cast it at his feet, and said, surely a bloody husband art thou to me. So he let him go: then she said, a bloody husband thou art, because of the circumcision.'

Here we are given a clear, instructive picture of how the deliverance of our souls is accomplished, a picture of God's method of grace toward sinners. I want to show you seven things in this passage that are essential to the salvation of our souls.

**A Gracious God**
Salvation begins with a gracious God. Salvation starts with the will of God, who declares, 'I will have mercy on whom I will have mercy'. Indeed, everything begins with the will of God. Israel went into Egypt according to the will of God. They remained there 400 years according to the will of God. And they were delivered from Egypt according to the will of God. Indeed, that is exactly how God the Holy Spirit explains this whole affair, applying it to the salvation of our souls in Romans 9:8-24. Salvation begins with God's will and his eternal purpose and covenant of grace to sinners in Christ, in election and in predestination (Ephesians 1:3-7; 2 Thessalonians 2:13, 14; Psalm 65:4).

**A Blood Sacrifice**
But the will of God in election and predestination is not all there is to salvation. The second thing required for the salvation of our souls is a blood sacrifice, the bloody sacrifice of our Lord Jesus Christ. It is written, 'Without shedding of blood is no remission' (Hebrews 9:22).

If we could have been saved without the sacrifice of God's Son, we would have been. Christ did not die for nothing. He died in our place upon the cursed tree because there was no other way God could save us. Justice must be satisfied; and the only way justice could be satisfied and mercy extended was by the sacrifice of Christ (Romans 3:25, 26).

This necessity of a blood sacrifice is portrayed in verses 24-26 in our passage by the rite of circumcision. Moses could not deliver Israel from Egypt until the sentence of death had experimentally passed upon him. He must have the sentence of death inscribed by the hand of God upon his nature. Sinful nature must be punished.

Paul wrote, 'We had the sentence of death in ourselves, that we should not trust in ourselves, but in God which raiseth the dead' (2 Corinthians 1:9). Every servant of God knows something about this. Moses was about to declare this solemn message to Pharaoh. 'Thus saith the Lord, Israel is my son, even my firstborn: and I say unto thee, Let my son go, that he may serve me: and if thou refuse to let him go, behold I will slay thy son, even thy firstborn.' His message to Pharaoh was a message of death, a message of judgment. At the same time, his message to Israel was a message of life and salvation. But the man who will speak on God's behalf of death and judgment, and life and salvation must experience these things in his own soul.

That is what Moses experienced here. 'And it came to pass, by the way in the inn, that the Lord met him, and sought to kill him. Then Zipporah took a sharp stone, and cut off the foreskin of her son, and cast it at his feet, and said, surely a bloody husband art thou to me. So he let him go: then she said, a bloody husband thou art, because of the circumcision'. It is evident that up to this point, Zipporah had shrunk from the application of the knife to that around which the affections of nature were entwined. She had avoided that mark which had to be set in the flesh of every member of the Israel of God. She was not aware that her relationship with Moses was one involving death to nature. She recoiled from the cross. This was natural. But Moses had yielded to her in the matter; and that explains this scene 'in the inn'. If Zipporah refused to circumcise her son, the Lord God was going to kill her husband. If Moses allowed the feelings of his wife to prevent him from circumcising his son, the Lord God was determined to kill him. The sentence of death must be written upon everything about our lives.

Zipporah is an instructive picture of the Church. She was married and united to Moses; but their union could not be complete until she was reconciled to him by blood. He must be made 'a bloody husband' to her. So it is with us. Though espoused, married, and united to Christ from eternity, we must be conformed to his death, and conformed to him in his death (Philippians 3:10). We must mortify our members which are on the earth, take up the cross daily, and follow him. Our relationship with Christ is founded upon blood, and the manifestation of that relationship, necessarily, involves death to nature.

'And ye are complete in him, which is the head of all principality and power: In whom also ye are circumcised with the circumcision made without hands, in putting off the body of the sins of the flesh by the circumcision of Christ: Buried with him in baptism, wherein also ye are risen with him through the faith of the operation of God, who hath raised him from the dead' (Colossians 2:10-12).

The sin atoning, blood sacrifice of our Lord Jesus Christ on the cross is that 'circumcision made without hands, in putting off the body of the sins of the flesh by the circumcision of Christ', by which the filth of our flesh, 'the body of the sins of the flesh', have been put away. In him, by his blood, we have the perfect remission of sin. We are made the righteousness of God in him, given complete acceptance, everlasting security, and full fellowship with Christ in all his glory. In a word 'Ye are complete in him.'

Nothing can be added to one who is 'complete in him'. Can 'vain philosophy', 'the tradition of men', 'the rudiments of the world', 'meats, drinks, holy days, new moons', 'Sabbaths', 'touch not' this, 'taste not' that, 'handle not' the other, 'the commandments and doctrines of men', 'days and months, and times, and years', can any of these things, or all of them together, add anything to one God has pronounced 'complete in him'? By no means!

This completeness by our 'Bloody Husband', the Lord Jesus Christ, is not something for which we must diligently strive. No, it is the present and everlasting portion of every believer. The very weakest saint is included in the apostolic 'ye'. All the people of God 'are complete' in Christ. The apostle does not say, 'ye will be', 'ye may be', 'hope that ye may be', or 'pray that ye may be'. No, he says, by God the Holy Spirit, in the most absolute and unqualified way possible, 'Ye are complete in him'! That is the starting point of faith and the end.

Some may ask, 'Are you saying we have no sin, no imperfection, no failure?' Of course not. 'If we say that we have no sin, we deceive ourselves, and the truth is not in us' (1 John 1:8). We have sin in us, but no sin on us. Our standing before God is not in ourselves, but in Christ. It is 'in him' that we 'are complete'. God says the believer in Christ is one with Christ, and exactly as Christ. This is our changeless condition, our everlasting standing in grace.

'The body of the sins of the flesh' has been 'put off by the circumcision of Christ'. The believer is not in the flesh, though the flesh is in us. We are united to Christ in the power of a new and an endless life; and that life is inseparably connected with the righteousness of God in which we stand before him 'accepted in the Beloved'. The Lord Jesus has put away everything that was against us; and he has brought us nigh unto God, in the self-same favour as that which he himself enjoys. Thus, Horatius Bonar could write,

> Near, so very near to God,
> Nearer I cannot be;
> For, in the person of His Son,
> I am as near as He!

In a word, Christ is our righteousness. That fact settles every question, answers every objection, silences every doubt. As it is written, 'Both he that sanctifieth and they who are sanctified, are all of one' (Hebrews 2:11).

Until we have the sentence of death passed in us in the experience of grace, until Christ becomes 'a bloody husband to us', we know nothing about these things. But once we experience in our souls 'the circumcision made without hands, in putting off the body of the sins of the flesh by the circumcision of Christ ... wherein also we are risen with him through the faith of the operation of God', we are brought out of Egypt's darkness and bondage, and made to experience freedom from sin, guilt and death in Christ (1 Peter 4:1-3).

## A Revealing Prophet

Third, this sweet experience of grace comes to us by a revealing Prophet. Moses was that prophet of God who typified our Lord Jesus Christ in his prophetic office, the Prophet of whom Moses said, 'unto him ye shall hearken' (Deuteronomy 18:15-18). Christ is that Prophet who has made known the will of God to us, without whom we could never know God or his will (John 1:14-18).

It is the clear teaching of the Word of God that our Lord Jesus Christ has a three-fold office: Prophet, Priest, and King. While others, as types of Christ, have held one, or perhaps two, of these offices, no one has ever been prophet, priest, and king except Christ. How good and gracious the Lord is to send among us so great a Prophet as the Son of God, Emmanuel, 'God with us' (Matthew 1:23; 17:5). He is a Prophet like no other. He came from heaven and is above all, having the Spirit without measure, fulfilling what others only talked about, declaring the whole counsel of God, and bringing life and immortality to light through his gospel (John 3:31-35; 2 Timothy 1:8-10). Without Christ as our Prophet, we would yet sit in darkness and be left to stumble in blindness (2 Corinthians 4:3-6). But his words are true and faithful; and to hear him is to hear God (John 12:48-50; Hebrews 1:1, 2).

How blessed are those who hear and believe him (John 5:24). God declares, 'I will put my words in his mouth' (John 7:16; 8:28; 17:6-8). His words are the words of life, not just true facts about God and the kingdom of heaven. When he speaks, sinners live (John 5:21, 24; James 1:18; 1 Peter 1:23), even as he spoke and Lazarus came forth. His words are the words of truth (John 1:14-17; 14:6; 18:37). His words are the words of grace. He is full of grace and truth. His words bring peace, pardon, life, and salvation from sin. Christ is that Prophet who came that we might have life, and have it more abundantly. If any man hear his words and believe on him, he shall never die (John 8:51; 14:23, 24).

**A Mediating Priest**
Fourth, we cannot be saved without a mediating priest; and that Priest, who is the God-man, our Mediator, is the Lord Jesus Christ, typically portrayed in Aaron, the High Priest of Israel. You will notice that Aaron, the mediating priest, met Moses, who symbolizes the law of God in Mount Horeb, and kissed him (v. 27).

That is what the Lord Jesus Christ did for us. He met God's law, magnified it, and made it honourable at Calvary. There Mercy met Justice, and kissed each other. Upon the basis of his finished work at Calvary, he mediates between God and men. He speaks to God for us and speaks to us for God (Hebrews 7:25; 1 John 2:1, 2).

**A Preached Gospel**
Still, something more is required. Deliverance must be proclaimed. Israel did not come out of Egypt until Moses and Aaron, symbolically the Law of God and the Priest of God, were sent to proclaim deliverance by the power of God. 'And Moses and Aaron went and gathered together all the elders of the children of Israel: And Aaron spake all the words which the LORD had spoken unto Moses, and did the signs in the sight of the people' (vv. 29, 30).

And this is the fifth point, there is no salvation bestowed upon men except by a preached gospel. 'It pleased God by the foolishness of preaching to save them that believed'. Every gospel preacher knows he has no power to deliver anyone. Yet, the preaching of the gospel is, by the will and decree of God, the means by which God saves chosen, redeemed sinners (Romans 1:15-17; 10:13-17; 1 Peter 1:23-25).

Without question, were it his pleasure to do so, God Almighty could have chosen to save sinners without the use of any means or agency of any kind. Had he chosen to do so, he could have sent angels to pull us into heaven by our noses, once atonement was made for us. But that is not his pleasure. The Lord God has chosen to regenerate and call chosen, redeemed sinners through the agency of gospel preaching. The fact that God has so ordained it makes the preaching of the gospel the catalyst necessary for the communication of his saving grace.

I know that many cry out against this and say, 'That limits God's sovereignty. That makes salvation depend upon man.' Do not be so foolish as to be found fighting against God. We must never force the Scriptures to mean what we want them to mean. We must never bend the Word of God to our doctrinal notions and theological system. Rather, we bow to God's Word. We cannot extol and honour God if we refuse to submit our reason to his revelation.

Carefully read the Scriptures once more. It is impossible to read the following passages in their context without concluding that regeneration and faith in Christ, gifts of God the Holy Spirit and operations of his irresistible grace, are communicated to chosen, redeemed sinners through the instrumentality of gospel preaching. Read Romans 1:15-17; 10:13-17; 1 Corinthians 1:21; Ephesians 1:13; 1 Timothy 4:12-16; James 1:18; 1 Peter 1:23-25. In each of these passages the Lord God plainly declares it is his purpose and pleasure to save his elect through the preaching of the gospel.

You might ask, 'What if one of God's elect is in a remote tribe in the jungles of New Guinea where no gospel preacher has ever been?' I can see how that would create a problem, except for one thing: There are no problems with God! He knows exactly how to get his prophet to the people to whom he has purposed to show his mercy. Just ask Jonah!

We preach the gospel with a sense of urgency, knowing that sinners cannot believe on Christ until Christ is preached to them. Yet, we preach with confidence of success, knowing our labour is not in vain in the Lord (1 Corinthians 15:58). God's Word will not return to him void. It will accomplish his will and prosper in the thing it is sent to do (Isaiah 55:11). Every chosen, redeemed sinner must be regenerated and called by the Holy Spirit. And that work will be accomplished through the preaching of the gospel.

### A Believing People

Salvation involves a gracious God, a blood sacrifice, a revealing prophet, a mediating priest, a preached gospel, and, sixth, a believing people. In verse 31 we are told that when they heard the message of deliverance from the mouths of God's servants, 'the people believed'.

There is no salvation apart from faith in Christ. Faith in Christ is as essential to salvation as God's decree, Christ's obedience, and the Spirit's efficacious grace. You cannot be saved except you believe on the Son of God. 'Without faith it is impossible to please him: for he that cometh to God must believe that he is, and that he is a rewarder of them that diligently seek him' (Hebrews 11:6). 'He that believeth and is baptized shall be saved; but he that believeth not shall be damned' (Mark 16:16). 'Believe on the Lord Jesus Christ, and thou shalt be saved' (Acts 16:31).

In John 6:37 our Saviour declares, 'All that the Father giveth me shall come to me'. Without question, those words declare the blessed doctrine of God's sovereign election, inasmuch as it asserts there are some who were given to Christ. Our Saviour's words are also an assertion of effectual calling and irresistible grace. He tells us all who were given to him in eternal election must and will come to him, being brought to him by the omnipotent grace of God the Holy Spirit. In this same sentence the Lord Jesus asserts the indispensable necessity of faith, declaring plainly that even those who are given to him are not saved except they come to him. They must come to him, for there is no other way to heaven but by the door, Christ Jesus. All that the Father gives to our Redeemer must come to him. None can come to heaven except they believe on the Lord Jesus Christ.

### A Divine Visitation

One more thing is absolutely essential to the salvation of our souls. One more thing is necessary for the accomplishment of deliverance. There must be a divine visitation, a visitation of grace. None will ever believe except the power of God the Holy Spirit accompanies the preaching of the gospel (1 Thessalonians 1:4-6). The power of God must be performed. That is portrayed in verses 30 and 31.

'And Aaron spake all the words which the LORD had spoken unto Moses, and did the signs in the sight of the people. And the people believed: and when they heard that the LORD had visited the children of Israel, and that he had looked upon their affliction, then they bowed their heads and worshipped.'

No sinner will ever believe on the Lord Jesus Christ, until God comes to him in the power of his Spirit. But when the day of visitation comes, salvation follows.

'And in that day thou shalt say, O LORD, I will praise thee: though thou wast angry with me, thine anger is turned away, and thou comfortedst me. Behold, God is my salvation; I will trust, and not be afraid: for the LORD JEHOVAH is my strength and my song; he also is become my salvation. Therefore with joy shall ye draw water out of the wells of salvation. And in that day shall ye say, Praise the LORD, call upon his name, declare his doings among the people, make mention that his name is exalted. Sing unto the LORD; for he hath done excellent things: this is known in all the earth. Cry out and shout, thou inhabitant of Zion: for great is the Holy One of Israel in the midst of thee' (Isaiah 12:1-6).

'And it shall be said in that day, Lo, this is our God; we have waited for him, and he will save us: this is the LORD; we have waited for him, we will be glad and rejoice in his salvation' (Isaiah 25:9).

# Chapter 37

## 'Who Is The LORD?'

'And afterward Moses and Aaron went in, and told Pharaoh, Thus saith the LORD God of Israel, Let my people go, that they may hold a feast unto me in the wilderness. And Pharaoh said, Who is the LORD, that I should obey his voice to let Israel go? I know not the LORD, neither will I let Israel go. And they said, The God of the Hebrews hath met with us: let us go, we pray thee, three days' journey into the desert, and sacrifice unto the LORD our God; lest he fall upon us with pestilence, or with the sword.'
Exodus 5:1-3

In chapter 3, when Moses asked the Lord to tell him who he is, the Lord Jesus gave his servant a short, but gracious and full answer, revealing himself as the God of life, grace, and redemption; the Covenant God of his covenant people. 'God said unto Moses, I AM THAT I AM: and he said, Thus shalt thou say unto the children of Israel, I AM hath sent me unto you. And God said moreover unto Moses, Thus shalt thou say unto the children of Israel, The LORD God of your fathers, the God of Abraham, the God of Isaac, and the God of Jacob, hath sent me unto you: this is my name for ever, and this is my memorial unto all generations (vv. 13-15). In verses 19 and 20 the Lord told Moses, 'And I am sure that the king of Egypt will not let you go, no, not by a mighty hand. And I will stretch out my hand, and smite Egypt with all my wonders which I will do in the midst thereof: and after that he will let you go'.

The fifth chapter opens with Moses and Aaron standing before Pharaoh. 'And afterward Moses and Aaron went in, and told Pharaoh, Thus saith the LORD God of Israel, Let my people go, that they may hold a feast unto me in the wilderness. And Pharaoh said, Who is the LORD, that I should obey his voice to let Israel go? I know not the LORD, neither will I let Israel go'.

The Egyptians were a pagan, idolatrous people, who worshipped over eighty gods. They had a god for everything. But he who is God alone was unknown to them. So when Moses stood before him as God's ambassador, and said, 'Thus saith the LORD God of Israel, Let my people go, that they may hold a feast unto me in the wilderness', Pharaoh insolently demanded, 'Who is the LORD, that I should obey his voice?' And God gave that defiant little imp an answer that goes all the way through chapter 14.

The Lord God was determined to harden Pharaoh's heart through a series of ten plagues (wonders) he would perform against him and all the land of Egypt, consummating in the complete overthrow of Pharaoh and his chariots with the armies of Egypt drowned in the Red Sea and his people singing his praise on the other side of the sea (Exodus 15).

**Singular Message**
The singular message and constant theme of Holy Scripture is that the Lord Jesus Christ is God our Saviour, the God who delivers his people, who sets them free from bondage, who redeems them. He finds them lost and ruined, without strength and helpless, in bondage and thick darkness, dead in trespasses and in sins, and saves them by his omnipotent grace. And he does so in such a way that all men are made to see that he who is our God is God alone, and beside him there is no other.

In Exodus 15:2, 3 Moses sang, 'The LORD is my strength and song, and he is become my salvation: he is my God, and I will prepare him an habitation; my father's God, and I will exalt him. The LORD is a man of war: the LORD is his name'. I want to tell you about his salvation, as it is set before us in his answer to Pharaoh's blasphemy. 'Who is the Lord, that I should obey his voice?'

## Pharaoh's Problem

Pharaoh's problem was the problem of all men since the fall of our father Adam. He thought he was god. That was the root of his blasphemy and unbelief. As stated above, the Egyptians worshipped over eighty gods. They looked upon lions, oxen, rams, wolves, dogs, cats, swans, vultures, falcons, hippopotami, crocodiles, cobras, dolphins, fish, trees, frogs, beetles, locusts, even flies and lice as divine things! Even men were worshipped as gods among the brilliant heathen. Among the men who were thought to be gods and deities were their Pharaohs.

The Pharaoh was always fabled to be the son of Amon-Ra, ruling as god upon the earth. He wore the falcon symbol of Horus, their solar god, on his head, with a snake rising from his forehead, as the symbol of wisdom and life, communicating magical powers to his crown. The Pharaoh was chief-priest of the Egyptians, prominently presiding over the festivals of their gods.

We laugh at such absurdities as being so foolish that we can hardly imagine they are historic facts; but facts they are. The same absurdities are found among religions in our day. Some countries are overrun with rats and other filthy pests, constantly subjecting the whole land to horrible filth and disease, because they foolishly imagine the pests to be divine.

Yet, the most foolish, most blasphemous form of pagan idolatry is practiced by the most refined, well educated people today! Every Sunday, all over the world, men and women gather in churches and set themselves up in the place of god, worshipping themselves and demanding they be worshipped as God.

## Pharaoh's Religion

Pharaoh is held before us throughout the Scriptures as a type of Satan and of antichrist, the man of sin. And the religion of man is the religion of Pharaoh. Pharaoh's religion is not dead. Turn to 2 Thessalonians, and you will see how God the Holy Spirit identifies it.

'Now we beseech you, brethren, by the coming of our Lord Jesus Christ, and by our gathering together unto him, that ye be not soon shaken in mind, or be troubled, neither by spirit, nor by word, nor by letter as from us, as that the day of Christ is at hand' (2 Thessalonians 2:1, 2).

While there are no visible signs or prophecies to be fulfilled before our Lord's return, the Apostle does tell us that before Christ's second advent there will be a wholesale, universal apostasy and departure from the faith.

Paul is not talking here about liberals, open heretics, and vile ungodliness. He talks about those things in other places. Here he is talking about a departure of men and women from the faith, who claim to be in the faith; a subtle, deceiving, damning departure from the faith by professed believers throughout the world. Look at this third verse.

'Let no man deceive you by any means: for that day shall not come, except there come a falling away first, and that man of sin be revealed, the son of perdition' (2 Thessalonians 2:3).

Here the Holy Spirit tells us that heresies must come. They had already begun in apostolic times, they are with us now, and they will only get worse as time passes.

'For there must be also heresies among you, that they which are approved may be made manifest among you' (1 Corinthians 11:19).

'Now the Spirit speaketh expressly, that in the latter times some shall depart from the faith, giving heed to seducing spirits, and doctrines of devils; Speaking lies in hypocrisy; having their conscience seared with a hot iron; Forbidding to marry, and commanding to abstain from meats, which God hath created to be received with thanksgiving of them which believe and know the truth' (1 Timothy 4:1-3).

'This know also, that in the last days perilous times shall come. For men shall be lovers of their own selves, covetous, boasters, proud, blasphemers, disobedient to parents, unthankful, unholy, without natural affection, trucebreakers, false accusers, incontinent, fierce, despisers of those that are good, traitors, heady, highminded, lovers of pleasures more than lovers of God; Having a form of godliness, but denying the power thereof: [i.e. denying the gospel, which is the power of God] from such turn away. For of this sort are they which creep into houses, and lead captive silly women laden with sins, led away with divers lusts, ever learning, and never able to come to the knowledge of the truth. Now as Jannes and Jambres, [Pharaoh's magicians], withstood Moses, so do these also resist the truth: men of corrupt minds, reprobate concerning the faith. But they shall proceed no further: for their folly shall be manifest unto all men, as theirs also was' (2 Timothy 3:1-9).

'Beloved, believe not every spirit, but try the spirits whether they are of God: because many false prophets are gone out into the world. Hereby know ye the Spirit of God: Every spirit that confesseth that Jesus Christ is come in the flesh is of God: And every spirit that confesseth not that Jesus Christ is come in the flesh is not of God: and this is that spirit of antichrist, whereof ye have heard that it should come; and even now already is it in the world' (1 John 4:1-3).

Next we are told that the man of sin, antichrist, will be revealed. Forget about what you see coming out of Hollywood. This man of sin will not be revealed to the world. He is not some hideous looking, green-eyed monster, with horns, a red suit and a pitch-fork, with 666 stamped on his forehead. He is so smooth and slick that unless God himself enables you to recognize him, you cannot recognize him. However, he shall be revealed to God's elect. Read on,

'Who opposeth and exalteth himself above all that is called God, or that is worshipped; so that he as God sitteth in the temple of God, showing himself that he is God' (2 Thessalonians 2:4).

Here the Apostle identifies the antichrist, this man of sin. The antichrist is not one man. I have no problem at all in stating as our forefathers did, in great faithfulness, that the pope is antichrist and the church of Rome is antichrist. I do not mean that is the way it used to be. I mean that his unholiness, the pope, is antichrist. I mean that Roman Catholicism is antichrist. It cannot be stated too often, or too emphatically.

However, it is a serious mistake to limit antichrist to one man, or one religious sect, or even to a specified period of time. Antichrist was already at work in the Apostolic age. John said many antichrists had gone out into the world. Paul had to contend with antichrists at Galatia, Colossae, Corinth, and Jerusalem. Abel contended with antichrist in his brother Cain. And Moses contended with antichrist in Pharaoh and the Egyptians.

Notice how Paul describes this thing called 'the man of sin, the son of perdition'. He is one who: opposes God, exalts himself above God and sets himself up in the Temple of God and is worshipped as God, showing that he is God.

The religion of Pharaoh is the religion of antichrist. And antichrist is any system of religion, any man, any preacher, any church, any denomination that puts man in the place of power over God, any religion that makes salvation to be dependent upon or determined by the will, works, and worth of man rather than the will, works, and worth of Christ. It does not matter whether that system of religion is conservative or liberal, a mainline Protestant Church or a wild cult, Baptist or Methodists, Pentecostal or Presbyterian. Any church, doctrine, preacher, or religious system that makes man the centre-piece is antichrist and the religion of Pharaoh and the Egyptians. Let me be understood:

Those who teach that God's will can be altered, hindered, or thwarted by man's will, are, according to Colossians 2:23, will worshippers, not God worshippers. They are antichrists. Such people, like Pharaoh, place on their heads the crown of deity and make themselves gods, demanding that men worship them as God.

Those who teach that the merit and efficacy of Christ's atonement resides in man's will, man's decision, and man's faith are antichrists. Such people, like Pharaoh, place on their heads the crown of deity and make themselves gods, demanding that men worship them as God.

Those who teach that the gracious operations of the Holy Spirit may be successfully resisted by man are antichrists. Such people, like Pharaoh, place on their heads the crown of deity and make themselves gods, demanding that men worship them as God.

Those who teach that grace can be forfeited or taken away as the result of something a man does are antichrists. Such people, like Pharaoh, place on their heads the crown of deity and make themselves gods, demanding that men worship them as God.

Now, look at 2 Thessalonians 2:5-7.

'Remember ye not, that, when I was yet with you, I told you these things? And now ye know what withholdeth that he might be revealed in his time. For the mystery of iniquity doth already work: only he who now letteth will let, until he be taken out of the way.'

Paul told these saints at Thessalonica that the Holy Spirit now restrains, or withholds, the power and influence of antichrist. However, the time shall come, he wrote, when the Lord God will turn all hell loose to deceive the nations of the world again. At the end of the age, he said, Satan shall be loosed for a little season. I fear we are living in that little season, right now.

'And I saw an angel come down from heaven, having the key of the bottomless pit and a great chain in his hand. And he laid hold on the dragon, that old serpent, which is the Devil, and Satan, and bound him a thousand years, and cast him into the bottomless pit, and shut him up, and set a seal upon him, that he should deceive the nations no more, till the thousand years should be fulfilled: and after that he must be loosed a little season. And I saw thrones, and they sat upon them, and judgment was given unto them: and I saw the souls of them that were beheaded for the witness of Jesus, and for the word of God, and which had not worshipped the beast, neither his image, neither had received his mark upon their foreheads, or in their hands; and they lived and reigned with Christ a thousand years. But the rest of the dead lived not again until the thousand years were finished. This is the first resurrection. Blessed and holy is he that hath part in the first resurrection: on such the second death hath no power, but they shall be priests of God and of Christ, and shall reign with him a thousand years. And when the thousand years are expired, Satan shall be loosed out of his prison' (Revelation 20:1-7).

'And then shall that Wicked be revealed, whom the Lord shall consume with the spirit of his mouth, and shall destroy with the brightness of his coming: Even him, whose coming is after the working of Satan with all power and signs and lying wonders, and with all deceivableness of unrighteousness in them that perish; because they received not the love of the truth, that they might be saved' (2 Thessalonians 2:8-10).

Read the Apostle's inspired words with care. Do not allow a single syllable to pass before your eyes without prayerful thought and consideration. Here are five things revealed in these three verses.

Like Pharaoh, antichrist arises, is revealed, consumed, and destroyed exactly according to the purpose of God.

As with Pharaoh, signs, wonders, and miracles are as certainly marks of antichrists in the last days as they were of Christ and his Apostles in the Apostolic era.

The deception of antichrist, like the darkness of Egypt, is tremendous, so tremendous that were it possible the very elect of God would be deceived.

Like the religion of Egypt, the idolatrous religion of antichrist, self-righteous, free-will, works religion, is 'unrighteousness!'

The reason for the delusion of men is their own, wilful rejection of truth. It is not that they do not receive the truth, theoretically, but that 'they received not the love of the truth, that they might be saved'.

It is not merely giving mental assent to truth that is evidence of saving faith. Saul of Tarsus had that. Judas had that. The demons who confessed Christ had that. Even Pharaoh gave assent to his sin and that which God revealed (Exodus 9:27; 10:16). Saving faith not only embraces truth, it loves the truth. We love Christ, the embodiment of truth; and we love the truth of the gospel revealed in and by him. All believers do!

**God's Purpose**
The Lord God tells us exactly what his purpose was in sending Israel down into Egypt, in raising up Pharaoh, in hardening Pharaoh's heart, and in bringing Israel out of Egypt.

First, the Lord God sent Israel down into Egypt as his covenant people that he might bring them out with greater substance than they could otherwise have obtained. So it is with us.

'And he said unto Abram, Know of a surety that thy seed shall be a stranger in a land that is not theirs, and shall serve them; and they shall afflict them four hundred years; And also that nation, whom they shall serve, will I judge: and afterward shall they come out with great substance. And thou shalt go to thy fathers in peace; thou shalt be buried in a good old age' (Genesis 15:13-15).

Second, the Lord God raised up Pharaoh to oppose his people, that he might show in that idolatrous tyrant his sovereign power and goodness, in the exercise of his saving mercy, and that his name might be declared in all the earth as God our Saviour. So it is today.

'For he saith to Moses, I will have mercy on whom I will have mercy, and I will have compassion on whom I will have compassion. So then it is not of him that willeth, nor of him that runneth, but of God that showeth mercy. For the scripture saith unto Pharaoh, Even for this same purpose have I raised thee up, that I might show my power in thee, and that my name might be declared throughout all the earth. Therefore hath he mercy on whom he will have mercy, and whom he will he hardeneth' (Romans 9:15-18).

The Psalms repeatedly emphasize the fact that Christ our God is God our Saviour. 'Salvation belongeth unto the LORD' (Psalm 3:8). 'The LORD is my rock, and my fortress, and my deliverer; my God, my strength, in whom I will trust; my buckler, and the horn of my salvation, and my high tower' (Psalm 18:2). He is 'the God of my salvation'

(Psalm 18:46). 'The Lord is my light, and my salvation' (Psalm 27:1). 'From him cometh my salvation' (Psalm 62:1). 'God is my King of old, working salvation in the midst of the earth' (Psalm 74:12). Christ our Saviour is the theme of the Psalms, the theme of all the hymns in the inspired hymnbook of God's Israel. When we read the prophets, we find the same recurring theme, particularly Isaiah 40, 45 and 53.

'Comfort ye, comfort ye my people, saith your God. Speak ye comfortably to Jerusalem, and cry unto her, that her warfare is accomplished, that her iniquity is pardoned: for she hath received of the Lord's hand double for all her sins' (Isaiah 40:1, 2).

'Why sayest thou, O Jacob, and speakest, O Israel, My way is hid from the LORD, and my judgment is passed over from my God? Hast thou not known? hast thou not heard, that the everlasting God, the LORD, the Creator of the ends of the earth, fainteth not, neither is weary? there is no searching of his understanding. He giveth power to the faint; and to them that have no might he increaseth strength. Even the youths shall faint and be weary, and the young men shall utterly fall: But they that wait upon the LORD shall renew their strength; they shall mount up with wings as eagles; they shall run, and not be weary; and they shall walk, and not faint' (Isaiah 40:27-31).

'I will go before thee, and make the crooked places straight: I will break in pieces the gates of brass, and cut in sunder the bars of iron: And I will give thee the treasures of darkness, and hidden riches of secret places, that thou mayest know that I, the LORD, which call thee by thy name, am the God of Israel' (Isaiah 45:2, 3).

'I am the LORD, and there is none else, there is no God beside me: I girded thee, though thou hast not known me: That they may know from the rising of the sun, and from the west, that there is none beside me. I am the LORD, and there is none else. I form the light, and create darkness: I make peace, and create evil: I the LORD do all these things' (Isaiah 45:5-7).

'Thus saith the LORD, The labour of Egypt, and merchandise of Ethiopia and of the Sabeans, men of stature, shall come over unto thee, and they shall be thine: they shall come after thee; in chains they shall come over, and they shall fall down unto thee, they shall make supplication unto thee, saying, Surely God is in thee; and there is none else, there is no God. Verily thou art a God that hidest thyself, O God of Israel, the Saviour' (Isaiah 45:14, 15).

'But Israel shall be saved in the LORD with an everlasting salvation: ye shall not be ashamed nor confounded world without end' (Isaiah 45:17).

'Assemble yourselves and come; draw near together, ye that are escaped of the nations: they have no knowledge that set up the wood of their graven image, and pray unto a god that cannot save. Tell ye, and bring them near; yea, let them take counsel together: who hath declared this from ancient time? who hath told it from that time? have not I the LORD? and there is no God else beside me; a just God and a Saviour; there is none beside me. Look unto me, and be ye saved, all the ends of the earth: for I am God, and there is none else. I have sworn by myself, the word is gone out of my mouth in righteousness, and shall not return, that unto me every knee shall bow, every tongue shall swear. Surely, shall one say, in the LORD have I righteousness and strength: even to him shall men come; and all that are incensed against him shall be ashamed. In the LORD shall all the seed of Israel be justified, and shall glory' (Isaiah 45:20-25).

'Yet it pleased the LORD to bruise him; he hath put him to grief: when thou shalt make his soul an offering for sin, he shall see his seed, he shall prolong his days, and the pleasure of the LORD shall prosper in his hand. He shall see of the travail of his soul, and shall be satisfied: by his knowledge shall my righteous servant justify many; for he shall bear their iniquities' (Isaiah 53:10, 11).

The universal message of the prophets is the testimony of Jonah. 'Salvation is of the Lord' (Jonah 2:9). Pharaoh asked, 'Who is the Lord, that I should obey his voice to let Israel go?' And the very first answer God gave to his sneering blasphemy, by the mouths of Moses, Aaron, and the elders of Israel, is the thing I am trying to convey to you.

'And they said, The God of the Hebrews hath met with us: let us go, we pray thee, three days' journey into the desert, and sacrifice unto the LORD our God; lest he fall upon us with pestilence, or with the sword' (Exodus 5:3).

Jehovah, the only true and living God, is, always has been, and ever will be 'the God of the Hebrews', 'our God', the Saviour of his people.

'O give thanks unto the LORD; call upon his name: make known his deeds among the people. Sing unto him, sing psalms unto him: talk ye of all his wondrous works. Glory ye in his holy name: let the heart of them rejoice that seek the LORD. Seek the LORD, and his strength:

seek his face evermore. Remember his marvellous works that he hath done; his wonders, and the judgments of his mouth; O ye seed of Abraham his servant, ye children of Jacob his chosen. He is the LORD our God: his judgments are in all the earth. He hath remembered his covenant for ever, the word which he commanded to a thousand generations' (Psalm 105:1-8).

'He suffered no man to do them wrong: yea, he reproved kings for their sakes; Saying, Touch not mine anointed, and do my prophets no harm. Moreover he called for a famine upon the land: he brake the whole staff of bread. He sent a man before them, even Joseph, who was sold for a servant: Whose feet they hurt with fetters: he was laid in iron: Until the time that his word came: the word of the LORD tried him. The king sent and loosed him; even the ruler of the people, and let him go free. He made him lord of his house, and ruler of all his substance: To bind his princes at his pleasure; and teach his senators wisdom. Israel also came into Egypt; and Jacob sojourned in the land of Ham. And he increased his people greatly; and made them stronger than their enemies. He turned their heart to hate his people, to deal subtly with his servants. He sent Moses his servant; and Aaron whom he had chosen. They showed his signs among them, and wonders in the land of Ham. He sent darkness, and made it dark; and they rebelled not against his word. He turned their waters into blood, and slew their fish. Their land brought forth frogs in abundance, in the chambers of their kings.

He spake, and there came divers sorts of flies, and lice in all their coasts. He gave them hail for rain, and flaming fire in their land. He smote their vines also and their fig trees; and brake the trees of their coasts. He spake, and the locusts came, and caterpillars, and that without number, and did eat up all the herbs in their land, and devoured the fruit of their ground. He smote also all the firstborn in their land, the chief of all their strength. He brought them forth also with silver and gold: and there was not one feeble person among their tribes. Egypt was glad when they departed: for the fear of them fell upon them' (Psalm 105:14-38).

'For he remembered his holy promise, and Abraham his servant. And he brought forth his people with joy, and his chosen with gladness: And gave them the lands of the heathen: and they inherited the labour of the people; that they might observe his statutes, and keep his laws. Praise ye the LORD' (Psalm 105:42-45).

The Lord God sent Israel down to Egypt that he might bring them out a richer people than they could otherwise have been. He raised up Pharaoh and overthrew him as he did so that he might be known by Israel in all the world as 'the God of the Hebrews', our God and Saviour.

'And I will take you to me for a people, and I will be to you a God: and ye shall know that I am the LORD your God, which bringeth you out from under the burdens of the Egyptians' (Exodus 6:7).

'And that thou mayest tell in the ears of thy son, and of thy son's son, what things I have wrought in Egypt, and my signs which I have done among them; that ye may know how that I am the LORD' (Exodus 10:2).

Third, he did all this to make Pharaoh and the Egyptians know that he is 'the God of the Hebrews', the Lord God our Saviour. So it is to this day.

'And the Egyptians shall know that I am the LORD, when I stretch forth mine hand upon Egypt, and bring out the children of Israel from among them' (Exodus 7:5).

'But against any of the children of Israel shall not a dog move his tongue, against man or beast: that ye may know how that the LORD doth put a difference between the Egyptians and Israel' (Exodus 11:7).

'And I will harden Pharaoh's heart, that he shall follow after them; and I will be honoured upon Pharaoh, and upon all his host; that the Egyptians may know that I am the LORD. And they did so ... And the Egyptians shall know that I am the LORD, when I have gotten me honour upon Pharaoh, upon his chariots, and upon his horsemen' (Exodus 14:4, 18).

'And the LORD shall be known to Egypt, and the Egyptians shall know the LORD in that day, and shall do sacrifice and oblation; yea, they shall vow a vow unto the LORD, and perform it' (Isaiah 19:21).

'But I will strengthen the arms of the king of Babylon, and the arms of Pharaoh shall fall down; and they shall know that I am the LORD, when I shall put my sword into the hand of the king of Babylon, and he shall stretch it out upon the land of Egypt. And I will scatter the Egyptians among the nations, and disperse them among the countries; and they shall know that I am the LORD' (Ezekiel 30:25, 26).

Throughout the Old Testament, the triune Jehovah is revealed as God our Saviour, 'the God of the Hebrews', our Redeemer. And the picture constantly held before us in Old Testament Scripture of election, redemption, grace and salvation by Christ is the deliverance of Israel from the bondage of Egyptian slavery and darkness after the determined 400 years of captivity.

## God's Reminder

The Lord God gave Israel a constant reminder of his great deliverance, of his great redemption by requiring Israel to observe the day of atonement and the feast of the passover every year, as the day that marked the beginning of life for them as God's ransomed people.

'This month shall be unto you the beginning of months: it shall be the first month of the year to you' (Exodus 12:2).

'And the blood shall be to you for a token upon the houses where ye are: and when I see the blood, I will pass over you, and the plague shall not be upon you to destroy you, when I smite the land of Egypt. And this day shall be unto you for a memorial; and ye shall keep it a feast to the LORD throughout your generations; ye shall keep it a feast by an ordinance for ever' (Exodus 12:13, 14).

'And it shall come to pass, when your children shall say unto you, What mean ye by this service? That ye shall say, It is the sacrifice of the LORD'S passover, who passed over the houses of the children of Israel in Egypt, when he smote the Egyptians, and delivered our houses. And the people bowed the head and worshipped' (Exodus 12:26, 27).

So it is with us today. 'Christ our Passover is sacrificed for us' (1 Corinthians 5:7); and he has given us the bread and wine of the Lord's Supper as the constant reminder of his wonders wrought for us in the earth.

'For I have received of the Lord that which also I delivered unto you, That the Lord Jesus the same night in which he was betrayed took bread: And when he had given thanks, he brake it, and said, Take, eat: this is my body, which is broken for you: this do in remembrance of me. After the same manner also he took the cup, when he had supped, saying, This cup is the new testament in my blood: this do ye, as oft as ye drink it, in remembrance of me. For as often as ye eat this bread, and drink this cup, ye do show the Lord's death till he come' (1 Corinthians 11:23-26).

Does anyone ask, 'Who is the Lord?' Let him hear the answer that God himself gives. He is 'the God'. Beside him there is none else. He is 'the God of the Hebrews'. The God of that people whom he has chosen, distinguished, and made to be his people, his covenant people, and for whom he does all things. He is 'our God'.

Do any ask, 'What is the God of the Hebrews' doing? The Word of God answers with unmistakable clarity, 'He is bringing his people out of Egypt.'

# Chapter 38

## I Can Smile At Satan's Rage

'And afterward Moses and Aaron went in, and told Pharaoh, Thus saith the LORD God of Israel, Let my people go, that they may hold a feast unto me in the wilderness ... Then the LORD said unto Moses, Now shalt thou see what I will do to Pharaoh: for with a strong hand shall he let them go, and with a strong hand shall he drive them out of his land.'
Exodus 5:1-6:1

Revelation 12 describes a great warfare that has been waged since the dawn of creation. It is not a warfare waged between men and nations, though it is the cause of all wars. The warfare of which John speaks in the twelfth chapter of the Revelation of Jesus Christ is a war waged against the Son of God by the prince of this world, a war between Satan and our Saviour, a war between the fiend of hell and the Friend of sinners, a war between the deceiver and our Deliverer.

The war John saw in his vision is described as a great 'wonder in heaven'. As soon as God's purpose of grace was revealed to the angels of heaven, as soon as the triune God announced to the angels of light that he had created them to be servants to men who would be the heirs of his salvation, servants to his chosen, Satan was enraged and led a revolt against the throne of God. One third of the heavenly angels followed him in his rebellion. As soon as Satan raised his head in pride, and sought to overthrow the throne and purpose of God, the Lord Jesus cast him and the fallen angels out of heaven, overturned their first estate, and reserved them 'in everlasting chains under darkness unto the judgment of the great day' (Jude 6).

Though his doom is sure, Satan's rage against God is relentless and ever increasing. He does not usually appear openly as one enraged. He is subtle and cunning, like a snake. That is how he deceived Eve in the Garden, when he launched his first attack against Christ upon the earth. But the fiend of hell is a fire-breathing dragon, bent upon the destruction of the Lord Jesus Christ, our God and Saviour.

He sought to devour our God-man Mediator as soon as he came into the world. He tried to destroy him in the wilderness of temptation. He stirred the wrath of the world against him all the days of his earthly ministry. Oh, how he assaulted our Substitute in Gethsemane with the prospect of being made sin for us! But he had no power against our Saviour. He who was born to rule all nations for the salvation of his people 'was caught up unto God, and his throne' (Revelation 12:5), and was given power over all flesh that he should give eternal life to blood-bought sinners everywhere.

### Warfare for Our Souls

The Saviour, being out of his reach, Satan turns his rage toward God's elect, usurping authority over the souls of chosen sinners who are by nature his willing captives, making war against the woman's seed and God's elect. Seeing these things John cried, 'Woe to the inhabiters of the earth and of the sea! for the devil is come down unto you, having great wrath, because he knoweth that he hath but a short time'. Yet, Isaac Watts wrote, 'I can smile at Satan's rage'. How? The answer is given in that same vision. Our Saviour has bound and cast out the devil by his success as our crucified Substitute (Revelation 12:7-10).

The warfare John describes in Revelation 12 is a warfare between the Lord Jesus Christ and Apollyon; and it is a warfare for the souls of God's elect. 'The angel of the bottomless pit' seeks to destroy our souls; but Christ is determined to save us by his omnipotent grace. I can smile at Satan's rage, because I know what the outcome of this warfare shall be. 'Israel shall be saved in the LORD with an everlasting salvation: ye shall not be ashamed nor confounded world without end' (Isaiah 45:17).

It is this warfare and its glorious outcome that is depicted in the Book of Exodus. Exodus chapter 5 gives a vivid picture of the war's commencement in the souls of men in the experience of grace, when the Captain of our Salvation, the Lord Jesus Christ, comes to bind the strong man and set captive sinners free.

**The Confrontation**

The Lord Jesus sent Moses and Aaron to Pharaoh, not to plead with him, but to confront him as the ambassadors of the King of heaven, and demand that he let his people go (vv. 1, 2).

'And afterward Moses and Aaron went in, and told Pharaoh, Thus saith the LORD God of Israel, Let my people go, that they may hold a feast unto me in the wilderness. And Pharaoh said, Who is the LORD, that I should obey his voice to let Israel go? I know not the LORD, neither will I let Israel go.'

'Pharaoh' was the title of the Egyptian rulers. It comes from a word that conveys the idea of 'one who is a destroyer'. And Pharaoh is held before us as a type of Satan, the great destroyer of men. Egypt, the place of Pharaoh's dominion, is typical of the world. And Israel's bondage in Egypt typifies the bondage of darkness, sin, and death, into which Adam plunged our race.

At God's appointed time, the Lord Jesus Christ comes to overthrow Satan's usurped dominion in the hearts of chosen, redeemed sinners by his omnipotent grace. But Satan will never willingly relinquish his captives. So a great struggle takes place in the City of Mansoul. That is the picture we have before us in Exodus 5.

The fact is, God never works like we think he should. He never does things the way we expect him to do them. Never is that fact more evident than it is in the exercise of his saving operations of grace (Deuteronomy 32:39; 1 Samuel 2:6-8; Job 5:18; Hosea 6:1).

The result of Moses' first meeting with Pharaoh was not very encouraging. The thought of losing Israel made Pharaoh more determined than ever to hold them. He tightened his grip and resolved to make their escape impossible. So it is in the initial experience of grace. When Satan's dominion is threatened, his rage increases.

That is what we see here. The fiery trial is about to be quenched by the hand of redeeming love; but, before it is, it blazes with greater fierceness and intensity than ever. Satan will never release his captives, until his grip is broken by Christ. Our Lord Jesus describes him as 'a strong man armed', and while he 'keepeth his palace, his goods are in peace'. But, blessed be God, there is 'a stronger than he', who has taken from him 'his armour wherein he trusted', and divided the spoils among the favoured objects of his everlasting love.

## God's Determination

The determination of the triune God is the complete deliverance, redemption, and salvation of his elect. Everything else is subservient to that great purpose and determination of our God. When he sent Moses and Aaron to Pharaoh, that was the message he gave, the command he issued. He identified himself as 'the Lord God of Israel'. The Lord God owned Israel as his own people, peculiarly and distinctly his people. He demanded that Pharaoh let his people go, so they might worship and serve him. 'That they may hold a feast unto me in the wilderness.'

That was Jehovah's message to Pharaoh. He demanded the full deliverance of Israel on the ground they belonged to him. And our Lord Jesus Christ, the Lord God who sent Moses to Pharaoh, demands the full deliverance of his elect from sin, Satan, the curse of the law, death, and hell on the ground that we belong to him exclusively. We are his by his own choice, by the Father's gift, and by lawful purchase. And nothing can ever satisfy God our Saviour in reference to his elect, but their entire emancipation from the yoke of bondage. His command is, 'Loose him, and let him go'! That is the command of omnipotent mercy and irresistible grace. Though held in bondage by Satan, God's elect are his, the objects of his eternal love, and they shall be loosed.

## Our Condition

Yet, when we see Israel working as slaves in the brick-kilns of Egypt, we have a graphic image of the condition of every child of Adam by nature, even God's chosen. There we were, crushed beneath Satan's galling yoke, having no power to deliver ourselves. The very thought of liberty in our minds made our bonds tighter and our burdens greater.

Fallen sinners are under the usurped tyranny and dominion of Satan, 'sold under sin', 'led captive by Satan at his will', bound in the fetters of their own hearts' lusts, 'without strength', 'without God', 'without Christ', 'without hope'! That is the condition of all men by nature. How, then, can they help themselves? What can they do? The sinner's thoughts, his words, his deeds, are the thoughts, words, and deeds of a slave. Should he weep and sigh for emancipation, his very tears and sighs are melancholy proofs of his slavery. He may struggle for freedom; but his very struggle declares his bondage.

If deliverance was to be obtained, it was absolutely necessary that it come from without. But from where? Where can ransom be found?

Where is the power to break our chains? Where can one be found with the price, power, and will to save our souls? Then, when we had no strength, without hope, and in utter despair, God the Holy Spirit turned us and caused us to look out of ourselves, to look away to Christ, in whom deliverance is found (Job 33:18-30; Psalm 89:19; Isaiah 45:22).

Job's 'friends' were miserable comforters who terribly misjudged God's servant Job. Still, these three often spoke the truth. Certainly, that is the case in Job 33, where Elihu speaks, declaring God's work. 'He keepeth back his' elect 'from the pit'. He chastens the object of his mercy 'with pain upon his bed ... So that his life abhorreth bread, and his soul dainty meat ... Yea, his soul draweth near unto the grave, and his life to the destroyers ... In his great mercy, the Lord God sends 'a messenger ... an interpreter' to the chosen sinner, 'to show unto man his uprightness', to reveal Christ as the Lord our Righteousness. 'Then he is gracious unto him, and saith, Deliver him from going down to the pit: I have found a ransom.' That is how chosen sinners are made new creatures in Christ in the experience of grace. When Christ is revealed in the chosen sinner, he prays unto God, and God shows himself 'favourable unto him'. Only then does the sinner see the glory of God in the face of his crucified Substitute 'with joy'. He sees Christ with the joy of faith, because God renders to the heaven-born soul 'his righteousness', delivers 'his soul from going into the pit', and causes 'his life' to 'see the light. Lo, all these things worketh God oftentimes with man, to bring back his soul from the pit, to be enlightened with the light of the living' (vv. 18-30). That is the way it is in every case. Christ is the Deliverer we must have. 'Neither is there salvation in any other: for there is none other name under heaven given among men, whereby we must be saved' (Acts 4:12).

**Our Nature**
Man's condition is slavery. But his slavery is not a mere outward, physical bondage. It is a moral, inward, spiritual bondage, the bondage of a radically corrupt, completely fallen, totally depraved nature, entirely enslaved to and under the power of Satan. Our nature, by birth, is the nature of one enslaved. Sinners need something more than a new condition. We need a new nature! If it were possible for the sinner to improve his condition, he would still be a slave. The Lord Jesus Christ freed his elect from Satan's clutches, freed us from sin and death, and

freed us from the curse of the law, when he died as our Substitute on Calvary's cursed tree (Colossians 2:10-15; Galatians 3:13). But our Saviour's work on the cross did not, in any way, change our nature. We were still 'dead in trespasses and in sins', walking 'according to the course of this world, according to the prince of the power of the air, the spirit that now worketh in the children of disobedience: Among whom also we all had our conversation in times past in the lusts of our flesh, fulfilling the desires of the flesh and of the mind; and were by nature the children of wrath, even as others' (Ephesians 2:1-3). We were still in bondage in our souls. We had to have a new nature imparted to us and created in us before we could live in liberty.

## Our Standing

The Lord Jesus Christ has, by the invincible power and grace of God the Holy Spirit, brought us experimentally into an entirely new condition, giving us a new nature to match the condition. By the new birth, we are free-born children! We stand before God in Christ and in grace. 'Who was delivered for our offences, and was raised again for our justification. Therefore being justified, by faith we have peace with God through our Lord Jesus Christ: By whom also we have access by faith into this grace wherein we stand, and rejoice in hope of the glory of God' (Romans 4:25-5:2).

We stand before God in Christ without sin, without guilt, without condemnation, 'complete in him', in a state of perfect and everlasting justification. That is to say, not only has the Lord God fully pardoned us from all sin (past, present, and future), he has made us completely and perfectly righteous in his Son, giving us in Christ such perfect righteousness that his infinite holiness cannot find a single stain upon us! He has taken us out of our former condition of guilt, and placed us, absolutely and eternally, in a new condition of unspotted righteousness.

Justification is not an improvement of standing. It is a totally new standing! And the new birth is not an improvement of our fallen nature! It is the creation of a new nature, 'a new creature' in Christ (2 Corinthians 5:17). 'That which is crooked cannot be made straight'. And what is unholy cannot be made holy. 'That which is born of the flesh is flesh.' The old man cannot be made clean. 'Can the Ethiopian change his skin, or the leopard his spots?' The new birth is Christ coming into us, 'Christ in you the hope of glory', by which we are made 'partakers of the divine nature'. It is the birth of a new man, 'created in righteousness and true holiness', who walks before God in freedom!

Man is born in slavery. Until he is 'born again', he cannot know anything else. You may try to improve yourself. You may resolve to be better in the future, 'turn over a new leaf', and live a better life. You may give up this vice or that, and begin to practise this or that virtue; but you can do nothing to change your condition as a sinner, a bondman, a slave to Satan and to sin. You may scream, 'No, I'm good!' But your heart and conscience screams back, 'You're a liar! The outside may be clean; but inside you are as vile as hell itself!'

You may get a little dose of religion, start going to church, reading your Bible, praying, and doing good things for other people. You may get baptized, join the church, take the Lord's Supper, teach Sunday School, preach, and become a zealous missionary. But 'ye must be born again', or perish in bondage under the wrath of God.

How can this new birth be had? It can be had only by the Son of God saying to Satan, 'Let my people go'! It can be had only by the Lord Jesus Christ coming to the dead, and saying, 'Live!' And when he does, the heaven born soul believes on the Son of God, receiving him gladly. Our faith in Christ is not the cause of the new birth, but the result of it (John 1:12, 13; 3:36; 5:24; 17:3; 1 John 5:11, 12).

**Our Sacrifice**

Upon what basis does the Lord God deal with sinners in such grace? On what basis dare any sinner hope he can walk before God in freedom, without guilt, fearing no condemnation, finding acceptance with him? Read Exodus 5:3. The only basis upon which anyone can ever entertain such hope is a blood Sacrifice, the sacrifice of our Lord Jesus Christ.

'The God of the Hebrews hath met with us.' It was God who came to Israel, not Israel that came to God. 'Let us go three days' journey'. I do not know all that is implied by those 'three days', but I do know that three days was the time between the death of Christ and his resurrection as our Substitute. 'And sacrifice unto the LORD.' The Lord God requires we bring a sacrifice to him, but only the Sacrifice he requires, the Sacrifice he provides, the Sacrifice he accepts, the Sacrifice who is 'The Lord Jesus Christ'! 'Lest he fall upon us with pestilence, or with the sword'. If we do not come to him and worship him in and by Christ, he will fall upon us in his wrath!

That is the plain, universal doctrine of Holy Scripture. Everything turns on, rests on, and depends upon this one thing. 'Jesus died and rose again.' Blessed are they who can truthfully say, 'We believe that Jesus died and rose again'. The ever-blessed Son of God came down into this world of guilt and sin, took on himself the likeness of sinful flesh, and died upon the cross, the Just for the unjust, under the full weight of his people's sins, being made sin for us, that we might be made the righteousness of God in him. By his one sacrifice, by his obedience and blood, the Lord Jesus Christ met all that was or could be demanded of us, and removed all that was or could be against us. He magnified the law and made it honourable. In his sacrifice 'Mercy and truth are met together; righteousness and peace have kissed each other'. Infinite justice was satisfied. And, from the crucified Son of God, infinite love flows in all its infinite fulness to poor needy sinners to set the captive free.

The crucified Christ is the Sacrifice God provided and God accepted, the Sacrifice that perfectly meets all the cravings of our needy souls and all the demands of a screaming conscience. The Lord Jesus, on the cross, died in our place. He died as our Representative, bearing our sins. He died our death to give us his life. We are forever linked to him by our Father's decree, by his own eternal espousal of our souls, by covenant union, and by the living union of grace, linking our souls and his. That is the great freedom of life and grace that belongs to every believer! 'As he is so are we in this world' (1 John 4:17).

That is our joy, our peace, our assurance, our hope, our confidence before God in the blessed experience of his saving grace. 'We also joy in God, through our Lord Jesus Christ, by whom we have now received the atonement' (Romans 5:11). What blessed power and beauty I see in those emancipating words of our Saviour! 'Let my people go, that they may hold a feast unto me in the wilderness'. He said, 'The Spirit of the Lord is upon me, because he hath anointed me to preach the gospel to the poor; he hath sent me to heal the brokenhearted, to preach deliverance to the captives, and recovering of sight to the blind, to set at liberty them that are bruised' (Luke 4:18).

The good news of grace is the announcement of full deliverance from every yoke of bondage. Peace and liberty are the boons Christ bestows upon his people in saving mercy.

## Determined Destroyer

But the liberty and freedom of grace does not come without pain. I do not know if babies suffer any pain during the process of birth, as they are passing through the birth canal; but I do know that God's children suffer much pain in the experience of grace, in the experience of all that is associated with the new birth. The conviction of sin, the conversion of our souls, repentance toward God, taking up the cross to follow Christ, losing our lives, and dying to self are all things that involve pain, pain that is deeply felt. If the seed of life is planted in the heart, the heart must be ploughed; and the ploughing of the heart is painful work.

Christ is determined to save, determined to set his people free; but Satan is determined to destroy. Christ will prevail; but Satan never relents. That is what we see in the rest of this chapter. Pharaoh, the Destroyer, refused to let Israel go. Instead, he acted like a tyrant who sensed he was losing control. The enraged little imp on Egypt's throne demanded the children of Israel make bricks without straw, and beat them when they could not produce the bricks required (Exodus 5:6-19).

'And Pharaoh commanded the same day the taskmasters of the people, and their officers, saying, Ye shall no more give the people straw to make brick, as heretofore: let them go and gather straw for themselves. And the tale of the bricks, which they did make heretofore, ye shall lay upon them; ye shall not diminish ought thereof: for they be idle; therefore they cry, saying, Let us go and sacrifice to our God. Let there more work be laid upon the men, that they may labour therein; and let them not regard vain words' (vv. 5-9). 'Go ye, get you straw where ye can find it: yet not ought of your work shall be diminished' (v. 11). 'And the taskmasters hasted them, saying, Fulfil your works, your daily tasks, as when there was straw. And the officers of the children of Israel, which Pharaoh's taskmasters had set over them, were beaten, and demanded, Wherefore have ye not fulfilled your task in making brick both yesterday and to day, as heretofore?' (vv. 13, 14). 'Go therefore now, and work; for there shall no straw be given you, yet shall ye deliver the tale of bricks. And the officers of the children of Israel did see that they were in evil case, after it was said, Ye shall not minish ought from your bricks of your daily task' (vv. 18, 19).

Pharaoh's severe measures illustrate the malignant efforts of Satan against the chosen sinner, when the Lord begins to deal with him in grace. When Satan sees Christ coming to spoil him of his goods, coming in mercy to a poor sinner, he puts forth every effort to hold his house and his goods intact. The fiend of hell is never more violently malicious than now. He spares no pain. Satan never gives up his prey without a fierce struggle. When a soul is convicted of sin, and brought to long after mercy and grace, pardon and righteousness, liberty and peace with God, the Devil endeavours, just as Pharaoh did with the Israelites, to expel all such desires from his heart.

Conditions for the Hebrews worsened before they were delivered, and when Christ comes to deliver his chosen, their condition gets worse before it gets better. There is a vivid example of this in Luke 9:42. 'And as he was yet a coming, the devil threw him down, and tare him.' As that poor soul was coming to Christ, the devil sought to destroy him. So long as a person has no desire for Christ, Satan pretty much leaves him alone; but once a sinner is awakened to know his need of the Saviour, and begins to seek him, Satan puts forth every effort to destroy him.

So it was with the Hebrews in Egypt. Just as hope was awakened, their misery was increased. Just when deliverance seemed at hand, their bondage was made more bitter. John Trapp observed, 'Things commonly go backward with the saints before they come forward, as the corn groweth downward ere it grow upward.' The most profound darkness and depressing gloom always precedes the rising of 'the Sun of Righteousness' from behind the thick clouds, with healing in his wings, to heal eternally, 'the hurt of the daughter of his people'.

The fiend of hell often seeks to destroy the souls of men by putting sinners who seek grace upon the footing of works. He takes the place of pretended holiness and righteousness, and demands that the sinner produce bricks, by which he can build steps to the altar of God, saying, 'Go, therefore, and work'. God requires righteousness. Produce some. God requires repentance. Where is yours? God requires you to believe. Produce a little faith. God demands mourning; but you have not really mourned. God requires a sincere heart; but your heart is full of deceit and hypocrisy. If he cannot keep sinners from Christ by convincing them they are too good to need a Saviour, the devil will try to convince them they are too bad to be saved, and persuade them they must first improve themselves. His doctrine is, 'Go therefore now, and work; for there shall no straw be given you, yet shall ye deliver the tale of bricks'. Indeed, that is ever the doctrine of Satan's ministers who transform themselves into ministers of righteousness (2 Corinthians 11:15).

## Messengers Despised

When guilt and oppression of soul increases, when bitterness increases, when the commandment comes and sin revives, the sinner, despairing of hope, often begins to despise the messenger of deliverance. I have seen it happen many times, just as it is described in Exodus 5:20, 21.

'And they met Moses and Aaron, who stood in the way, as they came forth from Pharaoh: And they said unto them, The LORD look upon you, and judge; because ye have made our savour to be abhorred in the eyes of Pharaoh, and in the eyes of his servants, to put a sword in their hand to slay us'.

Hunting dogs will often, in the heat of the hunt, snarl and bite their best friends. And sinners, when sin is made bitter to them, often snarl at and bite the man who delivers the message of redemption and grace to them.

## Moses' Prayer

We are told by the Spirit of God, 'The servant of the Lord must not strive; but be gentle unto all men, apt to teach, patient, in meekness instructing those that oppose themselves; if God peradventure will give them repentance to the acknowledging of the truth; and that they may recover themselves out of the snare of the devil, who are taken captive by him at his will' (2 Timothy 2:24-26). It was in that spirit that Moses, rather than striving with the people, turned to his Master. Speaking to the Lord God as a man speaks to his friend, he unburdened his heavy, breaking heart.

'And Moses returned unto the LORD, and said, Lord, wherefore hast thou so evil entreated this people? why is it that thou hast sent me? For since I came to Pharaoh to speak in thy name, he hath done evil to this people; neither hast thou delivered thy people at all' (vv. 22, 23).

Many have spoken severely of Moses for his words here. We are told by many that his faith should have been stronger, his will should have been more broken, or his resignation should have been more complete. And those are the nicer things men have said about the prophet. But there is no indication from God, before whom Moses poured out his soul, that he was displeased at all. In fact, we are encouraged, both by God's own command and by example, to do exactly what Moses did (Isaiah 37:14-16, 20; 43:25, 26; 45:11; Hebrews 4:16).

## God's Answer

I am sure the Lord God was not angered by Moses' honesty in opening his heart before him, because the answer the Lord gave him did not have the slightest hint of disapproval or rebuke. It was all grace. Moses came to the throne of grace to find mercy and grace to help in time of great need; and God gave him that which he sought. 'Then the LORD said unto Moses, Now shalt thou see what I will do to Pharaoh: for with a strong hand shall he let them go, and with a strong hand shall he drive them out of his land' (Exodus 6:1).

We often get in a hurry. God never does. There is no need for him to hurry. His delays, or what we think are delays, are always wise and good. He did not deliver Israel immediately; and he purposed that they must endure greater afflictions than they had known before, because he was determined to be gracious to them, and to do them the best good possible. He did not destroy Pharaoh until Pharaoh made it clear that justice demanded his overthrow. His tolerance of Pharaoh and Egypt for so long displayed his greatness as God who endures 'with much long-suffering the vessels of wrath fitted to destruction'. And, the more they were afflicted the more his people would appreciate deliverance when the appointed time arrived.

In all things, God's time is best. Let us wait for him. 'It is good that a man should both hope and quietly wait for the salvation of the LORD' (Lamentations 3:26). 'For the vision is yet for an appointed time, but at the end it shall speak, and not lie: though it tarry, wait for it; because it will surely come, it will not tarry' (Habakkuk 2:3). Wait, child of God, in all things wait on the Lord and 'smile at Satan's rage'!

'Why sayest thou, O Jacob, and speakest, O Israel, My way is hid from the LORD, and my judgment is passed over from my God? Hast thou not known? hast thou not heard, that the everlasting God, the LORD, the Creator of the ends of the earth, fainteth not, neither is weary? there is no searching of his understanding. He giveth power to the faint; and to them that have no might he increaseth strength. Even the youths shall faint and be weary, and the young men shall utterly fall: But they that wait upon the LORD shall renew their strength; they shall mount up with wings as eagles; they shall run, and not be weary; and they shall walk, and not faint' (Isaiah 40:27-31).

# Chapter 39

# No Compromise!

'And afterward Moses and Aaron went in, and told Pharaoh, Thus saith the LORD God of Israel, Let my people go, that they may hold a feast unto me in the wilderness ... And Pharaoh called for Moses and for Aaron, and said, Go ye, sacrifice to your God in the land ... And Pharaoh said, I will let you go, that ye may sacrifice to the LORD your God in the wilderness; only ye shall not go very far away: intreat for me ... And Moses and Aaron were brought again unto Pharaoh: and he said unto them, Go, serve the LORD your God: but who are they that shall go? And Moses said, We will go with our young and with our old, with our sons and with our daughters, with our flocks and with our herds will we go; for we must hold a feast unto the LORD. And he said unto them, Let the LORD be so with you, as I will let you go, and your little ones: look to it; for evil is before you. Not so: go now ye that are men, and serve the LORD; for that ye did desire. And they were driven out from Pharaoh's presence ... And Pharaoh called unto Moses, and said, Go ye, serve the LORD; only let your flocks and your herds be stayed: let your little ones also go with you. And Moses said, Thou must give us also sacrifices and burnt offerings, that we may sacrifice unto the LORD our God. Our cattle also shall go with us; there shall not an hoof be left behind; for thereof must we take to serve the LORD our God; and we know not with what we must serve the LORD, until we come thither ... And Moses said, thou hast spoken well. I will see thy face again no more.'
Exodus 5:1-10:29

In the political world compromise is, I suppose, a necessary evil. Were it not for compromise, nothing would ever be accomplished. In the business world the same is true. Corporations operate by compromise. Compromise is the settlement of differences by mutual concessions. That may be a good thing in politics and business; but in the church and kingdom of God, in all things spiritual, compromise is deadly.

We will begin this study in Exodus 5:1; but it will cover specific aspects of chapters 5-10. In these six chapters Pharaoh stands before us as an instructive type of Satan, the god of this world, proposing four compromises to Moses, compromises by which he attempted to keep Israel in subjection to himself, while allowing them to behave as free men, compromises which would have allowed Israel much freedom. Yet they would have remained Pharaoh's slaves still.

### God's Demand

Exodus 5 opens with a divine confrontation. The Lord God confronts Pharaoh. But the confrontation pictures one far more severe, with far greater consequences. It shows our Saviour's confrontation with Satan.

'And afterward Moses and Aaron went in, and told Pharaoh, Thus saith the LORD God of Israel, Let my people go, that they may hold a feast unto me in the wilderness' (Exodus 5:1).

God's servants Moses and Aaron stand before Pharaoh, the king of Egypt. They have only one thing to say. Their issue before the king of Egypt is the singular, unambiguous demand of the King of Heaven. 'Let my people go, that they may hold a feast unto me in the wilderness'!

What a volume of rich instruction those words contain! It is given in plain and forcible language. It sets before us the blessed purpose of the Lord God of Israel to have his people completely delivered from Egypt and separated unto himself, in order that they might feast with him in the wilderness. Nothing could satisfy his heart with regard to his covenant people, but their complete emancipation from the land of death and darkness. He would free them not only from Egypt's brick-kilns and taskmasters, but from its gods and its temples, from its altars and its customs, and from its people and their way of life. The Lord God was determined to deliver the chosen nation from Egypt, from the land of Egypt, the bondage of Egypt, the people of Egypt, and the life of Egypt. In a word, they had to be thoroughly separated from Egypt before they could worship him in the wilderness.

Thus it was with Israel, and thus it is with us. We, too, must be a fully and consciously delivered people before we can worship, serve, and walk with God. We cannot worship God until we are sanctified by him, separated from Egypt by his omnipotent grace. We must know the forgiveness of our sins, and our entire freedom from guilt, wrath, judgment, and condemnation. But there must also be a separation, a complete deliverance from this present evil world. The world is to us what Egypt was to Israel. As Israel left Egypt, we must leave the world. God demands a real, out-and-out, thorough separation of our hearts from Egypt. He says, 'Let my people go, that they may hold a feast to me in the wilderness.'

In a word, our God demands, and will not rest until he has accomplished the complete sanctification of his elect, the complete separation of his people unto Christ. This separation from the world may involve physical things; but it is not a physical separation. It is not a separation to be displayed before men by the clothes we wear, the things we eat and drink, or places in which we eat and drink. That kind of separation is nothing but a Pharisaical show of hypocrisy. The separation, or sanctification, of God's elect to Christ is a spiritual separation, a separation of our hearts to our Saviour. It is a separation touching every aspect of our lives. He says, 'Give me thine heart' (Proverbs 23:26). What does the husband want from his wife? Her heart. What does the wife want from her husband? His heart. And that which Christ wants, and will have from his people is their hearts. If he has my heart, he has everything. If my heart is not his, nothing about me, nothing possessed by me is his.

But Satan does not give up his captives easily. He must be driven by the force of our Saviour's omnipotent arms to do so. The fiend of hell will not lose his captives if he can help it. He will exercise all his subtlety, craft, cunning, and power to hold them. We are not ignorant of his devices. If the adversary fails to succeed with one device, he will try another. That is the picture drawn before us by the pen of Inspiration in Exodus 5-10. Like Pharaoh, Satan denies God's right to be God, saying, 'Who is the LORD, that I should obey his voice'? (v. 2). And he finds the hearts of all in agreement with him, 'because the carnal mind is enmity against God: for it is not subject to the law of God, neither indeed can be' (Romans 8:7). Every fallen sinner is, by nature, a disobedient rebel before God (Ephesians 2:2).

Satan looks upon the Word of God as a vain thing (v. 9). 'Yea, hath God said' (Genesis 3:1) is still his favourite device for man's ruin.

Again, he finds fallen man in agreement with his device. The Word of the living God, the message of grace, redemption, and deliverance is something men trample beneath their feet. 'The preaching of the cross is to them that perish foolishness' (1 Corinthians 1:18).

And, as Pharaoh required the Jews to make brick without straw, Satan ever puts sinners to the impossible task of doing something to make their deliverance possible. He seizes the notion in every depraved heart that man can and must do something to win God's favour. His messengers, appearing to be ministers of righteousness, teach sinners that they must obey the law and produce righteousness for themselves.

**First Compromise**
If Satan cannot succeed with open scorn and oppression, like Pharaoh, he will try to hold his captives with the snare of compromise. Pharaoh's proposals of compromise begin in Exodus 8:25. The Lord God had turned the water into blood; but Pharaoh's heart was hardened. God sent frogs upon the land; but Pharaoh's heart was hardened again. The Lord had filled the land of Egypt with lice; but Pharaoh's heart was hardened again. Then God caused swarms of flies to cover the land of Egypt, and Pharaoh offered a compromise. In verse 25 we read, 'And Pharaoh called for Moses and for Aaron, and said, Go ye, sacrifice to your God in the land'.

How crafty, how subtle, how cunning. Pharaoh's words were well calculated. 'Go ye, and sacrifice to your God in the land'. Moses might have plausibly argued, 'This is an uncommonly generous proposal. Pharaoh is willing to allow us to worship the Lord our God. There is no reason to proceed any further.' But he could not do so without betraying the trust God had given him and betraying the people God sent him to serve. Moses could not accept Pharaoh's proposed compromise without disobeying God's command. Read his answer to Pharaoh in vv. 26, 27.

'And Moses said, It is not meet so to do; for we shall sacrifice the abomination of the Egyptians to the LORD our God: lo, shall we sacrifice the abomination of the Egyptians before their eyes, and will they not stone us? We will go three days' journey into the wilderness, and sacrifice to the LORD our God, as he shall command us.'

At first glance it might appear that Pharaoh was at last bending, recognizing the futility of fighting against the Almighty. But a close look at his words show him a rebel still. God's command was crystal clear. He demanded the complete separation of his people unto himself. He demanded that his people go 'three days' journey' into the wilderness.

## A Resurrected People

God would have his people completely delivered from the land of darkness and death. And he demanded that Israel hold a feast unto him in the wilderness, not in Egypt. But they must do it as a resurrected people. They must go 'three days' journey' into the wilderness. Throughout the Scriptures, the third day speaks of the triune God and of the resurrection.

We cannot worship God except we worship him as a resurrected, heaven-born, regenerate people, as new creatures in Christ, standing before him on the lofty ground of accomplished redemption and the full-orbed light of the new creation.

Only by the power of God the Holy Spirit dwelling in us can we see where Christ has brought us by his sin atoning death and resurrection. Then we can call upon the name of the Lord, worshipping him in 'spirit and in truth' (John 4:24), presenting our 'bodies a living sacrifice, holy, acceptable unto God' (Romans 12:2), 'to offer up spiritual sacrifices, acceptable to God by Jesus Christ' (1 Peter 2:5).

Pharaoh said to Moses and Israel, 'Go ye, sacrifice to your God in the land'. But Egypt represents the world. And God's people have been delivered 'from this present evil world' (Galatians 1:4). Our Saviour said, 'Ye are not of this world, but I have chosen you out of the world' (John 15:19). And again, 'they are not of the world, even as I am not of the world' (John 17:16). James writes, 'The friendship of the world is enmity with God' (James 4:4). How can believers worship God 'in the land'? We cannot. God must be worshipped 'in spirit and in truth'. And to worship God 'in spirit' is to worship him in the new nature he gives. It is taking our place, by faith, outside of the world which crucified the Son of God. It is 'going forth without the camp, bearing his reproach' (Hebrews 13:13). God's requirement is the same today. 'Come out from among them, and be ye separate, saith the Lord' (2 Corinthians 6:17).

## The Sacrifice Required

There is another reason Moses could not accept this proposed compromise. To worship God 'in the land' would be to 'sacrifice the abomination of the Egyptians'. In Genesis 46:34 we are told that, 'every shepherd is an abomination unto the Egyptians'. If every 'shepherd' was an abomination to the Egyptians, certainly to offer a lamb in sacrifice to God would be equally abominable to them.

The Sacrifice required, if we are to worship God 'in spirit and in truth', is Christ our Lord, the Lamb of God; and Christ crucified is ever an abomination to the world. 'The preaching of the cross is to them that perish foolishness.' Christ crucified, is the condemnation of the flesh. Christ crucified reveals man's total depravity. The cross of Christ is an offence and a 'stumbling-block' to those who believe not the gospel.

Moses understood this. He said to Pharaoh, 'Shall we sacrifice the abomination of the Egyptians before their eyes, will they not stone us?'

Press upon men the necessity of redemption by Christ, declaring that the holy Lord God must and shall condemn all sin (Romans 8:3), that there is no other way by which sinners can approach God, that without the shedding of Christ's blood none can be saved (Hebrews 11:6), and that by the cross of Christ believers are crucified to the world (Galatians 6:14), and man's hidden enmity against God erupts in a rage. The Lord Jesus tells us plainly, 'If ye were of the world, the world would love his own; but because ye are not of the world, but I have chosen you out of the world, therefore the world hateth you. Remember the word that I said unto you, The servant is not greater than his Lord. If they have persecuted me, they will also persecute you; if they have kept my saying, they will keep yours also' (John 15:19, 20).

## God's Word

There was one more reason Moses gave for not accepting Pharaoh's compromise. It was contrary to God's plain command given in his word (8:27).

The Word of God settles all issues for believers. When God has spoken, there is no room for reason, debate, or even discussion. We bow to that which God declares in his Word. The Book of God, and the Book of God alone must determine our doctrine, regulate our worship, and govern our lives. In the church and kingdom of God the Word of God is our first and our final appeal for all things. We believe nothing, preach nothing, and practise nothing in the house of God except that which is plainly revealed in Holy Scripture. Human opinion, religious tradition, and social approval, or disapproval, are utterly insignificant.

When compromise is proposed, it must be flatly rejected by all who would worship God. Why would anyone consider compromising the Word of God? Compromise does nothing to honour God, but only dishonours him. Compromise does nothing for the good of men's souls, but only destroys them. Compromise does nothing to build God's church, but only corrupts it. No one benefits from compromise except the compromiser. And, ultimately, he will find his compromise destructive (1 Corinthians 3:11-17).

I press this matter because God's servants and his people are constantly pressed to compromise the things of God. We are constantly urged to do something to make the gospel more 'acceptable' to men; and our sinful flesh is always inclined to make concessions. Multitudes of churches today have what they like to call 'contemporary worship' services. In such services the music is more lively and the songs are less meaningful, but more emotional. Preaching gives way to sharing, and worship to clapping hands!

In the dictionary on my desk, just below 'contemporary' I find the word 'contemptible'. And the religion of this age is utterly contemptible! Let there be no compromise with Pharaoh in the Israel of God. To compromise our message is to destroy our message (Romans 11:6). And unless we are willing to compromise our message, we will not compromise our methods, our music, or our ministry in any way. Let men say what they will to justify themselves, I have never yet known any church or preacher who altered his methods who did not compromise his message.

## Second Compromise

Pharaoh's second proposed compromise was very much like his first. If he could not keep Israel in Egypt, he would keep them as near to Egypt as possible. He said, 'I will let you go, that ye may sacrifice to the Lord your God in the wilderness; only ye shall not go very far away' (8:28).

He was ready to lengthen the chain, but it was still a chain; and he still held the chain. Complete liberty he was not willing to grant. The point at issue was the complete separation of God's people from Egypt, typifying the world, and Pharaoh, representing Satan, fought against this to the bitter end.

'Only ye shall not go very far away' is one of Satan's most cunning devices. God saved me just before my seventeenth birthday. I had lived next door to a man I highly respected for most of my life. He was, as far as I know, a very moral, and highly respected man. I never knew exactly what his job was; but he was a government agent of some kind. He and I got along very well. We visited in his back yard frequently, talking about things that interest and amuse teenage boys. Though he knew a good many of my vices, he never once warned me of their consequences, or even suggested I should not engage in them. But, as soon as he learned that I had been baptized and had preached a few times, he called for me to come over for a talk. I cannot recall his exact words, but essentially he said, 'Don, I hear you have gotten religion. That is really good. But you want to be careful not to be extreme. Do not become narrow minded. You do not want to become so heavenly minded that you are of no earthly good.'

That is precisely the wisdom of this world. The world says, 'Avoid extremes. Do not become a fanatic. Beware of becoming dogmatic and narrow-minded. God does not want you to be long-faced and miserable. There is no need for religion to radically change your life. Do 'not go very far away.'

But our God has made the wisdom of this world foolishness. God sent Moses to Pharaoh to bring his people out of Egypt and into the land of Canaan. And in this Moses was typical of the Lord Jesus. The Son of God left heaven for earth that he might bring his people from earth to heaven. He tells us to set our affection upon things above (Colossians 3:1). And that is far away from this world! To that end, the Spirit of God says to every believer, 'Love not the world, neither the things which are in the world. If any man love the world the love of the Father is not in him' (1 John 2:15).

'God forbid that I should glory, save in the cross of our Lord Jesus Christ, by whom the world is crucified unto me, and I unto the world' (Galatians 6:14). The cross of Christ has crucified the world unto us and us unto the world. The world counts us dead. Dead people do not count. Dead people are meaningless. That is how the world looks upon us. But that is okay. If the world is crucified to me, that is how I look upon the world. It is a dead thing. It is meaningless. It does not count.

But how can we be happy if we turn our backs upon all the world? Where shall we find fulfilment and satisfaction? CHRIST. To any who have forsaken all and followed Christ I ask you what our Lord asked his disciples. 'Lacked ye anything?' The universal answer is, 'Nothing'

(Luke 22:35). Our very meat and drink is to hold a feast unto the Lord our God in this wilderness, to walk in fellowship with him who loved us and gave himself for us, to do the will of our Father (John 4:34).

As soon as the plague of flies was removed, Pharaoh 'hardened his heart neither would he let the people go' (8:32). Heavier judgments were then sent upon his land. They brought the rebel to his knees, but not in genuine repentance and submission.

## Third Compromise

Pharaoh's third compromise reveals another of Satan's cunning devices. He offered to let the 'men go and serve the Lord'. But, pretending to be concerned for the children and the dangers to which they would be exposed, he said, 'You do not want to take them with you, for evil is before you.'

'And Moses said, We will go with our young and with our old, with our sons and with our daughters, with our flocks and with our herds will we go; for we must hold a feast unto the LORD. And he said unto them, Let the LORD be so with you, as I will let you go, and your little ones: look to it; for evil is before you. Not so: go now ye that are men, and serve the LORD; for that ye did desire. And they were driven out from Pharaoh's presence' (Exodus 10:9-11).

If he could hold their children in Egypt, Pharaoh would retain a powerful hold upon the hearts of the Hebrews, holding that which was dearest to them. They could never be done with Egypt as long as Egypt held their children.

Our children represent the most tender objects of our care. This proposed compromise is the suggestion of half-hearted devotion. How crafty the serpent is! Satan knows that if he can hold that which is dearest to us, he will hold us. But our Saviour demands total, unreserved surrender. He demands that we forsake all, if we would follow him. 'If any man come to me, and hate not his father, and mother, and wife, and children, and brethren, and sisters, yea, and his own life also, he cannot be my disciple' (Luke 14:26).

The Lord Jesus does not demand that we treat our families or our lives with contempt, or wish harm upon them or ourselves. To do so, as John Gill wrote, 'would be contrary to the laws of God, to the first principles of nature, to all humanity, to the light of nature, to reason and divine revelation.' When the Lord God declares, 'Jacob have I loved, but Esau have I hated' (Romans 9:13), the essential intent of his words (if I am not mistaken) is, 'I am totally committed to Jacob, but to Esau I give no consideration.'

That is precisely what our Saviour requires of us, whole-hearted devotion. As we follow him, we must allow no one, not even husband or wife, or son or daughter, or mother or father to come into consideration. He will have no rival.

### Fourth Compromise

Pharaoh first tried to keep Israel in Egypt. Then he tried to keep them near the land. Third, he sought to keep that which was dearest to their hearts in Egypt. Finally, when he could not persuade Moses to accept any of those compromises, he proposed sending them out into the wilderness without any ability to serve the Lord. If he could not keep the servants, he would prevent them from having the ability to serve. If he could not induce them to sacrifice in the land, he would send them out of the land without sacrifices. That is the proposed compromise of Exodus 10:24-26, Pharaoh's last compromise.

'And Pharaoh called unto Moses, and said, Go ye, serve the LORD; only let your flocks and your herds be stayed: let your little ones also go with you. And Moses said, Thou must give us also sacrifices and burnt offerings, that we may sacrifice unto the LORD our God. Our cattle also shall go with us; there shall not an hoof be left behind; for thereof must we take to serve the LORD our God; and we know not with what we must serve the LORD, until we come thither.'

The flocks and herds of this pastoral people constituted the principle part of what they owned. They speak of our earthly possessions. The fact is nothing we possess is really ours. Everything we have, we have as that which God has trusted to our hands as stewards in his house. It is ours only to use at his will, for his glory, and in the interests of his house. Of old, God charged Israel with robbing him of his tithes and offerings (Malachi 3:8). And the same charge can justly be laid against multitudes today. Let us not be guilty.

As Moses said to Pharaoh, 'There shall not an hoof be left behind', let us bring all to our Saviour, serving him with everything he has entrusted to our hands. 'There shall not an hoof be left behind' means all that I have and all that I am belong to my Redeemer; I hold all at the disposal of my Lord.

But there is more to the picture. Inasmuch as Israel's deliverance was a picture of our redemption by Christ, a type of our Saviour's glorious accomplishments of redemption, Moses' response to Pharaoh gives us a very clear declaration of particular and effectual redemption. Every soul for whom a lamb was slain in Egypt came out of Egypt, and all came out with everything pertaining to their lives. 'Not a hoof' was 'left behind'. So, too, every sinner for whom Christ our Passover was sacrificed, every sinner for whom the Lamb of God was slain shall come out of Egypt. 'There shall not an hoof be left behind'!

# Chapter 40

# Wait, O My Soul, Thy Maker's Will

'And afterward Moses and Aaron went in, and told Pharaoh, Thus saith the LORD God of Israel, Let my people go, that they may hold a feast unto me in the wilderness ... And Moses returned unto the LORD, and said, Lord, wherefore hast thou so evil entreated this people? why is it that thou hast sent me? For since I came to Pharaoh to speak in thy name, he hath done evil to this people; neither hast thou delivered thy people at all.'
Exodus 5:1-23

How often God's providence appears to contradict his promise! Though his determination is our salvation, he often appears determined to destroy us. Though he has promised never to turn away from us to do us good, it often seems that he does us evil. In all such times we would be wise to reason thus with our souls. Benjamin Beddome wrote,

> Wait, O my soul, thy Maker's will
> Tumult'ous passions all be still!
> Nor let a murm'ring thought arise;
> His ways are just, His counsels wise.
>
> He in the thickest darkness dwells,
> Performs His work, the cause conceals;
> But though His methods are unknown,
> Judgment and truth support His throne.

In heav'n and earth, and air, and seas,
He executes His firm decrees;
And by His saints it stands confessed,
That what He does is ever best.

Wait, then, my soul, submissive wait,
Prostrate before His awful seat;
And 'midst the terrors of His rod,
Trust in a wise and gracious God.


In Exodus 5 we have a vivid picture of God's providence appearing to contradict his promise. The Lord Jesus appeared to Moses in the bush, and said, 'I have seen the affliction of my people ... And I am come down to deliver them ... I will send thee unto Pharaoh, that thou mayest bring forth my people the children of Israel out of Egypt' (Exodus 3:7, 8, 10). Then, he promised Moses that the children of Israel would believe his message and that Pharaoh would let his people go, assuring him of success.

Armed with the promise of God, Moses went back to Egypt with his brother, Aaron. They gathered together all the elders of Israel and delivered God's message of deliverance to the children of Israel, the message of redemption and salvation by the hand of the Lord. 'And the people believed: and when they heard that the LORD had visited the children of Israel, and that he had looked upon their affliction, then they bowed their heads and worshipped' (Exodus 4:31). Things were looking good. Moses was on his pastoral 'honeymoon'. Everything seemed very promising; but it was all about to change.

In chapter 5 he and Aaron go in and tell Pharaoh God's demands. This is a chapter full of instruction for our souls. May God the Holy Spirit teach us its message and apply it to our hearts.

## Men with a Message
The first thing that is obvious is this: God's prophets are men sent of God with a message that must be delivered.

'And afterward Moses and Aaron went in, and told Pharaoh, Thus saith the LORD God of Israel, Let my people go, that they may hold a feast unto me in the wilderness' (v. 1).

In this day of religious foolishness it must be stated that the gospel preacher is a man, never a woman. He is a man sent by God, called, gifted, equipped, and sent by God himself. He is sent with a message. Not a lesson, not a proposal, not an offer, but a message, a message that must be delivered. God's prophets are watchman set upon the walls of Zion. Their message is the message of redemption, grace, and salvation by Christ (Isaiah 52:4-10; Ezekiel 3:27). Notice, too, how Moses describes the believer's worship of God. In Exodus 4:23 the Lord Jesus calls it serving him. Here, Moses calls it keeping a feast. We worship our God and serve him as we feed upon Christ our Saviour by faith (Psalm 63:5; Isaiah 25:6; John 6:51, 53-58). 'This is the work of God, that ye believe on him whom he hath sent' (John 6:29).

**Some Believe Not**
We are, by the gospel we preach, to some a savour of life unto life, but to others a savour of death unto death. When we proclaim redemption by the blood of Christ, when we declare salvation accomplished by his out-stretched, omnipotent arm of grace, some believe and some believe not. The gospel is, to those who believe, the power of God unto salvation. But to those who believe not, it is foolishness. Moses' and Aaron's message was to Israel the power of God unto salvation. 'And the people believed: and when they heard that the LORD had visited the children of Israel, and that he had looked upon their affliction, then they bowed their heads and worshipped' (4:31). But to Pharaoh and the Egyptians it was foolishness. Look at Pharaoh's response in verse 2.

'And Pharaoh said, Who is the LORD, that I should obey his voice to let Israel go? I know not the LORD, neither will I let Israel go'.

Pharaoh knew not the Lord! What a dreadful state. To know Christ is eternal life. Not to know him is death. This lack of knowledge in the fallen sons of Adam is the cause of all the sin and contempt people have for Christ throughout the earth (Job 21:14, 15; 1 Corinthians 2:7, 8).

**God of the Hebrews**
Next we see that the Lord God of heaven and earth, the triune Jehovah, is distinctly and specially God of his people, 'The God of the Hebrews'.

'The God of the Hebrews hath met with us: let us go, we pray thee, three days' journey into the desert, and sacrifice unto the LORD our God; lest he fall upon us with pestilence, or with the sword' (v. 3).

He was the God over the Egyptians; but he is 'the God of the Hebrews'. He had distinctly attached himself to them by covenant and by revelation. He is also distinguished as 'the God of the Hebrews' to distinguish him from all the gods of the Egyptians.

So it is today. The Lord our God is unlike all the gods of men. He who is our God is God indeed, the only true and living God, holy and wise, gracious and good, faithful and true, sovereign and merciful. He is the God of his chosen, and he 'delighteth in mercy'! He has distinctly attached himself to us and us to him by sovereign, free grace. He is our God; and we are his people.

The word 'Hebrews' is used synonymously with both Israelites and Jews. I cannot find a definite meaning to the word translated 'Hebrews' in the Scriptures; but it conveys the idea of 'one from beyond', or 'one who passes over', or 'one who lives beyond'. That is a pretty good description of God's people. The child of God in this world is one from beyond, who passes over the earth, and lives beyond it. 'We are the circumcision which worship God in the spirit, and rejoice in Christ Jesus, and have no confidence in the flesh' (Philippians 3:3).

**A Slandered People**
Just as the children of Israel were falsely accused and slandered by Pharaoh, God's people in this world are constantly falsely accused of evil and slandered by those who despise our God.

'And the king of Egypt said unto them, Wherefore do ye, Moses and Aaron, let the people from their works? get you unto your burdens. And Pharaoh said, Behold, the people of the land now are many, and ye make them rest from their burdens. And Pharaoh commanded the same day the taskmasters of the people, and their officers, saying, Ye shall no more give the people straw to make brick, as heretofore: let them go and gather straw for themselves. And the tale of the bricks, which they did make heretofore, ye shall lay upon them; ye shall not diminish ought thereof: for they be idle; therefore they cry, saying, Let us go and sacrifice to our God. Let there more work be laid upon the men, that they may labour therein; and let them not regard vain words' (vv. 4-9).

Pharaoh knew his accusation against God's people was baseless and completely untrue. 'They built for Pharaoh treasure cities, Pithom and Raamses' (Exodus 1:11). Yet, he said, 'They be idle!' So it is to this day. God's saints have many faults, faults they readily confess and acknowledge. But they are falsely accused of evil and slandered by people who know their accusations are false (Romans 3:8). It is often slanderously reported that we say, 'Let us do evil that good may come'. Because we preach God's total sovereignty in all things, we are accused of living licentiously. Because we preach salvation by grace alone, we are slandered as promoters of wickedness. Because we preach the believer's complete freedom from the law, we are accused of being opposed to the law. Furthermore, those who would do us evil are often, if not most commonly, people who assert that they are our brethren.

'And the taskmasters of the people went out, and their officers, and they spake to the people, saying, Thus saith Pharaoh, I will not give you straw. Go ye, get you straw where ye can find it: yet not ought of your work shall be diminished. So the people were scattered abroad throughout all the land of Egypt to gather stubble instead of straw. And the taskmasters hasted them, saying, Fulfil your works, your daily tasks, as when there was straw. And the officers of the children of Israel, which Pharaoh's taskmasters had set over them, were beaten, and demanded, Wherefore have ye not fulfilled your task in making brick both yesterday and today, as heretofore?' (Exodus 5:10-14)

Those taskmasters were probably Egyptians; but their officers were Israelites. They were like the publicans of our Lord's day (Matthew 18:17), Jews who gained favour with the Romans by oppressing their brethren. Painful as it is to put up with, we are wise to leave such people alone. Just wait, never retaliate (Isaiah 10:1; 2 Thessalonians 3:1, 2; 1 Corinthians 4:3-5; James 5:8). We might think it too hard to be expected to put up with such behaviour, to bear it patiently. But we have good reason to do so. Our Master did. The Lord Jesus left us an example, that we 'should follow his steps' (Isaiah 53:7; 1 Peter 2:21-24; John 15:21).

It is true, 'we must through much tribulation enter into the kingdom of God' (Acts 14:22). But our tribulation here will soon be forgotten. John Trapp wrote, 'Things commonly go backward with the saints before they come forward'. See Revelation 7:13-17.

## A Foolish Mistake

The officers of the children of Israel pray to Pharaoh. 'Then the officers of the children of Israel came and cried unto Pharaoh, saying, Wherefore dealest thou thus with thy servants? There is no straw given unto thy servants, and they say to us, Make brick: and, behold, thy servants are beaten; but the fault is in thine own people. But he said, Ye are idle, ye are idle: therefore ye say, Let us go and do sacrifice to the LORD. Go therefore now, and work; for there shall no straw be given you, yet shall ye deliver the tale of bricks. And the officers of the children of Israel did see that they were in evil case, after it was said, Ye shall not minish ought from your bricks of your daily task.'

What a sad and foolish mistake they made! This was a presumptuous attempt to take the matter of their deliverance into their own hands. God had not performed his promise. So they decided to help him. Ignoring Moses and Aaron, God's messengers, they hoped to reason with Pharaoh! Perhaps they decided that Moses and Aaron had been unreasonable, demanding too much; hard, unbending, unwilling to compromise. They were ready, in their foolish pride, to modify God's Word, seeking compromise with the very man who was tormenting them! Christ is our Deliverer. He is mighty to save. We will be wise to wait upon him (Isaiah 63:1-5; Lamentations 3:25-33; Isaiah 40:31).

**God Blamed**
Jacob blamed Simeon and Levi, saying, 'Ye have troubled me to make me stink among the inhabitants of the land ... And I shall be destroyed' (Genesis 34:30). In verses 20, 21 we see the sons of Jacob blaming God's messengers for their woe.

'And they met Moses and Aaron, who stood in the way, as they came forth from Pharaoh: And they said unto them, The LORD look upon you, and judge; because ye have made our savour to be abhorred in the eyes of Pharaoh, and in the eyes of his servants, to put a sword in their hand to slay us.'

What a heart-piercing accusation that must have been! Remember, Moses and Aaron were merely God's messengers. They were really blaming God for their woe! In all things we ought to bow to our God. How sad it is when we blame him (Jonah 4:4-9).

Remember, also, these same people had believed God's promise of deliverance when they heard it. They bowed and worshipped before him (4:31). Here we see them not only relinquishing their confidence, but also murmuring against God and blaming him and his messengers, because their professed faith had brought them trouble. Yet we must not be too hard in our judgment concerning them. Are we not the same? Do we not blame God, when in times of darkness and displeasing providences we murmur and complain? God forgive our unbelief! May God the Holy Spirit give us faith and uphold us by his grace, enabling us to keep a steady eye fixed on our blessed Saviour, that like Abraham of old, we stagger 'not at the promise of God through unbelief', that we may be confident of his Word, his all-sufficient grace, and his salvation.

### Mercy Sought

How heart-broken Moses must have been! In verses 22, 23 he goes to God in prayer, and unburdens his heavy heart to the Lord his God.

'And Moses returned unto the LORD, and said, Lord, wherefore hast thou so evil entreated this people? why is it that thou hast sent me? For since I came to Pharaoh to speak in thy name, he hath done evil to this people; neither hast thou delivered thy people at all.'

What blessed instruction this portion of Holy Scripture gives! In all our troubles, in our distresses it is always right, wise, and best to return to the Lord, putting him in remembrance of his promise and seeking his mercy (Isaiah 43:26). The Lord sent Moses to deliver his people out of Egypt. He had heard their groanings, and graciously promised to deliver them. The people believed the Word of the Lord, bowed their heads and worshipped him, adoring his great goodness. But, then, the oppression and afflictions, under which they had groaned, instead of lessening, began to increase. Soon, they became desperate, and charged God foolishly. Moses, who had talked with God at the bush, who had seen 'the good will of him that dwelt in the bush', and saw the miracles God performed to confirm his commission, appears to have been tainted with the same spirit of unbelief. 'Moses said, Lord, wherefore hast thou so evil entreated this people? why is it that thou hast sent me? For since I came to Pharaoh to speak in thy name, he hath done evil to this people; neither hast thou delivered thy people at all'.

What a picture we have in this chapter of our poor souls and our corrupt, depraved hearts! In all they experienced the Lord God was pursuing nothing but good for his people. He was, even in their woes, performing his great purpose of grace. The deliverance he had promised, he was performing. There had been no alteration in his purpose, no amendment of his covenant, and no change in his love. The Lord God was performing his wise decrees in such a way as to make their emancipation the more blessed and glorious, and his distinguishing mercy, love, and grace more striking.

But Israel could see nothing but their pain and trouble. They experienced disappointment after disappointment, frustration after frustration, and heartache after heartache. All about them was darkness and gloom. And they forgot all that God had promised.

How is it with you? How is it with me? When the promises of God seem to clash with his providence, and, according to our limited view of things, seem to be impossible, how do we act? How do we respond? We are far too much like Israel, ever disposed to take counsel with flesh and blood, rather than believing God. How quickly unbelief engulfs us! The lusts we thought were completely subdued break out afresh in full force. We find ourselves, like Peter, sinking in the tempestuous sea. Then, the hand of our omnipotent Saviour is stretched out to catch us again and raise us up! Wondrous mercy! Yet, how soon it is forgotten!

Oh for grace, in the midst of dark providence, in trying times, to trust our ever gracious, ever faithful and true God and Saviour! Oh for grace to hear his voice in the whirlwind and the storm! It is our blessedness to wait upon the Lord, to depend upon him, to believe him, to trust his promise when everything seems to say, 'He has forsaken us, he has forgotten to be gracious, his mercy is clean gone forever.'

We do not expect too much when we expect God to do what he has promised. Moses had been preaching that God had visited his people to deliver them. But, instead of being delivered from their furnace, the furnace just got hotter. Where else should he go, but to the throne of grace? I recognize that his faith was mixed with unbelief. Yet, he turned to God in faith. It is the crowning grace of faith, 'against hope to believe in hope', and amid the most desperate circumstances, to cling to Christ as a sure Friend, when in his providence it appears he comes forth as a determined enemy. In such times he truly honours God who can confidently say with Job, 'Though he slay me, yet will I trust in him'.

'We roar all like bears, and mourn sore like doves: we look for judgment, but there is none; for salvation, but it is far off from us' (Isaiah 59:11). Such was the cry of God's saints of old.

And such is, and will be their cries until grace is consummated in glory. But our times of trouble and trial shall not last an hour, not even a moment beyond our Lord's appointment. Then, deliverance will come. When he sees that our power is gone, he will show himself gracious. May he give us grace to trust him!

# Chapter 41

## The Gospel According To Moses

'Then the LORD said unto Moses, Now shalt thou see what I will do to Pharaoh: for with a strong hand shall he let them go, and with a strong hand shall he drive them out of his land. And God spake unto Moses, and said unto him, I am the LORD: And I appeared unto Abraham, unto Isaac, and unto Jacob, by the name of God Almighty, but by my name JEHOVAH was I not known to them. And I have also established my covenant with them, to give them the land of Canaan, the land of their pilgrimage, wherein they were strangers ... And I will bring you in unto the land, concerning the which I did swear to give it to Abraham, to Isaac, and to Jacob; and I will give it you for an heritage: I am the LORD.'
(Exodus 6:1-8)

The Book of Leviticus is about redemption, redemption by the precious blood of Christ, the Lamb of God, our sin atoning Substitute. Before we can know anything of redemption accomplished for us, we must experience redemption. The redemption was accomplished before we came to experience it; but it is not known until it is experienced. By the arrangement of divine providence, we come to the Book of Exodus before we get to the Book of Leviticus. Exodus is about the experience of grace, the experience of redemption. Leviticus portrays redemption accomplished. Exodus portrays redemption applied. But no one can know he was redeemed at Calvary until Christ the Redeemer is revealed in him, causing him to believe. In other words, we come to know that Christ obtained eternal redemption for us when God the Holy Spirit makes the gospel effectual to us in the saving operation of his grace. That is precisely what we are taught in Ephesians 1:3-14.

The Lord God had a people in Egypt. They were his own elect people. They had been grievously oppressed, and had been brought into bitter and ignominious slavery, but his interest in their welfare had not diminished. God's purpose in sending Moses down into Egypt was to bring that specific, chosen people out from among the nations and make them a peculiar people unto himself, that he might give them an inheritance and cause them to possess the land of Canaan, that land which flowed with milk and honey, and that they might dwell there as witnesses of his boundless mercy, grace and covenant faithfulness. And what the Lord God was doing with Israel in the land of Ham is precisely what he is doing with his elect throughout the world.

**Object of Preaching**
The object of gospel preaching is to gather out of the nations a people loved, chosen, and predestined by the triune God from eternity, a people redeemed unto himself to be his peculiar heritage. Those people loved and chosen of God and redeemed by the precious blood of Christ, his covenant people, must and shall be fetched out of the nations by God the Holy Spirit, just as David fetched Mephibosheth out of Lodebar by his servant, Ziba (2 Samuel 9:4, 5). Every chosen, redeemed sinner must and shall be made, by the experience of grace, God's own. The elect shall obtain their covenant inheritance. They shall be brought into a distinct, covenant relationship with the eternal God as his peculiar people. They must be made a separated people and be brought into a distinct position and relationship with the Lord God. 'Lo, the people shall dwell alone, and shall not be reckoned among the nations' (Numbers 23:9). Ultimately, they shall be brought to a place for which they shall be distinctly prepared. 'And they shall be mine, saith the LORD of hosts, in that day when I make up my jewels; and I will spare them, as a man spareth his own son that serveth him' (Malachi 3:17).

**God's Work Alone**
This great work of grace is the work of the triune God alone. The same right hand of Jehovah, glorious in power, that brought the sons of Jacob out of Egypt, is stretched out to deliver his chosen today. And ransomed sinners in this Gospel Age, standing with Moses, Miriam, and the

children of Israel on the Canaan side of the Red Sea, sing the praises of Christ their Redeemer, saying, 'He hath triumphed gloriously, the horse and his rider hath he thrown into the sea' (Exodus 15:1, 21).

In fact, we are specifically told in Revelation 15:3, that in heaven's everlasting glory, we shall sing the song of Moses, the servant of God, and the song of the Lamb, because the redemption of Israel out of Egypt was always meant to be a delightful, instructive type of our redemption by our Lord Jesus Christ, who loved us and gave himself for us.

**Instruments Used**
This great work of deliverance is the work of God alone. 'Salvation is of the LORD'. None can perform it but God. In great, condescending grace, he has chosen to accomplish it by the instrumentality of men, just as he used Moses for Israel's deliverance from Egypt. 'It pleased God by the foolishness of preaching'. But he only employs instruments like Moses, who know they are poorly suited for the work, unworthy to speak in his name and incapable of the work they are sent to perform, 'that no flesh should glory in his presence' (1 Corinthians 1:26-29).

In the first eight verses of Exodus 6 the Lord God tells Moses to tell his people who he is, what he had done for his people, and all that he was about to do for them in the blessed experience of redemption.

**A Gracious Answer**
In the last two verses of chapter 5 we saw Moses unburdening his heart before the Lord. Here the Lord answers his servant, assuring him of his great grace, assuring him he would do all he had promised. First, the Lord God reminds Moses of his great Name, assuring him he would perform his word and purpose of grace to deliver his people (vv. 1-3).

'Then the LORD said unto Moses, Now shalt thou see what I will do to Pharaoh: for with a strong hand shall he let them go, and with a strong hand shall he drive them out of his land. And God spake unto Moses, and said unto him, I am the LORD: And I appeared unto Abraham, unto Isaac, and unto Jacob, by the name of God Almighty, but by my name JEHOVAH was I not known to them.'

Obviously, God's great redemptive name was made known to his people before this. From the day he made himself known to Abraham and made his covenant with him, the triune God was known and worshipped by his great, distinguishing name Jehovah (Genesis 15:6-

8; 26:2, 24; 28:13). But the triune Jehovah had not revealed himself as fully to the patriarchs as he had revealed himself to Moses in the bush, and would reveal himself in bringing Israel out of Egypt. Jehovah is the name by which the Lord God makes himself known to us distinctly as our eternal, immutable, self-existing, self-sufficient, life-giving, life-sustaining covenant God. He who is El-Shaddai, the Almighty God, is Jehovah our Saviour, our covenant God. The revelation of his name is the revelation of his character. His name is who he is.

Do you know him in this character, as your God and Saviour? If so, it is because he has made himself known to you. It is by this name, the very being of God our Saviour that we are encouraged to walk before him in confident faith (Isaiah 40:25-31). Connecting these two names together in the person of our great Saviour, Jehovah-Jesus, the Almighty God, we are doubly assured that what God has promised he will perform. How blessed we are to whom the triune God makes himself known in the saving revelation and operation of his grace in Christ (Exodus 14:18; Isaiah 44:6; Jeremiah 9:23, 24; John 17:3; Revelation 22:13). Others know about him. We know him, because he has established his covenant with us in the blessed experience of grace.

When we focus on ourselves, look to ourselves, seek satisfaction in ourselves, try to find a reason for hope in ourselves, and trust in ourselves we meet with disappointment and failure. Job 29 gives a picture of Job in his most pitiful state. Defending himself before Bildad, he gloried in what he had done. In twenty-five verses he used the words 'I', 'me', and 'my' thirty-nine times. In Ecclesiastes 2, Solomon spoke of all he had seen and learned. He used those same three words thirty-eight times. But it was all vanity, nothing but vanity. Our thoughts are terribly low when we think about ourselves. And our words are most vulgar when we begin to talk about ourselves. None but God can rightly and truly speak much of 'I'. When the Lord God speaks to his chosen in mercy, when he speaks of his salvation, we rejoice to hear him use those blessed words 'I', 'me', and 'my'! He used those words nineteen times in these eight verses to quieten Moses' fearful heart and assure him of his salvation. Our Saviour's 'fear nots' are always followed with 'I'. He says, 'Fear not, It is I'. 'Fear not, I have redeemed thee'. 'Fear not, I am with thee'. 'Fear not, I will help thee'. 'Fear not, I will uphold thee'. 'Fear not, I have loved thee'. 'Fear not, I will never leave thee, nor forsake thee'. 'Fear not, I will keep thee'. 'Fear not, I have blotted out, as a thick cloud, thy transgressions, and, as a cloud, thy sins'. 'Fear not, I, even I, am he that blotteth out thy transgressions for mine own sake, and will not remember thy sins'. I love to hear our God say, 'I'.

Second, having reminded Moses of his great and glorious Name, Jehovah, the Almighty God, he reminded his servant of all he had done for his people in the past (vv. 4, 5). 'And I have also established my covenant with them, to give them the land of Canaan, the land of their pilgrimage, wherein they were strangers. And I have also heard the groaning of the children of Israel, whom the Egyptians keep in bondage; and I have remembered my covenant.'

Put the name of our God to his promise, and add to that all that we have already experienced in his goodness, and all doubt should be driven from our hearts forever! O my fearful heart, remember these things, just these three things, and be still! The Lord declares, 'I have established my covenant with them' (Genesis 17:8; 2 Samuel 23:5). 'I have heard the groaning of the children of Israel' (Psalm 106:4). 'I have remembered my covenant' (Psalm 106:45; 105:8; 103:10-17).

**Seven Sure Promises**
After reminding Moses of his great Name and his great grace performed in the past, the Lord God gives him seven sure promises, seven 'I wills'. God's 'I wills' are as sure as his 'I haves'. God's word to his servant was, 'Now shalt thou see what I will do to Pharaoh'. Soon the strong hand of Pharaoh, which oppressed, enslaved, and tormented his people, would drive them out of his land. Pharaoh and his kingdom would be turned upside down; Israel would be free. Read these great 'I wills' of our God (vv. 6-8), and be assured, 'He which hath begun a good work in you will perform it' and bring it to its completion, because 'it is God which worketh in you both to will and to do of his good pleasure'.

'Wherefore say unto the children of Israel, I am the LORD, and I will bring you out from under the burdens of the Egyptians, and I will rid you out of their bondage, and I will redeem you with a stretched out arm, and with great judgments: And I will take you to me for a people, and I will be to you a God: and ye shall know that I am the LORD your God, which bringeth you out from under the burdens of the Egyptians. And I will bring you in unto the land, concerning the which I did swear to give it to Abraham, to Isaac, and to Jacob; and I will give it you for an heritage: I am the LORD'.

'I am the LORD, and I will bring you out from under the burdens of the Egyptians.' Israel had been forced to make bricks without straw. An impossible task! Rest was what they needed and wanted; and rest is what the Lord God promised to give. So with us (Matthew 11:28-30).

'I will rid you out of their bondage.' The Lord did not tell Israel to do anything to achieve this. He will do it. (Colossians 1:12-14; 2:8-17).

'I will redeem you with a stretched out arm, and with great judgments'. Notice this is a promise of redemption by power and by judgment. Deliverance and salvation can never be obtained except by judgment accomplished and by the power of omnipotent grace. Our redemption was accomplished by the judgment of our sin in Christ at Calvary. It is applied to us by the omnipotent power of God's sovereign grace in the effectual call of his Spirit (Galatians 3:13, 14).

'I will take you to me for a people'. Our Saviour has redeemed us unto himself as his own peculiar people, set apart from all others by grace. 'Ye are not your own. Ye are bought with a price. Therefore glorify God in your bodies and in your spirits, which are God's'.

'I will be to you a God: and ye shall know that I am the LORD your God, which bringeth you out from under the burdens of the Egyptians.' All who experience the blessed, saving operations of his grace know him, and are assured he alone is God who is their God; and they know all the work of their salvation is his work.

'I will bring you in unto the land, concerning the which I did swear to give it to Abraham, to Isaac, and to Jacob.' He who has chosen us, redeemed us, and called us will keep us; and he will bring us home to heaven, to sit down with Abraham, Isaac, and Jacob in his Kingdom.

'I will give it you for an heritage.' Not only will he bring us home at last, he will cause us to possess and enjoy all his kingdom and glory forever as our rightful heritage, as a people who are 'heirs of God and joint-heirs with Jesus Christ'.

Be sure you do not fail to observe that the Lord's first words in this string of promises were, 'I am the LORD' (v. 6). And his last words are, 'I am the LORD' (v. 8). That is because the whole thing is God's doing, not man's. He who is our Saviour is the Alpha and the Omega, the First and the Last, the Beginning and the End. In the whole business of salvation he is the Alpha and the Omega, the First and the Last, the Beginning and the End. And that is the gospel according to Moses.

# Chapter 42

## Believers In Their Lowest Condition

'And Moses spake so unto the children of Israel: but they hearkened not unto Moses for anguish of spirit, and for cruel bondage.'
(Exodus 6:1-30)

May God the Holy Spirit give us grace to apply the message of this chapter to ourselves. We should always read the Scriptures personally as God's Word to us. Solomon said, 'As in water face answereth to face, so the heart of man to man' (Proverbs 27:19). If we are honest, we must confess we see something of ourselves in all others, and something of our own hearts' depravity in the deeds of others. As we read the chapter, it is obvious that the children of Israel in Egypt were not unlike us.

We tend to look at the children of Israel as though we are better than they were, stronger than they were, and less carnal. But that is a great mistake. They were no more depraved and no weaker than we are. They were no more disinclined to believe God than we are. It is only our shameful pride and evil inclination to self-righteousness that makes us think we are better than they. This is obvious in their unbelief and ours.

'And Moses spake so unto the children of Israel: but they hearkened not unto Moses for anguish of spirit, and for cruel bondage.' Never was Israel in a lower condition than this. And you and I are in our lowest condition when we refuse to believe our God, when we are 'for anguish of spirit and cruel bondage' incapable of believing him. Nothing more dishonours our God than our unbelief. Yet, that is often the condition in which we find ourselves, incapable of believing him. Is it not?

## Moses' Message

'And Moses spake so unto the children of Israel.' The children of Israel had been groaning under the yoke of cruel bondage and oppression. The Lord God heard their cries and sent his servant, Moses, to deliver them. But, from the time that Moses arrived and announced God's purpose of grace toward them, their misery only increased. They complained to Pharaoh and blamed Moses for their increased troubles and afflictions.

Moses took the matter to God. And the Lord sent him to his people with a message of grace. It was a consoling, heart-cheering, assuring message of redemption and deliverance by God's own hand. The Lord God gave Moses his message; and Moses delivered it faithfully, exactly as he received it. What a message it was! It was the gospel of salvation from a cruel bondage, the gospel of hope, the gospel of glorious promise. It was the same message God's servants preach continually, the message of God's free and sovereign grace in Christ, the message of redemption, salvation, and grace for our needy souls (vv. 2-8).

First, Moses spoke to the children of Israel about their God (vv. 2, 3). He said, 'Your God is God indeed; and his name is Jehovah, the God of your fathers, the God of Abraham, of Isaac, and of Jacob.' But they looked up from their bricks, and seemed to say, 'God? What do we have to do with him? What does he have to do with us? We need straw to make our bricks! We are up to our necks in this filthy Nile mud making bricks, and you talk to us about God, his name, Jehovah, and his promises!' Their cruel bondage was so painful, their anguish of heart so heavy that they could think of nothing else; and 'they hearkened not unto Moses'. El-Shaddai, God Almighty, Lord Jehovah, was Israel's God; but they believed him not. He was their only hope; but they found no hope in him. Light was shining upon them, but their darkness was not dispelled. Why? 'For anguish of spirit and cruel bondage.'

How often that is the case with us! When we are overwhelmed with grief, crushed with affliction, cast down with care, God our Saviour bids us cast all our care upon him, assuring us he cares for us, but we cannot believe 'for anguish of spirit and cruel bondage'. It is not an excuse for our unbelief nor justification for it. It is a statement of fact. How often we have been forced to cry, 'Lord, I believe; help thou mine unbelief' (Mark 9:24). Like that poor soul whose son was grievously vexed with a devil, we hear our Saviour say, 'If thou canst believe, all things are possible to him that believeth'. But we are still filled with unbelief!

Is your life made bitter by trouble, made bitter with toil and heartache, so bitter you are in 'anguish of spirit'? Thank God, there is an inheritance above the grinding toil of this life. Child of God, there is a portion infinitely better than the killing care that seems to make your life a life of woe. Do not, because of the heaviness of your lot, refuse to hear God, your Maker, your Benefactor, and your Redeemer. Let the history of Israel encourage you to hope (Psalm 106; Psalm 103:1-14).

After reminding Israel of their God and Saviour, Moses went on to tell them about his covenant (v. 4). I am sure many of them had no idea what he was talking about. They knew no more of God's covenant with them than they did of the riches of Canaan. All they experienced made the thought of such a covenant laughable, but for one thing. It was true! It should never be so, but often covenant grace sounds like mockery to broken hearts. There are times when we are in such straits we dare not say what we feel. God says that his mercy endures forever; but we feel that his mercy is clean gone forever. God says that he will never leave us, nor forsake us; but we feel utterly forsaken.

Yet, God's word is true, and sure. If you are in such a state as God's people of old, if your 'anguish of spirit' is such that you cannot find comfort in God's covenant grace, let me tell you again, it is all true. The triune God has entered into covenant with you. He has bound himself to you for good by an everlasting covenant, ordered in all things and sure, a covenant of pure grace and everlasting mercy. Your deliverance is sure. Even your present 'anguish of spirit and cruel bondage' is a token of that covenant (Romans 8:28-39). Goodness and mercy have followed you all the days of your life, and shall follow you until those twin hounds of heaven have chased you into heavenly glory with Christ.

Moses went on to remind God's chosen ones of his great pity toward them (v. 5; Isaiah 63:9). Yet, when the hand of God lays heavily upon us we find it hard to believe he pities us. Oh, we have the idea firmly fixed in our minds, but our 'anguish of spirit' shuts it out of our hearts. Was it pity, was it mercy, was it the remembrance of his covenant that moved Joseph's brothers to sell him into bondage? Yes, it was. Was it his pity that made David's bones wax old through his crying, day and night? Yes, it was. Was it pity that put Peter in the sieve to be sifted by Satan? Yes, it was. Was it pity that refused to take away Paul's thorn in the flesh? Yes. It is his pity that leaves us in this body of flesh, to mourn and struggle with our corruptions of heart and our sins.

**Why am I thus?**

When Rebekah found two nations struggling in her womb, she asked the Lord what every believer is compelled by experience to ask, 'Why am I thus?' (Genesis 25:22). That is what Paul experienced (Romans 7:18-21). And it is exactly what I experience day by day. 'I know that in me (that is, in my flesh,) dwelleth no good thing. The evil which I would not, that I do ... When I would do good, evil is present with me'.

Why? 'Why am I in this condition?' 'Why is sin so prominent in my nature?' 'Why is evil always present with me?' 'Why is there a constant warfare in my soul?' These are questions I am frequently asked by concerned souls who honestly acknowledge their sin. And these are questions I frequently ask myself.

The Word of God alone supplies us with the answer to them. 'That which is born of the flesh is flesh; and that which is born of the Spirit is spirit' (John 3:6). It is as simple and as profound as that.

All true believers are people with two natures: 'Flesh' and 'Spirit'. Those two natures are constantly at war with one another. The spirit will never surrender to the flesh and the flesh will never bow to the spirit. We do not walk in the flesh. We walk in the Spirit. And those who walk in the Spirit do not fulfil the lusts of the flesh. Yet, we never escape those lusts. We will never be free from 'the body of this death', until we have dropped this body in death. Painful as this situation is, while we live in this world, it is best for us that we live in this condition for three reasons:

1. We must never forget that the only thing distinguishing us from other people is the distinguishing grace of God (1 Corinthians 4:7).

2. We must never forget that our only acceptance with God is the blood and righteousness of Christ (1 Corinthians 1:30).

3. We must never become content with our existence in this world (2 Corinthians 5:1-9).

**Grace Sufficient**

Then, in verses 6-8 Moses said to Israel the very same thing the Lord Jesus told Paul in 2 Corinthians 12:9, 'My grace is sufficient for thee!' In all the promises of grace that the Lord God commanded Moses to proclaim to Israel he reminded his chosen of his determination and resolve to do them good, to redeem them, deliver them, and save them. When God says, 'I will', he means it. We can and should depend upon it. He does not ask our permission, or wait for our help. God's 'I will' is omnipotence putting itself into words. And his promises are never 'yea and nay'. They are always, 'yea and amen' in Christ Jesus! Oh, may he give us grace to believe him! Spurgeon put it like this,

'These are great words, but they come from the mouth of the great God, who cannot lie. Wherefore believe them and take hope. God will take you, poor guilty ones, to be his children. He will promote you to be his willing servants. He will use you for his glory though now you dishonour his name. He will sanctify you and cleanse you, and he will bring you to heaven, even you who have lien among the pots and have been deified in the brick kilns of sin. He will never rest till he makes you sit upon his throne with him, where he is glorified, world without end … He will bring you out of bondage and guide you through the wilderness till you come into the eternal rest, even to a goodlier land than Canaan, though it flowed with milk and honey.'

## Israel's Unbelief

Still, after hearing this great and glorious gospel, we are told, 'The children of Israel harkened not unto Moses for anguish of spirit and cruel bondage'. The message was from the Lord, and it was full of hope, but they were too low to receive it, too heavy-hearted to believe it.

They could not receive Moses' gospel message because they had been terribly disappointed. They had expected to be set free at once, as soon as Moses went in unto Pharaoh. When that did not happen, they fell back into sullen despair. Insofar as they could see, like the Saviour's disciples after his death, their great expectation of deliverance had proved a great disappointment (Luke 24:13-21).

When Moses came to them and said that God had appeared to him at the bush, and had sent him to deliver them, they bowed their heads and worshipped. But after that, when Moses went in unto Pharaoh, and the tyrant doubled their labour by denying them straw, they could not believe God or his messenger. In my own experience I have found it so (Isaiah 28:12). I know exactly what they felt. I am ashamed to confess, but confess I must, that I have often found myself like Job of old, 'I will not refrain my mouth; I will speak in the anguish of my spirit; I will complain in the bitterness of my soul' (Job 7:11). 'Trouble and anguish have taken hold on me: yet thy commandments are my delights' (Psalm 119:143). I find life in this body of flesh to be 'the land of trouble and anguish, from whence come the young and old lion, the viper and fiery flying serpent' (Isaiah 30:6). 'Hope deferred maketh the heart sick: but when the desire cometh, it is a tree of life' (Proverbs 13:12).

Opening my heart's door, as best I can, entering into its most secret chambers, I see the most abominable and frightful things imaginable. In my sinful heart of flesh I see every foul and evil thing a man has ever done, or imagined against God and his fellowman. I make no exceptions (Matthew 15:19). I see evil thoughts, murderous imaginations, vile adulteries, fornications and perversions, deceit, thefts, lying, and blasphemies. Let other men talk of progressively getting more sanctified, holy and righteous, and less sinful, if they dare speak so proudly. As for me, 'I know', by the testimony of Holy Scripture and by painful experience, 'that in me (that is, in my flesh) dwelleth no good thing'. 'I am carnal, sold under sin.'

Before God saved me, I thought things would be different if ever God was pleased to save me. I knew my sins would not be eradicated. But I did think they would at least be fewer, weaker, and less troublesome. But things are not as I dreamed! I was shocked to wake up one day and realize I am just as sinful as ever by nature. My flesh is still flesh; and it always will be. Until this body of flesh dies, my sin will never die, or even diminish! The outward deeds are not so bad as they once were; but the inward corruptions are worse, far worse.

I am trying to be honest with you who read these lines, because I want you to be honest with yourself and with God. Before God saved you, did you ever imagine a saved person could be so vile as you are? I never thought a saved man could love Christ so little as I do, and love the world so much, trust God as little and fret so much, have such a cold heart of indifference to the things of God and such a lively spirit to the things of the world, have such a hard time praying and reading God's Word, and so impatient, grumbling, and resentful of God's providence.

In myself I honestly see nothing good, righteous, or holy. I pray; but my prayers are full of selfish desires. I read God's Word; but my mind runs to every evil thing. I love Christ; but my love for him is shameful. I trust my God; but my faith is mixed with unbelief.

This is my confession: I am a sinner, nothing else. My only hope is God's free grace in Christ. My only acceptance with God is the righteousness and shed blood of Christ, the sinner's Substitute.

**More Good News**

Exodus 6 begins with the declaration of the gospel, the good news of God's sure salvation. Then, in verse 9 we have that sad, sad picture of our unbelief because of our 'anguish of spirit' and continued bondage.

Israel's inability to believe Moses' message arose from the fact they were earthbound by heavy oppression. The mere struggle to exist exhausted their energy, and destroyed their hope. The hardness of their lot made them despondent. They had to work from morning to night. It was a daily question with them whether life was worth living under such cruel conditions. Therefore, they 'hearkened not unto Moses'.

Blessed be God, his promised grace and the performance of it do not in any way depend upon us, or even upon our faith in him. It seems the Lord ignored their inability, remembering they were but dust. In great mercy he met their great need by proclaiming more good news. As we read this chapter, if we were to leave out verse 9, it would not be missed at all. In the rest of the chapter the Lord God goes right on declaring his purpose of grace, his determination and resolve to save those very people of his choice, who were in such a low condition that they could not and would not believe him 'for anguish of spirit and cruel bondage'.

At first, Israel did not receive God's message of grace by reason of their anguish of soul; but the message was true and the promise was sure, nonetheless. I cannot begin to tell you how very thankful I am that God's grace is immutable! It does not wait or depend upon me for anything!

What did the Lord do when he found these people did not hearken to Moses 'for anguish of spirit, and for cruel bondage'? Did he give them up because of their wretched condition? Not on your life! He said, 'I will bring them out;' and he meant to do it.

The first thing the Lord did to prove his persevering grace was to renew his commission to Moses (Exodus 6:1; 7:2). Moses and Aaron had been greatly discouraged by the unbelief of Israel, and by seeing their anguish and cruelty increase. What did the Lord do? Did he tell his servants to wash their hands of them and go to another people? Oh, no! He simply renewed his charge to them, and gave them their marching orders again. No matter how impossible the task might appear, there was to be no backing out of it. Israel must be delivered, and must be delivered by the men God sent to deliver them (vv. 10-13). The God of heaven issued his royal decree, and refused to go back on his Word. Moses and Aaron were in water over their heads. They could not deliver Israel out of Egypt; but they did.

It is so with us today. We are called to perform the impossible. Ours is a labour and a task that requires unrelenting miracles of omnipotent mercy. I see before me a valley full of dry bones. God Almighty commands me go and say to them, 'Thus saith the Lord, Ye dry bones, Live.' What a preposterous thing! Someone once said, 'To preach the gospel to dead sinners is as preposterous as to wave a pocket-handkerchief over a grave.' I fully agree. But, if God has sent me to wave his handkerchief over the dead, as I wave it, I fully expect the dead to live.

One more thing. As we read the rest of the chapter, we see that the Lord began to count the heads of those he would redeem out of bondage. The rest of the chapter speaks of the children of Reuben, and the children of Simeon, and the children of Levi. God said, 'Pharaoh, let my people go!' Pharaoh replied, 'I will not.' And the Lord God made a roster, put it in Moses' hands, and said, 'Take this and shove it under Pharaoh's nose. These whose names are written in the Lamb's book of life, slain from the foundation of the world, shall go out. They shall be my people; and I will be their God.'

'The foundation of God standeth sure, having this seal, The Lord knoweth them that are his.' He has written their names in his book from eternity. And he declares, 'They shall be mine, saith the Lord, in that day when I make up my jewels.' Out of the mass of fallen humanity, a company shall come to him, and shall glorify his name, as it is written, 'This people have I formed for myself; they shall show forth my praise.'

How we ought to give thanks and rejoice to know that 'If we believe not, yet he abideth faithful: he cannot deny himself' (2 Timothy 2:13). The fact is, we cannot and will not believe our God except as he gives us faith to believe him. When he fulfils his Word, delivering us from the 'anguish of spirit and cruel bondage' that holds us in darkness, we will believe him (Psalm 106:4-12). If we believe, we shall see the glory of God; and we shall believe when God reveals his glory in the wonders of his grace before our eyes (John 11:40-45; Psalm 80:3, 7, 19).

# Chapter 43

# God's Work And Its Performance

'Then the LORD said unto Moses, Now shalt thou see what I will do to Pharaoh: for with a strong hand shall he let them go, and with a strong hand shall he drive them out of his land.'
(Exodus 6:1)

Every believer recognizes and rejoices in the fact that 'Salvation is of the LORD'. It is God's work and God's work alone. It is in no way dependent upon, conditioned upon, or determined by anything in man or done by man. We contribute nothing to the salvation of our souls; and we contribute nothing to the salvation of others. It is entirely God's work. 'Salvation is of the LORD'! That cannot be stated too strongly, too often, or too fully. None 'can by any means redeem his brother, nor give to God a ransom for him' (Psalm 49:7). And 'none can keep alive his own soul' (Psalm 22:29). Salvation is God's work (John 1:12, 13; Romans 9:16).

Every believer understands that salvation is God's work alone, but many fail to realize that, in his infinite sovereignty, the God of heaven condescends to use saved sinners to save lost sinners, to use the preaching of the gospel as the instrument by which he saves his elect, though this is clearly taught in Holy Scripture (Romans 1:14-17; 10:13-17; 1 Peter 1:23-25). 'It pleased God, by the foolishness of preaching, to save them that believe' (1 Corinthians 1:21).

**Grace Portrayed**

We have a beautiful, clear, instructive picture of God's use of human instrumentality in the salvation of his elect in the Book of Exodus. I keep repeating this because I want you to always read the Book of Exodus in this light, as a picture of God's saving operations of grace toward and upon his elect. Let me show you another aspect of the picture.

'Now shalt thou see what I will do.' The Lord God had a people in Egypt. They were the people of his choice and his covenant. They were enslaved in Egypt and horribly oppressed by Pharaoh. Yet, they were his people. God's purpose in sending Moses down into Egypt was that he might bring his people out of Egypt and make them a separate people to himself, that he might bring them into a land that flowed with milk and honey, that they might inherit that land and possess it as perpetual witnesses of his great goodness.

That which the Lord God did for Israel in bringing them out of the cursed land of Ham is precisely what he is doing today throughout the whole world by the preaching of the gospel. By the preaching of the gospel, God the Holy Spirit gathers out from among the nations a people chosen and predestinated by God the Father and redeemed by the Lord Jesus Christ to be his peculiar heritage. He fetches them out from among the fallen sons of Adam and makes them his own peculiar people by the distinct experience of his grace.

It is written, 'Lo, the people shall dwell alone, and shall not be reckoned among the nations' (Numbers 23:9). God's chosen shall be brought to heaven as a place specially prepared specifically for them from eternity, and a place for which they are prepared in time by the mighty operations of his grace. As Jehovah himself has declared, 'They shall be mine ... in that day when I make up my jewels' (Malachi 3:17).

Just as the Lord God sent Moses to deliver Israel out of Egypt, though the deliverance was his work alone, so he sends his servants to deliver his elect from sin and death by the preaching of the gospel, though the deliverance is his work alone.

**God's Voice**

First, I want you to see and see clearly that the salvation of God's elect is by his voice alone. It was not Moses' voice that brought Israel out of Egypt, but God's (Exodus 4:22, 23).

'And thou shalt say unto Pharaoh, Thus saith the LORD, Israel is my son, even my firstborn: And I say unto thee, Let my son go, that he may serve me: and if thou refuse to let him go, behold, I will slay thy son, even thy firstborn.'

It is not the voice of the gospel preacher that brings dead sinners to life and faith in Christ, but the voice of God alone (John 5:25; 6:63; 10:16, 27; 1 Thessalonians 1:4, 5). It is the power of God's voice that brings his people out of Egypt. Here are three specific things uttered by God himself, by which he brought Israel out of Egypt, three mighty words of grace, by which God saves his elect.

First, he said to Pharaoh, 'Israel is my son, even my firstborn'. It is written, 'The Lord knoweth them that are his'. The Lord God claims his inalienable right to his people, and asserts his unfailing interest in their welfare, saying, 'Israel is my son, even my firstborn'. Though they were slaves in Egypt, he said, 'Israel is my son, even my firstborn'. Though they were ground down, making bricks, he said, 'Israel is my son, even my firstborn'. Though they were terribly degraded, so degraded they could not even dream of deliverance, even when the day of deliverance dawned upon them, and could not believe 'for anguish of spirit and for cruel bondage', the Lord God said, 'Israel is my son, even my firstborn'.

They had no thought of liberty. They were sunk into the base idolatry of the Egyptians. They did not even know God by his great name, 'Jehovah'. Yet, the Lord said of those poor, wretched, hopeless people, 'Israel is my son, even my firstborn'. They were his all the while; and he owned them as his own. Though they forsook him, he never relinquished them. 'Israel is my son, even my firstborn.'

So it is with God's elect in this world. Though lost and ruined by the sin and fall of our father Adam, though dead in trespasses and in sins, up to our necks in mud, though we all went 'astray from the womb speaking lies', though we did not know him and did not want to know him, though we hated him and rebelled against him, and were by nature 'children of wrath even as others', the Lord God said of his chosen, 'Israel is my son, even my firstborn'.

Blessed be his name forever, our even then Saviour was not ashamed to call us his brethren. Even then, our Father was not ashamed to own us as his sons and daughters, his firstborn. He proclaims his great love wherewith he loved us, even when we were dead in trespasses and sin.

He loved us when we were cast out from our mothers' wombs, lying in our blood, unwashed, naked, and filthy. When no eye pitied us in the day of our nativity, and we were cast out in the open field, he passed by in the time of love and said unto us, 'Live'. Oh, wondrous grace! Does God own his people as his people even before they know him? Of course he does! If he did not, we would never have come to know him. We love him now because he first loved us. And had he not known us and loved us before we knew him, we could never know and love him.

When the Lord God said, 'Israel is my son', he was speaking in reference to the covenant he had made with Abraham 400 years before any of those now in Egypt had been born. Yes, the Lord knows his people, and shows favour to them, not because of any personal merit, worth, or work by which they recommend themselves to him. We have none. There was no superiority in our nature, no brightness in our minds, no beauty in our character that was pleasing in his sight.

The only title any sinner has to God's grace is that ancient covenant ordered in all things and sure, which he made not with Abraham, but with our Lord Jesus Christ, who stands from everlasting as our covenant Head and Surety. This is the great fountain from which the wells of salvation are continually filled with the living waters of grace.

This is the reason why God called Israel his son. Israel was made his son by an ancient covenant; and so were we. Some are so ignorant that they deny this blessed fact of Divine Revelation. I have often read and heard men say, 'God never calls anyone his son until he believes. We become the sons of God by believing in Christ.' Not true! It is true we come to know we are the sons of God by faith in Christ, his Spirit bearing 'witness with our spirit that we are the children of God' (Romans 8:16). But we were made the sons of God in eternal grace. We are born again in time, trust Christ in time, because we are the children of God from eternity. 'And because ye are sons, God hath sent forth the Spirit of his Son into your hearts, crying, Abba, Father' (Galatians 4:6).

It is because his people are really his sons before they know anything at all about it, that in due time God sends the Spirit of his Son to give them the nature of his Son, that they may enjoy the adoption of children, and say, 'Abba, Father'. Our faith in Christ does not make us God's children. Our faith in Christ is the fruit of us being his children from eternity. Faith in Christ does not give us birth. It is the result of our heavenly birth. The Lord God owned us as his own before the worlds were made. He loved us as 'his son, even his firstborn' with a love that cannot be measured and cannot be altered from everlasting.

He said to Pharaoh, 'Israel is my son. You, Pharaoh, may call him your slave, but he is my child. He was mine before he was yours. Israel is my son. You say, "No, he is my slave." I say, though he has fallen under your yoke, I maintain my right to him as my firstborn. He is a prince, and to that estate he shall be raised.' The long and short of it is this: the Lord God has a claim upon his elect as his own sons and daughters, the claim of the firstborn. All the claims of law and all the chains of sin, death and hell can never set this claim aside. Though we basely submitted to the claims of the wicked one, and made a covenant with death, and were in league with hell, Jehovah's claim stood firm. He said, 'Your covenant with death shall be disannulled, and your agreement with hell shall not stand' (Isaiah 28:18).

The Lord Jesus will not allow those he has made to be his own in everlasting love, and ransomed by the price of his precious blood poured out upon the cursed tree, to remain the slaves of sin and Satan. They are his. His Father gave them to him. He bought them. Their names are written on his hands and on his heart. He will not leave even one of them in bondage to the adversary. By owning us as his people, the Lord God exerts a positive claim upon us, one that makes all other claims null and void! With the bare assertion of his right, he demands our unconditional freedom. 'Thus saith the Lord, Israel is my son, even my firstborn: and I say unto thee, let my son go' (Exodus 4:22, 23).

What a great word from our God that is! What a blessed edict of absolute sovereignty! As God said, 'Let there be light: and there was light'. So too, these short words are launched with sovereign force, 'Let my son go'! Let us apply those words to ourselves. It is the reason they are written, that we may see and understand that our salvation is accomplished by the irresistible, sovereign edict of our God. The law held us under its curse; but God said; 'Let my son go'! Satan, the god of this world, claimed us as his subjects; but God said, 'Let my son go'! Death held us in its cold grip; but God said, 'Let my son go'! Hell grasped us in its clutches; but God said, 'Let my son go'!

In due time our Redeemer appeared. The Lord Jesus Christ came, identified himself with his enslaved brethren, bore all our curse, paid all our debt, fulfilled the law; and now, on the ground of simple justice, he demands for us full and perfect liberty and life everlasting. He who was made sin for us, and being made sin put away our sins by the sacrifice of himself, says to his own holy law, 'Let my son go'. God declares, 'As for thee also, by the blood of thy covenant I have sent forth thy prisoners out of the pit wherein is no water' (Zechariah 9:11).

The law, Satan, death, hell, and sin release the ransomed sons of God by the voice of God our Saviour! When he speaks, the chains that held us captive are snapped like dried twigs, and ransomed sinners go free! When he commands life, the dead come forth in life (John 11:43, 44).

Fast bound in our prison, as Peter in Acts 12, deliverance seemed impossible. The iron gates, one after another, shut us in the innermost ward of our dungeon prison. But at midnight, as we slept in senseless darkness, the Angel of the Lord smote us on the side. Around us there shined a great light. And Christ, the Angel of covenant mercy, led us through gate after gate with such ease that the iron gates seemed to open of their own accord; and we found ourselves free. At first, we could not believe it. It was as though we had seen a vision. But the freedom wherewith Christ has made us free filled our hearts with laughter. 'The Lord has done great things for me, whereof I am glad'.

That same omnipotent voice will continue to echo as long as we are in this world, 'Let my son go'! When troubles crush us down, tender omnipotence says, 'Let my son go'! When sin trips us, and we fall into the snare of the devil, omnipotent grace says, 'Let my son go'! When the law would accuse and condemn us, irresistible love says, 'Let my son go'! When our own conscience screams accusations against us, infinite goodness says, 'Let my son go'! When at last our bodies are laid in the grave, the day will come when our glorious, sovereign God and Saviour shall appear and say, 'Let my son go'!

There shall not a bone of a believer be left in the grave. As it was said of old, 'not a hoof shall be left behind', so nothing that belongs to the redeemed man shall be left in the grave either. Our Saviour's word to the Father is, 'Of all that thou hast given me I have lost nothing.' And nothing shall be lost! The voice of God claims us as his own, and demands our freedom. And that same voice, the eternal, unalterable voice of the Almighty, is what causes us to know and worship him by faith in Christ. 'Let my son go, that he may serve me' (Exodus 4:23).

We are no sooner set free from serving Pharaoh than we begin to serve Jehovah. 'Let my son go, that he may serve me.' How did Israel serve God? It was in the loftiest capacity possible. Israel became

Jehovah's priest. It was in Israel that the sacrifice was offered. In Israel the incense burned. From Israel, psalms of praise went up to heaven. Israel stood before the Lord in that high position of sacred privilege.

So it is with us. As soon as a sinner is brought out of bondage into liberty, he brings the sacrifice of Christ to God by faith, and presents himself a living sacrifice to God with his Saviour. His thanksgivings, his broken and contrite heart, his praises, even his every effort to honour his God are perpetual oblations and offerings of a sweet smelling savour acceptable to God by Jesus Christ. Israel was to be God's servant, serving him by faith. For forty years they walked through the wilderness, living on the word, promise, and power of God. Without sowing or reaping, they were fed day by day. Without wells, they were refreshed with water out of the Rock. They had no tailors, yet, they were perfectly clothed. They had no cobblers in their camp, yet, they were well shod. Their camp was well shaded by day, and lit well by night.

Israel in the wilderness had the blessed experience of having nothing and yet possessing all things. With no fertile fields or fruitful trees, Israel was made to live upon the fat of the earth, and to ride upon the high places of the earth. She had all things and she abounded. The Lord was her Shepherd, and she did not want. Is it not so with you? Enabling 'faith in Christ' is the work of God in us, and believing is the greatest work a man can do. Israel alone ate the passover. No one else had the sacrifice of God. Israel alone had a sabbath rest. God gave that blessed rest, typifying our rest of faith in Christ our Sabbath, to no other people. Israel alone walked with God. Israel alone lived upon Manna that fell from heaven. Israel alone drank from the Rock. Israel was brought up out of Egypt by the voice of God. And so it is today. 'Today, if ye will hear his voice, harden not your heart.'

### A Man's Voice
Second, the Scriptures show us that God's voice spoke Israel's deliverance out of Egypt by a man's voice. 'Thou shalt say unto Pharaoh, Thus saith the Lord ... Let my son go' (Exodus 4:22, 23). Why do you suppose the Lord did not say it himself? Why did he send Moses to say it? God made the work all the more glorious and all the more glorifying to him by using a man to do it. And in the salvation of his elect, in calling chosen, redeemed sinners from death to life in Christ by his Spirit, God has chosen to make his wondrous work of grace all

the more glorifying to himself by using men to preach the word of life to them (1 Corinthians 1:18-31). Why does God not speak to every sinner directly and save his chosen without the use of men? He could. But when he stoops to gather poor mortals, who have tasted his grace, he uses weak things to confound the mighty and foolish things to confound the wise, making his wonders of grace all the more admirable.

All the works of God redound to his glory; but when the instruments he uses appear to be totally inadequate to do the work he performs by them, our reverence is excited, while our reason is awed. We marvel at the power we cannot understand. It was by Moses that God brought Israel out of Egypt. It was by Moses alone that God led and instructed Israel. Every time they imagined that God spoke to them by another, they got into trouble. When they thought God spoke to them by Aaron, they found themselves dancing naked around a golden calf, pretending to worship Jehovah! When many of them looked upon Korah as God's prophet, the Lord killed them and their self-appointed prophet! So it is today. God saves his people, instructs, guides, edifies, and feeds them by the preaching of the gospel. He puts the treasure of his grace in earthen vessels of flesh to make the treasure shine more brightly (Ephesians 4:7-16; 1 Thessalonians 5:12, 13; Hebrews 13:7, 17).

Once Moses knew he was sent of God to carry God's Word to men, he was fearless before Pharaoh, Egypt, and Israel. Insignificant as he was in and of himself, the very fact God sent him to speak for him silenced his fears. Being sent of God he was assured of success. 'Then the LORD said unto Moses, Now shalt thou see what I will do to Pharaoh: for with a strong hand shall he let them go, and with a strong hand shall he drive them out of his land' (Exodus 6:1). With that sweet assurance, Moses steadily kept at his work until he saw God's salvation accomplished. He persevered with diligence in the work God sent him to perform until his work was done. In the end, he led the people of God out of Egypt and through the Red Sea, triumphing over Pharaoh.

**Divine Power**

Yet, third, the work was all God's. Without the power of God, Moses' voice would have been utterly meaningless. His work would have been complete vanity. It was not Moses, but God who plagued Pharaoh, filled the land of Egypt with lice, flies, frogs, and locusts. So it is with the preaching of the gospel (1 Thessalonians 1:5; 2 Thessalonians 3:1).

# Chapter 44

## Seven Covenant Promises

'Wherefore say unto the children of Israel, I am the LORD, and I will bring you out from under the burdens of the Egyptians, and I will rid you out of their bondage, and I will redeem you with a stretched out arm, and with great judgments: And I will take you to me for a people, and I will be to you a God: and ye shall know that I am the LORD your God, which bringeth you out from under the burdens of the Egyptians. And I will bring you in unto the land, concerning the which I did swear to give it to Abraham, to Isaac, and to Jacob; and I will give it you for an heritage: I am the LORD.'
(Exodus 6:6-8)

When I am discouraged because of some pressing distress, or cast down by the leanness of my own soul, when I am brought low by Satan's assaults, my own barrenness of heart, or the circumstances in which I find myself, nothing is more refreshing to my soul in such times of trial and temptation than the blessed assurance of covenant grace. Like David, when he was about to die, I find strength for my soul and joy for my heart, when I can find strength and joy nowhere else, in God's covenant grace and the stedfast and sure promises of that covenant (2 Samuel 23:5).

In Exodus 6:6-8 the God of heaven speaks of himself as the covenant God of his people. He encourages us to rest our souls upon him, to trust him implicitly, by reminding us of our covenant relationship with him, and of his covenant promises to us. The covenant of grace, so frequently portrayed in the covenants God made with his ancient people, is now confirmed and sealed to us in the blood of Christ and by the gracious gift of his Holy Spirit. And that which the Divine Writer of this blessed Book has said by his servant John (1 John 5:13) applies to this revelation of his covenant promises. 'These things have I written unto you that believe on the name of the Son of God; that ye may know that ye have eternal life, and that ye may believe on the name of the Son of God.' As Robert Hawker says, 'We can never trust ourselves too little, nor our God too much.'

### 'Wherefore'

Verse 6 begins with the word 'wherefore', indicating that everything to follow is directly connected with that which has just been stated. Here are four reasons the Lord our God gives for us to believe the promises he has made. Imagine that! The God of all grace stoops to reason with us. He whose name is Faithful and True stoops to give us reasons to believe his promises!

In verse 3 the Lord God pins his name to the promises he gives in verses 6-8. He who is God Almighty, El-Shaddai, Jehovah, the one and only God, who is our Saviour and Redeemer pins the honour of his name upon the fulfilment of his covenant.

In verse 4 he declares, 'I have established my covenant with them'. It is, as David said, 'ordered in all things and sure', because it is God's covenant. It is a covenant God has established. And it is a covenant God has established with his people, by his decree from eternity, by the death of Christ at Calvary, and by the seal of his Spirit in the new birth. Then in verse 5, the Lord God declares, 'I have heard the groaning of the children of Israel'. Our God is never ignorant of our needs. Our Father's ear is always open to our cries. Not only that, he hears our groans. Every tear we shed, he records in a book of remembrance (Psalm 56:8). He is touched with the feeling of our infirmities and sympathizes with our groans. He who hears the cries of the young ravens and responds to their cries in pity (Psalm 147:9) will hear our groans, even when we cannot put our cries into words.

'And', in the last line of verse 5, Jehovah our God, the Almighty, the triune God declares, 'I have remembered my covenant'. We may often forget his covenant; but he never does! He will 'ever be mindful

382

of his covenant' (Psalm 111:5). Therefore he is ever 'mindful of us' (Psalm 115:12).

## Bible Numbers

In the light of these four facts, let us believe the seven covenant promises our God gives in verses 6-8. I do not make as much of the numbers used in Scripture as some; but it is obvious that some numbers are used in Scripture for specific purposes.

The number 3 seems to refer to God, the Three-in-One Jehovah, and life. On the third day God caused the earth to bring forth life everywhere (Genesis 1:11-13).

The number 6 is used repeatedly for man. Man was created on the sixth day (Genesis 1:26-31). Six is the number of man, the number of weakness, frustration, and failure. The number of the beast is 666. And the Lord God appointed six cities of refuge for men.

The number 7 speaks of redemption, grace, perfection, completion, and rest. There were seven appointed feasts to be kept annually in the Old Testament. The sabbath day was the seventh day. The year of Jubilee to be kept every fiftieth year, after every seven weeks of years.

And the promises of the covenant are repeatedly set before us as seven promises. That indicates that the covenant of redemption and grace is perfect and complete. It is a covenant that brings rest. It is the Jubilee covenant of God's Israel.

## Genesis 17

In Exodus 6, the Lord God specifically tells us, in verse 3, that the covenant promises of verses 6-8 are the very promises he made to Abraham, Isaac and Jacob in Genesis 17. There God made seven distinct promises to Abraham.

1. 'And I will make thee exceeding fruitful' (Genesis 17:6).

2. 'And I will make nations of thee, and kings shall come out of thee' (Genesis 17:6).

3. 'And I will establish my covenant between me and thee and thy seed after thee in their generations for an everlasting covenant, to be a God unto thee, and to thy seed after thee' (Genesis 17:7).

4. 'And I will give unto thee, and to thy seed after thee, the land wherein thou art a stranger, all the land of Canaan, for an everlasting possession' (Genesis 17:8).

5. 'And I will be their God' (Genesis 17:8).

6. 'And I will establish my covenant with him for an everlasting covenant, and with his seed after him (Genesis 17:19).

7. 'My covenant I will establish with Isaac' (Genesis 17:21).

## Jeremiah 31

These promises are given again in Jeremiah 31, where God describes the 'new covenant' (31:31) of grace, by which he saves his elect. Again, the promises of the covenant are specifically set before us under the number of perfection, grace, completion, and rest.

1. 'After those days, saith the Lord, I will put my law in their inward parts' (Jeremiah 31:33).

2. 'And write it in their hearts' (Jeremiah 31:33).

3. 'And will be their God' (Jeremiah 31:33).

4. 'And they shall be my people' (Jeremiah 31:33).

5. 'And they shall teach no more every man his neighbour, and every man his brother, saying, Know the LORD: for they shall all know me, from the least of them unto the greatest of them, saith the LORD' (Jeremiah 31:34).

6. 'And I will forgive their iniquity' (Jeremiah 31:34).

7. 'And I will remember their sin no more' (Jeremiah 31:34).

## Seven Promises

Look at the seven covenant promises of our God in Exodus 6:6-8. These are God's promises to his elect. They are the sure and certain promises of his free grace in Christ, covenant promises that come to us by the merit of Christ's shed blood, 'the blood of the everlasting covenant'.

'Wherefore say unto the children of Israel, I am the Lord.' He is eternal in his being, immutable in his counsels, and faithful to his covenant. He is able to fulfil his promises. He can be trusted to do what he has purposed.

1. Deliverance. The Lord God has promised to deliver his people from all their burdens. 'I will bring you out from under the burdens of the Egyptians' (v. 6).

They may think nothing of this promise who know nothing of Egypt's burdens. But to weary, heavy-laden sinners, crushed beneath the load of sin and shame, better news can never be heard than this. 'I will bring you out from under the burdens of the Egyptians'! If ever you are brought so low before God that you cry, like Job, 'My soul is weary of my life; I will leave my complaint upon myself; I will speak in the bitterness of my soul' (Job 10:1), then you will rejoice to hear the God of all grace speak of sure deliverance. Truly, 'This is the rest wherewith ye may cause the weary to rest' (Isaiah 28:12). God himself declares, 'I will bring you out from under the burdens of the Egyptians'!

2. Liberty. The Lord promises to give the burdened soul in bondage the liberty of grace. 'And I will rid you out of their bondage' (v. 6).

Israel in Egypt was in bondage; heavy, oppressive bondage. But the Lord God promised to rid them of Egypt's bondage completely. And you and I were, by nature, in bondage in Egypt, in cruel bondage, under the heavy, oppressive yoke of the law. Just as Pharaoh required Israel to make bricks without straw, the law required us to produce righteousness, but gave us no aid and offered us no assistance. But just as the Lord God made a complete riddance of Israel's bondage to Pharaoh's yoke of oppression, our Lord Jesus Christ has made a complete riddance of our bondage by fulfilling all the law's demands as our Substitute (Romans 8:1-4; 10:4; Galatians 5:1-4).

> The law demands we pay our debt.
> (Justice cannot forgive one cent.)
> But grace points to the Lamb of God,
> And says our debt He paid with blood.
>
> The law provokes and stirs up sin,
> And makes more hard the hearts of men;
> But grace, (Almighty grace!), imparts
> Life and melts rebel sinners' hearts.
>
> 'Go, do the work', the law demands;
> Yet gives me neither feet nor hands.
> But grace the gospel's good news brings,
> Says, 'Fly to Christ', and gives me wings!
>
> With wings of love and wings of faith,
> Sinners awakened from their death,
> Fly to the throne of grace and see
> God in His Son is all mercy!

My soul, on wings of faith, now fly,
And soar aloft to God on High.
Faint not, nor falter in the race;
But run, and work, and sing, 'FREE GRACE!'

3. Redemption. This deliverance and liberty comes to us freely by the gift of grace; but it was obtained for us at a very great cost. It is deliverance and liberty bestowed upon us by redemption; redemption by power and by justice. 'And I will redeem you with a stretched out arm, and with great judgments' (v. 6).

The Lord God redeems his elect experimentally by the power of his omnipotent, irresistible grace in regeneration and effectual calling, giving life to the dead (Ephesians 2:1-9). But we could never have been redeemed by the power of our Saviour's out-stretched arm of grace, had he not redeemed us 'with great judgments', when he stretched out his arms upon the cursed tree as the Lamb of God, our sin atoning Sacrifice (Romans 3:24-28).

4. Acceptance. The Lord God has promised to give his chosen people everlasting acceptance with him. 'And I will take you to me for a people' (v. 7). But have we not been accepted in Christ from eternity? Indeed, we have (Ephesians 1:3-6). Yet, God promises to make each of his chosen accepted. How can both things be true? The fact is, everything God promises he will do for us in time, in the experience of grace, he has done for us from eternity in Christ our Surety (Romans 8:28-31; Ephesians 1:3-7).

5. Knowledge. Next, the Lord our God promises that the experience of his grace will come to his chosen people by knowledge of him. 'And I will be to you a God: and ye shall know that I am the Lord your God' (v. 7).

Salvation is knowing him (John 17:3). And the only way we can know him is by him revealing himself to us (2 Corinthians 4:6). This is not a bare promise of factual knowledge. The Lord God promises that all who are his shall be made to know he is theirs. What can be sweeter than the knowledge that Christ is my God, my Saviour, my Redeemer, my Righteousness and my Salvation? See Romans 9:25-28 and Jeremiah 9:23, 24.

6. Rest. Then, the Lord God promises to give his chosen rest; blessed, sweet rest in Christ. 'Ye shall know that I am the Lord your God, which bringeth you out from under the burdens of the Egyptians' (v. 7).

When the Lord God grants faith in Christ, he gives rest to the weary. This is that blessed rest that was portrayed in the legal, typical sabbath days of the Old Testament. It is rest from labour and fear, and rest from all our foes (Exodus 34:24). It is the joyful, jubilee rest of faith in Christ our Sabbath. As the sabbath of old was for Israel alone, so Christ our Sabbath belongs to none but God's elect; and all God's elect find rest in him (Hebrews 4:3-10; Colossians 2:16).

If ever you find rest in Christ our Sabbath, you will 'call the Sabbath a delight' (Isaiah 58:13), no longer going your own ways, serving the pleasures and lusts of the flesh, and observing the laws of men, but honouring him alone as your blessed and glorious Saviour (1 Corinthians 1:30, 31).

7. Inheritance. The Lord God has sworn and promised, in the covenant ordered in all things and sure before the world was made, that he will give his chosen an everlasting inheritance. That inheritance which is ours in Christ was typified by the land of Canaan. 'And I will bring you in unto the land, concerning the which I did sware to give it to Abraham, to Isaac, and to Jacob; and I will give it you for a heritage: I am the Lord' (v. 8).

Not only did the Lord bring his people out of the land of bondage, he brought them into the land he had sworn to give unto Abraham, Isaac, and Jacob. They were not consumed by the Amalekites (Exodus 17). Though Sihon, king of the Amorites, and Og king of Bashan, gathered all their people together and went out against Israel (Numbers 21), though Balak hired Balaam to curse Israel, no weapon formed against them could prosper. The Lord God who made the promise performed it; and Israel came into, and possessed, the promised land.

So it shall be with us! The Lord Jesus Christ shall, at last, bring every chosen, blood-bought sinner safely into Heaven's everlasting glory. The world, the flesh, and the Devil may array themselves against us; but not one sheep of Christ shall perish. We shall, every one of us, possess that blessed land of promise 'for an heritage' by the free gift of free grace. All God's elect shall possess it completely. All shall possess it freely. All shall possess it forever (Romans 8:16-18).

Did you notice, in reading these covenant promises in Genesis 17 and Exodus 6, how frequently the promise is prefaced by the two infinitely precious words 'I will'? The Lord God declares, 'I am the Lord. I will bring you out. I will rid you. I will redeem you'! Let our hearts reply, 'O Lord, do as you have said', and pray, that he may give us grace to believe him (1 John 5:10, 11).

John Kent wrote,

> We'll sing the vast unmeasured grace,
> Which from the days of old,
> Did all the chosen sons embrace,
> As sheep within the fold.
>
> The basis of eternal love,
> Shall mercy's frame sustain;
> Earth, hell, or sin the same to move,
> Shall all conspire in vain.
>
> Sing, O ye sinners bought with blood,
> Hail the great Three in One;
> Tell how secure the covenant stood,
> 'Ere time its race begun.
>
> Ne'er had ye felt the guilt of sin,
> Nor the sweets of pardoning love,
> Unless your worthless names had been,
> Enrolled to life above.
>
> Oh what a sweet, exulting song
> Shall rend the vaulted skies,
> When, shouting grace, the blood-washed throng,
> Shall see the Top Stone rise!'

# Chapter 45

# An Explosion Of Miracles

'And the LORD said unto Moses, See, I have made thee a god to Pharaoh: and Aaron thy brother shall be thy prophet. Thou shalt speak all that I command thee: and Aaron thy brother shall speak unto Pharaoh, that he send the children of Israel out of his land. And I will harden Pharaoh's heart, and multiply my signs and my wonders in the land of Egypt. But Pharaoh shall not hearken unto you, that I may lay my hand upon Egypt, and bring forth mine armies, and my people the children of Israel, out of the land of Egypt by great judgments. And the Egyptians shall know that I am the LORD, when I stretch forth mine hand upon Egypt, and bring out the children of Israel from among them. And Moses and Aaron did as the LORD commanded them, so did they. But the LORD hardened Pharaoh's heart, and he would not let them go. And Pharaoh said unto him, Get thee from me, take heed to thyself, see my face no more; for in that day thou seest my face thou shalt die. And Moses said, Thou hast spoken well, I will see thy face again no more.' (Exodus 7:1-10:29)

Exodus chapters 6–10 set before us an explosion of miracles performed by Moses and Aaron against Pharaoh and the Egyptians. They begin with Aaron's rod becoming a serpent, and proceed to describe the first nine plagues that God unleashed on Pharaoh and the people of Egypt. The whole land of Egypt was made to tremble beneath the successive strokes of God's rod. Everyone, from Pharaoh on his throne to the servant in the field, was made to feel the terrible weight of divine judgment.

'He sent Moses his servant; and Aaron whom he had chosen. They showed his signs among them, and wonders in the land of Ham. He sent darkness, and made it dark; and they rebelled not against his word. He turned their waters into blood, and slew their fish. Their land brought forth frogs in abundance, in the chambers of their kings. He spake, and there came divers sorts of flies, and lice in all their coasts. He gave them hail for rain, and flaming fire in their land. He smote their vines also and their fig trees; and brake the trees of their coasts. He spake, and the locusts came, and caterpillars, and that without number, and did eat up all the herbs in their land, and devoured the fruit of their ground' (Psalm 105:26-35).

That is an explosion of miracles. Yet, Pharaoh, in his arrogance of heart and enmity against God, defied the most high God. And, as a just consequence of his rebellion, he was given over to judicial blindness and hardness of heart.

'And the LORD hardened the heart of Pharaoh, and he hearkened not unto them; as the LORD had spoken unto Moses. And the LORD said unto Moses, Rise up early in the morning, and stand before Pharaoh, and say unto him, Thus saith the LORD God of the Hebrews, Let my people go, that they may serve me. For I will at this time send all my plagues upon thine heart, and upon thy servants, and upon thy people; that thou mayest know that there is none like me in all the earth. For now I will stretch out my hand, that I may smite thee and thy people with pestilence; and thou shalt be cut off from the earth. And in very deed for this cause have I raised thee up, for to show in thee my power; and that my name may be declared throughout all the earth' (Exodus 9:12-16).

What do we learn from the things recorded in these five chapters?

## Salvation Sure
The first thing that comes to my mind, as I read these chapters, is that the salvation of God's elect is sure. I am reminded of the inspiring visions given to John in the Book of Revelation. In that blessed book we see the last proud oppressor of Christ's people bringing down upon himself and upon all who follow him the seven vials of the wrath of the Almighty.

It is God's purpose to save his Israel. All who dare oppose the purpose of God and set themselves against his church shall be taken out of the way. Divine grace must find its object. All who stand in the way shall be removed from the way. Whether it be Egypt, Babylon, antichrist, or Satan himself, all shall be taken out of the way. God's providence clears the path for his grace. His enemies and ours shall reap, throughout the ages, the bitter fruit of having exalted themselves against 'the LORD God of the Hebrews'. He has promised his chosen, 'no weapon that is formed against thee shall prosper', and his infallible faithfulness will assuredly make good what his infinite grace hath promised. Every chosen redeemed sinner shall be saved. Every saved sinner shall be kept and brought at last into his heavenly glory to possess his predestined inheritance with Christ.

Thus, in Pharaoh's case, when he persisted in holding God's people in bondage, the vials of divine wrath were poured forth upon him. The land of Egypt was covered throughout its length and breadth with darkness, disease, desolation, and death. So will it be with the man of sin, that last great oppressor who has emerged from the bottomless pit, armed with satanic power, to crush beneath his 'foot of pride' the favoured objects of Jehovah's love. Satan and the man of sin shall be overturned, his kingdom devastated by the seven last plagues, and, finally, plunged, not in the Red Sea, but 'in the lake that burneth with fire and brimstone'. And all whose names are found in the book of life of the Lamb slain from the foundation of the world shall be found with Christ in his glory (Revelation 17:8; 20:10).

Not one jot or one tittle of what God has promised shall fail. He will accomplish all. Notwithstanding all that has been, is, and shall be said and done to the contrary, God remembers his promises, and he will fulfil them. They are all 'yea and amen in Christ Jesus'. No power of earth or hell can ever thwart, reverse, or even hinder God's purpose of grace. The eternal God has sworn, and the blood of the everlasting covenant has ratified the covenant. Who, then, shall make it void? Heaven and earth shall pass away; but God's eternal word of predestination and promise shall never pass away. Truly, 'there is none like unto the God of Jeshurun, who rideth upon the heaven in thy help, and in his excellence on the sky. The eternal God is thy refuge, and underneath are the everlasting arms, and he shall thrust out the enemy from before thee; and shall say, Destroy them. Israel then shall dwell in safety alone: the fountain of Jacob shall be upon a land of corn and wine; also his heavens shall drop down dew. Happy art thou, O Israel:

who is like unto thee, O people saved by the Lord, the shield of thy help, and who is the sword of thy excellency! and thine enemies shall be found liars unto thee; and thou shalt tread upon their high places' (Deuteronomy 33:26-29).

## Miracles and Revelation

Whenever we read about men performing miracles in the Word of God, the question arises, 'Should we expect such miracles today?'

The majority of people tell us the miracles described in the Bible never took place at all, or those things that appear to be miracles can be explained scientifically. Such people simply refuse to acknowledge that God really rules the universe. They may claim to be Christians and claim to believe in God; but their religion is a delusion. To deny that God rules the universe absolutely is to deny that God is. There is no difference between the denial of God's absolute sovereignty and atheism.

There are others who do not hesitate to say we should always 'expect a miracle'. They tell us that if we do not see miracles, if preachers do not perform miracles, it is because we do not have sufficient faith and the preacher lacks the anointing of the Holy Spirit.

A careful reading of Holy Scripture shows that all the miracles in Scripture fall into four distinct periods. They were all performed during Moses' era, or in the days of Elijah and Elisha, or in the time of the Babylonian captivity, or in the days of Christ and his apostles. These were all times of crisis in which God was moving in a special way to further his cause. Put them all together and they represent a very small portion of all the years covered by the Bible. In a word, miracles took place intermittently. Those who get caught up with the performance of miracles always miss the spiritual truths and messages they were performed to portray. It was not the miracle that was important, but the message conveyed by the miracle.

Having said that, let me be crystal clear in asserting that the apostolic age of miracles, signs and wonders, and speaking in tongues ceased with the fulfilment of divine revelation, with the full revelation of God given in Holy Scripture. Because we have the complete revelation of God in his Word, we have no need for and must not expect the performance of miracles today. We have something far better than miracles. We have God's inspired Word (2 Peter 1:16-21).

There have been none with the gift and ability to speak in tongues and perform miracles by the Spirit of God since the days of the apostles. Those who yet pretend to possess such supernatural gifts are nothing but pretenders. They are not the servants of Christ. The Holy Spirit tells us, with unmistakable clarity, that those who pretend to have prophetic and apostolic gifts today are not the servants of Christ, but of antichrist (2 Thessalonians 2:7-10). Let me show you what these wonders performed by Moses teach us about our God and his great salvation.

## Divine Sovereignty

When Moses and Aaron made their second appearance before Pharaoh, 'they were standing', as Roger Ellsworth puts it, 'on the front edge of one of history's most dazzling displays of God's sovereignty and glory'. The Lord God first demonstrated his sovereignty when Pharaoh demanded that Moses give him a sign (7:10-13). When Pharaoh made that demand, Aaron did 'as the Lord had commanded'. He threw his rod to the ground, and it immediately turned into a serpent. Pharaoh's magicians did the same thing with their rods by 'their enchantments'. But Aaron's serpent swallowed the serpents of Pharaoh's magicians.

Remember, the serpent was the emblem of Pharaoh's power. His head-dress featured a raised cobra. That Aaron's serpent devoured the other serpents amounted to nothing less than the Lord God declaring his supremacy over Pharaoh. The ten plagues were God's assertion of his supremacy over the gods of Egypt. The first plague consisted of the water of the Nile being turned to blood. The Egyptians worshipped the Nile. By turning its water to blood, God demonstrated his supremacy over the Nile, and made their own god repugnant and repulsive to them.

One after another more plagues came: frogs, lice, flies, diseased livestock, boils, hail and fire, locusts, and darkness that was felt. With each plague, the God of Israel declared himself to be the God of gods, in total control of the gods of Egypt that were powerless before him. The sovereign God, who demonstrated his might over the gods of Egypt, is the God with whom we have to do. We will either bow before him and worship him, or he will take us out of the way forever.

## Divine Justice

The plagues God sent upon Egypt demonstrated more than his sovereignty. They were his just judgments upon the Egyptians for their cruel treatment of the Israelites and for their slaughter of male babies (Exodus 1:22). Men commonly think that because God does not send judgment immediately, he never will (Psalm 10:11, 13; 59:7; 94:7). How foolish! No one ever gets away with sin. God's judgment will come. The wheels of justice grind slow; but they grind to powder!

The plagues the Lord sent upon Egypt were miniature pictures of that which he will send upon unbelievers at the last day (Revelation 16). In that day people will cry for the rocks and mountains to cover them and hide them from the face of the Lamb (Revelation 6:16); but there will be no escape. Divine judgment is always a matter of strict justice. It is always judgment executed upon each according to that which he has done.

We labour diligently, preaching the gospel, 'warning every man, and teaching every man in all wisdom; that we may present every man perfect in Christ Jesus' (Colossians 1:28), urging all to flee the wrath of God, urging all to flee to Christ the sinner's only Refuge. But, unless God by an act of omnipotent mercy prevents it, fallen man stops his ears and hardens his heart, just like Pharaoh. Soon, every rebel will discover, to his everlasting ruin, that 'the soul that sinneth, it shall die', that God 'will by no means clear the guilty', 'for the wages of sin is death; but the gift of God is eternal life through Jesus Christ our Lord.'

### Satan's Counterfeit

The chapters before us also remind us of the reality that Satan ever counterfeits the work of God. This is evident when we see Pharaoh's magicians turn their rods into serpents (Exodus 7:11). Satan is a powerful and clever foe. His servants perform signs and wonders by which they deceive many (2 Thessalonians 2:9). And they transform themselves into ministers of righteousness, teaching sinners to perform righteousness, rather than trust Christ for righteousness. This was a matter of great concern to Paul; and it should be a matter of great concern to us (2 Corinthians 11:3, 4, 13-15).

The most Satanic opposition to God's gospel is the imitation of it by a 'form of godliness', a form of godliness that denies 'the power thereof'. Yet, we must not fail to remember the blessed assurance God has given us concerning Pharaoh's magicians. The Spirit of God tells us their names in 2 Timothy, where Paul speaks of those perilous times that must come (2 Timothy 3:1-9), assuring us that 'as Jannes and

Jambres withstood Moses, so do these also resist the truth: men of corrupt minds, reprobate concerning the faith ... they shall proceed no further'. All they can do is oppose God's cause. They cannot overthrow, or even hinder it!

## Hardened Hearts

These successive miracles of the serpent and the plagues that followed display something else. They give us a vivid portrayal of the incredible hardness of the human heart. The hardness of Pharaoh's heart is described in three ways. In some places we are simply told that it 'was hardened', or grew hard (7:13, 22; 8:19; 9:7). In other places we are told that, 'Pharaoh hardened his heart' (8:15, 32; 9:24). And in yet other places we are told, 'the LORD hardened Pharaoh's heart' (9:12; 10:20, 27). Putting them together, this is what we are taught by these three things.

1. God has purposed all things, even the damnation of the wicked.

2. When people harden their hearts against Christ, God often judges them by hardening their hearts even more. And,

3. When sinners harden their hearts against him, they bring upon themselves the wrath of God.

God did not create the evil in Pharaoh. We dare not charge the holy Lord God with sin (James 1:13-16). What a solemn warning this is to all who hear the gospel and harden their hearts against it (Proverbs 1:23-33; 2 Corinthians 2:14-16; 5:20-6:2).

## God's Grace

We should be grateful that the accounts of Aaron's serpent and the plagues yield yet another truth. They show us God is gracious, always gracious toward his elect. Israel had been in such desperate conditions for such a long time that they must often have felt as if God had forsaken them and had forgotten them, and that he did not care about them. As the plagues began to unfold, Israel began to see that God was showing himself strong on their behalf.

You and I often have to deal with the same feelings. Do we not? How often we feel like crying, 'Is his mercy clean gone for ever? doth his promise fail for evermore? Hath God forgotten to be gracious? hath he in anger shut up his tender mercies?' (Psalm 77:8, 9). When evil mounts up around us and troubles seem to prevail over us, when our hearts are broken with heaviness and our souls are cast down, we want to cry out, 'O Lord God, Where are you?' In such times let us resist Satan's snare, remembering that our God is today exactly where he has always been, sitting on his throne (Psalm 115:1-3; 135:6). He is doing us good in his good pleasure, working out his everlasting purpose of grace toward us in Christ (Romans 8:28-31).

God never forgets his own. He will in his own time and way deliver us from all evil. It is not our responsibility to figure God out. It is ours to trust him and serve him while we wait for that day when dark things will be made plain (Isaiah 40:28-31).

# Chapter 46

## The Serpent, Serpents And Another Serpent

And the LORD said unto Moses, See, I have made thee a god to Pharaoh: and Aaron thy brother shall be thy prophet. Thou shalt speak all that I command thee: and Aaron thy brother shall speak unto Pharaoh, that he send the children of Israel out of his land. And I will harden Pharaoh's heart, and multiply my signs and my wonders in the land of Egypt. But Pharaoh shall not hearken unto you, that I may lay my hand upon Egypt, and bring forth mine armies, and my people the children of Israel, out of the land of Egypt by great judgments. And the Egyptians shall know that I am the LORD, when I stretch forth mine hand upon Egypt, and bring out the children of Israel from among them. And Moses and Aaron did as the LORD commanded them, so did they. And Moses was fourscore years old, and Aaron fourscore and three years old, when they spake unto Pharaoh. And the LORD spake unto Moses and unto Aaron, saying, When Pharaoh shall speak unto you, saying, Show a miracle for you: then thou shalt say unto Aaron, Take thy rod, and cast it before Pharaoh, and it shall become a serpent. And Moses and Aaron went in unto Pharaoh, and they did so as the LORD had commanded: and Aaron cast down his rod before Pharaoh, and before his servants, and it became a serpent. Then Pharaoh also called the wise men and the sorcerers: now the magicians of Egypt, they also did in like manner with their enchantments. For they cast down every man his rod, and they became serpents: but Aaron's rod swallowed up their rods. And he hardened Pharaoh's heart, that he hearkened not unto them; as the LORD had said.'
(Exodus 7:1-13)

## A God to Pharaoh

This chapter begins with a strange declaration. 'And the LORD said unto Moses, See, I have made thee a god to Pharaoh: and Aaron thy brother shall be thy prophet'.

Did the Lord God say to Moses, 'I have made thee a god to Pharaoh'? What does that mean? Look at the previous verse (Exodus 6:30). Being again commissioned of God to go to Pharaoh, Moses said, 'Behold, I am of uncircumcised lips, and how shall Pharaoh hearken unto me?' This is the Lord's next word to Moses. 'See, I have made thee a god to Pharaoh.' With that declaration, he assured Moses that he was sent with Divine authority as God's messenger, and that, as God's messenger, failure was an impossibility. Moses had been commissioned as God's messenger to Pharaoh. He was clothed with power and authority from God as God's representative to the King of Egypt. Civil magistrates are called 'gods' (Psalm 82:6, 7; John 10:34-36), because they are set over men by Divine authority, to whom we are responsible, and whose laws we are commanded to obey (Romans 13:1-7).

Here, Moses is called 'a god to Pharaoh' specifically because he was sent as God's ambassador, as a man with a message from God to deliver to Pharaoh. That is the position in which every man sent of God as his messenger stands before those to whom he is sent. God's servants are all sinful men, just like you, nothing but sinful men. Yet, that man who is sent of God, carrying God's message to you, is clothed with Divine authority. He is to be heard. His message is to be obeyed. The labour of such men is never in vain (Jeremiah 1:10; 2 Corinthians 5:20-6:2; Hebrews 13:7, 17; 2 Corinthians 2:14-17).

Moses received the message directly from God; but he did not personally deliver it to Pharaoh. He related God's message to Aaron, his brother, the man appointed by God to be high priest over the house of Israel. And Aaron delivered the message to Pharaoh.

What a vivid portrayal that is of true preaching. God's servants seek and obtain a message from him. Then, they deliver the message back into the hands of Christ, the only Mediator between God and men, and implore him to deliver his message by them in the power of his Spirit.

And those men who are sent of God to speak for him, true gospel preachers, studiously labour to know and to speak only that which God commands and all that God commands in his Word (Exodus 7:2; Jeremiah 23:28; Matthew 28:18-20; Acts 20:27).

Like Moses, God's servants are not free to preach what they desire, selecting what they think is appropriate. We are commanded and responsible to 'declare unto you all the counsel of God', to 'preach the word' (2 Timothy 4:2) in season and out of season, to 'hold fast the form of sound words' (2 Timothy 1:13). 'If any man teach otherwise, and consent not to wholesome words, even the words of our Lord Jesus Christ, and to the doctrine which is according to godliness; he is proud, knowing nothing' (1 Timothy 6:3, 4).

With this qualification, 'I have made thee a god to Pharaoh', Moses went forth, acting as God's representative. He ruled over Egypt's proud king, commanding him, controlling him, and punishing him for his disobedience.

Moses is no longer timid, hesitant, and discouraged. He never again mentions his own inability, but goes forth in the name of Christ, as God's messenger to men, full of confidence, not in himself, but in God whose servant he was. Let every man called and sent of God do likewise

## God's Purpose

In verses 3-5, the Lord God tells Moses plainly he will be to Pharaoh a messenger of death and of judgment. It was God's purpose in sending Moses to Pharaoh to harden Pharaoh's heart by his word and by the wonders he would perform before his eyes. 'And I will harden Pharaoh's heart, and multiply my signs and my wonders in the land of Egypt' (v. 3). Here we see the great sovereignty of our God displayed in wisdom and justice. God hardened Pharaoh's heart by every renewed declaration of his word, and by every wonder performed before his eyes. By these things the children of Israel were more and more convinced that the Lord was about to deliver them; but Pharaoh and the Egyptians became more and more hardened in their hatred of God. The same sun that melts the wax until it is flows, hardens clay into solid brick (2 Corinthians 4:3, 4; Hebrews 3:12, 13; Isaiah 6:9, 10; Romans 11:5-10; 2 Thessalonians 2:8-12; Romans 1:28-32).

Many try to blunt the keen edge of Holy Scripture in order to make it more acceptable to the carnal mind. Instead of acknowledging with fear and trembling that God's word teaches precisely what is here stated, that the Lord God actually hardened the heart of Pharaoh, most argue that he did nothing of the kind, that he simply permitted the Egyptian monarch to harden his own heart.

While it is true that Pharaoh did harden his own heart, the Scriptures specifically tell us the Lord God himself hardened Pharaoh's heart, and did so according to his own sovereign pleasure and eternal purpose. Pharaoh was responsible for hardening his heart. He did so because he hated God and refused to bow to him. Yet, even Pharaoh's hardness of heart was accomplished according to God's purpose (Romans 9:15-23).

## Two Great Ends

But God's purpose in hardening Pharaoh's heart was not an arbitrary, capricious whim. He raised up Pharaoh, hardened his heart, and dumped him in the Red Sea in order to accomplish two great ends: the glory of his own great name and the deliverance of his people. We see this clearly in verses 4 and 5 and in Psalm 105:2-28.

'But Pharaoh shall not hearken unto you, that I may lay my hand upon Egypt, and bring forth mine armies, and my people the children of Israel, out of the land of Egypt by great judgments. And the Egyptians shall know that I am the LORD, when I stretch forth mine hand upon Egypt, and bring out the children of Israel from among them (Exodus 7:4, 5).

The Lord God turned the Egyptians to hate his people, to deal subtly with his servants. Then, 'He turned their heart to hate his people, to deal subtilly with his servants. He sent Moses his servant; and Aaron whom he had chosen. They showed his signs among them, and wonders in the land of Ham. He sent darkness, and made it dark; and they rebelled not against his word' (Psalm 105:25-28).

And 'led them by the right hand of Moses with his glorious arm, dividing the water before them, to make himself an everlasting name … led them through the deep, as an horse in the wilderness, that they should not stumble. So didst thou lead thy people, to make thyself a glorious name' (Isaiah 63:12-14).

## The Men

In verses 6 and 7 the Spirit of God describes the men God chose to be his servants by whom he would deliver his people. He does so by declaring just two things about them (Exodus 7:6, 7). 'And Moses and Aaron did as the LORD commanded them, so did they. And Moses was fourscore years old, and Aaron fourscore and three years old, when they spake unto Pharaoh.'

First, Moses and Aaron were faithful men. God only requires one thing of his servants. 'It is required in stewards, that a man be found faithful' (1 Corinthians 4:2). 'And Moses and Aaron did as the LORD commanded them, so did they' (Exodus 7:6). They never again showed the slightest reluctance, or made any objection to any message they were commanded to deliver or any work they were commanded to do, but went about it at once, and performed it with all readiness of mind and cheerfulness of heart. May God the Holy Spirit give me grace to follow their example, for Christ's sake!

Second, they were old men; they were faithful old men. 'And Moses was fourscore years old, and Aaron fourscore and three years old, when they spake unto Pharaoh' (Exodus 7:7). I see several things here that are important. They were men of considerable experience. They were mature men, seasoned with the experience of life in this world. They had been in training for a long time. They were wise, prudent men of great age, sedate and composed. And they were weak, old men.

A. W. Pink wrote, 'This reference to the ages of Moses and Aaron seems to be brought in here in order to magnify the power and grace of Jehovah. He was pleased to employ two aged men as his instruments.'

## The Serpents

What is the significance of the serpents mentioned in verses 8-12?

'And the LORD spake unto Moses and unto Aaron, saying, When Pharaoh shall speak unto you, saying, Show a miracle for you: then thou shalt say unto Aaron, Take thy rod, and cast it before Pharaoh, and it shall become a serpent. And Moses and Aaron went in unto Pharaoh, and they did so as the LORD had commanded: and Aaron cast down his rod before Pharaoh, and before his servants, and it became a serpent. Then Pharaoh also called the wise men and the sorcerers: now the magicians of Egypt, they also did in like manner with their enchantments. For they cast down every man his rod, and they became serpents: but Aaron's rod swallowed up their rods' (Exodus 7:8-12).

After delivering God's message to him, Pharaoh demanded (as God said he would) that Moses show him a sign, a miracle. Like multitudes throughout the ages, he seems to have said, 'I will believe God, if you can prove that I should.' And God gave him a sign. But, remember, it was God who chose the sign. Aaron threw his rod to the ground; and it immediately turned into a serpent. Then Pharaoh's magicians did the same thing with their rods by 'their enchantments'. But Aaron's serpent swallowed up the serpents of Pharaoh's magicians.

The serpent was the emblem of Pharaoh and his power. As we have seen, his head-dress featured a raised cobra. That Aaron's serpent devoured the other serpents was the Lord God declaring his sovereignty, supremacy, and power over Pharaoh and his gods. But it showed more. This sign, by which God originally declared himself to Pharaoh, was a display of our Lord Jesus Christ and his dominion and triumph over Satan, by which he would accomplish our redemption and eternal salvation. Aaron's rod clearly represents Christ himself. It was the rod of power that budded with life. When it was thrown on the ground, it became a serpent. That is exactly what happened when our Lord Jesus Christ came into this world in human flesh. It was a serpent, Satan, who beguiled Eve and brought Adam into ruin. This was by God's design (Job 26:13; Isaiah 27:1). When our Lord Jesus Christ was portrayed in his redemptive power and grace, he was portrayed as a serpent (Numbers 21:9; John 3:14, 15).

The serpent Moses made and held up in the wilderness for the saving of the people was a serpent of brass, because brass has within it a toxin, or poisonous element; and our blessed Saviour, when he died in our place at Calvary made the toxin, the poison that ruined us, his own, when he bare our sins in his own body on the tree. The serpent was made of brass for another reason. Brass is the colour that most resembles the colour of the noxious reptile. And our Lord Jesus, in order to redeem and save his people from their sins, was made a curse for us. Therefore, when Moses portrayed him in his redemptive character, he made the image of a serpent, the only creature of God that is said to be under the Divine curse.

Pharaoh's magicians, 'with their enchantments', threw their rods on the ground and made them appear as serpents. It really does not matter, but I am inclined to think these magicians did not actually turn their rods into serpents, but they simply made them appear to be serpents, just as false prophets ever seek to imitate true prophets, and seek to give out imitations of Christ for Christ himself (2 Corinthians 11:13).

Then Aaron's rod swallowed up their rods. The rods of Jannes and Jambres were entirely consumed by Aaron's rod. God the Holy Ghost uses this great picture to assure his Church and his servants in all ages that our Lord Jesus Christ, his Church, and his gospel always prevail over the gates of hell (2 Timothy 3:1-9). Our Lord Jesus Christ has, by his sin atoning sacrifice, completely destroyed the devil and cast him out. 'The prince of this world is judged' (John 12:31-33; 16:11; Revelation 20:1-6).

Christ has bound the old serpent with the chain of his omnipotence, having utterly consumed every evil he brought upon God's chosen. Soon, just as 'Aaron's rod swallowed up their rods', our blessed Saviour shall completely rid the universe of the slime of Satan upon his creation! 'And there shall be no more curse!' Because Christ died and rose again, because he has swallowed up the curse, God's people have nothing to fear from the serpents spawned by Satan in this world (Isaiah 11:8, 9).

## A Hardened Rebel

Pharaoh's heart was hardened by that which, it would appear, should melt any heart. 'And he hardened Pharaoh's heart, that he hearkened not unto them; as the LORD had said' (v. 13). The fact is, so hard is the heart of man that it cannot be melted to repentance, except God himself melt it by his grace. But the primary emphasis of this statement is that our great God is in absolute control of all things, both the good and the evil (Psalm 76:10; Proverbs 21:1; Revelation 17:17; Romans 11:33-36). Let us worship and adore him.

> Our sov'reign God maintains,
> His universal throne;
> In heav'n, and earth, and hell He reigns,
> And makes His wonders known!
>
> His counsels and decrees,
> Firmer than mountains stand;
> He will perform whate'er He please;
> And none can stay his hand!
>
> All things His will controls;
> And His all-wise decree,
> Has fixed the destinies of all
> In matchless sov'reignty.

Jacob by grace He saved,
And gives no reason why;
But Esau's heart He left depraved.
And who shall dare reply?

What if the Potter takes
Part of a lump of clay,
And for Himself a vessel makes,
And casts the rest away?

Who shall resist His will,
Or say, 'What doest Thou?'
Jehovah is the Sov'reign still;
And all to Him must bow!

My soul, bow and adore
The Lord in all His ways;
His sov'reignty none can explore;
But I will trust His grace!

'For of Him and through Him
And to Him are all things:
To Whom be glory evermore!
Amen! Amen! Amen!'

Joseph Irons

# Chapter 47

## Water And Blood A Deadly Mixture

'And the LORD said unto Moses, Pharaoh's heart is hardened, he refuseth to let the people go. Get thee unto Pharaoh in the morning; lo, he goeth out unto the water; and thou shalt stand by the river's brink against he come; and the rod which was turned to a serpent shalt thou take in thine hand. And thou shalt say unto him, The LORD God of the Hebrews hath sent me unto thee, saying, Let my people go, that they may serve me in the wilderness: and, behold, hitherto thou wouldest not hear. Thus saith the LORD, In this thou shalt know that I am the LORD: behold, I will smite with the rod that is in mine hand upon the waters which are in the river, and they shall be turned to blood. And the fish that is in the river shall die, and the river shall stink; and the Egyptians shall loathe to drink of the water of the river. And the LORD spake unto Moses, Say unto Aaron, Take thy rod, and stretch out thine hand upon the waters of Egypt, upon their streams, upon their rivers, and upon their ponds, and upon all their pools of water, that they may become blood; and that there may be blood throughout all the land of Egypt, both in vessels of wood, and in vessels of stone. And Moses and Aaron did so, as the LORD commanded; and he lifted up the rod, and smote the waters that were in the river, in the sight of Pharaoh, and in the sight of his servants; and all the waters that were in the river were turned to blood. And the fish that was in the river died; and the river stank, and the Egyptians could not drink of the water of the river; and there was blood throughout all the land of Egypt. And the magicians of Egypt did

so with their enchantments: and Pharaoh's heart was hardened, neither did he hearken unto them; as the LORD had said. And Pharaoh turned and went into his house, neither did he set his heart to this also. And all the Egyptians digged round about the river for water to drink; for they could not drink of the water of the river. And seven days were fulfilled, after that the LORD had smitten the river.'
(Exodus 7:14-25)

In the opening verses of this chapter, the Lord God had demonstrated the power and dominion of Christ over Satan by causing Aaron's rod to become a serpent and making it devour the serpents Pharaoh's sorcerers made by their enchantments. Our Lord Jesus Christ would later be symbolized by the serpent of brass lifted up in the wilderness. Here, in Exodus 7, as throughout the Word of God, we are assured that he who was made a curse for us has all power. He has conquered Satan. He shall devour Satan and all that is spawned by him.

These things were demonstrated so clearly and irrefutably so there could be no mistake regarding them. Moses was God's prophet. The God for whom he spoke is God indeed. But Pharaoh hardened his heart, as God said he would. The Lord God hardened Pharaoh's heart so he might perform his wonders in the land of Egypt (v. 3). In the passage now before us, Exodus 7:14-25, God the Holy Ghost describes the first of God's wonders in the land of Ham. The waters of Egypt were turned into blood by the hand of God.

**The Place of Confrontation**
We should not fail to notice the place at which the Lord commanded Moses to confront Pharaoh. In verse 15, he told Moses to take his rod and meet Pharaoh at the Nile River. That is significant. Prior to this, Moses had gone into Pharaoh's palace to meet with the king; but now the Lord God compelled the king of Egypt to come down to the river to meet Moses. Pharaoh thought he was going out that morning to take a bath, or to observe his idolatrous devotions at the Nile. He had no idea what God was about to do.

Eighty years earlier Pharaoh's daughter had come down to that same river to bathe herself, only to find a helpless baby God would have her protect and raise as her own that he might deliver Israel at his appointed time. When I think of that fact, Revelation 12 comes to my mind.

God brought Pharaoh to the Nile River, which was for him both an object and a place of idolatrous worship, to confront him in divine judgment, judgment brought upon him by Moses, the representative of God, his law, and his justice, who was raised in the palace he occupied. Pharaoh looked upon the Nile River as the source of Egypt's life, power, and glory, the great benefactor of his land. The God of Glory was about to make his god and his religion a curse upon him and his land. As he later did by his prophet Elijah on Mount Carmel, God here mocked Pharaoh's god by his prophet Moses.

## Moses and Christ

There is an obvious and striking contrast between this first plague performed by Moses and the first miracle performed by the Lord Jesus, illustrating the fact that 'the law was given by Moses, but grace and truth came by Jesus Christ' (John 1:17). What a difference there is between the law that Moses represents and the grace that comes to sinners by Christ! All the law brings is death. Thus Moses turned water into blood, killing everything in the water. But Christ brings grace to our needy souls, grace that gives life to the dead and floods our hearts with joy. Grace and truth, like wine, make the heart glad. So the first miracle by which our Saviour began to show forth his glory was turning water into wine (John 2:1-11).

## Clear Message

The message God sent Moses to deliver was clear (vv. 16-18).

'And thou shalt say unto him, The LORD God of the Hebrews hath sent me unto thee, saying, Let my people go, that they may serve me in the wilderness: and, behold, hitherto thou wouldest not hear. Thus saith the LORD, In this thou shalt know that I am the LORD: behold, I will smite with the rod that is in mine hand upon the waters which are in the river, and they shall be turned to blood. And the fish that is in the river shall die, and the river shall stink; and the Egyptians shall loathe to drink of the water of the river'.

There was no offer of mercy, no appeal was made to Pharaoh, no indication of grace was given, and no compromise was offered, just a plain command and a stark declaration of what God was about to do.

407

**The Plague**

Now, look at the plague itself.

'And the LORD spake unto Moses, Say unto Aaron, Take thy rod, and stretch out thine hand upon the waters of Egypt, upon their streams, upon their rivers, and upon their ponds, and upon all their pools of water, that they may become blood; and that there may be blood throughout all the land of Egypt, both in vessels of wood, and in vessels of stone. And Moses and Aaron did so, as the LORD commanded; and he lifted up the rod, and smote the waters that were in the river, in the sight of Pharaoh, and in the sight of his servants; and all the waters that were in the river were turned to blood. And the fish that was in the river died; and the river stank, and the Egyptians could not drink of the water of the river; and there was blood throughout all the land of Egypt' (vv. 19-21).

Water was changed to blood. These two great elements of creation are essential to life. But here Moses turned both into a curse, a deadly mixture, by divine appointment. What a curse this was! What a terrible picture of divine judgment. When water is where blood ought to be, death is at hand (Luke 14:2). And when blood is where water is supposed to be death is at hand (Luke 8:41-48).

There are spiritual lessons to be drawn from this. As you know, in the Word of God blood speaks of life and death. It specifically refers to the sin atoning sacrifice of our Lord Jesus Christ. By the shedding of his blood, he poured out his life in death that he might give us life by his grace. Also, water is used in Scripture to represent the regenerating, sanctifying work of God the Holy Spirit (John 7:37-39).

Multitudes make the deadly mistake of putting the blood of Christ where God has put the work of the Spirit, or putting the work of the Spirit where God has put the blood of Christ. In doing so, they attempt to nullify the sin atoning work of Christ and the regenerating work of God the Holy Spirit. The fact is, both the work of Christ for us, as our Redeemer, and the work of God the Holy Ghost in us in the new birth are vital. We must be redeemed; and we must be born again. Our sins must be put away; and we must be given a new nature.

Sinners are saved by the works of the triune God: Father, Son and Holy Ghost (Ephesians 1:3-14). None are saved without, or apart from the work of God the Father in eternity. But the eternal election and predestination of God the Father is not all that is necessary for our salvation. The redemptive work of Christ at Calvary and the life-giving operations of God the Holy Spirit are as essential to our salvation as the eternal purpose of God the Father in predestination. We must be saved by blood and by water. Neither the blood (the work of Christ), nor the water (the work of the Spirit) alone can save us. We must have both.

We were saved, redeemed, justified, and sanctified when the Son of God died in our place at Calvary. When he arose from the dead, all God's elect were 'quickened together with him'. When our Mediator took his seat in heaven as our Forerunner, we sat down with him. When our Saviour cried, 'It is finished', salvation's work was done. Sin was put away. Righteousness was brought in. Atonement was made. The redemption of our souls was accomplished. The purpose of God the Father is not enough to save anyone. Blood must be shed. Christ had to die, for 'without shedding of blood is no remission' (Hebrews 9:22).

Still, something else is required. The precious blood of Christ is not enough to make us 'meet to be partakers of the inheritance of the saints in light'. If we are saved, if we are to enter into heaven's eternal glory, something else is necessary, just as necessary as the work of the Father and the work of the Son. We must be saved by the blessed work of God the Holy Spirit in the blessed experience of grace (Titus 3:5-7). The experience of grace gives the sinner hope before God. God's purpose made the salvation of his elect sure, but gives hope to no one. Christ's death is the singular basis of the sinner's hope, but gives hope to none. It is 'Christ in you', Christ formed in you by God the Holy Spirit in the experience of grace, God says 'is the hope of glory' (Colossians 1:27).

Christ is formed in us by the omnipotent mercy and almighty grace of God the Holy Spirit, in the experience of grace, granting us repentance toward God and giving us faith in Christ. He makes a complete reversal of all things, restoring that which he took not away, in the complete, perfect restoration of our souls to God. It is this reversal of all things, this perfect restoration that every chosen, redeemed sinner experiences in Christ in the sweet experience of God's saving grace.

When sinners are born of God, they are made new creatures in Christ, made 'partakers of the divine nature, having escaped the corruption that is in the world through lust' (2 Corinthians 5:17; 2 Peter 1:3, 4; 1 John 3:5-10). In the new birth God the Holy Spirit creates in us a new life. He gives chosen, redeemed sinners an entirely new nature. He forms Christ in us, puts righteousness in us, makes us righteous, pure and holy, puts in us a spirit in which there is no guile, and makes us 'meet to be partakers of the inheritance of the saints in light'. This new man is 'Christ in you, the hope of glory'. This is that 'holiness' we must have, 'without which no man shall see the Lord'. It is written, 'There shall in no wise enter into it anything that defileth, neither whatsoever worketh abomination, or maketh a lie: but they which are written in the Lamb's book of life' (Revelation 21:27). God the Holy Ghost does not regenerate the old man in the new birth; he creates a new man in the dead sinner 'in righteousness and true holiness' and that new man is 'Christ in you, the hope of glory'.

It takes both the precious blood of Christ and the water, or grace, of the Spirit to bring us to glory.

> Sinners are saved by sovereign grace,
> Abounding through the Son.
> And not by works of righteousness
> Which their own hands have done!
>
> It is the mercy of our God
> That gives us hope within;
> Both by the water and the blood
> Our souls are washed from sin.
>
> Raised from the dead, we live anew;
> And justified by grace,
> We shall appear in glory, too,
> And see our Saviour's face.

## The Magicians

Pharaoh's magicians also turned water into blood, or at least appeared to do so. Whether it was mere trickery and deception, or whether God gave them power to turn water into blood is really irrelevant. The fact is, God sent Pharaoh a strong delusion that he might be damned, just as he does today (2 Thessalonians 2:11-13). Though their sorcery produced a trivial thing, Pharaoh and his magicians used it as an excuse for rebellion and unbelief. They went on, vainly resisting the revelation of God and his power, though their hearts must have quaked within them. The fact is, no man can or will believe God except God the Holy Spirit create faith in him. Let us not forget our faith in Christ is the gift and operation of God's free grace. 'Thanks be unto God for his unspeakable gift!'

## Pharaoh Hardened

'And Pharaoh's heart was hardened, neither did he hearken unto them' (v. 22). He regarded not the work of the Lord and gave no thought to the work of his hands (Isaiah 5:12). 'As the Lord had said'. God still has mercy on whom he will have mercy; and he still hardens whom he will (Romans 9:16-18).

'And Pharaoh turned, and went into his house' (v. 23). He turned on his heels, turned his back against God, and went home to his palace in the darkness of a hardened heart, refusing to bow to the undeniable revelation of God. 'Neither did he set his heart to this also'. He had no more regard for this miracle of turning the waters into blood than he had to the former.

'And all the Egyptians digged round about the river for water to drink; for they could not drink of the water of the river' (v. 24). As the Israelites had been compelled by Pharaoh to seek straw where there was none, now the Egyptians, under the judgment of God, sought water where there was none. 'For the people turneth not unto him that smiteth them, neither do they seek the LORD of hosts' (Isaiah 9:13).

'And seven days were fulfilled, after that the LORD had smitten the river' (v. 25). All this was done in judgment upon Egypt; but let us never forget it was done in great mercy for Israel. Let us never forget that even when darkness appears to cover the earth, even when death and destruction are seen everywhere, our God and heavenly Father is working all things together for the salvation and everlasting good of his elect. He turned the water into blood that he might bring Israel out of Egypt. If Christ is ours, we have no reason to fear, though the very foundations of the earth crumble. If Christ undertakes our cause, our cause is sure. If he undertakes for our souls, we are safe and secure in his hands. Let us trust, and not be afraid. All is well!

# Chapter 48

# Frogs, Lice, Flies, And Pharaoh

'And the LORD spake unto Moses, Go unto Pharaoh, and say unto him,
Thus saith the LORD, Let my people go, that they may serve me …
And Pharaoh hardened his heart at this time also, neither would he let
the people go.'
(Exodus 8:1-32)

Seven days after the Lord God turned the water into blood in Egypt he
sent Moses back to Pharaoh. In this eighth chapter of Exodus three more
plagues are poured out upon the land of Egypt. Frogs, lice, and flies are
sent upon the land. By the command of God, Moses brought these three
successive plagues upon the land of Egypt. What is their significance?
Why are these things recorded in the Book of God? Are they written
here as mere records of history? I am sure they are not. Are they
recorded to demonstrate God's omnipotence? No. Moses was inspired
of God to perform these things and to record them for our benefit, for
our learning, to teach us patience, give us comfort, and encourage us to
believe God, that we 'might with one mind and one mouth glorify God,
even the Father of our Lord Jesus Christ' (Romans 15:4, 6).

The Book of Revelation makes clear that the plagues God wrought
upon the Egyptians were typical of the judgments God brings upon the
world today. As we read the description of those trumpet judgments we
cannot avoid seeing the similarity between them and the judgments of
God upon the Egyptians in the book of Exodus. As then, the plagues
were poured out upon Egypt, and Israel was unharmed; even so, the
judgments of God that fall upon the wicked today never harm God's

elect, but only assist in the accomplishment of their salvation! 'There shall no evil happen to the just' (Proverbs 12:21). May God the Holy Spirit be our Teacher as we observe that which he has recorded in these 32 verses about frogs, lice, flies, and Pharaoh.

### Frogs

In verse 1 the Lord God issues his command to Pharaoh a third time. 'And the LORD spake unto Moses, Go unto Pharaoh, and say unto him, Thus saith the LORD, Let my people go, that they may serve me.'

The command is the same as Pharaoh had heard before. He will hear it eight times. Though he harden his heart again and again, God's command will not be altered. He is determined to deliver his people out of Egypt. He is determined to prevail over Pharaoh. Israel must be saved. It is God's purpose to save his people; and save them he will (Romans 8:28-30). According to his eternal purpose, by the efficacy of his blood, by the work of his all-wise providence, and by the omnipotent power of his grace, 'all Israel shall be saved' (Romans 11:26).

Let us ever pray for grace to make us obedient to our God, to keep us from hardening our hearts like Pharaoh (Psalm 119:4-6). 'Today, if ye will hear his voice, harden not your heart!' Four times in the Book of God we are urged, 'harden not your heart', because we are constantly tempted to do so. Harden not your heart against the gospel of Christ, the doctrine of God our Saviour, the providence of God. Harden not your heart against the revelation of God. 'Thou hast commanded us to keep thy precepts diligently. O that my ways were directed to keep thy statutes! Then shall I not be ashamed, when I have respect unto all thy commandments.' All who harden their hearts against the revelation of God, either in obstinate rebellion or in attempts to compromise that which God has revealed, prove themselves reprobate and court the judgment of God. 'And if thou refuse to let them go, behold, I will smite all thy borders with frogs' (v. 2; Psalm 107:40; 7:12, 13; 78:45).

'And the river shall bring forth frogs abundantly, which shall go up and come into thine house, and into thy bedchamber, and upon thy bed, and into the house of thy servants, and upon thy people, and into thine ovens, and into thy kneadingtroughs: And the frogs shall come up both on thee, and upon thy people, and upon all thy servants. And the LORD spake unto Moses, Say unto Aaron, Stretch forth thine hand with thy rod over the streams, over the rivers, and over the ponds, and cause frogs to come up upon the land of Egypt. And Aaron stretched out his hand over the waters of Egypt; and the frogs came up, and covered the land of Egypt' (Exodus 8:3-6).

This second plague, like the first, was directed against the idolatry of the Egyptians. The Nile River was revered by them as the source of life. Frogs were worshipped by them as gods representing fertility. So the Lord God multiplied their ugly, croaking, smelly gods until he made their gods obnoxious to them. The frogs not only 'covered the land of Egypt', but invaded their homes, entered their bed-chambers, crawled into their ovens, and even filled their kneading troughs!

The only time these dirty creatures are mentioned in the New Testament is in Revelation 16. There the Holy Spirit shows us the significance of this plague. Frogs represent the corrupting influence of false religion, specifically as it opposes Christ, his gospel, and his people. They are 'the spirits of devils, working miracles'.

'And I saw three unclean spirits like frogs come out of the mouth of the dragon, and out of the mouth of the beast, and out of the mouth of the false prophet. For they are the spirits of devils, working miracles, which go forth unto the kings of the earth and of the whole world, to gather them to the battle of that great day of God Almighty' (Revelation 16:13, 14).

In verse seven, the Lord gives Pharaoh's magicians power to imitate his servants. 'And the magicians did so with their enchantments, and brought up frogs upon the land of Egypt'. 'The deceived and the deceiver are his' (Job 12:16). And he uses them as he will (2 Timothy 3:8 and 2 Thessalonians 2:7-11). He who is our God is 'the God of this world' who blinds the hearts and minds of those who will not bow to his Word (John 12:40; Romans 11:7, 25; 2 Corinthians 3:14; 4:3-5).

Read verses 9-15 and learn this. Judgment never brings repentance. Many, as Pharaoh, tremble when they are terrified by God's judgments; but judgment never brings repentance. 'And Moses said unto Pharaoh, Glory over me: when shall I entreat for thee, and for thy servants, and for thy people, to destroy the frogs from thee and thy houses, that they may remain in the river only? And he said, To morrow. And he said, Be it according to thy word: that thou mayest know that there is none like unto the LORD our God. And the frogs shall depart from thee, and from thy houses, and from thy servants, and from thy people; they shall remain in the river only. And Moses and Aaron went out from Pharaoh:

and Moses cried unto the LORD because of the frogs which he had brought against Pharaoh. And the LORD did according to the word of Moses; and the frogs died out of the houses, out of the villages, and out of the fields. And they gathered them together upon heaps: and the land stank. But when Pharaoh saw that there was respite, he hardened his heart, and hearkened not unto them; as the LORD had said.'

'The goodness of God leadeth thee to repentance' (Romans 2:4). 'For godly sorrow worketh repentance to salvation not to be repented of: but the sorrow of the world worketh death' (2 Corinthians 7:10). I do not say that God does not use acts of providential judgment to arouse, impress, subdue, and humble his elect and bring them to repentance. He does graciously use these things (Psalm 107:1-31; Luke 15:11-20). But divine judgment, in and of itself, will never produce repentance in the heart. The heart of man is so obstinate, proud, and hard that even in the torments of hell the damned will never repent (Revelation 16:9).

Until God the Holy Ghost comes into the heart by the mighty, saving operations of his grace, no affliction, judgment, or terrifying alarms, though they be ever so great, ever so heavy, and ever so multiplied, will reach the soul (Psalm 78:31-37). Not only is it true that judgment never produces repentance, even when favour is shown to the wicked, they will not repent, except God grant repentance by the saving revelation of Christ in them (Exodus 8:15; Isaiah 26:10; Zechariah 12:10).

**Lice**
'And the LORD said unto Moses, Say unto Aaron, Stretch out thy rod, and smite the dust of the land, that it may become lice throughout all the land of Egypt. And they did so; for Aaron stretched out his hand with his rod, and smote the dust of the earth, and it became lice in man, and in beast; all the dust of the land became lice throughout all the land of Egypt. And the magicians did so with their enchantments to bring forth lice, but they could not: so there were lice upon man, and upon beast. Then the magicians said unto Pharaoh, This is the finger of God: and Pharaoh's heart was hardened, and he hearkened not unto them; as the LORD had said' (Exodus 8:16-19). 'He spake, and there came divers sorts of flies, and lice in all their coasts' (Psalm 105:31).

There are several things here that demand attention. First, notice that Aaron smote the dust of the land 'and it became lice in man and beast' (v.17). In the judgment God pronounced upon fallen Adam we read that he said, 'Cursed is the ground for thy sake' (Genesis 3:17), and again, 'for dust thou art, and unto dust shalt thou return' (Genesis 3:19). When Aaron smote the 'ground', and its 'dust' became lice, and the lice came upon the Egyptians, what a graphic picture it was of fallen man under the curse of the holy Lord God.

Second, when Pharaoh's magicians tried to imitate God's servants by their enchantments, this time 'they could not' do so. God restrained them. Therefore, they were helpless. He permitted them to make it appear they could produce snakes like Aaron. He permitted them to make it appear they could turn water into blood, and bring forth frogs, just like Moses and Aaron. But, when God withheld their magical powers, they were helpless to deceive. So it is with Satan himself. Satan's power is limited, and controlled by the Almighty. He cannot wiggle without God's decree. God may permit him to bring forth uncleanness and deception, just as he permitted Pharaoh's magician prophets to deceive their king; but the curse of God, Satan and his messengers cannot remove. That is done only according to the gospel: only when God's law is satisfied by God's Priest.

Third, in verse 19 we read, 'Then the magicians said unto Pharaoh, This is the finger of God'. It is the last thing recorded in the Scriptures they say. With their final word, they were forced to acknowledge the hand of God. So it shall be in the last day. Satan, the beast, the false prophet, and all who follow their deception shall bow before and publicly confess that Jesus is the Christ, confessing him as God and Lord alone (Philippians 2:9-11).

Fourth, there is a striking correspondence between this third plague and what is recorded in the eighth chapter of John's Gospel. There we see a similar contest between the Lord Jesus and false religion. The Scribes and the Pharisees, using the woman taken in adultery as their bait, sought to ensnare the Saviour. His only response was to stoop down and write on the ground. After saying to them, 'He that is without sin among you, let him first cast a stone at her', we read that 'Again he stooped down and wrote on the ground'. Do you remember what happened next? 'They which heard, being convicted by their conscience, went out one by one ... and Jesus was left alone, and the woman standing in the midst'. As the Lord Jesus wrote in the dirt, by their action, they acknowledged 'this is the finger of God'.

Fifth, I find it striking that God was pleased to use something as small, weak, insignificant, and dirty as lice to subdue these false prophets who withstood Moses. He might have turned dust into lions or scorpions; but he chose to use lice. He still uses weak things to confound the mighty (1 Corinthians 1:18-31; Psalm 64:5-10).

'They encourage themselves in an evil matter: they commune of laying snares privily; they say, Who shall see them? They search out iniquities; they accomplish a diligent search: both the inward thought of every one of them, and the heart, is deep. But God shall shoot at them with an arrow; suddenly shall they be wounded. So they shall make their own tongue to fall upon themselves: all that see them shall flee away. And all men shall fear, and shall declare the work of God; for they shall wisely consider of his doing. The righteous shall be glad in the LORD, and shall trust in him; and all the upright in heart shall glory' (Psalm 64:5-10).

### Flies
'And the LORD said unto Moses, Rise up early in the morning, and stand before Pharaoh; lo, he cometh forth to the water; and say unto him, Thus saith the LORD, Let my people go, that they may serve me. Else, if thou wilt not let my people go, behold, I will send swarms of flies upon thee, and upon thy servants, and upon thy people, and into thy houses: and the houses of the Egyptians shall be full of swarms of flies, and also the ground whereon they are. And I will sever in that day the land of Goshen, in which my people dwell, that no swarms of flies shall be there; to the end thou mayest know that I am the LORD in the midst of the earth. And I will put a division between my people and thy people: to morrow shall this sign be. And the LORD did so; and there came a grievous swarm of flies into the house of Pharaoh, and into his servants' houses, and into all the land of Egypt: the land was corrupted by reason of the swarm of flies' (Exodus 8:20-24).

'He sent divers sorts of flies among them, which devoured them; and frogs, which destroyed them' (Psalm 78:45). 'He spake, and there came divers sorts of flies, and lice in all their coasts' (Psalm 105:31).

The plague of flies was a striking display of divine sovereignty. The Egyptians worshipped Beelzebub as the god of flies. What could be more admirably suited to show God's contempt for their idol than the use of flies, the very objects of their idolatry, to punish them? That which they worshipped devoured them. 'Dead flies cause the ointment of the apothecary to send forth a stinking savour' (Ecclesiastes 10:1).

God used flies again to punish those who despised and rejected his darling Son (Isaiah 7:14, 17, 18). Flies are most abundant where manure is thickest. That is exactly how God would have us look upon all free will, works religion. Like Paul, we are to count it but dung.

Let us ever give thanks to our God for that great mercy by which he has set us free from all the dunghill deities of false religion. Notice, there were no flies in the land of Goshen, where the children of Israel dwelt (v. 22). The Lord God said, 'I will put a division between my people and thy people' (v. 23). Thank God for distinguishing, free grace! Thank God for the difference he makes by election, redemption, and effectual calling! 'Thanks be unto God, for his unspeakable gift' (2 Corinthians 9:15). He who is our God is God indeed. 'For God is my King of old, working salvation in the midst of the earth' (Psalm 74:12).

## Pharaoh

Pharaoh is set before us again in verses 25-32.

'And Pharaoh called for Moses and for Aaron, and said, Go ye, sacrifice to your God in the land. And Moses said, It is not meet so to do; for we shall sacrifice the abomination of the Egyptians to the LORD our God: lo, shall we sacrifice the abomination of the Egyptians before their eyes, and will they not stone us? We will go three days' journey into the wilderness, and sacrifice to the LORD our God, as he shall command us. And Pharaoh said, I will let you go, that ye may sacrifice to the LORD your God in the wilderness; only ye shall not go very far away: entreat for me. And Moses said, Behold, I go out from thee, and I will entreat the LORD that the swarms of flies may depart from Pharaoh, from his servants, and from his people, tomorrow: but let not Pharaoh deal deceitfully any more in not letting the people go to sacrifice to the LORD. And Moses went out from Pharaoh, and entreated the LORD. And the LORD did according to the word of Moses; and he removed the swarms of flies from Pharaoh, from his servants, and from his people; there remained not one. And Pharaoh hardened his heart at this time also, neither would he let the people go' (Exodus 8:25-32).

Pharaoh pretended to repent, but his pretence only demonstrated the greater hardening of his heart. He tried to get Moses and Aaron to compromise with him. Let me call your attention to just four things in these verses.

The Lord Jesus Christ, our God and Saviour, demands absolute surrender. Multitudes, like Pharaoh, vainly imagine that God will accept them on their terms. He will not. He demands complete surrender (Luke 14:25-33).

That sacrifice by which we worship and serve our God, the crucified Lamb of God, is now, always has been, and ever shall be an abomination to this world. 'But God forbid that I should glory, save in the cross of our Lord Jesus Christ, by whom the world is crucified unto me, and I unto the world' (Galatians 6:14).

We cannot worship and serve our God by compromise. Any compromise of the gospel, any compromise with God's enemies is damning, both to the compromiser and to those who follow him.

Hardened hearts will only continue to be hardened, until God, by his great mercy and grace, breaks them. From hardness of heart and contempt of his Word, may God ever deliver us!

But let us remember, all these things were done, not merely as acts of judgment upon the Egyptians, but also as acts of grace toward Israel. God sent the frogs, and the lice, and the flies, and hardened Pharaoh's heart, for the salvation of his chosen people. When we see that all things are ordained of God and work the salvation of our souls by his sovereign hand, such a view of heavenly mercy ought to endear our faithful, gracious, covenant God to our hearts. Oh, how we ought to rejoice in and give thanks for our heavenly Father's love, our great Redeemer's grace, and the Holy Spirit's unrelenting mercy!

How blessed we are to have the God of heaven and earth as our Saviour and Friend at all times! Such insignificant things as frogs, lice, and flies, and even such mighty things as the king of Egypt are employed by our God for the saving of our souls. How joyful we ought to be, knowing we live always under the smile of divine favour. How peaceful, how confident, we ought to be of whom the God of heaven says, 'I will make a covenant for them with the beasts of the field, and with the fowls of heaven, and with the creeping things of the ground. No weapon that is formed against thee shall prosper, and every tongue that shall rise against thee in judgment thou shalt condemn. This is the heritage of the servants of the LORD, and their righteousness is of me, saith the LORD'.

# Chapter 49

# The Will Of God Absolute, Irresistible, Sure

'And the LORD spake unto Moses, Go unto Pharaoh, and say unto him, Thus saith the LORD, Let my people go, that they may serve me ... And Pharaoh hardened his heart at this time also, neither would he let the people go.'
(Exodus 8:1)

The Lord God had determined he would deliver Israel at the precise time he had appointed. When the appointed time of deliverance arrived, he sent his servant Moses to Pharaoh demanding, 'Let my people go, that they may serve me'. This was not a request, but a command. With those words, the God of Israel revealed his will by issuing a command to his creature. His command, 'Let my people go', was a word of power, like, 'Let there be light'. Pharaoh was not inclined to let Israel go; but that was meaningless. The God of Glory said, 'Let my people go, that they may serve me'. Thus, Pharaoh was compelled to release his grasp. God's command came with irresistible force to the king of Egypt.

Then, the Lord revealed the reason behind his command. It was 'that they may serve me'. He did not need to give a reason, yet he chose to do so. In giving the reason for his command, he revealed both his claim upon Israel as his people and his claim upon Pharaoh as his servant, a tool in his hand by which he would both thrust Israel out of Egypt and display his glory and greatness as the one true and living God. God's authority over man is perfectly reasonable. He is the Creator. We are his creatures. He is the Potter. We are the clay. He makes no claim of sovereignty our own consciences do not justify. He has a claim upon us, a claim none can deny, resist, or rival. We must and shall serve him. While this claim is here specifically spoken regarding his chosen, it applies to every creature equally. All must and shall serve him, either willingly or unwillingly. The Lord God said to Pharaoh, 'You will let my people go'. He says, with regard to his chosen, 'They shall serve me'.

## Spiritual Application

That which is here spoken concerning Pharaoh and Israel applies to all God's creation with regard to the salvation of his elect. It is the intent of God the Holy Ghost that we make this application (Romans 9:15-28). With regard to his elect, his church, the Holy One of Israel says to his enemies and theirs, to those who hold them in bondage, the Pharaohs of the world, to Satan, the demons of hell, and indeed to all creation, 'Let my people go, that they may serve me'. When he does, he speaks with absolute, irresistible force. It is the will of God that his people be delivered out of all earthly bondage into 'the glorious liberty of the children of God', delivered from the bondage of Satan into the liberty of Christ, that we may serve him forever.

## Liberty and Service

Salvation is the deliverance of our souls both to the liberty of grace and to the service of our God. These two things are inseparable. We are not called to liberty alone, but to liberty and service. And we are not called to service alone, but to service that involves and arises from liberty. Liberty is mentioned first, because service is impossible without liberty. Without question, there can be and is service in Egypt, such service as may be demanded by and may satisfy the gods of Egypt; mechanical, self-righteous, legal, Pharisaical service, the service of the outer man, a form of godliness; but there can be no serving God with the heart and from the heart, without the liberty of grace.

It is the will of God that every chosen, redeemed sinner be brought into the blessed liberty of grace that we may serve him forever; and God's will is absolute, irresistible and sure.

## God's Irresistible Will

The very first thing to be considered is that which is the first thing, and the cause of all things: the will of God. Let me repeat what I have just stated. God's will is absolute, irresistible, and sure. We are assured in the Book of God that all things obey the will of God. The will of God is his eternal purpose; and all things obey it, either willingly or unwillingly (Deuteronomy 29:29; Romans 11:33-36).

God has purposed, decreed, and ordained all things that ever have come to pass and all things that ever shall come to pass, without exception (Psalm 115:3; 135:6; Isaiah 46:10; Daniel 4:35; Acts 2:23; 4:27, 28; 13:48; Romans 8:28-30; 9:15-18; 2 Corinthians 5:18; Ephesians 1:11). Everything that is, has been, or shall be, is the will of God. Here are five distinct things revealed in the Scriptures that it pleased God to do.

It pleased God to put all fulness in Christ, to give his Son pre-eminence in all things (Colossians 1:18, 19).

It pleased God to bruise the Lord Jesus Christ in the place of his people (Isaiah 53:10).

It pleased God to make his chosen his people (1 Samuel 12:22).

It pleased God to reveal his Son in chosen, redeemed sinners and call them by his grace (Galatians 1:15, 16).

It pleased God to reveal his Son in and call his elect by his grace through the instrumentality of the preaching of the gospel (1 Corinthians 1:21; Romans 10:17).

All that comes to pass in time comes to pass by the will of God to accomplish the great purpose of God (Isaiah 46:9-11; Daniel 4:34, 35; Acts 2:23; 4:27, 28; 13:48; Romans 8:28-30; 11:33-36; 2 Corinthians 5:18; Ephesians 1:11).

God is absolutely sovereign in directing the affairs of the universe. His will includes all things, evil as well as good, sin as well as salvation, error as well as truth. And God's will is always, perfectly accomplished in and by all things. Whatever he does in providence, God willed from eternity. 'He is in one mind, and who can turn him? and what his soul desireth, even that he doeth' (Job 23:13; Ephesians 1:11). He acts voluntarily in all he does. He is never compelled to do anything. God does in providence exactly what he willed to do from eternity (Acts 15:18). If he could will, desire, or purpose to do anything that he failed to accomplish, he would not be omnipotent. God's will of purpose includes all things (Psalm 76:10; Proverbs 16:4). It is his eternal, immutable, sovereign, unconditional, and irresistibly effectual will, ever holy, wise, and good.

Because carnal men are ever bent upon perverting the things of God, I must give a word or two of caution regarding the will of God's purpose. The sovereignty of God's purpose does not destroy man's responsibility. The universality of God's purpose does not make God the author of sin (James 1:13). God is not the author of sin; but he is the author of the good which he accomplishes by overruling sin. Without question, Adam's fall was ordained of God; but God did not force Adam to do what he did. Yet, he used the fall to accomplish his good pleasure toward his elect for the glory of his own great name (1 Corinthians 15:21, 22). The Lord God certainly ordained the crucifixion of his Son in the place of his people (Acts 2:23). Yet, he did not compel wicked men to crucify him. He simply overruled their wicked deeds to accomplish his purpose, which is the salvation of his elect for the everlasting praise of his name. When we hear God say regarding all things, 'I will do all my pleasure', we rejoice to bow before him and say, 'thy will be done', knowing that the accomplishment of God's will is the salvation of his elect, to the praise of his glory.

## Our Bondage
'And the LORD spake unto Moses, Go unto Pharaoh, and say unto him, Thus saith the LORD, Let my people go, that they may serve me.'

Our natural condition, as the fallen sons and daughters of Adam, is one of bondage. We are born in Egypt, not in Canaan. We were born in prison, born in shackles and irons, born slaves, and born under the curse of the law. Our wills were in bondage. Our faculties were in bondage. Our affections were in bondage. Our wills, our minds, our thoughts, and our hearts were in bondage. Our souls were in bondage. Bondage characterises everything about us.

There is no free motion or free action in any part of fallen man. All is constrained by our fallen, depraved nature. Men in bondage act under the sense of terror, or for a reward, or in order to obtain pardon, but never freely. Work done in chains is no service to God at all. Work done in order to purchase liberty is not acceptable work. It is not worshipping and serving God.

## Created for Liberty

We were all born in bondage; but God's elect were made for liberty. Though Egypt was made for Israel, Israel was not made for Egypt. Though God raised up Pharaoh to be lord over Israel for a specified period of time, Israel was not made to be a servant to Pharaoh.

So, too, God's elect were not created for bondage and the prison-house. God's will from eternity was, and is, that his people shall be free, free in the entirety of our beings, free in all our faculties, free in all our affections, free in all our works, free in our hearts, free in our souls, free in Christ. He created us to make us free, completely free, serving him without any constraint of any kind, except the constraint of our hearts, the constraint of Christ's love revealed and shed abroad in our hearts by the Holy Ghost. He created us to be his voluntary bond-slaves, serving him willingly. Religion, all human religion, all freewill and works religion operates upon the principle of bondage, and holds people in bondage. Christ sets sinners free. As soon as he raises a chosen, redeemed sinner from the dead in the new birth, he says, 'Loose him, and let him go'! And every faithful servant of God, by the preaching of the gospel, proclaims liberty, not bondage, to all who trust the Son of God.

## No Liberty No Service

Here is another thing clearly implied in our text. We cannot serve God without liberty. 'And the LORD spake unto Moses, Go unto Pharaoh, and say unto him, Thus saith the LORD, Let my people go, that they may serve me.'

We may do many things without liberty. The body can labour in a prison, in shackles and irons; but the soul must be free in order to serve, completely free, without constraint, without force, without coercion of any kind from without.

In the worship and service of God, nothing is done by constraint. Everything is done willingly (2 Corinthians 8:12). Religion forces people into service against their will, threatening punishment or promising reward; but God's service must be performed freely. He will accept nothing that does not arise from a willing heart. We must be free that we may serve him. We do not serve him in order to get liberty. We are liberated to serve our God. Until we are free, we cannot serve God.

## Called to Liberty

Let me show you one more thing. Christ calls us to liberty (John 8:32, 36; Galatians 5:1-5, 13). 'Ye have been called unto liberty.' The Son of God came to open our prison doors, to bring us out of the house of bondage. He came to break our chains, and to make us wholly free. The Son makes us free. Liberty comes directly from Christ.

The truth makes us free. It is through the truth that Christ gives us liberty. He is the Truth and he liberates. His Spirit is truth and his Spirit liberates. His word is truth and his word liberates. With our fetters broken by his touch, and our souls receiving his truth, being filled with his Spirit in the gift of life, we go forth as freed men to serve our God. Now, we sing with David, 'I will walk at liberty', because we are in Christ, where bondage cannot exist (Romans 8:1-15).

Have you been set free? Are you walking at liberty? Has the gospel brought peace into your soul? Is the Spirit of adoption teaching you to cry, Abba, Father? Perhaps you say, 'I am trying to serve the Lord'. By what spirit do you seek to serve him? In the Spirit of love or the spirit of dread? In the Spirit of gladness or the spirit of terror? In the Spirit of light or the spirit of gloom?

Has Christ made you free? Then let no man bring you again into bondage. Walk at liberty and serve God your Saviour forever (Galatians 5:1-4).

# Chapter 50

## God: The Great Divider Of Men

'And I will sever in that day the land of Goshen, in which my people dwell, that no swarms of flies shall be there; to the end thou mayest know that I am the LORD in the midst of the earth. And I will put a division between my people and thy people: tomorrow shall this sign be. And the LORD did so; and there came a grievous swarm of flies into the house of Pharaoh, and into his servants' houses, and into all the land of Egypt: the land was corrupted by reason of the swarm of flies.' (Exodus 8:22-24)

God is the great divider of men. When the Lord sent Moses and Aaron to Pharaoh, he commanded Moses to tell Pharaoh he would divide his people from the Egyptians in a demonstrably clear and undeniable way. He would make the division so apparent that the king of Egypt would be made to know that he is God alone in the midst of the earth.

God has always put a difference between men. He has from everlasting put a difference between Israel and Egypt. He has maintained that division throughout the ages of time. And he will maintain it forever. He always puts a distinction between Israel and Egypt. Every time he sent Moses to Pharaoh, he spoke of Israel as 'my people'. The Egyptians he called 'thy people'.

The Lord God said, 'I will put a division between my people and thy people ... And, blessed be his name, the LORD did so!' There is a continual and eternal distinction observed in the Word of God between the chosen seed of promise and the world, between God's elect and the children of the wicked one, between Christ's seed and the serpent's seed. It is a distinction God made and a distinction God maintains.

Who can trace out the wonders of distinguishing grace? What a vast distinction God has made, and makes daily between the sons of men, between his people and the rest of Adam's fallen race! How vast that difference will be in the world to come! We ought to make this a matter of unceasing meditation and thanksgiving. You cannot awake in the morning, walk through the day, or lay down at night without experiencing the difference God puts between Israel and Egypt. Everything proclaims it. Every event confirms it. Our God says, 'Against any of the children of Israel shall not a dog move his tongue, against man or beast: that ye may know how that the Lord doth put a difference between the Egyptians and Israel' (Exodus 11:7).

God's object and purpose in everything he did with Egypt and Pharaoh was the deliverance of his people for the praise of his glory. He raised up the nation, that he might use that nation to protect, provide for, and increase his people Israel, until the appointed time came for him to fulfil his covenant with Abraham and glorify himself in delivering his chosen from their cruel oppressors, for the glory of his own great name. No mercy was intended for Egypt. No blessing was bestowed upon Egypt. Furthermore, Israel suffered no harm, but only great good, by their 400 years in Egypt. So it is to this day. That is exactly what God is doing with the world now. He is gathering his elect out of the nations of the earth, just as he gathered his Israel out of Egypt. He is separating the precious from the vile. He is separating the wheat from the tares, gathering his wheat into his barn and binding the tares in bundles for the burning. Egypt will always be Egypt, the world will always be the world, and God's elect will always be his Israel. Between the two, between Egypt and Israel, God has made, and constantly makes, a division.

**Not Obvious**
Though the division was made between Israel and Egypt long before Israel went down into Egypt, and though the division was made and maintained in Israel's favour, until the appointed day of deliverance came, it appeared to greatly favour the Egyptians. Judging by everything the eye could see and reason could observe, it appeared Egypt must have been God's chosen nation and Israel the reprobate people. Egypt had the whip, and Israel felt the lash. Egypt owned everything. The Israelites performed the labour. The sons of Jacob

made bricks and built houses. The Egyptians lived in them. The Egyptians drank wine from golden goblets. The children of Israel drank water from clay cups.

But that all changed in a heartbeat. God turned the tables in one night. Even before he brought Israel out of Egypt, he made it obvious Egypt was marked for destruction and Israel was divinely protected. When the Lord God wrought his plagues in Egypt, the land of Goshen was spared. He sent thick darkness over all the land, felt darkness; but in the land of Goshen there was light. He sent swarms of flies and lice through all the borders of Egypt; but there was not a fly nor any lice to be seen in Goshen. God sent hail and a murrain upon all the cattle of the Egyptians; but the cattle of the children of Israel were spared, and on their fields fell no desolating curse from heaven. At last, when the destroying angel unsheathed his glittering sword to smite his final decisive blow, in every house throughout the land of Egypt there was weeping and wailing, because the firstborn was killed in every dwelling of Egypt; but not one died in Israel that night. God provided a sacrifice for Israel; but for the Egyptians, no sacrifice was provided.

The Lord God led the chosen nation forth like sheep, like a huge flock through the wilderness, by the hands of Moses and Aaron. When they came to the Red Sea, he divided the sea and made a path for his chosen. They sang his praise, rejoicing in his salvation. The flood stood upright like a wall. The depths were congealed in the heart of the sea. Israel passed through the depths as through a wilderness, and the Egyptians were drowned in the flood. In all things, the Lord God put a glorious division between Israel and Egypt. The fiery, cloudy pillar gave light to Israel and darkness to the Egyptians. In everything God blessed Israel; and in everything he cursed Egypt. So it ever has been. So it is now. So it shall ever be, to the praise of the glory of his grace.

### The Division

The Lord God said to Pharaoh, 'I will put a division between my people and thy people … And the LORD did so'. The Lord God Almighty has put a division between those who are his people and those who are not his people. There are many divisions among men that will one day be blotted out; but this is an eternal division that is immutable and abiding. This division is so wide we may truly say, 'Between Israel and Egypt there is a great gulf fixed; and none can pass from one side of the chasm to the other'. It is a division of unimaginable proportion made by the infinite God from eternity. That which distinguishes God's elect from the reprobate of this world is the distinguishing grace of God. It is written, 'The LORD doth put a difference between the Egyptians and Israel'. The distinction which grace makes is a fivefold distinction.

### The Distinction of God's Sovereign Election
'Ye have not chosen me, but I have chosen you, and ordained you, that ye should go and bring forth fruit, and that your fruit should remain: that whatsoever ye shall ask of the Father in my name, he may give it you' (John 15:16).

'But we are bound to give thanks alway to God for you, brethren beloved of the Lord, because God hath from the beginning chosen you to salvation through sanctification of the Spirit and belief of the truth: Whereunto he called you by our gospel, to the obtaining of the glory of our Lord Jesus Christ' (2 Thessalonians 2:13, 14).

In the eternal covenant of grace the Lord God wrote the names of his elect in the book of life. The Lord Jesus Christ, God's darling Son, became their Surety, and stood forth as our substitute to suffer in our room and stead. Covenant engagements were made for Israel, and for Israel alone. Our names were of old inscribed in the book of God and engraved upon the precious stones of our High Priest's breastplate. Before the starry sky was spread, or the foundations of the earth were dug, the Lord made a division between Israel and Egypt. Hear this, and rejoice, child of God, 'God hath from the beginning chosen you'!

### The Distinction of Christ's Blood Redemption
'And they sung a new song, saying, Thou art worthy to take the book, and to open the seals thereof: for thou wast slain, and hast redeemed us to God by thy blood out of every kindred, and tongue, and people, and nation' (Revelation 5:9).

As the Lord God made a division between Israel and Egypt in his eternal decrees of election and predestination, so too he made a division at Calvary. There, upon the cursed tree, as the Lord Jesus Christ hung between two thieves, he divided the two. For one he made atonement; for the other none. For one he made intercession; for the other none. To the one he gave a promise; to the other none.

## The Distinction of the New Birth

Our God has made another division, a vital one. It is an essential distinction of nature. Some imagine the only division God makes between men is outward. That is not the case. If sinners are saved a distinction of nature must be made. We cannot enter into heaven with the nature that caused God to drive Adam out of the garden. 'Flesh and blood cannot inherit the kingdom of God' (1 Corinthians 15:50; Revelation 21:27). Concerning all his chosen, the Lord Jesus says, 'Ye must be born again!' But the division and distinction of grace does not end with the new birth. This distinction is carried out in providence.

## The Distinction of God's Gracious Providence

'And we know that all things work together for good to them that love God, to them who are the called according to his purpose. For whom he did foreknow, he also did predestinate to be conformed to the image of his Son, that he might be the firstborn among many brethren. Moreover whom he did predestinate, them he also called: and whom he called, them he also justified: and whom he justified, them he also glorified. What shall we then say to these things? If God be for us, who can be against us?' (Romans 8:28-31)

To the naked eye of flesh, all things appear to happen to Israel and Egypt alike. The righteous suffer as well as the wicked. We all must soon go to the grave. But there is a vast difference. God's providence draws a line like a laser between the sons of men. To his chosen, every act of providence is a blessing. A blessing is wrapped up in all our conflicts and all our crosses. Our cups are often bitter; but they are always healthy. We are never losers by our losses; but we grow rich towards God when we become poor toward the world (Psalm 57:2).

To Egypt, all things work together for evil. Is he prosperous? He is as the beast fattened for slaughter. Is he healthy? He is as the blooming flower soon to be mowed down. Does he suffer? His sufferings are the first drops of the eternal hail-storm of divine vengeance. Everything is blackness and darkness (Psalm 73:18).

'O LORD, how great are thy works! And thy thoughts are very deep. A brutish man knoweth not; neither doth a fool understand this. When the wicked spring as the grass, and when all the workers of iniquity do flourish; it is that they shall be destroyed forever' (Psalm 92:5-7).

## The Distinction of Resurrection Glory

'Marvel not at this: for the hour is coming, in the which all that are in the graves shall hear his voice, And shall come forth; they that have done good, unto the resurrection of life; and they that have done evil, unto the resurrection of damnation' (John 5:28, 29).

That division will be manifest to all in the last day. Then, when he shall sit upon the throne of his glory, God our Saviour shall divide Israel from Egypt, as a shepherd divides the sheep from the goats. He shall cry unto his angels, and say, 'Gather out of my kingdom all things that offend and them that do iniquity'. Then, with the sharp sickle in his hand, will the angel fly through the midst of heaven and reap the tares, and gather them together in bundles to burn. But, stepping from his throne, not delegating the delightful task to an angel, the King himself, the crowned Reaper, shall take his own golden sickle, and shall gather the wheat into his barn. Then, hell shall open its mouth and swallow up the impenitent, they shall go down alive into the pit, as Korah, Dathan, and Abiram did of old. Then, they shall see the righteous flowing up to heaven, like a stream of light in bright garments, shouting hymns in one glorious symphony of praise. Then, shall it be seen that the Lord has put a division between Israel and Egypt. When across the impassable gulf, the rich man shall see Lazarus in Abraham's bosom, when from the lowest pit of hell, the condemned one shall see the accepted one glorified in bliss, then shall the truth stand out written in letters of fire 'The LORD hath put a difference between the Egyptians and Israel'.

## The Division Manifest

But is the division unknown until the last day? Oh, no. God makes the division manifest day by day. We see it manifest in the deliverance of his chosen in the sweet experience of grace. Two sinners come into the house of God. They take their seats side by side. Both hear the gospel preached. But one goes down to his house justified, the other goes home like he came, unmoved, unbroken, unbelieving. Why? Because God made a difference (2 Timothy 1:9, 10). The division God makes is manifest in his gracious preservation of his chosen. It is manifest in the sweet restoration of his fallen saints. It is manifest upon the death-beds of his chosen (1 Corinthians 4:7). And, that which he has begun in me, he will finish 'to the praise of the glory of his grace'.

# Chapter 51

## 'Take Away The Frogs'

'Then Pharaoh called for Moses and Aaron, and said, Entreat the LORD, that he may take away the frogs from me, and from my people; and I will let the people go, that they may do sacrifice unto the LORD.' (Exodus 8:8) 'And Pharaoh sent, and called for Moses and Aaron, and said unto them, I have sinned this time: the LORD is righteous, and I and my people are wicked. Entreat the LORD (for it is enough) that there be no more mighty thunderings and hail; and I will let you go, and ye shall stay no longer' (Exodus 9:27, 28). 'Then Pharaoh called for Moses and Aaron in haste; and he said, I have sinned against the LORD your God, and against you. Now therefore forgive, I pray thee, my sin only this once, and entreat the LORD your God, that he may take away from me this death only. And he went out from Pharaoh, and entreated the LORD. And the LORD turned a mighty strong west wind, which took away the locusts, and cast them into the Red sea; there remained not one locust in all the coasts of Egypt. But the LORD hardened Pharaoh's heart, so that he would not let the children of Israel go' (Exodus 10:16-20).

The Apostle Paul speaks of the sorrow of the world that produces a repentance to be repented of, a repentance not unto salvation, but a repentance that is unto death. Three times Pharaoh, the king of Egypt, displayed a vivid picture of repentance that is to be repented of, repentance that is unto death. Three times Pharaoh asked Moses to entreat the LORD for him. Three times he was so overwhelmed by the judgment of God that he repented, acknowledged the LORD Jehovah is

God indeed, and confessed his sin. Yet, his heart was hardened; he refused to repent, he refused to acknowledge God as God, and he refused to confess his sin. Pharaoh's repentance was a repentance to be repented of, repentance that at last brought forth death, everlasting death under the wrath of God in the torments of hell. Oh, may God save you from such repentance, for Christ's sake!

'Pharaoh called for Moses and Aaron, and said, Entreat the LORD, that he may take away the frogs from me'. Again, 'Pharaoh sent, and called for Moses and Aaron, and said unto them, I have sinned this time: the LORD is righteous, and I and my people are wicked. Entreat the LORD, for it is enough!' And a third time, 'Pharaoh called for Moses and Aaron in haste; and he said, I have sinned against the LORD your God, and against you. Now therefore forgive, I pray thee, my sin only this once, and entreat the LORD your God, that he may take away from me this death!' Is this the same Pharaoh that said, 'Who is the LORD, that I should obey his voice?' Is this the same man who has been scoffing at God and his servants, and tormenting his people? Yes, it is the same man, the same Pharaoh, the same rebel. He is terrified; but he is the same. Three times he begged Moses to entreat the Lord for him. Three times Moses did so. But, as soon as the cause of Pharaoh's terror was gone, he hardened his heart the more.

What was wrong with Pharaoh's repentance? He said the right things. He felt the judgment of God. He confessed his sin. He acknowledged Christ as the Lord God of heaven and earth. He acknowledged the necessity of worshipping and serving God by the sacrifice of Christ, as Moses had declared God must be worshipped and served by his people. He even acknowledged that only the Lord God who had brought judgment upon him could take it away. Yet, Pharaoh's heart was hardened by the very act of repentance; and he is in hell today because of it. So, what was wrong with his repentance?

**An Unregenerate Man**
Pharaoh's repentance was that of a natural, unregenerate man, a man without life and faith in Christ. True repentance, like true faith, arises from the gift of life by the Spirit of God. It is the result of the new birth, not a prelude to it. We turn to God in repentance, trusting Christ as Lord and Saviour, when we have been turned to God by the Spirit of grace. 'Turn thou me, and I shall be turned; for thou art the LORD my God.

Surely after that I was turned, I repented; and after that I was instructed, I smote upon my thigh: I was ashamed, yea, even confounded, because I did bear the reproach of my youth' (Jeremiah 31:18, 19).

'Repentance to salvation not to be repented of' (2 Corinthians 7:10) is not the cause of salvation, but the result. Christ is the captain, cause, and author of salvation. Repentance, like faith, is the means through and by which salvation is brought home to our souls in the sweet experience of grace; and both repentance and faith come to us by 'the gift of God' the Holy Ghost in regeneration, flowing to us in the river of his sovereign grace by the blood of Christ (Ephesians 2:8). As he 'that believeth and is baptized', trusting Christ as his righteousness, is saved, so he that repents of sin 'shall be saved' (Mark 16:16).

Repentance is the gift of the triune God bestowed upon chosen sinners by grace. It is the covenant gift of God the Father to chosen sinners. He commands his servants, in meekness, to instruct 'those that oppose themselves, if God peradventure will give them repentance, to the acknowledging of the truth' (2 Timothy 2:25). It is bestowed upon us as the gift of God the Son, our Lord Jesus Christ, as the Mediator of the covenant, who is exalted as a Prince and Saviour 'to give repentance unto Israel, and forgiveness of sins' (Acts 5:31; 11:18). And it is the gift of God the Spirit, who convinces redeemed sinners of sin, righteousness, and judgment, and works repentance in them (John 16:8). Repentance is the work and operation of God the Holy Spirit in omnipotent mercy and saving grace, 'who hath mercy on whom he will have mercy, and whom he will he hardeneth' (Romans 9:18).

What tremendous words those are! He 'hath mercy on whom he will have mercy, and whom he will he hardeneth!' If God has granted us repentance, let us ever praise him and extol him for his free grace and sovereign mercy. Yet, we must not fail to see and acknowledge that 'whom he will he hardeneth', just as he did Pharaoh, whose heart he hardened with false repentance.

## Pharaoh's Trouble

Pharaoh's repentance, like the repentance of countless multitudes in our day, was the mock repentance of a sinner terrified by a sense of divine judgment. Such repentance counterfeits true repentance, but has features by which it betrays itself. Three times we see Pharaoh visibly and deeply troubled. He was alarmed. He knew he was under the wrath and judgment of God. He confessed his sin. He promised obedience. But his repentance was unto death. There is a difference between being in trouble and being humbled, being alarmed and being awakened, between the fear of going to hell and knowing you deserve to go to hell.

When the Holy Spirit works repentance in a sinner, he brings down his heart with labour and brings him to his wits' end with guilt and felt judgment in his soul, because he knows he is justly condemned before God. His bones wax old through roaring. Day and night the hand of God lays heavily upon him. His moisture is turned into the drought of summer (Psalm 32:3, 4). The guilty sinner has a sense of hell in his soul! But Pharaoh was not crushed with guilt, only with judgment; and the judgment of God never brings repentance (Revelation 16:8-11).

Let me be clear. I do not say that God never uses providential acts of judgment to arouse, impress, subdue, and humble his elect and bring them to repentance. He often uses outward, temporal acts of judgment to graciously bring sinners to Christ (Psalm 107:1-31; Luke 15:11-20). But I do say that divine judgment, in and of itself, will never produce repentance in the heart of a man. The heart of man is so obstinate, proud, and hard that even the torments of hell will never cause the damned to repent. They gnaw their tongues for pain, but will not shed a tear for the cause of their pain. And if there is no repentance in hell, where God's greatest judgments are executed, the lesser judgments of providence certainly will not change the sinner's heart and produce repentance. Judgment does not soften the sinner's heart; it hardens it. Wrath will never convert a man. It is grace that saves. Any repentance produced by God's acts of providential judgment or by legal fear is a false repentance. Pharaoh, Cain, Herod and Judas all repented of the evil they had done, because they saw the judgment of God upon them. But they were not saved. They all perished under the wrath of God.

Only the revelation of Christ in the heart can produce true repentance (Zechariah 12:10). Repentance is the tear that drops from faith's eye (Job 42:5, 6). No one will ever truly repent until he is converted by the grace of God, and looks to and sees Christ crucified as his only, all-sufficient, sin atoning Substitute. Repentance is the response of faith to the promises of God in the gospel (Isaiah 55:7; Jeremiah 3:11-13). Repentance is the result, not the cause, of God's converting grace, the fruit of faith in Christ (Jeremiah 31:19).

## Pharaoh's Requests

Look at the requests this terrified man made to Moses. Three times the king of Egypt called for Moses and cowered before him, begging him to entreat the Lord for him. The God of heaven made himself known to Pharaoh by the judgments he executed upon him. And Pharaoh cowered before God's servant Moses, whom he had despised, acknowledging that none but God could have brought the frogs and none but God could remove them. He begged Moses and Aaron to intercede for him, that the Lord might remove the plague of frogs from him and his people.

When men are in great distress, they often greatly value and honour God's servants, whom before they treated with contempt. When the man of God prophesied against the altar Jeroboam erected at Bethel, the king put forth his hand and said, 'Lay hold on him. And his hand, which he put forth against him, dried up, so that he could not pull it in again to him. The altar also was rent, and the ashes poured out from the altar, according to the sign which the man of God had given by the word of the LORD. And the king answered and said unto the man of God, Intreat now the face of the LORD thy God, and pray for me, that my hand may be restored me again' (1 Kings 13:4-6). When King Saul was forsaken and the Philistines threatened to destroy him, he went to the witch of Endor and said, 'Bring me up Samuel' (1 Samuel 28:11). The rich man in hell, places a great value upon Lazarus, whom he despised upon the earth (Luke 16). The Philippian jailor laid great store upon the words of Paul and Silas, when he was driven to utter despair and ready to kill himself (Acts 16). Pharaoh begged God's servant Moses to pray for him, when he thought God was about to kill him. Unlike preachers of our day, who bow and scrape before little men, and applaud them if they happen to mention God's name in an honourable way, Moses saw through Pharaoh's show of humility and demanded the king of Egypt glory over him before all the people. Moses demanded that Pharaoh acknowledge publicly that he was indeed the prophet of the only true and living God. Pharaoh did as Moses demanded, and God removed the frogs. But Pharaoh hardened his heart.

'And Moses said unto Pharaoh, Glory over me: when shall I entreat for thee, and for thy servants, and for thy people, to destroy the frogs from thee and thy houses, that they may remain in the river only? And he said, Tomorrow. And he said, Be it according to thy word: that thou mayest know that there is none like unto the LORD our God. And the frogs shall depart from thee, and from thy houses, and from thy servants, and from thy people; they shall remain in the river only. And Moses and Aaron went out from Pharaoh: and Moses cried unto the LORD because of the frogs which he had brought against Pharaoh. And the LORD did according to the word of Moses; and the frogs died out of the houses, out of the villages, and out of the fields. And they gathered them together upon heaps: and the land stank. But when Pharaoh saw that there was respite, he hardened his heart, and hearkened not unto them; as the LORD had said' (Exodus 8:9-15).

When we get to chapter 9, after enduring the plagues of lice, flies, a grievous murrain, boils and blain upon men and beasts, pestilence and grievous hail, Pharaoh's terrors were renewed and intensified. So, he called for Moses and Aaron again. He made three confessions that are, in this day of easy-believism thought to be evidences of saving faith.

'And Pharaoh sent, and called for Moses and Aaron, and said unto them, I have sinned this time: the LORD is righteous, and I and my people are wicked. Entreat the LORD (for it is enough) that there be no more mighty thunderings and hail; and I will let you go, and ye shall stay no longer' (Exodus 9:27, 28).

'I have sinned this time', as if to say, Moses, I know I was not sincere before, but this time I am really sincere. I know, this time, I have sinned. 'The LORD (Jehovah, the self-existent, eternal God) is righteous'. I acknowledge God's judgment is righteous and just. If he destroys us he will only be doing what is right. 'I and my people are wicked.'

With that last confession, Pharaoh betrayed his insincerity. True repentance deals with personal sin, not the sins of others. A self-righteous man, pretending to be humble, merges his guilt with the guilt of others. In doing this, Pharaoh was saying, 'I am a wicked man, but so is everyone else. Moses, you know we are all sinners'.

Then, the terrified king of Egypt begged Moses and Aaron to pray for him. 'Entreat the Lord, for it is enough.' I have suffered enough. The hail, thunder, and lightning has convinced me. I have now heard God's voice. If he will take away my punishment, 'I will let you go, and ye shall stay no longer; go the three days' journey into the wilderness'.

But Moses knew Pharaoh's hypocrisy. In verse 30 he said, 'I know that ye will not yet fear the LORD God'. 'And when Pharaoh saw that the rain and the hail and the thunders were ceased, he sinned yet more, and hardened his heart, he and his servants. And the heart of Pharaoh was hardened, neither would he let the children of Israel go; as the LORD had spoken by Moses' (vv. 34, 35).

Pharaoh confessed he had done wrong, but never confessed his sin. He never acknowledged the evil of his heart. He needed help; but he was not helpless. He still thought he was in control. He said, 'If the Lord will take away this judgment, I will let Israel go. If he refuses my demand, I will continue to refuse his.' Pharaoh sought mercy on the footing of works. He asked Moses (the law) to intercede for him, promising to do better. When he said, 'I have sinned this time', he was saying, 'I promise to do better, if the Lord will take away his wrath. I will let you go.' Once the thundering and lightning and hail stopped, his fear subsided; he hardened his heart the more.

Then, in chapter 10 God sent the plague of locusts. Armies of locusts marched in unbroken ranks through the land of Egypt at God's command, until they covered the whole country. The swarms were so great that they darkened the sky, devoured every herb of the land, the fruit of every tree, and every green thing that grew in Egypt. Pharaoh was more terrified than ever. He was sure he was about to die. So, he called for Moses and Aaron to pray for him again (Exodus 10:16, 17).

Pharaoh, terrified with the fear of imminent death, sent messengers in haste to fetch God's prophet and priest to him. This time, his confession was more thorough. He said, 'I have sinned against the LORD your God, and against you', but it was nothing but the ranting of a terrified man. 'Now therefore forgive, I pray thee, my sin, only this once'. Pharaoh was pretending he would never offend again, if the Lord would forgive him. He acknowledged God had sent the plague of locusts and God alone could remove it. 'Entreat the LORD your God, that he may take away from me this death only'. Here, again, Pharaoh betrayed his heart. He wanted only to escape the death he feared. The fear gone, his heart was hardened. 'But the LORD hardened Pharaoh's heart, so that he would not let the children of Israel go' (v. 20).

## Pharaoh's Knowledge

As we read these three passages and hear Pharaoh speak, it is obvious he was convinced of many things and was informed of more. He knew he had sinned. He was convinced the Lord our God, the triune Jehovah, is God alone. He had been informed by Moses that God has a chosen people for whom he had made a covenant, a people he would surely deliver, and that he would be worshipped and served by them through the blood sacrifice of a sacrificial lamb. And he knew that God had the power to save him or destroy him. But Pharaoh's knowledge was altogether carnal. He learned all those facts; but they were just facts. He knew he had sinned, but had no idea he was a sinner. He knew God is, and that God is the sovereign Lord of the universe. He had no trouble with divine sovereignty, as a matter of fact. But the Lord God had not conquered his heart. Instead, he hardened it. Pharaoh was terrified of God; but there was no fear of God before his eyes. He knew about God's covenant with his people, but knew nothing of covenant mercy, love, and grace. He knew about the lamb Moses spoke of, but did not know the Lamb. Pharaoh knew much; but he knew nothing in his heart. He knew nothing experimentally, knew nothing in his heart, except fear.

**Dying Convictions**
Pharaoh's acts of repentance were acts of repentance to be repented of, because the convictions from which they sprang were dying convictions. Once God took away the frogs, Pharaoh had no more need of God. Once the Lord removed the locusts, he was no longer terrified of judgment. Once God's thunder silenced and the hail ceased, Pharaoh's fears were silenced, and his need for God's mercy ceased.

There are multitudes just like Pharaoh in this world: often trembling but never turned, often convicted but never converted, often bent but never broken, often looking to God in fear but never looking to Christ in faith (Hosea 6:4, 5). Multitudes, upon hearing the gospel preached in the power of the Holy Spirit, experience deep religious convictions which soon die away, like the morning dew. Lot's wife (Genesis 19:15, 16), Israel at the Red Sea (Exodus 15:2, 22-24), the rich young ruler (Luke 18:18-23), Felix the Roman Governor (Acts 24:24, 25), and King Agrippa (Acts 26:28) all heard God speak and were moved toward repentance by the Word, just like Pharaoh. But, like Pharaoh, their convictions did not last long. Many others went further than these. Under deep conviction, Ananias and Sapphira, Simon Magus, Demas, and Diotrephes professed faith in Christ, united with his people, and served his cause for a while. But in time their convictions died.

Most people who sit under the sound of the gospel are, at one time or another, moved by it. They hear God's voice in the gospel. Yet, they harden their hearts. They push aside the claims of Christ in the gospel, like Felix, saying, 'At a more convenient season I will call for thee'. Like morning mist before the rising sun, their convictions fade away. Be warned. The road to hell is paved with good intentions. Multitudes in hell today once wept and prayed over their souls (Proverbs 29:1).

How many there are who once stood as pillars in the visible church of God whose convictions died away in time. They began well. But they are no longer among us. They did much, moved by legal conviction. They gave much, moved by legal principles. But, where are they now? What happened? The convictions they once felt strongly died away. Why do the convictions of many die? I have preached to many who wept, but repented not. I have preached to many who appeared to be truly penitent, who appeared to be people of strong, firm conviction, but whose convictions faded away. How does this happen? Why do the convictions of many die? Here are four answers to those questions:

1. They never knew their own guilt, depravity, sin, and helplessness before God. You may see the doctrine of total depravity very clearly, without having any personal knowledge of inward corruption.

2. They never saw the beauty, glory, and fulness of Christ. Many know the doctrine of Christ who never embrace Christ. Many see his doctrine who never see him and love his doctrine who never love him.

3. They never bowed to the rule and dominion of Christ as their Lord. Many want a Saviour to keep them out of hell who refuse to bow to Christ as Lord to rule over them. But Christ will not be your Saviour if he is not your Lord.

4. They still love the world. If you love the world, the love of God is not in you. Nothing is more deadly than the care and pleasures of the world and the deceitfulness of riches. Sooner or later, the love of the world will cause conviction to die. Materialism will destroy conviction.

Dying convictions are natural, legal convictions. Saving faith is the result of Holy Spirit conviction (John 16:8-11). But dying convictions are seldom corrected. God will not always speak to those who refuse to hear. He will not always call those who refuse to obey. There is such a thing as judicial reprobation. Pharaoh was reprobate. God hardened his heart. God fixed it so he could not repent. And God has not changed. 'He hath mercy on whom he will; and whom he will he hardeneth!'

God Almighty will fix it so that those who will not obey the gospel cannot obey. If you harden your heart, God will harden your heart (Proverbs 1:23-33; Luke 13:23-27). Be warned! Take heed! If you reject the gospel, you reject life. Convictions that are put off tend to make the heart harden. Just as iron is hardened by being melted and cooled again, so is the heart of man.

## Harden Not Your Heart

'Today if ye will hear his voice, harden not your hearts.' 'Incline your ear, and come unto me: hear, and your soul shall live; and I will make an everlasting covenant with you, even the sure mercies of David.' 'Ho, every one that thirsteth, come ye to the waters, and he that hath no money; come ye, buy, and eat; yea, come, buy wine and milk without money and without price.' 'Today if ye will hear his voice, harden not your hearts.'

Sinner, the day of darkness and judgment is coming. It is rapidly coming. In that day, your sin and guilt will be too heavy for you to bear! In that day, men will pray. A very strange prayer meeting will take place on the day of judgment.

'And I beheld when he had opened the sixth seal, and, lo, there was a great earthquake; and the sun became black as sackcloth of hair, and the moon became as blood; And the stars of heaven fell unto the earth, even as a fig tree casteth her untimely figs, when she is shaken of a mighty wind. And the heaven departed as a scroll when it is rolled together; and every mountain and island were moved out of their places. And the kings of the earth, and the great men, and the rich men, and the chief captains, and the mighty men, and every bondman, and every free man, hid themselves in the dens and in the rocks of the mountains; And said to the mountains and rocks, Fall on us, and hide us from the face of him that sitteth on the throne, and from the wrath of the Lamb: For the great day of his wrath is come; and who shall be able to stand?' (Revelation 6:12-17)

Flee away to the only Refuge there is for your guilty soul. Flee to Christ. Go not to Moses or Aaron. Go not to a preacher or a priest. Go straight to Christ, and straight to God by him. Go at once to the Saviour. Go, with all your sins, all your guilt, all your helplessness. Go now. He will receive you, and save you. He has said, 'Him that cometh unto me I will in no wise cast out!' May God grant you repentance not to be repented of, for Christ's sake!

# Chapter 52

## Living In Goshen
## Or Blessedness In The Midst Of Trouble

'Then the LORD said unto Moses, Go in unto Pharaoh, and tell him, Thus saith the LORD God of the Hebrews, Let my people go, that they may serve me ... And the heart of Pharaoh was hardened, neither would he let the children of Israel go; as the LORD had spoken by Moses.' (Exodus 9:1-35)

God's saints in this world are like the children of Israel living in Goshen. Goshen was in Egypt, the place of Israel's long sojourn, and the place of her terrible bondage and great trouble. Egypt was the land of Israel's enemies, persecutors, and tormentors. There, in Goshen, the chosen nation was preserved, provided for, and increased for four hundred years. There, in Goshen, the children of promise lived, worked, raised their families, educated their children, buried their dead, and died themselves. There, in Goshen, God's covenant people multiplied. And there, in Goshen, they lived in the midst of great trouble and sorrow. They got sick; but their sickness was not the sickness of the Egyptians. They had trouble; but theirs was not the trouble of the Egyptians. The land of Goshen, though in Egypt, was under the special care of God's watchful eye, because the children of Israel dwelled in Goshen. That tiny little spot of ground is mentioned by name only twice in the Book of Exodus (8:22; 9:26). In both places, the Lord God declares his special, distinct care for that spot of ground where his people dwelled.

'And I will sever in that day the land of Goshen, in which my people dwell, that no swarms of flies shall be there; to the end thou mayest know that I am the LORD in the midst of the earth' (Exodus 8:22). 'Only in the land of Goshen, where the children of Israel were, was there no hail' (Exodus 9:26).

In this chapter Moses continues to give his inspired and instructive record of the plagues God brought upon Pharaoh and the Egyptians for the twofold purpose of punishing them for their sins and the deliverance and salvation of Israel. The water was turned to blood; but Pharaoh refused to hearken to God's word. The land was filled with frogs; and Pharaoh still refused to listen. Lice filled the land of Egypt; and, still, Pharaoh hardened his heart. Swarms of files covered all the land of the Egyptians; yet the king of Egypt was obstinate in his rebellion. In chapter 9, three more plagues are brought upon Egypt: a murrain (deadly disease) broke out among their cattle; boils and blains (hemorrhoids) broke out both upon man and beast, and a terrible, terrifying storm of thunder, lightning, and rain destroyed all that was in the field. Again, Pharaoh pretended to repent; but as soon as the plagues were removed, he was hardened the more, and refused to let Israel go.

**Pharaoh Warned**
'Then the LORD said unto Moses, Go in unto Pharaoh, and tell him, Thus saith the LORD God of the Hebrews, Let my people go, that they may serve me' (v. 1). God always warns before he strikes. Here he gave Pharaoh the very same message he had given him before. Five times in the Book of Leviticus (26:14, 18, 21, 23, 27), God warns he will punish all who disregard his Word. How often he has warned you, who believe not, of impending judgment! He has done so by his Word, by your screaming conscience, and by his providence. May he give you grace to hear his voice and flee to Christ for refuge!

'Ho, every one that thirsteth, come ye to the waters, and he that hath no money; come ye, buy, and eat; yea, come, buy wine and milk without money and without price ... Seek ye the LORD while he may be found, call ye upon him while he is near: Let the wicked forsake his way, and the unrighteous man his thoughts: and let him return unto the LORD, and he will have mercy upon him; and to our God, for he will abundantly pardon' (Isaiah 55:1, 6, 7).

'For if thou refuse to let them go, and wilt hold them still ... ' (v. 2). What God declared to Pharaoh for the temporal deliverance of Israel, he declares to all the enemies of his people. His people will be eternally delivered. When the year of the Lord's redeemed is come, when the appointed time of love has arrived for the salvation of God's elect, he will break the power of their enemies (Isaiah 43:3, 4; 60:12; 63:4, 5). If, like Pharaoh, you are left to your will, it will be your hell!

'Behold, the hand of the LORD is upon thy cattle which is in the field, upon the horses, upon the asses, upon the camels, upon the oxen, and upon the sheep: there shall be a very grievous murrain' (v. 3). 'Murrain' is a disease in livestock, something like foot-and-mouth disease, or anthrax, or even mad-cow disease. How far reaching the consequences of sin are, no mortal can imagine. Man sins and creation groans, groans for the complete salvation of God's elect in the resurrection (Romans 8:22, 23).

### Goshen Severed

'And the LORD shall sever between the cattle of Israel and the cattle of Egypt: and there shall nothing die of all that is the children's of Israel' (v. 4). I ask, with Paul, 'Doth God take care for oxen? Or saith he it altogether for our sakes? For our sakes, no doubt, this is written' (1 Corinthians 9:9, 10). Here, again, we are graciously reminded by the Spirit of God that it is God himself who separates the precious from the vile, by his sovereign, free, discriminating grace (Malachi 3:11, 18).

### Set Time

'And the LORD appointed a set time, saying, Tomorrow the LORD shall do this thing in the land' (v. 5). 'There is a time to every purpose under the heaven' (Ecclesiastes 3:1). All comes to pass according to the time appointed by God. 'Boast not thyself of tomorrow; for thou knowest not what a day may bring forth' (Proverbs 27:1).

'And the LORD did that thing on the morrow, and all the cattle of Egypt died: but of the cattle of the children of Israel died not one' (v. 6). Again, we are reminded of God's discriminating grace. This is something the Lord would have us keep before our minds and cherish in our hearts continually (1 Corinthians 4:7). Though the cattle of Israel were in the same climate, breathed the same air, ate of the same grass, and drank of the same water, yet the murrain upon the cattle of Egypt was not found on one calf in Goshen. Thank God for his special care for our poor souls (Psalm 36:6; Luke 12:6, 7).

## Pharaoh Hardened

'And Pharaoh sent, and, behold, there was not one of the cattle of the Israelites dead. And the heart of Pharaoh was hardened, and he did not let the people go' (v. 7). 'Who hath hardened himself against him, and hath prospered?' (Job 9:4). Yet, the heart of man is so obstinate and hard that it cannot be broken, except by grace (Zechariah 7:11, 12).

## Boils and Blains

'And the LORD said unto Moses and unto Aaron, Take to you handfuls of ashes of the furnace, and let Moses sprinkle it toward the heaven in the sight of Pharaoh. And it shall become small dust in all the land of Egypt, and shall be a boil breaking forth with blains upon man, and upon beast, throughout all the land of Egypt. And they took ashes of the furnace, and stood before Pharaoh; and Moses sprinkled it up toward heaven; and it became a boil breaking forth with blains upon man, and upon beast. And the magicians could not stand before Moses because of the boils; for the boil was upon the magicians, and upon all the Egyptians' (Exodus 9:8-11).

These boils and blains or haemorrhoids were the 'blotch' of Egypt (Deuteronomy 28:27). They specifically refer us to the curse of God that falls upon men because of false religion (Revelation 16:2). That is probably the reason we are told that Pharaoh's magicians suffered it with the rest of Egypt. Forced to admit these plagues were 'the finger of God' (8:19), they still opposed God's messenger and did their utmost to harden Pharaoh's heart against him (Acts 13:8-11; 2 Timothy 3:8, 9).

## Marked for Ruin

'And the LORD hardened the heart of Pharaoh, and he hearkened not unto them; as the LORD had spoken unto Moses' (v. 12). Pharaoh had hardened his heart; and now the Lord hardened Pharaoh's heart. God gave him up to a reprobate mind. He was marked for ruin. When God gives a sinner up, hell is his everlasting portion. What solemn words these are 'And the LORD hardened the heart of Pharaoh'. More solemn words were never written. They describe the most awful state of a soul this side hell (Hosea 4:17; Romans 1:28; 2 Thessalonians 2:11, 12).

'And the LORD said unto Moses, Rise up early in the morning, and stand before Pharaoh, and say unto him, Thus saith the LORD God of the Hebrews, Let my people go, that they may serve me' (v. 13). Six times before, the Lord had spoken, only to have his word despised. Yet, he speaks again. 'For I will at this time send all my plagues upon thine heart, and upon thy servants, and upon thy people; that thou mayest know that there is none like me in all the earth' (v. 14). Pharaoh and the Egyptians were marked for ruin. They could not be saved from God's wrath. The Lord God warns, and warns, and warns, 'Therefore also will I make thee sick in smiting thee, in making thee desolate because of thy sins' (Micah 6:13). Sinners are often, like Pharaoh, terrified by his warnings and by his providential judgments; but none will repent except God himself work repentance in us (Deuteronomy 28:66, 67).

The Holy Spirit tells us these acts of judgment were done according to God's sovereign, eternal purpose (Exodus 9:15, 16; Romans 9:17).

'For now I will stretch out my hand, that I may smite thee and thy people with pestilence; and thou shalt be cut off from the earth. And in very deed for this cause have I raised thee up, for to show in thee my power; and that my name may be declared throughout all the earth.'

## Hail Storm

'As yet exaltest thou thyself against my people, that thou wilt not let them go? Behold, to morrow about this time I will cause it to rain a very grievous hail, such as hath not been in Egypt since the foundation thereof even until now. Send therefore now, and gather thy cattle, and all that thou hast in the field; for upon every man and beast which shall be found in the field, and shall not be brought home, the hail shall come down upon them, and they shall die. He that feared the word of the LORD among the servants of Pharaoh made his servants and his cattle flee into the houses: And he that regarded not the word of the LORD left his servants and his cattle in the field' (Exodus 9:17-21).

'He suffered no man to do them wrong: yea, he reproved kings for their sakes; Saying, Touch not mine anointed, and do my prophets no harm' (Psalm 105:14, 15). Some of the livestock of Egypt would be needed for the chariots and horsemen to carry Pharaoh and his armies to destruction in the Red Sea, as they pursued Israel. Therefore, the Lord inclined some of the Egyptians to believe his servant; and they took their cattle to shelter.

'And the LORD said unto Moses, Stretch forth thine hand toward heaven, that there may be hail in all the land of Egypt, upon man, and upon beast, and upon every herb of the field, throughout the land of

Egypt. And Moses stretched forth his rod toward heaven: and the LORD sent thunder and hail, and the fire ran along upon the ground; and the LORD rained hail upon the land of Egypt' (Exodus 9:22, 23). 'Fire, and hail; snow, and vapours; stormy wind fulfilling his word' (Psalm 148:8). 'He destroyed their vines with hail, and their sycamore trees with frost. He gave up their cattle also to the hail, and their flocks to hot thunderbolts' (Psalm 78:47, 48). 'At the brightness that was before him his thick clouds passed, hail stones and coals of fire. The LORD also thundered in the heavens, and the Highest gave his voice; hail stones and coals of fire' (Psalm 18:12, 13).

'So there was hail, and fire mingled with the hail, very grievous, such as there was none like it in all the land of Egypt since it became a nation. And the hail smote throughout all the land of Egypt all that was in the field, both man and beast; and the hail smote every herb of the field, and brake every tree of the field. Only in the land of Goshen, where the children of Israel were, was there no hail' (Exodus 9:24-26).

'And Pharaoh sent, and called for Moses and Aaron, and said unto them, I have sinned this time: the LORD is righteous, and I and my people are wicked. Entreat the LORD (for it is enough) that there be no more mighty thunderings and hail; and I will let you go, and ye shall stay no longer' (Exodus 9:27, 28).

You can mark it down. This will be the language of the ungodly in the final day of retribution. The damned will be forced from their own mouths to confess God's righteousness in their condemnation.

'And Moses said unto him, As soon as I am gone out of the city, I will spread abroad my hands unto the LORD; and the thunder shall cease, neither shall there be any more hail; that thou mayest know how that the earth is the Lord's. But as for thee and thy servants, I know that ye will not yet fear the LORD God. And the flax and the barley was smitten: for the barley was in the ear, and the flax was bolled. But the wheat and the rie were not smitten: for they were not grown up. And Moses went out of the city from Pharaoh, and spread abroad his hands unto the LORD: and the thunders and hail ceased, and the rain was not poured upon the earth. And when Pharaoh saw that the rain and the hail and the thunders were ceased, he sinned yet more, and hardened his heart, he and his servants. And the heart of Pharaoh was hardened, neither would he let the children of Israel go; as the LORD had spoken by Moses' (Exodus 9:29-35).

**Goshen Favoured**

Israel, though living in the midst of a crooked and perverse people, though living among a wicked people under the judgments of God, was favoured. Living in Goshen, they found nothing but blessedness in the midst of trouble. May it be your happiness and mine, as we read the things recorded in this chapter, to follow the design of God the Holy Ghost in recording them. Oh, may he make us 'wise unto salvation through the faith which is in Christ Jesus', effectually applying this portion of his Word to our hearts. Though God's judgments upon the earth in this day are great, his mercies to his chosen are greater still. O my soul, never forget this! He that severed the cattle of Israel from the cattle of Egypt still separates the precious from the vile. 'The Lord knoweth how to deliver the godly out of temptation!' The Lord Jesus Christ, our great Saviour, is still the 'hiding place from the storm, and the covert from the tempest'. And when the Lord hides his saints, he shows himself. Though he hides his church in Goshen, he promises, 'I the Lord do keep it, I will water it every moment lest any hurt it, I will keep it night and day' (Isaiah 27:3).

There were storms surrounding Goshen; but Israel was not harmed by them. The Lord turned the waters of the Egyptians into blood; but the Lord graciously turns cursed water into wine for his chosen to show forth his glory in our crucified Saviour (Exodus 7:19-21; John 2:7-11; 2 Corinthians 5:21). When the Lord sent the swarms of flies, filling the houses of Egypt, in the land of Goshen, there were none (Exodus 8:21, 22). In the murrain God destroyed the cattle of the Egyptians; but 'of the cattle of the children of Israel died not one' (Exodus 9:6). In the darkness that covered the whole land of Egypt the Israelites had perfect day (Exodus 10:21-23). In the destruction of the firstborn, as the blood sprinkled on the door posts and lintels of Israel's houses preserved the whole alive, we read concerning Egypt, 'that there was not an house where there was not one dead' (Exodus 12:30.)

These things mark and identify for us all the history of divine providence, from the beginning to the end of time. Every plague on Egypt taught Israel to see spiritual blessings flowing to them. May God teach us by his Spirit to judge him and his works in this same way.

Solomon tells us all things happen alike to all men, both the righteous and the wicked (Ecclesiastes 9:2). That is true, with regard to the outward circumstances and experiences of our lives. But they do not happen for the same reason, or produce the same effects. Goshen was spared the plagues of Egypt, and Israel was made better by them because they were God's chosen people, they were God's covenant people, they were God's redeemed people and they were God's blessed people; and the blessing of God cannot be reversed.

They were a people kept safe and secure by the promise of God their Saviour (Exodus 15:26).

Yes, God's elect suffer all the evils that come upon men as the result of sin; but we suffer them not as acts of divine judgment or for punishment. We suffer them for the everlasting benefit of our souls. And we suffer all these things in the immediate presence of our great God, Redeemer, and Saviour. May God give us grace to quit living our lives in survivalist mode, and teach us to live as men and women to whom God has said,

'But now thus saith the LORD that created thee, O Jacob, and he that formed thee, O Israel, Fear not: for I have redeemed thee, I have called thee by thy name; thou art mine. When thou passest through the waters, I will be with thee; and through the rivers, they shall not overflow thee: when thou walkest through the fire, thou shalt not be burned; neither shall the flame kindle upon thee. For I am the LORD thy God, the Holy One of Israel, thy Saviour: I gave Egypt for thy ransom, Ethiopia and Seba for thee. Since thou wast precious in my sight, thou hast been honourable, and I have loved thee: therefore will I give men for thee, and people for thy life' (Isaiah 43:1-4).

'Rejoice in the Lord alway: and again I say, Rejoice. Let your moderation be known unto all men. The Lord is at hand. Be careful for nothing; but in everything by prayer and supplication with thanksgiving let your requests be made known unto God. And the peace of God, which passeth all understanding, shall keep your hearts and minds through Christ Jesus' (Philippians 4:4-7).

# Chapter 53

## Not A Hoof Left Behind

'And the LORD said unto Moses, Go in unto Pharaoh: for I have hardened his heart, and the heart of his servants, that I might shew these my signs before him: And that thou mayest tell in the ears of thy son, and of thy son's son, what things I have wrought in Egypt, and my signs which I have done among them; that ye may know how that I am the LORD ... There shall not an hoof be left behind ... But the LORD hardened Pharaoh's heart, and he would not let them go. And Pharaoh said unto him, Get thee from me, take heed to thyself, see my face no more; for in that day thou seest my face thou shalt die. And Moses said, Thou hast spoken well, I will see thy face again no more.'
(Exodus 10:1-29)

No doctrine of Holy Scripture is more clearly stated than the blessed, soul cheering, gospel doctrine, commonly called limited atonement. Concerning this foundation truth of Holy Scripture, there can be no compromise. No preacher, pastor, missionary, or local church who does not whole-heartedly embrace and faithfully preach limited atonement should be embraced by us as our brethren in Christ. We must align ourselves with no religious organization or ministry that is not of like mind in this matter. Deny limited atonement and you deny the gospel.

All for whom Christ shed his precious blood at Calvary shall be saved by his almighty grace, or none shall be saved by him. Either he is an almighty, omnipotent, effectual Saviour, or he is no Saviour at all.

There is no in-between ground. God the Holy Ghost gives us a clear picture of the glorious efficacy of Christ's salvation in Exodus 10.

The Lord our God said to Pharaoh, 'In very deed for this cause have I raised thee up, for to show in thee my power; and that my name may be declared throughout all the earth' (Exodus 9:16). God was determined, in mercy and grace, to deliver his people Israel from the bondage of Egypt and from the tyranny of Pharaoh. Both the time of their bondage and the time of their deliverance were appointed by God in the covenant he made with Abraham (Genesis 15:13, 14). And, as you well know, the whole affair typically represents the redemption, salvation, and complete deliverance of God's elect from sin and Satan by the Lord Jesus Christ.

## By Divine Purpose

Though God ordained Israel's bondage in Egypt, he did not force Israel to go down into Egypt. Jacob sent his sons down into Egypt willingly, freely, voluntarily, without any constraint but this: 'Jacob saw that there was corn in Egypt' (Genesis 42:1). Even so, God ordained the fall of our father Adam and the fall of the race in him; but God did not force Adam to sin. Adam, with full awareness of what he was doing (1 Timothy 2:14), willingly, freely, voluntarily took the fruit of the tree of the knowledge of good and evil, because his wife gave it to him. Eve was deceived, but not Adam. He wilfully chose rebellion against God over strife with his wife. By his wilful act of rebellion against God, our race was plunged into the bondage of sin, Satan, and death (Genesis 3:1-24).

Long before Israel went into Egypt, God provided a Saviour, by whom he would both preserve and deliver his chosen people. When Joseph was a young man, his brothers hated him. In their jealousy, they would have killed him; but God prevented it. Instead, they sold him to a caravan of Ishmaelites going down to Egypt, for twenty pieces of silver (Genesis 37:23-28). Joseph himself tells us that his being sold into the hands of the Egyptians was the work of God. He said to his brothers, 'I am in the place of God. As for you, ye thought evil against me: but God meant it unto good, to bring to pass, as it is this day, to save much people alive' (Genesis 50:19, 20).

Joseph is a beautiful type of our Saviour, the Lord Jesus Christ, who was sold into the hands of the Jewish priests by his own familiar friend for thirty-pieces of silver. And just as Joseph was provided as a Saviour for Israel long before Israel came into bondage, the Lord Jesus Christ was provided by the triune Jehovah as the Saviour of his people long before the fall of our father Adam. Before there was a sinner, there was a Saviour. Before we fell in Adam, we stood in Christ. Before we transgressed, the sacrificial Lamb was provided. Christ is 'the Lamb slain from the foundation of the world' (Revelation 13:8). Before we came under the curse of the law, a ransom was found. Even before the world was made, the Lord God was gracious to his elect, and said, 'Deliver him from going down to the pit: I have found a ransom' (Job 33:24). Long before we fell in bondage in Adam, our complete deliverance was secured and accomplished by Christ in the covenant of grace (Ephesians 1:3-6; 2 Timothy 1:9).

Then, at the time appointed, God graciously brought all the children of Israel out of Egypt (Exodus 12:40, 41). Not one day early, not one day late, but exactly on the day appointed of God, Israel was delivered from their bondage.[2] They were redeemed by the blood of the paschal lamb and delivered by the power of God's almighty arm. All who were chosen of God had a lamb. All who had a lamb were redeemed from judgment. And all who were redeemed by blood were delivered across the Red Sea by the power of God. And it was all God's work. Well did Moses say, 'Stand still, and see the salvation of the LORD!'

The picture is clear. Is it not? In precisely the same manner, all of God's elect are delivered at the appointed time of mercy from the bondage of sin and the curse of the law. At God's appointed time, Christ died in the place of his people, to deliver us from the curse of the law (Romans 5:6; Galatians 4:4, 5; Acts 2:23). And, at the time of mercy, the Spirit of God delivered us from the bondage of sin by his almighty, irresistible grace (Galatians 4:6; Ezekiel 16:6-8). All who were chosen of God in eternity were redeemed by Christ at Calvary. All who were redeemed by Christ are called by the Spirit. And all who are called by the Spirit of God are completely delivered from the bondage of sin and the curse and condemnation of the law (Galatians 3:13, 14; Romans 8:29, 30).

God appointed the time of Israel's bondage. God provided for Israel's deliverance. And God accomplished Israel's salvation. God's

---

[2] Israel dwelt in Egypt 430 years, but the time of their affliction was 400 years.

purpose in all of this was the glory of his own great name, so all men might know that he alone is God, both sovereign and gracious (Romans 9:15-18; Psalm 106:8). Had there been no bondage, there would have been no deliverance. Had there been no wicked Pharaoh on the throne, there would have been no mighty conquest at the Red Sea. Had there been no pursuing army and no Red Sea, there would have been no song of redemption. But God ordained all that he might be glorified. The same is true with us.

God wisely and sovereignly ordained the fall of all men in Adam and the redemption of his elect in Christ, 'to the praise of the glory of his grace' (Ephesians 1:6). As God raised up Pharaoh and hardened his heart, so that he might drown his wicked carcass in the sea for the glory of his own great name, even so, he ordained the fall of Lucifer and made him the prince of the power of the air, that he might glorify himself by the overthrow of Satan and the destruction of his kingdom in the sea of his wrath. In the end, like the overthrow of Pharaoh and his armies, the final overthrow of Satan and his armies shall show forth the praise of our God. Like Pharaoh, the defeated fiend of hell will be an everlasting monument to the greatness and power of our God (Revelation 15:2-4). Then, the words of David will be fulfilled, 'All thy works shall praise thee, O Lord; and thy saints shall bless thee' (Psalm 145:10).

## Context

Look at this in the context of this tenth chapter. Pharaoh tried repeatedly to conciliate God, and tried repeatedly to get Moses to compromise. At last, he said to Moses, 'Go ye, serve the Lord; only let your flocks and your herds be stayed: let your little ones also go with you'. In other words, he said, 'All right, I give in. You may go out of the land. You can even take your wives and children. You've got what you wanted. I only require that you leave your sheep and cattle with me.' But he soon found out that man does not bargain with God, and God's prophets will not be induced to compromise. Hear Moses' response to Pharaoh in verse 26, 'Our cattle also shall go with us; there shall not an hoof be left behind; for thereof must we take to serve the Lord our God'.

Pharaoh's heart has not been changed; and Moses commission has not been changed. Sooner or later, something must give; but it will not be God or his servant. In this chapter Moses is sent by the Lord God to inflict the eighth and ninth plagues upon Egypt. First, locusts are sent upon the land until it is covered with them, and the vegetation is completely devoured; then, three days of felt darkness.

We will miss the beauty, the purpose, and the message of this passage altogether if we fail to understand it spiritually as a type and allegory of our deliverance from sin and its bondage by the glorious conquests of our Lord Jesus Christ. What great comfort there is here for our souls (Psalm 107:7; Job 23:10). We who have experienced God's deliverance are to tell in the ears of our children and our children's children, generation after generation (vv. 1, 2).

'And the LORD said unto Moses, Go in unto Pharaoh: for I have hardened his heart, and the heart of his servants, that I might show these my signs before him: And that thou mayest tell in the ears of thy son, and of thy son's son, what things I have wrought in Egypt, and my signs which I have done among them; that ye may know how that I am the LORD.'

When Moses told Pharaoh what God was about to do, Pharaoh's servants said, 'Let Israel go. Egypt is destroyed.' But Moses refused to compromise with the king of Egypt; and Pharaoh drove Moses and Aaron from his presence in anger. So God brought the locusts and everything in Egypt was devoured by them (vv. 3-20). Pharaoh was hardened the more, and God sent the darkness (vv. 21-23). How horrible it must have been! Yet, that great darkness was nothing compared to the darkness awaiting the damned in hell!

Again, we are reminded of God's distinguishing grace upon his chosen. The darkness upon Egypt was so great it was felt, so thick that one man could not even see another for three days. 'But all the children of Israel had light in their dwellings' (v. 23, Psalm 97:11). At last, Moses said to Pharaoh, 'Our cattle also shall go with us; there shall not an hoof be left behind; for thereof must we take to serve the Lord our God' (v. 26). The Lord our God demands complete surrender and he accomplishes complete deliverance.

## Total Surrender

The Lord Jesus Christ demands total surrender. I know in this day of easy-believism, decisional regeneration, kneel-at-the-altar salvation, this is strange doctrine; strange to those who are yet strangers to God. But faith in Christ is nothing less than the willing, voluntary surrender and commitment of your heart to Christ as your Lord. Christ will have the whole man, or none of the man. All or none! There is no middle ground. Christ will reign without a rival in our hearts, or he will not dwell in our hearts. Without the complete reconciliation of the heart, there is no salvation. Spurgeon said, 'Christ will not be part-proprietor of any man. He will not have one part of the man, and leave the other part to be devoted to Satan.' Moses said to Pharaoh, 'There shall not an hoof be left behind.'

These flocks and herds represented everything the Israelites had. All their property, all their possessions, all their livelihood must be brought out of Egypt and consecrated to the service of God. Our Lord Jesus puts it this way, 'Whosoever will save his life shall lose it; but whosoever shall lose his life for my sake and the gospel's, the same shall save it' (Mark 8:35). If you would have Christ, the Treasure of heaven, you must sell all that you have to get him. If you would have Christ, the Pearl of great price, you must sell all that you have to buy that Pearl (Matthew 13:45, 46).

Saving faith is something more than saying a little prayer, believing a few facts, embracing a religious creed, and changing your habits of life. Faith is trusting Christ alone for acceptance with God. His righteousness is all my righteousness. His blood is all my pardon. His grace is all my keeping. I have no hope of anything before God except the Lord Jesus Christ (1 Corinthians 1:30). Faith surrenders to Christ's righteousness, justice, and sovereignty as Lord (Matthew 8:1, 2; 15:21-28). And saving faith consecrates everything to Christ. Faith gives up all rights to everything (Luke 14:25-33). Either you and I will be servants under the dominion of King Jesus, voluntarily giving up all to his claims, or we will go to hell. 'There shall not a hoof be left behind!'

All true believers willingly surrender everything to Christ in the intent and purpose of their hearts. I do not for a moment suggest that it is possible for us to be perfectly consecrated to God while we live in this world. I know, by painful, long, and bitter experience it is not. Sin is mixed with all we do. Sin mars our best actions and best ambitions. Sin besets us constantly. But with the will and determination of the heart, every believer is entirely devoted to Christ. Our baptism is a public confession of our faith in and allegiance to Christ as Lord (Romans 6:4-6).

From the crown of my head to the soul of my foot, I belong to Christ, or I do not belong to him at all. All my property, all my time, all my talents, all my family, all that I am, all that I possess, I willingly lay at his feet, or else, I do not know him.

And what is true in our hearts shall soon be true in the reality of heavenly glory. Child of God, in a little while, after a few more struggles against the flesh, after a few more conflicts with sin, after a few more warrings with old Adam, you will put your foot upon the neck of the enemy. Sin and self shall both be slain and you shall reign triumphantly with Christ forever. One day soon, we shall be made altogether perfect (1 John 3:2). As we have born the image of the earthly, we shall bear the image of the heavenly. Our God will see to it (Jude 24, 25). Once we have dropped this robe of flesh, our spirits will be among 'the spirits of just men made perfect' (Hebrews 12:23). And in the resurrection these bodies of ours shall also be glorified (Romans 8:18-23). 'There shall not an hoof be left behind!' 'And the God of peace shall bruise Satan under your feet shortly' (Romans 16:20).

## Total Deliverance

Our great, all-glorious Saviour, the Lord Jesus Christ accomplishes total deliverance. Moses typically represents Christ. Israel represents God's elect. Egypt represents the world. And Pharaoh represents the devil. Christ Jesus says, with regard to the deliverance of his people out of this sin cursed world and out from under the power of Satan, 'There shall not an hoof be left behind!' What does that mean? Two things:

First, our Lord Jesus Christ will save all his people. There is a people in this world for whom Jesus Christ is Surety, Substitute, and Representative. Christ is not the Mediator, Redeemer, and Advocate of all men, but of some men. He did not come to save all men from their sins. But he shall save his people from their sins (Matthew 1:21). All of those given to Christ in the covenant of grace shall be saved at last. All for whom the Saviour died, all who were redeemed by his blood at Calvary will be with him in heaven (John 6:37-40, 44, 45; 10:16). The notion of universal redemption is as blasphemous as it is heretical. Our Lord Jesus Christ made infinite satisfaction to God's justice for us. His intention in dying was the eternal salvation of God's elect; his intention can never be frustrated. His intention and his accomplishments are the same (Isaiah 53:8-12). All for whom he died shall be saved.

The Lord Jesus Christ died for a particular people. And the death of Christ effectually accomplished the eternal redemption of those people

(Hebrews 9:12). Three hundred years ago, John Owen presented three statements in defence of the doctrine of Particular Redemption, which no reasonable man can deny. Owen wrote …

'Either Christ atoned for all the sins of all men, which means that all men will be saved, for if all sin has been atoned, there is no grounds for punishment, and universalism is true, which is contrary to Scripture.'

'Or Christ atoned for some of the sins of all men, which means that there are some sins for which we must make atonement ourselves. If that is received as truth, then we must conclude that salvation is by works and not by grace alone. Such doctrine we know is false.'

'Or else, Christ made atonement for all of the sins of some men, which is the doctrine of Holy Scripture.'

All of those who were given to Christ in eternal election and redeemed by Christ's effectual atonement shall be saved by Christ at last. Not one of Christ's redeemed ones can be lost. 'There shall not an hoof be left behind.' The Good Shepherd will seek his sheep 'until he find it'. When he has found it, he will lay it upon his back, holding it in the strong hands of his omnipotent grace, and carry it all the way home. To deny the eternal salvation of all for whom Christ died is to deny the doctrine of Christ altogether.

Universal atonement is a denial of the gospel, because it essentially denies the divine character of Christ. Let me show you how. If any of those for whom Christ died at Calvary perish in hell under the wrath of God, then his grace would be frustrated, his will and purpose would be nullified, his love would not be eternal, his power would be defeated, his justice would be perverted, and his cross would be discovered a miscarriage, his travail meaningless, and his blood would be shed in vain! He could never see of the travail of his soul and be satisfied. He would necessarily undergo some change, which God cannot do. If Christ is not immutable in all things, he is not God (Malachi 3:6). He would suffer shame and failure forever, having failed to finish what he came to do. He would have to give up his claim to his throne. If one for whom he died, if one for whose salvation he reigns were to perish, then the King of Glory would be forced to abdicate his throne in shame!

That man who says he believes in Christ and yet proclaims that some for whom Christ made atonement shall perish at last, blasphemes God, mocks the souls of men, and treads the blood of Christ under the foot of man's free-will! With every fibre of my being, I stand in stern protest against the heresy of universal atonement. I say with Moses, concerning all the hosts of God's elect, 'There shall not one hoof be left behind!'

## Blessed Bondage

Not only is it true that Christ will save all God's elect, he will also win back for us all that we lost in our Father Adam. When Israel came out of Egypt, they were far better off than they were when they went down into that dark land. I do not hesitate to declare that we shall gain far, far more in Christ than we lost in Adam. As Israel was better off for having been in bondage, God's elect shall be better off for having fallen in Adam.

In Adam we lost fellowship with God. In Christ we gain union with God. In Adam we lost innocence. In Christ we gain holiness. In Adam we lost acceptance. In Christ we gain adoption. In Adam we lost peace. In Christ we gain pardon. In Adam we lost the right to natural life. In Christ we gain the right to eternal life. In Adam we lost goodness. In Christ we gain grace. In Adam we lost the crown of creation. In Christ we gain the crown of glory. In Adam we lost daily communion with God. In Christ we gain eternal communion with God. In Adam we lost the Garden of Eden. In Christ we gain heaven.

Well may we look upon the ruins of Adam's fallen race, and weep. 'How art thou fallen, O mighty man!' But, child of God, rejoice. The Son of God looks upon us in our barren, fallen, depraved, deprived condition, and says, with regard to all we lost in the fall, 'There shall not an hoof be left behind'.

Abandon yourself now to Christ and you will never be abandoned by Christ. If you lay yourself down at his feet, he will take you into his arms. I call on you now to surrender to Christ. Surrender or destruction, which will it be? Not a hoof left behind. Child of God, daily consecrate yourself to Christ (Romans 12:1, 2; 1 Corinthians 6:19, 20). Not a hoof left behind! Let us labour on in the cause of Christ, with the sweet assurance of success. 'There shall not a hoof be left behind!'

# Chapter 54

## Three Felt Things

'And the LORD said unto Moses, Stretch out thine hand toward heaven, that there may be darkness over the land of Egypt, even darkness which may be felt. And Moses stretched forth his hand toward heaven; and there was a thick darkness in all the land of Egypt three days: They saw not one another, neither rose any from his place for three days: but all the children of Israel had light in their dwellings.' (Exodus 10:21-23)

The basis of our faith is the Word of God, and the Word of God alone. I fully agree with Martin Luther who wrote:

> Feelings come and feelings go,
> And feelings are deceiving.
> My warrant is the Word of God;
> Naught else is worth believing!

With David, I say, 'My soul fainteth for thy salvation: but I hope in thy word'. 'Thou art my hiding place and my shield: I hope in thy word'. 'Remember the word unto thy servant, upon which thou hast caused me to hope'. 'I wait for the LORD, my soul doth wait, and in his word do I hope' (Psalm 119:81; and also 49, 114). Our feelings are no basis for hope. Our hope is in that which God has caused to be written in Holy Scripture. If I have 'a good hope through grace', I ought to be able to turn to some text, or fact, or doctrine of God's Word as the source and basis of it. Our confidence must arise from something God has said in his Word, that we have received and believed with our hearts. 'The heart is deceitful above all things' (Jeremiah 17:9). 'He that trusteth in his own heart is a fool' (Proverbs 28:26). Good feelings are deceiving, unless we can point to 'thus saith the Lord' as the basis of our hope. Our hope is found in, arises from, and is based upon the Book of God. 'For whatsoever things were written aforetime were written for our learning, that we through patience and comfort of the scriptures might have hope' (Romans 15:4). The Book of God was written specifically to give believing sinners an assured hope of grace, salvation, and eternal life in Christ (1 John 5:1-3).

The basis of hope is the Word of God. And that which is revealed in the Word of God, which gives us hope, is the Person and work of the Lord Jesus Christ, our Substitute (Romans 8:34, 35; 2 Corinthians 5:17-21). Christ is the Foundation upon which we are built. 'Jesus Christ, which is our Hope' (1 Timothy 1:1). We 'hope in our Lord Jesus Christ' (1 Thessalonians 1:3). 'The LORD is my portion, saith my soul; therefore will I hope in him' (Lamentations 3:24). Our hope is in Christ, our Covenant Surety, our blessed, sin atoning Redeemer, our Advocate and High Priest in heaven, our Righteousness. 'I know whom I have believed, and am persuaded that he is able to keep that which I have committed unto him against that day' (2 Timothy 1:12).

The basis of our hope is the Word of God. That which is revealed in this Book that gives us hope is the Person and Work of the Lord Jesus Christ. And I want you to see that the good hope of grace and salvation God gives to his elect is something that is felt in us, felt inwardly in our hearts. The Apostle Paul speaks of God's saints as people 'rejoicing in hope' (Romans 12:12). We read in Romans 5:5, 'Hope maketh not ashamed, because the love of God is shed abroad in our hearts by the Holy Ghost which is given unto us'.

I would not give a nickel for any religion that is nothing but feeling. Emotionalism and religious excitement is not grace. But I would not give a cent for religion without feeling. Religion that has no feeling, that is all intellect, is always cold and dead. The hope that has been begotten in us is called 'a lively hope'. And I say with Peter, 'Blessed be the God and Father of our Lord Jesus Christ, which according to his abundant mercy hath begotten us again unto a lively hope by the resurrection of Jesus Christ from the dead' (1 Peter 1:3). When Lazarus was raised from the dead, he felt it! A prisoner released from prison, delivered from the hole of the pit in which no water could be found, feels it. You may not feel a pardon; but if ever you experience forgiveness, you will feel forgiveness!

Christianity is a matter of the heart. A man believes with his heart. He repents in his heart. Prayer is found in and comes from the heart. The things that are found in the heart are felt things. It is 'Christ in you' whom the Spirit of God calls, 'the Hope of Glory' (Colossians 1:27). If Christ is in you, he will stick out. If he sticks out, you will feel it.

There are three things specifically spoken of in Holy Scripture as things people felt. All three are things experienced and felt. They are all physical things; but they are physical things that vividly portray spiritual things. The first is found here in Exodus 10:21-23.

## Felt Darkness

When the Lord God brought his ninth plague upon the land of Egypt, by which he destroyed the land, that is to say by which he destroyed the strength and confidence of the Egyptians, it was a plague 'of thick darkness ... even darkness which may be felt'. And when God the Holy Spirit comes in the mighty operations of his grace to save a sinner, his first task is to destroy all creature strength in the sinner. He does so by bringing into the soul of the chosen sinner the thick darkness of guilt. When he comes to convince a sinner of his sin, he brings into the land of man's soul 'thick darkness ... even darkness which may be felt'. Darkness is often used in Scripture in this symbolic way (Isaiah 9:2; 29:18; 42:5-7; 50:10; Matthew 4:16; 2 Corinthians 4:6; Ephesians 5:8; Colossians 1:12-14).

This conviction of sin is something felt in the soul. Jeremiah wrote, 'I am the man that hath seen affliction by the rod of his wrath. He hath led me, and brought me into darkness, but not into light' (Lamentations 3:1, 2). Before God reveals grace, he causes grief; and both the grief and the grace that follows are according to God's sovereign, eternal purpose. Salvation is obtained by simple, childlike faith in the Lord Jesus Christ; but faith that does not arise from a felt need of Christ and is not accompanied by a genuine conviction of sin is not true faith. Where there is no conviction there is no conversion. Where there is no misery there is no mercy. Where there is no grief there is no grace. 'But though he cause grief, yet will he have compassion according to the multitude of his mercies' (Lamentations 3:32). Jeremiah describes the darkness he felt in his soul in Lamentations 3:3-20.

'Surely against me is he turned; he turneth his hand against me all the day. My flesh and my skin hath he made old; he hath broken my bones. He hath builded against me, and compassed me with gall and travail. He hath set me in dark places, as they that be dead of old. He hath hedged me about, that I cannot get out: he hath made my chain heavy. Also when I cry and shout, he shutteth out my prayer. He hath inclosed my ways with hewn stone, he hath made my paths crooked. He was unto me as a bear lying in wait, and as a lion in secret places. He hath turned aside my ways, and pulled me in pieces: he hath made me desolate. He hath bent his bow, and set me as a mark for the arrow. He hath caused the arrows of his quiver to enter into my reins. I was a derision to all my people; and their song all the day. He hath filled me with bitterness, he hath made me drunken with wormwood. He hath also broken my teeth with gravel stones, he hath covered me with ashes. And thou hast removed my soul far off from peace: I forgat prosperity. And I said, My strength and my hope is perished from the LORD: Remembering mine affliction and my misery, the wormwood and the gall. My soul hath them still in remembrance, and is humbled in me.'

All who know the Lord God in the experience of his saving operations of grace freely acknowledge and frankly confess that God is strictly righteous in the exercise of his grace and truly gracious in his righteous judgments. These are the things that Jeremiah learned by deep, painful experience and recorded in this third chapter of Lamentations for our learning and comfort.

Jeremiah was a man who had experienced terrible grief in his soul; but, being a man of God-given faith, he understood and acknowledged that the cause of all his grief was the Lord his God. He acknowledged God in all his ways and owned him as the origin of all things. Twenty-two times, referring to his woes in verses 1-17, he said, 'God did it'. When he was afflicted, he said it was by the rod of God's wrath (v. 1). When his soul was brought into bondage, he said God had hedged him about and put a chain upon him (v. 7). When he was overwhelmed with grief, he said, he 'hath pulled me in pieces' (vv. 8-19). When he was, by these things brought to utter hopelessness in himself, he found hope in the Lord God (vv. 21-31). Oh, blessed, blessed, blessed are those sinners who have been brought down to utter hopelessness in themselves that they might find hope in the Lord God!

Jeremiah said, 'He hath set me in dark places, as they that be dead of old'. 'He discovereth deep things out of darkness, and bringeth out to light the shadow of death'. He makes 'darkness his secret place'. 'Clouds and darkness are round about him: righteousness and judgment are the habitation of his throne.'

'Such as sit in darkness and in the shadow of death, being bound in affliction and iron; Because they rebelled against the words of God, and contemned the counsel of the most High: Therefore he brought down their heart with labour; they fell down, and there was none to help. Then they cried unto the LORD in their trouble, and he saved them out of their distresses. He brought them out of darkness and the shadow of death, and brake their bands in sunder. Oh that men would praise the LORD for his goodness, and for his wonderful works to the children of men! For he hath broken the gates of brass, and cut the bars of iron in sunder' (Psalm 107:10-16).

When Jeremiah was, by these things, brought to utter hopelessness in himself, he found hope in the Lord God.

'This I recall to my mind, therefore have I hope. It is of the LORD'S mercies that we are not consumed, because his compassions fail not. They are new every morning: great is thy faithfulness. The LORD is my portion, saith my soul; therefore will I hope in him. The LORD is good unto them that wait for him, to the soul that seeketh him. It is good that a man should both hope and quietly wait for the salvation of the LORD. It is good for a man that he bear the yoke in his youth. He sitteth alone and keepeth silence, because he hath borne it upon him. He putteth his mouth in the dust; if so be there may be hope. He giveth his cheek to him that smiteth him: he is filled full with reproach. For the Lord will not cast off for ever: But though he cause grief, yet will he have compassion according to the multitude of his mercies' (Lamentations 3:21-32).

The sinner's only hope is the Lord God himself (vv. 21-25). The only thing an utterly helpless, hopeless sinner can do for God's salvation is wait (v. 26). The place where a sinner must wait for God's salvation is in the dust of repentance before the throne of grace (vv. 27-31). The sinner must bear the yoke of his guilt under Holy Spirit conviction (v. 27). Each must do business with the Almighty personally (v. 28), making his headquarters in the dust (v. 29), justifying God in his own condemnation (v. 30), looking to God in Christ for mercy (v. 31). 'Though he cause grief, yet will he have compassion according to the multitude of his mercies.'

This is what Jeremiah is teaching us. I cannot explain it to people who have not experienced it; but this is the experience of every heaven-born soul. There is a felt darkness and confusion in the soul when God convinces a sinner of his personal vileness and hell worthiness. This is the grief Jeremiah is talking about. It is a spiritual grief caused in the soul by God. We recognize that every event of providence that brings grief is God's work. He brings the cloud over the earth as well as the sunshine (Genesis 9:14). If there were no clouds, you would never see a rainbow. He makes peace and creates evil in the earth (Isaiah 45:7).

The eye of faith sees also that spiritual grief and sorrow are the works of God's hands. God's holy displeasure with sin is everywhere seen. It must be experienced and acknowledged. When Adam sinned in the garden, God made him feel his hot displeasure (Genesis 3:17-19). When God gave his law at Sinai, the thunder and the darkness, and the trembling made known his displeasure with sin in such a way that Israel felt it and heard it. And when God comes to a sinner in saving operations of grace, the very first thing he does is make that sinner to know his displeasure. God will never give grace where he does not cause grief (John 16:8-12).

I once heard Pastor Harry Graham say, 'When God deals with a sinner in mercy, he takes him to hell first.' This is God's strange work. He causes grief so he may bestow grace! Thomas Bradbury put it like this, 'Where sin is not felt and hated, salvation will never be enjoyed. Where wrath has not been dreaded, love will not be experienced. The heart that is a stranger to misery must be a foreigner to mercy.' God creates 'the waster to destroy' (Isaiah 54:16) all earthly, creature comfort to bring us down to hell (Psalm 107), so we might look to the crucified Christ and find all comfort for our souls in him alone. Those who are grieved by God, God alone can gladden. 'Blessed are they that mourn: for they shall be comforted' (Matthew 5:4). 'Though he cause grief, yet will he have compassion according to the multitude of his mercies.'

## Felt Healing

The first thing the Holy Spirit does in the sinner in the experience of grace is to bring felt darkness into his soul by the conviction of sin. Then, he brings felt healing by the conviction of righteousness. He convinces the sinner of righteousness, because Christ has returned to the Father, having accomplished what he came into the world to accomplish. He brought in everlasting righteousness. The bringing in of righteousness involved two things: obedience and satisfaction (2 Corinthians 5:21; Galatians 3:13; 1 Peter 2:24; 3:18).

'Wherefore, as by one man sin entered into the world, and death by sin; and so death passed upon all men, for that all have sinned ... For if by one man's offence death reigned by one; much more they which receive abundance of grace and of the gift of righteousness shall reign in life by one, Jesus Christ. Therefore as by the offence of one judgment came upon all men to condemnation; even so by the righteousness of one the free gift came upon all men unto justification of life. For as by one man's disobedience many were made sinners, so by the obedience of one shall many be made righteous. Moreover the law entered, that the offence might abound. But where sin abounded, grace did much more abound: That as sin hath reigned unto death, even so might grace reign through righteousness unto eternal life by Jesus Christ our Lord' (Romans 5:12, 17-21). If ever God gives you, a poor sinner, faith to touch Christ's clothes, his righteousness, 'the garments of salvation' (Isaiah 61:10), you will feel the healing of his grace in your soul. Then you will discover he has made you whole, righteous before God. We see this beautifully illustrated in Mark 5:25-29.

'And a certain woman, which had an issue of blood twelve years, and had suffered many things of many physicians, and had spent all that she had, and was nothing bettered, but rather grew worse, when she had heard of Jesus, came in the press behind, and touched his garment. For she said, if I may touch but his clothes, I shall be whole. And straightway the fountain of her blood was dried up; and she felt in her body that she was healed of that plague'.

## Felt No Harm

In Acts 28 we see a third felt thing.

'And when they were escaped, then they knew that the island was called Melita. And the barbarous people shewed us no little kindness:

for they kindled a fire, and received us every one, because of the present rain, and because of the cold. And when Paul had gathered a bundle of sticks, and laid them on the fire, there came a viper out of the heat, and fastened on his hand. And when the barbarians saw the venomous beast hang on his hand, they said among themselves, No doubt this man is a murderer, whom, though he hath escaped the sea, yet vengeance suffereth not to live. And he shook off the beast into the fire, and felt no harm' (Acts 28:1-5).

When Paul was bitten by that viper, 'he shook off the beast into the fire, and felt no harm'. Like Paul, you and I have been bitten by a viper, the viper of hell, that old serpent, the devil. What pain the viper's bite has caused us and is causing us! But as soon as the poor, perishing sinner is convinced by God the Holy Spirit (John 16:11) that judgment has been forever removed from him by the sacrifice of Christ, because justice has been satisfied on his behalf by the death of God's dear Son, he looks to Christ in faith, shakes off the serpent, and soon feels no harm in his soul.

'There is therefore now no condemnation to them which are in Christ Jesus, who walk not after the flesh, but after the Spirit. For the law of the Spirit of life in Christ Jesus hath made me free from the law of sin and death. For what the law could not do, in that it was weak through the flesh, God sending his own Son in the likeness of sinful flesh, and for sin, condemned sin in the flesh: That the righteousness of the law might be fulfilled in us, who walk not after the flesh, but after the Spirit' (Romans 8:1-4).

'What shall we then say to these things? If God be for us, who can be against us? He that spared not his own Son, but delivered him up for us all, how shall he not with him also freely give us all things? Who shall lay any thing to the charge of God's elect? It is God that justifieth. Who is he that condemneth? It is Christ that died, yea rather, that is risen again, who is even at the right hand of God, who also maketh intercession for us. Who shall separate us from the love of Christ?' (Romans 8:31-35).

I cannot imagine a more glorious felt thing than 'no harm'. Can you? Yet, this is something that cannot be fully felt until that great day (and it can't be too soon!), when we shall at last shake off the beast of hell, that old serpent, the devil, into the fire of hell, and so completely and thoroughly triumph over him that we shall feel no harm! It is written,

'And God shall wipe away all tears from their eyes; and there shall be no more death, neither sorrow, nor crying, neither shall there be any more pain: for the former things are passed away' (Revelation 21:4). 'He will swallow up death in victory; and the Lord God will wipe away tears from off all faces; and the rebuke of his people shall he take away from off all the earth: for the Lord hath spoken it' (Isaiah 25:8).

Notice the very slight, but very significant difference in the way those two texts (speaking of the same promise) are worded. Isaiah tells us that God will wipe away 'tears from off all faces'. He promises us that God will wipe tears from the faces of all who possess eternal life with Christ in everlasting glory. But in Revelation 21:4 the apostle John tells us that, 'God shall wipe away all tears from their eyes'. By divine inspiration, he gives an added touch of grace. He tells us our God is not only going to wipe tears from the eyes of all his people, but also 'God shall wipe away ALL TEARS from their eyes!' In other words, when we have at last shaken the serpent into the fire, we shall feel no harm from his bite!

Put the two texts together and you have the glorious promise of God in the gospel to every believing sinner. It is this. When our great and glorious God is finished with all things, he will have so thoroughly and completely saved all his people from all sin, and from all the evil consequences of sin forever that there will never be a tear in our eyes again. We shall feel no harm from the serpent's bite!

Imagine that! Who can grasp the fulness of this promise? It is too great, too broad, too incomprehensible for our mortal brains. Yet, it is gloriously true! Our great God shall in heaven's glory remove us from all sin, remove all sin from us, and remove us from all the evil consequences of sin. He will remove us from every cause of grief. He will bring us at last into the perfection of complete salvation; and every desire of our hearts will be completely gratified. God's salvation is so perfect and complete that when he is finished, we will not even have the slightest tinge of sorrow for anything. We will feel no harm!

In heaven's glory our God will wipe all tears from our eyes. Impossible as it is for us to imagine, there is a time coming when we shall weep no more, when we shall have no cause to weep, when we shall feel no harm from the serpent's bite! Heaven is a place of sure, eternal, ever-increasing bliss; and the cause of that bliss is our blessed Christ! Heaven is a place of joy without sorrow, laughter without weeping, pleasantness without pain! In heaven there are no regrets, no remorseful tears, no second thoughts, no lost causes, no sorrows of any kind!

If God did not wipe away all tears from our eyes, there would be much weeping in heaven. We would surely weep much over our past sins, unconverted loved ones forever lost in hell, wasted opportunities while we were upon the earth, our many acts of unkindness toward our brethren here, and the terrible price of our redemption! But God will wipe away all tears from our eyes. In heaven's glory there will be no more death to part loving hearts. There will be no more sorrow of any kind. There will be no more crying for any reason. There will be no more pain of any sort. Why? How can these things be? 'The former things are passed away!' We will feel no harm!

Yes, our great God shall in heaven's glory remove us from all sin, remove all sin from us, and remove us from all the evil consequences of sin. He will remove us from every cause of grief. He will bring us at last into the perfection of complete salvation; and every desire of our hearts will be completely gratified. Then, we shall be like Christ. We shall be with Christ. We shall see Christ. We shall love Christ perfectly. We shall serve Christ unceasingly. We shall worship Christ without sin. We shall rest in Christ completely. We shall enjoy Christ fully. We shall have Christ entirely. These things will be our everlasting experience, without interruption! And we shall feel no harm!

# Chapter 55

## Divine Attributes Revealed

'But the LORD hardened Pharaoh's heart, and he would not let them go. And Pharaoh said unto him, Get thee from me, take heed to thyself, see my face no more; for in that day thou seest my face thou shalt die. And Moses said, Thou hast spoken well, I will see thy face again no more. And the LORD said unto Moses, Yet will I bring one plague more upon Pharaoh, and upon Egypt; afterwards he will let you go hence: when he shall let you go, he shall surely thrust you out hence altogether. Speak now in the ears of the people, and let every man borrow of his neighbour, and every woman of her neighbour, jewels of silver, and jewels of gold. And the LORD gave the people favour in the sight of the Egyptians. Moreover the man Moses was very great in the land of Egypt, in the sight of Pharaoh's servants, and in the sight of the people. And Moses said, Thus saith the LORD, About midnight will I go out into the midst of Egypt: And all the firstborn in the land of Egypt shall die, from the firstborn of Pharaoh that sitteth upon his throne, even unto the firstborn of the maidservant that is behind the mill; and all the firstborn of beasts. And there shall be a great cry throughout all the land of Egypt, such as there was none like it, nor shall be like it any more. But against any of the children of Israel shall not a dog move his tongue, against man or beast: that ye may know how that the LORD doth put a difference between the Egyptians and Israel. And all these thy servants shall come down unto me, and bow down themselves unto me, saying, Get thee out, and all the people that follow thee: and after that I will go out. And he went out from Pharaoh in a great anger. And the LORD said unto Moses, Pharaoh shall not hearken unto you; that my wonders may be multiplied in the land of Egypt. And Moses and Aaron did all these wonders before Pharaoh: and the LORD hardened Pharaoh's heart, so that he would not let the children of Israel go out of his land.' (Exodus 10:27-11:10)

The Lord told Moses that he hardened Pharaoh's heart, that he might perform all his wonders in Egypt, so that his people might know that he alone is the LORD (Exodus 10:1, 2). This knowledge of the triune God is seen in the revelation of his divine attributes in the salvation of his people, putting 'a difference between the Egyptians and Israel' (Exodus 11:7). No mortal on this earth can know all the wonders of God's distinguishing grace toward his people. We will have to wait until we see things more clearly in the light of heaven's eternal glory to see such things fully. Yet, even now, the great, distinguishing grace by which our God has revealed himself to our souls is a matter of unceasing amazement and wonder to us. It is by the grace we have experienced in the saving revelation of our Lord Jesus Christ that we are made to know that the triune Jehovah is God alone. Beside him there is no God!

What a vast difference grace has made between Egypt and Israel! What a difference grace makes in this world 'between the righteous and the wicked, between him that serveth God and him that serveth him not' (Malachi 3:18). What an everlasting difference grace will make in the world to come! 'For who maketh thee to differ from another? and what hast thou that thou didst not receive? now if thou didst receive it, why dost thou glory, as if thou hadst not received it?'(1 Corinthians 4:7).

Oh, how we ought to lift our hearts with unceasing praise to our God for his distinguishing grace! We cannot awake in the morning, walk down the street, go out to work, eat our bread, come into the house of God, or lay down at night without experiencing God's distinguishing mercy, love, and grace upon us. May God the Holy Spirit give us grace ever to observe and lay to our hearts all the vast and numberless dispensations of divine providence and grace going on in life by which our God constantly puts a difference between Egypt and Israel! Everything proclaims it. Every event confirms it. Oh for grace to be always on the watch-tower to see and acknowledge it! 'Oh the depth of the riches both of the wisdom and knowledge of God! How unsearchable are thy judgments, and his ways past finding out!'

## Divine Sovereignty

The first thing we see in this passage is a display of divine sovereignty. We begin in Exodus 10:27, because the last verses of chapter ten should be read in connection with the eleventh chapter. Here we see our great God is God alone, he is God who purposes all things (Ecclesiastes 3:1, 17; 8:6; Isaiah 14:24-27; 46:10, 11; Romans 11:33-36). Specifically, God's purpose is twofold. He has purposed salvation for all his chosen vessels of mercy, whom he prepares for glory, and destruction for all the vessels of wrath, who are in this world, fitted for just destruction by their own obstinate rebellion (Exodus 10:27-29; 11:10; Romans 9:13-23). Is this not what we see in God's dealings with Pharaoh?

'But the LORD hardened Pharaoh's heart, and he would not let them go. And Pharaoh said unto him, Get thee from me, take heed to thyself, see my face no more; for in that day thou seest my face thou shalt die. And Moses said, Thou hast spoken well, I will see thy face again no more' (Exodus 10:27-29). 'And Moses and Aaron did all these wonders before Pharaoh: and the LORD hardened Pharaoh's heart, so that he would not let the children of Israel go out of his land' (Exodus 11:10).

Essentially, Moses said to Pharaoh, as the Prophet of God did to king Amaziah, 'I know that God hath determined to destroy thee, because thou hast done this, and hast not hearkened unto my counsel'. Pharaoh 'mocked the messengers of God, and despised his words, and misused his prophets, until the wrath of the LORD arose against his people, till there was no remedy' (2 Chronicles 25:16, 36:16).

Be sure you understand the teaching of Scripture in this matter. Pharaoh's heart was hardened by the Lord our God, so that the Lord God might reveal himself in saving mercy to Israel. Yet, he was fitted to destruction by his own wilful rebellion, by his obstinate rejection of divine revelation, as are all those who perish under the wrath of God. He went to hell according to the purpose of God; but he went to hell because he despised the counsel of the Most High. Yet, the deliverance of the children of Israel was an act of free grace and sovereign mercy bestowed on them according to God's covenant with Abraham (Genesis 15). The salvation of God's elect is an act of free grace and sovereign mercy bestowed upon us according to God's covenant with Christ our Surety before the world was made (2 Samuel 23:5).

Yes, God eternally decreed the damnation of the reprobate, just as surely as he has decreed the salvation of his elect; but the damnation of the wicked is always presented in Holy Scripture as an act of divine justice (Proverbs 1:23-33; 29:1). Every sinner who goes to hell perishes because of his own determination not to bow to God as God, because he deserves the wrath of God. Every sinner who enters into life everlasting is saved because God loves him freely with an everlasting love, because God has chosen to be gracious to him. This is what we see in Exodus 11:5-7.

'And all the firstborn in the land of Egypt shall die, from the firstborn of Pharaoh that sitteth upon his throne, even unto the firstborn of the maidservant that is behind the mill; and all the firstborn of beasts. And there shall be a great cry throughout all the land of Egypt, such as there was none like it, nor shall be like it any more. But against any of the children of Israel shall not a dog move his tongue, against man or beast: that ye may know how that the LORD doth put a difference between the Egyptians and Israel.'

Why did God make a distinction between these two nations? Why did he hate Egypt, but love Israel. Why did he afflict Egypt, but spare Israel? Why did he choose Israel alone among all the nations of the earth to be the object of his love? Why was Israel alone favoured, being told, 'You only have I known of all the families of the earth' (Amos 3:2)? The Lord God said to Israel, 'Thou art an holy people unto the LORD thy God: the LORD thy God hath chosen thee to be a special people unto himself, above all people that are upon the face of the earth' (Deuteronomy 7:6).

Why? Was Israel a more outwardly desirable nation? Not at all! 'The LORD did not set his love upon you, nor choose you, because ye were more in number than any people; for ye were the fewest of all people' (Deuteronomy 7:7). Was Israel a more inwardly deserving nation? Not at all! Israel was just as wicked as Egypt. 'For all have sinned and come short of the glory of God' (Romans 3:23). God chose Israel from among the nations in his absolute sovereignty. 'It pleased the Lord to make you his people' (1 Samuel 12:22; Psalm 115:3; Ephesians 1:3-6).

Because God loved Israel, because he loved us with an everlasting love, he declares, 'Against any of the children of Israel shall not a dog move his tongue, against man or beast: that ye may know how that the LORD doth put a difference between the Egyptians and Israel'. Blessed security! Thank God for his great sovereignty, and his distinguishing mercy! He not only delivered Israel, he made the Egyptians supply what they needed for their journey. 'Speak now in the ears of the people, and let every man borrow of his neighbour, and every woman of her neighbour, jewels of silver, and jewels of gold' (Exodus 11:2). This silver and gold would later be used to adorn the tabernacle in the wilderness. Ever remember, both the creation and government of the whole world is for the glory of our God and the salvation of his people.

Robert Hawker wrote, 'Blessed God! Let it be my happiness to record thy praises, and to speak of all the signs and wonders which thou hast wrought in a way of redeeming my soul, and the souls of all thy people, from the house of spiritual bondage, in the accomplishment of which thou hast subdued Egypt and destroyed it, and scattered thine enemies abroad with a mighty hand. Oh, may it be written upon my heart with the pencil of the living God, that it is not by might, nor by power in ourselves, that thou hast brought us out; but by thy right hand, thine arm, and the light of thy countenance. Salvation belongeth unto the Lord, and thy blessing is upon thy people!'

The God of all grace, our heavenly Father, set his love upon such undeserving sinners as we are from eternity (Jeremiah 31:3). He appointed his own dear Son to bring us salvation (John 17:2). The Lord Jesus Christ has fulfilled his commission (John 17:4, 6, 9), saving his people from their sins. Many self-righteous 'dogs' (Philippians 3:2) object and attempt to thwart God's sovereign purpose of grace (Psalm 22:16, 20), but to no avail (Revelation 22:15). Our blessed Saviour will without fail bring all his people to eternal glory (John 6:37, 39; 10:28).

## Divine Justice

The second thing we see before us is a display of God's justice. In verse 5 the Lord declares, 'all the firstborn in the land of Egypt shall die'. I find that statement striking. Throughout the Levitical dispensation constant reference was made to the firstborn. It seems that even in the destruction of enemies, as well as in the salvation of his elect, God's eye is fixed upon the sacrifice of Christ, the Firstborn. Let ours be fixed upon him as well. Just as Pharaoh and the Egyptians were slain by an act of divine justice, God's elect are saved by the work of God's justice.

Our God declares himself 'a just God and a Saviour' (Isaiah 45:21). In asserting that he is both 'a just God and a Saviour', the Lord God shows us two facts regarding his character that must be recognized, if we are to understand anything revealed in Holy Scripture. You do not know God, you do not understand his works, and you do not know the message of Holy Scripture, until these things have been established in your heart. God is just! He is holy and righteous. 'God is light; in him is no darkness at all!' Because he is righteous, just, and good, because he cannot compromise his character, he must punish sin. And this just God is also a Saviour! God is love. God is mercy. God is grace. He will be gracious. He will be merciful. He will save sinners. He must do so, because he cannot compromise his character.

When Adam sinned, he was cast out of the garden, because God is just; but he went out with the promise of a Redeemer, wearing the garments of an innocent victim who was slain in his stead, because our God is a Saviour. The world was once destroyed by a flood, because God is just; but 'Noah found grace in the eyes of the Lord', and was saved in an ark God had provided, because God is a Saviour. The Lord destroyed Sodom in the fires of his wrath, because he is just; but Lot was snatched out of the city of destruction, because he is a Saviour. The law was given on Mount Sinai in thunderings, lightnings, and thick darkness, bringing with it condemnation and death, because God is just, but there was given, in the holy of holies, the mercy seat, covered with sin atoning blood, where God promised to meet with sinners, because he is a Saviour.

This is the message of the cross of our Lord Jesus Christ. When Christ was made sin for us, the wrath of God fell upon the Son of his love, because God is just! Yet, by that very act, we are saved, because he is a Saviour! Here is the answer to the question of the ages. How can God be just and yet justify the sinner? It all happened at Calvary! Christ died 'that God might be just and the Justifier of all who believe on Jesus Christ' (Romans 3:24-26). At Calvary, mercy and truth met together, righteousness and peace kissed each other! 'By mercy and truth iniquity is purged' (Proverbs 16:6). That mercy, truth, and purging of iniquity is found only in the death of Christ as the sinners' Substitute. There is no other way for a holy God to save fallen man.

**God's Longsuffering**
Third, in Exodus 11:1 we see the longsuffering of God. 'And the LORD said unto Moses, Yet will I bring one plague more upon Pharaoh, and upon Egypt; afterwards he will let you go hence: when he shall let you go, he shall surely thrust you out hence altogether.' That is a terrible

declaration of justice and wrath. After all the plagues of Egypt, there yet remained one more in the death of the firstborn. Even so, after all the sorrows of the ungodly in this world are finished, there remains one more in their final destruction in the world to come (Psalm 9:17, 18). 'After this, the judgment'!

God would have been just in destroying Pharaoh the first time he refused to obey his command (5:2). Instead, he sent plague after plague upon him and the Egyptians. In each plague he revealed his power and mercifully granted Egypt space for repentance (Revelation 2:21). It is written, 'God, willing to shew his wrath, and to make his power known, endured with much longsuffering the vessels of wrath prepared for destruction' (Romans 9:22). So it is today. God would be absolutely just in destroying us the first time we refuse to obey his command to 'repent, and believe in the gospel' (Mark 1:15). Instead, he gives sinners warning after warning and opportunity after opportunity to comply with his command. Yet, man despises 'the riches of his goodness, forbearance, and longsuffering, not knowing that the goodness of God leadeth thee to repentance' (Romans 2:4).

Why is God so patient, forbearing, and longsuffering? It is because his love is set upon his own from eternity, and he is not willing that any of his loved ones perish. His longsuffering, like his sovereignty, is our salvation (2 Peter 3:9-15, 17, 18).

**Divine Supremacy**
Fourth, God's purpose in all he did in Egypt, as we saw in Exodus 10:2, was to display his supremacy as God, 'that ye may know how that I am the Lord'. Pharaoh was about to learn it. He was about to learn the same lesson learned by King Nebuchadnezzar of Babylon, the greatest ruler of his own day (Daniel 4:34-37). God said, 'When I get done he will not only let you go, he will throw you out of the land'.

The Lord Jesus Christ, our God and Saviour, is still supreme, 'over all God, blessed forever!' He has 'purposed, and who shall disannul it? and his hand is stretched out, and who shall turn it back?' (Isaiah 14:27).

'Behold, the nations are as a drop of a bucket, and are counted as the small dust of the balance: behold, he taketh up the isles as a very little thing. Lebanon is not sufficient to burn, nor the beasts thereof sufficient for a burnt offering. All nations before him are as nothing; and they are counted to him less than nothing, and vanity' (Isaiah 40:15-17).

God our Saviour has defeated his adversary and ours, the Devil. He is delivering his elect from him (John 17:2; Revelation 20:1-3; Matthew 12:27-29; Luke 10:17; John 12:31). Let us ever adore and praise our great God and Saviour for his free grace and distinguishing mercy toward us. The only difference between the believer and the unbeliever, between the righteous and the wicked, between the seed of Christ and the seed of the serpent is the difference grace has made. This every heaven-born soul gladly acknowledges. 'By the grace of God I am what I am!' God's grace is always particular, distinctive, and distinguishing. Those who are saved are distinguished from those who are lost by five marvellous acts of grace.

The first distinguishing act of God's grace is his eternal election. If you can, with the eye of faith, trace every spiritual blessing you now enjoy, and those you hope to enjoy, back to their original source, the place of their origin would be spelled 'E-L-E-C-T-I-O-N' (Ephesians 1:3, 4; 2 Thessalonians 2:13; Jeremiah 1:5; 31:3).

The second act of grace by which God has distinguished his elect from the rest of mankind is effectual redemption. By his precious blood, poured out unto death upon the cross, the Lord Jesus Christ has effectually ransomed God's elect from the hands of divine justice, by satisfying the claims of justice against us (Isaiah 53:8-11; Galatians 3:13; Hebrews 9:12).

The third act of grace by which the Lord has distinguished us from the rest of the world is his adorable providence. Our God governs all the affairs of this world; and he has governed all the affairs and circumstances of our lives to bring us to the place where we now are, and to eternal glory in Christ (Matthew 10:29-31; Romans 8:28).

The fourth act of grace by which we are distinguished from all other men is God's sovereign work of regeneration. The only thing that makes you different from any other being on this planet, if you are born again, is the fact God has saved you. He gave life and faith in Christ to you by the irresistible power of his Spirit (Ephesians 2:1-10).

The fifth act of grace by which God distinguishes his elect from the unbelieving is his merciful preservation. The only thing that keeps us in grace is grace itself. The only thing that holds us to Christ is Christ himself (Jeremiah 32:38-40).

# Chapter 56

# God's Distinguishing Grace

'But against any of the children of Israel shall not a dog move his tongue, against man or beast: that ye may know how that the LORD doth put a difference between the Egyptians and Israel.'
(Exodus 11:7)

God did all that he did to Pharaoh and the Egyptians and all that he did to and for Israel for this specific purpose 'that ye may know how that the LORD doth put a difference between the Egyptians and Israel'. The Word of God teaches us, repeatedly, whatever differences there are between believers and unbelievers, between God's elect and the reprobate, they flow from the distinguishing grace of God alone.

### Pride
Such is the depraved nature of man that we all naturally cherish, nurture, cling to, and promote, in ourselves and in one another, that which is most abhorrent to God, and most certain to bring us at last to utter ruin. The evil I speak of is the original sin of the universe, the persistent sin of our race, the most abominable of all sins in the sight of God, and the sin with which I have to battle every day, every waking hour, the sin of pride.

Pride was the sin of Lucifer in the beginning (Isaiah 14:13-15). Pride was the problem Adam had in the garden. Pride rises like an ugly, monstrous, thousand-headed serpent in the heart. As soon as you think you have cut one of the monster's heads off, dozens rise in its place. There is no such thing as a truly humble man by nature. Man's pretence of humility is just another expression of pride calling attention to itself. It is pride that hardens the heart and keeps sinners from coming to Christ (Daniel 5:20). 'The wicked, through the pride of his countenance, will not seek after God: God is not in all his thoughts' (Psalm 10:4). Nothing but pride causes a person to reject the Word of God (Jeremiah 43:2). The root and cause of all carnal strife, division, whisperings, backbiting, and slander is pride, showing itself in envy and jealously. Pride is the great deceiver of men. It makes men and women behave in cruel, mean-spirited self-righteousness, under the guise of doing God's service. Be warned my friends! Be warned, O my soul! Be warned, 'Pride goeth before destruction, and an haughty spirit before a fall' (Proverbs 16:18). O Holy Spirit of God, teach me what I am that I may truly walk humbly with my God, trusting Christ alone for all my righteousness and all my salvation.

### Three Questions

1 Corinthians 4:7 is a very familiar text. I quote it with great regularity, and preach from it frequently, and do so deliberately, because we need to constantly be reminded that all the differences there are between believers and unbelievers, between God's elect and the reprobate, must be traced to the distinguishing grace of God alone. 'Who maketh thee to differ from another? And what hast thou that thou didst not receive? Now if thou didst receive it, why dost thou glory, as if thou hadst not received it?' The three questions raised here by God the Holy Ghost may be and should be applied to any and all differences which appear among men. Oh, may God the Holy Ghost graciously burn these three questions into our hearts and cause us never to forget them.

'Who maketh thee to differ from another?' This question compels us to recognize three things which are true of all who are born of God.

### Sinners Still

First, we must acknowledge there is a sense in which God's elect do not differ from other people at all; and we know it. Though we have been chosen by God the Father, redeemed by the precious blood of the Lord Jesus Christ, and called by the blessed Holy Spirit of promise, though we are saved by God's adorable and amazing grace, the people of God in this world are sinners still. This is a sad fact, but a fact nonetheless, and a fact we must never forget. Grace does not eradicate, or even change the believer's old, Adamic, sinful nature. Grace subdues it. Grace rules it. Thank God, one day grace will destroy it! But grace does not change our old nature.

We know something about the depravity of our hearts (Matthew 15:19). Early in the life of every heaven-born soul this is made real by bitter experience. Perhaps the most shocking thing the believer discovers in this world, and usually discovers shortly after God saves him, is the fact that the raging monster of sin in his heart has not been slain or even tamed. The sad fact is, we are, every day, made aware of the depths of our depravity. Yet, we have not even begun to discover the hideous enormity of our sinfulness!

I know that my best deeds of righteousness are just filthy rags in God's sight (Isaiah 64:6; 1 John 1:8, 10). I have sinned. I do sin. I am sinning. But the worst of it is this, I am sin! When I would do good, evil is present with me. So, I cannot do the things that I would. All that I am, and all that I do, is sin.

Let me state the matter clearly. There is nothing in all the world more delightful to me than prayer; but there is nothing more difficult. There is absolutely nothing in the world that I desire like I desire to believe God; but nothing is more troublesome to me than my unbelief. There is nothing in the world I more want to do than to worship Christ and walk with him in sweet communion; but nothing appears to be further out of my reach. There is nothing in this world which I strive harder to attain than conformity to Christ in thought, word, and deed; but the more I strive after it the more elusive it appears to be. The fact is, I am a man at war with himself (Romans 7:14-24; Galatians 5:17).

> If I pray, or hear, or read, sin is mixed with all I do.
> You who love the Lord indeed, tell me, is it thus with you?

Without question, there is a very real sense in which believers are no different from other people, so long as we live in this world in this body of flesh. We still have the nature of our father Adam. We are sinners still!

## Saved Sinners

Yet, the second thing that is made obvious by Paul's question ('Who maketh thee to differ from another?') is that God's saints are, indeed, different from other people. We are sinners still; but we are saved sinners, men and women with a new nature, one which is born of God. 'The Lord doth put a difference between the Egyptians and Israel'. The question, 'Who maketh thee to differ', would be redundant if there were no difference. God's people do differ from other people. Believers are different from unbelievers. God's saints are a peculiar people.

Believers are men and women who have undergone a marvellous change (1 Corinthians 6:9-11; 2 Corinthians 5:17). We have been 'washed' from our sins by the blood of Christ. Our old record is gone, expunged, cleared. We are 'sanctified' by the Spirit of God, given a new nature in the new birth. Righteousness was imputed to us for justification; and a new, righteous nature was imparted to us in regeneration. There is in every heaven-born soul 'a new man created in righteousness and true holiness'. All saved sinners are made 'partakers of the divine nature'. We are 'justified', made righteous in Christ. This is mentioned last because it is experienced and perceived last. We were justified when Christ redeemed us; but we had no knowledge of our state until God the Holy Ghost called us and gave us faith in Christ.

Grace changes a person's life. You may change your way of life without grace; but you cannot experience the grace of God that brings salvation without also experiencing that change of life that causes us to live soberly, righteously, and godly in this present, evil world. 'If any man be in Christ, he is a new creature: old things are passed away; behold, all things are become new'. We have a new Master over our lives. The Lord Jesus Christ. We have a new motive in life. The Will of God and the Glory of God! We have a new manner of life. Godliness (Titus 2:1-14). Every person in this world who is born again by the grace and power of God the Holy Spirit bears the fruit of the Spirit (Galatians 5:22, 23). Love, joy, and peace toward God. Longsuffering, gentleness, and goodness toward one another. Faith, meekness, and temperance within.

Believers are people who live by faith in Christ, who trust the Son of God. It is written, 'The just shall live by faith.' We trust Christ our God and Saviour in his glorious person, in all his redemptive work. We trust his goodness and faithfulness, his providential rule, and his heavenly intercession. And God's people love each other (1 Corinthians 13:1-8; 1 John 4:7, 8). Believers are not mean-spirited, hateful, malicious, and cruel, but gracious, kind, and forgiving.

Believers are people who have been and are continually taught of God to live soberly, righteously, and godly in this world. I stress this because it needs stressing. Do not tell me that so long as a person believes the gospel it does not matter how he lives, that his character and conduct are insignificant. God's people do differ from unregenerate worldlings (Titus 2:11, 12; Ephesians 4:17-24).

## Distinguishing Grace

Those are the facts; but the question is, 'Who maketh thee to differ?' Paul answers the question himself in Philippians 2:13. 'It is God which worketh in you both to will and to do of his good pleasure.'

Here is the third thing that is made obvious by Paul's question. What distinguishes God's elect from the reprobate of this world is the distinguishing grace of God. It is written, 'The LORD doth put a difference between the Egyptians and Israel'. Let us ever adore and praise our great God and Saviour for his free grace and distinguishing mercy toward us. Josiah Conder wrote,

> 'Tis not that I did choose Thee,
> For, Lord, that could not be.
> This heart would still refuse Thee,
> Hadst Thou not chosen me.
> My heart owns none before Thee;
> For Thy rich grace I thirst,
> This knowing, if I love Thee,
> Thou must have loved me first!

'Who maketh thee to differ from another?' Only God. 'By the grace of God I am what I am'. Noah had to learn this. David had to learn this. Peter had to learn it. Paul had to learn it (2 Corinthians 12:3-10). And, one way or another, we must and shall learn it.

## God's Gift

All that we are in Christ, all that we have in Christ, and all that we do in the worship and service of our Lord Jesus Christ is the gift and operation of God. 'What hast thou that thou didst not receive?' Nothing! Nothing in nature! Nothing in grace! Nothing in time! Nothing in eternity! If I have life, God gave it. If I have faith, it is God's operation.

If I have forgiveness, Christ obtained it. If I have righteousness, God performed it. If I am justified, God did it. If I am sanctified, God sanctified me. If I have peace, God gives it. If I have assurance, God gives it. If I am of any usefulness, in any way, to anyone, it is the Lord's doing. If I am saved, God saved me.

## Boasting Excluded

'Now, if thou didst receive it, why dost thou glory, as if thou hadst not received it?' John Gill wrote:

'To glory in any mercy, favour, or blessing received from God, as if it was not received from him, but as owing to human power, care, and industry, betrays wretched vanity, stupid, and more than brutish ignorance, horrid ingratitude, abominable pride, and wickedness; and is contrary to the grace of God, which teaches men humility and thankfulness. To God alone should all the blessings of nature, providence, and grace be ascribed. He ought to have all the glory of them; and to him, and him only, praise is due for them.'

> Boasting excluded, pride I abase;
> I'm only a sinner saved by grace!

Pride, envy, and jealousy are totally contrary to the grace we profess to believe. We are nothing but sinners saved by grace! There is no room for pride in the house of grace.

'Not unto us, O LORD, not unto us, but unto thy name give glory, for thy mercy, and for thy truth's sake' (Psalm 115:1).

'For ye see your calling, brethren, how that not many wise men after the flesh, not many mighty, not many noble, are called: But God hath chosen the foolish things of the world to confound the wise; and God hath chosen the weak things of the world to confound the things which are mighty; And base things of the world, and things which are despised, hath God chosen, yea, and things which are not, to bring to nought things that are: That no flesh should glory in his presence. But of him are ye in Christ Jesus, who of God is made unto us wisdom, and righteousness, and sanctification, and redemption: That, according as it is written, He that glorieth, let him glory in the Lord' (1 Corinthians 1:26-31).

'Thus saith the LORD, Let not the wise man glory in his wisdom, neither let the mighty man glory in his might, let not the rich man glory in his riches: But let him that glorieth glory in this, that he understandeth and knoweth me, that I am the LORD which exercise lovingkindness, judgment, and righteousness, in the earth: for in these things I delight, saith the LORD' (Jeremiah 9:23, 24).

Satan desires to have us that he may sift us as wheat. And our Saviour sometimes runs us through the sieve, to separate the precious from the vile, teaching us to trust him (Luke 22:32-34; John 13:36-14:1).

When I read these three, humbling questions, 'Who maketh thee to differ from another? And what hast thou that thou didst not receive? Now if thou didst receive it, why dost thou glory, as if thou hadst not received it?' My heart is humbled within me before my God and Saviour, and cries, 'By the grace of God, I am what I am', and I rejoice to add confidently, 'His grace was not bestowed upon me in vain'. That which he has begun in me, he will finish 'to the praise of the glory of his grace', that all creation shall know and forever acknowledge 'that the LORD doth put a difference between the Egyptians and Israel'.

Not all the blood of beasts
On Jewish altars slain
Could give the guilty conscience peace,
Or wash away the stain.

But Christ, the heavenly Lamb,
Takes all our sin away,
A Sacrifice of nobler name
And richer blood than they!

Isaac Watts

# Chapter 57

# Christ Our Passover

'And the LORD spake unto Moses and Aaron in the land of Egypt, saying, This month shall be unto you the beginning of months: it shall be the first month of the year to you ... And it came to pass the selfsame day, that the LORD did bring the children of Israel out of the land of Egypt by their armies.'
(Exodus 12:1-51)

Our Lord Jesus said, 'Moses wrote of me' (John 5:46). Indeed, 'To him give all the prophets witness, that through his name whosoever believeth in him shall receive remission of sins' (Acts 10:43). As we read the twelfth chapter of Exodus, all who are taught of God are compelled to say, as Phillip did to Nathaniel, 'We have found him, of whom Moses in the law, and the prophets, did write, Jesus of Nazareth, the son of Joseph' (John 1:45). The best commentary ever written upon this passage is 1 Corinthians 5:7, 8.

'Christ our passover is sacrificed for us: Therefore let us keep the feast, not with old leaven, neither with the leaven of malice and wickedness; but with the unleavened bread of sincerity and truth.'

Everything that took place on that memorable night when God brought Israel out of Egypt with a high hand and stretched out arm, and everything involved in the Jews' annual feast of the passover in the Old Testament, was designed and intended by God to be a typical representation and picture of our Lord Jesus Christ and the redemption of our souls by him. As Israel was preserved from death and delivered out of Egypt by the blood of the paschal lamb and the mighty arm of

God, so God's true Israel, all the host of his elect, has been delivered from death and hell by the sacrifice of Christ our Passover, and shall be delivered from all bondage by the arm of God's omnipotent and irresistible grace.

Following the Holy Spirit's commentary on this passage in 1 Corinthians 5, I want to show that 'Christ our Passover is sacrificed for us'. We are not in any way tied to those Old Testament laws, ceremonies, feasts, holy days, and sabbath days. To observe those things today is to say that Christ has not yet come, and redemption is not yet accomplished. The practice of Old Testament, ceremonial, legal ordinances in this gospel age is nothing short of idolatry. We worship God in the Spirit, trusting Christ alone as our Saviour, the true Passover Lamb, who is sacrificed for us! By his one sacrifice, we are sanctified.

### Christ our Passover

The Lord Jesus Christ, the Lamb of God, is our Passover. The purpose of the Old Testament Scriptures was and is to set forth the Lord Jesus Christ in his glorious person and work as our Substitute and Saviour in pictures and prophecies. Without question, one of the clearest and most instructive pictures of Christ in the Old Testament is the paschal lamb. The Lord Jesus Christ is the Lamb of God, by whose death all God's elect are delivered from sin and bondage and death forever.

The passover victim was a lamb. 'Speak ye unto all the congregation of Israel, saying, In the tenth day of this month they shall take to them every man a lamb, according to the house of their fathers, a lamb for an house' (v. 3). This is a picture of our Lord Jesus in his humiliation. He who is the eternal, almighty God became a lamb, the Lamb of God, that he might redeem us with his blood. 'Behold, the Lamb of God that taketh away the sin of the world.' Throughout the Scriptures our Saviour is presented to us under the figure of a lamb (Genesis 4:4; 22:8; Isaiah 53:7; John 1:29; 1 Peter 1:18-20; Revelation 5:12).

The lamb slain had to be a male of the first year and a lamb without blemish. 'Your lamb shall be without blemish, a male of the first year: ye shall take it out from the sheep, or from the goats' (v. 5). It had to be a male, a ram of the sheep or of the goats, not a ewe, a ram. By man came sin. By man righteousness must be established. A man brought death. A man must obtain life. It must be a ram of the first year (v. 5), in the prime of life. It had to be without spot. None but that Mighty One chosen of God (Psalm 89:19) could accomplish redemption for us. But might alone could not redeem our souls. The sin atoning Saviour must be holy, harmless, undefiled, and separate from sinners.

This lamb of sacrifice had to be separated from the rest of the flock. 'And ye shall keep it up until the fourteenth day of the same month: and the whole assembly of the congregation of Israel shall kill it in the evening' (v. 6). Christ was set apart in the counsel and decree of God as the Lamb slain from the foundation of the world (Revelation 13:8). He is the Lamb chosen out of the flock (Psalm 89:19). Four days before he was crucified he rode into Jerusalem (the place of sacrifice), and was set apart from men. Upon examination, he was found even by his enemies to be a Lamb with no fault in him.

The paschal lamb had to be slain in the evening of the fourth day after its separation (v. 6). It must die a violent death in the evening of the fourteenth day of the month. At the appointed time (Romans 5:8; Galatians 4:4), in the fourth day of time, the fourth millennia since creation, Christ died for the ungodly. The lamb had to be killed at Jerusalem (Deuteronomy 16:5, 6). So Christ set his face like a flint to go up to Jerusalem as the time of the passover drew nigh. It had to be violently slaughtered. So our Saviour was violently slaughtered for us under the fury of God's holy wrath. The lamb had to be roasted with fire (v. 8); and the Lamb of God was roasted in the fire of divine justice. Not a bone of the lamb could be broken (v. 46); and not a bone of the Lamb of God was broken (John 19:33-36). In every detail of our Saviour's death, the Scriptures were fulfilled. The types, promises, and prophecies of the Old Testament are so minute and given in such detail that none, except those who choose to deny the recorded facts of history, can dispute the fact that the Lord Jesus Christ fulfilled them (Acts 2:23; 3:18; 4:23-28; 13:26-30).

The blood of the slain lamb had to be sprinkled upon the doorposts and the lintel (v. 7). As the father of every household in Israel sprinkled the blood upon the door of his house for the salvation of his family, so our heavenly Father, by the power and grace of his Spirit, applies the blood of Christ to the hearts of his elect at the appointed time of deliverance (Hebrews 9:14; 10:22). What a striking picture this is of the sprinkling of the blood of the Lord Jesus (Hebrews 12:24), teaching us that his precious blood must be applied as well as shed, personally applied to each of God's elect, just as the blood of the lamb was to be applied to every house of the children of Israel (Romans 5:11). Robert Hawker rightly observed, 'The blood of the sacrifice must be applied as well as spilt. An unapplied ransom is no ransom. An unapplied Saviour is no Saviour (Hebrews 9:19, 20).'

Only God the Holy Spirit can do that for us. When he sprinkles the guilty conscience with the blood of Christ, guilt is removed from the conscience, because he makes us to see and know the Saviour's blood is enough, that by his blood alone justice is satisfied and iniquity is purged. The blood sprinkled speaks peace to our souls.

Yet, every person in the house was required to eat the roasted lamb for himself (v. 8). Only those who ate the lamb were delivered from death. All who ate the lamb were delivered. All for whom blood was shed ate the lamb and walked out of Egypt. Moses, who represented the law of God, led the way.

God commands us to eat the Lamb. That means it is all right for us to do so. God commands us to believe on Christ (1 John 3:23). That means it is all right for you to believe! If you eat the Lamb, his blood was shed for you; but this is something only you can do. You must eat the Lamb for yourself (John 6:51-56).

Every soul under the blood was saved by the blood. 'And the blood shall be to you for a token upon the houses where ye are: and when I see the blood, I will pass over you, and the plague shall not be upon you to destroy you, when I smite the land of Egypt' (v. 13). Someone died in every house in Egypt that night, 'for there was not a house where there was not one dead' (v. 30). But the destroying angel did not enter a single house where the blood stained the door. None of those for whom blood was shed died in Egypt that night. Yet, 'there was not a house where there was not one dead'. The firstborn of every house died, either personally or representatively.

The firstborn represents the whole family. And this is God's law concerning the firstborn. The Lord God declares, 'All the firstborn are mine' (Exodus 22:29; 34:18-20; Numbers 3:13). As it was in Egypt, so it is now. Justice passes by none. All must suffer the wrath of God. All must die. Either personally or representatively, we must face the hot wrath and cold justice of the holy Lord God. Someone must die, either me or a Substitute, either you or a Substitute! The blood of Christ, the Lamb of God, stops the destroying angel, the executioner of divine justice, at our door. The blood says, 'Touch not this house!' The blood atoned for our sin. The blood pacifies the wrath of God. The blood satisfies divine justice. The holy, infinite justice of God cannot require more than the life's blood of the Lamb of God (Romans 8:1-4; 5:9-11).

The Lord God said, 'When I see the blood I will pass over you'. When were we delivered from the wrath of God? When God saw the blood upon the Door (Christ) of our house! How long will this thing last? As long as God sees the blood on the Door! When did God see the blood on the Door? He saw the blood long before we saw it. He sees the blood when we see it. He sees the blood even when we cannot see it. His eye is always on the blood. Always! Blessed be his name forever! He will still see the blood in the Day of Judgment. Christ is our Passover.

**Is Sacrificed**
'Christ our Passover is sacrificed.' Notice, not was sacrificed, but is sacrificed. That means his one sacrifice is enough, that its effects are lasting and perpetually meritorious and effectual, and no other sacrifice will ever be made. The Jews of old had only the picture, the promise, and the prophecy. We have the Passover. The type, being fulfilled, is abolished forever. The law, being fulfilled, is abolished forever (Romans 10:4). The sins of God's elect, being nailed to the tree, are abolished forever! Justice, being satisfied, demands the deliverance of all for whom the Paschal Lamb is sacrificed. Our God declares to his chosen, 'Fury is not in me' (Isaiah 27:4). All God's elect are now redeemed forever (Hebrews 9:12; Galatians 3:13; 1 Peter 3:18). Being redeemed means we are delivered from the curse of the law, forgiven of all sin, made righteous and reconciled to God.

This is not a fanciful dream, but the blessed reality of grace! Christ, the Paschal Lamb, died; and all for whom he died are redeemed and delivered from all possibility of curse or condemnation (Galatians 3:13; Romans 8:1, 33, 34).

**For Us**
'Christ our Passover is sacrificed.' But for whom was this great sacrifice made? The Holy Spirit answers the question emphatically in the last two words of 1 Corinthians 5:7, 'FOR US'. 'Christ our Passover is sacrificed for us.' No lamb was provided, no sacrifice was made, no blood was shed for the Egyptians, only for Israel, for all Israel, but only

for Israel, God's chosen people whom he had purposed to redeem, promised to redeem, and came to redeem.

Blood was shed only for those who came out of Egypt that night. Even so, the Lord Jesus Christ, the Lamb of God, is not a Passover Lamb slain for all the world, but 'for us' who are delivered by his blood. The Son of God did not in any way, or to any degree, die to redeem and save those who yet suffer the wrath of God in hell. His sacrifice was made for and secured the eternal salvation of all for whom he died.

There is not a hint of universal redemption in the Book of God. Every text referring to the redemptive work of Christ, every type of redemption in the Old Testament, and every statement about the consequences of our Lord's death at Calvary declares plainly that he died for a specific people, and that all for whom he died were effectually redeemed by his blood. 'Christ our Passover is sacrificed for us.' 'For us' whom he came to save (Matthew 1:21). 'For us' who are God's elect (Romans 8:29). 'For us' his church (Ephesians 5:25-27). 'For us' his sheep (John 10:11, 15, 26). 'For us' who believe on him. 'For us' who shall be with him at last in heaven (Romans 5:9, 10).

**Just Suppose**
Why are we so dogmatic and insistent in declaring that the Lord Jesus Christ actually redeemed all for whom he died? Why do we so dogmatically assert the doctrine of particular, effectual redemption? Why do we insist, in the teeth of universal opposition from the religious world around us, on this doctrine of limited atonement? Why must we constantly denounce as heresy the hellish doctrine of universal (useless) redemption? Just suppose it was true that Jesus Christ died for the purpose of redeeming every person in the world, and that some of those for whom he died perished in hell!

Where is the love of God? Does God not love his own elect any more than the rest of the world? Does he not love Jacob more than Esau, and Peter more than Judas? Universal redemption reduces the love of God to nothing. What kind of love must that be which does not save men from hell, when it is able to do so?

Where is the wisdom of God? The sacrifice of Christ in the place of his people is 'the manifold wisdom of God'. But what wisdom is there in the plan of saving sinners by the death of Christ, if some of those for whom Christ died are not saved?

Where is the justice of God? The death of Christ in the place of sinners was the satisfaction of divine justice. But what justice is it that demands a double payment for the same crime? Can God in justice slay his Son in my place and slay me, too?

Where is the power of God? If Jesus Christ, God the eternal Son, tried by his death upon the cross to save every person in the world, and some of them go to hell, in spite of his best efforts, what power does he have? Does not God Almighty have power to forgive sin, take away unbelief, and give faith to whom he will?

Where is the immutability of God? Can God at one time love a man so greatly that he gave his only begotten Son to die in his place, and at another time burn with such hatred, wrath, and anger against that same man that he sends him to hell? Did he not say, 'I am the Lord, I change not'?

Where is the glory of God? The ultimate end of God in redemption is his own glory; but if some of those for whom Christ died suffer in hell eternally, God is robbed of his glory.

Know this, if Jesus Christ died in the place of any man who suffers the wrath of God in hell for his own sins, then that awful absurdity must follow, that 'Christ died in vain'! Perish the thought! The Son of God did not fail in his work. He accomplished an effectual redemption. Every soul for whom Christ died shall believe the gospel; and all who believe shall have eternal life.

The Lord God specifically commanded that the blood of the passover lamb was to be sprinkled upon 'the two side posts and the upper door post' of each house in Israel (v. 7), but not a drop was to be spilled upon the threshold. Why? Because the blood must never be trampled underfoot as a common, or unholy thing (Hebrews 10:29).

### Keep the Feast

'Christ our Passover is sacrificed for us. Therefore let us keep the feast.' 'Purge out therefore the old leaven, that ye may be a new lump, as ye are unleavened. For even Christ our passover is sacrificed for us: Therefore let us keep the feast, not with old leaven, neither with the leaven of malice and wickedness; but with the unleavened bread of sincerity and truth' (1 Corinthians 5:7, 8).

The passover feast was in many ways similar to the Lord's Supper. Indeed, our Lord Jesus Christ used the symbolism of the last passover supper to establish the gospel ordinance of the Lord's Supper. However, 1 Corinthians 5 does not refer to the Lord's Supper. 1 Corinthians 11 tells us plainly that the Lord's Supper is not a feast, and it is not to be kept as a feast. The passover feast was a picture of the life of faith. The keeping of the feast referred to here is a spiritual thing. Believing on the Lord Jesus Christ, we feed upon him as our Passover Sacrifice. We eat his flesh and drink his blood, constantly, by faith (John 6:51-57).

A feast implies both plenty and joy. In Christ there is plenteous redemption. In him there is an infinite supply of grace. Let us therefore feast upon him with the joy of faith. The feast of faith must be eaten with bitter herbs of godly sorrow and true repentance (Zechariah 12:10), as the passover was (v. 8).

This feast of faith cannot be kept with the old leaven of malice and wickedness, or enmity and hypocrisy. It must be kept with the unleavened bread of sincerity and truth. The old leaven of nature must be purged. Being born again by God the Holy Spirit, we must put off the old man and put on the new. God cannot be worshipped, except by those who worship him in the Spirit and in the Truth (Ephesians 4:21-24; Titus 3:3-5; John 4:24; Philippians 3:3).

As leaven sours the loaf, so malice sours the life. As leaven ruins, so wickedness destroys. As leaven swells, so hypocrisy swells the hearts of men with pride. Let us put away the leaven of malice and wickedness, putting off our old, carnal Adamic passions. Spirit of God, sweep the leaven of nature away, that we may worship God with the unleavened bread of sincerity and truth.

This feast of faith is a feast of expectation and hope. The Jews ate the passover with their coats on their backs, their shoes on their feet, and their staff in their hands. They ate it expecting to go out of Egypt that night. That is what it is to keep the feast. It is living upon Christ with the expectation of deliverance, having our loins girt about with the girdle of truth, our feet shod with the gospel of peace, the coat of Christ's righteousness upon our backs, and the staff of faith in our hands. We keep the feast by reckoning ourselves dead indeed unto sin, but alive unto God. We keep the feast with an eye upon eternity and the land of promise. 'Christ' is 'our Passover'. 'Christ our Passover is sacrificed for us.' 'Therefore let us keep the feast.'

# Chapter 58

## 'The LORD'S Passover'

'And the LORD spake unto Moses and Aaron in the land of Egypt, saying, This month shall be unto you the beginning of months: it shall be the first month of the year to you. Speak ye unto all the congregation of Israel, saying, In the tenth day of this month they shall take to them every man a lamb, according to the house of their fathers, a lamb for an house: And if the household be too little for the lamb, let him and his neighbour next unto his house take it according to the number of the souls; every man according to his eating shall make your count for the lamb. Your lamb shall be without blemish, a male of the first year: ye shall take it out from the sheep, or from the goats: And ye shall keep it up until the fourteenth day of the same month: and the whole assembly of the congregation of Israel shall kill it in the evening. And they shall take of the blood, and strike it on the two side posts and on the upper door post of the houses, wherein they shall eat it. And they shall eat the flesh in that night, roast with fire, and unleavened bread; and with bitter herbs they shall eat it. Eat not of it raw, nor sodden at all with water, but roast with fire; his head with his legs, and with the purtenance thereof. And ye shall let nothing of it remain until the morning; and that which remaineth of it until the morning ye shall burn with fire. And thus shall ye eat it; with your loins girded, your shoes on your feet, and your staff in your hand; and ye shall eat it in haste: it is the LORD'S passover. For I will pass through the land of Egypt this night, and will smite all the firstborn in the land of Egypt, both man and beast; and against all the gods of Egypt I will execute judgment: I am the LORD.

And the blood shall be to you for a token upon the houses where ye are: and when I see the blood, I will pass over you, and the plague shall not be upon you to destroy you, when I smite the land of Egypt. And this day shall be unto you for a memorial; and ye shall keep it a feast to the LORD throughout your generations; ye shall keep it a feast by an ordinance forever.'
(Exodus 12:1-14)

Exodus 12 describes the last night of Israel's bondage in the land of Egypt. The Lord's captives had suffered much and suffered long in the land of bondage. The fiery furnace in which Israel was refined had been heated by the hatred of Ishmael's seed against the seed of promise. But God's appointed time had come for the deliverance promised in his covenant with Abraham. When the appointed day of deliverance dawned, no power could hold God's chosen captive. Mad opposition was utterly helpless before Jehovah's outstretched arm of omnipotent mercy. The chosen people must go free.

Child of God, rest your soul upon this rock: The purposes and promises of our God are as sure, as immutable, and as dependable as God himself. Like the gifts and callings of God, they are without repentance. At God's appointed time we shall march triumphantly into our Canaan!

**New Beginning**
'And the LORD spake unto Moses and Aaron in the land of Egypt, saying, This month shall be unto you the beginning of months: it shall be the first month of the year to you' (Exodus 12:1, 2).

The Lord commanded the children of Israel to celebrate the passover as a time of new beginning (Deuteronomy 16:1). The month Abib was in the spring of the year, corresponding to our March or April. It is the time of new life springing forth in the earth. How blessed it is to know that there is a new beginning for our souls! On that great day of grace when Christ brought deliverance to our souls, all things were made new for us (2 Corinthians 5:17).

**The Lamb**
'Speak ye unto all the congregation of Israel, saying, In the tenth day of this month they shall take to them every man a lamb, according to the

house of their fathers, a lamb for an house' (v. 3). How fitting that the first thing mentioned with regard to this new life, and that which is most prominent is the lamb. Who can miss the reason for this? Throughout the Book of God, our Lord Jesus Christ, who is our life, is set before us as 'the Lamb of God' (Revelation 13:8; 5:6-9, 12; John 1:29). He is,

The Lamb Provided in Predestination
The Lamb Portrayed in the Sacrifices of the Old Testament
The Lamb Promised (Genesis 22:8)
The Lamb Prophesied (Isaiah 53:1-12)
The Lamb Presented and Sacrificed (Romans 3:24-26)
The Lamb Proclaimed in the Gospel (John 1:29)
The Lamb Pursued by Faith (Philippians 3:3-14)
The Lamb Praised Forever (Revelation 5:8-14; 14:1)

'And if the household be too little for the lamb, let him and his neighbour next unto his house take it according to the number of the souls; every man according to his eating shall make your count for the lamb' (v. 4). As one family they 'did all eat the same spiritual meat' (1 Corinthians 10:3). So it is to this day, and shall be forever. God's saints are one family, feasting on one Sacrifice, worshipping one Saviour, 'of whom the whole family in heaven and earth is named' (Ephesians 3:15).

'Your lamb shall be without blemish, a male of the first year: ye shall take it out from the sheep, or from the goats' (v. 5). The lamb sacrificed that night in Egypt had to be a lamb without blemish, a male of first year (Leviticus 1:3-10). Again, our Lord Jesus Christ is held before us in the picture. We have been redeemed 'with the precious blood of Christ, as of a Lamb without blemish and without spot' (1 Peter 1:19). And our Saviour, like the lamb sacrificed in Egypt, was slain in the prime of his life, when he was full of strength.

The sacrificial lamb could be taken from among the sheep or from among the goats. I have often wondered why the Lord made that specific declaration. As a lamb of the sheep we see that our Saviour was an innocent victim. As a kid of the goats we are given a picture of him being made sin. John Trapp observed that a kid of the goats shows that Christ 'was made a sinner' (2 Corinthians 5:21).

'And ye shall keep it up until the fourteenth day of the same month: and the whole assembly of the congregation of Israel shall kill it in the evening' (v. 6). Does this command seem strange to you? Why did God specifically require that the 'the whole assembly of Israel' have a hand in killing the sacrifice? It seems obvious to me that everything in this verse was prophetic of three things.

First, the whole nation of Israel slaughtered the Lord Jesus Christ (Luke 22:1, 2). The whole nation's hands drip with the blood of the Son of God. This was done according to the purpose of God (Acts 2:22, 23).

Second, all the congregation of God's true Israel are the beneficiaries of Christ's sacrifice. Though our hands drip with his blood, we live by him whom we have killed!

Third, as the lamb here must be killed in the evening, so our blessed Saviour, the Lamb of God, was sacrificed for us in the evening of time, in the end of the world (Hebrews 9:26). Christ came in the evening of the world (Hebrews 1:2), in the last hour of the world's time (1 John 2:18), when all was buried in the darkness of sin and death.

**Blood Applied**

'And they shall take of the blood, and strike it on the two side posts and on the upper door post of the houses, wherein they shall eat it' (v. 7) What a striking allusion this is to the sprinkling of the blood of the Lord Jesus (Hebrews 12:24). The teaching is as obvious as the nose on your face, Christ's precious blood must be personally applied to us as well as shed for us (Romans 5:5-11).

When God the Holy Spirit comes in the saving operations of his grace he takes the things of Christ and shows them to his people. He shows redeemed sinners what the Saviour has done for them (2 Timothy 1:9, 10). Giving us the hyssop of faith, showing us what Christ has accomplished for us, we are made to see that the righteousness of Christ is sufficient for our souls, that by his blood we are justified and cleansed from all sin. It is by this application of the blood that we 'have peace with God through our Lord Jesus Christ', by whom we have received the atonement.

**Lamb Eaten**

'And they shall eat the flesh in that night, roast with fire, and unleavened bread; and with bitter herbs they shall eat it' (v. 8). This, too, is a picture of that faith by which we live before God. Faith is eating the Sacrifice (John 6:51-57).

The lamb had to be roasted with fire. That is a portrait of our Saviour's agonies on the cross, when he endured all the fire of God's holy wrath due to our sins when they were made his. He called this the consuming of his bones (Psalm 31:10). The unleavened bread to be eaten with the sacrifice portrays that Christ is received, believed and trusted, by a new man, by one who is born of God, and faith mixes nothing of the flesh with the sacrifice of Christ (1 Corinthians 5:7, 8). The bitter herbs with which the sacrifice was eaten speak of contrition of soul and bitterness and sorrow of heart, the godly sorrow of true repentance, which always accompanies faith in Christ, as we look on him whom we have pierced (2 Corinthians 7:10; Zechariah 12:10).

'Eat not of it raw, nor sodden at all with water, but roast with fire; his head with his legs, and with the purtenance thereof' (v. 9) The whole lamb had to be eaten. So it is with us. We need the whole Christ. We trust the whole Christ. We receive the whole Christ. We live by the whole Christ. Nothing short of the Lord Jesus Christ will suffice for our souls' needs.

But the lamb was not to be eaten raw, or merely boiled in water. It had to be thoroughly roasted with fire. Christ is not received rashly, in a cold, lukewarm manner, with indifference. And nothing can be mixed, added, or joined to him. Christ alone must be trusted for our acceptance, justification, and salvation. This is emphasized again in verse 10. 'And ye shall let nothing of it remain until the morning; and that which remaineth of it until the morning ye shall burn with fire.'

'And thus shall ye eat it; with your loins girded, your shoes on your feet, and your staff in your hand; and ye shall eat it in haste: it is the LORD'S passover' (v. 11). This is a great picture of sinners trusting Christ. Our loins are 'girt about with truth' (Ephesians 6:14). Our feet are 'shod with the preparation of the gospel of peace' (Ephesians 6:15). And the staff of faith is in our hands.

'For I will pass through the land of Egypt this night, and will smite all the firstborn in the land of Egypt, both man and beast; and against all the gods of Egypt I will execute judgment: I am the LORD. And the blood shall be to you for a token upon the houses where ye are: and when I see the blood, I will pass over you, and the plague shall not be upon you to destroy you, when I smite the land of Egypt' (vv. 12, 13) The blood sprinkled upon the door, not merely the blood spilt, but the blood applied, was the token of God's favour by which Israel was assured of God's salvation. Robert Hawker observed, 'An unapplied ransom is no ransom. An unapplied Saviour is no Saviour' (Hebrews 9:19, 20; 1 John 1:7).

## A Memorial

'And this day shall be unto you for a memorial; and ye shall keep it a feast to the LORD throughout your generations; ye shall keep it a feast by an ordinance forever' (v. 14). This ordinance of our God, the Lord's passover, is an ordinance to be kept forever in God's Israel, because 'it is the Lord's Passover' (v. 11). No, we do not keep the carnal feast; but we do keep the feast, as we live by faith upon Christ our Passover, who is sacrificed for us.

Never was there such a display of wrath and judgment as that displayed in the sacrifice of our Christ at Calvary. Never was there such a display of mercy, love, and grace. There is no death, but only life in the house sprinkled with Christ's precious, sin atoning blood. Let there be no fear in our souls, but only a holy feasting upon the table and the sacrifice God has spread for us. As Israel was ready to go out of Egypt because of the blood sprinkled, so we who trust the Son of God are ready to go out of this world because of the blood sprinkled (Colossians 1:9-14).

If you dwell safely, dwell beneath the blood, justice cannot drag you to execution. The curse cannot be upon you. The law cannot condemn you. Vengeance cannot slay you. The blood upon you cries 'Away! Stand back! No foe can touch, where I protect!'

Are you thus marked by the blood as one of Christ's redeemed? If not, arise and flee to the wounded Lamb. The day is far spent; the night of ruin is at hand. The destroyer is at your heels. Each house unmarked with blood was a house not spared. Each soul unwashed will be a soul undone. Only the blood applied can heal. Only the blood applied can stand as a token upon the door. May God give you faith in the crucified Lamb!

Let none forget, 'it is the Lord's passover'. Everything about the work of redemption and grace is his. 'Salvation is of the LORD'! He is the Father of his house. He chose the Lamb to be slain. He slew the Lamb. His is the hyssop, the gift of faith, by which the blood is applied. His is the application of the blood. He sees the blood. He passes over the blood-sprinkled soul. His is the glory, both now and forever.

500

# Chapter 59

## The Token Of The Blood

'And the blood shall be to you for a token upon the houses where ye are: and when I see the blood, I will pass over you, and the plague shall not be upon you to destroy you, when I smite the land of Egypt.' (Exodus 12:13)

The Scriptures constantly speak about the blood. It is written in the books of the law, 'The life of the flesh is in the blood'. God told Moses, 'The blood shall be to you for a token'. He said, 'When I see the blood, I will pass over you'. When the high priest went into the holy of holies on the Day of Atonement, he went in with blood. No man can come to God without blood atonement.

When our Saviour instituted the Lord's Supper, he took the cup of wine, held it before his disciples, and said, 'This is the blood of the New Testament, shed for many for the remission of sins'. In Hebrews 9:22, we read, 'Without shedding of blood is no remission'. That makes the blood a matter of infinitely immense importance.

These days, it is common for preachers, churches, theologians, and hymnwriters to say as little as possible about the blood. We have become so educated, refined, and sophisticated that talking about blood is considered improper, rude and unsophisticated. But it is still true that 'without shedding of blood is no remission'. The whole of God's revelation of himself, the whole of the gospel, the whole of salvation is wrapped up in the blood, the precious, sin atoning blood of the Lord Jesus Christ (Hebrews 9:12; 1 Peter 1:18-21).

The shedding of Christ's blood was and is absolutely essential to the saving of our souls. Let us ever cherish the blood of Christ as that which is precious above all things. 'The blood shall be to you for a token'. Because of the blood; the precious, sin atoning blood of the Lord Jesus Christ, the blood represented and typified in the paschal lamb, the Lord God here issues the greatest promise a man on earth can have from God, the greatest promise God ever gave to a sinner.

'And the blood shall be to you for a token upon the houses where ye are: and when I see the blood, I will pass over you, and the plague shall not be upon you to destroy you, when I smite the land of Egypt.'

What is God saying? He is saying, 'When I deal in judgment with Egypt, I will deal in mercy with you.' That is what he is saying to us in this passage: 'When I deal in judgment with the world's sin, when I come in wrath, judgment, and condemnation upon this world; I will cover you with my grace.' The holy, just, and true God is saying to chosen, redeemed sinners, sinners in whose hearts and consciences God the Holy Ghost has sprinkled the Saviour's blood, 'When I execute wrath for sin, I am going to extend my mercy to you.' 'When I see the blood, I will pass over you.'

When this promise was given, an angry God was walking through the streets of Egypt. Someone said, 'God, with sword drawn and sharpened for the conflict, was walking through the streets of Egypt that midnight and slaying on either hand the firstborn in every home'. God came in judgment, in wrath, in condemnation, falling upon the land of Egypt, and God destroyed the pride of every home, the joy of every house, and the firstborn of every family, from Pharaoh's palace to the servant in the mill, to the cattle in the barn and the cattle in the field.

Will God smite all? Will he condemn all? Will he destroy all? No. In wrath, he remembers mercy! With the voice of mercy, he speaks. 'When I see the blood, I will pass over you.' God in judgment, walking through the streets of Egypt, God in wrath, God dealing with sin, and God in mercy dealing with men, speaks to a few among many, a nation within a nation, and says, 'When I see the blood, I will pass over you.'

### Saved and Safe

God's people are safe. God's people, chosen, redeemed, and called, are saved; and they are safe. They are secure. No judgment can come upon them. Why are God's people safe? Paul said, 'There is therefore now no condemnation to them which are in Christ Jesus, who walk not after the flesh, but after the Spirit ... Who shall lay anything to the charge of God's elect? It is God that justifieth. Who is he that condemneth? It is Christ that died, yea rather, that is risen again, who is even at the right hand of God, who also maketh intercession for us' (Romans 8:1, 33, 34). Here are four things that demand the absolute safety of God's elect.

God's people are safe because they are in his heart. He said, 'I have loved you with an everlasting love. In lovingkindness I have drawn you.' God's people are safe because they are in his heart. It is in his heart to save them. It is in his heart to keep them. It is in his heart to sustain them. It is in his heart to protect them.

Not only are they in his heart but they are also in his hand. Our Lord Jesus Christ said; 'My sheep hear my voice and I know them and they follow me and I give them eternal life and they shall never perish. My Father which gave them me is greater than all and no man is able to pluck them out of my hand. My Father which gave them to me is greater than all and no man can pluck them out of my Father's hand.' They are in his hand. No one can get to them. They are secure and they are safe. God's people are safe. When the angry God stalked the land of Egypt at midnight, and the horrible, bitter, wail of grief rose to a crescendo, a cry never been heard before or since, God's people were safe because they were in his heart and in his hand. Not only that, they were in his covenant. He said, 'I will make a covenant with you and I will write my law in your hearts and on your minds and your sins and iniquities I will remember no more.' We are in his heart, in his hand, and in his covenant, but God's people are safe because they are in his Son. 'There is no condemnation to them who are in Christ Jesus.'

When the Lord God comes in judgment, in providential judgment to any nation, any house, or any age, or when he comes in the final judgment of that great day when the elements being on fire shall melt with a fervent heat, God's people are safe. He has promised ...

'The blood shall be to you for a token upon the houses where ye are: and when I see the blood, I will pass over you, and the plague shall not be upon you to destroy you, when I smite the land of Egypt.'

## Blood Spilled
God's people are safe because, only because, they are 'under the blood'. Our salvation, our safety, our security is in the blood, only in the blood

of Christ, the blood spilled by the hand of divine justice at Calvary. The blood of the Lamb had to be spilt, violently spilt, or we could never be saved. The Lord God said,

'Speak ye unto all the congregation of Israel, saying, In the tenth day of this month they shall take to them every man a lamb, according to the house of their fathers, a lamb for an house: And if the household be too little for the lamb, let him and his neighbour next unto his house take it according to the number of the souls; every man according to his eating shall make your count for the lamb. Your lamb shall be without blemish, a male of the first year: ye shall take it out from the sheep, or from the goats: And ye shall keep it up until the fourteenth day of the same month: and the whole assembly of the congregation of Israel shall kill it in the evening' (vv. 3-6).

Without question, the most wondrous of all God's works is the work of redemption. When we attempt to consider what that work involved, we are lost in astonishment. When we think of the unutterable depths of shame and sorrow into which the Lord of Glory entered to save us, we are awed and staggered. A. W. Pink rightly wrote:

'That the eternal Son of God should lay aside the robes of his ineffable glory and take upon him the form of a servant, that the Ruler of heaven and earth should be 'made under the law' (Galatians 4:4), that the Creator of the universe should tabernacle in this world and 'have not where to lay his head' (Matthew 8:20), is something which no finite mind can comprehend; but where carnal reason fails us, God-given faith believes and worships.'

As we trace the path of our Saviour from the throne of life to the tomb of death and behold him who was rich, for our sakes, becoming poor, that we through his poverty might be made rich, we cannot fathom the depths of the wonders before us. We know every step in the path of our Redeemer's humiliation was ordained in the eternal purpose of God. Yet, it was a path of immeasurable sorrow, unutterable anguish, ceaseless ignominy, bitter hatred, and relentless persecution; a path that brought the Beloved Son of God, the Darling of heaven, to suffer the painful, shameful death of the cross! Who could have imagined such things as these? Standing at the foot of the cross, as I behold the Holy One nailed to the cursed tree, covered with his own blood and the spit of an enraged mob, made to be sin, forsaken and cursed of God his Father, yet, realizing this is the work of God's own hand, I am lost in astonishment! I am filled with reverence and awe (2 Corinthians 5:21; Galatians 3:13).

But, awed as I am with reverence for my crucified Lord, still there is a question I cannot suppress, a question that reason and sound judgment cannot fail to ask. The question is, Why? Why did the Son of God suffer such a death? Why did God so torment his beloved Son, and kill him in such a way? Was it to save my soul? I know he did so that I might live. He suffered, the Just for the unjust, that he might bring me to God. But was there no other way for the omnipotent God to save me? Was all this done to demonstrate the greatness of God's love to me? I know it was (Romans 5:8; 1 John 3:16; 4:9, 10). But God could have revealed his love to me another way. Why did he slay his Son? What necessity was there for the Son of God to suffer and die on the cross?

Only one answer can be found to that question. The justice of God had to be satisfied. There was no necessity for God to save anyone. Salvation is altogether the free gift of his grace. But, having determined to save his elect from the ruins of fallen humanity, the only way God could save his people, and forgive their sins, was by the death of Christ. 'Without shedding of blood is no remission' (Hebrews 9:22). The justice of God had to be satisfied in order for God to save his people; and the only thing that could ever satisfy the justice of God is the blood of Christ. The blood must be spilt, or sinners cannot be saved.

### Blood Sprinkled

And the blood spilt must be sprinkled. In verse seven the Lord God said:

'And they shall take of the blood, and strike it on the two side posts and on the upper door post of the houses, wherein they shall eat it'

There is a striking allusion here in the sprinkling of blood, to that of the blood of the Lord Jesus (Hebrews 9:19, 20; 12:24). The blood had to be sprinkled upon the two doorposts of every house, because no one can get into the house and family of God but by blood. And the blood had to be sprinkled upon the lintel, overhead, because sinners must have a mediator between us and the holy Lord God. But the blood must not be sprinkled on the threshold, because the blood of the covenant, the precious, sin atoning blood of Christ must never be looked upon as a common thing, as something to be trampled upon (Hebrews 10:29).

Our Redeemer's precious blood must be applied as well as shed. It had to be sprinkled in heaven, accepted by God; and it must be sprinkled upon, personally applied to each ransomed soul (Romans 5:11). When the Holy Ghost, whose office it is to take of the things of Christ and show them to his people, thereby giving the heaven-born soul faith in Christ, he sprinkles the conscience from dead works and declares justification in the soul. So every sinner, taught of God, has the testimony from God himself that Enoch had, 'that he pleased God' (Hebrews 9:12-14; 11:5, 6). Lord, grant that our souls may fully feel the blessed application of Jesus' blood and righteousness, in this soul-refreshing way, to the glory of God in Jesus Christ!

Then, the Lord commanded the children of Israel go inside the house and eat the lamb, all of it; leaving nothing until the morning (vv. 8-11). This is, of course, a vivid picture of faith in Christ. Faith receives, embraces, and trusts the whole Christ. He is our Prophet, our Priest, and our King. He is our Wisdom, our Righteousness, our Sanctification, and our Redemption. And, the Lord God said, 'When I see the blood I will pass over you'. God's people are safe only through the blood. 'It is the blood that maketh atonement for the soul.' That is what Scripture says. 'Without the shedding of blood there is no remission of sin'.

> Under the blood of Jesus
> Safe in the shepherd's fold
> Under the blood of Jesus
> Safe while the ages roll.
> Safe, though the world may crumble
> Safe, though the stars grow dim
> Under the blood of Jesus
> We are secure in Him.

God spared Israel that fearful night in Egypt. God spared the firstborn in the home of every Israelite. Why? He said; 'When I see the blood I will pass over you.' Because the blood was on the door, the firstborn of every Israelite household was spared. Where there was no blood on the door, God visited in wrath. There may have been flowers out there. There may have been anything out there, but if there was no blood on the door, then death struck. God visited in wrath.

So it is with us. In the day when God shall judge the world, when God shall come forth in wrath against sin, we will be secure, we will be kept, and we will be safe if we are covered with the Saviour's blood.

It is the blood of Christ that makes atonement for the soul. Peter said. 'We are not redeemed with corruptible things, such as silver and gold, from the vain conversation received by tradition from our fathers, but with the precious blood of Christ as of a lamb without spot or blemish.'

> What can wash away my sin?
> Nothing but the blood of Jesus.
> What can make me whole again?
> Nothing but the blood of Jesus.

This is what the Bible teaches. 'When I see the blood I will pass over you'. That is what God said to Israel; and that is what he says to you and me. 'When I see the blood.' Not your church membership, not your morality, not your self-righteousness, not your religious deeds, not even your decision. God says, 'When I see the blood I will pass over you'.

'For the life of the flesh is in the blood: and I have given it to you upon the altar to make an atonement for your souls: for it is the blood that maketh an atonement for the soul' (Leviticus 17:11).

In Old Testament days under the types, and shadows, and symbols, and pictures, almost all things were sanctified by blood. The priest was sprinkled with blood, the book was sprinkled with blood, and the altar was sprinkled with blood. The tabernacle was sprinkled with blood; everything was sprinkled with the blood.

Without the shedding of blood there is no forgiveness. Isaac asked his father Abraham, after they started up that mountain of sacrifice, Mount Moriah, 'Behold the fire and the wood: but where is the lamb for a burnt offering? And Abraham said, My son, God will provide himself a lamb for a burnt offering.' Christ is the Lamb God provided, the Lamb God sacrificed, and the Lamb God accepted. There can be no worship of God without blood, no acceptance by God without blood and no redemption by God without blood. There can be no sin offering without blood. A bloodless religion is just religion. It has no salvation and no hope. It has no promise. Without blood, religion is blasphemy.

## Seen Blood
The blood by which we are redeemed, justified, and saved is blood that is seen by God with approbation, approval, and satisfaction. Our seeing

the blood by faith is not redemption. It is God's seeing the blood that is our redemption and salvation. Those Israelites inside their houses could not see the blood. It is God's eye upon the blood that is salvation. And the Lord God saw the blood from everlasting, accepted it from everlasting, and accepted us by the blood from everlasting. Christ is the Lamb of God slain from the foundation of the world (Revelation 13:8; 17:8), and all for whom he was slain from eternity were saved by him from eternity (Romans 8:29, 30; Ephesians 1:3-5; 2 Timothy 1:9, 10).

**Four Things**
Let me call your attention to four things we need to have in the forefront of our minds continually. Here is God passing through the land of Egypt in wrath, judgment, and condemnation. Men are dying on every hand. The scream is going up from the land of Egypt at midnight. God has fallen upon the people in wrath.

**The Blood**
God said, 'When I see the blood I will pass over you'. What kind of blood is it? The blood on that door was the blood of a divinely-appointed victim. It was not just any blood. God said to Israel; 'Take a lamb'. God designated what it was to be, a lamb. God has designated our sin offering, our sacrifice.

John the Baptist came preaching, 'Prepare the way of the Lord'. Salvation is coming. He pointed to the Lord Jesus Christ and said, 'Behold the Lamb of God'. There he is, the ordained, appointed, designated victim, the sacrifice, the Lamb of God. He was led as, 'a lamb to the slaughter, and as a sheep before her shearers is dumb, he opened not his mouth'. In the fulness of the time God sent his Son to be the propitiation for our sins. He was ordained and appointed of God.

It was the blood of a divinely appointed victim; and it must be a spotless victim. They could not take a lamb that was diseased or had broken bones or was sickly. They had to take a lamb, the firstling of the flock, in its first year, full of strength, without spot or blemish. They put it in a pen for four days and observed it to ensure there was no spot.

Our Lamb, the Lord Jesus Christ, is without sin. He knew no sin. He had no sin. He did no sin. No guile was in his mouth. Our Lord Jesus Christ was tempted in all points, like as we are, yet without sin. He was holy, harmless, and undefiled. He had no sin.

Their lamb was an animal. The blood of animals cannot put away sin. Hebrews 10 tells us that the blood of goats and calves can never take away sin. No human sacrifice, or work, or gift can make atonement for the soul. Those carnal sacrifices were types and pictures.

This blood is the blood of God himself. Let it be understood what I am saying; I want you to understand exactly what I am saying. Back in Old Testament days when Aaron and the sons of Levi brought and killed a lamb, and put its blood on the mercy seat, it was a picture. The blood did not put away anyone's sin. If it could have done so, 'those sacrifices would have ceased to be offered'. They repeated the sacrifices again, and again, and again. Christ came, and this man, who is himself God, offered one sacrifice for sins. And, with his one sacrifice, he perfected forever those that are sanctified. By his one sacrifice, all his elect, all for whom he died, were saved.

Jesus Christ of Nazareth, who died on the cross, is God Almighty in human flesh. He is not just a representative, or a messenger. He is not just an ambassador. He is not even a son of God. He is God the Son, the Son of God, God in our nature (Matthew 1:20-23; John 1:1-3, 14).

The Lord Jesus said, 'I and my Father are one. He that hath seen me hath seen the Father'. Paul said, 'Feed the church of God which God purchased with God's own blood'. Our heavenly Father said of Christ, 'Thy throne O God is forever'.

If Jesus Christ is a mere man, he is the biggest liar, the greatest imposter and phony that ever walked on this earth. His soul is in hell at this moment, his bones are rotting in a grave in Jerusalem. But he is not a mere man. He is the God-man. When Jesus Christ came to this earth, God walked among men. When he went to the cross in human flesh, God Almighty reconciled the world to himself by providing himself a sacrifice. He provided the sacrifice to himself and of himself.

The blood spoken of in Exodus 12 is the blood of a divinely appointed victim. It is the blood of a sinless victim. It is the blood of God himself. Can you imagine the value of it? Can you imagine the power of it? Can you imagine the glory of it? That night in Egypt, each family had its own lamb, but now all believers have the same Lamb.

## Its Efficacy

I have to remind you of the efficacy of the blood! God said, 'When I see the blood I will pass over you'. What do I mean by efficacy? I mean that the blood of Christ, the blood of the Son of God, is effectual blood. 'He is able to save to the uttermost them that come to God by him.' It accomplished and accomplishes all it was intended to accomplish. We know its efficacy because God has accepted the sacrifice. God is satisfied with the sacrifice. How do we know that God Almighty accepted Christ's sacrifice for his people? How do I know that God is satisfied with him? First, we know it by his Word. In Ephesians 1:7, we are told that in Christ, 'we have redemption through his blood, the forgiveness of sin'. Second, we know God's offering and sacrifice of Christ is accepted because 'he raised him from the dead' (Romans 4:25). On that Sunday morning, after three days in the tomb, the angel came down from heaven and touched that stone and it rolled away. Our Lord Jesus Christ came out of the tomb, ascended back to the Father, and sat down at the right hand of the Majesty on High. That's how we know God accepted his sacrifice for us. He was declared to be the Son of God by his resurrection from the dead.

**The Condition**
One condition was fixed to the promise. God said, 'When I see the blood'. The one condition of grace and salvation is God, the triune Jehovah, seeing the blood. He saw the blood long before I saw it. He saw it from eternity. He saw the blood when it was spilt by the sword of his own holy fury and justice on Calvary's hill. He saw the blood when I saw it, sprinkled upon my heart by the Spirit of God. And he sees the blood even if the time comes when I cannot see it.

**The Token**
The Lord God tells us that the blood sprinkled is to us for a token. 'The blood shall be to you for a token upon the houses where ye are: and when I see the blood, I will pass over you, and the plague shall not be upon you to destroy you, when I smite the land of Egypt.'

A token is a sign of something. Of what is the blood, the precious blood of Christ a sign, or token? It is a token of God's infinite love (1 John 4:9, 10), of covenant blessedness (Ephesians 1:3-6), of perfect satisfaction (Romans 3:24-26), of complete forgiveness (Isaiah 43:25; 44:22), of free access (Hebrews 10:19-22), and of blessed safety (Exodus 11:7; Psalm 91:10).

# Chapter 60

## 'What Mean Ye By This Service?'

'Seven days shall ye eat unleavened bread; even the first day ye shall put away leaven out of your houses: for whosoever eateth leavened bread from the first day until the seventh day, that soul shall be cut off from Israel. And in the first day there shall be an holy convocation, and in the seventh day there shall be an holy convocation to you; no manner of work shall be done in them, save that which every man must eat, that only may be done of you. And ye shall observe the feast of unleavened bread; for in this selfsame day have I brought your armies out of the land of Egypt: therefore shall ye observe this day in your generations by an ordinance forever. In the first month, on the fourteenth day of the month at even, ye shall eat unleavened bread, until the one and twentieth day of the month at even. Seven days shall there be no leaven found in your houses: for whosoever eateth that which is leavened, even that soul shall be cut off from the congregation of Israel, whether he be a stranger, or born in the land. Ye shall eat nothing leavened; in all your habitations shall ye eat unleavened bread. Then Moses called for all the elders of Israel, and said unto them, Draw out and take you a lamb according to your families, and kill the passover. And ye shall take a bunch of hyssop, and dip it in the blood that is in the basin, and strike the lintel and the two side posts with the blood that is in the basin; and none of you shall go out at the door of his house until the morning. For the LORD will pass through to smite the Egyptians; and when he seeth the blood upon the lintel, and on the two side posts, the LORD will pass over the door, and will not suffer the destroyer to come in unto your houses to smite you. And ye shall observe this thing for an ordinance to thee and to thy sons forever. And it shall come to pass, when ye be come to the land which the LORD will give you, according as he hath promised, that ye shall keep this service. And it shall come to pass, when your children shall say unto you, What mean ye by this service? That ye shall say, It is the sacrifice of the LORD'S passover, who passed over the houses of the children of Israel in Egypt, when he smote the Egyptians, and delivered our houses. And the people bowed the head and worshipped. And the children of Israel went away, and did as the LORD had commanded Moses and Aaron, so did they.' (Exodus 12:15-28)

In this passage Moses conveyed to the children of Israel the instructions God had given him with regard to the passover, telling them both of God's promised deliverance of his chosen out of Egyptian bondage and of the way in which they were to observe the ordinance of the Passover throughout their generations. This whole affair was, by God's design, a type and picture of Christ our Passover, who was sacrificed for us, and of our redemption and deliverance by his blood (1 Corinthians 5:7).

### Highlights

This chapter is bursting with meaning. It is one of those passages where you do not have to look for Christ. You have to look away to miss him! Here are a few delightful highlights, which are obvious to anyone who reads these verses with spiritual understanding.

As this was the beginning of months to the Jews, the changing of their calendar, so the experience of redemption and grace in Christ is the beginning of an altogether new life for the believer. Faith in Christ is a new beginning (Exodus 12:2; 2 Corinthians 5:17).

Every man in Israel had to have a lamb of sacrifice (vv. 2-6, 21). The father of each household had to seize a lamb and kill it for his family with his own hands. Even so, we must have a lamb of sacrifice, even Christ the Lamb of God. The lamb was selected, provided, and slaughtered by the father of the house. So our heavenly Father selected, provided, and slaughtered his own dear Son as the Lamb of sacrifice for us. The lamb had to be a male of the first year, in the prime and full vigour of life. The lamb had to be without spot or blemish of any kind.

And the lamb had to be slain. It had to be slaughtered. It had to die a violent death. It had to be slaughtered by the father's hand. In all these things our blessed Saviour is portrayed.

The blood of the paschal lamb had to be applied to every house in Israel. This is where most people misinterpret this passage, and miss the beauty and glory of it. They talk about the application of the blood as something we do for ourselves. But that is not the case. The blood was applied by the one who chose and killed the lamb. And it was applied to the house for which it was provided and slaughtered. As it was with the type, so it is with the antitype. The blood of Christ is applied to chosen sinners by God himself, by the power and grace of his Spirit, through the bunch of hyssop he has chosen, by the preaching of the gospel. The blood was applied to all the children of Israel, and none but the children of Israel, and effectually secured the deliverance of all for whom it was spilled.

We saw, in verses 7-11, that the paschal lamb had to be eaten. That portrays faith in Christ. Yet, even this faith, by which we personally receive and feed upon our Lord Jesus, is not our work, but God's work in us. Faith is the gift and operation of God the Holy Spirit in us (Ephesians 2:8; Colossians 2:12). Faith in Christ is eating the true Passover (John 6:53-58).

Christ our Passover must be eaten roasted with fire, being convinced of sin punished, righteousness established, and judgment finished by the doing and dying of the Son of God, the Lord Jesus Christ, the Lamb of God (John 16:8-11). Christ our Passover must be eaten with unleavened bread, with sincerity and honesty before God. He must be eaten with the bitter herbs of repentance. He must not and cannot be eaten raw, or sodden with water. Christ cannot be eaten carnally, with a carnal heart and mind, or by carnal reason. He must be eaten spiritually, by faith.

The whole Sacrifice must be eaten by faith. Faith trusts Christ as he is revealed in the gospel, in the totality of his being, offices, and works. He is all our Wisdom, all our Righteousness, all our Sanctification, all our Holiness, all our Redemption, and all our Salvation.

And we eat our true Passover in expectation, with our loins girded, our shoes on our feet, and our staff in our hand in the good hope and expectation of eternal life. As it was on that night in Egypt, Christ must be trusted now. The Passover must be eaten in haste! 'Today, if ye will hear his voice, harden not your hearts.' 'Behold, today is the day of salvation.' Judgment is coming (v. 12).

The most important aspect of this whole affair was the blood, the precious life blood of the paschal lamb (vv. 13, 22, 23). 'The blood shall be to you for a token', a token of righteousness established, justice satisfied, sins forgiven, a covenant fulfilled; infinite, eternal, unchanging mercy, love, and grace! God's eye is always on the blood; and the God of all grace says, 'When I see the blood, I will pass over you'.

This was an ordinance to be kept forever by the children of Israel, perpetually, throughout their generations, in remembrance and celebration of their redemption and deliverance out of the land of Egypt (vv. 14-17). It was a memorial feast in celebration of redemption, a hopeful feast in anticipation of the true Passover, and a covenant feast celebrating redemption accomplished at God's appointed time (vv. 40-42). The passover was ordained and ordered by God to be a sabbath feast. No work could be done during the feast (v. 16). That, too, portrays faith in Christ. Faith in Christ is true sabbath keeping, a complete cessation of work (Hebrews 4:9, 10). To trust Christ is to rest in him. And this was a family feast. No stranger was allowed to eat the feast (v. 43); and all the congregation of Israel was required to keep it (v. 47). Only the circumcised, and all the circumcised kept the passover. Even so, only those who are born of God, and all who are born of God, all the true circumcision, feast upon Christ our Passover (Philippians 3:3).

### The Lord's Supper
In verse 26 we read, 'And it shall come to pass, when your children shall say unto you, What mean ye by this service?' In gospel churches God's saints regularly gather around the Lord's Table to eat the bread and drink the wine of the Lord's Supper, as our Saviour commands. This is, like the Old Testament passover, a celebration of redemption; true redemption by our Lord Jesus Christ. As we eat the bread and drink the wine of the Lord's Supper, we celebrate the deliverance of our souls by the blood and grace of our all-glorious Christ, the true Passover, remembering him.

What a blessing it would be if our children would show enough interest in the worship of our God to ask, 'What mean ye by this service?' In spiritual worship everything must be understood. Those who worship God must worship him in spirit and in truth. And we cannot worship him in truth unless we understand what we are doing in our acts of worship. The mere religious ritualist is content with the form and ceremony, with acts of outward worship, the form of godliness. The believer worships with understanding. Our understanding is neither perfect nor complete; but we worship God our Saviour with spiritual understanding, discerning the body of Christ, knowing our need of him and knowing what he has done for us as the Lamb of God.

The Jews, with the many outward symbols of carnal ordinances, had a terrible tendency toward empty, meaningless, religious ritualism. Therefore, the Lord carefully taught them the meaning and significance of their ordinances. We have the same problem. We all naturally gravitate toward ritualism, ceremonialism, and idolatry. But this tendency must not be tolerated. The observance of any ordinance merely as a religious ritual without recognizing and understanding the meaning of the ordinance is nothing less than idolatry, and will never be accepted by God (Isaiah 1:10-14). We must know the meaning of what we do; otherwise our worship and observance of the ordinances of God are no more than the blessing of an idol! That is exactly the meaning of Isaiah 66:3.

We do not observe the Jewish passover. But in the church of God we observe the Lord's Supper regularly. If we would truly worship our God in the observance of this gospel ordinance, we must know why we observe it. We must understand its spiritual significance. What has God the Holy Spirit recorded in the Sacred Volume about the meaning of this ordinance of public worship?

## No Sacrament

The Lord's Supper is not a sacrament. Sacraments are part of the pope's tapestry. We do not keep sacraments. There are no sacraments mentioned anywhere in the Bible. The only place you find sacraments is in the church of Rome and in the creeds and confessions of those who are her children. The word 'sacrament' means 'a visible sign of inward grace', 'a means of grace', or 'that by which grace is conferred'. Protestant, Reformed, and Reformed Baptist churches all refer to the ordinances of Christ as sacraments, because they really do believe that keeping the 'sacraments' is a means by which grace is conveyed to the soul. Any sensible person must see that such rubbish is contrary to the

515

gospel of the grace of God. But that is typical Catholic, Protestant, and Reformed doctrine.

Baptism is not a sacrament by which grace is conferred, but an ordinance by which redemption is confessed (Romans 6:4-6). The Lord's Supper is not a sacrament by which grace is given, but an ordinance by which the sacrifice of Christ is remembered (1 Corinthians 11:23-26). These gospel ordinances do not speak of inward grace, but of accomplished redemption, redemption without which grace could never come to, be conferred upon, or bestowed upon sinners.

## Act of Obedience
The eating and drinking of the bread and wine at the Lord's Table is an act of obedience to our Master (1 Corinthians 11:24, 25). It is to be observed by all believers. And it is to be observed regularly.

Our worthiness to observe this ordinance is Christ. Those who are unworthy to eat the bread and drink the wine of the Lord's Supper are those who do not trust Christ as their Saviour. They do not trust him because they do not discern the Lord's body. They do not know who Christ is and what he accomplished for sinners by his obedience unto death. They do not discern their need of a sin atoning substitute. All believers are not only permitted, but commanded to observe this blessed ordinance of worship. Our worthiness to do so is Christ our Saviour.

## Memorial Feast
The Lord's Supper is a memorial feast (1 Corinthians 11:24, 25).

> In memory of the Saviour's love,
> We keep the sacred feast,
> Where every humble, contrite heart
> Is made a welcome guest.

## An Exhibition
The Lord's Supper is an exhibition of our Saviour's death as our Redeemer and Substitute. 'For as often as ye eat this bread, and drink this cup, ye do shew the Lord's death till he come' (1 Corinthians 11:26). The unleavened bread symbolizes our Saviour's holy humanity, his body. The bread broken portrays the crushing of his body under the horrid fury of God's holy wrath, when he was made sin for us. The wine

represents his blood, his precious, sin atoning blood. The bread and the wine separated, his body and his blood separated speak of certain death.

## Communion Table
The Lord's Table is a table of communion (1 Corinthians 10:16, 17). We come together, as redeemed sinners saved by grace, at the Lord's Table to share intimate family thoughts and emotions.

'The cup of blessing which we bless, is it not the communion of the blood of Christ? The bread which we break, is it not the communion of the body of Christ? For we being many are one bread, and one body: for we are all partakers of that one bread' (1 Corinthians 10:16, 17).

## Covenant Token
The Lord's Supper is a token of his covenant (Matthew 26:27, 28). Redemption, grace, and salvation by Christ come to sinners through 'the blood of the everlasting covenant' (Hebrews 13:20).

'And he took the cup, and gave thanks, and gave it to them, saying, Drink ye all of it; For this is my blood of the new testament, which is shed for many for the remission of sins' (Matthew 26:27, 28).

## Thanksgiving Feast
The Lord's Supper is a feast of thanksgiving (Luke 22:15-20). As we remember our blessed Saviour, taking the bread in our mouths, lifting the cup to our lips, we give thanks to our God for his unspeakable gift.

'And he said unto them, With desire I have desired to eat this passover with you before I suffer: For I say unto you, I will not any more eat thereof, until it be fulfilled in the kingdom of God. And he took the cup, and gave thanks, and said, Take this, and divide it among yourselves: For I say unto you, I will not drink of the fruit of the vine, until the kingdom of God shall come. And he took bread, and gave thanks, and brake it, and gave unto them, saying, This is my body which is given for you: this do in remembrance of me. Likewise also the cup after supper, saying, This cup is the new testament in my blood, which is shed for you' (Luke 22:15-20).

## Picture of Faith
The Lord's Supper is a picture of faith in Christ (John 6:53-58). As each believer takes the bread and wine of the Lord's Table for himself, and

eats and drinks for himself, so too, in the experience of grace, each individual born of God takes Christ for himself by the hand of faith. Eating his flesh and drinking his blood, all that he is becomes ours.

'Then Jesus said unto them, Verily, verily, I say unto you, Except ye eat the flesh of the Son of man, and drink his blood, ye have no life in you. Whoso eateth my flesh, and drinketh my blood, hath eternal life; and I will raise him up at the last day. For my flesh is meat indeed, and my blood is drink indeed. He that eateth my flesh, and drinketh my blood, dwelleth in me, and I in him. As the living Father hath sent me, and I live by the Father: so he that eateth me, even he shall live by me. This is that bread which came down from heaven: not as your fathers did eat manna, and are dead: he that eateth of this bread shall live forever' (John 6:53-58).

### Symbol of Hope

The Lord's Supper is a symbol of hope (1 Corinthians 11:26; Exodus 12:11). We are to eat the bread and drink the wine upon the tip-toe of faith, looking for Christ, expecting him to appear in his glory for our consummate deliverance by him in resurrection glory.

'And thus shall ye eat it; with your loins girded, your shoes on your feet, and your staff in your hand; and ye shall eat it in haste: it is the LORD'S passover' (Exodus 12:11).

'For as often as ye eat this bread, and drink this cup, ye do show the Lord's death till he come' (1 Corinthians 11:26).

'And ye shall observe this thing for an ordinance to thee and to thy sons forever. And it shall come to pass, when ye be come to the land which the LORD will give you, according as he hath promised, that ye shall keep this service. And it shall come to pass, when your children shall say unto you, What mean ye by this service? That ye shall say, It is the sacrifice of the LORD'S passover, who passed over the houses of the children of Israel in Egypt, when he smote the Egyptians, and delivered our houses. And the people bowed the head and worshipped. And the children of Israel went away, and did as the LORD had commanded Moses and Aaron, so did they' (Exodus 12:24-28).

# Index Of Bible Verses